The
Content Analysis Reader

Dedicated to our families
Marge, David, Rosie, and Emily, for their support and patience
&
To human coders everywhere . . .

The Content Analysis Reader

Klaus Krippendorff
The Annenberg School for Communication, University of Pennsylvania

Mary Angela Bock
The Annenberg School for Communication, University of Pennsylvania

Los Angeles • London • New Delhi • Singapore

For information:

SAGE Publications, Inc.
2455 Teller Road
Thousand Oaks, California 91320
E-mail: order@sagepub.com

SAGE Publications Ltd.
1 Oliver's Yard
55 City Road
London EC1Y 1SP
United Kingdom

SAGE Publications India Pvt. Ltd.
B 1/I 1 Mohan Cooperative Industrial Area
Mathura Road, New Delhi 110 044
India

SAGE Publications Asia-Pacific Pte. Ltd.
33 Pekin Street #02-01
Far East Square
Singapore 048763

Printed in the United States of America

Library of Congress Cataloging-in-Publication Data

The content analysis reader/Klaus Krippendorff, Mary Angela Bock, editors.
p. cm.
Includes bibliographical references and index.
ISBN 978-1-4129-4965-1 (cloth)
ISBN 978-1-4129-4966-8 (pbk.)
1. Content analysis (Communication) I. Krippendorff, Klaus. II. Bock, Mary Angela.

P93.C65 2009
401′.41—dc22 2008003529

This book is printed on acid-free paper.

08 09 10 11 12 10 9 8 7 6 5 4 3 2 1

Acquisitions Editor: Todd R. Armstrong
Editorial Assistant: Aja Baker
Production Editor: Astrid Virding
Copy Editor: Gillian Dickens
Typesetter: C&M Digitals (P) Ltd
Proofreader: Gail Naron Chalew
Cover Designer: Klaus Krippendorff
Marketing Manager: Carmel Schrire

CONTENTS

INTRODUCTION

Welcome to our *Content Analysis Reader,* a collection we hope captures the myriad ways this valuable and adaptable methodology has been, is, and might be used to answer questions from careful examinations of all kinds of communications—texts, images, interviews, and observational records. Here you will find applications of the method to a variety of data—from science fiction stories to Nazi films, from comics to music videos. Some of the articles are highly theoretical; others are more practical. Diversity is what keeps content analysis current—but also makes it difficult to standardize. It is our hope that the readings included here will be of use to anyone struggling to design a content analysis or use its results.

Some of the articles are also of historical significance in that they broke new ground or revealed uses of content analysis that were novel at the time of their publication. Gordon Allport, for example, applied content analysis to personal letters, redirecting the psychological community's attention to individual cases, Nathan Leites et al. used the method innovatively for traditional "Kremlin watching," and George Gerbner's influential reports on network television violence were based on careful and longitudinal content analyses. The availability of texts in electronic form and computers to process large volumes of them has made it possible to undertake larger studies. We have included examples of these and other uses of content analysis to show how the field has evolved.

We start with a look at the history and conceptualization of the method; how did it start? The remaining parts of the book reflect the decisions required when one designs a content analysis: defining units of analysis, choosing a sample, conceptualizing analytical constructs, and developing coding categories, whether working with human coders or "training" computer software to aid the process. We have also included a key word list that we hope will help the reader navigate the book according to questions about applications or methodological considerations. Whether you are using this book in conjunction with Klaus Krippendorff's (2004) *Content Analysis* text, as part of a methods course, or to get ideas for designing a study, we believe you will find inspiration in these pages.

We would like to thank our editor Todd Armstrong and everyone at Sage Publications who assisted with producing this anthology. We appreciate collaborations with many scholars who granted us the permission to include their work. Thanks, too, is due to several generations of students at the University of Pennsylvania's Annenberg School for Communication, who, studying content analysis with Klaus, waded through the wealth of readings and offered valuable feedback of their usefulness. We are finally grateful to our families for their help and patience with the time-consuming project. Mary is particularly thankful to her husband and daughters for pitching in when it was time to count words and organize bibliographies.

REFERENCE

Krippendorff, K. (2004). *Content analysis: An introduction to its methodology* (2nd ed.). Thousand Oaks, CA: Sage.

PART 1

History and Conception of Content Analysis

Consider this commentary, published by *The New Hampshire Spy,* November 30, 1787:

> *A* RECEIPT *for an* ANTIFEDERAL ESSAY
>
> WELL-BORN, nine times — *Ariſtocracy,* eighteen times — *Liberty of the Preſs,* thirteen times repeated – *Liberty of Conſcience,* once – *Negro ſlavery,* once mentioned — *Trial by Jury,* ſeven times — *Great Men,* ſix times repeated — Mr. WILSON, forty times — and laſtly, GEORGE MASON's *Right Hand in an a Cutting-Box,* nineteen times — put them altogether, and diſh them up at pleaſure. Theſe *words* will bear boiling, roaſting or frying — and, what is remarkable of them, they will bear being ſerved, after being once uſed, a dozen times to the ſame table and palate.

Part political commentary, part literary criticism, and part effort to objectify an argument, the above stab at antifederalist writers during the early history of the United States is also part of what content analysts do today. While the research technique surfaced within communication studies during the 20th century, analytical interests in text go back to the beginning of writing. It shaped ancient disciplines—philosophy, rhetoric, and the arts—and became the focus of religious inquisitions, legal disputes, and political controversies. Karin Dovring discovered such roots when studying the reception of a book of religious hymns in 18th-century Sweden. The use of this book pitched the Swedish State Church against the growing popularity of religious dissenters who used these hymns in their sermons. Her article shows how various approaches to analyzing these hymns evolved during that controversy. Although these analyses were politically motivated, it is remarkable that notable scholars entered the dispute by debating the validity of various ways of counting words, images, analogies, and contexts to speculate about the source of these hymns and infer the reason for their surprising popularity. These counts anticipated several methods that are now a main staple of communication research, well before content analysis had a name.

Max Weber's address to the first congress of German sociologists in 1910 was prescient in a number of ways. He called for analyzing newspapers by "measure[ing] with scissors and compasses, how the contents of newspapers have quantitatively shifted during the last generation, especially in the advertising section, in the feuilleton." Weber not only recognized the virtue of quantifying newsprint, but he also embedded the proposed effort in qualitative, critical, and comparative research questions, presaging the political-economic approach to the content analysis of print media.

That same year and worlds apart, a Byron Mathews published "A Study of a New York Daily," which reflects the then rampant dissatisfaction with sensationalist journalism. His was a period during which the educated elite had lost control over the news media, and commercialism, advertising, and mass circulation started to drive newspaper content. Note how Mathews categorized content and that he had no idea about sampling, reliability, and alternative methods of inquiry. He did not even say which newspaper he examined. Quantification served merely to legitimize even the most ludicrous findings—perhaps not so uncommon today. His results say more about Mathews's role in society than about the press he sought to evaluate. This may serve as a warning against using content analysis self-servingly.

Alvan Tenney, a Columbia University journalism professor, was the first to call for a comprehensive and global content analysis of the press to get a sense of how public concerns change in various parts of the country—analogous to, as he suggested, how the U.S. Weather Bureau collects its data. His proposal far exceeded what in 1913 was technologically possible. Three decades later, his ideas resurfaced in Harold Lasswell's world attention survey* and another 30 years later in George Gerbner's cultural indicators project**; on a smaller scale, they are now implemented in David Fan's computational content-analytic alternative to public opinion research.***

Alexander George describes the use of content analysis in the service of extracting military intelligence from enemy domestic propaganda during World War II. These efforts shifted the concept of content analysis from purely descriptive accounts of content, naively conceived, to making reliable and valid inferences from textual matter. It also suggested that content analysis, much as anticipated by Weber, is most informative when used in conjunction with other data, particularly with reasonable assumptions about the motives and theory underlying the sources of texts. George's article describes one example of how British and U.S. propaganda analysts assessed the reality behind enemy lines and predicted the deployment of a weapon system.

Since then, content analysts increasingly have focused their attention on the inferences one could make from texts to their contexts of use. This has rendered the naive notion of content as an objectively describable entity no longer tenable. The psychological states of authors, the worlds that the mass media present to their audiences, the political leanings of a newspaper, ethnic

---

*See reading 5.3, this volume.

**See reading 6.6, this volume.

***See reading 7.6, this volume.

prejudices, and so on are not observable as such, but they may well be inferred from the physicality of communications, images, and texts. Justifying such inferences became a methodological necessity, to which ends content analysts had to adopt what we call "analytical constructs." An analytical construct is a means to render inferences from texts to the contexts of their use conclusive. In George's article, the analytical construct consists of knowledge of how an elite's use of preparatory propaganda responded to events not under its control. The following article by Gordon Allport relies on psychological constructs.

Allport, a pioneer in modern psychology, realized the possibilities of making valid inferences from personal documents, such as letters, and introduced the method into psychology, heretofore preoccupied with making experiments. His "Letters From Jenny" reproduces a large collection of remarkable personal letters by one woman, written over the course of several years and saved by her correspondents. Following this collection, Allport discusses various approaches (analytical constructs) to infer different aspects of the psychological makeup of the writer and her experienced world. We chose just a few of these letters and his discussion of two content analyses, one undertaken by Alfred Baldwin, who traced the flow of her ideas throughout her life, and another, using the General Inquirer computer program to identify her personality traits.

While making specific inferences from text to their contexts is now the defining feature of content analysis, informs its methodology, and has guided our selections in this volume, there are analyses of textual matter that do not go as far. "Impressionistic content analyses," such as the brief account from the *New Hampshire Spy* in Figure 1, and Mathews's article, published largely for nonacademic readers, do not tell their audience how and why categories were chosen and offer no compelling inferences. Mary Bock describes three contemporary examples. One offers a comparison of the 100 most frequent content words in four books of well-known authors, routinely provided by Amazon.com to potential buyers. The other is a frequency account of the words used during the interview of a celebrity. The third is an account published by the *New York Times* of the frequency of selected words used by George W. Bush in his State of the Union addresses, delivered between 2001 and 2007. While such counts do not reach the level of an analysis, they do offer a view of texts that differs from what one would obtain by reading them. Obviously, without some background knowledge of the authors and contexts of their texts, word frequencies or rank orders say little. Words, when taken out of their contexts, have many more meanings than in the text from which they were taken. In the absence of well-articulated analytical constructs, the authors of such accounts leave it to the reader to infer anything they please from them. Nevertheless, raw word counts can be suggestive, and content analysts often use word counts to get a sense of the vocabulary they are facing.

1.1

QUANTITATIVE SEMANTICS IN 18TH CENTURY SWEDEN

KARIN DOVRING*

In 1743, a collection of 90 hymns, entitled *Songs of Zion,* was published in Sweden, This publication soon became the storm center of a religious controversy which is of particular interest to the social scientist because in the course of it there were foreshadowed many of the methods of content analysis, which have found systematic expression only during the past decades. In fact, if not in name, participants in this debate were concerned with many of the problems, which concern today's content analyst: the identification of key symbols, the division of content into favorable, unfavorable and neutral categories, the coding of values, and other related problems. Indeed, the controversy revolved around the formula, which has become so familiar to students of communication: Who said what to whom, how and with what effect?

The *Songs of Zion* appeared at a time when the powerful State Church (Lutheran) was struggling against German pietistic influences. Pietism, stressing faith rather than ritual, was making substantial inroads among the orthodox in Sweden, when the influences of still another German religious movement began to be felt. This movement was that of the Moravian Brethren, led by the Count von Zinzendorf. At first, the orthodox Lutheran clergy welcomed the Moravian ideas, believing that they might provide a spiritual means of bringing the pietistic dissenters back into the fold. It was not long, however, before the State Church recognized the Moravians as enemies rather than allies.

Publication of the first edition of the *Songs of Zion* seems to have occurred without appreciable controversy. The Swedish State Censor found the hymns to be somewhat odd, and neither beautiful nor superior to those in the *Hymnal* of the Established Church, but since they were already being used in manuscript form he allowed them to be printed. Nobody seemed disturbed that the authors of these hymns were unknown.

---

*Dovring, K. (1954–1955). Quantitative semantics in 18th century Sweden. *Public Opinion Quarterly 18*, 4:389–394. Substantially taken from the author's dissertation (Dovring, 1951a, 1951b).

In 1774, application was made to the Swedish authorities for permission to publish a second edition. By this time, however, the State Church had become alarmed by the effects, which they believed the *Songs* were having on the public. Three important developments indicated that something was wrong. First, the public filled the churches where the clergy were influenced by the Moravian Brethren, leaving the orthodox pastors with fewer listeners, in spite of the fact that according to the law every citizen had to attend church in the district where they resided. Second, frequent reports had been received that the *Songs* were being used at private religious meetings, although meetings of this character were illegal. Finally, themes reminiscent of the Count von Zinzendorf, German leader of the Moravian Brethren, could be heard from many pulpits, and by this time the orthodox clergy had become convinced that this movement was unlikely to bring pietistic dissenters back to the established church.

Despite the hostility of the ecclesiastical authorities, a new edition of the *Songs* was permitted to appear in 1745, and both the old and the new editions were reprinted in 1747 and 1748. The last two printings were wholly unlicensed, and the authorities discovered many changes of wording in them.

During this later period, public debate of the religious issues involved became acrimonious. The orthodox clergy called the Moravian movement "the contagion" and identified the *Songs* as "the nest of the contagion." The Archbishop of Sweden demanded that the contagion be rooted out, while the Minister of Justice commented darkly that "recent developments may have disastrous consequences for the whole Swedish state." Before the controversy was concluded some of the Moravian supporters were forced to deny their convictions. Others, refusing to recant, were exiled from their native land.

Who Says What to Whom and With What Effect?

It is apparent from the historical record that the 18th century disputants approached their problem by asking questions, which are thoroughly familiar to present-day students of communications. *Who said* the debatable things in these songs? The Orthodox clergy tried to find out, and caused many investigations of suspected persons. And *what* was said? This was the most important question. What did these songs say which influenced people to break the law and threaten the power of the State Church? Some of the advocates of the *Songs* pointed out that the subject matter contained in them was substantially the same as in the official hymnal. This argument was considered by the orthodox clergy, but they observed that the response of the public to the two collections of hymns was different. Perhaps, some of them concluded, it was a question of *to whom* the *Songs of Zion* were directed. Were these publications used only in those circles, which were already infected with the ideas of the Moravians? Other investigators observed that this was not the case. Many people had been influenced who previously had known nothing about the "dangerous ideas" being disseminated. The behavioral and attitudinal *effects* attributed to the songs—the enthusiasm for preachers with Moravian ideas and the incidence of private religious meetings—have already been referred to.

Some of the most interesting contributions to the debate were made not by the clergy, but by intellectuals. In 1746 a perceptive article in the Swedish *Learned News,* a journal discussing the current progress of science, had, in a tolerant manner, examined the doctrine of the Moravian Brethren. This article concluded that the Moravian movement embodied the essential principles of Lutheranism but that the movement might become dangerous because it seemed to preach only a part of the orthodox doctrine. It stressed the words and ideas, which referred to the redemption of man by Christ, at the expense of those words and ideas that referred to the efforts of men to live as Christians. It gave a new meaning to familiar expressions, thus influencing public opinion in a new direction. The article gave specific examples of the way in which a new meaning was produced by emphasizing one value at the expense of another, and concluded that it was not enough only to possess the truth. The truth must also be presented in a manner that will elicit the desired effect.

Many dissenters agreed with this analysis to the extent that they argued that the whole dispute was essentially not about doctrine, but simply about the manner of presentation. Clergymen influenced by the Moravian Brethren held that since people were not educated enough to understand the whole doctrine, preachers should present the correct doctrine in a manner which the public could understand.

To this, the orthodox clergy replied that there were dangers in simplification. The content of what was said would not really be distinguished from the manner of presentation. Clear and simple presentation would not necessarily lead the public to proper understanding; instead, it might give rise to oversimplified ideas. This, the orthodox clergy suspected, was true in the case of the *Songs of Zion.*

Another contribution, which combined both an interest in semantics with a rough content analysis procedure, was made by the learned and well-read orthodox clergyman Kumblaeus. From the German literature, which had been written in opposition to the Moravian movement, Kumblaeus learned that Count Zinzendorf and his adherents used a special language in the dissemination of their unorthodox ideas. Their ideas were dressed in the ordinary vocabulary of each country's language, but new meanings were given to well-known words, themes and symbols. Furthermore, the public was not aware that they were being exposed to a new way of thinking because of the familiarity of the words and phrases (used by) the Moravians. Kumblaeus felt that this use of language made it possible for the Moravians to conceal dangerous, false doctrines, and create "a state within a state."

To show the way in which the followers of Count Zinzendorf altered the orthodox doctrine, Kumblaeus subjected Moravian writings to a quantitative analysis. He counted the symbols referring to the Trinity in Moravian writings and found that these writings tended to ignore two of the three persons in the Trinity and concentrate on Jesus in his role as a savior. In the *Songs of Zion* Kumblaeus observed that symbols describing Jesus as a bleeding and loving savior occurred far more frequently than those dealing with other Christian values cherished by orthodox Lutheranism. He also distinguished other categories of content and showed that the frequency with which they were treated deviated from ordinary practice. Kumblaeus concluded on the basis of his analysis that the exclusion of certain essential Christian themes and emphasis on certain others tended to create new conceptions, which threatened the doctrine of the established church.

The Swedish dissenters hastened to reply to this criticism. In addition to expressing general indignation at Kumblaeus' allegations, they attacked his method of analysis. One anonymous reply—printed abroad and smuggled into Sweden—pointed out that one was not limited to a single terminology in expressing the meaning of the Bible. The fact that Kumblaeus had found few specific mentions of the Holy Ghost was not significant, since this same concept could be expressed in other words. Furthermore, many of the words criticized by Kumblaeus as being "unbiblical" were in fact used both in the Bible and by Luther. Other replies took Kumblaeus to task for not considering the context in which the expressions he criticized had appeared.

Kumblaeus, for his part, continued repeating his accusations and went on to compare the debatable words in the *Songs of Zion* with the same actual words as used in their context in the Bible. He found that certain words and expressions, which were presented as having a negative value in the Biblical context, were given a positive direction when used in the *Songs.* In this way a new meaning was given to them. Kumblaeus followed this new approach throughout the rest of the debate.

Here the matter stood until a scholarly government official, Johan Breant, introduced a trend into the discussion, which was more favorable to the defenders of the *Songs.* The Moravians had been accused of overemphasizing symbols referring to Jesus' blood and wounds, but Breant pointed out that frequent use of these symbols was not peculiar to the *Songs of Zion.* In order to demonstrate this contention he tabulated the frequency with which the same symbols occurred in the Official Hymnal of the Swedish Established Church and was able to show that the number of references to them was very large.

Now it was the turn of the ecclesiastical authorities to protest. They were irritated by Breant's research and informed the Swedish government that "the words were interpreted without considering the context." Breant replied by suggesting that the government undertake an analysis which took account of context, a proposal which met with little agreement on either side.[1] The state authorities, too, were bewildered by the fact that the same words which were condemned when they appeared in the *Songs of Zion* were praised when they appeared in other hymnals. They had, moreover, just received an anonymous study showing that the frequency of expressions, which Kumblaeus had condemned in the *Songs,* was identical with the frequency of the same expressions in other non-official hymnals. Many orthodox clergymen were confused by these developments and asked the advice of their superiors. They said that nobody now dared to sing about the blood and wounds of Jesus for fear of being accused of Moravian tendencies. These superiors had nothing to say except that an expression standing in the Official Hymnal was right, but that the same expression in the *Songs of Zion* was dangerous.

In trying to determine who had collaborated in writing the *Songs of Zion* and who had been influenced by them, Swedish authorities made further use of content analysis. Adherents of the orthodox point of view listened intently to sermons in the churches and noted all "ways of expression" that seemed revolutionary. These expressions were compared with the symbols and themes from the *Songs* and from German writings by the Moravian Brethren, and often a connection was clear. The authorities investigated everyone suspected of Moravian propaganda, using tests well-known to every expert of modern propaganda analysis (Berelson & de Grazia, 1947). Numerous scientists, schoolteachers and pastors were found to have been influenced by the "dangerous thoughts" of the German dissenters, and some of the writers who had contributed to the *Songs* were disclosed as well.

Quantitative Semantics in Historical Research

The use . . . of content analysis techniques in 18th century Sweden lacked certain refinements from the modern scientific point of view. Since the investigations were undertaken to serve a pressing purpose they were often rushed to conclusion with insufficient care. Nor did all those attempting to use quantitative techniques have sufficient insight to use these techniques correctly. Above all, the investigations did not make use either of the universe of content or of scientifically chosen samples. And finally, the researchers found it difficult to interpret statistical data. After presenting their symbol lists and frequency tables they described their results using terms such as "more than," "not so much as," and other equally imprecise expressions. Nevertheless, the results of these quantitative analyses did in fact influence the decisions of the power-holders of that time.[2]

Consideration of this 18th century controversy is of interest not only because it anticipated certain trends in modern content analysis, but also because it suggests a method of study which may be applied to other historical situations. We have spoken here about the influence of certain German ideas in Sweden. The history of Europe as a whole can be regarded largely as a series of struggles among different ideas. These ideological debates are customarily described in a qualitative way, but it would be illuminating to make a quantitative analysis of them as well. Such an approach might prove to be useful in connection with the discussion of qualitative *versus* quantitative content analysis, since quantity itself is one of the qualities of any text which ought to be described.

A quantitative approach would help to free investigators from the predispositions of their own time when analyzing conflicting ideologies from other periods of history. Quantitative investigation reveals the most frequent ideas in a text—ideas that because of the frequency of their occurrence must have been of importance to writers of the document, as well as to the vast majority of their audience. Looking at other ages through one's own glasses has been a mistake made by too many historians. A quantitative approach will allow the sources themselves to define the key symbols, which were at the focus of attention at a given period. The publicist of today knows that the meaning and effect of what is said or shown are determined in part by what receives public attention. And the propagandists of other ages knew it as well. A quantitative approach to ideological struggles thus provides additional insight into the processes by which history has been determined.

Notes

1. Breant did, in fact, attempt to analyze the *Songs* in such a manner as to take both meaning and context into account. This analysis was of debatable value, however, since it involved attempts to guess the meanings that both the communicator and the public assigned to the symbols used.

2. A quantitative investigation that made use of the universe of the texts in question gave interesting results, confirming the correctness of many of the accusations made by the orthodox clergy (Dovring, 1951a, 1951b).

References

Berelson, B., & de Grazia, S. (1947). Detecting collaboration in propaganda. *Public Opinion Quarterly 11,* 2:244–53.

Dovring, K. (1951a). *Striden Kring Sions Stinger* (2 vols.). Lund, Sweden (English summary).

Dovring, K. (1951b). *Striden kring Sions sånger och närstående sångsamlingar. En idé- och lärdomshistorick studie,* I-II (dissertation) Lund.

1.2

Towards a Sociology of the Press

An Early Proposal for Content Analysis

Max Weber*

Gentlemen, the first topic that the Society** deemed suitable for a purely scientific exploration is a sociology of the press. We need to realize that this is an enormous undertaking, an effort that will require not only very large material support for doing the preliminary work, but also the trust and goodwill of those interested in the press. . . . A committee will have to assure the cooperation of experts and theoreticians of the press. We already have numerous brilliant theoretical works on this topic (let me remind you of Löbl's*** (1903) book, which deserves to be known better than it is)—and practitioners of the press whose collaboration is needed. There is also hope that preliminary talks will interest the associations of newspaper publishers and editors. . . .

One does not need to speak here about the magnitude and importance of the press. . . . Think about what modern life would be without the kind of publicity created by the newspaper. Antiquity had its publicity as well. Jakob Burckhardt (1898) described the horrors of publicity in Hellenistic life, which encompassed all and the most intimate details of Athens' citizen. This kind of publicity does not exist today, and it would be interesting, indeed, to inquire into what contemporary publicity is like and what it will be in the future; what is published by the newspaper and what is not? One hundred

*From Max Weber (1924, pp. 434–441), a speech delivered at the first Congress of Sociologists, meeting in Frankfurt, 1910. Translated by Klaus Krippendorff. For quoting, see the original text.

**The (German) Society of Sociologists meeting 1910 in Frankfurt/Main.

***Emil Löbl (1861–1935). Austrian journalist and editor at the Wiener Zeitung, later of the Neues Wiener Tageblatt. His *Kultur und Presse* offers an elaborate system of categories for studying newspaper contents. His work influenced what later became "Publizistik," the science of publishing, especially newspapers, a name used mainly in Germany.

fifty years ago, the British Parliament forced journalists to apologize on their knees for breach of privilege by reporting about its sessions. Today the mere threat by the press *not* to print the speeches of representatives forces Parliament to its knees. . . . Evidently, the idea of parliamentarianism, as well as the position of the press, has changed. . . . And so have local differences. For instance, until recently, some American stock market exchanges used frosted glass windows to prevent market fluctuations from being signaled to its outside. Yet, almost all relevant facets of newspaper production are influenced by public information about the stock market. . . . When an English lord marries an American woman, the American press publishes details of her physical and psychological attributes, including her dowry, while a respectable German newspaper, following views prevailing here, would spurn such publicity. Where do such differences originate? . . . Which worldview underlies the one tendency or the other?

Our task will be to study the power inequalities that specific newspaper publicity creates. Publicity about science, for example, seems far less important than about the accomplishments of actors and conductors, evidence of which disappears with the passing of the day. . . . Theatre and literature reviewers can easily establish existences or destroy them. . . . The relations between the newspaper and political parties, here and elsewhere, and its relations to the business world and numerous groups and interests that influence and are influenced by the public is an enormous area for sociological inquiry, but currently in its infancy.

Speaking sociologically about the press also requires acknowledging that today's press is not only a necessarily capitalistic and private business enterprise, but also occupies a unique position in contrast to any other business. It has two very different types of "customers:" One consists of newspaper buyers who in turn are either subscribers or single-copy buyers, a difference that, in advanced societies, results in decisively different characteristics of the press. The other consists of advertisers. Between these two groups exists the most peculiar interrelationships. For instance, for a newspaper to attract many advertisers, it is certainly important that it also has many subscribers, and to some extent vice versa. Not only is the role that the advertiser plays in the press budget much more important than that of the subscriber, one can say that a newspaper can actually never have too many advertisers. However, and this is in contrast with any other seller of goods, it can have too many buyers, namely, when it is unable to raise advertising revenues to cover the costs of an expanded circulation. . . .

Whether the increasing need for capital means an increasing monopoly of the already existing enterprises has not yet been determined. The best-informed experts disagree. This leads to the question: Regardless of the growing capital needs, how does the strength of the monopolistic position of already existing newspapers differ, depending on whether the press relies on regular subscriptions or on single sales? In the latter case, readers choose individual issues among several papers, which makes the emergence of new papers easier. . . . An examination of this phenomenon might answer the question: Does the increase in investment also mean an increase in the power to mold public opinion? Or, inversely, does it mean an increase in sensitivity to fluctuations in public opinion?

I am raising these issues mainly to show how the business side of press enterprises must be taken into account. We must ask: How does the (economic) development of newspaper publishing influence the sociological position of the press in general and its role in the process of public opinion formation in particular? . . .

Much has been said "for" and "against" the anonymity of what appears in the press. We do not take sides but ask: . . . How does it happen that (neutrality) is favored, for example, in Germany and England, whereas the conditions in France are different. . . ? This may have something to do with how conflicts of interests are resolved between the interest of individual journalists to become well known and the interest of newspapers not to become too dependent upon the cooperation of individual journalists. These differences may well depend on commercial interests, on whether or not single sales dominate, but also on the political predisposition of a population. One nation—as is the case of Germany—tends to be impressed by the institutional powers of a newspaper, acting like a "supra-individual," more than by the opinions of individuals—or whether it is free of this type of metaphysics.

These questions lead into the area of how the press acquires its material for publication. Who writes for the newspapers? What? What not? And why not? Part-time journalism, for example, is a phenomenon that is more common in England and in France than in Germany. . . . How have the conditions of professional journalists shifted in different countries? . . . News services not only strain the budgets of the press but increasing reliance on them raises the question of what a news source actually is. . . . Is the steady increase in the importance of purely factual accounts here (in Germany) a general phenomenon or a culture specific one? Frenchmen seem to want primarily an opinion sheet. But why? . . .

Finally, what are the effects of this mass product, whose paths we need to investigate, on the reader? There exists an enormous amount of literature, partly valuable but also containing extreme contradictions. . . . As we know, there have been attempts to examine the effects of the press on the human brain, questioning what it means when modern humans have become accustomed to take in a journalistic hodgepodge, leading them through many areas of cultural life before pursuing their daily work. That this makes a difference is obvious. It is easy to talk in general terms about these effects, but far from so to advance our understanding beyond its infant state of knowledge. . . .

You will ask now: Where is the material to begin such studies? This material consists of the newspapers themselves, and, to be specific, we will now start to measure, with scissors and compasses, how the contents of newspapers have quantitatively shifted during the last generation, especially in the advertising section, in the feuilleton,* between feuilleton and lead editorials, between editorials and news, between what is actually carried as news and what is no longer made available. In these regards, conditions have changed drastically. Available studies are only beginning.

From these quantitative accounts, we will proceed to qualitative considerations. We will have to study the stylization of newspapers, how the same problems are discussed inside and outside the newspapers, the apparent repression of the emotional in the newspapers, which always provides the basis of their ability to exist and pursue things. Then, we may finally approach the point where we have reasons to hope for a slow approximation to our wide-ranging questions. It is our goal to answer them.

References

Burckhardt, J. (1898). *Griechische Kulturgeschichte.* Berlin: W. Spemann.

Löbl, E. (1903). *Kultur und Presse.* Leipzig: Duncker und Humblot.

Weber, M. (1924). *Gesammelte Aufsätze zur Soziologie und Sozialpolitik.* Tübingen: J.C.B. Mohr.

*Originally French, part of a European newspaper or magazine devoted to entertain the general reader, including fiction catering to popular taste (Webster).

1.3

A Study of a New York Daily

Byron C. Mathews*

The press is often mentioned as one of the great educational agencies of our day. It certainly is a great agency, but whether it is an educational agency depends upon what is meant by education. The public school system is unquestionably the great educational agency in this country and in the leading European countries. Its purpose is educational and nothing else. Its purpose is to improve the character and the condition of the people in every desirable way. Its entire machinery and all its methods have the accomplishment of this purpose as their one and only end. Its methods are those approved by students of educational problems. If the purpose of the public school system were private profit instead of public welfare, its methods and hence the results would be wholly different from what they are now. The thoughts of those who determine methods would be on dollars instead of on improved human beings, and the methods would point toward dollars, and the results would be dollars. Exactly so it is with any institution. The purpose for which it exists determines the methods employed in accomplishing that purpose and the character of the results that follow from its methods. The press is no exception to this principle. As far as its purpose is to improve the character and conditions of human beings and as far as its methods are bent toward the accomplishment of this purpose, the press is truly an educational agency.

There are good reasons for thinking that this is true, in greater or less degree, of some of our monthly magazines, of some of our weekly reviews, and possibly of some of our dailies. On the other hand, there is a mass of convincing evidence that the chief purpose of the daily press is dollars. Its methods point toward dollars and evidently, the results are dollars. The daily press is generally owned by individuals or corporations who are not its editors or contributors. The owner is the power behind editors to determine its purpose and character. The object of ownership, exactly as in any other business enterprise, is private profit. Editors are usually hired agents to accomplish the purposes of owners, and are allowed

*From Mathews, B. C. (1910). A study of a New York daily. *Independent 68:*82–86.

to determine methods to be employed only as far as these will accomplish the purposes of owners. Under these conditions, the methods employed and the results accomplished will not be such as to entitle the daily press to be ranked as one of the great educational agencies. Its influence is great and far extended. But this does not make it an educational agency. . . . [I]t is able to impress upon the public what is positively bad, or what is positively good, to improve the race or to degrade it, and whether it is doing the one or the other is a matter of grave concern. It is impossible for a man interested in social improvement to read the daily papers, even the best of them, and not regret that so small a percentage of the news given is devoted to what ennobles and improves character, and so much is devoted to the trivial and demoralizing.

With a view of determining about what percentage of the news items are to be approved from an educational point of view, the writer has made a study of one of our best New York dailies. It would not be fair to judge the daily press as a whole by the results of a study of any of the so-called yellow journals, or even of the more sensational which are not quite yellow, but the sensationals and the yellows certainly cannot complain if judged by the results of a study of one of the few that are universally acknowledged to be the best of our daily papers. The writer wishes to say that the paper selected is the one, which, during the last ten years, he has bought and read more than all other New York dailies together. He has tried at least half a dozen others, but invariably comes back to the one chosen for this study. It certainly holds a place among the first.

This study . . . embraces the daily issues for a period of three months of the current year. Attention has been given to the *news* items only. The editorial page, devoted to criticism and the expression of opinion on the part of editors and contributors, has not been included, except as news items were occasionally found on that page. All advertising matter has, of course, been eliminated. An attempt has been made to classify all news items under such headings as will indicate their character, such, for example, as art, accident, blackmail, benevolence, catastrophe, club life, social functions, engineering, forgery, humanitarian, judicial, literary, matrimonial, military, murder, musical, religious, robbery, etc. Under 177 such headings, 13,330 news items were classified. These items include the markets, which are news items, although intended for a particular class of readers, and any study of the news items would be incomplete without them, but they do not figure in our final conclusions. This number, 13,330, does not include many short, unimportant items occupying less than an inch of space, nor does it include any items which regularly appear on the news pages generally read under set captions like matrimonial, died, maritime, weather, etc. . . .

. . . [T]he headings under which the items had been classified were arranged in four groups.* From this arrangement in groups the market items were eliminated, since they are the expected thing from day to day. So, of course, were the unclassified items eliminated. These omissions left a fairer basis for judgment. After these omissions were made, 173 headings, embracing 10,029 items, were grouped. In studying these headings, together with the character of the items under them, with a view of grouping them, one is constantly impressed that much of the matter is trivial, that much of it is really demoralizing, and that another portion of it, while not positively demoralizing, is nevertheless depressing and unwholesome. A considerable portion of it is, of course, worthwhile. So the groups we decided upon were the "Trivial," the "Unwholesome," the "Demoralizing," and the "Worth While." Under these four groups the case may be tabulated as follows:

Our effort has been to use these terms as they are used by intelligent people in ordinary parlance. By the "Trivial" is meant the light, inconsequential matter, such as is a loss of time for one to read if he has anything to do

*It is important to keep in mind that this article was written well before the concept of content analysis was known. The lack of methodological considerations, starting with the absence of a reference to the newspaper studied and especially the categories of analysis chosen here, speaks of the concerns at that time.

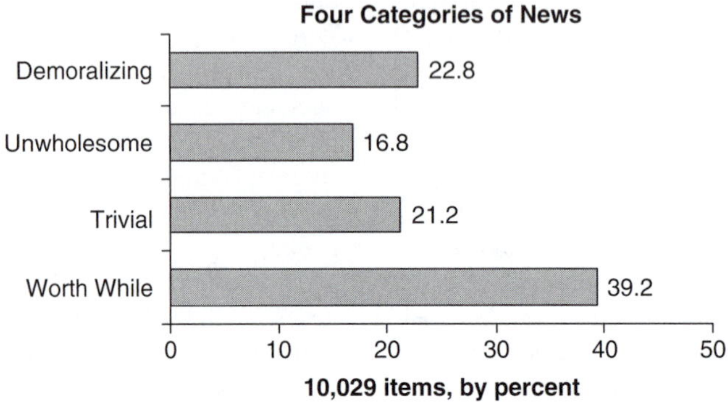

Figure 1

that is worth doing. It may not be harmful per se, it may not have enough meaning to have real influence, yet it may serve the purpose of entertainment for idle people of small brain caliber whose only function in life is existence. This trivial kind of news is illustrated by a caption that appeared on the front page of one of our morning dailies of a recent issue, "Alfonso Grows Whiskers." On the front page of the next issue, we were told that the "King Loses His Whiskers." These two items of tremendous significance to the American people were given prominent places on the front pages of two successive issues, where they occupied seven and one-half inches of space. We would not object so strenuously to the publication of such news if it could be segregated in a journal published especially for the idle and the feeble-minded, but it is very annoying to busy, serious men, who want and need a newspaper made up of matters that are worth while. According to our classification of the items under consideration 21.2 percent were of this trivial order.

We have called one group the "Unwholesome" and the other "Demoralizing." The word demoralizing is used to embrace all such items as when read will leave one's character not quite as clean as it was before reading. This influence on character of a single item or, of a half dozen items is imperceptible, but nevertheless real. Its reality is seen in the case of one who is a habitual reader of such literature, whether found in newspapers or printed in books. Many items do not have exactly the effect of soiling one's character, but rather of depressing his spirits. They tend to demoralize in the sense of throwing out of order, or putting into disorder, as we say a holiday demoralizes the work of a school. All such items were classed as "Unwholesome." The distinction we make is seen by illustration. To read about disasters and catastrophes is not necessarily demoralizing in the sense of injuring character, but it certainly is depressing and unwholesome, while to read of assaults and prizefights is positively demoralizing, even brutalizing. Likewise, to read about insanity and disease is depressing and so unwholesome, yet not demoralizing, while to read of wars and murder and suicides and divorce suits is demoralizing. According to our classification and grouping of the 10,029 items, 16.8 percent were unwholesome and 22.8 percent were demoralizing. It is a conservative estimate, therefore, that one-fifth of the items that appeared during the three months under consideration were positively demoralizing. In this estimate, we are eliminating the items of news of the stock and bond markets, which formed 15 percent of the whole 13,330 items. It is true that much of this 15 percent is legitimate and deserves a place, but it is just as true that much of it is harmful and ought to be cut out. . . .

If we had an endowed press and the function of the modern daily were truly and entirely educational, the unwholesome news even then could not be wholly eliminated, as that which is demoralizing could and ought to be. Much that is unwholesome ought to be eliminated. There is absolutely nothing gained, but much is lost in publishing the repulsive and nauseating details of railroad disasters and lynchings, of the horrors of cyclones and earthquakes. However, in this day of injustice, much that is depressing ought to be published, so that those who are living in comfort and plenty may know what their fellows in life are suffering because of wrong economic conditions. . . .

After we have deducted the trivial, the unwholesome and demoralizing from our 10,029 news items, we have a little more than 39 percent left, made up of that which is "worth while," clean, wholesome news freed from scandals, murder trials, suicides, divorce proceedings, and all other news for the publication of which there is never any excuse.

The character of the news contained in the 13,330 items considered can be seen in contrasts. For example, there were six items pertaining to the peace movement of the nations and 227 pertaining to war and military operations. There were 178 items devoted to benevolence and philanthropy, to making the other fellow comfortable, and 2,228 devoted to self-gratification in one form or another. While 129 were concerning art, 1,011 pictured the details of disasters and calamities. While 157 pertained to educational affairs, 1,683 presented some form of lawlessness. While 12 items pertained to ethical matters, 720 were given to matrimonial affairs, divorce and inane society life. The number of items devoted to business was 4,221 out of the total of 13,330. Of this same total 9,143 were devoted to business, lawlessness, personal gratification, horrors and disasters, while 827 pertained to art, science, travel, things literary, education, benevolence, philanthropy, natural phenomena and reform movements.

In these days, when scientific psychological research has demonstrated the power of suggestion from without over the functions of both the human body and of the human mind, it becomes a fearful responsibility for any man to determine to put before his tens of thousands of readers day after day, for three hundred and sixty-five days in the year, the unwholesome and demoralizing stuff that appears in most of our daily papers. The proprietors of these papers cannot excuse themselves on the ground of the freedom of the press. Neither reason nor national or State constitution gives any man freedom to do throughout all the days of the year that which is so obviously and positively harmful to the public. Neither can they excuse themselves on the ground that they are giving the public what the public wants, without at the same time confessing that their chief aim in life is pelf* even at the cost of public degradation. The character of the modern daily is simply one phase of the modern economic problem. It is one manifestation of the frenzy for wealth accumulation, which has become a menace to the permanency of American democracy. When or how this frenzy will terminate the future must disclose. It seems not unreasonable to hope that the still sober portion of the people will take some step toward raising the standards of our daily newspapers, all of them. . . .

*Pelf (slang): money.

1.4

The Scientific Analysis of the Press

Alvan A. Tenney*

The effectiveness of the various forms of government was long ago ascertained with some degree of accuracy. Within limits, one knows what to expect from a despot, a constitutional monarchy or a democracy. The public has learned also how to distinguish a Tweed from a reformer. The various forms of government and the various kinds of individuals who govern are recognized as types that function with some degree of regularity.

Analysis has to go back to the forms of government and the personalities of the individuals who govern. In those municipalities where ignorant and heterogeneous populations live, we expect the boss. In communities composed of an intelligent and alert body of citizens, whose desires are many but reasonably harmonious, we expect thorough discussion and efficient public action. There are known conditions that produce good government.

In similar general fashion, we know what conditions are necessary for the production of an intelligent body of citizens. Among these conditions are prosperity, schools and the means for public discussion. To discover the road to prosperity, economics is applying scientific method. To discover how to obtain the best schools educators are also applying scientific method.

To discover how to obtain the best means for public discussion, however, no thoroughgoing investigations have yet been made. What is actually known, for example, concerning the net stimulus to public opinion given by the 25,000 daily papers of this country? Practically nothing.

Most citizens are acquainted merely with the character of not more than one or two newspapers and half-dozen magazines. A few experts know in a general way the "policy" of possibly a hundred periodicals. Nobody, however, knows in exact terms even such a simple quantitative fact as the relative proportion of attention paid by the newspapers of the country as a whole to matters of cultural interest compared with the amount of attention paid to topics of a political or business nature. Even in the political field, no one can state just how much increased attention has been

*From Tenney, A. A. (1912). The scientific analysis of the press. *Independent 73:*895–898.

given by the press of the nation during the past few years to the subject of socialism. Yet it would be of practical value to know the facts. It would then be possible to investigate the truth of such a proposition as that the vote of the socialist party rises and falls in proportion to the degree of attention paid to socialism in the press. More important still would be the opportunity to prove whether increased attention to socialism by the press precedes an increased socialist vote or *vice versa.* As socialism in this country has thus far made its chief gains in particular municipalities, the possession of facts by which to show whether or not the same degree of press attention has uniformly preceded an increased socialist vote in those particular municipalities might throw some light on at least one of the possible factors producing change. It might be possible thus to advance the exact analysis of social causation to another step.

Similar exact knowledge concerning the relation of press attention to other matters, such as civic reform, legislation on finance, taxation, labor and business, the commission of particular forms of crime and other topics of public concern might also throw some light on the problem of social causation.

To anticipate fairly close correlations pointing to causal connections on such topics as have been mentioned is no more unreasonable than to expect definite results from advertising. Advertisers know from careful bookkeeping when, where and how advertising pays. By analyzing their effects, they learn both the best method and the exact cost of producing certain definite changes in the public mind. Advertisers thus obtain accurate knowledge of how to make people think what they desire them to think.

Why should not a society study its own methods of producing its various varieties of thinking by establishing an equally careful system of bookkeeping?

The first step in the investigation of such questions as have been suggested is to obtain data concerning the degree of attention paid by the press to the various topics it actually notices. Equipment for continuous analysis of the press of the entire country, or even for analysis of the material sent out by the chief news-supplying agencies each day, would require the continuous services of paid investigators. That an extended trial of such continuous analysis should be made, however, is perhaps a justifiable conclusion from the results of an experiment made by certain students of sociology in Columbia University last year.

The first part of this experiment consisted in measuring the number of linear column inches of space devoted on the average by various newspapers to each of the various classes of articles or items published. For example, it was ascertained concerning a prominent New York City daily that, out of a total of 16,572 column inches devoted to news in 13 issues, cultural topics occupied 2,194 linear column inches, economic matters 5,107 inches, political 5,514, other topics 3,757. The amount of space devoted to various subdivisions of these main classes was also ascertained.

By applying the same categories and method to several periodicals, material for a number of comparisons was obtained. The periodicals studied were 17 New York City daily newspapers. The choice of individual newspapers was made partly in accordance with the preferences of the volunteers who did the work of the classification and enumeration. Of the 17 New York City dailies, five were published in English, three in German, five in Italian and four in Yiddish. With the exception of a slight study of advertising in one Italian paper, attention was directed exclusively to the news—defined as everything printed except editorials, illustrations and advertising. Of the papers published in English, 13 issues each were examined, of the German, six, Italian, six, Yiddish, seven. The total news space measured was for papers in English, 98,497 inches, German 13,099, Italian, 14,218, Yiddish, 33,768. For purposes of comparison, the figures of gross space devoted to the various classes of news were reduced to percentages of the total news space. For example, the 2,194 inches of news space devoted to cultural topics in the 13 issues of the New York daily previously mentioned constituted 13% of the 16,572 inches of news in those issues; economic news occupied 31% and political 33%.

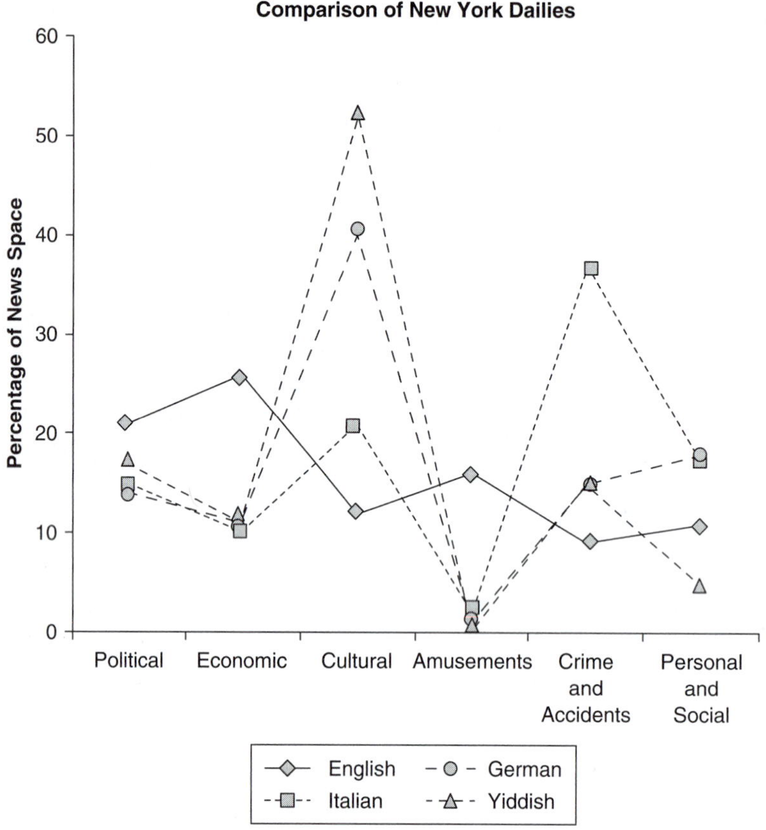

Figure 1 A Comparison of New York Dailies

NOTE: This figure shows the high rank of dailies printed in English in political and economic news, the low rank of non-English papers in these subjects, the extraordinarily high rank of German and Yiddish journals in cultural news and the high proportion of news of crime and accidents in the Italian journals. Of the 52% cultural news in Yiddish journals, however, 20 units were serial story; of the 41% cultural in German papers 12 units were serial story. The percentage of news of crime alone for the Italian journals was 37, of which less than six units were due to the Viterbo trial.

In Figure 1, such percentages are represented graphically for the news topics: Governmental, economic, cultural, amusements, crime and accidents, and personal, derived from the total figures for each topic in each class of journals studied.

The most striking facts reflected in this figure are the high rank of dailies published in English in political and economic news; the low rank of the non-English-language papers in these categories; the extraordinarily high rank of German and Yiddish dailies in cultural news; and the extremely high proportion of crime and accident news in the Italian dailies. It is true that there was considerable variation among the individual papers composing the various classes represented in the graph. Nevertheless, if each of the seventeen papers were to be represented by a separate line, even the extreme variations, with but few exceptions, would not in any category be found to remove any member of a class from the relative rank of the average of that class. This simply means that the individual papers did not vary so much from the average of their respective classes as to render the comparison of averages misleading.

The five papers printed in English were less alike than were the representatives of any other class. For these five papers, the variation from the highest percentage to the lowest was: for political news, from 33% to 16%;

economic, 32% to 16%; cultural, 23% to 12%; amusements, 26% to 8%; accidents and crime, 16% to 4%; personal, 14% to 7%. These variations, even though they do not invalidate the comparison of average rank, are nevertheless great enough to be significant.

Comparison of figures in more detailed news divisions than the six represented in the graph yielded some curious results. It so happens that, of the five New York dailies printed in English, the paper that published the maximum proportion of financial news had next to the minimum percentage of labor news, whereas the paper giving the minimum financial news, published, with one exception, the maximum of labor news. The paper publishing the maximum labor news was next to the lowest in financial news. It would be interesting to discover by further investigation whether this relationship of financial and labor news would hold true for a larger number of papers over a longer period, or is merely a somewhat peculiar coincidence. It would be desirable also to test further the somewhat unexpected result that the paper, in English, giving the maximum to sporting news was found well to the front in cultural news, and that it actually printed more than the proportion devoted to that topic by the paper paying the least proportionate attention to sports. These results throw doubt upon the truth of the popular idea that much attention to sports accompanies little attention to cultural topics.

For the Yiddish and German dailies the 52% and 41% cultural news shown in the figure comprehended the following percentages in subclasses: Serial story, 20% and 12%, respectively; education, 14% and 6%; anecdotes and verse, 2% and 11%; drama, 6% and .5%; music, 1% and 4½%; religion, 2% and 1%; letters, 2% and 0%; other cultural, 5% and 6%. In the Italian papers, the 21% of cultural news divided as follows: Serial story, 10%; science and education, 5%; art, 5%; philanthropy, 1%. These figures reflect the known interest of Hebrews in education and drama, the German's love of music and the Italians of art.* A further analysis of the type of serial story published by each class of journals would doubtless show the influence of further characteristic traits.

The category "crime and accidents" revealed the most startling facts of the whole investigation. For the Italian dailies, the figure was 38%. Of this, only one of the units was "accidents," leaving 37% as the average for crime alone. Of these 37 not more than six units were due to the Viterbo trial, and as far as known there was nothing else to render the 37% other than typical. This class of news in the various Italian papers of New York City ranged from a maximum of 45% of the entire news space to a minimum of 25%. Thirteen issues of a standard daily, published in Italy at about the same dates, showed only 8% "crime" news. The 37% of "crime" news was subdivided as follows: Trials, 16%; arrests, 4%; fights and brawls, 3½%; bomb and black hand, 3½%; murder and suicide, 3%; other crime, 7%. Such figures seem to sustain the opinion of a leading New York Italian, that "the Italian press of the city has no more constructive value than a band of brigands." In the advertising columns of a single issue of one of the Italian dailies there were 187 insertions of "physician's" cards. Of these 90 were Italian names, 97 non-Italian. In the same issue there were also 69 items advertising medicines.

The necessarily limited experiment which produced these results did not constitute an adequate test of the method. What is needed, as was earlier indicated, is the continuous analysis of a large number of journals. Data would then exist for discovering the exact relation, which may obtain between press attention and public action. The records in themselves would constitute a series of observations of the "social weather" comparable in accuracy to the statistics of the Unites States Weather Bureau.

There is, however, still another use to which the data could be applied that alone might justify an extended trial to discover whether the method here employed will prove valuable when analysis of a much

*It is important to remember that this article was published in 1912, before ethnic and gender stereotypes were questioned, studied, and challenged as they are today.

larger number of publications is attempted. If newspapers were compelled by law conspicuously to publish the weekly, monthly and yearly averages of the percentage of attention, which, upon continuous analysis of space, they found they were actually giving to various specified subjects, they might soon be advertising their relative rankings, in kinds of news published, as they now advertise circulation. This might lead eventually to more detailed comparisons involving discussion of the treatment, style and social value of the news as printed. Without raising the question of values, however, if the percentage of news attention to a definite set of subjects were continuously obtained a long step toward the scientific analysis of the press would be taken. At any rate, the *New York Times* could then inform us in exact terms what news, on the average, it really does consider "all that's fit to print," and the New York *Evening Post* could tell how nearly, in reality, it is utilizing its space in accordance with the ideals it professes.

1.5

Propaganda Analysis

A Case Study From World War II

Alexander L. George*

Background

For over a year prior to the launching of the V-1** in mid-June 1944, German leaders and propagandists had threatened reprisals with a new offensive weapon. The British High Command was sufficiently concerned to undertake extensive exploratory reconnaissance and bombing missions. Their concern was strengthened by intelligence reports, which confirmed the existence of secret-weapon factories. Aerial reconnaissance showed the construction of an unusual type of concrete installation in northern France pointed toward England.

The British Air Ministry was certain that the installations in Pas de Calais were launching-sites for a new type of weapon. "But the missiles were so long in coming," writes Gen. Walter Bedell Smith, Chief-of-Staff to Eisenhower during the war, "that some of our officers—highly placed, too—advanced the theory that the platforms were a gigantic hoax, constructed by the Nazis with great cunning to divert our bombers from vital targets" (Smith, 1956). The opposite point of view prevailed, however, and a certain weight of the Allied bombing offensive was directed to suspected factories and launching-sites of the secret weapons.

"The development and employment of these [secret] weapons," wrote Eisenhower, "were undoubtedly greatly delayed by our Spring [1944] bombing campaign against the places where we suspected they were under manufacture . . . [and] the suspected launching sites" (Eisenhower, 1948:259). A sober reminder of the consequences of an incorrect appraisal of the German secret weapons is contained in Eisenhower's further appraisal:

> It seemed likely that, if the German had succeeded in perfecting and using these weapons six months earlier than he did, our invasion in

*From George, A. L. (1959). *Propaganda analysis: A study of inferences made from Nazi propaganda in World War II.* Evanston, IL: Row, Peterson & Co. Excerpt represents pp. 140–150 from Chapter 11, "Prediction of an Elite's Actions."

**"V" for the German "Vergeltungswaffe," a rocket developed to retaliate for Allied mass bombings of German cities. V-1, a flying bomb, was later followed by V-2, a rocket.

> Europe would have proved exceedingly difficult, perhaps impossible. I feel sure that if he had succeeded in using these weapons over a six-month period, and particularly if he had made the Portsmouth-Southampton area one of his principal targets, Overlord [the cross-Channel invasion in 1944] might have been written off. (p. 260)

How good was Allied intelligence on the German secret weapons? "During this long period," reports Eisenhower,

> the calculations of the Intelligence agencies were necessarily based upon very meager information and as a consequence, they shifted from time to time in their estimates of German progress. Nevertheless, before we launched the invasion, Intelligence experts were able to give us remarkably accurate estimates of the existence, characteristics, and capabilities of the new German weapons. (p. 230)

What contribution did propaganda analysis make toward the correct assessment of German V-weapons? This question is difficult to answer. Many different types of intelligence activities contributed data for over-all assessments, but none of the accounts examined clearly distinguish the weight of each. On the other hand, it is possible today to note at least the accuracy of the propaganda-analysis reports, whatever their utility at the time. The British report, to be examined here, is without doubt one of the most skillful of the propaganda analyses undertaken during (World War II). The U.S. Federal Communications Commission's (FCC) analyses of this problem, on the other hand, were markedly less successful. A comparison of the two, therefore, serves to spotlight elements in procedure and analysis, which make for more or less successful inferences.

The British Report

A special propaganda analysis of German V-weapon propaganda was issued in early November 1943, by the British Political Warfare Executive. It listed a number of inferences about a German secret weapon drawn solely from analysis of German propaganda.

Inferences

The British analyst's systematic approach and his ability to identify the precise components of the inferential problem are impressive in themselves. Equally striking is the clear-cut manner in which degrees of plausibility are assigned to different inferences.

In close paraphrase, the report stated that:

1. It is beyond reasonable doubt that Germany possesses an offensive weapon, which her leaders believe:
   - (a) Is of a type unknown to the Allies.
   - (b) Cannot be countered within a short period.
   - (c) Will be used for the first time on a scale sufficient to produce very striking results.
   - (d) Will create in British cities havoc at least as great as that in German cities, and probably much greater.
   - (e) Will have a more shocking effect upon civilians than air-bombing on present scales.
2. It is further highly probable that
   - (f) By the end of May, preparations for the use of this weapon were past the experimental stage.
   - (g) Something occurred on or a little before August 19th, which substantially postponed D-day.
3. It is further probable that:
   - (h) Something occurred between the 3rd and about the 10th of September which further postponed D-day.
   - (i) The schedule for the offensive weapon has lagged in relation to that for a type or types of defensive weapon, and Germany's leaders now expect a diminution in the weight of Allied air attacks to precede German retaliation.
4. It may be tentatively estimated that Germany's leaders expect this offensive weapon to come into use *not before the middle of January, 1944, and not later than the middle of April.* There is unlikely to be an error of more than a month each way in the first of these estimated dates, but there might well be an error of two months either way in the latter.

The estimate for the earliest date of use is based partly upon estimates of the schedule existing in June, in early August, and in early September. If these estimates from propaganda can be confirmed by independent evidence, it would be possible to regard the final estimate (mid-January) with slightly less caution.

The estimated schedule at these earlier periods was:

In June:	Earliest use, mid-September
In early August:	Earliest use, beginning October
In early September:	Earliest use, beginning December

Reasoning and Verification of British Report

Many of these inferences, it turns out, were remarkably accurate and well reasoned.

(The British analyst's reasoning is reproduced here only in part.)

Inferences 1, *a–e,* appear to have accurately described the German leaders' estimate of their new weapon. Hitler was particularly gratified by the fact that the V-1 flying bombs did not depend upon radio beams for their aiming, a fact which made it technically impossible for Allied defense to deflect them from their course (Lochner, 1948:467).

That the Germans had some sort of new weapon, and were not merely bluffing, was firmly believed by the propaganda analyst. This inference rested upon the fundamental assumption, confirmed on many past occasions, that *German propaganda never deliberately misled the German people in questions involving an increase of German power.* (Excluded from this were relatively petty instances, such as figures of losses.) In view of this, the British analyst felt it necessary to accept at face value the repeated statement in German home propaganda that Germany was preparing, and expected to employ, a new weapon of reprisal.

A number of characteristics of the propaganda in question permitted insight into the nature of the new weapon. Thus, the British analyst noted that references to forthcoming "retaliation" by German propagandists seemed to be predicated on the idea that something new existed, that retaliation would not be carried out by normal air attack, and that German scientists, engineers, and constructors were playing a particularly important part.

Inference *f* cannot be verified, but *g* and *h* appear to be quite accurate. These two inferences rested upon an interpretation of the fact that propaganda references to reprisal weapons ceased abruptly for a period of time after August 19 and again after September 10. (A fuller account of this interpretation is given below.) To be sure, direct evidence that German propagandists were ordered to cease all references to the secret reprisal weapon for a while after August 19 and September 10 is lacking. But that such orders were given in response to events occurring approximately on or before these two dates, events which caused substantial postponements in the scheduled use of the V-weapon, seems to be a safe assumption in view of Hitler's remarks to Goebbels on the latter date to the effect that:

> Unfortunately the English raids on Peenemünde and on our OT work in the West [presumably the launching-sites for the new weapons in the Boulogne-Calais area] have thrown our preparations back four and even eight weeks, so that we can't possibly count on reprisals before the end of January. (Lochner, 1948:435–436)

The analyst's reasoning on behalf of inferences *g* and *h* is discussed below.

Inference *i* was based upon the observation that after August 19 German propagandists spoke of coming defensive measures against Allied air bombardment in such a manner as to suggest that these would precede the use of the secret weapon against England. (Prior to August 19 the development of new defensive countermeasures had *not* been mentioned in the same breath as preparations for retaliation.) These subtle shifts in propaganda, reasoned the analyst, could hardly be accounted for except on the premise that the relative schedules for defensive and offensive weapons had changed after August 19 in favor of the former. The hypothesis that the offensive weapon had been delayed was more plausible to the analyst than the hypothesis that the schedule for the defensive weapon had been speeded up. For, unless this were the case, there would have been no need for German propagandists to make, as they did, an excuse for not having the offensive weapon ready. Once again, direct verification of this inference is lacking, but new German antiaircraft defense measures, which proved to be effective against Allied night bombing raids, were applied in the early spring of 1944, several months before the use of the V-1.

Finally, the British analyst's tentative estimate, *made in early November, 1943,* that *at this time* German leaders expected to have the new offensive weapon ready for use sometime between mid-January and mid-April, 1944, proved to be amazingly accurate. For, on *September 22, 1943,* Hitler gave Goebbels his estimate that the V-weapon could be used by the end of January or the beginning of February; and in late November, 1943, Speer, Minister of Armaments and War Production, told Goebbels that reprisals could begin only in March.

The British analyst's remark that his second estimated date—i.e., mid-April, 1944—might be off by two months in either direction was the basis for Wallace Carroll's observation that the British propaganda analysts predicted D-day for the new weapon right on the nose—i.e., June 15 (Carroll, 1948:154). However, at the time of the British report (November 8, 1943), as is clear in the two entries in Goebbels Diary, German leaders expected to have the V-weapons ready at an earlier date, which was well within the narrower range of time predicted by the British analyst. In other words, the British estimate in November, 1943, was even better than Carroll's assessment implies. At the time of the report, events which would further delay the German timetable for V-weapons had not yet occurred. As British Air Marshals Sir Arthur Harris and Lord Tedder both note, in December, 1943, the launching-sites for the V-weapons were so effectively destroyed by Allied bombing that the Germans were forced to improvise new sites, inferior to the first (Harris, 1947:198; Tedder, 1948:95–96). In the estimate of Harris and Tedder, this delayed the V-weapons' timetable another six months.

The deduction concerning the German leaders' private estimate of the timing of the V-weapon was based upon ingenious use of a general observation about Nazi propaganda practice. The British analyst reasoned that Goebbels would be careful not to give the German public a promise of retaliation too far ahead of the date on which the promise could be fulfilled. For Goebbels had shown himself to be astute enough to realize that, if a promise of this sort were not made good within a reasonable time, the public would become disillusioned, skepticism and hostility toward German leaders and propaganda would set in, and Goebbels would have aggravated the very morale problem which his retaliation promises were designed to allay. Taking a number of factors into account, the British analyst reckoned that Goebbels would give himself about three months as the maximum period for which it would be safe to propagandize forthcoming retaliation in advance.

While this estimate cannot be checked directly today on the basis of available verification material, indirect evidence supporting it was available at the time and was cited in the British report. Goebbels' propaganda commitment on new reprisal weapons was launched in June, 1943; and by mid-August, some two and a half months later, local Nazi speakers were finding it necessary to deal with skeptics. By mid-September, public skepticism was a considerable problem; and in October, Nazi party speakers were devoting a large part of their time to reassuring doubters that retaliation would come, after all.

FCC Analyses

FCC analyses of the same German V-weapon propaganda have been examined in order to discern, if possible, why the results were of lower caliber than those made by the British analyst. Three major explanations for this divergence emerge.

1. The FCC analysts, in contrast to the British analyst, were reluctant to tackle the main inferential problems growing out of

German propaganda on retaliation and secret weapons. Assuming that other intelligence specialists with techniques more appropriate than propaganda analysis were at work on the problem, the FCC analysts stuck pretty closely to description of the content of German V-weapons propaganda. They ventured few inferences—and these cautiously and sporadically—on such crucial questions as whether secret weapons for reprisal actually existed, what the nature of such weapons was, how soon the Nazis expected to use them, against which targets, and with what expected effects.

Moreover, the FCC analysts worked on their own and were not asked to co-ordinate their analysis of German V-weapons propaganda with that of other intelligence specialists. This may be contrasted with the experience of the British analyst, whose report of November 8, 1943, was clearly in reply to a request, and who was taken into the confidence of his superiors and asked to match his inferences against information about the presumed significance of targets attacked by the R.A.F. at Peenemünde and by Allied aircraft in the Pas de Calais area. The FCC analyses, on the other hand, were made on a week-to-week basis; a systematic retrospective analysis of all preceding propaganda on this subject was not undertaken. It is obvious today that such a retrospective analysis, had it been made, would have sharpened the FCC analysts' insights and analytical procedures.

2. *The FCC analysts did not develop analytical techniques and hypotheses of sufficient refinement for this problem.* It is, or should be, a truism in propaganda analysis that the investigator is likely to develop more discriminating and fruitful analytical techniques only in the process of stating and attempting to assess alternative inferences when confronted with a concrete problem. As the following paragraphs will indicate, the reluctance of the FCC analysts to attempt inferences on the subject of German secret weapons kept them from making optimum use and needed refinements of the analytical equipment they brought to the task.

The fundamental proposition employed by the British analyst—that German propaganda never deliberately misled the German people in questions involving an increase of German power—was not unknown to the FCC analysts. Reluctant to make inferences about the V-weapons, however, the FCC analysts apparently overlooked the relevance of this proposition as a basis for evaluating Goebbels' propaganda commitment on retaliation by means of secret weapons.

Another deficiency of the FCC's procedure was its failure to make use of systematic, quantitative procedures in evaluating certain aspects of Nazi V-weapon propaganda. The British analyst, it may be noted, employed highly systematic procedures for a trend analysis of the occurrence and volume of such Nazi reprisal threats. The FCC analyst used only impressionistic methods.

It is because of this, no doubt, that the British analyst, but not the FCC, discovered several *time intervals in which reprisal propaganda dropped almost to the zero point.* Unknown to the public and to the propaganda analysts, the R.A.F. attack of August 17, 1943, upon Peenemünde had the German experimental secret-weapons station as its target. Similarly, Allied air raids of September 7–8 between Boulogne and Calais had as their secret target the installations suspected of being launching-platforms for new German weapons. The purpose of these two raids became known to the British analyst only later. He did notice, however, that references to retaliation suddenly dropped out of German propaganda for ten days, beginning August 19. Similarly, for a week after September 11 not a single item on retaliation appeared in German domestic propaganda.

Some time later, in preparing his report of November 8, the British analyst was apprised of the significance of the targets in these two raids. His problem, therefore, was to consider alternative explanations for the gaps he had noted in German reprisal propaganda and for possible shifts in the character of this propaganda following resumption of reprisal threats. For this purpose, he took into account and attempted to explain the following: (1) the *suddenness* with which the gap began; (2) any *change in the quality* of propaganda on retaliation and on the forthcoming new weapon *after the gap* in attention passed; (3) the *coincidence* of the beginning of the gap with events which might have been *connected with retaliation* and/or a new weapon; and (4) the *coincidence* of the gap with other events or with changes in the war situation which might be expected to cut off the flow of reprisal propaganda.

It was discovered that the gap beginning August 20, 1943, had been sudden, that it was followed by a watering-down of the propaganda commitment on reprisal (i.e., propaganda allusions now put the date of use of the V-weapons further into the future than they previously had), and that the gap in propaganda on the new reprisal weapon did not coincide with other events. (Other events, those not directly connected with German preparations of the reprisal weapon, might be, for example, Allied air raids on Germany, and German morale.) References to reprisal usually occurred either in propaganda diatribes against Allied air raids or in conjunction with propaganda efforts to salve the poor morale of the German public. Therefore, an absence of reprisal talk might be correlated with an absence of Allied air raids on Germany or an improvement in German morale. *Only when these possibilities were ruled out was it reasonable so deduce that not other events but some consideration directly connected with the retaliation weapon itself was responsible for the gap in reprisal propaganda.*

The necessary explanation, then, was that something must have happened just before August 20, which was connected with the preparation and schedule of the new reprisal weapon. (This, of course, confirmed the effectiveness of the Peenemünde raid.)

Another gap, beginning September 11, 1943, also fulfilled these criteria, but not so clearly. Therefore, the analyst inferred that it was only slightly less probable that something had occurred in early September, which further postponed the Nazi schedule for the use of the reprisal weapon. Thus, once again, confirmation was obtained of the effectiveness of the Allied air raids, this time of those on Boulogne and Calais.

The four considerations listed above were not articulated by the FCC analysts, an omission which followed from their failure to do a systematic time analysis of trends in reprisal propaganda.

The FCC analysts, however, were not insensitive to the possible significance of shifts in propaganda commitments as to the date of reprisal. They were aware . . . that shifts toward *increased ambiguity* in setting the time of reprisal meant that D-day for use of the new weapon, as estimated by the Nazi leaders, had been further deferred. This type of reasoning was essentially the same as that employed by the British analyst but was applied less systematically and less boldly. Thus, in late November, 1943, an FCC analyst noted that Goebbels' current reprisal threat remained "undated"; "in fact, the wording makes the prospect of realization seem less definite than in many previous announcements which have come from German leaders and, in particular, from Goebbels himself."

3. The FCC and British analysts both recognized the connection between reprisal propaganda and the German elite's preoccupation with internal morale. But only the British analyst explored this relationship to its logical conclusion and, thereby, formulated an assumption crucial for the high-grade inferences that he made.

The FCC noted as early as did the British that public disillusionment in Germany with Nazi propaganda promises of reprisal was beginning to set in. Increasing public skepticism on this issue was noted in subsequent FCC reports, but its significance in terms of Goebbels' astuteness as a propagandist was never squarely faced by the FCC. It was certainly not beyond the analytical proficiency of FCC analysts to note that Goebbels' propaganda promises (of reprisal by means of new weapons) must have been made in the expectation that they would be realized in time to save him from severe embarrassment. For Goebbels, of all Nazi leaders, was known by the FCC to be most cautious about making propaganda commitments to the German people which could not be fulfilled and which might, therefore, prejudice public attitudes toward their leaders.[1]

Given this appraisal of Goebbels, the FCC analysts too might have concluded that the propaganda commitment on reprisal would not have been made by Goebbels too soon before the date on which he expected reprisals to take place. And, accordingly, when the continued deferment of D-day for reprisals created increasingly difficult morale problems for the Nazi leadership, the inference should have followed that something had happened to delay the timetable for the reprisal weapon. The closest an FCC analyst came to making such inferences was in mid-November, 1943, when heavy Allied raids on Germany made retaliation even more urgent from a morale point of view. Taking note of the fact that Nazi propaganda promises of retaliation to the German public were continuing, the FCC analyst commented:

> The propaganda intent clearly appears to be to help tide German morale over its severest crisis. . . . In the interest of home morale, a realized threat would seem a matter of utmost urgency. . . . Delay may be attributable to unfinished technical preparations, or retaliation may be timed for a certain strategic moment, which has not arrived yet. But this much is certain; Nazi propagandists could hardly risk taking so many chances with an impatient domestic audience, were it not for cogent reasons. (FCC, 1943:A-10)

Had this general hypothesis been further refined, and, especially, had it been applied to the whole history of the V-weapons propaganda, the FCC would doubtlessly have approximated the findings of the British analyst more closely.

Note

1. Toward the end of the war, Goebbels departed from this otherwise invariable rule only to the extent of reluctantly permitting Party propagandists to use the idea of a miracle weapon in word of mouth propaganda. He made this concession in part because he felt that he, as official propagandist, would not be compromised by such irresponsible rumors, the official inspiration of which could not be traced: "No one will ever be able to reproach us for having circulated this rumor. No one will ever be able to nail us down for having made such a prediction, because we never did make it" (Riess, 1948:303).

References

Carroll, W. (1948). *Persuade or perish.* Boston: Houghton-Mifflin.

Eisenhower, D. D. (1948). *Crusade in Europe.* Garden City, NY: Doubleday.

FCC, Analysis Division, German Section: *Central European Analysis ("CEA") #45,* Nov. 19, 1943.

Harris, A. (1947). *Bomber offensive.* London: William Collins & Sons.

Lochner, L. P. (Ed.). (1948). *The Goebbels diaries, 1942–1943.* Garden City, NY: Doubleday.

Riess, C. (1948). *Joseph Goebbels.* Garden City, NY: Doubleday.

Smith, W. B. (1956). *Eisenhower's six great decisions.* New York: Longmans, Green & Co.

Tedder, A. W. (1948). *Air power in war.* London: Hodder & Stoughton.

1.6

Letters From Jenny

Gordon W. Allport*

Three Letters

Chicago, Illinois. 3/10/26

My dearest Glenn and Isabel:

There is a matter of considerable importance that worries me, and I earnestly desire you two children to discuss it with me, if you will be so very kind—and I feel sure that you will.

In order to make myself clear I must write you a series of letters. . . .

This is No. 1—Ross.

We were in New York—Ross roomed with an artist who had an apartment—I was in the cubby hold on 16th St. No heat, no window. Ross was out of employment. I was ill—dreadfully ill. I tried to work in fits and starts, my salary once so low as $14 a week, but I insisted on Ross' coming to my room often—2 or 3 times a week, and I cooked good porterhouse steaks for him, and bought him good cigars. I practically starved to do it. Weighed 96 pounds.

Then Ross found a position—he was quite delighted—it was such a good position with fine prospects, salary $50 a week. He offered to cover my rent—$25 a month, and I said it would be a great help. He paid 1 month ($25). The next month slipped by until the 15th. My rent was due on the first. Ross said he was "rather pressed for money" and could only spare $20. I was stung to the quick, but took it. The 3rd month he was again late, but he offered me $25. He called at my room when I was out, and left the money, with a note.

I sent it back to him—said he evidently needed it worse than I and that I refused to accept anything at all from so niggardly a giver.

I got no more—he offered none. Six months slipped by—Ross lost his position and was again out of employment. He had little or no money and I again filled in the gap insisting on setting good meals, cigars, etc. When his tooth showed signs of decay I gave

*From Allport, G. W. (1965). *Letters From Jenny.* New York: Harcourt. Excerpt represents pages 7–8, 20, 126–127, and Chapter Eight, 191–205. Allport's book is based on 301 letters from 1926 to 1937, nearly all of them to her son Ross's friend from college, Glenn, or Glenn's wife, Isabel. We have chosen three examples as a preface to Allport's use of content analysis as a psychoanalytic tool.

him $10. He failed to go to a Dentist, and believing he had used the money, I supplied another 10—I gave $30 for the Dentist, but he never had the tooth attended to. When he got that position in Brooklyn, he wanted to go out there to room and asked me for *the loan* of 10. I emptied my purse that evening as we sat on my bed together, gave him my entire savings—$30 and kept 2.50 for myself to carry me over until my next pay. At that time, I was receiving $18 a week.

It was in Brooklyn that he met the old maid with money who bought and married him. He never even mentioned money to me again. Never once offered to help me in any way.

I am a strongly intuitive person, am subject to impressions—beliefs—prejudices etc. not founded on any basis of reason.

It was my "feeling" for a long time that Ross was lying to me—when he said he could not come to see me because he was so very busy, I felt that he lied. When he spoke of his low salary, I felt that he lied. Yet I was ashamed: I never tried to prove, or disprove, anything. I thought "the boy is all right—every word he says is probably true—it is I who am mean, suspicious, and hateful—forget it," and so the time went by.

The day he was married he said he could not keep his appointment with me to put up a shelf I needed because he had to stay at the store and help take inventory. I knew he lied that day and was angry—I asked why should an efficiency man in a Dept. Store take inventory. He said it was mean of me to doubt him, and that all I had to do was telephone the 7th floor of the store and ask for him. He knows I would not do that. He ran his bluff—he just lied.

The last day I spent in New York before coming here, last September, I went to Jersey and saw the General Mgr. of the place where Ross had such splendid prospects. I wanted to know why Ross left, and what salary he had received. He left because they asked him to leave, his work was not satisfactory. He received *$75* a week for 6 mos. *$75*. Think of it! Ross was too "hard pressed" for money to spare $25 a month, and gave only 20 and even that for only 2 months. And he received over *three hundred dollars a month* for *six months.*

When at the store only a very short time he borrowed from the Co. $150.00 and said he was married and his wife had to undergo an operation. He finally repaid the loan. He actually had the nerve to take to the office a sporting woman and her illegitimate child whom he introduced as his wife. The men laughed behind Ross's back for the woman was stamped, as they all are, and they knew he lied.

Ross brought this same woman and her brat to my house on Sunday evening and I was angry and told him that if he ever brought any more prostitutes to my house I would have them both arrested. Anyone, short of a fool, would know what she was at one glance.

This is my first letter (I am all trembling) . . .

Au revoir,

Lady Masterson
N.Y.C. Sept. 2/26

My dearest:

I hope to be among the first to wish you happiness in your new home.

Such a lot of things have happened since you, Glenn dear, and Ross stood in the college office waiting to write on your exam. Tall, thin, pale boys, the world and life all before you—anxious, tense—a long time ago.

If anyone had said then the day would come when you, Glenn dear, the pale slim boy, would be the only protection of the other boy's mother, you would have been considerably surprised. And then meeting Isabel, and knowing Isabel, and your marriage, and your sweet little nest—it is all wonderful.

The last time I wrote I knew there was something special I wanted to say to you, Isabel dear, but could not, for the life of me, recall what it was, so I just babbled away about something else.

It's your hair. I really think you ought to bob your hair. For one thing, almost everyone, old and young, is bobbed now, and one looks peculiar with long hair; and another thing is it is less trouble. Of course, Mary Pickford is not bobbed, but pretty near everyone else it.

Best love,

J.G.M.
N.Y.C. Sunday Oct. 13/35

My dearest Boy:

. . . I have been around trying to hunt up some class, or lectures, for the winter. There are, of course, plenty, but they are all too expensive for me. Columbia charges $15 for the Winter Extension Course, or $1.50 for each single lecture, and when I found they have such lecturers on their program as Amelia Earhart, I pass them all up. The very sight of the woman is disagreeable to me. Then the Met. Museum charges $10 for 3 mos. and all their free lectures are by *women.* I don't like to see women on a platform—never saw one yet I would want to see again, and then their thin squeaky voices give me a pain. I always feel kind of ashamed when I see a woman stand up to speak. Last time I went to the Met, the woman speaker kept *laughing* all the time, and heaven only knows what she saw funny about it, for the subject was on tapestries and their making. Women are like that.

. . . I have now no hope of getting out of here, and so accept my fate in a stupid, stolid manner as one would if at the bottom of a well. This also applies to many of the half-witted stupid old women who hang around here for years and years—their minds (if they ever had any) have ceased to work, they have gone to seed.

. . . I am greatly interested in the war and read all the papers, altho' I don't suppose that any of the reports are reliable. I seems the whole world is mad—every line of life in every country is upset. I have now reached the point, like the old Quaker, twirling my thumbs, and nodding at you, say "Except me and thee"—thee will always stand out, and alone, to me. I would be lost without you—I often feel that I am the loneliest woman in the world, but I can never be that while I have you, and that will be "till all friendships die."

Often I do not speak one word for weeks at one time—it is hard to be alone.

Lady M.

Jenny's Traits

Some psychologists find fault with the depth approach, regarding it as elaborate, speculative, and largely un-verifiable. Better not manufacture for Jenny, they would say, an unconscious, which in fact she may not possess. . . .

If we say that Jenny's habits are the key to her nature the question arises, how shall we identify and classify these habits? What is the structural composition of her personality?

To answer this question with scientific precision is difficult—at the present time impossible. And yet, no approach to personality analysis is more direct, more commonsensical than this. Almost always we think about, and talk about, people in terms of their *traits,* which are nothing other than clusters of related habits. (Ordinarily we use the term *habit* to designate a limited and specific formation, such as Jenny's habit of taking long walks, or quoting poetry, or making trips to the sea. A *trait* is a family of habits, or a widely generalized habit-system, illustrated by Jenny's solitariness, aestheticism, love of nature.)

To start our analysis we asked thirty-six people to characterize Jenny in terms of her traits. They used a total of 198 trait names. Many of the terms, of course, turn out to be synonyms, or else clearly belong in clusters.

Loose as this approach is, we present a codification of the terms used, arranged in order of frequency of occurrences. Under each of the central trait designations are listed some of the equivalent or related terms employed.

1. Quarrelsome/Suspicious	**2. Self-Centered**	**3. Independent/Autonomous**
distrustful	selfish	self-reliant
paranoid	jealous	scrupulous
rebellious	possessive	hardworking
prejudiced	egocentric	frugal
bellicose	proud	courageous
opinionated	snobbish	persistent
tactless	martyr complex	stubborn
misogynous	self-pitying	reclusive
etc.	over-sacrificial	calculating
	etc.	solitary
		etc.

4. Dramatic/Intense	**5. Aesthetic/Artistic**	**6. Aggressive**
emotional	intuitive	ascendant
rigid	fastidious	indomitable
serious	literary	domineering
temperamental	cultured	self-assertive
vigorous	appreciative	autocratic
violent	expressive	forceful
voluble	poetic	recalcitrant
self-dramatizing	lover of nature	*etc.*
etc.	*etc.*	

7. Cynical/Morbid	**8. Sentimental**	**Unclassified** (13 terms out of 198)
pessimistic	retrospective	intelligent
sarcastic	loyal	predictable
disillusioned	affectionate	incestuous
humorless	dweller in the past	witty
despondent	maternal	whimsical
frustrated	*etc.*	*etc.*
insecure		
hypochondriacal		
fixation on death		
etc.		

Having employed this method of listing we note a few interesting results. (a) Nearly all judges perceive as most prominent in the structure of Jenny's personality the traits of suspiciousness, self-centeredness, autonomy; and the majority remark also her dramatic nature, her aestheticism, aggressiveness, morbidity, and sentimentality. (b) While there may be disagreement concerning the classification of any given trait name, the main clusters are not difficult to identify. (c) The reader, however, feels that these clusters are not independent of one another; they interlock; thus her sentimentality and her artistic nature seem somehow tied together, and her quarrelsomeness is locked with her aggressiveness. For this reason we cannot claim by the trait-name approach to have isolated separate radicals in her nature. (d) The few terms marked as "unclassified" seem to belong somewhere in the total picture, although our method does not readily absorb them. (e) While there is noteworthy agreement among judges there are occasional contradictions, such as witty/humorless, voluble/reclusive, self-pitying/courageous. But at this point, we accept Jung's assurance that every human being harbors opposites in his nature.

Let us return to the problem raised by item (c). Since the traits as listed manifestly overlap, is there some way of finding more inclusive themes? Surely, her personality is not an additive sum of eight or nine separate traits.

We asked the judges whether they perceived any one unifying theme that marks all, or almost all, of her behavior. We received such answers as the following:

> "Her life centers around the Jungian archetype of motherhood."
>
> "If one considers her possessiveness toward Ross to be the central object of Jenny's life, then almost all of her interests and behavior fall into place. In Ross's early years her life was completely unified around this goal. In later life, this unity is lost; Jenny then "falls to pieces."
>
> "I think the leading theme in her life is the need for self-vindication; everything seems to be constellated here."
>
> "Since her behavior is continuously self-defeating I see as central the need for self-punishment, due to repressed guilt."
>
> "While I cannot discover any single unifying theme, I would submit that *five* (not wholly separate) themes are dominant: extreme possessiveness of Ross, hatred of women, importance of money, aesthetic interests, preoccupation with death."

Such attempts to discover unity in Jenny's personality are suggestive though inconclusive. Just where the center of emphasis should fall we still cannot say. Yet the fact that there is clear overlap among these diagnoses leads us to conclude that there is definite structure (if only we could pin it down), and that this structure is dynamic, leading us toward a true explanation of her behavior.

A convinced depth analyst, of course, would say that this approach is too much "on the surface," too phenotypical. The root themes, the genotypes, lie completely buried—perhaps in the confusion of sex-identity or other early Oedipal conflict.

Whether we favor unconscious genotypes or whether we believe that her learned dispositions are themselves genotypical, we mark in either case an essential firmness in the structure of her personality. After reading the first few letters we find ourselves forecasting what will happen next. We predict that her friendship with (a woman named) Mrs. Graham will turn to sawdust, and so it does; "The more I know of Mrs. Graham the less I like her. . . ." At first Jenny likes (a woman named) Vivian Vold, but we know she will soon become just another "chip." The Home first appears bright to her; soon it becomes the "Prison." Her journeys to other cities start with hope but end in despair. The predictability of Jenny, as with any mortal, is the strongest argument for insisting that personality is a dependable hierarchy of sentiments and dispositions, possessed of enduring structure.

Take the evidence of her stylistic traits. Her handwriting is remarkably stable over time, even allowing for a slight unsteadiness with increasing age. Her prose is invariably direct, lively, urgent, and with a sharpness of metaphor. Whatever she says or does, she will do or say with vigor. While she is predictably affectionate toward Glenn and Isabel, we know that her chief interest is in her own needs and feelings. Any outsider who enters her monologue is on the distant periphery or else is doomed to be sucked into the vortex of her resentments.

Two Content Analyses

Thus far, our structural approach has been grounded in simple common sense. We have read the Letters, "understood" them, and formed an impression of Jenny's make-up. The procedure is essentially intuitive. The only check on our impressions is what other people report from their own intuitive reading. We incline to put more weight on interpretations given frequently by many readers, but we have no objective or quantitative standard to follow.

Stricter methodologists would ask, "Can we avoid such gross subjectivism? Is there not some way in which we can objectify and quantify the structure of Jenny's personality?" The answer is, Yes—by the method of *content analysis.*

Virtually all that we know of Jenny comes from her own pen. As published here the Letters contain 46,652 words. From these discrete semantic units content analysis would seek to reconstruct a more pointed, better organized, and, therefore, more meaningful account of the structure of her personality.

There are various ways in which content analysis can proceed. On the simplest level we might count the separate mentions of Ross, or of money, or art, and from such a simple tally infer the relative prominence of different topics in her thought life (as revealed in the Letters). But we need not stop with such a simple count of subject matter (nouns); we can count also the expressions of favor or disfavor, or of other feelings in relation to subject matter. Such a further step is sometimes called "value" or "thematic" analysis (Baldwin, 1942).

Two rather ambitious content studies have already employed Jenny's Letters.

Personal Structure Analysis

Using the whole unabridged series of Letters, Alfred Baldwin set himself the task of studying the organization of the flow of Jenny's ideas (White, 1951). For example, when she spoke of Ross, how frequently was he mentioned in a context of money, of art, of women, of favor, of disfavor? When she spoke of money how frequently was this topic associated with Ross, with health, with jobs, with death?

The method selects, somewhat arbitrarily, prominent topics and themes and plots the frequency of their coexistence in the same context of thought. Also, it connects these topics with basic attitudes and value judgments made by her. Since Jenny was careful in her paragraphing, a single unit of thought was often a paragraph from a letter, although in some cases the unit might be longer or shorter. Statistically Baldwin used a variation of the Chi-square test to determine the significance of each association.

The accompanying diagram represents the principal clusters (co-occurrences) of ideas and feelings that emerge by this method of analysis. The diagram is based on the unabridged series of letters, but only from their beginning until November 2, 1927.

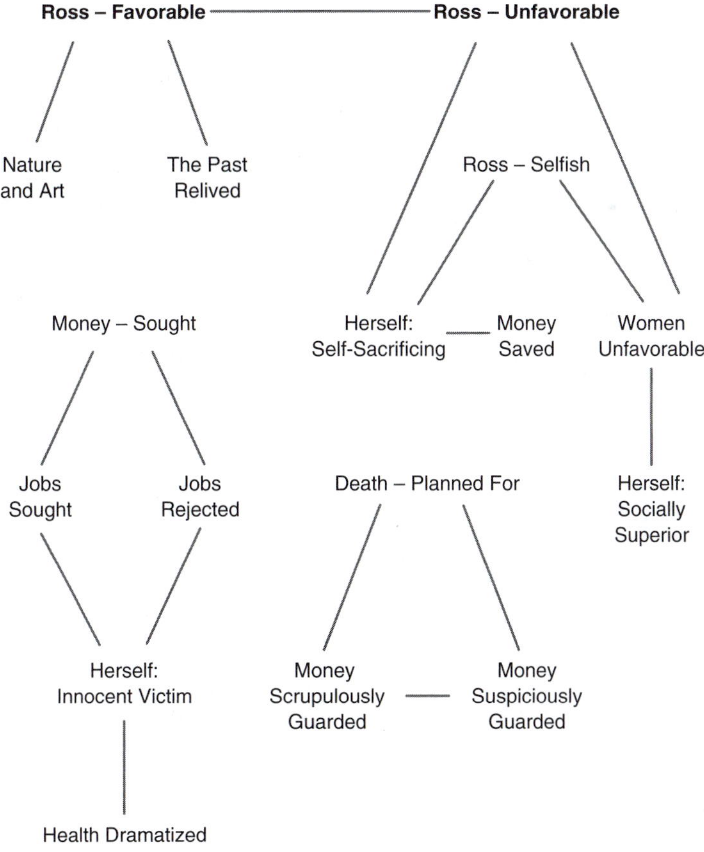

Figure 1

The reader can judge whether this rather laborious mode of classifying ideational clusters adds anything new to the interpretations reached through a common-sense reading of the material. Perhaps the frequency with which she mentions money may come as a surprise, especially the fact that money enters into all three major contexts of her discourse. It is related to her ideas of self-sacrifice which fall into the ROSS-UNFAVORABLE cluster; also to her search for jobs and concern for health; finally to the context of her death. Interesting is the fact that these three major topics of concern are not themselves tied closely together.

The analysis in the diagram does not cover the entire series of letters. Had it done so we might find the patterns change. For example, mentions of art and nature would no longer be tied almost completely to ROSS-FAVORABLE, but might well form a self-sufficient cluster of values.

For our present purposes it is sufficient to present this brief account of Baldwin's method to show that quantification of the *V* structure of a single personality is possible by means of statistical aids applied to content analysis.

Computer Aided Content Analysis

Some years after Baldwin's study was published advances in computer techniques invited a more elaborate analysis of Jenny's personality. Instead of using relatively few categories for coding and cross-tallying, it became possible to work on a wider base, using more categories and making more complex calculations.

In both methods, the first step is similar. The content of her letters must be coded; that is, what she says must be classified into categories. At this stage, there is always subjective judgment involved on the part of the analyst, who must decide what basic categories to employ. Jenny's vocabulary is large; she uses many different words to express the same essential idea. A loose woman may be a "chip," a "prostitute," a "sex-starved old maid," or some other type of wanton.* What we need then is a lexicon of "basic English" to which her rich discourse may be reduced.

Jeffrey Paige (1964) had at hand such a lexicon in a dictionary of concepts relevant to social science, developed for use by the General Inquirer computer system (Stone, Bales, Namenwirth, & Ogilvie, 1962).

This dictionary contains approximately 3000 entries, which form the initial basis for a coding system. The Letters are first translated into this lexicon, and then can be recast into a smaller number of "tag" words. To give an example, the many terms Jenny uses to express aggression, hostility, opposition, are finally coded together under the tag ATTACK.

The method allows not only for a wide base of categories, but also permits the coder to indicate when each tag word represents the subject, verb, or object in a sentence. When the material has been appropriately punched on cards and tagged by the computer, a great variety of retrieval operations becomes possible. The program will print out all sentences bearing upon the question the investigator has in mind. For example, if the query concerns Jenny's retentiveness of money and possessions, the analyst might ask for the co-occurrence of SELF, POSSESS, and ECONOMIC. In order to avoid retrieving irrelevant sentences, the analyst specifies that only the sentences in which SELF is subject, POSSESS is verb, and ECONOMIC is object are sought. In this way, an accurate count of the frequency of this particular ideational structure is obtained.

The General Inquirer and associated statistical procedures permit coding, retrieval, correlations, and computations. With this automated assistance Paige reaches certain conclusions regarding Jenny's personality structure.

For example, the frequency with which various tag words in a given letter are associated with all others in the same letter forms a basis for factor analysis. The first 56 letters—up to the death of Ross—are employed for this purpose, since they are on the average longer than the later letters. By this statistical method, Paige extracts eight factors, which he considers to be Jenny's "most prominent traits." They are listed here in decreasing order of frequency.

*See reading 5.2, this volume, on dictionary building.

Table 1

Trait	*Mode of Expression*
Aggression	Deprecatory invective, especially directed at Ross and women; anger; arguments with Ross. Indirectly expressed in travel and job hunting.
Possessiveness	A combination of nurturant and retentive needs; expressed in Jenny's joy in caring for children, including Ross when he was younger, and in her later attempts to bind her son to her by legal and financial means.
Need for Affiliation	Expressed directly by telling Glenn and Isabel how much they are depended upon, by praising them and their home, by writing of the joy she takes in their friendship. Indirectly expressed by exaggerated descriptions of her distress, intended (probably unconsciously) to invoke sympathy.
Need for Autonomy	Optimism and happiness in being able to support herself despite poverty and lack of skills. Pride in ability to find work and perform hard jobs. Frustrated by supervision, especially during the period of the nursery.
Need for Familial Acceptance	Attempts to return to Canada and be reconciled with Betty, to visit and live with her. Indirectly expressed by associating family values with herself and Ross.
Sexuality	Jenny's romantic descriptions of her relationship with her son; rides by moonlight, trips to the country; indirectly by her vicarious sharing (by identification with Isabel) in the affection of Glenn's family.
Sentience	Jenny's love of art, literature, and natural beauty. Also expressed by her need to be dependent on Glenn and Isabel.
Martyrdom	The nobility of Jenny's sacrifices for others, particularly for Ross. Also expressed by complaints that her sacrifices are unappreciated and bring her only grief and descriptions of the burdens she must bear.

Although the list of traits derived from factor analysis is not identical with our earlier list (of traits), there is much overlap and similarity.

With three exceptions, the parallel is close. It seems likely that the use of tag words binds the factorial method more closely to actual situations; whereas the intuitive reader perceives stylistic and expressive dispositions more readily and thus selects the *cynical-morbid* and *dramatic-intense* traits in her nature.

It would be wrong, however, to assume that the computer method cannot deal with stylistic variables. A special code permits the retrieval of words tagged by OVERSTATE (such words as *always, never, impossible,* etc.). Words tagged UNDERSTATE indicate reserve, caution, qualification. Jenny's Letters throughout the series score much higher on OVERSTATE than on UNDERSTATE. Thus, we find the common-sense diagnosis of "dramatic-intense" is confirmed (and quantified) by automated content analysis.

Besides aiding in the search for central structural units, the method turns up several additional insights, some new, some old.

It confirms our impression that Jenny's feelings about her own sex are consistently negative (except toward Isabel). Women are associated with the tag words DISTRESS and BAD, almost never with PLEASURE or GOOD. They score high on DEVIATION, meaning that they violate culturally accepted standards; and they score zero on FOLLOW, meaning that Jenny never respects them nor becomes submissive toward them. Her statements about women score especially high on OVERSTATE.

Her attitudes toward men are generally less unfavorable. Her score for AVOID is high (except for Glenn), but there are some

Table 2

Factorial Traits	*Common-Sense Traits*
aggression	quarrelsome-suspicious aggressive
possessiveness	self-centered
need for affiliation need for family acceptance	sentimental
need for autonomy	independent-autonomous
sentience	aesthetic-artistic
martyrdom	self-centered
sexuality	(no parallel)
(no parallel)	cynical-morbid
(no parallel)	dramatic-intense

associations with GOOD, AFFECTION, and PLEASURE—a pattern virtually nonexistent for women. A close analysis shows that Jenny expresses more affection for Glenn than for Isabel, and makes more requests of him for advice and help. She tends to share her experiences with Isabel but her worries and dependency needs with Glenn. Both, of course, are idealized, seldom spoken of in any but glowing terms. Because she rarely sees them in person, she is better able to maintain her conception of their respective roles. Even granted the conventions of correspondence it is still noteworthy that Jenny tends to see people in unrealistic extremes—Glenn and Isabel as all good, others as all bad. And we recall that the same extremism marked her attitudes toward Ross. Evaluative tags of BAD are more frequent than tags of GOOD, but she does occasionally express love for Ross, and once declares that he is a "first-rate neighbor." But among the statements tagged GOOD we find several that are sarcastic—"I have truly a noble son, an honor to his college, his friends, his family." (Let us note that the computer is not able to identify sarcasm.)

Jenny was surely not a discriminating judge of character. It is interesting to compare her personal qualities with those of a "poor judge of character" emerging from the research of Cottrell and Dymond (1949:355–359). These investigators conclude that a poor judge is rigid, introverted, lacking self-insight, inhibited emotionally, subject to emotional outbursts. The research discovered further that poor judges "experienced difficulty in interpersonal relations, mistrusted others, were less well integrated, and had had unsatisfactory family relationships in childhood." For the most part Jenny fits this picture.

Confirming our impression that Jenny is given to self-pity we note (by the method of retrieval) that in 289 sentences she refers to herself in distressing situations of one sort or another. Her preoccupation with death is indicated over and over again, more often than a casual reading of the Letters might suggest.

Every reader notes the aesthetic sensitivity in her nature. By computer count there are 114 sentences dealing with PLEASURE or AFFECTION in relation to objects of art, nature, and literature. "I love the sunset over the Jersey hills." "I find real pleasure in our old time books." "One day a customer brought in a lovely nude picture to be framed": Now this region of her life seems to be free from conflict. Even when Ross enters the aesthetic sphere all her associations are favorable. Therefore, we discover here a point of considerable importance for our structural analysis. This sentient trait in Jenny's nature has considerable dynamic force, and for the most part it is segregated from the major aspects of her existence. Thus, the computer helps us to discover that her aestheticism is a prominent secondary disposition, relatively independent of the central or cardinal (trouble giving) trends in her nature.

Suppose we now ask the computer to examine the allegation of depth psychology that guilt is an important factor. It does so by retrieving sentences involving SELF, BAD, DEVIATION, GUILT. It turns out that virtually none of Jenny's statements seems to be self-deprecations. She does admit that "mothers certainly are a nuisance when they are old, and had not sense enough when young to remember that they would not always be young." Also she states that "I was ashamed, ashamed to have doubted him [Mr. Barter]." But for the most part the retrievals are extropunitive in character: "I always feel kind of ashamed when I see a woman stand up to speak"; or to Betty,

"I have always been labeled the lawless one, the family disgrace, the black sheep who married a divorced man." From this exercise in retrieval we must conclude that Jenny consciously feels little guilt; hence if guilt is a major psychodynamic force in her behavior it must be of the unconscious and repressed order.

Automated content analysis confirms our impression of change in her personality toward the end of her life. More and more she concentrates on herself and her isolation. Memories of Ross seem to fade, especially after she casts his ashes into the sea and burns his photographs. To find support she increasingly, but vainly, turns to her aesthetic values. Her dislike of authority becomes more and more intense. She openly insults the superintendent and battles physically with nurses and inmates. Her fury is so great that the Home feels that she must soon be committed to an institution for the insane.

Summary

Content analysis (whether by hand or computer) provides no golden key to the riddle of Jenny. It does, however, objectify, quantify, and to some extent purify common-sense impressions. By holding us close to the data (Jenny's own words) it warns us not to let some pet insight run away with the evidence. And it brings to our attention occasional fresh revelations beyond unaided common sense. In short, by bringing Jenny's phenomenological world to focus it enables us to make safer first-order inferences concerning the structure of personality that underlies her existential experience.

It is well to remember, as Berelson (1954) says, that content analysis (whatever form it takes) deals primarily with the "manifest content of communication." It does not directly reveal structure in depth, unless this structure does in fact correspond to the traits we identify by first-order inference—a possibility that the present study tends to affirm.

References

Baldwin, A. L. (1942). Personal structure analysis: A statistical method for investigating the single personality. *Journal of Abnormal and Social Psychology 37:*163–183.

Berelson, B. (1954). Content analysis. In G. Lindzey (Ed.), *Handbook of social psychology* (Vol. 1). Reading, MA: Addison-Wesley.

Cottrell, L. A., & Dymond, R. F. (1949). The emphatic response: A neglected field for research. *Psychiatry 92:*355–359.

Paige, J. M. (1964). *Automated content analysis of "Letters from Jenny."* Unpublished thesis, Harvard University: Library of Social Relations.

Stone, P. J., Bales, R. F., Namenwirth, J. Z., & Ogilvie, D. M. (1962). The General Inquirer: A computer system for content analysis and retrieval based on the sentence as a unit of information. *Behavioral Science 7:*1–15.

White, R. K. (1951). *Value analysis: The nature and use of its methods.* Glen Gardner, NJ: Libertarian Press.

1.7

Impressionistic Content Analysis

Word Counting in Popular Media

Mary Angela Bock

As text in electronic form is more readily available and optical character reading and textual analysis software have become cheaper and more accessible, so too have word counts in popular media. These counts make no scientific claims or inferences; instead, they offer their readers the possibility of unconstrained interpretations, based solely on the assumption that word frequencies mean something.

In 2005, Amazon.com added a concordance to the "Inside the Book" portion of its Web sites, alongside other textual analysis features such as a readability index,* a citation index, and a "words to the dollar" index. Senior Product Manager Brian Williams hopes that shoppers might find it fun and return to the site. The concordance simply lists the top hundred most frequent words in a book, using larger fonts to represent the higher frequencies. Simple as it is, says Williams, "People love the concordance."

Typically, he says, customers like to look at the concordance for books they've read before because it's fun to try to guess what will show up. For instance, in our examples, it's no surprise that "*dream*" shows up in a big way on the concordance for Freud's *Interpretation of Dreams.* Freud was a writer with a rich vocabulary and, as can be seen in the concordance for his book, used its words almost uniformly. But look at the concordance for *War and Peace* by Tolstoy: The word *war* is quite small by comparison, and *peace* doesn't show up at all. Readers with political interests might find interesting differences between the concordances of the memoirs of two very unlike former U.S. presidents: Richard Nixon and Bill Clinton.

Time magazine published a similar graphic in 2007 following the television appearance of society diva Paris Hilton, who had just been released from prison. The Web page version is interactive: Users could pass their mouse over a word to find the exact frequencies of words from her interview on CNN with Larry King. Each word turned red as a callout displayed the frequency: "285" for *I,* "4" for *scary,* and "16" for *jail.* This simple word count of her interview on CNN with Larry King made it appear that Hilton is remarkably self-centered—though, in

*See reading 3.9, this volume.

Freud's *Interpretation of Dreams*

already analysis another between cannot case certain child childhood children come connection content course day does dream dreamer during elements even example experience explanation expression fact father find first following found friend give however ideas impression interpretation itself know life little long man material may meaning means memory might mother must myself new night now occur often once order own part patient person place point possible process psychic quite relation second see seems sexual shall should show since sleep something state still system take therefore though thought thus time two unconscious upon waking whom whose wish without words work years

Tolstoy's *War & Peace*

again always andrey another army asked away came come count countess day denisov down emperor even everything eyes face father feeling felt first french general go going good great hand head heard himself horse house know kutuzov left let life little long look looked looking love man marya men moment moscow must napoleon natasha new nikolay nothing now officer old once own people pierre prince princess put right room rostov round russian saw say see seemed side smile soldiers something sonya still take tell thing though thought time told took tsar two voice war went whole without words yes young

Clinton's *My Life*

again against america american arkansas asked big bill bush called came campaign come congress country day democrats done down economic election end even family few first friends gave get go going good got government governor help hillary home house including job knew know last later law leaders left life little long lot man months mother national new next night now office old peace people percent political president problems republicans right school see senator several should since state still support tax things though thought three time told took two united vote wanted war washington week went white work world years young

Nixon's *Memoirs*

against agreement american asked called came campaign case come committee communist country day dean decided decision down during eisenhower election end even fact felt few first get go going government great haldeman house however issue johnson kissinger knew know later long man may meeting might mitchell must new next night north now office own party pat people point policy political president press problem public put question republican right say see should south soviet speech staff states still support take talk thing think thought time told two united vietnam vietnamese want wanted war washington watergate weeks went whether white world years

Figure 1 Amazon.com's Concordances of Four Books

fairness, she was being interviewed about her own experience and could hardly avoid frequent use of the first-person pronoun *I*.

The *New York Times* occasionally has included word counts for material such as commencement speeches, ads on the popular Internet bulletin board Craig's List, and presidential State of the Union addresses. In 2007, the *Times* offered the feature interactively for its online readers, allowing them to explore the way words ebbed and flowed in the State of the Union addresses by George W. Bush. The seven State of the Union addresses Bush had delivered to date* averaged about 5,000 words each, about 34,000 words in all. Some words have appeared frequently, others sporadically, and their patterns of use make for interesting conjecture.

Figure 3 presents not only the distribution of a selected word in his speeches, indicating where, in which paragraphs, that word occurred, but also simple word frequencies of several selected words. The *Times* thereby not only provided examples of word frequencies

*As the *Times* points out, in 2001, Mr. Bush was a newly elected president and did not deliver a formal State of the Union address. His speech to a joint session of Congress on February 27, 2001, is used for purposes of the word-counting feature because it served essentially the same political function.

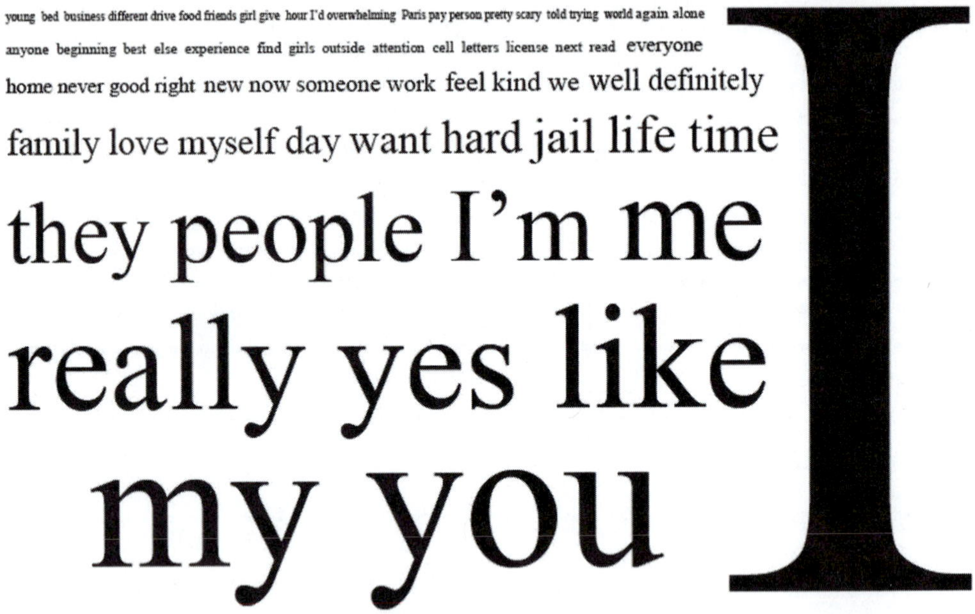

young bed business different drive food friends girl give hour I'd overwhelming Paris pay person pretty scary told trying world again alone
anyone beginning best else experience find girls outside attention cell letters license next read everyone
home never good right new now someone work feel kind we well definitely
family love myself day want hard jail life time
they people I'm me
really yes like
my you
I

Figure 2 This graphic was created by Fielding Cage for Time.com. Some common words, including pronouns, were excluded from the graphic, which was interactive when viewed on an Internet browser. When users moused their cursor over a particular word, its actual count was displayed. For instance, a callout display of "48" appeared when the mouse passed over the word *like.*

and location but also put a rather sophisticated text analysis software in the hands of anyone with access to the Internet.

In contrast to Amazon's static presentation of concordances, the creator of the *Times* word counter, Ben Werschkul, added an interactive feature which allows users to suggest words to search (personal communication, March 6, 2007). We entered the word THEY—the pronoun used to refer to others* not *I,* not *us.* The *Times* interactive feature shows us graphically that word in the context of Bush's speeches and quotes the context of its first occurrence. In 2001, THEY were the critics of his educational initiatives. In 2007, the THEY was dominated by terrorists. With that in mind, we typed two more words into the *Times* Web site—EDUCATION and ENEMY—and found, as can be seen in Figure 3, them inversely related (negatively correlated) over time.

Useful claims in content analysis require contextual understanding, formal analytical constructs, appropriate sampling, and the possibility of testing validity. Simple word counts may not be scientifically useful, but they can be suggestive, surprising, and fun.

*For a motivation of this choice, see reading 7.7, this volume.

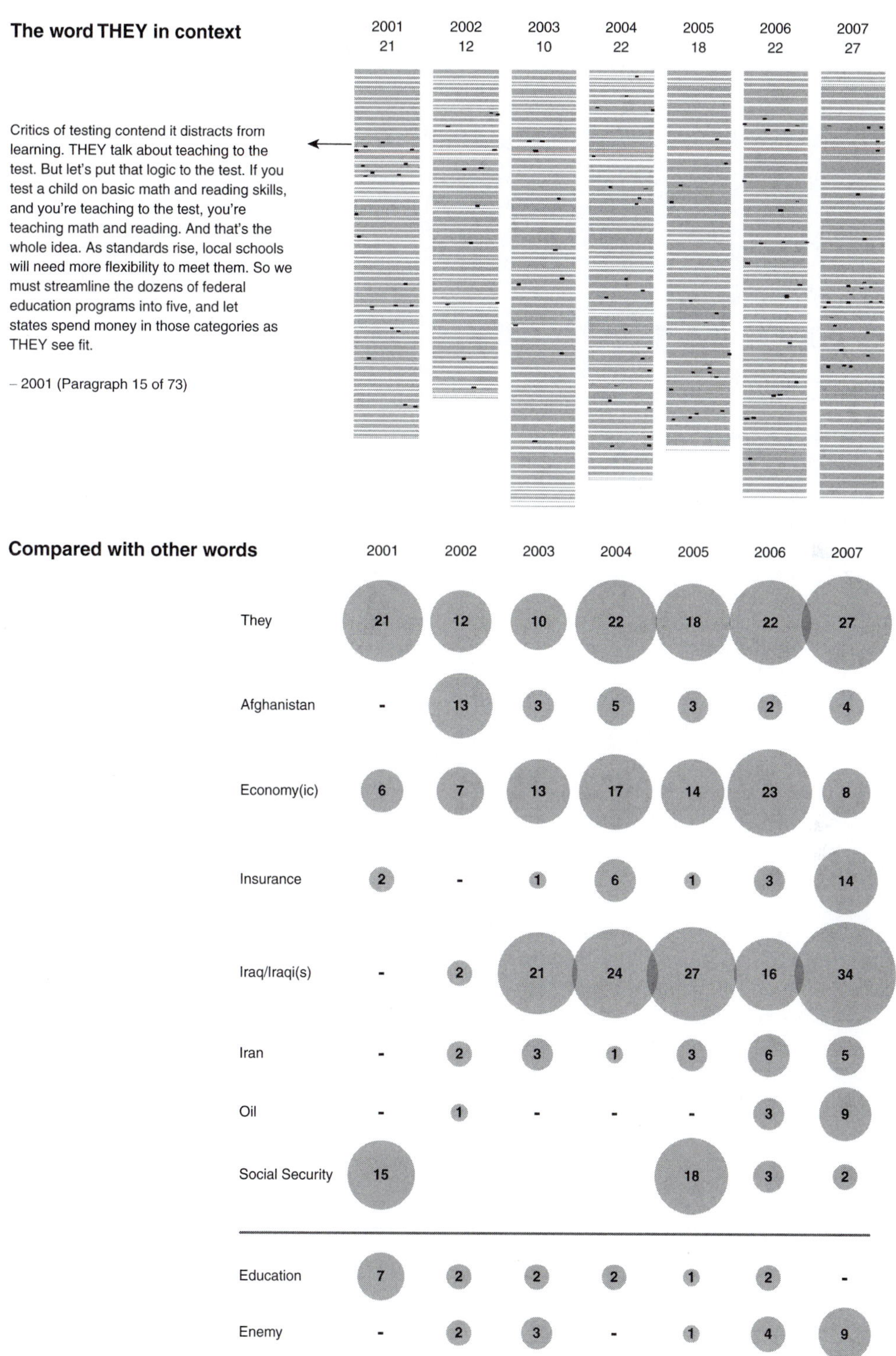
The word THEY in context
2001 21
2002 12
2003 10
2004 22
2005 18
2006 22
2007 27
Critics of testing contend it distracts from learning. THEY talk about teaching to the test. But let's put that logic to the test. If you test a child on basic math and reading skills, and you're teaching to the test, you're teaching math and reading. And that's the whole idea. As standards rise, local schools will need more flexibility to meet them. So we must streamline the dozens of federal education programs into five, and let states spend money in those categories as THEY see fit.
– 2001 (Paragraph 15 of 73)
Compared with other words
2001 2002 2003 2004 2005 2006 2007
They 21 12 10 22 18 22 27
Afghanistan - 13 3 5 3 2 4
Economy(ic) 6 7 13 17 14 23 8
Insurance 2 - 1 6 1 3 14
Iraq/Iraqi(s) - 2 21 24 27 16 34
Iran - 2 3 1 3 6 5
Oil - 1 - - - 3 9
Social Security 15 18 3 2
Education 7 2 2 2 1 2 -
Enemy - 2 3 - 1 4 9

Figure 3 *New York Times*' Account of Word Frequencies and Locations in Texts

PART 2

UNITIZING AND SAMPLING

Quantitative assertions presuppose units of enumeration. Even qualitative content analysts who avoid counting and measuring, they cannot bypass issues of unitization—for example, when sampling textual matter for inclusion in a study, selecting relevant features of text for attention, or coding and sorting pieces of text into interpretable categories.

Statistical sampling theory offers systems for selecting the very units on which generalizations about them are tested. In content analysis, however, sampling is rarely as simple. For example, when one wants to draw inferences about populations of people, events, or happenings, samples need to be representative of these populations, not of the texts that lead to such inferences—unless there is a one-to-one correspondence between textual units and the phenomenon of interest. Moreover, institutions tend to systematically presample the texts they generate or keep and, in the case of the mass media, disseminate to their audiences. Consequently, content analysts who wish to use available texts as data need to know and undo their statistical biases.

We start this section with an article by Harold Garfinkel, who looked into the recordkeeping practices of a mental health hospital. He and his colleagues found its patient records to be incomplete and hard to comprehend by outsiders; nothing like what the term *record* leads one to expect. However, Garfinkel found good institutional and sociological reasons for a hospital to create records that satisfy internal demands but are far from being consistent, complete, and statistically representative of patients and their treatments—echoing Dibble's analysis of historical texts as "social bookkeeping."* His observations point to the importance of context, the institutional position of the recorders, and the value attached to particular data. Content analysts cannot sample the texts created by institutions without understanding their institutional roles.

Rather than simply applying the assumptions of sampling theory Daniel Riffe and colleagues report the results of sampling experiments conducted to determine useful sample sizes and constructed weeks of newspapers for analysis. Sampling periodicals is a special problem—periodicals show periodicity, seasonal variations, and uneven distributions of relevant content that sampling must acknowledge. Random sampling, which does not specifically acknowledge periodicities, turns out to require larger sample sizes than constructed weeks in order to achieve the same significance. While their findings might not be generalizable to all media, this article should encourage content analysts to experiment with media-specific sampling methods, especially where the statistical significance of inferences becomes an issue.

The Internet, of course, is of great interest to contemporary media researchers. Yet, unlike printed matter or material recorded on tape, Web sites never "stand still." The sheer number of pages available on the Internet, with their rapid turnover and changes, creates a challenge for

*See reading 3.2, this volume.

content analysts who need to sample in order not to be overwhelmed with what is available. In her article, Sally McMillan examines various approaches that have been used to contend with Web pages as analyzable text.

Sociologist David Phillips's article uses straightforward correlations to prove a rather chilling point: that news coverage of suicides of well-known people is followed by dramatic increases in multifatality plane crashes. We have included it here because of the care with which Phillips selected airplane fatality statistics in the area of newspaper coverage of suicides, drawing on a wealth of previous findings regarding other suicides recorded as accidents. Here, sampling closely followed his hypotheses.

Besides the importance of *sampling units,* units in content analysis serve other purposes as well. We distinguish between *recording units,* the units actually described or coded, and *context units,* the units from which information about recording units is allowed to enter their description. The use of context units acknowledges the fact that textual units are rarely ever entirely independent of each other. Indeed, by themselves, words may have many meanings, but in the context of coherent narratives, they usually are unambiguous. Coding units of text without considering their context inadvertently discards valuable information, and simple word counts offer only the roughest picture of a text.*

Robert Bales's work is a good example of how this problem has been addressed. Bales was famous for his studies of small groups. He recorded group processes in fixed intervals of time, distinguished by a mechanical clock—rather unnatural for conversations. Observers were carefully trained to describe each interval in interaction categories (shown in his article), taking account of what *preceded* that interval. Had these intervals been coded out of context, they may not have made much sense, not to speak of the unreliability of coding them meaningfully. While the book from which we excerpted the article is more than a half-century old, Bales's way of studying group activity remains exemplary and relevant today.

Siegfried Kracauer's pioneering analysis of Nazi propaganda films is as useful today for content analysts interested in visual communication. His article describes a method for analyzing film into sequential units in parallel "tracks." By subsequently relating these units to each other over time, Kracauer lays the foundation of what one may call a visual rhetoric. He accounts for the manipulability of audio and visual information with the analytical construct of propaganda, which leads him to infer otherwise hidden intentions. His conception of content analysis—without using this name—may strike the current reader as prescient, being applicable to contemporary film and video productions, not only in the political realm, but in entertainment and advertising as well.

We end this section with a portion of the seminal agenda-setting article by Max McCombs and Donald Shaw. To cross-tabulate what they called "major and minor items" in the press with audience knowledge involved juggling several kinds of units at once—audience members, the media they followed, and units of text. Their research led to the historic claim that the media do not merely reflect but crucially participate in determining what is important to the public, what is being discussed.

Further outstanding examples of how units are definable, especially for using computers, may be found in Osgood's contingencies,** Holsti's and Kleinnijenhuis's articles concerning elementary propositions,*** Best's computation of memes,**** and Bengston and Xu's value-relevant words.*****

---

*See reading 1.7, this volume.

** See reading 3.1, this volume.

***See reading 3.5 and 7.5, this volume.

****See reading 3.6, this volume.

*****See reading 5.2, this volume.

2.1

"Good" Organizational Reasons for "Bad" Clinic Records

Harold Garfinkel*

Normal, Natural Troubles

The troubles that an investigator can encounter in using clinic records can be roughly divided into two types. We may call the first type general methodological troubles, and the second, "normal, natural troubles."

General Methodological Troubles furnish the topic of most published discussions about the use of clinic records for research purposes. Interest in these troubles is directed by the task of offering the investigator practical advice on how to make a silk purse out of a sow's ear. Instead of "silk purse," we should say a container of sorts that might, with the investigator's sufferance, be permitted to hold a usable percentage of the sorry and tattered bits that are removed from the files and put into it. Such discussions attempt to furnish the investigator with rules to observe in bringing the contents of case folders to the status of warranted answers to the research questions. What is generally involved here is the rephrasing of actual folder contents so as to produce something like an actuarial document that hopefully possesses the desired properties of completeness, clarity, credibility and the like. The transformed content of the record lends itself more readily than the original to various kinds of social scientific analyses on the assumption, of course, that there exists a defensible correspondence between the transformed account and the way the information was meant in its original form.**

*From Garfinkel, H. (1967). "Good" organizational reasons for "bad" clinic records. In *Studies in ethnomethodology* (pp. 189–207). Englewood Cliffs, NJ: Prentice Hall.

**Ideally, the transformed account compensates for known institutional biases. Correcting known biases in textual matter is a general problem in analyzing mass media content. Not only are images and text representative of phenomena outside them, they are also made available by institutions with interests in the consequences of producing them. See Krippendorff, K. (2004:318ff) for semantic and sampling validity.

Any investigator who has attempted a study with the use of clinic records, almost wherever such records are found, has his litany of troubles to recite. Moreover, hospital and clinic administrators frequently are as knowledgeable and concerned about these "shortcomings" as are the investigators themselves. The sheer frequency of "bad records" and the uniform ways in which they are "bad" were enough in itself to pique our curiosity. So we were led to ask whether there were some things that could be said by way of describing the great uniformity of "bad records" as sociological phenomenon in its own right.

We came to think of the troubles with records as "normal, natural" troubles. We do *not* mean this ironically. We are *not* saying "What more can you expect?!" Rather, the term "normal, natural" is used in a conventional sociological sense to mean "in accord with prevailing rules of practice." Normal, natural troubles are troubles that occur because clinic persons, as self-reporters actively seek to act in compliance with rules of the clinic's operating procedures that for them and from their point of view are more or less taken for granted as right ways of doing things. "Normal, natural" troubles are troubles that occur because clinic persons have established ways of reporting their activities; because clinic persons as self-reporters comply with these established ways; and because the reporting system and reporter's self-reporting activities are integral features of the clinic's usual ways of getting each day's work done—ways that for clinic persons are right ways.

The troubles we speak of are those that any investigator—outsider or insider—will encounter when consulting the files in order to answer questions that depart in theoretical or practical import from organizationally relevant purposes and routines under the auspices of which the contents of the files are routinely assembled in the first place. Let the investigator attempt a remedy for shortcomings and he or she will quickly encounter interesting properties of these troubles. They are persistent, they are reproduced from one clinic's files to the next, they are standard and occur with great uniformity as one compares reporting systems of different clinics, they are obstinate in resisting change, and above all, they have the flavor of inevitability. This inevitability is revealed by the fact that a serious attempt on the part of the investigator to remedy the state of affairs convincingly demonstrates how intricately and sensitively reporting procedures are tied to other routinized and valued practices of the clinic. Reporting procedures, their results, and the uses of these results are integral features of the same social orders they describe. Attempts to pluck even single strands can set the whole instrument resonating.

When clinic records are looked at in this way the least interesting thing one can say about them is that they are "carelessly" kept. The crux of the phenomenon lies elsewhere, namely in the ties between records and the social system that services and is serviced by these records. There is an organizational rationale to the investigator's difficulties. It is the purpose of this paper to formulate this rationale explicitly. Toward that end, we shall discuss several organizational sources of the difficulties involved in effecting an improvement in clinic records.

Some Sources of "Normal, Natural Troubles"

One part of the problem, a part to which most efforts of remedy have been directed, is contributed by the marginal utility of added information. The problem for an enterprise that must operate within a fixed budget involves the comparative costs of obtaining alternative information. Because there are comparative costs of different ways of keeping records, it is necessary to choose among alternative ways of allocating scarce resources of money, time, personnel, training, and skills in view of the value that might be attached to the ends that are served. The problem is in strictest terms an economic one. For example, information about age and sex can be had almost at the cost of glancing at the respondent; information about occupation puts a small tax on the time and skill of the interviewer; occupational history is a high-cost piece of information. The economic problem is summarized in the question that is almost invariably addressed to any recommended change of reporting procedure: "How much of the nurse's (or the resident's or the social worker's, etc.) time will it take?"

If the troubles in effecting an improvement amounted entirely to how much information the clinic could afford on a strict time cost basis, the remedy would consist of obtaining enough money to hire and train a large staff of record keepers. But it is enough to imagine this remedy to see that there are other troubles in effecting "improvements" that are independent of the number of record keepers.

Consider a part of the trouble, for example, that is contributed by the marginal utility of information when the information is collected by clinic members according to the procedures of an archive—*i.e.,* where uniform information is collected for future but unknown purposes. An administrator may be entirely prepared to require of persons in his establishment that whatever is gathered be gathered consistently. But that administrator must be prepared as well to maintain their motivation to collect the information in a regular fashion knowing that the personnel themselves also know that the information must be gathered for unknown purposes that only the future can reveal. Over the course of gathering the information such purposes may vary in their appearances to personnel, from benign to irrelevant to ominous, and for reasons that have little to do with the archives.

Further, partisans in the clinic for one reporting program or another are inclined to argue the "core" character of the information they want gathered. Administrators and investigators alike know this "core" to be a troublesome myth. Consider, for example, that a sociologist might urge the regular collection of such minimum "face sheet" information as age, sex, race, marital status, family composition, education, usual occupation, and annual income. The question he must argue against competitors to archive rights is not *"Is* the information worth the cost?" but *"Will it have been* worth the cost?" One need not be a trained investigator to understand that by addressing almost any definitive question to the archives one can reveal the shortcomings of the collection enterprise. Whether or not it turns out that what has been gathered will not do after all, and will have to be gathered all over again, will depend upon what constraints the investigator is willing to accept that are imposed by the necessity of his having to frame questions for which the archives will permit answers. For such reasons, an administrator with an eye to the budgeted costs of reporting procedures is apt to prefer to minimize the burden of present costs and to favor short-term peak load operations when the investigator has decided what is needed in a formulated project.

There are the further difficulties of ensuring the motivation to collect "core" information that occur when "good reporting performance" is assessed according to research interest. Such standards frequently contradict the service interests of professional persons within the organization. Moreover, founded priorities of occupational responsibility may motivate vehement and realistic complaints as well as—and with greater likelihood—informal and hidden recording practices that permit the recorder to maintain the priority of his other occupational obligations while keeping the front office appropriately misinformed.

This point touches on a related source of troubles in effecting improvement, troubles having to do with ensuring compliance of self-reporting personnel to record-keeping as a respectable thing for them to be doing from their point of view. The division of work that exists in every clinic does not consist only of differentiated technical skills. It consists as well of differential moral value attached to the possession and exercise of technical skills. To appreciate the variety and seriousness of troubles contributed by this organizational feature one need only consider the contrasting ways in which records are relevant to the satisfactory accomplishment of administrative responsibilities as compared with professional medical responsibilities and to the wary truce that exists among the several occupational camps as far as mutual demands for proper record-keeping are concerned.

Clinic personnel's feelings of greater or lesser dignity of paper work as compared with the exercise of other skills in their occupational life are accompanied by their abiding concerns for the strategic consequences of avoiding specifics in the record, given the unpredictable character of the occasions under which the record may be used as part of the ongoing system of supervision and review. Records may be used in the service of interests that those higher up in the medical-administrative hierarchy are probably not able, but in any case are neither required nor inclined beforehand, to specify or give warning about. Inevitably, therefore, informal practices exist which are known about by everyone, that as a matter of course contradict officially depicted and openly acknowledged practices. Characteristically, the specifics of who, what, when, and where are well-guarded team secrets of cliques and cabals in clinics, as they are in all bureaucratically organized settings. From the point of view of each occupational team, there are the specifics that facilitate the team's accomplishment of its occupational daily round, which is none of the business of some other occupational team in the clinic. This is not news of course, except that any investigator has to confront it as a fact of investigative life when, for example, in order to decide the import of what is in the record, it's necessary to consult materials that are not in the record but are nevertheless known and count to someone.

Another source of troubles: clinic personnel know the realities of life in the clinic in their capacity as socially informed members, whose claims to "have the actual account of it" derive in good part from their involvements and positions in the social system, involvements and positions which carry, *as a matter of moral obligation,* the requirement that incumbents make good sense of their work circumstances. Because of that moral obligation there is the long standing and familiar insistence on the part of self-reporters: "As long as you're going to bother us with your research why don't you get the story right?" This occurs particularly where standard reporting forms are used. If the researcher insists that the reporter furnish the information in the way the form provides, he runs the risk of imposing upon the actual events for study a structure that is derived from the features of the reporting rather than from the events themselves.

A closely related source of trouble stems from the fact that self-reporting forms—whatever they may consist of—provide not only categories with which clinic personnel describe clinic events, but simultaneously and inevitably, such forms constitute rules of reporting conduct. The self-reporting forms consist of rules that for personnel define correct self-reporting conduct as a work obligation. It is not startling that the investigator can obtain a description of clinic events precisely to the extent that the reporting form is enforced as a rule of reporting conduct upon reporting personnel. But then, it should also come with no surprise that the information the investigator can or cannot have is subject to the same conditions that investigators are aware of in other areas of rule-governed conduct: namely, that well-known differences and well-known sources of differences occur between rules and practices, differences that are notoriously recalcitrant to remedy.

Such differences are not understandable let alone remediable by attempting to allocate blame between reporters and investigators. Consider, for example, the case where a staff member may seek to report in compliance with what the investigator's forms provide, and, precisely because in taking the reporting form seriously, finds it difficult to reconcile what he or she knows about what the form is asking with what the form provides as a rule for deciding its relevance. For example, consider a question which provides the staff member with fixed alternative answers, *e.g.,* "Yes" or "No," yet in a particular case the staff member is convinced that a "Yes" or "No" answer will distort the question or defeat the inquirer's aim in asking it. Taking the study seriously, the reporter might wonder whether a marginal note will do it? But then, will writing it invite trouble? Perhaps it would be better to wait for an encounter with the investigator and mention this case? He should wait until he encounters the investigator and then remind him of this case? And why only *this* case? Staff members and other reporters know of many cases and of many places throughout the reporting form, so that such a complaint is entirely a realistic one that by making marginal jottings, there might be innumerable remarks to make for many items in many cases.

The investigator wants nothing more of the self-reporter than that he treat the reporting form as the occasion to report what the self-reporter knows *as he knows it.* Thus, we find that the self-reporter may distort the reality of the case precisely in an attempt to be helpful and thereby complies with the reporting form. The staff member may know it is distorting and resent it or otherwise suffer it. One can easily imagine the resentment and suffering are matched on the investigator's side.*

Further, while the terminology in self-reporting forms is fixed, the actual events that these terms refer to, as well as the ways in which actual events may be brought under the jurisdiction of the form's terminology as descriptions are highly variable. The relevance of the reporting form's terminology to the events it describes is subject to the stability of the on-going clinic operations and depends upon the self-reporter's grasp and use of the regular features of the clinic's operation as a scheme of linguistic interpretation. Upon any change of clinic policy, organization, personnel, or procedure the terms on the reporting forms may change in their meaning without a single mimeographed sentence being altered. It is disconcerting to find how even small procedural changes may make large sections of a reporting form hopelessly ambiguous.

Difficulties that are introduced either because the clinic members are reporting on their own activities or because the self-reporting activities are carried on with the use of prepared forms, may be extended and illuminated by considering that candor in reporting carries well known risks to careers and to the organization. Speaking euphemistically, between clinic persons and their clients, and between the clinic and its environing groups, the exchange of information is something less than a free market.

A Critical Source of Trouble: Actuarial Versus Contractual Uses of Folder Contents

. . . [T]o think of such troubles as a managerial problem of bringing record-keeping performances under greater or more consistent control, overlooks a critical and perhaps unalterable feature of medical records as an element of institutionalized practices. We propose that the enumerated troubles—and obviously our enumeration is by no means complete—either explicate or themselves consist of properties of the case folder as a reconstructable record of transactions between patients and clinic personnel. This critical feature of clinic records brings the enumerated troubles under the jurisdiction of their status as "structurally normal troubles" by relating reporting systems to the conditions of the clinic's viability as a corporately organized service enterprise. We shall now endeavor to show that clinic records, such as they are, are not something clinic personnel get away with, but that instead, the records *consist of procedures and consequences of clinical activities as a medico-legal enterprise.*

In reviewing the contents of case folders it seemed to us that a case folder could be read in one or the other of two contrasting and irreconcilable ways. On the one hand it could be read as an *actuarial record.* On the other hand it could be read as the *record of a therapeutic contract* between the clinic as a medico-legal enterprise and the patient. Because our understanding of the term "contract" departs somewhat from colloquial usage, but not from the understanding that Durkheim taught, a brief explanation is in order.

Ordinarily "contract" refers to a document containing an explicit schedule of obligations, the binding character of which is recognized

*One needs to realize that, on the investigator's side, coders experience similar frustrations when categorizing text in terms of categories that serve the purpose of a research project but do not quite fit the interpretations of the text by typical readers. Scientific research is an institutional practice as well (see Part 5).

by identifiable parties to the agreement. In contrast, and because we are talking specifically about clinics, we use the term "contract" to refer to the *definition* of normal transactions between clientele and remedial agencies in terms of which agencies' services are franchised and available to clients. One of the crucial features of remedial activities is that their recipients are socially defined by themselves and the agencies as incompetent to negotiate for themselves the terms of their treatment.

Thus it is the socially acknowledged normal course of affairs that a patient "puts himself in the hands of a doctor" and is expected to suspend the usual competence of his own judgment about his well being, what he needs, or what is best for him. The same applies to the criminal, *mutatis mutandis,* who is the sole person barred from contributing his opinion to the formulation of a just sentence. Despite these limitations of competence, neither patients nor criminals lose their right to the "treatment they deserve." This is so because treatment consists of occasions for performances that in the eyes of participants accord with a larger scheme of obligations. The larger scheme of obligations relates the authorization in terms of which a remedial agency is deputized to act to the technical doctrines and practical professional ethics, which govern the operations of the agency. By assuming jurisdiction in specific cases, medical and legal agencies commit themselves to honoring legitimate public claims for "good healing" and "good law." An indispensable though not exclusive method whereby clinics demonstrate that they have honored claims for adequate medical care consists of procedures for formulating relevant accounts of their transactions with patients.

Sociologically, . . . legal contracts are only one variant of the class of contracts. The larger conception of contract, namely, its power to define normal relations, also requires that questions of competent readership be considered. Thus, we were obliged to consider how the designations, terms, and expressions contained in the clinic folders were read to make them testify as answers to questions pertaining to medico-legal responsibility. In our view, *the contents of clinic folders are assembled with regard for the possibility that the relationship may have to be portrayed as having been in accord with expectations of sanctionable performances by clinicians and patients.*

By calling a medical record a "contract," we are not claiming that the record contains only statements of what should have happened as opposed to what did happen. Nor are we proposing that a contractual reading of the medical record is even the most frequent reading, let alone the only reading that occurs. Clinic records are consulted upon many different occasions and for many different interests. But for all the different uses which records may be put and for all the different uses that they serve, considerations of medico-legal responsibility exercise an overriding priority of relevance as prevailing structural[1] interests whenever procedures for the maintenance of records and their eligible contents must be decided.

Although folder materials may be put to many uses different from those that serve the interests of contract, *all* alternatives are subordinated to the contract use as a matter of enforced structural priority. Because of this priority, alternative uses are consistently producing erratic and unreliable results. But also because of this priority, every last suggestion of information in a medical record can come under the scope of a contractual interpretation. Indeed, the contract use both addresses and establishes *whatsoever* the folder might contain as the elements of a "whole record" and does so in the manner that we shall now describe.

When any case folder was read as an actuarial record its contents fell so short of adequacy as to leave us puzzled as to why "poor records" as poor as these should nevertheless be so assiduously kept. On the other hand, when folder documents were regarded as unformulated terms of a potential therapeutic contract, *i.e.,* as documents assembled in the folder in open anticipation of some occasion when the terms of a therapeutic contract might have to be formulated from them, the assiduousness with which folders were kept, even though their contents were extremely uneven in quantity and quality, began to "make sense."

We start with the fact that when one examines any case folder for what it actually contains, a prominent and consistent feature is the occasional and elliptical character of its remarks and information. In their occasionality, folder documents are very much like utterances in a conversation with an unknown audience, which, because it already knows what might be talked about, is capable of reading hints. As expressions, the remarks that make up these documents have overwhelmingly the characteristic that their sense cannot be decided by a reader without his necessarily knowing or assuming something about a typical biography and typical purposes of the user of the expressions, about typical circumstances under which such remarks are written, about a typical previous course of transactions between the writers and the patient, or about a typical relationship of actual or potential interaction between *the writers and the reader.* Thus the *folder contents, much less than revealing an order of interaction, presuppose an understanding of that order for a correct reading.* The understanding of that order is not one, however, that strives for theoretical clarity, but is one that is appropriate to a reader's pragmatic interest in the order.

Further, there exists an entitled use of records. The entitlement is accorded, without question, to the person who reads them from the perspective of active medico-legal involvement in the case at hand and shades off from there. The entitlement refers to the fact that the full relevance of the clinician's position and involvement comes into play in justifying the expectancy of having proper business with these expressions, that they will be understood and put to good use. The specific understanding and use will be occasional to the situation. The entitled reader knows that just as understanding and use is occasional to the situation in which one finds oneself, so the expressions that one encounters are understood to have been occasional to the situations of their authors. The possibility of understanding is based on a shared, practical, and entitled understanding of common tasks between writer and reader.

Occasional expressions are to be contrasted with "objective" expressions, *i.e.,* expressions whose references are decided by consulting a set of coding rules that are assumed, by both user and reader, to hold irrespective of any characteristics of either one, other than their more or less similar grasp of these rules.

A prototype of an actuarial record would be a record of installment payments. The record of installment payments describes the present state of the relationship and how it came about. A standardized terminology and a standardized set of grammatical rules govern not only possible contents, but govern as well the way a "record" of past transactions is to be assembled. Something like a standard reading is possible that enjoys considerable reliability among readers of the record. The interested reader does not have an edge over the merely instructed one. That a reader is entitled to claim to have interpreted the record correctly, *i.e.,* a claim to competent readership, does not depend on any particular characteristics, previous transactions or interest on the part of the reader.

To recite investigators' troubles in the use of clinic folders is to remark on the fact that a negligible fraction of the contents of clinic folders can be read in an actuarial way without incongruity. An investigator who attempts to impose an actuarial reading upon folder contents will fill a notebook with recitation of "shortcomings" in the data, with complaints of "carelessness," and the like.

However, the folder's contents *can* be read, without incongruity, by a clinic member if, in the way that an historian or a lawyer might use the same documents, he is developing a *documented representation* of what the clinic-patient transactions consisted of as an orderly and understandable matter. The various items of the clinic folders are tokens—like pieces that will permit the assembly of an indefinitely large number of mosaics—gathered together not to describe a relationship between clinical personnel and the patient, but to permit a clinic member to formulate a relationship between patient and clinic as a normal course of clinic affairs when and if the question of normalizing should arise as a matter of some clinic member's practical concern. In this sense, we say that a folder's contents serve the uses of contract rather than description, for a contract does not and is not used to describe a relationship. Rather it is used to normalize a relationship, by which is meant that the *quid pro quo* of exchanges is so ordered in an account of the relationship as to satisfy the terms of a prior and legitimate agreement, explicit or implicit.

Folder contents are assembled against the contingent need, by some clinic member, to construct a potential or a past course of transactions between the clinic and the patient as a "case," and thereby as an instance of a therapeutic contract, frequently in the interests of justifying an actual or potential course of actions between clinic persons and patients. Hence, whatever their diversity, a folder's contents can be read without incongruity by a clinic member if, in much the same way as a lawyer "makes the brief," the clinic member "makes a case" from the fragmented remains *in the course* of having to read into documents their relevance for each other as an account of legitimate clinic activity.

In contrast to actuarial records, folder documents are very little constrained in their present meanings by the procedures whereby they come to be assembled in the folder. Indeed, document meanings are disengaged from the actual procedures whereby documents were assembled, and in this respect the ways and results of competent readership of folder documents contrast, once more, with the ways and results of competent actuarial readership. When and if a clinic member has "good reason" to consult folder contents, his or her purpose at the time defines some set of the folder's contents as constituent elements of the formulated account. If, in the course of consulting the folder, the purpose should change, nothing is suffered since the constituent set of documents is not completed until the reader decides that there is enough. The rounds for stopping are not formulated beforehand. Thereby, the list of folder documents is open ended and can be indefinitely long.

Most important, the competent reader is aware that it is not only that which the folder contains that stands in a relationship of mutually qualifying and determining reference, but parts that are not in it belong to this too. These ineffable parts come to view in the light of known episodes, but then, in turn, the known episodes themselves are also, reciprocally, interpreted in the light of what one must reasonably assume to have gone on while the case progressed without having been made a matter of record.

The scheme for interpreting folder documents may be drawn from anywhere at all. It may change with the reading of any particular item, change with the investigator's purposes in making a case of the documents he encounters, change "in light of circumstances," change as the exigencies require. . . . [W]hether or not there is continuity, consistency, coherence between the sense of one document and another is for the reader to see. In no case are constraints placed upon the reader to justify beforehand or to say beforehand what in the folder counts for what, or what he is going to count or not count for what.

In order to read the folder's contents without incongruity a clinic member must expect of himself, expect of other clinic members, and expect that as he expects of other clinic members they expect him to know and to use a knowledge (1) of particular persons to whom the record refers, (2) of persons who contributed to the record, (3) of the clinic's actual organization and operating procedures at the time the folder's documents are being consulted, (4) of a mutual history with other persons—patients and clinic members—and (5) of clinic procedures, including procedures for reading a record, as these procedures involved the patients and the clinic members. In the service of present interests, he uses such knowledge to assemble the folder's items as a documented representation of the relationship.[2]

The clinic that we studied is associated with a university medical center. By reason of the clinic's commitment to research as a legitimate goal of the enterprise an actuarial record has high priority of value in the clinic's usual affairs. But the contract character of the contents of case folders has a competing priority of value which is associated with practical and prevailing necessities of maintaining viable relationships with the university, with other medical specialties, with the state government, with the courts, and with the various publics at large by making out its activities to be those of a legitimate psychiatric remedial agency in the first place.

Between the two commitments there is no question on the part of the many parties concerned, patients and researchers included, as to which of the two takes precedence. In all matters, starting with considerations of comparative economics and extending through the tasks of publicizing and justifying the enterprise, the conditions for maintaining contract folders must be satisfied. Other interests are necessarily lesser interests and must be accommodated to these.

Notes

1. By calling interests "structural" we wish to convey that the interest is not governed by personal considerations in advancing a cause but is related to demands of organized practice, which the member treats as his real circumstances.

2. It is important to emphasize that we are not talking of "making some scientific best of whatever there is." Organizationally speaking, any collection of folder contents whatsoever can, will, even must be used to fashion a documented representation. Thus, an effort to impose a formal rationale on the collection and composition of information has the character of a vacuous exercise because the expressions that the so ordered documents will contain will have to be "decoded" to discover their real meaning in the light of the interest and interpretation that prevail at the time of their use.

Reference

Krippendorff, K. (2004). *Content analysis: An introduction to its methodology* (2nd ed.). Thousand Oaks, CA: Sage.

2.2

Effectiveness of Random, Consecutive Day and Constructed Week Sampling

Daniel Riffe, Charles F. Aust, and Stephen R. Lacy*

Two decisions confronting content analysts involve defining the population and determining how many issues to sample. While both depend on research objective and design, sample size also is constrained by resources at hand. The researcher's goal is to sample enough issues to achieve an "acceptable" estimate of unknown population parameters, while maximizing efficiency of time and effort. Selecting too few issues may produce unreliable data and invalid result; selecting too many may be a wasteful misuse of coding resources. But in the case of newspapers, maximum sampling efficiency involves sampling procedure (e.g., simple random sampling, constructing a week to represent all days of the week or selecting a convenient sample of seven consecutive days) as well as sample size.

Simple random sampling requires no assumptions about variation in newspaper content; particularly large newsholes (e.g., Sundays) could by chance be over- or underrepresented in a sample. However, constructed week sampling assumes cyclic variation of content for different days of the week and requires that all the different days of the week be represented (Stempel, 1989). For example, sports sections are larger on weekends when more sports take place. Ad space is greater on Wednesdays and Thursdays and the newshole larger—in many papers when grocery and department store ads run. In a constructed week sample, all Sundays are identified and one is then randomly selected, as is a Monday, a Tuesday, etc., until all seven days of the week are represented. In more convenient samples using sets of consecutive days, all weekdays may be present in a seven day sample, but the procedures ignores between-week differences.

Research on sampling is limited. Studying 1941 Pravda headlines, Mintz used one month as a population and drew a whole week sample, a three-day sample (5th, 10th and 25th of the month), a six-day sample (the 5th, 10th, and 25th of the month), a six-day sample (the 5th, 10th, 20th, 25th, and 30th of the month)

*Riffe, D., Aust, C. F., & Lacy, S. R. (1993). The effectiveness of random, consecutive day and constructed week sampling in newspaper content analysis. *Journalism Quarterly 70:*133–139.

and an every-other day sample of 15 days (Mintz, 1949). Only the six-day and 15-day samples did not differ significantly from the population mean. But a six-day sample draw from a population of only one month is a 20% sample, and a 15-day sample is a 50% sample. With larger populations, 20% and 50% become unmanageable. Further, a fixed-interval, six-day sample drawn from one month must exclude one day of the week. And while a 15-day sample guaranteed each day of the week was present at least twice, one was present three times. Mintz, however had concluded that "frequencies of headlines per day in Pravda were not subject to cycles," so representing all days of the week equally was unnecessary (Mintz, 1949:133).

Stempel examined front-page photographs in a six-issue a week (no Sunday edition) Wisconsin newspaper in 1951, comparing the population (a year) mean with means for different sample sizes. He drew 10 samples each of 6, 12, 18, 24, and 48 issues, using a random starting point and selecting every nth issue. With samples of these sizes (multiples of six) and a six-edition-a-week paper, his sampling interval guaranteed a different day of the week was selected with each choice, thus acting "as a stratification for days of the week"[1] as in constructed week sampling. He found 12 days-two constructed weeks sufficient to represent the year, and that "increasing sample size may be a poor investment of the researcher's time." He was, however, cautious about the effect of Sunday editions on sampling and he examined only front-page photographs.

Davis and Turner tested every-sixth day sampling of crime news in four newspapers with Sunday editions, drawing six six-day samples (the first sample included the 1st of the month, the 7th, the 13th, etc.; the second sample included the 2nd, the 8th, the 14th etc.) from each of two months, for four papers (Davis & Turner, 1951). Even though each six-day sample excluded one day of the week (e.g., if the first of the month was Saturday, no Sunday would be in the sample), they found no significant differences between sample means and population means in 48 samples. Note again that each sample included 20% of the one-month population.

In 1959 Jones and Carter constructed 30 separate weeks from a population of 21 days in examining four papers' newsholes.[2] Of the resulting 120 "tests" of the samples 85% were within 2% of the papers' "true" population newsholes. But a constructed week drawn from three weeks includes one-third of the population.

Most of these studies sampled small populations and compared sample means to population parameters, a useful comparison. But the efficiency gained by constructed week sampling might be more apparent in direct comparisons among constructed week, simple random and consecutive day samples.

This study addresses two research questions about sampling local news content:

1. What is the minimum number of constructed weeks needed to estimate the average number of local news stories per day, including Sundays?
2. Is a constructed week more efficient than simple random or consecutive day samples of comparable size?

Method

Testing efficiency of different sampling approaches requires knowledge of population parameters to compare with obtained sample statistics. This study used data from content analysis of a group-owned evening and Sunday newspaper (approx. 39,000 circ.). Three trained coders had examined every local news item in every issue in a six-month (182-day) period (February–July 1988). A total of 2,774 local items were coded across the 182 days. For this study the 182 days were treated as a population, each day having a local story count of from 6 to 27 items. The population mean was 15.2 local stories per day, the mode 8, the median 15, and standard deviation 6.18.

The first step involved drawing sets of 20 samples for different sample sizes using simple random sampling. Twenty seven-day samples were randomly selected, as were 20 14-day samples and 20 28-day samples. The second step involved drawing comparable sets of 20 samples using the constructed week method. Twenty samples of one constructed week (n = 7) were drawn, as were 20 samples of two constructed weeks (n = 14), 20 samples of three constructed weeks (n = 21) and 20 samples of four constructed weeks (n = 28). In the third step we drew comparable sets of 20 sample weeks using the consecutive day method. Twenty random starting points were generated and, for each, seven consecutive days selected to form a sample week. Then 20 two-week (14-consecutive days) samples were drawn using random starting points, as were 20 three-week (21 consecutive days) and four-week (28 consecutive days) samples. Finally, we examined how often—as a percentage of each set of 20—sample means fell within one or two standard errors of the population mean of 15.2.

Results

The basis for constructed week sampling—that newsholes vary by day of week—is supported by Table 1, showing average number of local stories for each of the seven days of the week. Sundays had the largest local newshole, averaging 24.77 stories, while Saturday's average of 9.81 was fewer than the population average. Wednesdays and Thursdays were slightly above the population average, and Tuesdays, Mondays and Fridays were below it.

The distribution is not surprising; newshole cycles follow advertising space cycles. Sunday is the week's largest issue because of increased retail, real estate and classified advertisings, and Sunday's extended leisure/reading time. Saturday's newshole is smaller because less ad space is bought, and Wednesdays and Thursdays have more space than all but Sunday issues because of grocery ads. Table 2 shows, for simple random, constructed week and consecutive day sampling, the range of sample size and sampling technique. As sample size increased, the range of sample means in the sets of samples declined, for all three sample types. For constructed week samples, the ranges were narrowest; for consecutive day samples, the ranges were widest.

The first research question asked how many constructed weeks were necessary to estimate the population mean for local stories. Table 3 shows the percentage of sample means in each set of 20 that fell within one and two standard errors of the population mean. For example, of the 20 samples of one constructed week 100% of sample means were within two standard errors of the population means, exceeding the 95% predicted by the Central Limits Theorem.[3] By contrast, only 85% of the 20 one-week consecutive day samples were within two standard errors.

Table 1 Mean Number of Local Stories and Standard Deviation by Day of the Week

	Mean Number of Stories	*Standard Deviation*	*Number of Days*
Monday	12.00	4.91	26
Tuesday	14.42	3.81	26
Wednesday	16.39	4.78	26
Thursday	16.15	4.78	26
Friday	12.81	3.46	26
Saturday	9.81	2.40	26
Sunday	24.77	5.41	26
Population	15.20	6.18	182

Table 2 Low and High, and Range of Mean Number of Local Stories for Sets of 20 Samples, by Type and Size of Sample

	Simple Random	*Constructed*	*Consecutive Day*
Days in Sample	*Low—High (range)*	*Low—High (range)*	*Low—High (range)*
7	**12.3–20.4** (7.8)	**13.6–17.4** (3.6)	**11.6–19.9** (8.3)
14	**11.4–17.5** (6.1)	**12.9–17.3** (4.4)	**11.4–18.4** (7.0)
21	**12.6–17.5** (4.9)	**14.1–17.0** (2.9)	**12.2–19.0** (6.9)
28	**12.9–16.9** (4.0)	**14.3–16.8** (2.5)	**13.3–18.5** (5.2)

To estimate average daily number of local stories with 95% confidence, one constructed week would suffice for this population. Of course 95% of the means for simple random samples of $n = 7$ also fell within two standard errors, a higher percentage than for the 14-day or 21-day simple random samples, or for any size of consecutive day sample.

The precision of constructed week sampling becomes even clearer with examination of results for one standard error. The Central Limits Theorem predicts that 68% of random sample means fall within one standard error of the population mean. Here, means for 85% of one- and four-constructed-week-samples, and 90% of two- and three-constructed-week samples were within that narrow set of bounds. Only the 28-day simple random sample, but none of the consecutive day sample sizes, was within one standard error. Precision is increased slightly with two or three constructed weeks, but may not merit the increased resource commitment, which would be doubled or tripled. The drop in precision from three to four constructed weeks may be a "blip" in the pattern due to the error of random sampling.

The second research question asked whether constructed week sampling is more efficient than simple random or consecutive day sampling. Tables 2 and 3 indicate the answer is "yes." Table 2 shows that the range of sample means was always smaller for the sets of constructed week samples than for consecutive day or simple random samples of the same size. The range of the 20 simple random

Table 3 Percentage of Sample Means in Sets of 20 Samples Falling Within One and Two Standard Errors of Population Mean by Type and Size of Sample

	Simple Random		*Constructed Week(s)*		*Consecutive Day Week(s)*	
Within	*2 S.E.*	*1 S.E.*	*2 S.E.*	*1 S.E.*	*2 S.E.*	*1 S.E*
Days in Sample	*%*	*%*	*%*	*%*	*%*	*%*
7	95	55	100	90	85	65
14	85	60	100	90	80	40
21	90	65	100	90	70	45
28	95	75	75	100	80	35

NOTE: Each percentage is based on the 20 samples in each combination of sampling technique and sample size.

sample means of $n = 7$ was 7.8 stories, compared to 8.3 for 20 samples of seven consecutive days, and only 3.8 for 20 sample sizes increased. Table 3 shows that percentages of constructed week sample means falling within one or two standard errors of the population mean always exceeded percentages for the simple random samples and consecutive day samples of same size. Percentages of simple random sample means that fell within two standard errors of the population mean ranged from 85% to 95%, compared to 70% to 85% for consecutive day samples, while 100% of constructed week sample means fell within two standard errors of the population mean. The percentage of simple random sample means that fell within one standard error of the population mean ranged from 55% to 75% while the range of the percentages for constructed weeks ranged from 85% to 90%. Only 35% to 65% of consecutive day samples were within one standard error.

Simple random sampling of newspaper editions will give a reliable estimate of the population mean, if sample size is large enough. That is true, generally speaking, of sampling from most other types of populations (e.g., people, acreage). The Central Limits Theorem allows researchers to use random sampling to estimate sampling error when a population distribution is unknown. But relying on the Central Limits Theorem—and simple random sampling—becomes comparatively inefficient when the population distribution is known and not normal. In such cases, stratification based on that known and non-normal population distribution—as in the case of days of the week—yields better estimates with smaller samples.

This study has shown by direct comparisons between simple random, consecutive day and constructed week sampling that a smaller sample stratified for day of week will give just as good as an estimate, if not better. The distribution of newspaper stories is simply not normal. Constructed weeks produce better estimates that purely random samples of days because they avoid the possibility of oversampling Sundays or Saturdays. Our comparisons with consecutive day sampling, which may also avoid oversampling individual weekdays, demonstrate the further importance of sampling across weeks (as in constructed week sampling) if one seeks generalizability beyond the consecutive day period itself. Consecutive day samples are very easy and convenient to use, and different weekdays may be represented, but they are not a reliable means of estimating content for a six-month period or longer.

Of course, the study is limited by its focus only on local stories from six months of a single newspaper. But showing that a constructed week procedure is more efficient than pure random or consecutive day sampling does not reveal how many constructed weeks are most efficient. This study found that for a population of six months of editions, one constructed week was as efficient as four, and its estimates exceeded what would be expected based on probability theory. By extension, two constructed weeks would allow reliable estimates of local stories in a year's worth of newspaper entire issues, a conclusion consistent with Stempel's findings on front-page photographs in a six-day-a-week paper. If this study of sampling of local news stories supports and extends the finding of Stempel and Carter and Jones, we hope it also serves an additional heuristic purpose of showing "how" constructed week sampling works.

Notes

1. Stempel (1952) reported that his approach also stratified for month of the year, though how that worked with samples of $n = 6$ is unclear.
2. The researchers also stipulated that all three population weeks must be represented in each constructed week.
3. The Central Limits Theorem states that the distribution of sample means approaches a normal distribution as the size of the sample increases, no matter what the distribution of the population, and is the basis for making inferences to unknown populations from randomly selected samples. See Blalock Jr., H. M. (1979) *Social Statistics,* rev. 2nd ed. McGraw Hill, NY, pp. 183–186.

References

Davis, F. J., & Turner, L. W. (1951). Sample efficiency in quantitative newspaper content analysis. *Public Opinion Quarterly 15:*762–763.

Jones, R. L., & Carter, R. E., Jr. (1959). Some procedures for estimating 'news hole' in content analysis. *Public Opinion Quarterly 23:*399–403.

Mintz, A. (1949). The feasibility of the use of samples in content analysis. In H. Lasswell, N. Leites, & Associates (Eds.), *Language of politics* (pp. 127–152). New York: George W. Stewart, Publishers.

Stempel, G. H., III. (1952). Sample size for classifying subject matter in dailies. *Journalism Quarterly 29:*333–334.

Stempel, G. H., III. (1989). Content analysis. In G. H. Stempel III & Bruce H. Westley (Eds.), *Research methods in mass communication,* (2nd ed., pp. 119–131). Englewood Cliffs, NJ: Prentice Hall.

2.3

THE CHALLENGE OF APPLYING CONTENT ANALYSIS TO THE WORLD WIDE WEB

SALLY J. MCMILLAN*

Content analysis has been used for decades as a microscope that brings communication messages into focus. The World Wide Web has grown rapidly since the technology that made it possible was introduced in 1991 and the first Web browsers became available in 1993 (Leiner et al., 2000). The Commerce Department estimates that one billion users may be online by 2005, and the growth in users has mirrored growth in content (Commerce Department, 2000). More than 320 million home pages can be accessed on the Web and some Web sites are updated almost constantly (Koehler, 1999).** This growth and change make the Web a moving target for communication research. Can the microscope of content analysis be applied to this moving target?

The purpose of this article is to examine ways that researchers have begun to apply content analysis to the World Wide Web. How are they adapting the principles of content analysis to this evolving form of computer-mediated communication? What are the unique challenges of content analysis in this environment? This review of pioneering work in Web-based content analysis may provide researchers with insights into ways to adapt a stable research technique to a dynamic communication environment.

METHODOLOGY

The author took several steps to identify both published and unpublished studies that have applied content analysis to the Web. First, a search of the electronic Social Sciences Citation Index was conducted searching for key words "Web" and "content analysis." The SSCI

*From: McMillan, S. J. (2000). The microscope and the moving target: The challenge of applying content analysis to the World Wide Web. *Journalism and Mass Communication Quarterly* 77:80–98.

**The Web, of course, has expanded since then and continues to do so.

was also searched for "Internet" and "content analysis." Selected communication journals were also reviewed for any articles that applied content analysis to the Web. The author also sought out papers from communication conferences (e.g., Association for Education in Journalism and Mass Communication, and International Communication Association) that applied content analysis to the Web. Finally, bibliographies were checked for all studies that were identified using the above techniques. Any cited study that seemed to apply content analysis to the Web was examined.

Eleven studies were identified that applied content analysis to computer-mediated communication technologies other than the Web. In addition to the studies that examined computer-mediated communication forms such as e-mail and ListServs, nineteen studies were found that focused specifically on content analysis of the World Wide Web. These nineteen studies are listed in Table 1 and examined in the Findings section of this article. The five steps in content analysis identified in the literature are the basis for examination of how these nineteen studies applied the microscope of content analysis to the moving target of the World Wide Web.

Findings

The first step in content analysis is to formulate research questions and/or hypotheses. The majority of these studies were descriptive in nature. However, a few of these studies do seem to be moving more toward hypothesis testing and theory development. For example, McMillan (1998) proposed four models of funding for Web content based in part on level of interactivity that was determined by analysis of Web site features. Wassmuth and Thompson (1999) suggested that their study might be a first step in developing a theory that explains relationships between specificity of banner ad messages and the goal of information tasks.

The second step in conducting a content analysis is to select a sample. Table 1 summarizes information about samples for the nineteen studies that analyzed content of Web sites. The sampling frame from which sites were drawn varied widely: One common way of defining a sampling frame was to use an online list of sites in a given category. A second popular technique was to use search engine(s) to identify sites that met criteria related to the purpose of the study. Two studies used off-line sources to identify Web sites (Frazer & McMillan, 1997; Liu, Arnett, Capella, & Beatty, 1997) and two studies combined online and off-line listings of Web sites (Clyde, 1996; Massey & Levy, 1999:138–151). Finally, one site analyzed three newspaper Web sites with no discussion of the sampling frame (Li, 1998).

After defining the sampling frame, researchers typically draw a sample for analysis. Nine of the nineteen studies did not sample; instead they analyzed all sites in the sampling frame. The goals of these studies were typically to describe and/or set a benchmark for analysis of a given type of Web sites.

Among studies that used sampling, use of a table of random numbers was the most common sampling technique. McMillan (1998) pointed out challenges of applying a table of random numbers to an online listing or search engine results. Most lists generated in this way are not numbered, leaving the researcher a tedious hand-counting task. Search engine listings may be presented in multiple hypertext sub-menus that further complicate the task of assigning random numbers.* However, few of the studies cited here provided much, if any discussion, of how to address sampling difficulties that arise from using online sources to identify the sampling frame. The sample size for these nineteen studies varied dramatically from three to 2,865. The majority of the studies (14) analyzed between 50 and 500 sites.

The third step in content analysis is defining categories. In content analysis of

*It is important to know as much as possible about how a search engine chooses and prioritizes its selections before deciding how to use it for sampling.

Table 1 Sampling

Study	*Sampling Frame*	*Selection Method*	*Sample Size*
Aikat (1995)	Master list of 12,687 WWW addresses	Random selection of about 10% of sites	1,140
Alloro et al. (1998)	Online biomedical journals	All found using multiple search tools	54
Bar-Ilan (1998)	6,681 documents retrieved using seven search engines	Examined all that made reference to Paul Erdos	2,865
Bates & Lu (1997)	The People Page Directory orig; http://www.peoplepage.com	The first five entries under each letter	114
Clyde (1996)	413 library Web sites from multiple sources	Randomly selected	50
Elliott (1999)	All World Wide Web sites that met four criteria	All sites found using links & search engines	356
Esrock & Leichty (1998)	Fortune 500 Companies on the Pathfinder* Web site	Every fifth site after a random start	90
Frazer & McMillan (1997)	Web sites mentioned in first year of Web coverage in *Advertising Age*	All sites mentioned that were still functioning at time of study	156
Gibson & Ward (1998)	U.K. political party Web sites	All listed in one or more of four indexes	28
Ha & James (1998)	Web Digest for Marketers (online)	Census of all business Web sites during given time	110
Ho (1997)	Representative sites found using Yahoo & Alta Vista	Stratified random sample of business categories	1,400
Li (1998)	Online editions of three major newspapers	Arbitrary	3
Liu et al. (1997)	Fortune 500 Companies	All that could be found using multiple search tools	322
Massey & Levy (1999)	Daily, general-circulation, English-language newspapers in Asia that publish companion Web editions	All that could be found using multiple search tools	44
McMillan (1998)	Yahoo listing of health-related Web sites	Random-number table selection of sites	395
McMillan & Campbell (1996)	City.net list of Web sites*	Random-number table selection of site	500
Peng, Tham & Xiaoming (1999)	Web newspapers published in the U.S.	Stratified sample of national newspapers, metropolitan dailies and local dailies	80
Tannery & Wessel (1998)	Association of Academic Health Science Libraries	All medial libraries listed in online list of libraries	104
Wassmuth & Thompson (1999)	Editor and Publisher listing of online U.S. newspapers	Every ninth site after a random start	75

*As if to underscore the premise of this article, these Web sites have changed or no longer exist as of March 2007.

traditional media, one of the first steps is to define the time period of the study (e.g., a constructed week of newspaper issues). But, in analysis of Web sites, study authors placed emphasis on the time frame (e.g., April 1997) of the study. As noted earlier, changes in the content of Web sites necessitate rapid collection of data. The most rapid data collection reported was two days and the longest was five months. Most studies collected data in one to two months.

After identifying the time frame of the study, researchers need to identify context units for coding. The most common context unit used for these studies was the "Web site." Many of the studies did not specify what was meant by the Web site. However, some did limit analysis to the "home page" or initial screen seen upon entering the site while others specified examination of all pages that could be found at a given site and others indicated that they had searched sites in "sufficient detail" to identify key features.

Given the magnitude and changing nature of sites, some creativity would seem to be needed in defining the context unit. Wassmuth and Thompson (1999) devised one creative approach in their analysis of banner ads that were encountered when the coder performed a specific task at a newspaper Web site (find a classified ad for a BMW). Another approach was to have coders analyze all sites for a specific length of time—about ten minutes (Frazer & McMillan, 1997; McMillan, 1998; McMillan & Campbell, 1996). This helps to reduce bias that might be involved in coding sites of varying lengths. However, it might introduce "error" in that different coders may choose to examine different parts of a Web site during the ten-minute examination period.

These nineteen studies varied widely in terms of coding units used by the researchers. The most common coding unit was "content categories." However, no standard list of categories emerges from these studies. Nor do they rely on established lists such as the fifty categories identified by Bush (1951). Instead, content categories seem to be specifically related to the goals of the given study. For example, Bar-Ilan (1998) developed content categories related to a specific historical figure, and McMillan and Campbell (1996) developed content categories related to the community-building features of city-based Web sites.

Another common coding unit is structural features of the Web site (e.g., links, animation, video, sound, etc.). Two studies used Heeter's (1989) conceptual definition of interactivity as a frame for organizing analysis of Web site features (Massey & Levy, 1999; McMillan, 1998). One study conducted an in-depth analysis of e-mail links (Gibson & Ward, 1998). Many of the other sites also coded e-mail links as a structural element. Tannery and Wessel (1998) developed a three-level categorization system for evaluating overall sophistication of Web sites based on both content categories and structural features. Some studies also reported on "demographic" characteristics of sites such as country of origin and type of institution that created the site while others explored the nature and/or purpose of the sponsoring organization in more detail. The Wassmuth and Thompson (1999) study is unique in its analysis of banner advertisements in Web sites.

The fourth step in content analysis is training coders and checking the reliability of their coding skills. One of the primary reasons for this attention to training and checking coders is that, as Budd, Thorp, and Donohew (1967:66) noted, an important requirement for any social-science based research is that it be carried out in such a way that its results can be verified by other investigators who follow the same steps as the original researcher. Krippendorff (1980:74) wrote that at least two coders must be used in content analysis to determine reliability of the coding scheme by independently analyzing content. Eight of the nineteen studies did not report any information about coders. Of those that did report on coders, the number of coders used ranged from two to twelve with an average of about five coders. Only seven studies reported on training of coders and most said little about how training was done.

Eleven studies reported cross-coding techniques. Most cross-coded a percentage (10 to 20%) of all sampled sites. Elliott had all sites crosschecked by two coders (1999) while Li (1998) had two coders crosscheck all the data collected in the first three days of a ten-day sample. Ha and James (1998) used a pre-test/post-test design that enabled them to correct coding problems prior to the start of data collection as well as to check reliability of collected data. Ten studies reported reliability of the coding. Formulas used for testing reliability included Holsti's reliability formula, Perreault and Leigh's reliability index, the Spearman-Brown Prophesy Formula, and Scott's Pi. Bar-Ilan (1998) did not indicate what type of test was used to generate a 92% reliability score for her study. Reliability scores ranged from .62 to 1.00.

The fifth stage of content analysis is to analyze and interpret data. As noted earlier, the purpose of most of these studies was descriptive in nature. Therefore, it is not surprising that key findings are also descriptive in nature.

One theme that emerged from several of these studies was the diversity found at Web sites. For example, Bates and Lu (1997) found that the "personal home page" is an evolving communication form, Clyde (1996) found variety in the structure and function of library Web sites, and McMillan (1998) concluded that the Web has diversity of content, funding sources, and communication models.

A second theme found in these studies is commercialization of the Web. Some studies view commercialization as positive for marketers and/or consumers while others express concern about impacts of commercialization on public life and/or academic expression. As a counterpoint to these concerns, Gibson and Ward (1998) found the Web offered a forum for minor political parties to have a voice.

A third major theme was the fact that many site developers are not using the Web to its full potential as a multi-media interactive environment. Researchers found many sites made limited use of interactivity, graphics and motion video, and search functions. And Elliott's (1999) study suggested that there is still significant room for development of new content in important areas such as family life education.

Recommendations for Future Researchers

The studies reviewed above found that the stable research technique of content analysis can be applied in the dynamic communication environment of the Web. But using content analysis in this environment does raise potential problems for the researcher. Some of these studies exhibit creative ways of addressing these problems. Unfortunately, others seem to have failed to build rigor into their research designs in their haste to analyze a new medium. Future studies that apply content analysis techniques to the Web need to consider carefully each of the primary research steps identified in the literature: formulating research questions and/or hypotheses, sampling, data collection and coding, training coders and checking the reliability of their work, and analyzing and interpreting data.

For the first step, formulating the research questions and/or hypotheses, content analysis of the Web is both similar to and different from traditional media. Content analysis of traditional media, such as newspapers and broadcast, assumes some linearity or at least commonly accepted sequencing of messages. Hypertext, a defining characteristic of the Web, defies this assumption. Each individual may interact with content of a Web site in different ways. Furthermore, the Web is both "like" and "unlike" print and broadcast as it combines text, audio, still images, animation, and video. These unique characteristics of the medium may suggest unique research questions. However, in some fundamental ways, the first step in the research process remains similar. Researchers should build on earlier theoretical and empirical work in defining their Web-based research. Approaches taken by the authors cited above tend to be consistent with Holsti's first purpose of content analysis: describing the characteristics of communication. This is appropriate for early studies of an emerging medium. However, researchers also need to move on to the other two purposes identified by Holsti (1969): making inferences as to antecedents of communication and making inferences as to the effects of communication.

The second step in content analysis research, sampling, presents some unique challenges for Web-based content analysis. As noted earlier, a key concern in sampling is that each unit must have the same chance as all other units of being represented. The first challenge for the researcher is to identify the units to be sampled. This will be driven by the research question. For example, if the researcher wants to examine a sample of Web sites for Fortune 500 companies, it may be fairly simple to obtain a list of these sites and apply a traditional sampling method (e.g., a table of random numbers, every *n*th item on the list, etc.). But, if one seeks a different kind of sample (e.g., all business Web sites) the task may become more difficult. Essentially, the researcher has two primary sources from which to develop a sampling frame: offline sources and online sources.

If the researcher draws a sample from offline sources (e.g., directories, lists maintained by industry groups, etc.) then drawing a random sample is fairly non-problematic. Because the sample universe exists in a "set" medium, traditional methods of sampling can be used. However, a major problem with offline sources is that they are almost certainly out of date. Given the rapid growth and change of the Web, new sites have probably been added since the printed list was created while others have moved or been removed.

Online sources can be updated more frequently, and thus help to eliminate some of the problems associated with offline sources. And, in many cases (e.g., directories, lists maintained by industry groups, etc.), the list can appear in the same kind of format that is found in an offline source, making sampling fairly straightforward. But, human list-compilers are less efficient than search engines for identifying all potential Web sites that meet specific criteria. And in some cases no compiled list may exist that directly reflects the criteria of a study. In these cases, search engines may be the best way of generating a sample frame. However, care must be taken in using search engine results. First, authors must make sure that they have defined appropriate key words and that they understand search techniques for the search engine that they are using. If they do not, they run the risk of either over registration or under registration. Human intervention may be needed to insure that the computer-generated list does not include any spurious and/or duplicate items. Once a list has been generated, the researcher needs to determine the best way to draw a random sample. One way to ease the problem of random assignment may be to generate a hardcopy of the list. Then the researcher can assign random numbers to the list and/or more easily select every *n*th item. However, if a hierarchical search engine (such as Yahoo!) is used, special care must be taken to ensure that all items in subcategories have an equal chance of being represented in the sample. In some cases, stratified sampling may be required.

Research needs to be done to test the validity of multiple sampling methods. For example, does the use of different search engines result in empirically different findings? What sample size is adequate? How can sampling techniques from traditional media (e.g., selection of "representative" newspapers or broadcast stations) be applied to the Web? A key concern is that sampling methods for the Web not be held to either higher or lower standards than have been accepted for traditional media.

The rapid growth and change of the Web also lead to potential problems in the third stage of content analysis: data collection and coding. The fast-paced Web almost demands that data be collected in a short time frame so that all coders are analyzing the same content. Koehler (1999) has suggested some tools that researchers can use to download Web sites to capture a "snapshot" of content. However, as Clyde (1996) noted, copyright laws of some countries prohibit, among other things, the storage of copyrighted text in a database system. Whether or not the site was downloaded prior to analysis, researchers must specify when they examined a site. Just as newspaper-based research must indicate the date of publication, and broadcast-based research must indicate which newscast is analyzed, so Web-based content analysis must specify the time-frame of the analysis. For sites that change rapidly, exact timing may become important.

Researchers must also take care in defining units of analysis. The coding unit can be expected to vary depending on the theory upon which the study is based, the research questions explored, and the hypotheses tested. However, some standardization is needed for context units. For example, analyses of traditional media have developed traditional context units (e.g., the column-inch and/or a word count for newspapers; time measured in seconds for broadcast), but no such standard seems to have yet emerged for the Web. The fact that multiple media forms are combined on the Web may be one of the reasons for this lack of a clear unit of measurement. The majority of the studies reviewed above simply defined the context unit as the "Web site." Future studies should specify how much of the Web site was reviewed (e.g., "home page" only; first three levels in the site hierarchy, etc.). But as analysis of the Web matures, entirely new context units may need to be developed to address phenomena that are completely nonexistent in traditional media. For example, Wassmuth and Thompson (1999) measured the ways in which the content of the Web was "adapted" in real-time to become more responsive to site visitors' needs.

The fourth step in content analysis, training coders and checking the reliability of their work, involves both old and new challenges on the Web. Given the evolving nature of data coding described above, training may involve "learning together" with coders how to develop appropriate context and coding units. But the rapid change that characterizes the Web may introduce some new problems in checking inter-coder reliability.* This does not mean that well-developed tools for checking reliability should be abandoned. Rather, the primary challenge is to make sure that coders are actually cross-coding identical data. If Web sites are checked at different times by different coders and/or if the context unit is not dearly defined, false error could be introduced. The coders might not look at the same segment of the site, or data coded by the first coder might be changed or removed before the second coder examines the site. Only one of the studies reviewed above directly addressed this issue. Wassmuth and Thompson (1999) carefully defined a task to be performed at a site and had two coders perform that identical task at exactly the same date and time. This is one viable alternative. However, if the content of the site is changing rapidly, this control may not be sufficient. Another alternative is to have coders evaluate sites that have been downloaded. These downloaded sites are "frozen in time" and will not change between the coding times. However, as noted earlier, there may be some legal problems with such downloaded sites. Furthermore, depending on the number of sites being examined, the time and disk-space requirements for downloading all of the studied sites may be prohibitive.

The Web does not seem to pose any truly new challenges in the final step in content analysis: analyzing and interpreting the data. Rather, researchers must simply remember that rigor in analyzing and interpreting the findings is needed as much in this environment as in others. For example, some of the studies reported above used statistics that assume a random sample to analyze data sets that were not randomly generated. Findings and conclusions of such studies must be viewed with caution. Such inappropriate use of analytical tools would probably not be tolerated by reviewers had not the Web-based subject matter of the studies been perceived as "new" and "innovative." But new communication tools are not an excuse for ignoring established communication research techniques.

In conclusion, the microscope of content analysis can be applied to the moving target of the Web. But researchers must use rigor and creativity to make sure that they don't lose focus before they take aim.

References

Aikat, D. (1995). *Adventures in cyberspace: Exploring the information content of the World Wide Web pages on the Internet.* Unpublished dissertation, University of Ohio, Athens.

Alloro, G., Casilli, C., Taningher, M., & Ugolini, D. (1998). Electronic biomedical journals: How they appear and what they offer. *European Journal of Cancer 34,* 3:290–295.

*A separate issue, not directly addressed in this study, is the use of computer-based content analysis for examining the digital content of Web sites. None of the studies examined in this article utilized this technique. With computerized analysis of content, reliability is ensured but validity and relevance become even more important.

Bar-Ilan, J. (1998). The mathematician, Paul Erdos (1913–1996) in the eyes of the Internet. *Scientometrics 43:*257–267.

Bates, M. J., & Lu, S. (1997). An exploratory profile of personal home pages: Content, design, metaphors. *Online and CDROM Review 21:*332.

Budd, R. W., Thorp, R. K., & Donohew, L. (1967). *Content analysis of communications.* New York: The Macmillan Company.

Bush, C. R. (1951). The analysis of political campaign news. *Journalism Quarterly 28:*250–252.

Clyde, L. A. (1996). The library as information provider: The home page. *The Electronic Library 14:*549–558.

Commerce Department. (2000). *The emerging digital economy.* Retrieved from http://www.ecommerce.govdanintro.html

Elliott, M. (1999). Classifying family life education on the World Wide Web. *Family Relations 48:*7–13.

Esrock, S. I., & Leichty, G. B. (1998). Social responsibility and corporate Web pages: Self-presentation or agenda-setting? *Public Relations Review 24,* 3:305–319.

Frazer, C., & McMillan, S. J. (1997). Sophistication on the World Wide Web: Evaluating structure, function, and commercial goals of web sites. In E. Thorson & D. Schumann (Eds.), *Advertising and the world* (pp. 119–134). Hillsdale, NJ: Lawrence Erlbaum.

Gibson, R. K., & Ward, S. J. (1998). U.K. political parties and the Internet: 'Politics as usual' in the new media? *Press/Politics 3:*14–38.

Ha, L., & James, E. L. (1998). Interactivity re-examined: A baseline analysis of early business web sites. *Journal of Broadcasting & Electronic Media 42:*457–474.

Heeter, C. (1989). Implications of new interactive technologies for conceptualizing communication. In J. L. Salvaggio & J. Bryant (Eds.), *Media use in the information age: Emerging patterns of adoption and consumer use* (pp. 217–235). Hillsdale, NJ: Lawrence Erlbaum.

Ho, J. (1997). Evaluating the World Wide Web: A global study of commercial sites. *Journal of Computer Mediated Communications 3,*3. Retrieved from http://jcmc.indiana.edu/v013/issue1/ho.html

Holsti, O. R. (1969). *Content analysis for the social sciences and humanities.* Reading, MA: Addison-Wesley.

Koehler, W. (1999). An analysis of web page and web site constancy and permanence. *Journal of the American Society for Information Science 50:*162–180.

Krippendorff, K. (1980). *Content analysis: An introduction to its methodology.* Thousand Oaks, CA: Sage.*

Leiner, B. M., Cerf, V. G., Clark, D. D., Kahn, R. E., Kleinrock, L., Lynch, D. C., Postel, J., Roberts, L. G., & Wolff, S. (2000). *A brief history of the Internet.* Retrieved from http://www.isoc.org/internet-history/brief.html

Li, X. (1998). Web page design and graphic use of three U.S. newspapers. *Journalism & Mass Communication Quarterly 75:*353–365.

Liu, C., Arnett, K. P., Capella, L. M., & Beatty, R. C. (1997). Web sites of the Fortune 500 companies: Facing customers through home pages. *Information & Management 31:*335–345.

Massey, B. L., & Levy, M. R. (1999). Interactivity, online journalism and English-language web newspapers in Asia. *Journalism & Mass Communication Quarterly 76:*138–151.

McMillan, S. J. (1998). Who pays for content? Funding in interactive media. *Journal of Computer-Mediated Communication 4.* Retrieved from http://jcmc.indiana.edu/v014/issue1/mcmillan.html

McMillan, S. J., & Campbell, K. B. (1996). *Online cities: Are they building a virtual public sphere or expanding consumption communities?* Paper presented at the AEJMC Annual Conference, Anaheim, CA.

Peng, F. Y., Tham, N. I., & Xiaoming, H. (1999). Trends in online newspapers: A look at the U.S. web. *Newspaper Research Journal 20,* 2:52–63.

Tannery, N., & Wessel, C. B. (1998). Academic medical center libraries on the Web. *Bulletin of the Medical Library Association 86:*541–544.

Wassmuth, B., & Thompson, D. R. (1999, March). *Banner ads in online newspapers: Are they specific?* Paper presented at the American Academy of Advertising annual conference, Albuquerque, NM.

*Krippendorff, K. (2004). *Content analysis: An introduction to its methodology* (2nd ed.). Thousand Oaks, CA: Sage.

2.4

AIRPLANE ACCIDENT FATALITIES AFTER NEWSPAPER STORIES ABOUT MURDER AND SUICIDE

DAVID P. PHILLIPS*

Earlier research (Phillips, 1974, 1977) showed that (a) suicides and motor vehicle accidents increase after publicized suicides, and (b) the more publicity given to the suicide, the greater the increase in suicides and in motor vehicle accidents. These findings suggest that suicide stories help to trigger a rise in suicides, some of which are disguised as motor vehicle accidents.

In this report, I will examine the impact of murder-suicide stories. I will present quantitative evidence for a large geographic area suggesting that murder-suicide stories trigger subsequent murder-suicides.

Many murderers may try to disguise murder-suicides as accidents to protect their survivors from insurance problems and from social stigma. One type of disguised murder-suicide may occur when a pilot deliberately crashes an airplane with passengers on board. If murder-suicide stories trigger subsequent murder-suicides, fatal aircraft accidents should increase abruptly and briefly just after such stories are published.

In this report, I will examine only noncommercial aircraft accidents, an exhaustive list of which is available[1] (National Transportation Safety Board). The murder-suicide stories to be studied consist of all stories meeting five criteria, which were established to ensure that the circumstances described in the story were as widely publicized as possible and as similar as possible to the circumstances obtaining for the pilot of a noncommercial plane. The five criteria were:

> The story must concern deaths occurring in the United States. This criterion was established because a U.S. pilot should be more likely to identify with 'American' deaths than with foreign ones.
>
> The story must concern one murderer acting alone, because a pilot bent on murder-suicide should

---

*Phillips, D. P. (1978). Airplane accident fatalities increase just after newspaper stories about murder and suicide. *Science 201*:748–750.

be more likely to identify with a single murderer than with several murderers acting together.

The story must concern a murderer and victims who died within a short time.[2] This type of murder-suicide is the most likely to affect a pilot bent on murder-suicide, because a pilot who deliberately crashes his plane is likely to kill himself and his passengers nearly simultaneously.

The story must concern a murderer who killed two or more victims. This type of story is likely to be heavily publicized, in contrast to the more routine murder-suicide, in which only one victim is killed.

The story must be carried on the front page of *The New York Times* or the *Los Angeles Times* or appear on the ABC, CBS or NBC network evening news programs, between 1968 and 1973. The period under study ended in 1973 because that was the last year before the Arab oil embargo markedly changed aircraft traffic patterns. The study period began on 5 August 1968 because systematic recording of network television news coverage began on this date. In all, 18 stories met the five criteria.[3]

Nonsystematic, exploratory study of airplane fatalities before 1968 suggested that airplane fatalities behave like motor vehicle fatalities (Phillips, 1977) and rise to a sharp peak on day three after a publicized death. Based on these earlier results, I predicted that a day-three peak should also be found in the study period, 1968 to 1973. As predicted, aircraft fatalities increased sharply on day three after publicized murder-suicides (Fig. 1, curve A).[4]

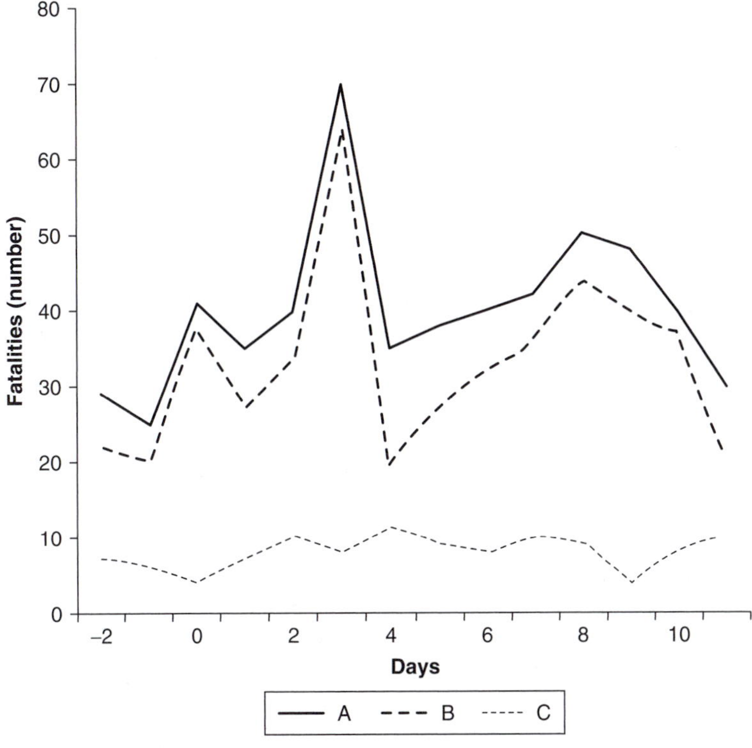

Figure 1 Daily fluctuation of U.S. noncommercial plane fatalities for a 2-week period before, during (day 0), and after publicized murder-suicides. (Curve A) Fluctuation of fatalities for all noncommercial plane crashes; (curve B) fluctuation of fatalities for multi-fatality noncommercial plane crashes; and (curve C) fluctuation of fatalities for single-fatality noncommercial plane crashes. Noncommercial flying refers to "the use of an aircraft for purposes of pleasure, personal transportation, . . . private business, in corporate/executive operations, and in other operations, wherein there is no direct monetary fee charged" (NTSB). Planes owned in the United States but crashing outside the 50 states are excluded from this analysis.

A single-fatality plane crash cannot imply both murder and suicide. Hence, this type of crash should not be triggered by murder-suicide stories. As expected, fatalities from this type of crash did not increase after publicized murder-suicides (Fig. 1, curve C). In contrast, however, fatalities resulting from multi-fatality crashes increase steeply (Fig 1, curve B).

These multi-fatality crashes resulted in 461 fatalities in the 14-day period under study. Of these, one fourteenth (32.93) would be expected on day 3, given the null hypothesis (H_0) of no relationship between the publicized murder-suicide and airplane fatalities. The observed number of deaths on day 3 (63) is almost twice the number expected.

One cannot test the statistical significance of this peak in terms of fatalities, however, because the appropriate significance test requires the assumption that the timing of each fatality is independent of the timing of every other. This assumption is obviously untenable for multi-fatality plane crashes. Instead, the significance of the day-three peak can be assessed in terms of crashes rather than fatalities. These can be treated as independent of one another, provided one counts a midair collision between two planes as only one crash. In the 14-day period under observation, there were 15 multi-fatality plane crashes. Under H_0, one fourteenth of these (11.14) would be expected to occur on day three, but 19 crashes actually occurred at this time. The binomial distribution can be used to evaluate the probability of 19 or more crashes when $p = 1/14$; $n = 156$. This probability is .0160. Hence, there is a statistically significant day-three peak in multi-fatality crashes.[5]

If murder-suicide stories do indeed help to trigger some fatal airplane accidents, then the more publicity given to a murder-suicide, the more airplane accidents should increase just after the murder-suicide. This hypothesis will be tested after an index of newspaper publicity is described.

In the midpoint of the study period, there were 1838 daily newspapers in the United States;[6] thus, it is not easy to measure the total amount of newspaper publicity devoted nationwide to a murder-suicide. The measurement procedure adopted here seems plausible and is convenient. Almost half of all the operative civilian aircraft in the United States are concentrated in only nine states.[7] The largest newspaper from each of these states was examined to determine which murder-suicide stories were carried on the front page.[8] The publicity devoted by these newspapers (Table 1) could then be used as an index of the total amount of publicity devoted by all newspapers. For any given story, the value of this index was calculated from

$$\sum_{i=1}^{9} x_i y_i$$

where x_i is the circulation of newspaper i at the time of the story and y_i is the number of days that story stayed on the front page. Five stories were not carried by any or the newspapers examined, only by the television networks. For these five stories, the value of the newspaper index was of course zero.

As predicted, the amount of newspaper publicity devoted to a murder-suicide was strongly correlated with the number of multi-fatality crashes following the story ($r = .637$; $p < .005$, one-tailed test).[9] In contrast, television publicity does not seem to be significantly correlated with the occurrence of multi-fatality plane crashes. The number of networks covering a murder-suicide story on the network evening news programs (Table 1) was taken as an index of the amount of network television publicity devoted to the story. This index was non-significantly correlated ($r = .379$; $p = .082$; one-tailed test; $n = 14$) with the number of multi-fatality plane crashes occurring after each story.[10] For the 14 stories for which information on both television and newspaper coverage is available (Table 1), the correlation between newspaper coverage and crashes ($r = .734$) was almost as high as the multiple correlation between newspaper-television coverage and crashes ($R = .737$). Evidently, newspaper coverage alone predicts multi-fatality crashes almost as well as newspaper and television coverage combined.[11]

Thus far I have shown that (a) multi-fatality crashes increased after murder-suicides and (b) the more newspaper publicity devoted to a story, the more plane crashes followed it. I will now show that (c) the increase in

Table 1 Relationship between publicity devoted to a murder-suicide and number of fatal noncommercial plane crashes in the week after that story. The date of the murder-suicide was the date of the murder (the first murder if more than one was described in the story).

Murderer	*Date of Murder-Suicide*	*Newspaper Circulation*	*Networks Carrying Story*	*Multi-Fatality Plane Crashes (N)*
F. Chegwin	08/07/68	856, 621	unknown	6
S. Kline } C. Bray[a]	12/18/68 } 12/19/68	1,032,655	unknown } 1	6
R. McLachlan	01/01/69	3,470,925	unknown	5
C. Stein	02/10/69	0	1	3
T. Walton	02/21/69	0	3	3
C. Gish	05/14/70	0	1	4
J. White	09/23/70	440,570	3	7
E. Pruyn	01/26/71	634,371	1	2
R. Putnam	07/13/71	1,044,660	2	4
G. Giffe	10/04/71	3,220,174	3	8
G. Logan	11/26/71	966,293	0	8
R. Cowden	12/13/71	404.957	1	4
J. Van Praag	03/07/72	981,661	0	4
H. McLeod	05/29/72	3,764,339	3	8
D. Tolstet	10/06/72	0	1	2
R. Jordan	01/23/73	0	1	2
S. Cloud	10/18/73	823,935	0	4

a. The bracketed murder-suicide stories occurred at almost the same time and were treated as one story.

multi-fatality plane crashes occurred mainly in the states where the murder-suicide was publicized. This result would be expected if multi-fatality plane crashes were triggered by publicized murder-suicides.

Some definitions must be supplied. The "experimental period" consisted of the 7 days (0 to 6 days) after the publicized murder-suicide. The "control period" was the remaining 7 days designated in Figure 1. For any given story, the "publicity area" was the state or states known to be receiving newspaper publicity about the story.[12] The "non-publicity area" consisted of all the remaining states.

If plane crashes increase mainly in the area where the murder-suicide is publicized, there should be a disproportionately large number of crashes in the publicity area in the experimental period. On the other hand, given H_0, the publicity area should not differ from the entire United States with respect to the probability that a crash would occur in the experimental period. In the 14-day interval under study, there were 121 multi-fatality crashes in the entire United States; of these, 63 (or .52) were in the experimental period. In the publicity area there were 20 multi-fatality crashes; 15 of these were in the experimental period. Given H_0 the probability of 15 or more crashes in the experimental period in the publicity area can be evaluated with the hypergeometric distribution, one-tailed (Hoel,

1965:116–117; Mosteller, Rourke, & Thomas, 1970: Table 3–3)[13] where:

$$P(x \geq 15) = \sum_{x=15}^{20} \frac{\binom{Np}{x}\binom{N-Np}{n-x}}{\binom{N}{n}}$$

$$= \sum_{x=15}^{20} \frac{\binom{63}{x}\binom{58}{20-x}}{\binom{121}{20}}$$

$$= .0213$$

Hence, multi-fatality plane crashes increased disproportionately in the areas where the murder-suicides were publicized.

The evidence thus suggests that (a) some persons are prompted by newspaper stories to commit murder as well as suicide, and (b) noncommercial airplanes are sometimes used as instruments of murder and suicide. Taken in conjunction with previous research (Phillips, 1974, 1977), the results suggest that the impact of newspaper stories may be at once more general and more grave than was previously suspected.[14]

Notes

1. I know of no large-scale, quantitative studies suggesting that noncommercial planes are sometimes used as instruments of both murder and suicide. There are some case studies suggesting a suicidal (but not a homicidal component in some noncommercial plane crashes: Gibbons, Plechus, & Mohler, 1967; Yanowitch, Bergin, & Yanowitch, 1973; Stevens, 1970). Jones (1977) reviewed earlier work and provided a case study. In addition, indirect evidence of a suicidal component in some crashes might perhaps be inferred from toxicological findings (Lacefield, Roberts, & Blossom, 1975) and possibly from personality tests of pilots involved in accidents (Sanders & Hofmann, 1975: 186; Sanders, Hofmann, & Neese, 1976:177). However, the two last-named studies present mutually contradictory evidence.

2. This time period was defined arbitrarily as 48 hours. However, in practically all cases, the deaths of the murderer and his victims occurred within 24 hours of each other. In almost all cases the murderer shot himself, but in a few cases (i.e., *McLachlan, Stein, Putnam,* and *Cloud*) the murderer was killed by the police after refusing to surrender. These four cases have been treated as suicide, because the murderer could have avoided death had he so desired. Cases like these, in which the victim precipitates his own death, have long been considered by some researchers to be a type of suicidal behavior. See, for example Wolfgang (1968:90–104).

3. Two of these stories (*Kline* and *Bray*) occurred at almost the same time. In accord with previous procedure (Phillips, 1977) they were treated as one to avoid problems of statistical dependence. Information on television network evening news coverage was provided by Vanderbilt Television News Archives (Joint University Libraries, Nashville, periodic issues). Weekend stories before July 1970 were excluded from the analysis, because until then weekend broadcasts were not recorded in the archives.

4. The particular 2-week period studied was chosen to make Figure 1 comparable with earlier results for automobiles (2). The graph of airplane accidents after murder-suicide stories resembles that of automobile accidents after suicide stories. In both, there is a primary peak on day 3 after the publicized death and a secondary peak on day 8. This secondary peak is at present unexplained.

5. An alternative approach to testing statistical significance would be to use one or another variant of the t-test to determine whether the number of crashes on day 3 is significantly larger than the number to be expected from an analysis of the crashes in the other 13 days studied. This approach is probably not valid, because the data do not meet the assumptions of the t-test. For the reader who wishes, nonetheless, to use the t-test, the following are the number of multi-fatality crashes from 2 days before to day 11 after the story: 7, 8, 12, 6, 10, 19, 9, 10, 13, 12, 14, 15, 12, 9.

6. *Ayer Directory of Publications* (Ayer, Philadelphia, yearly volumes).

7. The top nine states with respect to ownership of operative U.S. civil aircraft are (in order) California, Texas, Ohio, Illinois, Florida, Michigan, New York, Pennsylvania, and Washington [Department of Transportation, 1971. *Census of U.S. Civil Aircraft 1970–1971* Government Printing Office, Washington, D.C., 1971, table 7].

8. The nine newspapers examined are *Los Angeles Times, Dallas News, Cleveland Plain Dealer, Chicago Tribune, Miami Herald, Detroit News, New York Times, Philadelphia Bulletin,* and *Seattle Press Intelligencer.* For three states (Texas, New York, and Washington), the largest newspaper was not easily available, and the second-largest paper was used.

9. This significance level is valid only under the assumption that the joint distribution of the two variables is bivariate normal. I do not know whether this assumption holds for these data. The assumption is not required for assessing the significance of the Spearman *p* ($p = .707$, $p < .005$, one-tailed correlation, corrected for ties, for the data in Table 1).

10. Because of the failure of recording equipment and other factors, the Vanderbilt Television News Archives does not have information on the total number of networks covering the stories about Chegwin, Kline, or McLachlan. Consequently, these stories were excluded in the calculation of the correlation between the television publicity devoted to a story and the number of crashes after that story. The correlation with television publicity may be weak because the networks almost never reported the murder-suicides as lead stories. In contrast, the newspapers studied did treat the murder-suicides under examination as lead stories and carried them, very visibly, on page 1.

11. For these stories, the partial correlation between newspaper coverage and the number of multi-fatality crashes (correcting for television coverage) is .683. Single-fatality crashes should not be triggered by murder-suicide stories; hence, the fluctuation of single-fatality crashes after a story should not be correlated with the amount of newspaper publicity devoted to that story. This prediction is consistent with the data ($r = -.050$).

12. Because television publicity seems to be non-significantly related to plane crashes, television news coverage was ignored in this analysis, and stories receiving no newspaper coverage (only television publicity) were excluded from the analysis.

13. In this analysis, $N = 121$ rather than 156 as in the binomial analysis, because the present analysis omits crashes associated with five stories publicized only on television and three missing planes that crashed in unknown locations. One would prefer to code crashes by "place of take-off" rather than by "place of crash," but this is not possible because the publication describing the crashes studied often does not provide information on place of take-off.

14. The day-3 peak might be argued to result from a fortuitous association between a day-of-the-week cycle in murder-suicide stories and a day-of-the-week cycle in multi-fatality plane crashes. For example, if most murder-suicides occurred on Wednesday and most plane crashes occurred on Saturday, crashes would peak 3 days after murder-suicides, even if murder-suicides had no effect on plane crashes. However: (i) If the day-3 peak were due to a day-of-the-week cycle in plane crashes, the peak in crashes on day 3 should be followed by an equally large peak 1 week later (on day 10), 2 weeks later, and so on. There is no evidence of a peak on a day 10. In fact, the number of crashes on this day (12) was almost precisely equal to 11.14, the number to be expected if crashes are uniformly distributed from day –2 to day +11. (ii) More generally, if the "day-of-the-week" argument were correct, there should be a strong, positive correlation between the number of multi-fatality crashes on day x and the number of multi-fatality crashes on day x + 7. If this argument is not correct, then *r* should be approximately zero. For the data displayed in (8), $r = -.0206$. This does not support the "day-of-the-week" argument. (iii) If the "day-of-the-week" argument were correct, there would be no causal connection between publicized murder-suicides and plane crashes; hence, there should be no correlation between the amount of publicity given to a murder-suicide story and the number of crashes thereafter. In addition, there should be no correlation between the location of the publicity devoted to the murder-suicide and the location of the plane crashes occurring just afterward. Both of these predictions are inconsistent with the data.

References

Gibbons, H. L., Plechus, J. L., & Mohler, S. R. (1967). Consideration of volitional acts in aircraft accident investigation. *Aerospace Medicine 38,* 10:1057–1059.

Hoel, P. (1965). *Introduction to mathematical statistics.* New York: Wiley.

Jones, R. (1977). Suicide by aircraft: a case report. *Aviation, Space & Environmental Medicine 4:*454.

Lacefield, D. L., Roberts, P. A., & Blossom, C. W. (1975). Toxicological findings in civil aviation accidents, fiscal years 1968–1974. *Aviation, Space & Environmental Medicine 46:*1030.

Mosteller, F., Rourke, R. E. K., & Thomas, G. B. (1970). *Probability with statistical applications.* Reading, MA: Addison-Wesley.

Phillips, D. P. (1974). *American Sociological Review 39:*340.

Phillips, D. P. (1977). Motor vehicle fatalities increase just after publicized suicide stories. *Science 196:*1464–1465.

Sanders, M. G., & Hofmann, M. A. (1975). Personality aspects of involvement in pilot-error accidents. *Aviation, Space & Environmental Medicine 47,*2:186–190.

Sanders, M. G., Hofmann, M. A., & Neese, T. A. (1976). Cross-validation study of the personality aspects of involvement in pilot-error accidents. *Aviation, Space & Environmental Medicine 47,* 2:177–179.

Stevens, P. J. (1970). *Fatal civil aircraft accidents.* Bristol, England: Wright.

U.S. National Transportation Safety Board Briefs of accidents US. Civil Aviation (Government Printing 001cc, Washington. DC, periodic issues).

Wolfgang, M. (1968). Suicide by means of victim-precipitated violence. In H. Resnik (Ed.), *Suicidal behaviors* (pp. 90–104). Boston: Little, Brown.

Yanowitch, R. S., Bergin, J. R., & Yanowitch, S. A. (1973). Aircraft as an instrument of self-destruction. *Aerospace Medicine 44,* 6: 675–678.

2.5

INTERACTION PROCESS ANALYSIS

ROBERT F. BALES*

SMALL GROUPS

A small group is defined as any number of persons engaged in interaction with each other in a single face-to-face meeting or a series of such meetings, in which each member receives some impression or perception of each other member distinct enough so that they can, either at the time or in later questioning, give some reaction to each of the others as an individual person, even though it be only to recall that the other was present.

According to this definition, a number of persons who have never interacted with each other do not constitute a small group. A number of persons who may be physically present at the same event (such as a lecture) but do not interact with each other enough for each to be able to form any distinct impression of every other, or for the observers to produce some data concerning the relation of each member to every other, do not constitute a small group in the present sense. A number of persons so large or scattered that they interact with each other only indirectly as unknown members of sub-groups or through intermediary persons or impersonal means of communication (such as an industrial organization as a whole) is too large, too complex, and indistinct to fall within the definition. Some collections of people, which initially appear to fall within the definition, may prove, when techniques are applied, to fall outside the definition as a total group because one or several of the members may prove not to have been aware in any discernible way of the presence of one or more of the others. In this case, only that nucleus of persons, each of whom recognizes or remembers each of the others, and is in turn recognized or remembered by each of the others, constitutes the small group.

THE PROCESS OF INTERACTION

Here, we carry the analysis of the content of action . . . [into] the process of action . . . by presenting concepts in terms of which the observer can think about [that] process . . . not simply as a target object, but as a context within which acts may be placed or located. . . .

The . . . total process of action is complex in [three] ways. First, we assume that it

*Excerpts from Bales, R. F. (1950). *Interaction process analysis: A method for the study of small groups.* Chicago: University of Chicago Press. (pp. 8–11, 14–19, 34, 37–38, 49-50, 54, 66, 72–73)

involves a distribution of phases, or parts, or aspects in the time dimension. This assumption made, we find that we have to think of the process as having an internal complexity at any given point in time. Finally, we find that the process is complex in that it involves a distribution of parts or phases between persons. All three of these assumptions are interlocking, and in certain respects identical.

With regard to time involvement, the total process of action as a system of acts is conceived as proceeding from a beginning toward an end, from a felt need or problem toward a solution, from a state of tension toward tension reduction, from a state of heightened motivation toward motivation reduction, or in an instrumentally oriented or meaningful way which may be described in terms similar to these. Action is conceived to have a sense or direction such that any given act is relevant, either logically or causally to what has gone before, what the actor expects to come, or both. A given act is thus regarded as a part of a larger context, which is distributed in the time or process dimension, and the act is given its character in certain measure by its particular location in this context.

This forward and backward reference of action in the time dimension is assumed to rest largely on the ability of normally socialized human beings to deal with their situation by the manipulation of symbols. This ability, we postulate, makes it possible to remember the consequences of their past action and to foresee the consequences of their present activity, or rather, to build up expectations as to what the consequences will be. In human action, we assume, both the remembered consequences and the expected consequences can become a part of the effective causation of action. The manipulation of symbols is conceived to be not simply an epiphenomenon, but an aspect of action as "real" as any other in its causal role. The manipulation of symbols, we assume, can operate to steer the ongoing act; it is through the manipulation of symbols that the present act can bear a *meaningful* as well as a causal relation to what has gone before, and that the anticipated future can play a *causal* as well as a meaningful role in the present. In short, the manipulation of symbols or the imputation of meaning on the part of the actor is, insofar as it is present, a part or an aspect of the causal process.

From the assumption that the process of action is a process which goes on between social objects (actor and other, where more than one individual is involved, or actor and self, in the case of the single individual) we conclude that *communication* between the two foci is an indispensable feature of the process if it is to proceed in other than expressive ways. Communication between the two or more foci, however, as we view it, is in itself an achievement, i.e., it is a result of interaction and requires interaction if it is to be maintained or sustained. This seems to imply that at least in some sense, interaction is prior to communication. This indeed is what we do imply, along the lines suggested by George H. Mead, but this is an area of problems which we can by-pass by assumptions for the present.

If we by-pass for the moment the problem of how communication is achieved, and assume that at some given time it has been achieved and that action is proceeding in a small group as a joint or shared process, we also assume that insofar as communication does exist, the essential elements of the process are reproduced, repeated, or represented symbolically, separately in the minds of each of the participants. We also assume that each person proceeds with an awareness, or at least an assumption, that the process is being shared with the other. The "sense" (i.e., the intuition of appropriate cognitive, expressive, or instrumental consonance) of the activity of each of the participants, from both their own point of view and (that) of each of the others, depends upon the way the present act fits into the total shared process. Insofar as the process is shared or is felt to require a sharing by each participant, any failure of sufficiently exact reproduction in the mind of any one of the participants (as to the thinking, feeling, or intention of the others) may be felt by him, her, and by the others to constitute an impairment of the integrity of the total process and may constitute the occasion for one of the sudden modifications of the total process . . . in an effort to restore the shared integrity.

The Interaction Categories in the Context of Problem-Solving

The present set of categories is concerned with what we call interaction content or process content as distinguished from topical content. In other words, it is concerned with content that can be detected . . . in the process of interaction in any small group. The observer assumes that all small groups are similar in that they involve a plurality of persons who have certain common task problems arising out of their relation to an outer situation, and certain problems of social and emotional relationships arising out of their contact with each other. The possibility of a generalized set of categories like that presented here rests upon this assumption. Another important assumption involved is that each act of each individual in the group can be analyzed with regard to its bearing on these problems. This kind of abstract analysis we call *interaction process analysis.* The present set of categories is an attempt to provide a systematic framework in terms of which this kind of analysis can be made.

At its own level of abstraction, the type of analysis described here may be called inclusive and continuous. The set of categories is meant to be completely inclusive in the sense that every act, which can be observed, can be classified in one positively defined category. The method is continuous in that it requires observers to make a classification of every act they can observe, as it occurs in sequence, so that their work of classification and scoring for any given period of observation is continuous. No observed acts in a given period are omitted from classification except by error.

The twelve major categories in terms of which the scoring is done are shown in Figure 1. Perhaps the simplest way to conceive an idealized problem-solving sequence is in terms of the four sections of the chart, labeled A, B, C, and D. Section C constitutes a group of activities, which can be characterized very generally as Questions. Section B constitutes a group of Attempted Answers. Section A contains several varieties of Positive Reactions, and Section D contains a similar group of Negative Reactions. Using this conception, one might hypothesize that the interaction process consists of Questions, followed by Attempted Answers, followed by either Negative or Positive Reactions. This, however, is an idealized conception, which is largely formal in attire and ignores most of the important empirical characteristics of interaction in which we are interested.

Another way of describing the relations of the categories to each other is to regard the middle area of the system, Sections B and C, as constituting an area of Task Problems, while the terminal sections, A and D, constitute an area of Social-Emotional Problem. The idealized interaction process would then be described as one of alternating emphasis on the two types of problems. When attention is given to the task, strains are created in the social and emotional relations of the members of the group, and attention then turns to the solution of these problems. So long as the group devoted its activity simply to social-emotional activity, however, the task is not being done, and attention would be expected to turn again to the task area.

A somewhat more abstract way of describing this alternation is to regard the problems in the task area as primarily Adaptive-Instrumental in significance, while the problems in the Social-Emotional area are primarily Integrative-Expressive in significance. With this terminology, one can hypothesize that the necessity of adaptation to the outer situation leads to instrumentally oriented activity, which in turn tends to create strains in the existing integration of the group. When these strains grow acute enough, activity turns to the expression of emotional tensions and the reintegration of the group. While reintegration is being achieved, however, the demands of adaptation wait, and activity eventually turns again to the Adaptive-Instrumental Task. This is still a very generalized and abstract way of conceiving the problem-solving nature of social interaction, but we believe, one of very great theoretical relevance and power.

A more concrete and differentiated conception of the problem-solving sequence, which appears to be at a strategic level of abstraction, may be outlined in terms of pairs of categories. It will be noticed that there is a

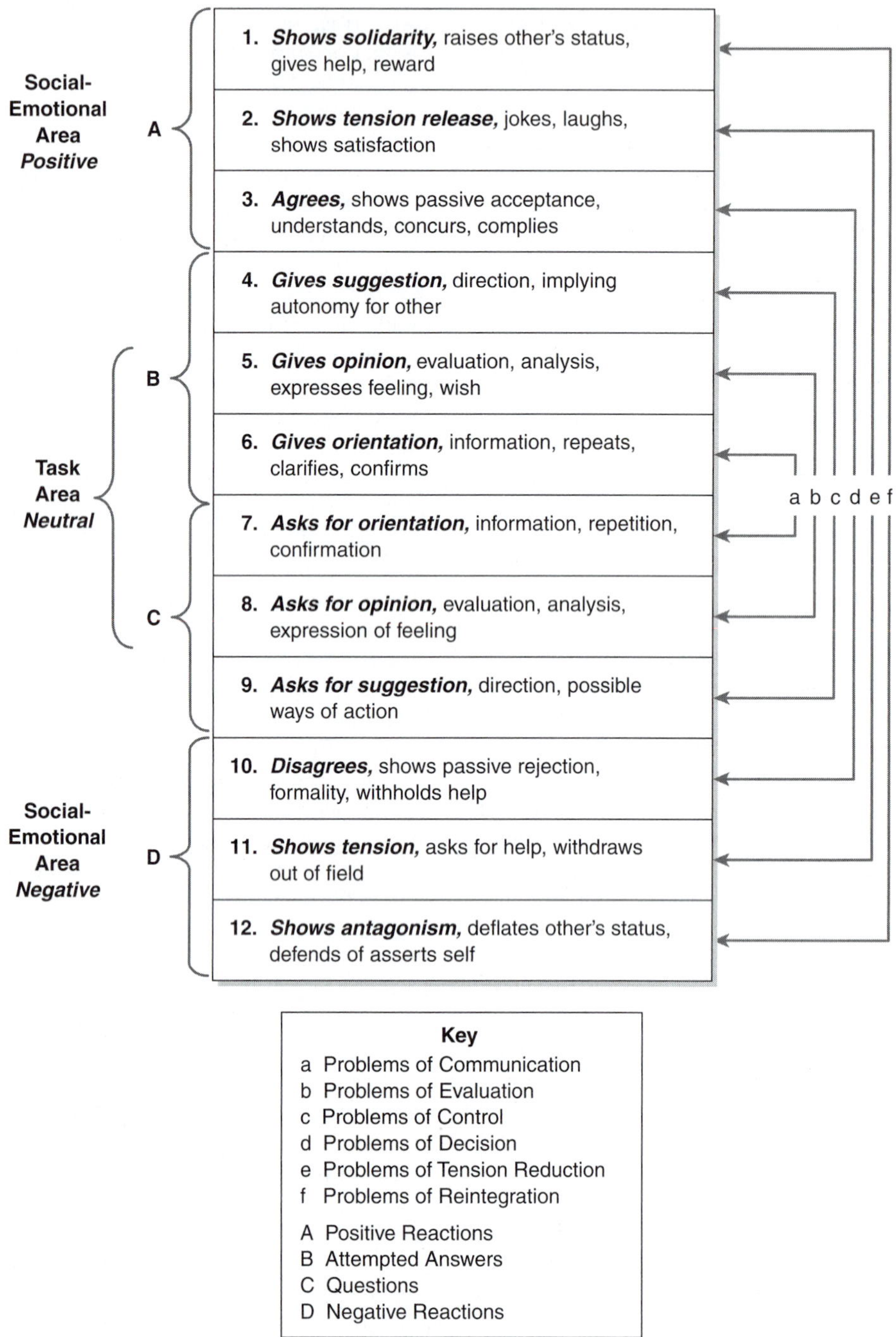

Figure 1 The System of Categories Used in Observation and Their Major Relations

symmetrical relation between the top half and the bottom half of the list of categories, with the middle line between Categories 6 and 7 taken as the starting point. To illustrate, Category 7 is concerned with activities that indicate a need for factual orientation of some kind and Category 6, its companion category, [that] appear to be intended to answer needs of this kind. Similarly, Category 5, giving opinion, etc, answers Category 8, asking for opinion, etc. The other categories have a similar relation. For each category below the line there is a companion category above the line, in a position symmetrical with it as to distance removed from the middle line.

Each pair of categories can be regarded as concerned with a particular aspect or phase of the complete problem-solving process. The successful transition through any particular phase may be regarded as one of the functional prerequisites to the maintenance of the interaction system in a kind of equilibrium. By equilibrium, we mean a turnover of the continuing process in a more or less regular pattern and emphasis of phases. For present purposes, these functional prerequisites may be formulated positively and given one-word designations that indicate roughly their kind of relevance to the successful and complete problem-solving sequence. In these one-word terms, Categories 7 and 6 are concerned with the functional problem of communication. The next pair, 8 and 5, is concerned with problems of evaluation, and following in order, Categories 9 and 4 with problems of control, 10 and 3 with problems of decision, 11 and 2 with problems of tension reduction, and 12 and 1 are concerned with problems of reintegration.

In conceiving the problem-solving process according to this model, then, we assume that there is a general tendency toward equilibrium; that is, a more or less regular turnover of phases back to a steady state. In order to maintain or regain the moving steady state, problems of communication must be solved as they arise, and so must be problems of evaluation, control, decision, tension reduction, and reintegration. It may be that through time there is a differing emphasis on each of these types of functional problems, so that there is an actual temporal order of "agenda topics," as it were, in the course of a group meeting.

The Units of Analysis

It has been taken as a general principle in the construction of the set of categories that all of the categories included should assume essentially the same time span; that is, they should all refer to single acts of communication or expression. This is not to deny that there are significant categories of analysis, which require longer contexts for application. . . .

The unit to be scored is the smallest discriminable segment of verbal or nonverbal behavior to which the observer, using the present set of categories after appropriate training, can assign a classification under conditions of continuous serial scoring. This unit may be called an act, or more properly, a single interaction—since all acts in the present scheme are regarded as interactions. The unit as defined here has also been called the single item of thought or the single item of behavior.

Often the unit will be a single simple sentence expressing or conveying a complete simple thought. Usually there will be a subject and predicate, though sometimes one of these elements will only be implied. As an example, if the actor in a conversation says "What?", the observer translates "What was that?" or "I do not understand you" or "Would yon repeat that?", thus filling out both subject and predicate. Complex sentences always involve more than one score. Dependent clauses are separately scored. If a series of predicates are asserted of a single subject, a separate score is given for each additional predicate on the reasoning that each one constitutes a new item of information or opinion. Compound sentences joined by "and," "but," etc., are broken down into their component simple parts, each of which is given a score. As an example of the foregoing points, the following sentence would be analyzed into four units: "This problem which we talked about for three hours yesterday / impresses me as very complicated / difficult / and perhaps beyond our power to solve. /" (Ends of units are indicated by slashes.)

In addition to speech centered on the issue being discussed, interaction includes facial expressions, gestures, bodily attitudes, emotional signs, or nonverbal acts of various kinds, either expressive and nonfocal, or more definitely directed toward other people. These expressions and gestures can be detected by the observer, given an interpretation in terms of the categories, and recorded.

Observers should remain as alert as possible; keeping their eyes on the group constantly, they should canvass the separate members for nonobtrusive expressive reactions at least once each minute and put down a score each time they can make a discrimination. The Interaction Recorder* is equipped with a warning light which flashes on once each minute as a signal for the observer to canvass the entire group for nonobtrusive and nonfocal expressive reactions, such as out of field symptoms. This kind of activity, which tends to be continuous and, unlike speech, does not break up naturally into units, is broken into units arbitrarily by the one-minute signal. If the observer notes the beginning of such continuous activity in the period between lights, he should record it when it starts and add a score each time the light goes on, for as long as the behavior continues.

Examples of Interaction Analysis

Figure 2 shows an example from the field of counseling. Mr. William Perry of the Harvard Bureau of Study Counsel has developed a hypothesis which, roughly, is this: If the counselor takes an essentially non-directive role in this type of student counseling for a period averaging somewhere around forty minutes, a relationship can often be established such that students cease to expect the counselor to take

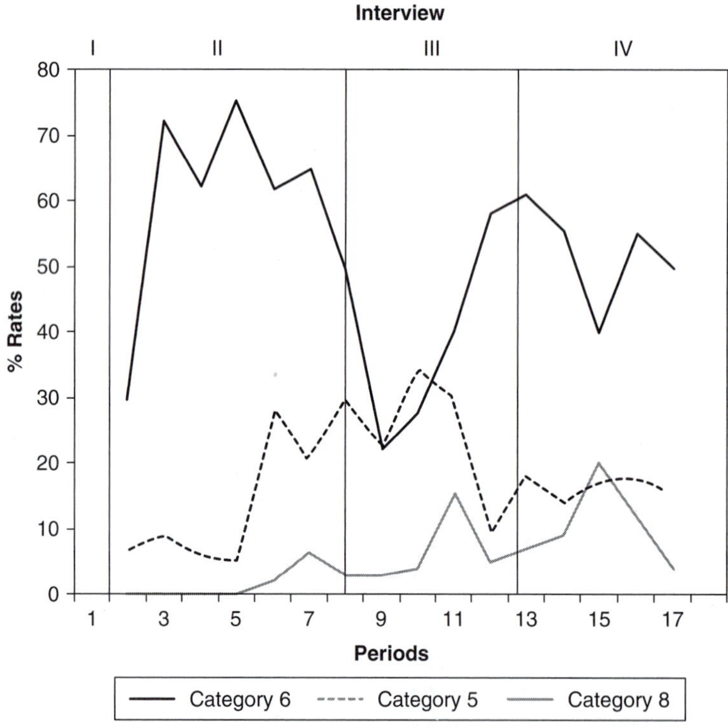

Figure 2 Counselor's Rate of Activity in Categories 6, 5, and 8, by Ten-Minute Periods Through Four Interviews With Students

*A mechanical device that marks time intervals, as discussed, and allows coders to record the appropriate category of the ongoing interactions—according to Bales "like a skilled typist or telegrapher."

the initiative and responsibility for solving their problems, but rather undertake initiative and responsibility themselves. Once this relationship is established, the counselor can then begin to introduce interpretations and otherwise play a more active role in hastening the achievement of the ends of the counseling, with a minimum of that impairment of client integrity and freedom which so often accompanies counselor activity.

In testing a hypothesis of this sort, a rather skillful and sensitively timed change of role is required of the counselor. Mr. Perry has been conducting interviews with this hypothesis in mind, and desires first of all to know if he has been doing what he thinks he has been doing. The problem is to delineate the balance between the non-directive role and the more active or interpretive role in various periods of the interviews. The investigator selects a sample protocol from regular practice and subjects it to an interaction process analysis. Figure 2 shows the counselor's rates of activity in three categories immediately relevant to the hypothesis. Category 6 . . . is the non-directive type of activity par excellence. On the chart, it may be seen that this type of activity formed a very large proportion of the counselor's total activity until very near the end of the second interview. (The first interview was a very brief conversation to arrange a meeting.) It begins a general decline at about the forty-minute mark and continues to decline thereafter. On the other hand, Category 5, in this case the interpretation and analysis of the student's problem, remains at the desired very low level until the forty-minute mark, and continues thereafter to increase. Its companion category, 8, in this case asking the student to make an interpretation or analysis of some part of his problem, remains at zero until the fifty-minute mark, when it shows a slight rise just before the counselor's rate of interpretation rises. This sequence—asking the student to interpret before offering to interpret—occurs again in the third interview and in general, the rate rises with its companion category. From this analysis, it can be said that insofar as the desired features of the counselor's role can be represented by rates of these particular categories, he succeeded in maintaining the required role for the required time and thereafter modified it slowly to a very different type of role, as required to test the hypothesis.

Figure 3 shows another way of arranging data, namely, in terms of "profiles." Profiles for a meeting or a series of meetings, or for individual members within any given period, can be obtained by making a breakdown of the total activity to show the percentage of the total falling in each category of activity. These percentages we speak of as "rates." A plotting of these rates as a frequency polygon attached to the system of categories, as in Figure 3, will show by inspection whether the rate of agreement exceeds the rate of disagreement, whether the rate of integrative status behavior exceeds the rate of malintegrative status behavior, and similar items of interest for technical analysis, feedback to group members, and training.

In a recent exploratory study, two different roles, which the leader was required to take in two similar training groups, were defined explicitly in terms of the categories of activity permitted and activity denied to him in each. His success in preserving the required role in each group was checked and controlled by the interaction profile through the course of the study. The results were made known to him after each meeting. Figure 3 shows the profile of the leader's activity in one group where he was supposed to maintain a role similar to that taken by a non-directive therapist, as nearly as that can be approximated in a group leadership situation. Figure 3 shows the profile of the same leader's activity in a second group where he was supposed to take a more directive (though definitely not an "autocratic") role.

Perhaps the most striking difference is in the gross amount of leader activity. In the "non-directive" training group, the leader accounted for only about 14% of the total activity. In the "directive" training group, the leader alone accounted for about 52% of the total activity. Furthermore, the quality of activity differed. In his non-directive role, the leader had very low rates in all categories except Category 6 and Category 3, both of which were permitted to him as strictly consonant with his defined role. In his directive role, although Category 6 is still his most frequent type of activity, he is relatively much higher in

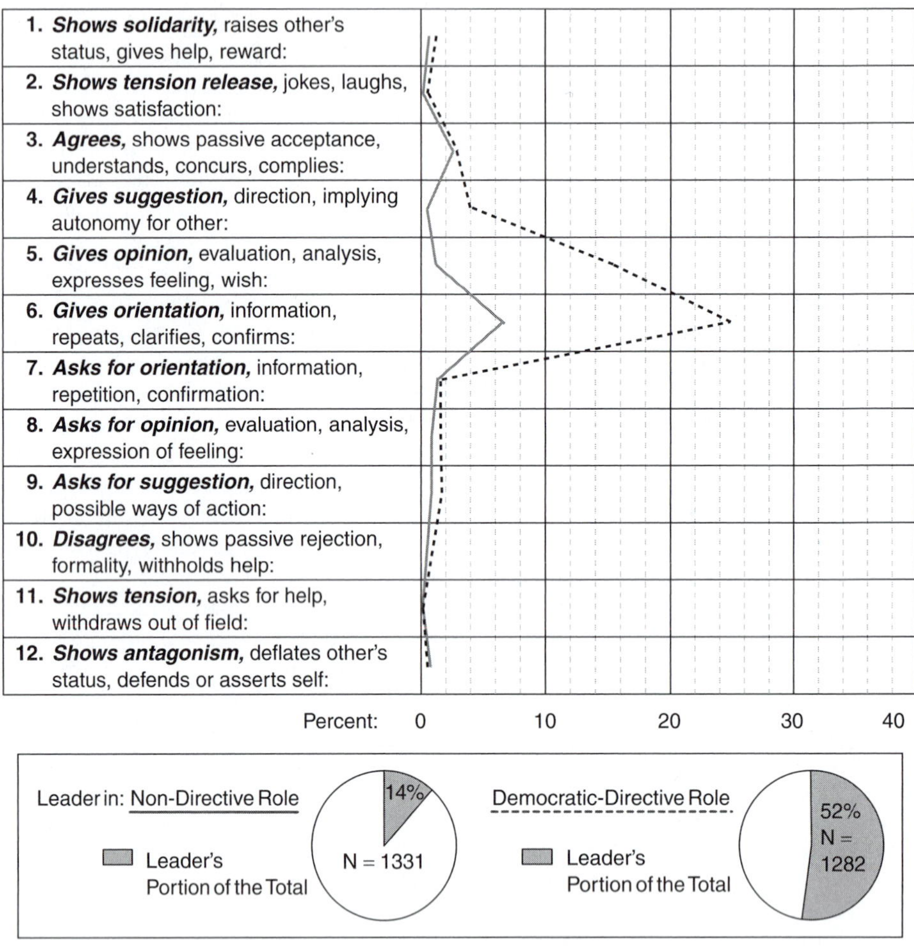

Figure 3 Interaction Profile of Leader in a Non-Directive Role and Democratic Director Role

Categories 5 and 4, both defined as consonant with his role, and somewhat higher in Categories 8, 9, and 1, all of which were permitted. In neither role did the leader disagree or display the negative types of social-emotional activity with any significant frequency.

Towards Theory

At this point, we have to recognize explicitly that all of the small groups we are theorizing about are made up of persons who come into the group with abilities of symbolizing and communicating already formed. They have had experience in social interaction before, and presumably come into the group with certain generalized ideas or stereotypes as to the kinds of relationships persons can have with each other, or as to the kinds of roles that they can play, or would like to play, or feel they should play. In short, we assume, they bring with them a frame of reference, however diffuse, about the main dimensions of social relationships; they tend to fit their activity into this frame of reference and to conceive of themselves as having or seeking a position in a differentiated range of possible positions and relationships from the very first, even before their interaction together in this particular group has become definitely institutionalized. We recognize that these relationships in their concrete totality are to a certain extent idiosyncratic from group to group and culture to culture, but we assume that there are certain features of the process of action and the situation so general as always to find their reflection in the way social relationships become arranged or structured. It is these most general and universal features or dimensions that we wish to formulate.

The observer's point of view [must be addressed here as well]. Observers attempt to take the "role of the generalized others" with regard to the (observed) actor at any given moment. That is, observers try to think of themselves as . . . group members, as those to whom the actor is talking, or toward whom the actor's behavior is directed, or by whom the actor's behavior is perceived. [Observers] . . . classify the act of the actor according to its instrumental or expressive significance to that other group member [while attempting] to put themselves in the shoes of the person the actor is acting toward and then asks himself: "If this fellow (the actor) were acting toward me (a group member) in this way, what would his act mean to me?" That is, what is he or she is trying to do . . . or what does his or her act reveal to me about him or his present emotional or psychological state. . . . Moreover, observers assume that in any given interaction the group members to whom the actor is talking are trying to put themselves in the actor's shoes, and by this process . . . help themselves to arrive at an understanding of what the actor is trying to do or what he or she is feeling. In other words, the observer assumes that the other, or group member, is attempting to empathize with the actor and, at the same time, is testing his own reaction to what he perceives—all of this is a basic process in communication. The observer carries the complication one step further by trying to empathize with the other or group member, as the group member perceives the actor. All categories are described in terms that assume the point of view of the group members toward whom the action is directed. . . . Although this point of view is theoretically complicated, in practice there seems to be little confusion.*

---

*See Poole and Folger (reading 6.4, this volume), who, 30 years after Bales, distinguish categories of analysis in terms of different degrees of observer involvement with their observed others, taking experienced, experiencer, and experiencing perspectives, respectively.

2.6

Structural Analysis of Film

Siegfried Kracauer*

Definition of Concepts

A *film* as a rule is divided into sequences, scenes and shots. This division, however, cannot be used here, for it would unnecessarily complicate the task of eliciting from the Nazi films all their propagandistic functions.

Since the analysis of a whole presupposes the analysis of its elements, we have to trace the smallest units that—either isolated or in relation to other units—imply intended propagandistic functions. They may be called basic units.

Complexes of these basic units compose what we call sections, passages and parts.

To begin with, the basic units, they appear in the three media of which each . . . film consists. These media are:

- The commentary—including both verbal statements and occasional captions;
- The visuals—including camera reality and the numerous maps;
- The sound—composed of sound effects and music, including songs (words spoken by characters on the screen are so rare that they can be ignored).

In the medium of the *commentary*, the basic unit may be called a verbal unit or, more specifically, a

> *Statement.* Each statement consists of one or more sentences. The whole commentary of a propaganda film is a succession of such explicit verbal statements, each separated from the other by an interval during which visuals appear or continue to appear.

Example 1: *Baptism of Fire*** opens with the

Statement: "As far back as the time of the Templars, the city of Danzig used to be a German stronghold against the East. The Hanseatic League, a merchant guild of Free

*From Kracauer, S. (1947). Propaganda and the Nazi war film. In *From Caligari to Hitler: A psychological history of the German film* (pp. 308-331). Princeton, NJ: Princeton University Press.

***Feuertaufe*, a.k.a. *Baptism of Fire* (1940). A Nazi propaganda film justifying the invasion of Poland in the fall of 1939 and showing the German mechanization of war.

German towns formed to protect their trade in the Baltic region, developed the city into an important and beautiful trade center. Beautiful old houses and gates still bear witness to a proud past, and today as ever demonstrate the Germanic character of the place."

FUNCTION: The intended propagandistic function of this statement is to emphasize Germany's historical right to Danzig.

In the medium of the *visuals*, we call the basic unit a

> *Picture unit.* The picture unit consists of one or more shots. Shots form a picture unit if they represent a unity of subject, of place, of time, of action, a symbolic unity or any combination of several of these factors.

Example 2: Maps are sometimes represented through one and the same traveling shot, which then constitutes a picture unit.

PICTURE UNIT: constituting a symbolic unity.

Example 2A: The statement of Example 1 is synchronized with a picture unit.

PICTURE UNIT: A number of shots showing old Danzig houses from different angles. These shots represent a unity of subject and place. Its intended propagandistic

FUNCTION: A romantic-aesthetic appeal.

In the medium of the *sound* the basic unit may be called a

> *Sound unit:* The sound unit consists of a uniform noise or a musical motif—a sad tune, a gay song, a terrifying bombardment.

These three kinds of basic units cover whatever is communicated within the three media. Since their propagandistic function originates in the content of the commentary, the visuals and the sound, they may be called *content units.*

In addition to the content units, there are basic units whose functions do not originate in any content, but in the relations between content units. These units may be called *relation units.* But before defining them, we have once more to examine the content units.

Each explicit statement (verbal unit) is usually synchronized with one or more picture units and/or sound units. We call such a complex a *section.* Each section normally extends over all three media.

Example 3: The statement about the German character of Danzig—Example 1—and the picture unit representing old Danzig houses—Example 2—are accompanied by a sound unit. These three synchronized content units form a section

For practical purposes, we assign to the commentary the leading role within any section. Since the commentary differs from the other media in that it is composed of explicit verbal statements, its propagandistic functions are less ambiguous. This methodological preference, however, does not imply that the commentary's propagandistic appeal is more important than that of the visuals or the sound. The contrary will frequently prove true.

To sum up: each statement determines a section.

> A *section* is composed of one statement, one or more picture units and possibly one or more sound units.

We now revert to the relation units, which can be divided into three types: the *linkage*, the *synchronization*, and the *cross-linkage*.

> A *linkage* is the relation between successive content units within one and the same medium. Such linkages may also occur between already-linked content units.

Example 4: taken from the visual part of *Baptism of Fire.*

We shall consider two successive sections of this film.

SECTION I

STATEMENT: "Hundreds of thousands of Polish prisoners are assembling for transportation into the camps." Synchronized with:

PICTURE UNIT: About eight shots representing moving Polish prisoner columns. The last shot shows a prisoner column retreating towards the rear.

SECTION II

STATEMENT: "The German troops are still following the retreating enemy on all fronts, advancing steadily eastward."

PICTURE UNIT: Several shots representing a moving German infantry column. The first two shots show the column moving towards the foreground.

FUNCTION: The intended propagandistic function of this linkage between two picture units is to emphasize symbolically the contrast of German advance with Polish retreat.

Synchronization is the relation between simultaneous content units or linkages of different media within one section.

Example 5: taken from the historical part of *Victory in the West.**

STATEMENT: (dealing with the events in Germany after the First World War) "The tributes extorted by the enemy, inflation and unemployment dragged the German people into the deepest kind of want. Exhausted, disrupted and in need of a leader, they drifted towards extinction" This statement is synchronized with one

PICTURE UNIT: consisting of about three shots:

1. Demonstrating worker processions with banners and signs: "Revolution Forever."
2. Same, with signs claiming "General Strike."
3. Crowd with signs: "Dictatorship of the Proletariat." A (Jewish-looking) speaker instigating the crowd.

FUNCTION: The intended propagandistic function of this synchronization of a picture unit with a simultaneous statement is obviously to identify the moral collapse, emphasized in the commentary, with the "Marxist Revolution" for the purpose of slandering this revolution.

A *cross-linkage* is the relation between a content unit in one of the three media of a section and a content unit in another medium of a neighboring section.

Example 6: taken from the media of the commentary and the visuals of *Victory in the West.* Towards the end of this film the following two successive sections appear:

**Sieg im Westen,* a.k.a. *Victory in the West* (1941). A Nazi propaganda film documenting Hitler's conquest of Holland, Belgium and France in the spring of 1940, using panzers, aircraft and infantry in what came to be known as blitzkrieg.

SECTION I

STATEMENT: "Up to the last moment the heavy forts of the Maginot Line are fighting." (This statement is followed by another one that can be neglected here.)

PICTURE UNIT *a:* A shot of a French gun-crew in a fort of the Maginot Line.

PICTURE UNIT *b:* Several shots exemplifying the German attack against the fort and its surrender.

SECTION II

STATEMENT: It sums up the balance of the campaign: almost two million prisoners have been taken, and there is no end of captured material.

PICTURE UNIT: It consists of four shots:

1. Two captured French officers
2. Pan-shot over a multitude of prisoners
3. Close shot of encamping Negroes
4. A group of Negroes, picked out in medium close-up.

DESCRIPTION: There is a distinct relation between the statement of Section I praising French bravery, and the picture unit of Section II pointing to the number of Negroes in the French army.

FUNCTION: The intended propagandistic function of this cross-linkage between the statement of Section I and the picture unit of the subsequent Section II is presumably to invalidate the praise of French bravery by the pictorial suggestion that the same French army is so decadent as to rely on Negroes. Thus, Germany's triumph appears to be the outcome of moral as well as military superiority.

We have yet to define the concepts of passage and part.

> The *passage* is composed of two or several successive sections, the number of which depends upon the length of the linkages and cross linkages connecting these sections. If a cross-linkage covers two sections and a simultaneous visual linkage of three sections, the passage is determined by the linkage comprising three sections. (It must be noted, however, that only linkages within the media of the commentary and the visuals determine the length of a passage; linkages in the medium of sound serve also as linkages of passages.)

SCHEME OF ANALYSIS

A scheme has to be established through which all basic units of . . . propaganda films can be analyzed. Since any large unit is not merely the sum of its components, such an analysis does not anticipate that of the "parts" of a film or of the film as a whole. On the other hand, this scheme will enable us to discover all film devices within the dimension of basic units.

The scheme is designed to be followed through any propaganda film from beginning to end.

In applying the scheme, for instance, to the analysis of a passage, one has first to consider the units within each medium of this passage—i.e., the content units (statements, picture units and sound units) and the linkages (relations between content units within each of the three media). Only then, can the basic units that connect media, i.e., synchronizations and cross-linkages, be taken into account.

Units Within Each Medium

The commentary being the starting-point for the analysis of a section, the media will have to be considered in the following order: commentary—visuals—sound.

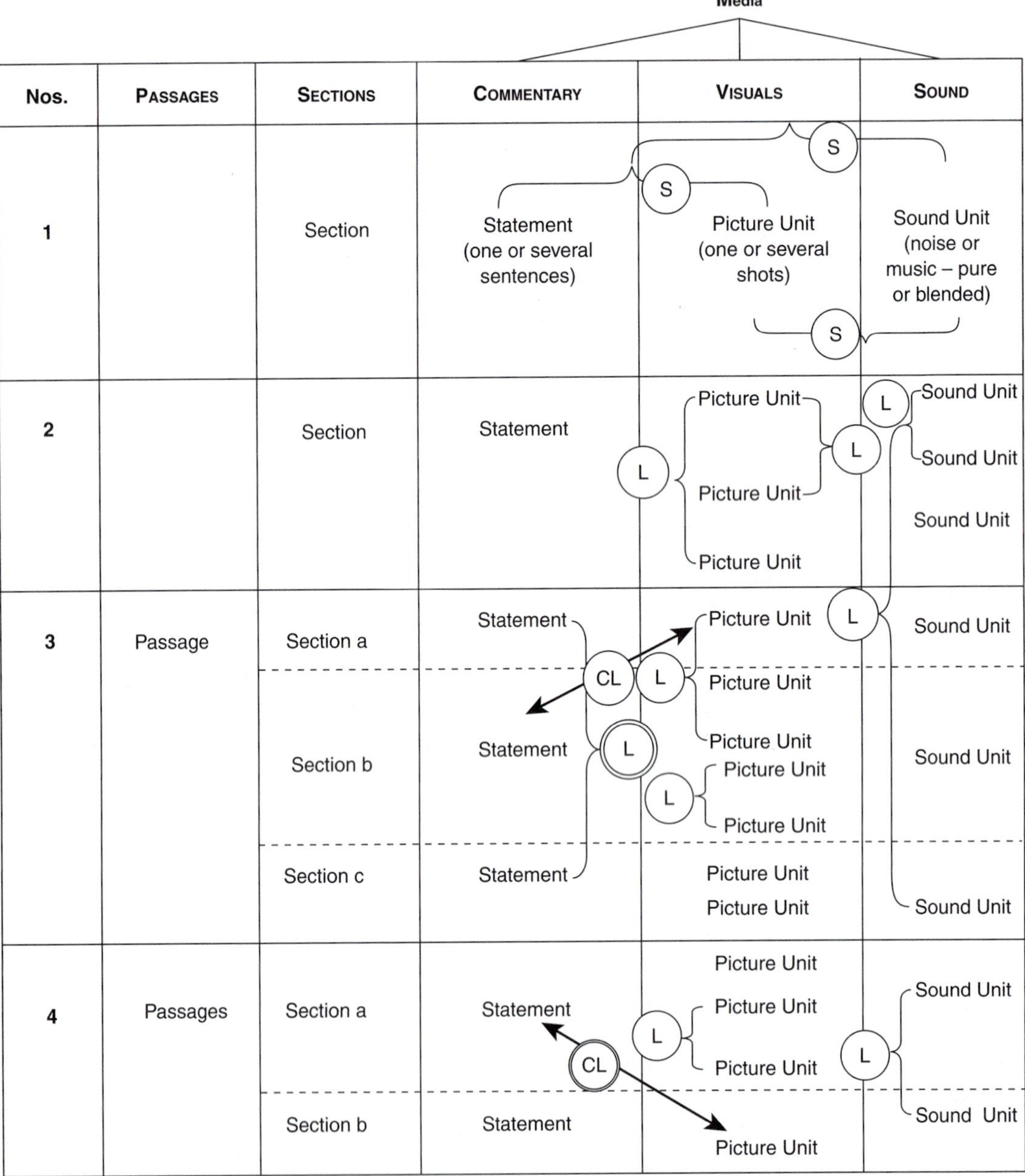

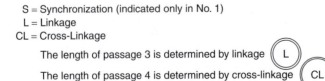

Figure 1 Concepts of Structural Analysis

COMMENTARY

The commentary includes statements and linkages of statements.

> *Statements:* Each statement has to be listed. Sometimes a statement is followed by one or several others that simply exemplify it. These exemplifying statements will be put in parentheses to indicate their subordinate character.

Example 7: taken from *Baptism of Fire*

STATEMENT: "Reconnaissance flights are producing valuable information, and snapshots are taken of the movements and positions of the enemy." This statement is followed by
STATEMENT: ("The snapshots are developed immediately, and form the basis for decisive operations initiated on account of information received.")

It is advisable to summarize, by means of generalization, the propagandistic content of most statements. This will be done under the [next] heading
CONTENT

The intended propagandistic function of the statement is pointed out in the subsequent column
FUNCTIONS

This column appears, of course, in each division of the scheme. It should never contain anything but the presumed function of the basic unit under consideration.

Like Nazi propaganda in general, Nazi film propaganda attempts to reduce the intellectual faculties of audiences, so as to facilitate the acceptance of its appeals and suggestions. Many basic units—particularly linkages—assume such preparatory functions. Others are intended to enlist sympathies for Nazi Germany or to terrify audiences through a demonstration of the German army's striking power. Whenever necessary, we characterize the type of the function.
REMARKS

This column is reserved for all such remarks as may prove valuable later.

Example 8: taken from the historical part of *Victory in the West:*

STATEMENT: "Willingly the Belgian customs guards open the frontier barriers to the troops of the Western Powers."
CONTENT: Belgium actually violating neutrality.
FUNCTIONS: Statement serves as moral justification of Germany's attack against Belgium. (Vindication motif.)
REMARKS: Falsification of facts.
LINKAGES: They have to be considered under the headings *Description* and *Functions.*

VISUALS

The visuals include picture units and linkages of picture units.

PICTURE UNITS: The shots of which each picture unit consists have to be listed and described. (See Examples 4, 5 and 6.)

As in the case of most statements, it is useful to summarize the propagandistically effective content of most picture units. This will be done in the column:
CONTENT

Note on "additional" picture units: Frequently, a statement is synchronized with a series of picture units, several of which are not covered by the statement. These "additional" picture units, which may elaborate on it or take a course of their own, seem to refer to a statement omitted in the commentary. The summary of their content, as listed in the column *"Content,"* can be considered a substitute for this missing statement. Such implicit statements will be put within quotation marks.

Example 9: taken from *Victory in the West*

STATEMENT: "In the gray light of dawn the German armies advance along a wide front." The following picture units are synchronized with this statement:
PICTURE UNIT *a:* About eight shots, showing several running soldiers and moving tanks that, like the soldiers, clear away obstacles.
CONTENT: Actions necessitated by the advance of the armies.
PICTURE UNIT *b:* Several shots of soldiers running across a field swept by enemy fire, seeking cover and machine-gunning.
CONTENT: "Soldiers crossing a field under enemy fire." (Implicit statement.)
PICTURE UNIT *c:* Several shots of an empty village street, with soldiers running and machine-gunning.
CONTENT: "Soldiers taking possession of a village." (Implicit statement.)

Linkages:

Like the linkages of statements, the linkages in the medium of the visuals have to be taken into account under the headings *Description* and *Functions.*

SOUND

The sound includes sound units and linkages of sound units.

Sound units:

They have to be examined in the column
CHARACTERIZATION.

Many sound units are definitely associated with certain images or ideas. Marching music, for instance, conveys the idea of military life, dance music that of festive occasions. In addition, if a musical unit is synchronized once or twice with picture units representing scenes of advance, it will later serve as a "leitmotif," and this leitmotif will automatically evoke the notion of advance. We mention all such fixed associations in the column *Characterization.*

Example 10: taken from *Victory in the West* and supplementing Example 8.

STATEMENT: (of Example 8) "Willingly the Belgian customs guards open the frontier barriers to the troops of the Western Powers," determines a section composed of two picture units not to be listed here. The second picture unit is synchronized with two sound units:
SOUND UNIT a: Music imitating the chatter in a chicken-yard.
CHARACTERIZATION: Funny.
SOUND UNIT b: English song, "The Siegfried Line," thinly instrumented and sung by a chorus.
CHARACTERIZATION: Satirical variation of a popular British soldiers' song. Here, we have an exception: the music alone assumes the function of ridiculing English soldiers.

Since, as a rule, sound alone does not impart propaganda messages, the column FUNCTIONS is omitted here.

Linkages:

Linkages of sound are not considered in this scheme.

Units Connecting Media

SYNCHRONIZATIONS. There are three kinds of synchronizations (i.e., relations between simultaneous content units or linkages of different media within one section):

- Relation of the visuals to the commentary
- Relation of the sound to the commentary
- Relation of the sound to the visuals.

We consider first, the

Relation of visuals to commentary:

Picture units or linkages in the medium of the visuals refer to statements in different ways, each of which may assume a specific propagandistic function. We characterize these different relations under the heading
CHARACTERIZATION:

With regard to the statement to which they refer, picture units (or linkages) may he symbolic, exemplificative, illustrative or explicative. The exemplification is either clear or indistinct. All kinds of representation can be elaborative.

As to the "additional" picture units, we refer to the note, above. The relations of these "additional" picture units to their "implicit" statements can be characterized, of course, in exactly the same manner as the relations to explicit statements.

Relation of sound to commentary and visuals:

These relations need only be examined with respect to their intended *functions.*

CROSS-LINKAGES

They have to be checked in tile columns
DESCRIPTION and
FUNCTIONS.

The scheme will be completed by the division

COMPOSITION OF THE SECTIONS AND PASSAGES

Within this division, we define the role each medium plays in producing the total effect of the section or passage under discussion.

Three Elaborate Examples

Preliminary remark: In case several basic units and their functions are intermingled, it is only the most important function that counts.

Example I: Taken From *Victory in the West*

Statements:	*Picture Units:*	*Sound Units:*
1) "The German Command has received information that a strong enemy force in the vicinity of Lille, consisting of a large number of French and English divisions, has been ordered to advance against the lower Rhine and on into the Ruhr District, in violation of Belgian and Dutch neutrality."	1) One shot of a map representing this intention. Arrows symbolizing enemy groups cross Belgium's boundaries and begin to advance towards a point marked "Ruhr."	
2) ("Willingly the Belgian customs guards open the frontier barriers to the troops of the Western Powers.") The beginning of this statement coincides with the shot of Belgian customs guards in picture Unit 2a.	2a) About 19 shots representing the advance of various French army units: motorcyclists, cyclists, artillery, moving tanks, soldiers in a freight train.—One of the first shots shows Belgian customs guards opening the barriers. The final shots represent marching French infantry, mostly Negroes, from different angles.	
	2b) British troops: – Shot 1: Medium shot of two English officers standing together. – Shot 2: Close-up of an English tank moving towards the left. – Shot 3: English infantry column advancing towards the left. – Shot 4: Same from another angle. – Shot 5: English infantry slowly moving in Indian file towards the rear. – Shot 6: Close shot of moving tank.	2b) Sound unit synchronized with Shots 1 and 2: music imitating the chatter in a chicken-yard. 2b) Sound unit synchronized with Shots 3-6: variation of the English soldiers' song, "The Siegfried Line," thinly instrumented and sung by chorus.

Analysis of Example I

Commentary

Statements

1) CONTENT: Enemy's intention to violate Belgium's neutrality and to invade the Ruhr on the point of being realized.
FUNCTIONS: Enemy stigmatized as aggressor.
REMARKS: Statement a falsification.

2) CONTENT: Belgium actually violating neutrality.
FUNCTIONS: Hint at Belgium's guilt implies moral German attack against Belgium.
REMARKS: Statement a falsification.

Linkages

None

Visuals

Picture Units

1) CONTENT: See description of picture unit.
FUNCTIONS: Threat to Ruhr symbolically stressed.
REMARKS: Moving map

2a)
and
2b) CONTENT: Through linkage with map (see Linkages) and relation of map to Statement 1 (see *Synchronizations*), content is defined as "Enemy enters Belgium" (Implicit statement).
FUNCTIONS: a) Aggression is a fact.
b) Shots of Negro troops intended to arouse race bias and deprecate French racial behavior.
REMARKS: Arrangement of captured French and English film material.

Linkages

DESCRIPTION: Immediately following the map in Picture Unit I, Picture Unit 2 seems to substantiate the symbolic advance of the arrows. Both picture units linked.
FUNCTIONS: See Function a) of Picture Units 2a and b.

Sound

2b) CHARACTERIZATION: Funny.
2b) CHARACTERIZATION: Satirical variation. In ridiculing English soldiers, music assumes a propagandistic function—an exceptional case.
REMARKS: Use of the popular English song, "The Siegfried Line."

Synchronizations

Relation of visuals to commentary

1) CHARACTERIZATION: Map symbolizes Statement 1.
FUNCTIONS: Symbolic representation gives the impression that enemies were already about to carry out intentions denounced by statement.

2) CHARACTERIZATION: Illustrative with reference to implicit statement "Enemy enters Belgium.
FUNCTIONS: See *Function a)* of *Picture Units 2a* and *2b*.

Relation of sound to visuals

2b) Functions: Ridiculing big English tank.
2b) Functions: Ridiculing English soldiers.

Composition of Passage

Commentary:	Enemy intending aggression. Moral justification of German attack.
Visuals:	They mark enemy aggression as a fact and arouse race bias (through relation of map to commentary, linkage and picture units).
Sound:	Ridiculing English arms and troops (through sound alone and relation of sound to visuals).

Example II: Opening of *Baptism of Fire*

Statements:	*Picture Units:*
1) "As far back as the time of the Templars, the city of Danzig used to be a German stronghold against the East. The Hanseatic League, a merchant guild of Free German towns formed to protect their trade in the Baltic Region, developed the city into an important and beautiful trade center. Beautiful old houses and gates still bear witness to a proud past, and today as ever demonstrate the Germanic character of the piece."	1) A series of shots of Danzig architecture: – Façades behind the river—among them a granary – Close-up of the upper part of this granary – Parts of an old fountains in close-up – Traveling around the fountain and its fence towards a steeple – Another steeple – Upper parts of several patrician houses – Tilting up to the upper part of an old house – Tilting down façade to the portal.
2) "This memorable German town was cut off from the mother country by the Treaty of Versailles and was formed into a so-called 'Free State' under the control of the League of Nations. Various restrictions and obligations were imposed upon this new political structure such as exportation customs, postal and railway sovereignty allotted to Poland within the Green Line. A district especially needed for the Territory of the Free State, the Westernplatte, guarding the entrance to Danzig's harbor, was equipped with extensive munition dumps, and the little fishing village of Gdynia, in a direct contradiction to the agreement underlying the constitution of the Danzig Free State, was enlarged into a harbor admitting seagoing ships, thus aiming at gradually averting and battling the trade connections of Danzig property."	2a) Map representing the Danzig territory. Camera travels up from the map. At the left appears the territory of Poland colored entirely black and thus contrasted with the little white Danzig region. The word *"Polen"* appears white on the black ground. Then we see the boundaries of the Free State region and the words, *Freistaat Danzig. Westernplatte, Gdingen.* 2b) Map representing Eastern Europe. At the right of the Free State region the black Polish territory with the word *"Polen"* in White letters. Camera travels up from the map, so as to encompass almost all Europe with England and France. The words *"England"* and *"Frankreich"* appear against black background.

Statements:	*Picture Units:*
3) "The German fraction among the conglomerate of nationalities was ruthlessly persecuted, German schools were closed, industries and landowners expropriated and large parts of the German populace were driven from the country. In steadily growing numbers, they tried to escape from Polish terror and seek protection in Reich territory. Hundreds of thousands of worn-out, distressed and panic-stricken people poured daily into German refugee camps."	3) Picture unit representing German refugee procession: – German refugees with bags and baggage moving through woods – They advance (about 20 to 30) towards the foreground. – A big column of refugees moving on road towards the rear, where, at one point, there is a sign with inscription, *"Lager Rummeslburg"* – Medium shot of a refugee group moving towards the foreground – Medium close-up: Refugees getting out of buses – Two or three shots of a go-cart handed down from the deck of a bus – Medium shot: group of refugees standing, a crying woman with child in their midst. Then a similar group – Another group with a man with a child in his arms; at his left a crying girl.

Analysis of Example II

Commentary

Statements

1) Content: Statement puts emphasis on Germanic character of Danzig and on beauty of its architecture.
   Functions: Germany a civilized nation (Appeal of culture). Her historical right to Danzig.
2) Content: Germany wronged by Versailles and the Poles.
   Functions: To arouse sympathy for Germany's sufferings.
3) Content: Germans victimized by Polish terror.
   Functions: Same as above, with emphasis on Poland's guilt.
   Remarks: Use of statistics.

Linkages

A) Descriptions: Statements 1 and 2.
   Functions: Contrast between Germany's economic and cultural achievements in Danzig (Statement 1) and Germany's sufferings (Statement 2) assumes the preparatory function of stirring emotions. Thus the spectator's intellectual faculties will be somewhat weakened. This kind of manipulation, found also in the opening part of *Victory in the West,* is the more needed here as

the subsequent Statement 3 invites unprejudiced audiences to think of the millions Nazi Germany herself drove away from their homes.

B) DESCRIPTIONS: Statements 2 & 3.
FUNCTIONS: Intensification of the propagandistic effect of each statement.

VISUALS

Picture Units

1) CONTENT: See description of picture unit.
FUNCTION: Romantic-aesthetic appeal.
REMARKS: Two steeples.

2) CONTENT: Representation of Danzig's predicament and Poland's dependence on England and France,
FUNCTIONS: Black and enormous, Poland is made to appear an uncanny threat to the tiny Free State region which, through its white color, is marked as the innocent victim. The later appearance of black England and France symbolizes these powers as pulling the strings from behind.
REMARKS: Moving maps.

3) CONTENT: See description of picture unit.
FUNCTIONS: To arouse pity for German refugees.

Linkages

Same as verbal linkages, with same functions.

SYNCHRONIZATIONS

Relation of visuals to commentary

1) CHARACTERIZATION: Illustrative, with reference to mention of Danzig's beauty.
FUNCTIONS: Collaboration with statement.

2) CHARACTERIZATION: Symbolic and elaborative.
FUNCTIONS: Collaboration with statement,

3) CHARACTERIZATION: Clearly exemplificative, with reference to mention of German refugees.
FUNCTIONS: Collaboration with statement.

COMPOSITION OF PASSAGE

COMMENTARY: Appeal of culture. Historical right to Danzig. Demanding understanding of Germany's sufferings (through statements).—Stirring emotions and thereby reducing intellectual faculties. Intensification of propagandistic effects (through linkages).

VISUALS: Picture units and linkages supporting statements and linkages of statements. Moreover: Romantic-aesthetic appeal. Poland an uncanny threat. England and France pulling the strings (through picture units).

Example III: Taken From *Baptism of Fire*

Statements:	*Picture Units:*
"After the fortifications have been covered by steady fire, a debarkation corps is sent ahead to attack. The men spread out in a hand-to-hand fight."	– Shot 1: Soldiers looking through peep-holes in a well at the right. – Shot 2: Close shot of several soldiers passing from left to right. The harbor of Gdynia in the background, with a battle-ship. – Shot 3: Soldiers running around a ruined building. – Shot 4: Soldiers moving through woods towards the rear. – Shot 5: Infantry with hand grenades moving towards the rear, through smoking wood. – Shot 6: Same from another angle. – Shot 7: Long shot of same, with much smoke. – Shot 8: Woods. White smoke rising. Explosion in a remote glade. – Shot 9: Same, with river in the foreground.

Remark: The sound consists of noise without particular significance.

Analysis of Example III

Commentary

Statement:

Content: Description of a military operation.
Functions: —

Visuals

Picture Unit:

Content: Soldiers—action indistinct.
Functions: —

Synchronizations

Relation of picture unit to statement:

Characterization: Indistinctly exemplifying.
Functions: It is of course difficult for filmmakers to cope with what has been called the intangibility of modern war. A battle covers enormous space, and there is no longer a general's hill from which to survey and direct operations. In addition, the mechanization of warfare has contributed much towards transforming the battlefield into a vacuum. However, all these difficulties do not prevent the British film *Target for Tonight* from offering exhaustive information about a bomber

raid. Similarly, the air-attack episode in *Baptism of Fire* proves that the Nazis themselves are quite able to enlighten the audience if they want to do so. But, as a matter of fact, they do want just the opposite, as can be inferred from the preponderance of edited battle scenes. Blurred depictions of military actions, these scenes seem designed to confuse the mind, so as to prepare it for the acceptance of propaganda suggestions.

Composition of Section

Synchronization of Picture Unit with Statement: Preparatory function of weakening intellectual faculties.

2.7

THE AGENDA-SETTING FUNCTION OF MASS MEDIA

MAXWELL E. MCCOMBS AND DONALD L. SHAW*

METHOD

To investigate the agenda-setting capacity of the mass media in the 1968 presidential campaign, this study attempted to match what Chapel Hill voters *said* were key issues of the campaign with the *actual content* of the mass media used by them during the campaign. Respondents were selected randomly from lists of registered voters in five Chapel Hill precincts economically, socially, and racially representative of the community. By restricting this study to one community, numerous other sources of variation for example, regional differences or variations in media performance were controlled.

Between September 18 and October 6, 100 interviews were completed. To select these 100 respondents a filter question was used to identify those who had not yet definitely decided how to vote—presumably those most open or susceptible to campaign information. Only those not yet fully committed to a particular candidate were interviewed. Borrowing from the Trenaman and McQuail strategy, this study asked each respondent to outline the key issues as he [or she] saw them, regardless of what the candidates might be saying at the moment.[1] Interviewers recorded the answers as exactly as possible.

Concurrently with the voter interviews, the mass media serving these voters were collected and content analyzed. A pretest in spring 1968 found that for the Chapel Hill community almost all the mass media political information was provided by the following sources: Durham *Morning Herald,* Durham *Sun,* Raleigh *News and Observer, Raleigh Times, New York Times, Time, Newsweek,* and NBC and CBS evening news broadcasts.

The answers of respondents regarding major problems as they saw them and the news and editorial comment appearing between September 12 and October 6 in the sampled newspapers, magazines, and news broadcasts were coded into 15 categories representing the key issues and other kinds of campaign news. Media news content also was divided into "major" and "minor" levels to

*From McCombs, M. E., & Shaw, D. L. (1972). The agenda-setting function of mass media. *The Public Opinion Quarterly, 36:*176–187.

see whether there was any substantial difference in mass media emphasis across topics.[2] For the print media, this major/minor division was in terms of space and position; for television, it was made in terms of position and time allowed. More specifically, *major* items were defined as follows:

1. Television: Any story 45 seconds or more in length and/or one of the three lead stories.

2. Newspapers: Any story which appeared as the lead on the front page or on any page under a three-column headline in which at least one-third of the story (a minimum of five paragraphs) was devoted to political news coverage.

3. News Magazines: Any story more than one column or any item which appeared in the lead at the beginning of the news section of the magazine.

4. Editorial Page Coverage of Newspapers and Magazines: Any item in the lead editorial position (the top left corner of the editorial page) plus all items in which one-third (at least five paragraphs) of an editorial or columnist comment was devoted to political campaign coverage.

Minor items are those stories which are political in nature and included in the study but which are smaller in terms of space, time, or display than major items.

Findings

The over-all *major* item emphasis of the selected mass media on different topics and candidates during the campaign is displayed in Table 1. It indicates that a considerable amount of campaign news was *not* devoted to discussion of the major political issues but rather to *analysis of the campaign itself.* This may give pause to those who think of campaign news as being primarily about the *issues.* Thirty-five percent of the major news coverage of Wallace was composed of this analysis ("Has he a chance to win or not?"). For Humphrey and Nixon the figures were, respectively, 30 percent and 25 percent. At the same time, the table also shows the relative emphasis of candidates speaking about each other. For example, Agnew apparently spent more time attacking Humphrey (22 percent of the major news items about Agnew) than did Nixon (11 percent of the major news about Nixon). The over-all minor item emphasis of the mass media on these political issues and topics closely paralleled that of major item emphasis.

Table 2 focuses on the relative emphasis of each party on the issues, as reflected in the mass media. The table shows that Humphrey/Muskie emphasized foreign policy far more than did Nixon/Agnew or Wallace/Lemay. In the case of the "law and order" issue, however, over half the Wallace/Lemay news was about this, while less than one-fourth of the Humphrey/Muskie news concentrated upon this topic. With Nixon/Agnew it was almost a third—just behind the Republican emphasis on foreign policy. Humphrey of course spent considerable time justifying (or commenting upon) the Vietnam War; Nixon did not choose (or have) to do this.

The media appear to have exerted a considerable impact on voters' judgments of what they considered the major issues of the campaign (even though the questionnaire specifically asked them to make judgments without regard to what politicians might be saying at the moment). The correlation between the major item emphasis on the main campaign issues carried by the media and voters' independent judgments of what were the important issues was +.967. Between minor item emphasis on the main campaign issues and voters' judgments, the correlation was +.979. In short, the data suggest a very strong relationship between the emphasis placed on different campaign issues by the media (reflecting to a considerable degree the emphasis by candidates) and the judgments of voters as to the salience and importance of various campaign topics.

But while the three presidential candidates placed widely different emphasis upon different issues, the judgments of the voters seem

Table 1 Major Mass Media Reports on Candidates and Issues, by Candidates

	Quoted Sources						
	Nixon	*Agnew*	*Humphrey*	*Muskie*	*Wallace*	*Lemay*[a]	*Total*
The issues							
Foreign policy	7%	9%	13%	15%	2%	—	10%
Law and order	5	13	4	—	12	—	6
Fiscal policy	3	4	2	—	—	—	2
Public welfare	3	4	(*)[b]	5	2	—	2
Civil rights	3	9	(*)[b]	0	4	—	2
Other	19	13	14	25	11	—	15
The Campaign							
Polls	1	—	—	—	1	—	(*)[b]
Campaign events	18	9	21	10	25	—	19
Campaign analysis	25	17	30	30	35	—	28
Other candidates							
Humphrey	11	22	—	5	1	—	5
Muskie	—	—	—	—	—	—	—
Nixon	—	—	11	5	3	—	5
Agnew	—	—	(*)[b]	—	—	—	(*)[b]
Wallace	5	—	3	5	—	—	3
Lemay	1	—	1	—	4	—	1
Total percent	101%[c]	100%	99%[c]	100%	100%	—	98%[c]
Total number	188	23	221	20	95	11	558

a. Coverage of Lemay amounted to only 11 major items during the September 12–October 6 period and are not individually included in the percentages; they are included in the total column.

b. Less than .05 percent.

c. Does not sum to 100% because of rounding.

to reflect the *composite* of the mass media coverage. This suggests that voters pay some attention to all the political news *regardless* of whether it is from, or about, any particular favored candidate. Because the tables we have seen reflect the composite of *all* the respondents, it is possible that individual differences, reflected in party preferences and in a predisposition to look mainly at material favorable to one's own party, are lost by lumping all the voters together in the analysis. Therefore, answers of respondents who indicated a preference (but not commitment) for one of the candidates during the September–October period studied (45 of the respondents; the others were undecided) were analyzed separately. Table 3 shows the results of this analysis for four selected media.

The table shows the frequency of important issues cited by respondents who favored Humphrey (D), Nixon (R), or Wallace (W) correlated (a) with the frequency of all the major and minor issues carried by the media and (b) with the frequency of the major and minor issues oriented to *each party* (stories with a particular party or candidate as a primary referent) carried by each of the four media. For example, the correlation is .89 between what Democrats see as the important issues and the *New York Times*'s emphasis on the issues in all its major news items. The correlation is .79 between the Democrats' emphasis on the issues and the

Table 2 Mass Media Report on Issues, by Parties

	Republican			Democratic			American		
	Nixon/Agnew			Humphrey/Muskie			Wallace/Lemay		
Issues	*Major*	*Minor*	*Total*	*Major*	*Minor*	*Total*	*Major*	*Minor*	*Total*
Foreign policy	34%	40%	38%	65%	63%	64%	30%	21%	26%
Law and order	26	36	32	19	26	23	48	55	52
Fiscal policy	13	1	6	10	6	8	—	—	—
Public welfare	13	14	13	4	3	4	7	12	10
Civil rights	15	8	11	2	2	2	14	12	13
Total percent	101%[a]	99%[a]	100%	100%	100%	101%[a]	99%[a]	100%	101%[a]
Total number	47	72	119	48	62	110	28	33	61

a. Some columns do not sum to 100% because of rounding.

Table 3 Intercorrelations of Major & Minor Issue Emphasis by Selected Media With Voter Issue Emphasis

	Major Items		Minor Items	
Selected Media	*All News*	*News, Own Party*	*All News*	*News, Own Party*
New York Times				
Voters (D)	.89	.79	.97	.85
Voters (R)	.80	.40	.88	.98
Voters (W)	.89	.25	.78	–.53
Durham Morning Herald				
Voters (D)	.84	.74	.95	.83
Voters (R)	.59	.88	.84	.69
Voters (W)	.82	.76	.79	.00
CBS				
Voters (D)	.83	.83	.81	.71
Voters (R)	.50	.00	.57	.40
Voters (W)	.78	.80	.86	.76
NBC				
Voters (D)	.57	.76	.64	.73
Voters (R)	.27	.13	.66	.63
Voters (W)	.84	.21	.48	–.33

emphasis of the *New York Times* as reflected only in items about the Democratic candidates.

If one expected voters to pay more attention to the major and minor issues oriented to their own party—that is, to read or view *selectively*—the correlations between the voters and news/opinion about their own party should be strongest. This would be evidence of selective perception. If, on the other hand, the voters attend reasonably well to all the news, *regardless* of which candidate or party issue is stressed, the correlations between the voter and total media content would be strongest. This would be evidence of the agenda-setting function. The crucial question is which set of correlations is stronger.

Considering both major and minor item coverage, Table 3 shows that in 18 of 24 possible comparisons voters [are] more in agreement with all the news rather than with news only about their own party/candidate preference. This finding is better explained by the agenda-setting function of the mass media than by selective perception.

There also is a high degree of consensus among the news media about the significant issues of the campaign, but again there is not perfect agreement. Considering the news media as mediators between voters and the actual political arena, we might interpret the correlations in Table 4 as . . . indicating the extent of agreement among the news media about what the important political events are. To the extent that the coefficients are less than perfect, the pseudo-environment reflected in the mass media is less than a perfect representation of the actual 1968 campaign.

Two sets of factors, at least, reduce consensus among the news media. First, the basic characteristics of newspapers, television, and newsmagazines differ. Newspapers appear daily and have lots of space. Television is daily but has a severe time constraint. Newsmagazines appear weekly; news therefore

Table 4 Intercorrelation of Mass Media Presidential News Coverage for Major and Minor Items

	Newsweek	*Time*	*New York Times*	*Raleigh Times*	*Raleigh News and Observer*	*Durham Sun*	*Durham Morning Herald*	*NBC*	*CBS*
					Major Items				
Newsweek		.99	.54	.92	.79	.81	.79	.68	.42
Time	.65		.51	.90	.77	.81	.76	.68	.43
New York Times	.46	.59		.70	.71	.66	.81	.66	.66
Raleigh Times	.73	.66	.64		.85	.89	.90	.72	.62
Raleigh News and Observer	.84	.49	.60	.74			.93	.82	.60
Durham Sun	.77	.47	.47	.70	.80		.94	.91	.77
Durham Morning Herald	.89	.68	.68	.80	.93	.73		.89	.76
NBC News	.81	.65	.38	.87	.73	.84	.75		.82
CBS News	.66	.60	.83	.88	.79	.76	.78	.72	
					Minor Items				

cannot be as "timely." Table 4 shows that the highest correlations tend to be among like media; the lowest correlations, between different media.

Second, news media do have a point of view, sometimes extreme biases. However, the high correlations in Table 4 (especially among like media) suggest consensus on news values, especially on major news items. Although there is no explicit, commonly agreed-upon definition of news, there is a professional norm regarding major news stories from day to day. These major-story norms doubtless are greatly influenced today by widespread use of the major wire services—especially by newspapers and television—for much political information. But as we move from major events of the campaign, upon which nearly everyone agrees, there is more room for individual interpretation, reflected in the lower correlations for minor item agreement among media shown in Table 4. Since a newspaper, for example, uses only about 15 percent of the material available on any given day, there is considerable latitude for selection among minor items.

In short, the political world is reproduced imperfectly by individual news media. Yet the evidence in this study that voters tend to share the media's composite definition of what is important strongly suggests an agenda-setting function of the mass media.

Notes

1. See Trenaman, J., & McQuail, D. (1961). The survey question was: "What are you most concerned about these days? That is, regardless of what politicians say, what are the two or three main things which you think the government should concentrate on doing something about?"

2. While recent reviews of the literature and new experiments have questioned the validity of the selective perception hypothesis, this has nevertheless been the focus of much communication research. For example, see Carter, Pyszka, and Guerrero (1969) and Sears and Freedman (1967).

References

Carter, R. F., Pyszka, R. H., & Guerrero, J. L. (1969). Dissonance and exposure to arousive information. *Journalism Quarterly 46:*37–42.

Sears, D. O., & Freedman, J. L. (1967). Selective exposure to information: A critical review. *Public Opinion Quarterly 31:*194–213.

Trenaman, J., & McQuail, D. (1961). *Television and the political image.* London: Methuen & Co

PART 3

INFERENCES AND ANALYTICAL CONSTRUCTS

While collecting data for content analysis can be labor intensive, justifying the inferences that content analysts wish to make is the intellectually most demanding task. In this section, we offer examples that show how such inferences can be justified. To appreciate what is involved, it is important to realize that such inferences are neither inductive (moving from particulars to generalizations) nor deductive (moving from general truths to particular incidences) but abductive (moving from one kind of incidences, here readable text, to another kind of incidence, here phenomena in the typically nonlinguistic context of the text). We call the model of the relationship between textual matter and the empirical domain of the desired inferences an *analytical construct.* Analytical constructs connect the data of a content analysis to the answers it hopes to provide. In the first article featured here, the analytical construct is established experimentally. The second describes four analytical constructs as proven practices. The third is an operationalization of expert knowledge. The fourth compares the inferential powers of quantitative and qualitative analytical constructs. The fifth is a formalization of a theory. While all texts lend themselves to numerous kinds of inferences, content analysts need to be explicit about the logical basis of the inferences that would answer their research questions: the analytical constructs they adopt.

Charles Osgood, a leading psycholinguist of his time, saw content analysis as a technique for inferring characteristics of authors or audiences from the words, concepts, elements of speech, or contents they either send or receive. We selected an article in which Osgood develops his now widely used contingency analysis. It counts not words or symbols but their *co-occurrences* and infers the association structures in their sources or receivers. Contingency analysis underlies many contemporary methods, for example, the computer program CATPAC* and automated content analyses claiming to mine meanings—all of them based on the same kind of empirical evidence, originally provided in this article.

Historians can be thought of being in the business of inferring events from surviving texts. As their efforts conform to our definition of content analysis, one can learn from how historians justify their claims. Vernon Dibble's article distinguishes four kinds of evidence that historians tend to rely on when justifying their inferences: testimony, social bookkeeping, correlates, and direct indicators. These invoke different models—analytical constructs—of how texts relate to the

*See reading 7.3, this volume.

contexts that produced them. Historians may well address questions that differ from those answered by content analysts such as Osgood, but their inferences are based on the same logic. Content analysts can learn a great deal from how historians work with texts.

Content analysis is perhaps the only method to study the politics of relatively closed regimes. Nathan Leites and his group of Sovietologists were interested in the likely succession within the Kremlin. They had at their disposal the speeches by members of the Politburo delivered at the occasion of Stalin's 70th birthday. As would be expected in a dictatorship, all of their speeches expressed the same adulation of Stalin. Sameness would make inferences about succession impossible. However, as Sovietologists, the researchers knew of two distinct culturally and politically appropriate ways Russians could speak of authorities. This gave rise to a useful analytical construct and set of categories that enabled Leites and his colleagues to determine how close individual Politburo members were to Stalin. History proved their ranking correct. One group consisting of Molotov, Malenkov, and Beria, who later succeeded Stalin, turned out to be on top of the ranging, and another group, including Khrushchev, who eventually challenged Stalinism, below.

Alexander George's piece addresses an old schism that has divided content analysts since its beginning: whether the method should be quantitative or allow qualitative inferences as well. Coming with experiences in propaganda analysis during World War II, he showed that these differences are best resolved by looking at the analytical constructs either proponent prefers and the kind of inferences they respectively enable or prevent. What he calls "direct content indicators" are established by correlations and are hence limited to phenomena that correlate statistically with available texts. Indirect indicators, by contrast, enable inferences that reach deeper in the sources of given texts, calling for models of the source that allow different kinds of data to enter the inferences they provide.

Ole Holsti renders Osgood's* evaluative assertion analysis accessible. This analysis incorporates dissonance theory as its analytical construct. Dissonance theory defines pairs of attitude objects or concepts (manifest in nouns) that are associated or dissociated with each other in a given text as either evaluatively consonant or dissonant, and it asserts that authors as well as readers prefer consonant accounts and read the valuation of objects or the relation between them accordingly. There is considerable evidence for the human preference for consonance (consistency or balance)—not reviewed in Holsti's piece. The theory leads to simple calculations that allow one to infer implicit valuations from their relations to explicit ones.**

Can texts "infect" group mind? If so, how do they travel and take hold of our imaginations? Internet researcher Michael Best from MIT's Media Lab forges two computational paradigms from biology into an analytical construct for the way ideas behave in Internet newsgroups. He considers electronic text as a collection of memes (the cultural analog of genes), which enter the mind of newsgroup members and either selectively reproduce there and reenter their conversations or die. Memes are distinguished from accidental pieces of text by so reproducing themselves. Drawing on an artificial intelligence approach, called ALIVE, Best observes how memes cooperate or compete with each other for the attention of the newsgroup members.***

---

*Osgood, C. E., Saporta, S., & Nunnally, J. C. (1956). Evaluative assertion analysis. *Litera 3:*47–102.

**See reading 7.5, this volume, for further development of these ideas.

***Incidentally, the authors of reading 7.6 (this volume) also use an analytical construct from biology, in their case from epidemiology, to model how attitudes travel through a population.

Content analysis has also been used to determine authorship of unsigned documents, perhaps most famously by Mosteller and Wallace (1964) in their statistical study of *The Federalist Papers.* We include an article by William Paisley, who conceptualizes as "minor encoding habits" what has been proven to be most successful in distinguishing among texts of different authors and attributing authors to unsigned literary texts, musical compositions, and pieces of art to their sources.

Sociologist Zvi Namenwirth studied American political party platforms over the course of centuries. After quantifying these texts, using Harold Lasswell's value categories,* he adopted an analytical construct that viewed political development as cyclical. Searching for autocorrelations, he found a recurrent pattern in the issues and concerns of the American electorate, which predicted each other with different periodicities. His work supports the old aphorism that "everything old is new again."

If your word processor gives you "readability statistics," it has in fact performed a particular content analysis, inferring readability from the textual characteristics of your writing. Inferring readability has a long history. During over a century of readability studies, conducted largely in educational but also in business and military settings, numerous readability statistics were proposed, tested, and revised. The formulas that survived this research amount to analytical constructs that are successful in bridging the properties of a text to its readers' interest in reading and ability to comprehend it. We conclude this section with Klaus Krippendorff's review of contemporary readability formulas.

Reference

Mosteller, F., & Wallace, D. L. (1964). *Inference and disputed authorship: The Federalist Papers.* Reading, MA: Addison-Wesley.

*See reading 5.3, this volume.

3.1

CONTINGENCY ANALYSIS

Validating Evidence and Process

CHARLES OSGOOD*

INFERENCES AND INDICATORS

Making an inference (or prediction) in content analysis involves at least the following: (1) some indicator or class of indicators that can be identified in the message sequence, (2) some state or process in the individuals producing or receiving the message, and (3) some dependency between these two such that the presence, absence, or degree of the former is correlated more than by chance with the presence, absence, or degree of the latter.** The events in messages that *might* serve as indicators (correlate unspecified) are practically infinite—the frequency or locus of occurrences of the first-person singular pronoun "I," the sheer magnitude or rate of output in word or other units, pitch and/or intensity oscillation of the voice in various message segments, the probability level of the syntactical alternatives chosen, and so on ad infinitum. Similarly, the states of individuals that one *might* make inferences about (again, correlate unspecified) are as infinite as the classificatory ingenuity of all of the members of the American Psychological Association put together—the intelligence, communicative facility, or racial origin of the speaker, his anxiety, aggressive, or sexuality level, his association, attitude, or value structure, his semantic or formal language habits, and so on. Most (if not all) of the characteristics of an individual, in one way or another, probably influence what happens in his communications. But the rub lies in (3) above—some indicator having a non-chance relation to the characteristic in which we are interested must be isolated—and so far, psycholinguistics has had little more than suggestions or hunches to offer.

[Content analysts] . . . are likely to be most interested in *specific inferences;* for instance, does country A intend to attack country B and

*From Osgood, C. K. (1959). The representational model and relevant research methods. In I. de Sola Pool (Ed.), *Trends in content analysis* (pp. 33–88). Urbana: University of Illinois Press. (Excerpt represents pp. 33–37, 54–71, and 73–77).

**When this text-context relationship is operationalized for use in a content analysis, we call it an "analytical construct." See Krippendorff, K. (2004:34–35, 171–187). *Content analysis: An introduction to its methodology* (2nd ed.). Thousand Oaks, CA: Sage.

when? Driven by internalized demands for scientific rigor, the academically oriented user of content analysis is likely to be most interested in *general inferences;* for instance, is there a general lawful relationship such that increase in the drive level of the speaker is accompanied by simplification and normalization of his semantic and structural choices? . . . [T]here is no necessary incompatibility here: just as the validation of many specific inferences by practically oriented users may provide insights into general relations, so the gradually accumulating generalities of the academician may enrich the inference base for the practical content analyst. The ideal situation is probably that in which "tool makers" and "tool users" work in close association.

Of all . . . source or receiver characteristics, which might be inferred from the content of their communications, . . . four (are outstanding. *Attention* or interest, inferred from the relative frequencies with which lexical items are produced; *Attitudes*, inferred from the use of evaluative terms; *Language correspondences* or linguistic habits, inferred from context dependent expectations; and *Association structures*, inferred from the contingencies between content items in a source's messages, regardless of either frequency of usage or evaluation. This chapter concerns the latter.)

Associations and Dissociations

An inference about the "association structure" of a source—what leads to what in its thinking—may be made from the contingencies (or co-occurrences of symbols) in the content of a message. This inference is largely independent of either "attention level" (frequency) or "evaluation" (valence). One of the earliest published examples of this type of content analysis is to be found in a paper by Baldwin (1942) in which the contingencies among content categories in the letters of a woman were analyzed and interpreted.

If there is any content analysis technique, which has a defensible psychological rationale, it is the contingency method. It is anchored to the principles of association, which were noted by Aristotle, elaborated by the British Empiricists, and made an integral part of most modern learning theories. On such grounds, it seems reasonable to assume that *greater-than-chance* contingencies of items in messages would be indicative of *associations* in the thinking of the source. If, in the past experience of the source, events A and B (e.g., references to FOOD SUPPLY and to OCCUPIED COUNTRIES in the experience of Joseph Goebbels) have often occurred together, the subsequent occurrence of one of them should be a condition facilitating the occurrence of the other: the writing or speaking of one should tend to call forth thinking about and hence producing the other. It also seems reasonable to assume that *less*-than-chance contingencies of items in messages would be indicative of *dissociations* in the thinking of the source. If, in the experience of the source, events A and B (e.g., MOTHER and SEX in a psychotherapy case) have often been associated, but with fear or anxiety, the occurrence of one of them should lead to the inhibition of the other. Such inhibition might be either central (unconscious and involuntary) or peripheral (conscious and deliberate).

An Experimental Test of the Basic Assumptions[1]

In applying contingency analysis to real problems, such as propaganda study and psychotherapy, we would like to use the data about what things co-occur in messages to make inferences about a person's association structure and also about what things have gone together in his (or her) experience; that is, about the experiential basis for his or her association structure. Unfortunately, however, in such application situations we seldom if ever have any data with which to validate our inferences. Usually we have only the messages produced, not the source who produced the messages (and who could give us other indices of his association structure) and certainly not the history of his experience. In order to test the basic assumptions of this method, therefore, it is necessary to develop a controlled experimental situation in which (1) the experiential history can be approximately known, and (2) the association structure can be estimated independently of the message structure. The following experiment provides such conditions.

Hypotheses and General Design

Our general assumption is that (1) *contingencies in experience* come to be represented in (2) *an individual's association structure* by patterns of association and dissociation of varying strengths, which help determine (3) *the contingencies in messages* produced by this individual. We require a simple situation in which we can measure

(1) $\mathbf{F_a(b) > F_a(c) > F_a(d) \ldots > F_a(n)}$ — the varying frequencies (F) in experience with which an event (a) is followed by other events (b, c, d . . . n);

(2) $\mathbf{P_a(b)}$, $\mathbf{P_a(c)}$, $\mathbf{P_a(d) \ldots P_a(n)}$ —the varying probabilities (P) with which subjects exposed to the above experience will associate items b, c, d . . . n when *some other person* (the experimenter) gives a, thus providing a measure of association structure (associational probability); and

(3) $\mathbf{P^*_a(b)}$, $\mathbf{P^*_a(c)}$, $\mathbf{P^*_a(d) \ldots P^*_a(n)}$ —the varying probabilities with which subjects exposed to the above experience will produce items b, c, d . . . n after *they themselves* have produced a. This provides a measure of message contingency (transitional probability). If we think of the subject in this experiment as a communicating unit in the information theory sense, $\mathbf{F_a(b)}$ is the input to the unit and $\mathbf{P^*_a(b)}$ is the output. The experimenter determines the input in such a way that $\mathbf{F_a(b) > F_a(c) > F_a(d)}$. (It is assumed that before this experience the associations between these items are random across subjects, and materials for the experiment are selected to approximate this condition.) The theory, which we are testing, may be stated more formally as a series of hypotheses.

Hypothesis I. Exposure to a sequence of paired events such that $\mathbf{F_a(b) > F_a(c) > F_a(d)}$ will result in a non-chance association structure among these events such that $\mathbf{P_a(b) > P_a(c) > P_a(d)}$.

Hypothesis II. Given an association structure such that $\mathbf{P_a(b) > P_a(c) > P_a(d)}$ in a set of subjects, sequential messages by these subjects limited to these events will display contingencies (transitional probabilities) such that $\mathbf{P^*_a(b) > P^*_a(c) > P^*_a(d)}$.

Hypothesis III. Given exposure to a sequence of paired events such that $\mathbf{F_a(b) > F_a(c) > F_a(d)}$ and subsequent production of sequential messages limited to these events, message contingencies will be such that $\mathbf{P^*_a(b) > P^*_a(c) > P^*_a(d)}$. This dependency relation between input and output assumes mediation via the subject's association structure.

Hypothesis IV. The dependency relation between association structure and message contingency (described in Hypothesis II) will be greater than the dependency relation between input contingency and message contingency (described in Hypothesis III). This derives from the assumption that message contingencies depend directly upon the association structure of the subject and only mediately upon his experience; to the extent that individual subjects have prior associative experience with the items, these associations will also influence the final structure.

Hypothesis V. The degree of dependence (1) of association structure upon experiential contingency and (2) of message contingency upon experiential contingency will be a direct function of the frequency of experiential contingency, $\mathbf{F_a(b)}$. In other words, we assume that modification of association structure (and hence transitional message structure) varies with the frequency with which events are paired in experience—a straightforward psychological association principle. With respect to measurement, this implies that the more frequent pairings in experience have been, the more significant will be the deviations of associational and transitional probabilities from chance.

Hypothesis VI. The degree of dependence between association structure and message contingency will be relatively independent of the frequency of experiential contingency. This assumes that whatever pre-experimental associations between items exist in individual subjects will determine both associative and transitional (message) contingencies; hence dependency relations here should be relatively independent of experimental inputs.

The burden of this analysis, if substantiated in the results, would be that contingency content analysis provides a valid index of the association patterns of the source, but only a mediate and tenuous index of his life history. It is realized, of course, that this "laboratory" approach side-steps many of the problems that arise in practical applications of contingency analysis; some of these will be considered later under a critique of the method.

Method

Two groups of 100 subjects each were shown 100 successive frames of a single-frame film strip. On each frame was a pair of girls' names, for example BEATRICE-LOUISE. There were only ten girls' names altogether, but these were so paired that (1) each name would appear equally often on the left and on the right, (2) the ordering of frames with respect to names was random, and (3)—the main experimental variable—each name appeared with others with different frequencies. The pattern of input pairing shown below for JOSEPHINE was duplicated for each of the ten names (with different specific names, of course):

JOSEPHINE-BEATRICE	6			LOUISE-JOSEPHINE	6
JOSEPHINE-CYNTHIA	3			GLADYS-JOSEPHINE	3
JOSEPHINE-HAZEL	1			ESTHER-JOSEPHINE	1
		with SARAH	0		
		with ISABELLE	0		
		with VALERIE	0		

Subjects were asked simply to familiarize themselves with the names. Following viewing of the 100 frames, two different measures were taken. (1) *Association test.* Each of the girls' names was shown separately on the screen for eight seconds, and subjects were instructed to write down the first other girl's name that occurred to them. Here the experimenter provides the stimulus—associative probability. (2) *Transitional contingency test.* Subjects were given little booklets and instructed to write one girl's name successively on each page, filling in as many pages as they could and not looking back. Here the stimulus for each response is the subject's own previous behavior.

The group that had the associational test first and the transitional last will be referred to as Group I; the one that had the transitional test first and the associational last will be called Group II. Three tables were formed for each group. The *input table,* the same for both groups, gave the relative frequency (percent) with which each name had been paired with every other name on the presentation frames, without regard to the forward or backward direction of association. Since each name appeared on 20 frames, an item paired six times with another would have this noted as 30 percent of its appearances, three times, 15 percent, and one time, 5 percent. The *association table* gave, for each stimulus name, the relative frequency (percent) of subjects giving each of the ten possible response names. Thus, if 16 of the 100 subjects wrote BEATRICE when they saw JOSEPHINE, 16 per cent was entered in the appropriate cell. The *transitional table* gave, for each self-produced stimulus name, the relative frequency (percent) of subjects giving each of the ten possible response names. Thus, if JOSEPHINE appeared in the booklets of 79 subjects and was followed immediately by the name HAZEL in the booklets of 11 of these subjects, 14 per cent was entered in the appropriate cell.[2]

Results

Table 1 gives the correlations obtained among input, association structure, and message contingency. With regard to the first hypothesis, it can be seen that the *r* between input frequency and associative probability is .58 for Group I and .37 for Group II—these are both significantly greater than zero and in the expected direction. The fact that the correlation is considerably higher for Group I than Group II may reflect the effect of interpolating the transitional test and the consequent greater remoteness of the stimulus input from the act of producing the association in Group II.

Relations between input frequency and transitional (message) contingency are both in the predicted direction but are not significantly different from zero. Hypothesis III is thus not confirmed at a satisfactory level of significance. It is interesting to note, however, that (1) the input/transitional *r* is actually lower in Group II, where the transitional test immediately followed the input, than in Group I, and (2) the relation between input and transitional probabilities seems to vary with that between input and associational probabilities—as if (as hypothesized) the transitional contingencies depended upon the associative structure.

Regarding Hypothesis II, it may be seen that the *r* between associational and transitional probabilities is positive and significant for both groups. That the degree of relation between associational and transitional probabilities is approximately the same (particularly when the continuous raw data are correlated, .46 and .42) for both groups substantiates Hypothesis VI; as is shown, despite the gross differences between Groups I and II in degrees of correlation between input frequencies and both measures, the relation with association structure and transitional message structure is the same. With regard to Hypothesis IV, it can be seen that for both groups the correlations between associational probabilities and transitional probabilities are higher than those between input frequencies and transitional probabilities, as anticipated.

Finally, there is Hypothesis V—that the degree of dependency of both associational and transitional probability upon the input frequencies varies with the absolute frequency of input pairing. To test that we examine whether the predictability of a response name from knowing the stimulus name varies with the frequency of pairing in the input. For each subject the number of "correct" responses given in each frequency category was recorded. (A Dixon-Mood sign test was used to determine significance.) For all conditions except the backward direction of association on the transitional test, six pairings yielded significantly more "correct" associations than either three or one pairings. The lower frequencies of pairing, three and one, were not significantly different from each

Table 1

Dependency Relations	*Group 1*	*Group II*
Input/Associational	.58[a]	.37[a]
Input/Transitional	.19	.09
Associational/Transitional[b]	.39[a] (.46)[a]	.48[a] (.42)[a]

a. Significantly greater than zero at the 5 percent level or better.

b. The bracketed values for associational/transitional in this table were computed from the continuous raw data prior to transformation into discrete stepwise values.

other or from zero pairing. As might be expected in a culture that reads from left to right, "forward" associations were significantly stronger than "backward" associations.

Conclusion

This experiment was designed to test certain assumptions that seem to give value to a contingency method of content analysis: (1) that the association structure of a source depends upon the contingencies among events in his life experience, and (2) that inferences as to the association structure of a source can be made from the contingencies among items in the messages he produces. This experiment provided conditions in which the contingencies among events occurring to human "sources" could be at least partly manipulated and hence known. It also provided conditions in which the resultant association structures of these "sources" could be determined independently of the contingencies in the "messages" (transitional outputs) they produced. Both of the major assumptions above were supported by the results, association being shown to be dependent upon input contingencies and transitional output contingencies upon association structure to significant degrees. The results also indicate that whereas "message" contingencies are dependent upon association structure, they are only remotely dependent upon experienced input within the experiment itself; that is, non-chance associations between items existed prior to the experimental input manipulation and also influenced transitional contingencies. In general, the degree to which input influences both association structure and transitional contingency is a function of the frequency of input pairing.

Nature of Contingency Analysis

In the application of the contingency method as a kind of content analysis, in contrast to the experimental situation just described, we are limited to events in messages, and from them try to make inferences about the association structure of their source. The message is first divided into units, according to some relevant criterion. The coder then notes for each unit the presence or absence of each content category for which he is coding. The contingencies or co-occurrences of categories in the same units are then computed and tested for significance against the null (chance) hypothesis. Finally, patterns of such greater-than- or less-than-chance contingencies may be analyzed. This may be done by a visual model, which gives simultaneous representation to all of the relationships. Let us take up these stages of analysis one by one.

Selection of Units

Often the message materials to be analyzed will fall into natural units. One would normally take each day's entry in a personal diary, for example, as a single unit. Or in analyzing the association structure of "Republicans" *vs.* "Democrats," where a sample of individuals in each class have written letters to an editor, the letter from each individual would be a natural unit. Similarly, in studying the editorials in a certain newspaper, each editorial might be a unit. On the other hand, one may wish to analyze the contingencies in a more or less continuous message, for example in James Joyce's *Ulysses,* and here it would be necessary to set up arbitrary units.

If the unit is too small (a single word, for example), then nothing can be shown to be contingent with anything else; if it is too large (the entire text or message, for example), then everything is completely contingent with everything else. There seems to be a broad range of tolerance between these limits within which approximately the same contingency values will be obtained. . . . In one small-scale investigation, . . . we found contingency values to be roughly constant between 120 and 210 words as units.

Selection of Coding Categories

Here, as in most other types of content analysis, the nature, number, and breadth of categories noted depend upon the purposes of the investigator. If the analyst has a very specific purpose, he will select his content categories around this core. In our own work, which has been methodologically oriented, we have merely taken those interesting contents most frequently referred to by the source. The same categorizing problems faced elsewhere are met here as well; for example, whether references to RELIGION in general, CHRISTIANITY, and the CHURCH should be lumped into a single category or kept separate. Of course, the finer the categories used, the larger must be the sample in order to get significant contingencies. We do run into one special categorizing problem with the contingency method, however: if one were to code two close synonyms like YOUNG WOMEN and GIRLS as separate categories, he would probably come to the surprising conclusion that these things are significantly dissociated in the thinking of the source; being semantic alternatives, the source tends to use one in one location and the other in another location. If such closely synonymous alternates are treated as a single category, the problem does not arise.

Raw Data Matrix

Armed with a list of the content categories . . ., the coder inspects each unit of the material and scores it in a raw data table such as that shown as Figure 1A.

Each row in the table represents a different unit (1, 2 . . . n) and each column a different content category (A, B . . . N). The coder may note merely the presence or absence of references to each content category; if present in unit 1, category A is scored plus, and if absent in unit 1, category A is scored minus—how often A is referred to (within a unit) is irrelevant in this case. One may also score in terms of each category being above or below its own median frequency; if above, plus, if

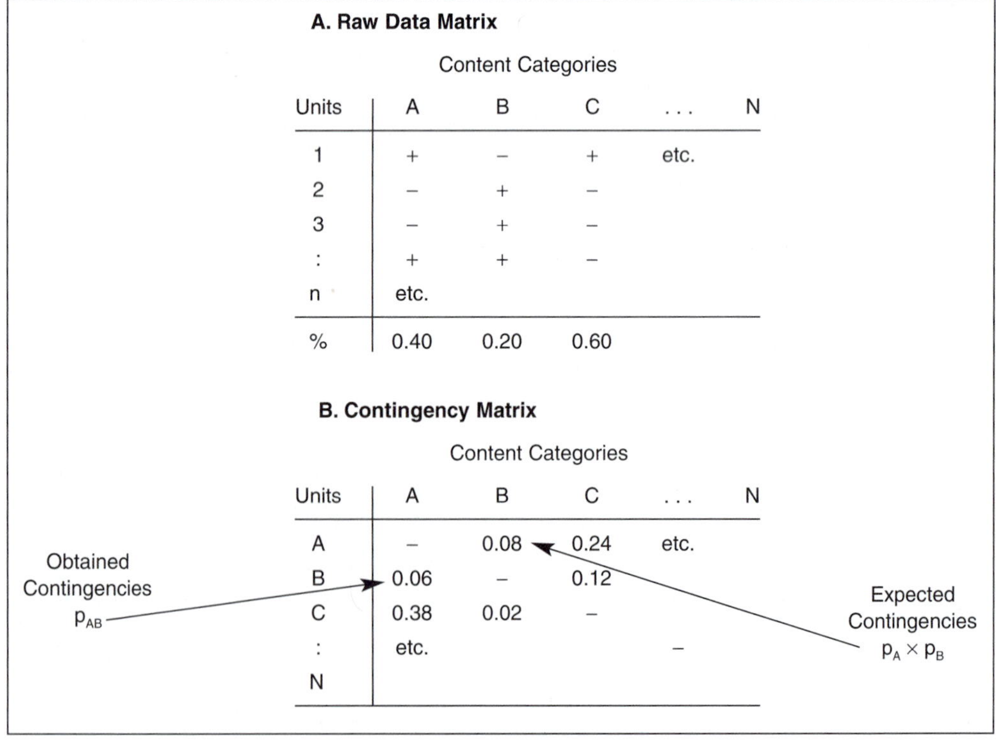

A. Raw Data Matrix

Content Categories

Units	A	B	C	. . .	N
1	+	–	+	etc.	
2	–	+	–		
3	–	+	–		
:	+	+	–		
n	etc.				
%	0.40	0.20	0.60		

B. Contingency Matrix

Content Categories

Units	A	B	C	. . .	N
A	–	0.08	0.24	etc.	
B	0.06	–	0.12		
C	0.38	0.02	–		
:	etc.			–	
N					

Figure 1 (A) Raw Data Matrix and (B) Contingency Matrix

below, minus. This method needs to be used when units are relatively large and many categories tend to occur in most units (as can be seen, the presence/absence method in this case would show everything contingent on everything else). In this case, one first enters the actual frequencies of reference in the cells of Figure 3A, computes the median for each column, and then assigns each cell a plus or a minus depending on whether its frequency is above or below this median.

Contingency Matrix

The contingency matrix, as illustrated in Figure 2B with entirely hypothetical data, provides the information necessary for comparing expected or chance going-togetherness of categories with actual obtained going-togetherness. The expected or chance contingency for each pair of columns is obtained by simply multiplying together the sheer rates of occurrence of these two categories, that is, p_A times p_B in analogy with the probability of obtaining both heads (HH) in tossing two unbiased coins whose P_H are both .50. We find the probabilities or relative rates of occurrence for each content category in the row labeled "percent" at the bottom of the raw data matrix. Thus, since A occurs in 40 per cent of the units and B in 20 per cent, we would expect A and B to occur together (be contingent) in only 8 per cent of the units on the basis of chance alone. Extending this to all possible pairs of categories, we fill in the upper right cells of the matrix, A/B, A/C, B/C, etc.

In the corresponding lower left cells of this matrix, for example B/A, C/A, C/B, etc., we then enter the actual or obtained contingencies; these are simply the percentages of units where plusses occur in both of the columns being tested. For example, in the part of the matrix shown in Figure 2A there is one such double plus between columns A and B.

If the obtained contingency is greater than the corresponding expected value (e.g., C/A .38, A/C .24), these events are co-occurring more often than by chance; if the obtained contingency is less than the corresponding expected value (e.g., C/B .02, B/C .12), these events are co-occurring less often than by chance.

Significance of Contingencies

The significance of the deviation of any obtained contingency from the expected value can be estimated in several ways. Baldwin (1942) utilized the chi-square test, in which a two-by-two frequency table (AB, A but not B, B but not A, neither A nor B) is arranged from the data in each pair of columns in the original data matrix and where the total N equals the number of units. This becomes pretty laborious with a large number of units. . . . [F]urthermore, the frequency of entries in the AB cell may often be below five, a number usually given as a lower limit in applying chi-square. We have used the simple standard error of a percentage,

$$\sigma_p = \sqrt{\frac{p(1-p)}{N}},$$

where p is the expected value in the upper right half of the contingency table and N is the total number of units sampled. This gives us an estimate of how much an obtained percentage may be anticipated to vary about its expected value; for example, if the sigma is .07 then a difference between the expected and obtained of .14 (two sigma) would only occur about five times in a hundred (two-tail test, direction of difference unspecified) by chance alone. . . . [W]ith large numbers of units, the size of p may become so small that some correction (e.g., an arc-sin transformation) must be made. . . . This method of estimating significance is not altogether satisfactory, and some work on a better method is needed. . . .

Representation of Results

There are a number of ways in which the results of a contingency analysis can be represented, all of them being matters of convenience and efficiency in communicating rather than rigorous quantitative procedures in themselves. (1) *Table of significant contingencies.* The simplest summary picture is a table which simply lists, for each category, the other categories with which it has significant associations or dissociations. (2) *Cluster analysis.* From the total contingency matrix, one may by inspection select sets of categories which form clusters by virtue of all having either significant plus relations with each other or at least include no significant minus relations. All such sets may be represented in an ordinary two-dimensional surface as overlapping regions (see Figure 2, the Goebbels diary data).

(3) *Models derived from the generalized distance formula.* Where the plusses and minuses in the raw data matrix represent frequencies above and below the median frequencies for each column, one may use the generalized distance formula

$$D = \sqrt{\sum d^2},$$

where d represents the difference in each unit between values (+ or –) in any two columns (zero where they have the same sign, 2 where different signs). If all signs between two columns are identical, D equals zero; if there is no correspondence, D is maximal.

We may now construct a new matrix similar to the contingency matrix (Fig. 1B) in which we enter D for every pair of categories. If no more than three factors are required to account for the relations in the D matrix, the entire set of distances can be represented in a solid (three-dimensional) model. If more factors are involved, a three-dimensional (representation) can only approximate the true distance relations (even though the values in the D matrix are valid for any number of dimensions) (see Osgood & Suci, 1952). (The reason the D method cannot be applied where mere presence and absence is recorded is that in this case pairing of minuses between columns merely indicates lack of relation or independence between categories.)

Illustrative Applications of the Contingency Method

Cameron's Ford Sunday Evening Hour Talks

A sample of 38 talks given by W. J. Cameron on the Ford Sunday Evening Hour radio program, each talk running to about 1,000 words, was studied by this method.[3] Each talk was treated as a unit. Based on a preliminary reading, 27 broadly defined content categories were selected in terms of frequency of usage. The analyst then went through these materials noting each reference to these categories. The median frequency of appearance of each category was computed and a matrix of units (rows) against categories (columns) was filled. A plus sign was entered for frequency of category above the median for a unit and a minus for frequencies below. Applying the formula for D given above to each pair of content columns, a D matrix showing the distance of each category from every other category was computed.*

. . . [Those] familiar with Cameron's talks [have acknowledged] that the pattern of relationships produced here had considerable face validity. References to FACTORIES, industry, machines, production, and the like (FAC) tended to cluster with references to PROGRESS (PRO), FORD and Ford cars (FD), free ENTERPRISE and initiative (ENT), BUSINESS, selling, and the like (BUS), and to some extent with references to RUGGED INDIVIDUALISM, independence (RI), and to LAYMEN, farmers, shopkeepers, and so on (LAY). But when Cameron talked about these things he tended *not* to talk about (i.e., to dissociate them from) categories like YOUTH, our young people (YTH), INTELLECTUALS, "lily-livered bookmen," etc.

*This can be represented in three dimensions; see Krippendorff, *Content Analysis,* 207.

(INT), and DISEASE, poisoned minds, unhealthy thoughts, and the like (DIS), which form another cluster. This relation in Cameron's thinking between YOUTH (always favorable) and DISEASE notions (obviously unfavorable) was unsuspected by the analyst until it appeared in the contingency data, which suggests one of the potential values of the method.

Also tending to be dissociated from the FORD, FACTORIES, ENTERPRISE cluster, and more or less independent of the YOUTH, INTELLECTUALS, and DISEASE one, we find an interesting collection of superficially contrary notions: on one hand we have SOCIETY in abstract, civilization (SOC), CHRISTIAN, God, and church (CHR), our ELDERS, mature minds (ELD), TRADITION and basic values (TRAD), and to some extent the PAST of our forefathers (PAS) and our HOMES, fireside, and families (HOM)—all things favorably drawn; but on the other hand, in the same cluster, we find DESTRUCTION and violence (DES), assorted ISMS like Communism, Fascism, and totalitarianism (ISM), FEAR, bewilderment, and dismay (FEAR), and sundry EVILS (EVL). Apparently, when he thinks and writes about the solid, traditional things that hold society together, he immediately tends to associate them with the things he fears, the various isms that threaten destruction of his values. References to the FUTURE (FUT) and to our HOPES and confidence in the New World (HOP) tend to be associated with references to AMERICA (AM), but also ISMS again. The allocation of a few other notions, including references to the general PUBLIC (PUB), to FREEDOM and democracy (FREE), and human NATURE, what is instinctive or natural (NAT), may be studied by the reader himself.

Goebbels' Diary

Using a table of random numbers to select pages and then lines-on-page, 100 samples, each approximately 100 words in length (beginning and ending with the nearest full sentence), were extracted from the English version of Goebbels' diary and typed on cards. An example would be:

> #38. Spieler sent me a letter from occupied France. He complained bitterly about the provocative attitude of the French, who continue to live exactly as in peacetime and have everything in the way of food that their hearts desire. Even though this is true only of the plutocratic circles, it nevertheless angers our soldiers, who have but meager rations. We Germans are too good-natured in every respect. We don't yet know how to behave like a victorious people. We have no real tradition. On this we must catch up in the coming decades.

In terms of a rough frequency-of-usage analysis made previously, 21 content categories were selected for analysis. An independent coder went through the 100 units in a shuffled order noting simply the presence or absence of reference to these 21 categories, generating a raw data table like that illustrated in Figure 1A. The data were then transformed into a contingency table of the sort shown as Figure 1B, and significance tests were run (utilizing the arc-sin transformation). References to GERMAN GENERALS were significantly contingent upon references to INTERNAL FRICTIONS (in the inner circle about Hitler) at the one per cent level; references to GERMAN PUBLIC were associated with those to BAD MORALE at the 5 per cent level, as were contingencies between RUSSIA and EASTERN FRONT; negative contingencies, significant at the 5 per cent level, were obtained between RUSSIA and BAD MORALE, between references to ENGLAND and references to GERMAN SUPERIORITY as a race, and between references to the GERMAN PUBLIC and references to RUSSIA. Such negative contingencies are at least suggestive of repressions on Goebbels' part; that is, avoiding thinking of Russia when he thinks of the bad home-morale situation, avoiding thinking about England when he thinks about the superiority of the German race, and so on. These are merely inferences, of course.

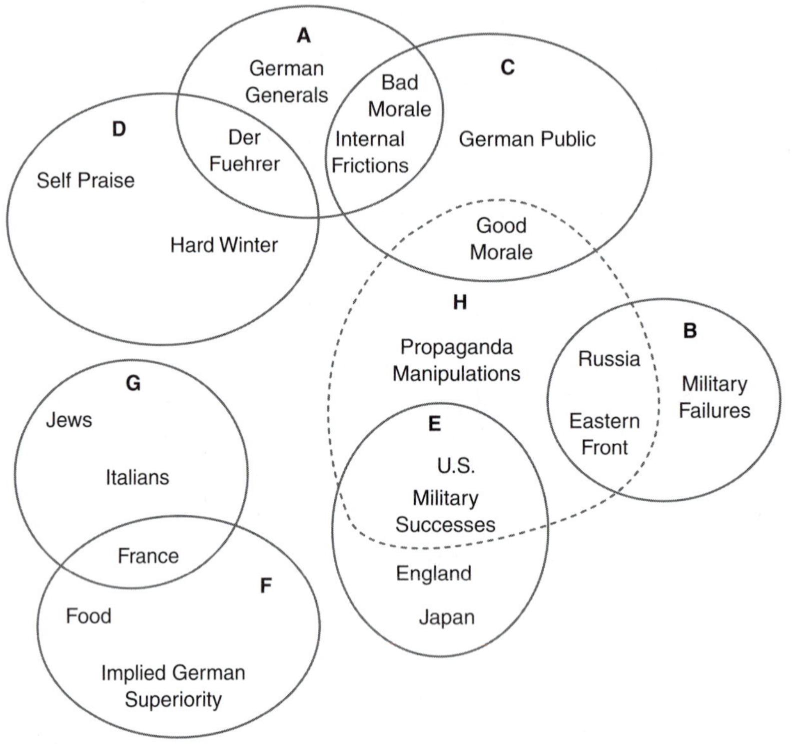

Figure 2 Clusters of Contingencies; Goebbel's Diary

A cluster analysis was made of these data, with the results shown in Figure 2. The content categories included within regions have mainly plus relations and no minus relations. Numerous inferences might be made from this chart. For example: (D) that Goebbels defends himself from thoughts about the HARD WINTER with SELF PRAISE and thoughts about his closeness to DER FUEHRER; (A) that ideas about BAD MORALE lead promptly to rationalizations in terms of the INTERNAL FRICTIONS brought about by GERMAN GENERALS, which in turn bring up conflicts between himself and others in securing the favor of DER FUEHRER; (C) that thoughts about his job of maintaining GOOD MORALE among the GERMAN PUBLIC lead to thoughts about BAD MORALE and INTERNAL FRICTIONS; (H) that his problem-solving ideas about PROPAGANDA MANIPULATIONS may lead him alternatively to the GOOD MORALE cluster of associations, to the dismal RUSSIA-EASTERN FRONT-MILITARY FAILURES cluster, or to the more encouraging cluster in which his ally, JAPAN, is having MILITARY SUCCESSES against ENGLAND and the U.S.; and finally (G and F), that when he thinks about the subject peoples, JEWS and ITALIANS, and FRANCE, he tends also, particularly in the case of FRANCE, to think about difficulties of maintaining FOOD supplies, leading quite naturally to ideas about GERMAN SUPERIORITY in withstanding hardships, and the like. These are inferences, of course; there are alternative interpretations possible as to why any cluster of symbols shows positive or negative contingency. But the inferences have the advantage of resting on demonstrable verbal behavior, which may even be unconscious to the source. They do not necessarily depend upon explicit statements of relation by the source.

Critique of the Contingency Method

The use of the contingency method is based upon a very general inference between messages and those who exchange them. . . . [C]ontingencies . . . in messages are indicative of the association structure in the source and predictive of the association structure that may result in the receiver (given sufficient frequency of [exposure]). But under what conditions is this general inference . . . valid?

If we are dealing with spontaneous informal messages from a single known source (e.g., personal diaries, . . . letters to friends and family, . . . extemporaneous speech, as in psychotherapeutic interviews, etc.) then attribution of the association structure to this source is probably most defensible. When dealing with deliberately planned messages, particularly when the source is an institution, as . . . in propaganda (or mass media content) analysis, it would probably be safer to speak of the "policy" of the source rather than its association structure.

(What does the contingency method yield when language use is instrumental or cynical, as can be expected when the analyst faces a clever rhetorician, a propagandist, an advertiser, a client in therapy, or a candidate for a political office? Those who question the use of the contingency method under such conditions assume that the results must represent message contents. This is not so.) The fact that references to YOUTH and DISEASE by Cameron are significantly associated says nothing (about Cameron's belief system) about the direction of the assertions between them. . . . Cameron's typical statement would be that "Our young people are *not* susceptible to the diseased ideologues of our times." What the method tells us, however, is that there is a greater-than-chance tendency for ideas about DISEASE to occur in the environment of ideas about YOUTH—quite apart from what assertions he may make relating these two.

[We] assume that a significant contingency, whether positive or negative, is evidence for an underlying association (not for whether they are habitual or deliberate). If the contingency is negative (i.e., a significant dissociation) it presumably means that these ideas are associated with some kind of unpleasant affect. (Intentionally avoiding certain associations, for example, in order not to offend somebody, to hide something, or in compliance with a taboo, suggests that the concepts are close in the mind of the source—not much else.)

The contingency method . . . does not take into account the (expressed) intensity with which assertions are made—if the source says "The French are *definitively* like the Italians in this respect," the method only records an instance of contingency between the categories of French and Italian. On the other hand, reflecting the basic psychological principle relating habit strength to frequency of response, the method does indirectly reflect the strength of an association (or dissociation).

. . . [A]ssociation is not indicative of semantic similarity. References to COMMUNISM may frequently lead to reference to CAPITALISM, but this does not necessarily imply that these concepts are either similar in reference or in psychological meaning. (They exhibit a contrast within a common linguistic domain, as in GOD and DEVIL, SOLDIER and SAILOR (or BUYER and SELLER).*

*Another example for the fact that associations have little to do with semantic similarities is synonyms. Synonyms rarely co-occur near each other, and lacking contingency might give the impression of dissociation. In contingency analysis, as presented here, this problem does not arise as it is applied to categories that subsume synonyms. When applied to raw words (see reading 7.3, this volume) this becomes a distraction.

Notes

1. This experiment was done by the author in collaboration with Mrs. Lois Anderson (1957).

2. These tables and certain details of statistical treatment will be found in Osgood and Anderson (1957).

3. It is instructive to compare the results of this contingency analysis with an earlier frequency analysis of speeches by the same speaker by Green (1939). The clusters spotted in the present study seem to have been largely overlooked in Green's more conventional analysis. The studies were independent of each other. The earlier one was not known to the present author.

References

Baldwin, A. L. (1942). Personal structure analysis: A statistical method for investigating the single personality. *Journal of Abnormal and Social Psychology 37:*163–183.

Green, Jr., T. S. (1939). Mr. Cameron and the Ford House. *Public Opinion Quarterly 3:*669–675.

Osgood, C. E., & Anderson, L. (1957). Certain relations between experienced contingencies, association structure, and contingencies in encoded messages. *American Journal of Psychology 70:*411–420.

Osgood, C. E., & Suci, G. J. (1952). A measure of relation determined by both mean difference and profile information. *Psychological Bulletin 49:*251–262.

3.2

Four Types of Inference From Documents to Events

Vernon K. Dibble*

Many of the intellectual procedures used by historians can be viewed in terms of the dichotomy between documentary evidence and facts or events that are external to the documents themselves. At some moments, historians work on only one side of this divide. Where the meaning of a document is not clear, for example, they sometimes use one phrase in order to infer the meaning of another. Or, working only on the other side of this dichotomy, once a given fact is established, they use it in order to make inferences about other facts. Although such inferences are almost completely neglected by manuals of historical method, they are very common in the works of historians. Chrimes (1952:15–16) writes, for example, that "from the time of Cnut at least we begin to see men who began their careers as Scribes in the king's service blossoming forth to be bishops and abbots—a sure sign of their growing importance and favor." The rules for making inferences of this type, whatever they might turn out to be when adequately codified, are quite different from rules for the use of documents. Once the first fact is established (e.g., the career lines of royal scribes), the historian's inference to the second fact (e.g., the importance of the royal secretariat) has nothing to do with documentary techniques.

At other moments historians move from one side of the dichotomy to the other. Moving from fact to document, they often use the former in order to make inferences about the provenance, age, authenticity, or authorship of the latter. And, of course, they also move in the opposite direction, using documents in order to make inferences about external events.

Although these various procedures are used in conjunction with one another, and although the resulting conclusions often stand or fall together, this article is concerned only with inferences from *documents to events*. It identifies four quite different ways in which historians make such inferences, as illustrated in recent historical literature, and discusses some of the problems which each of the four entails. Manuals of historical method also concentrate on inferences from documents to

*From Dibble, V. K. (1963). Four types of inference from documents to events. *History and Theory 3*:203–221.

events. But they hardly reflect the procedures that historians actually use. To judge by most manuals, historians establish facts from documents primarily by examining *testimony* to events, which is recorded by witnesses who have seen or heard about these events. This article is concerned not only with testimony but also with three other categories, which may be termed *social bookkeeping, correlates,* and *direct indicators.*

These four categories are based on two very different criteria of classification. First, the distinction between testimony and social bookkeeping is a classification of sources. Of all documents used by historians, some purport to record information about things that happen, and some do not. Codes of law, pieces of pottery, and poems, for example, do not. Documents, which do purport to record information, can in general be classified further as testimony or social bookkeeping, depending upon the circumstances under which they are produced. Since the procedures appropriate to testimony are not identical with those appropriate to social bookkeeping, this classification of sources is simultaneously a classification of techniques. Second, the distinction between correlates and direct indicators refers only to techniques. For all documents, both those that purport to record information and those that do not, are potential correlates and potential indicators. This double-edged scheme of classification must be kept in mind as we proceed further.

Testimony

The manuals give a number of familiar rules for evaluating testimony. Many historians do not care for generalizations or formal methodology and prefer to regard masterful documentary criticism as "a sort of sixth sense that will alert you to the tell-tale signs."[1] But most of these rules can be stated as general laws in one or another social science, although they are all probability laws and many are definitely of the armchair variety. Some rules turn out to be general laws governing the psychology of cognition: testimony about specific details is likely to be more accurate than testimony about general conditions.[2] Others are laws governing the psychology of memory: testimony recorded shortly after an event took place is likely to be more accurate than testimony recorded long afterwards. Other rules can be stated as general laws, which govern communication: testimony about ideologically relevant events, which is addressed to people who share the witness's beliefs and values, is likely to be more accurate than testimony addressed to audiences that do not share the witness's ideology. Some rules turn out to be laws governing cultural processes in cognition: the rule of thumb that the ancients grossly overestimated numbers would be such a law, if we were able to state in what kinds of societies or cultures people overestimate numbers and in what kinds they underestimate them.

In using such rules, historians implicitly construct syllogisms that include probability statements. That is, they begin with premises, which are stated in terms of likelihood rather than certainty and, therefore, proceed to conclusions, which are likely rather than certain to be true. This logical structure of inferences from testimony to events is seen more clearly when historians choose between n conflicting accounts than when they evaluate a single piece of testimony. . . .

Historians reach an overall conclusion at such points by engaging in a peculiar kind of arithmetic without numbers. They assign weights to each syllogism and to its conclusion, usually assigning greater weight to some than to others. . . . The different weights, or estimates of probable accuracy, are compared with one another, and out of the probabilities ascribed to each syllogism, an aggregate probability for each of the possible overall conclusions is arrived at. These combinations of probabilities, and comparisons between them, are carried out despite the fact that they are never stated with quantitative precision. For the logic of inferences from testimony to events is the logic of qualitative probabilities.

But while the notion of probability or likelihood may apply to the historian's assessments and conclusions, it does not apply to the single event in question. Patrick Henry either did or did not profess his loyalty to the king, and there is no probability about it. To say historians infer from documents to events by the logic of qualitative probabilities is to say that if they make inferences about hundreds of events by the simultaneous application, to each event in question, of a number of syllogisms which include probability statements, then they will reach the correct conclusion more often than not. But since their premises are probability laws, the most rigorous evaluation of testimony can lead to the incorrect conclusion in any single case. If, as the manuals suggest, historians relied primarily on witnesses, if document equaled testimony and internal criticism equaled the evaluation of testimony—then historians would seldom be able to spot those instances where rigorous evaluation of testimony leads to the wrong inference. But the impression conveyed by the manuals is fortunately incorrect. Historians infer from documents to events in ways that have nothing to do with the evaluation of testimony. Other types of inferences are sometimes used without reference to testimony and sometimes supplement testimony. The first of the three remaining types to be considered here is the use of social bookkeeping.

Social Bookkeeping

When the manuals speak of witnesses and their testimony and of the rules for evaluating testimony, there is always the implicit assumption that documents are produced by individuals and not by social systems. The secluded monk, the diarist alone in his room at the end of the day, and the solitary traveler are the classic examples of the historian's witness. But if one were to enumerate the sources used by, say, fifty representative historians, then one would probably find that documents produced in individualized circumstances make up only a small percentage of the total and are outnumbered by social bookkeeping. Groups and organizations in all literate societies have institutionalized procedures for recording facts and events. The term *social bookkeeping* refers to all documents which purport to record information and which are the product of groups and organizations. The term includes such diverse sources as transcripts of parliamentary debates, calendars of saints, bankbooks, tax returns, inventories of estates, the Domesday Book, court records, crime statistics, censuses, reports by subordinates in hierarchies to their superiors, and the list of graduates of Harvard University.

Testimony is the work of individuals. Historians have accordingly evolved a psychology and social psychology of documents that guide them in their use of testimony. Social bookkeeping is the work of social systems. But historians have not yet evolved a sociology of documents to guide them in their use of such sources. One does find in the manuals a few stray reminders that documents of this type must be read in the light of the social system that produces them. Students are reminded, for example, that the *Congressional Record* is not a literal transcript of Congressional debates. The *Record* is an inaccurate transcript not because recording clerks have faulty hearing, or political biases, or any other failing to which witnesses are prone. It is an inaccurate transcript because of one simple feature of the social system that produces it: members of Congress are free to amend their remarks before the *Record* goes to press.

It is possible to state a few general principles for the use of social bookkeeping. The *Congressional Record* reminds us that different forms of social bookkeeping vary in the extent to which interested parties have a hand in producing the record. In some societies, inventories of estates are compiled by heirs and in others by disinterested parties. The *Record* also reminds us that different forms of social bookkeeping vary in the extent to which interested parties are likely to check the record after it is first set down. People are more likely to check certificates of inheritance or deeds to their land than the information about themselves, which is collected by census enumerators. Different forms of social bookkeeping, which are checked by interested parties, vary in the extent to which the interested parties are free to alter the record. Lords of manors could presumably alter records, which were compiled by their own overseers, more easily than they could alter records compiled by tax officers. Different forms of social bookkeeping, which can be altered by interested parties, vary in the extent to which such alteration makes for greater accuracy or for less. Transcripts of some legal proceedings are less complete than they would be otherwise because interested parties can sometimes have remarks "stricken from the record." In contrast, alterations initiated by an interested party to his own advantage are likely to make for a more complete and a more accurate record if the record-keeper is in a position to make his own independent check on the accuracy of the suggested alteration. The professor who asks his chair(person) or dean to add missing items to his bibliography is an obvious example. If the record-keeper is not in a position to make an independent check, as with compilations of research allegedly in progress, the interested party is free to embellish veracity.

Some forms of social bookkeeping are provided with built-in checks, apart from interested parties, while others are not. The Bollandist fathers provide the Catholic Church with an institutionalized check on the record of saints: there is no built-in check on the biographies submitted to the editors of *Who's Who.* Different forms of social bookkeeping vary in the extent to which the events recorded are visible to the record-keeper or in the extent to which communication between observers and record-keepers is assured. They also differ in the number of steps between observer and record-keeper. There are no steps between observer and record-keeper when, as with court stenographers, the two jobs are performed by the same person. There are many steps in the hierarchy of a corporation between a sales(person)'s weekly reports to an immediate supervisor and the record of sales in the corporation's annual report, with communication steps in the sales department paralleled by different steps in accounting and billing departments. Different examples of social bookkeeping, which do come into being only after many steps between observer and record-keeper, vary in the extent to which distortion or suppression of information takes place along the way. Staff officers in contemporary American corporations get line personnel to innovate by agreeing to distort budget reports in order to make line personnel look better than they really are; no matter how many steps there might be between graduate students, dissertation supervisors, departmental secretaries, deans' offices, and printers of commencement programs, carelessness is not the only thing which might distort or suppress information along the way.

Some of these general observations, or others like them, have been concretely applied in the works of historians who have had to come to terms with particular kinds of social bookkeeping in particular historical societies . . . Kosminsky's criticism of the survey of 1279 and of certain other forms of social bookkeeping in thirteenth-century England is an example (Kosminsky, 1956). He asks who initiated the survey, and why. To whom would the returns be valuable and who might be hurt by them? Who carried it out, and how? What did the officers of the king do when they arrived in a county? How did the local juries acquire their information? Did the royal officers check on the local juries or simply accept their returns as given? Was new machinery devised for gathering the information required for the surveyor or established and tried machinery used? In what respects did the questions presented to the local juries force them to simplify the facts? What was most visible to the juries and what was least visible?

Many of the questions posed by Kosminsky have exact parallels in the criticism of testimony. Comparisons between descriptions of a manor in the survey of 1279 and in an *Inquisition post mortem* are analogous to comparisons between the testimonies of two witnesses to the same event. In some cases, however, we do not really have two independent records, since the information given by local juries was sometimes copied from another source. This is, of course, parallel to the difference between two independent witnesses and two witnesses, one of whom reports what the other had told him. Kosminsky's examinations of the vocabulary of the survey and of its internal consistency also have their parallels in the evaluation of testimony. For other questions, however, there is no parallel with the evaluation of testimony. The difference between improvised and established machinery for acquiring information, questions concerning the flow of communications and commands between different people involved in gathering the data, and questions concerning the extent to which some people checked up on other people, all point to the distinctly social character of social bookkeeping. In such questions as these the historian is concerned not with the veracity or eyesight of individuals, but with the operation of social systems.

As with criticism of testimony, historians criticize social bookkeeping in order to make decisions about the probable accuracy or completeness of the record. But, of course, historians are not interested only in accurate social bookkeeping. Inaccurate social bookkeeping can be just as valuable as testimony known to consist of lies and distortions. Whatever the survey of 1279 tells us or fails to tell us about manors and villages, it also tells us something about the administrative mechanisms of the medieval English state. Documents, which purport to record information, to be useful to historians, need to be accurate only when historians are concerned with the information they purport to record. But testimony is not always used qua testimony and social bookkeeping is not always used qua social bookkeeping. Documents of both types are used as correlates or direct indicators of facts or events other than those they purport to record. And, of course, documents that do not purport to record information can be used in the same way.

Documents as Correlates

Historians are often able to make inferences from documents to events in the absence of testimony or social bookkeeping that tells them about the events in question. One way of doing so is to use documents whose characteristics are known to be correlated with the events in question. Haskins (1918) provides a particularly striking example of the use of documents as correlates, supplementing the use of testimony.

In *Norman Institutions,* Haskins demonstrates that the governmental machinery of Robert Curthose (1087–1096 and 1100–1106) was weak, ineffective, and underdeveloped, but that the more highly developed institutions of the Conqueror were "in some measure maintained even during the disorder and weakness of Robert's time" (Haskins, 1918:84). Among his sources are the narratives of Odericus Vitalis, the charters of Robert Curthose, and the charters of William Rufus, who ruled Normandy between 1096 and 1100 while his brother Robert was on a crusade. The narratives of Odericus are, of course, an example of testimony. His descriptions of Normandy under Robert are "a dreary tale of private war, murder, and pillage, of perjury, disloyalty, and revolt . . ." (Haskins, 1918:62). Of William Rufus, in contrast, "Odericus tells us that . . . under his iron heel Normandy at least enjoyed a brief period of order and justice to which it looked back with longing after Robert's return" (Haskins, 1918:80).

Haskins is less concerned with private war and public peace than with the institutions of Norman government. The testimony of Odericus is not adequate for his purpose, since the witness was not close to Robert's governmental machinery and since his perceptions were colored by his geographical location and by his position as a monk. Haskins makes inferences about organs of government from the testimony of Odericus and from certain other narratives but then gives reasons not to rely on these inferences:

> Amidst these narratives of confusion and revolt, there is small place for the machinery of government, and we are not surprised that the chroniclers are almost silent on the subject. Robert's reliance on mercenaries [reference to Odericus and to another witness] shows the breakdown of the feudal service, which may also be illustrated by an apparent example of popular levies [reference to Odericus]; his constant financial necessities [reference to Odericus and to another witness] point to the demoralization of the revenue. The rare mention of his curia [reference to Odericus] implies that it met but rarely. Still, these inferences are negative and to that extent inconclusive, and even the detailed account of Odericus is largely local and episodic, being chiefly devoted to events in the notoriously troubled region of the south, and is also colored by the sufferings and losses of the church. (Haskins, 1918:64)

Thus far, Haskins could be following the injunctions of the manuals concerning the use of testimony. His next step, however, has not been dreamt of in the manuals. Having found his star witness wanting, he turns to the charters and similar documents of Robert's reign and uses certain of their characteristics as correlates of the nature of Robert's government. He notes that the number of surviving charters is small, relative to the length of the reign and in comparison with other Norman dukes. Perhaps only thirty-nine survive because "later times were indifferent to preserving charters of Robert Curthose, but it is even more likely that his own age was not eager to secure them. As confirmation at his hands counted for little, none of these charters consist of general liberties or comprehensive enumerations of past grants; they are all specific and immediate. Furthermore, so far as can now be seen, the surviving documents are all authentic; privileges of the Conqueror, Henry I, or Henry II were worth fabricating but no one seems to have thought it worth while to invent a charter of Robert" (Haskins, 1918:71).[3] Seventeen of the existing charters were issued in Robert's name, while twenty-two were drawn up by interested parties for him to attest. The seventeen issued in Robert's name are not uniform in size, style, or method of authentication. Of the seven, which are preserved in the original, each is in a different handwriting. Seals were used on only some of the charters, and were not used in uniform fashion. There are nine variations on the title *dux Normannorum.* To these varying titles there is sometimes added one of three variations of *filius Willelmi gloriosi regis Anglorum.* Robert signs sometimes as *dux* and sometimes as *comes.* Some charters invoke the Trinity while others do not.

From these and similar observations, Haskins concludes "the range of variation in style and form precludes the existence of an effective chancery and indicates that the duke's charters were ordinarily drawn up by the recipients" (Haskins, 1918:74). The decline of the ducal chancery is accompanied by a decline in the *curia.* The lists of witnesses on charters show little continuity in the ducal entourage and "still less any clearly marked official element" (Haskins, 1918:76), and a meeting of the *curia* is mentioned only once in the surviving documents. In short, the characteristics of Robert's charters confirm the inferences about the nature of his rule made on the basis of testimony in the chronicles. A similar examination of the writs and charters issued in or about Normandy by William Rufus during his reign there also confirms the testimony of Odericus. Under William Rufus, Haskins infers, we see "the regular mechanism of Anglo-Norman administration at work" (Haskins, 1918:83).

Haskins's use of ducal charters has nothing to do with the evaluation of testimony. And although charters are a form of social bookkeeping, since they record information about grants and privileges given by the crown, Haskins is not using them as such. He is not primarily concerned with the information about grants and privileges they contain. Haskins's procedure illustrates the making of inferences from documents to events by the use of documents as correlates of the events in question. As with testimony and social bookkeeping, the logic of such inferences can be stated syllogistically: Norman dukes known to have effective organs of government issued charters with the characteristics a, b, and c; Duke Robert's charters have characteristics which are the opposite of a, b, and c; therefore, Robert's rule must have been weak.

There are, of course, a number of syllogisms here, one for each characteristic in question. And, as with testimony and social bookkeeping, historians somehow combine the differently weighted conclusions of each syllogism in order to reach an overall conclusion, even though the weights to be given to each conclusion are not precisely known. It should be noted further that Haskins's major premises are not strictly adequate to the conclusion. Ideally, he should have grounds for his major premise that Norman dukes known to have effective organs of government issued charters with given characteristics while Norman dukes known to have ineffective organs issued charters with the opposite characteristics. Haskins actually has grounds only for making the first part of the statement, simply because there were not enough weak dukes to provide the evidence for the second part. The problem is hardly serious, however. Our knowledge of Norman government and society, and of the functions of charters in such a system, allows us to state why the characteristics of ducal charters should be correlated with the strength of ducal governments.

It may some day be possible to state general rules for the use of documents as correlates, just as there are rules in the manuals for the use of testimony. But most of these rules are likely to be quite different from the rules concerning testimony. The latter are, in effect, psychological or social psychological laws governing such phenomena as cognition, memory, and communication. Although a few similarly general principles might one day be stated for the use of documents as correlates, it is usually possible to use documents in this way only because of historically specific knowledge about the institutions of particular societies or types of societies. It was such knowledge, and not general laws, which enabled Haskins to use charters as correlates of the nature of Robert's regime.

Documents as Direct Indicators

The fourth type of inference from document to event might appear to entail no inference at all. This is the case when all or part of the document itself, as opposed to external events which are recorded by or correlated with the document, is the datum under investigation. If one wants to know, say, what the British ambassador in Berlin reported to the Foreign Office on the day Bismarck moved against France, then one simply finds and reads whatever messages he sent. His cables or dispatches are direct indicators. What is more, if no records have been lost and if there were no oral messages that were never recorded, then the documents themselves provide an exhaustive answer to the historian's question. There is no need to infer from documents to events. Direct indicators, surely, have nothing to do with inferences.

The matter is not quite so simple, however. The example given illustrates the methodologically uninteresting case in which the content of the documents and the answer to the historian's question are completely coterminous with each other. Documentary research comes closer to absolute certainty in such cases than in any other. There is no need for probabilistic syllogisms, which might lead to incorrect conclusions even when most rigorously applied. But this certainty is possible only in special cases, and sometimes requires that only trivial questions be asked. The documents at hand and the answer to the historian's question are coterminous only when two conditions are met. First, it must be possible to answer the question by reference to the documents themselves, as the historian's subjects happened to produce them, and without reference to their accuracy concerning, or correlation with, events external to the documents. Two sorts of questions meet this condition. (1) To continue with the example of Norman charters, one might ask questions about the formal characteristics of documents. What were Robert Curthose's charters like? (2) One might ask questions, which, in effect, simply state the content of the documents in interrogative form. What rights or privileges were granted to what monasteries in which of Robert's charters? Since a ducal grant of privileges in Norman society may be defined as the emission or attestation by the duke of a charter which states that he is making such a grant, charters can be used as direct indicators of the events in question. There is no need to argue the contention that historians cannot limit themselves to questions of these two types.

Second, even though the historian might be posing questions of these two types, the documents at hand and the answers to his questions are rarely if ever coterminous unless the questions call for purely descriptive answers. Such answers are not sufficient when historians conceptualize. And, as Marc Bloch has taught us, historians conceptualize all the time, even when they deny all interest in concepts and claim to deal only with unique particulars. A glance at one example of conceptualization in the work of a historian will indicate why conceptualization usually makes it impossible to pose questions whose answers are coterminous with the documents themselves.

As everyone knows, to conceptualize is to classify a number of relatively less general items under some relatively more general rubric. Instead of limiting themselves to specific items, on the one hand, and a single general rubric, on the other, historians and other social scientists often find it useful to specify conceptual rubrics of intermediate generality. Heckscher, for example, defines "mercantilist economic policy" in terms of five intermediate rubrics; mercantilism as an agent of unification, as a system of power, as a protectionist system, as a monetary system, and as a conception of society (Heckscher, 1955). Each of these intermediate rubrics or "five aspects of mercantilism," not to speak of the more general rubric under which they are all subsumed, sums up an enormous variety of concrete details. Each of them refers to a vast number of books or treatises, acts of parliament, royal decrees, instructions sent down through administrative hierarchies and arguments over economic policy. If the problem were one of economic practice, such sources would not necessarily tell us what people actually did and it would be necessary to make inferences from documents to events external to the documents. But since policy is defined by what people say and not only by what people do, such sources may in most cases be taken as direct indicators of mercantilist economic policy.

Implicit in Heckscher's definition of mercantilist policy is the empirical assertion that these "five aspects of mercantilism" were in fact correlated with one another, either because they were effects of the same cause or because some of them were causes of others. Also implicit in Heckscher's definition, however, is the empirical assertion that the correlation between the five aspects of mercantilist policy is less than perfect and is not always observed. Although the first two components of mercantilism, "unification and power, were well suited to each other . . . it is . . . important to draw attention to the opposite point, that the two were not inseparable. That there were two separate aspects becomes clear in considering *laissez-faire,* for this policy usually combined a unification which was almost complete in every respect with a remarkable indifference to considerations of power" (Heckscher, 1955:24).

This formulation betrays a notion which Heckscher did not spell out explicitly: the five components of his definition could all be subsumed under the same concept because they tended to go along together empirically, but there were five "separate aspects" because they did not necessarily go along together completely or in all times and places. And if the correlation between these five general rubrics is less than perfect, what are we to think of the enormous number of details which each of these rubrics sums up? If we look at the details under any single rubric, under monetary policy let us say, would we expect to find that a highly mercantilist royal decree is necessarily followed by other decrees which are equally mercantilist? And that as royal decrees become more mercantilist all judicial decisions, opinions of high officials, books published, and instructions sent down to subordinates by administrative superiors will follow along? Of course not. There is more free floating among the details, among the specific indicators of the general concept, than is seen when we deal with conceptual classifications that are established by adding up the general tendency of the details.[4]

The lesson is clear. If historians want to use direct indicators in order to answer limited factual questions, which call for purely descriptive answers, then there is no problem. The ambassador's cables are direct indicators of what he told the Foreign Office. But when historians use concepts that sum up a large number of details, the answers to their questions can rarely if ever be coterminous with any single document or set of documents. For any single item mayor may not be a reliable indicator of a concept, depending upon the way in which such items are inter-correlated with other items that are also subsumed under the same concept. A mercantilist treatise published in France in 1690 is sufficient to indicate that France was a mercantilist nation, only if we know that the characteristics of all books on economic policy were highly correlated and that the characteristics of such books were in turn correlated with the characteristics of royal decrees, memoranda by high officials, and all the rest. When information on all items subsumed under the concept is available, or when adequate samples are possible, there is no particular difficulty. When neither is possible, the problem may be handled in one of two ways. First, the indicators available might include such a large portion of all items included under the concept that we need not worry about the missing indicators. Whatever they might look like, if ever located, they could not radically change the original judgment. Second, even though the available indicators be a small portion of all items included under the concept, the historian might know or might be able to infer the ways in which they must have been inter-correlated with the missing items. The difference between these two situations is nicely illustrated in one of the most imaginative examples of the use of direct indicators that can be found in historical literature, V. H. Galbraith's guide to the Public Record Office in London (Galbraith, 1934).

Galbraith's task is to find order in collections that fell into disorder during centuries of neglect. In order to do so, he argues, one must regard documents as secretions of the organizations that issued them. Hence, he must reconstruct the issuing organizations and the relationships between them. His reconstruction of the various organs of government in medieval England illustrates the second situation described above. With hardly a glance at the substantive content of any document, he uses differences in seals, parchment, filing practices, systems of dating, language, and handwriting as indicators of the existence of separate organs of government and of their emergence at various points in time. Now, when one speaks of separate organs of government, and of the boundaries and differences between them, one refers primarily to patterns of interaction between officials or clerks and to the actions they perform. Characteristics of pieces of paper or of the way in which they are filed are only a small part of what one means. But the indicators that Galbraith uses must have been so highly correlated with the social systems within which officials and scribes did their jobs that we do not worry if they are only a small part of everything that is meant by "distinct organ of government" or "separate organization."

Galbraith's reconstruction of the changing channels of communication between the various organs of government in medieval England illustrates the first situation described above. Among fourteenth- and fifteenth-century documents, for example, he finds warrants under the Royal Signet, which were filed among the records of the Privy Seal office, and warrants under the Privy Seal, which were filed among the Chancery records. These documents indicate a flow of communication from the King through the office of the Privy Seal to the Chancery, a more complex system than is seen in earlier records. The documents indicate a similar flow of communication from the Council and other departments through the office of the Privy Seal and then on to the Chancery. The office of the Privy Seal was a great clearing house, the center of a system that placed the Great Seal, in the custody of the Chancery, at the disposal of all departments. But certain notations on Chancery documents, such as *per ipsum regem* or *per consilium,* indicate that these normal channels were sometimes circumvented. The King or other officials sometimes communicated directly with the Chancery. Communication between departments is indicated in other ways as well. The Exchequer's *Originalia* Rolls are extracts of Chancery Rolls dealing with fines payable, and duplicate copies of the Chancery's Inquisitions post mortem are found in the Exchequer archives.

"Channels of communication" includes oral communications which were never recorded and perhaps the less important, illicit, or informal communications which were not preserved. Some traces of oral communications are found in the documents, and written communications not destined for preservation are less of a problem when scarce parchment rather than plentiful paper was used. For these reasons, we need not worry too much about the missing indicators. Those, which are available to Galbraith, cover such a large portion of the phenomena in question that additional evidence could not change his judgments by very much. To speak of cooperation between departments is quite another matter (Galbraith, 1934:24). The sending of documents from one office to another is only a small part of what is meant by "cooperation" and all the other things meant by the term would not necessarily go along with the transmission of documents. The indicators used are not sufficient for this purpose because we do not know, without looking at other evidence, how they might have been correlated with other indicators of cooperation. When Galbraith reconstructs the channels of communication, however, he is on sure ground.

The use of documents as indicators must not be confused with the use of facts or events as indicators. The events that took place on May 30, 1765, in the House of Burgesses, along with numerous other events throughout the colonies, are indicators of, let us say, the degree of tension between the colonies and England. But in order to know what took place on that day in the House of Burgesses, historians must first confront documents and then make inferences about events that are external to the documents. Only then can the events be used as indicators. And, of course, historians must go through similar steps in order to use events as correlates of other events. The use of external facts as correlates or as indicators, in other words, the making of inferences from established facts to other facts, is among the procedures that historians share with social scientists generally. In contrast, although the four types of inference from documents to events, which have been identified here, are sometimes found in the works of other social scientists, these four procedures are among the distinctive features of the historian's craft.

In some cases, historians simultaneously use all of these four procedures in order to answer a single question. Testimony, social bookkeeping, correlates, and direct indicators are all used by Homans (1942) in order to establish the geographical location and boundaries between champion land and woodland in medieval England. Homans deals with four characteristics by which woodland and champion land differed from each other: size of fields, open or closed fields, certain agricultural practices, and the distribution of settlements. For the first of these characteristics, he relies on testimony. For the second he relies on testimony and on a correlate, enclosure acts. For both the first and second, he also uses a direct indicator. If you go out and look you "can see that Devonshire, with its small squarish fields and big walls, has not the same landscape as Oxfordshire, though today the fields of both counties are, in the technical sense of the word, enclosed" (Homans, 1942:16). (This direct indicator would be even more telling if the book were written today, for the more sensitive eyes of aerial photography have since been used for this purpose.) For the third characteristic Homans cites documents of the social bookkeeping type, medieval surveys and extents. For the fourth, he again relies on testimony. While some of the evidence, when taken singly, may be called into question, the consistency with which these four types of evidence all point to the same conclusion answers all objections.

Although it is possible to classify neatly the evidence and procedures used by Homans in terms of the four categories presented here, it is not possible to do so in all cases, which the reader might think of. For example, those portions of the letters sent to Versailles by the French colonial governors in Quebec that purport to record information about events are a cross between testimony and social bookkeeping. One must read them in both lights. Perhaps such documents are common to similar situations, those in which one person reports to another in an official capacity but, instead of being one link in a complex and formally organized system of communication, is free to decide what he reports and how he reports it. Similarly, the distinction between correlates and indicators may not always be neat, and readers with experience in such matters can undoubtedly remember using procedures that fit into neither category. This is all to the good. For the methodological analysis of research situations which cannot be unambiguously classified in terms of the categories set forth here will not only define the limits within which these categories are useful, but will also force us towards greater clarity and precision. The further refinement of the categories presented here, and the identification of still further types of inference from documents to events, will provide historians and all social scientists who use documents with a greater measure of self-conscious control over their materials and techniques.

The greatest historians may not need self-conscious control. Haskins did not need the general category "correlates." Kosminsky did not need the category "social bookkeeping." But few are blessed with their historical intuition. And among those who are not, only some can apply general methodological categories to the details of their specific problems. That is something, which the categories themselves cannot do for us. In short, while many may need methodological investigations such as this, perhaps only a few can make use of them. But if historians are willing to grant that there is any problem of methodology at all, then they must also welcome all steps toward methodological refinement.

Notes

1. The phrase is from Gray, W. (1959). *Historian's handbook: A key to the study and writing of history* (p. 36). Boston: Houghton Mifflin.

2. The consistent application of this rule to early Spanish accounts of the Incas has led one author to a reconstruction of Inca society very different from those presented by earlier writers who had accepted the general descriptions given in the Spanish accounts. Cf. Moore, S. F. (1958). *Power and property in Inca Peru.* New York: Columbia University Press.

3. Decisions about authenticity are, of course, an example of "external criticism" and not of inferences from documents to events. Once the decision about authenticity is made, however, the fact of authenticity or lack of authenticity is a characteristic of the document, which, in this case, is used as a correlate of external events.

4. This discussion has profited from Lazarsfeld (1959). So far as the writer knows, most historians become painfully aware of this fact—that the specific indicators of general concepts are not perfectly correlated with one another—only when they attempt to periodize. By the age of laissez-faire, or some such concept, historians refer to a thousand and one specific items. When they attempt to set the temporal boundaries of an age, however, they confront the fact that the specific indicators of the concept do not all change in equal degree with equal speed.

References

Chrimes, S. B. (1952). *An introduction to the administrative history of mediaeval England.* Oxford: Blackwell.

Galbraith, V. H. (1934). *An introduction to the use of the public records.* Oxford: Clarendon Press.

Haskins, C. H. (1918). *Norman institutions.* Cambridge, MA: Harvard University Press.

Heckscher, E. F. (1955). *Mercantilism* (M. Shapiro, Trans., & E. F. Soderlund, Ed., Vol. 1, rev. ed.). New York: Macmillan.

Homans, G. C. (1942). *English villagers of the thirteenth century.* Cambridge, MA: Harvard University Press.

Kosminsky, E. A. (1956). *Studies in the agrarian history of England in the thirteenth century* (R. Kisch, Trans., & R. H. Hilton, Ed.). New York: Kelly & Millman.

Lazarsfeld, P. F. (1959). Latent structure analysis. In S. Koch (Ed.), *Psychology: A study of a science* (Vol. 3, pp. 476–543). New York: McGraw-Hill.

3.3

Politburo Images of Stalin

Nathan Leites, Elsa Bernaut, and Raymond L. Garthoff*

Hypotheses regarding differences (or lack of differences) in policy-orientation or in degrees of influence between the various members of the Soviet Politburo have always been of great interest to students of politics. Thus there have been frequent speculations regarding alleged differences in foreign policy lines and on the problem of succession. The absence of confirming or disconfirming data for any of these hypotheses is striking, and obvious in view of the secrecy that enshrouds the internal operations of the Politburo. Published statements of any kind by members of the Politburo have become infrequent in recent years. Such statements as are available for analysis have usually dealt with different subjects and have been made at different dates, so that they were difficult to compare from the point of view of testing hypotheses regarding differences in policy of influence.

Through Stalin's seventieth birthday, December 21, 1949, however, a rare opportunity for comparative analysis did occur. *Pravda* published articles by Politburo members Malenkov, Molotov, Beria, Voroshilov, Mikoyan, Kaganovich, Bulganin, Andreyev, Khrushchev, Kosygin, and Shvernik (in this order), preceded by a joint message to Stalin from the Central Committee of the Party and the Council of Ministers of the USSR. These articles were reprinted in *Bolshevik,* the Party organ, and the Soviet press in general.[1] In addition, the anniversary issue of *Pravda* (but not *Bolshevik*) contained two articles on Stalin by persons who are not members of the Politburo, M. Shkiryatov (a Party Secretary) and A. Poskrebyshev (presumably Stalin's personal secretary), thus treating their statements on a par with those made by the members of the Politburo. This body of materials will be examined as to what it may reveal regarding the distribution of influence and attitudes within the Politburo.

While all the statements mentioned appear at first glance to express the same adulation of Stalin, they do contain nuances in style and emphasis. These nuances could more easily be dismissed as matters of individual rhetoric, of little relevance to political analysis, if the statements had been made by non-Soviet writers. But nuances in the political language

*From Leites, N., Bernaut, E., & Garthoff, R. L. (1951). Politburo images of Stalin. *World Politics 3:*317–339.

used by members of the Politburo when talking about Stalin are of a different nature. Stalinism is not afraid of monotony and does not shun repetitiveness. Lack of complete uniformity of language is therefore possibly of political interest. It is worthwhile to examine the materials intensively in order to determine whether or not the differences in language, however subtle, fall into any patterns, and to explore the meaning of differentiations between groups or individuals in the Politburo. It seemed especially useful to approach the material with a view to investigating the degree of maintenance (or disuse and replacement) of earlier Bolshevik terms and themes.

Two major types of statements about the image of Stalin which can be discerned in the articles are analyzed in this paper. Table 1 gives the total frequencies of statements[2] concerning these ideas: first, Stalin in comparison to Lenin; and second, characterizations of Stalin's dominant role, as "perfect Bolshevik" or "ideal Father." A third image, "Stalin" as person or symbol, is not presented in this table or discussed in detail because the difference between images is a more qualitative classification derived from analysis of the context within the articles; it is briefly discussed at the close of this article.

The frequencies of statements, when read across, indicate the weight given to "popular image" of Stalin. The articles were not uniform in length: Malenkov's article was approximately 3,500 words; those of Shvernik, Andreyev, Kosygin, Khrushchev, and Shkiryatov were each about 2,500 words; the others were each approximately 5,000 words. However, since the relative weight given to characterizations within each article is the subject of our attention here, no "weighing" of frequencies has been made in the table, and absolute figures have been used. . . .

Table 1 References to Stalin in the Birthday Speeches December 21, 1949

	Stalin: Lenin's Pupil or Equal?			*Stalin: Perfect Bolshevik or Ideal Father?*		
Politburo Member	*Bolshevik Image*	*Ambiguous*	*Popular Image*	*Bolshevik Image*	*Ambiguous*	*Popular Image*
Molotov	5	1	0	12	3	0
Malenkov	4	0	2	11	3	0
Beria	13	3	1	15	1	2
Shvernik	4	0	5	2	2	2
Voroshilov	0	0	1	1	2	4
Mikoyan	2	2	9	3	0	5
Andreyev	1	0	2	3	0	15
Bulganin	0	1	6	0	0	3
Kosygin	1	0	3	0	0	8
Khrushchëv	0	1	4	0	0	7
Kaganovich	0	3	6	0	3	21
Shkiryatov	0	3	6	0	0	6
Poskrebyshev	2	1	3	0	0	10

Stalin: Lenin's Pupil or Lenin's Equal?

In current Soviet public discourse, the "great" Lenin is not called "greater" than the "great" Stalin; nor is it affirmed explicitly that Lenin and Stalin are equal in "greatness." It is, however, possible to adopt formulations that suggest the former or the latter of these emphases.

In the articles on Stalin's birthday, the differences of stress fall into the pattern of tendencies toward what we have termed the "popular" and the "Bolshevik" images of Stalin; the popular image emphasizes Stalin's equality (and in some instances even primacy) in relation to Lenin, while the Bolshevik image lays more stress on Stalin as Lenin's "pupil," or the "continuer" of his work and ideas.

In the treatment of this point, the Bolshevik image characterizes the articles of the top group of the Politburo: Malenkov, Molotov, and Beria. In a "middle" position, using both images, are the joint article of the Central Committee and the Council of Ministers and Shvernik's article. Tendencies toward the popular image are expressed by Kosygin and Voroshilov (each of whom makes only two comparisons), Andreyev, and Poskrebyshev. The popular image is most frequently and clearly presented by Mikoyan, Kaganovich, Bulganin, Khrushchev, and Shkiryatov.

Beria uses the Bolshevik image, illustrated in the following examples, most frequently:

> From his first steps of revolutionary activity Comrade Stalin stood unwaveringly *under* Lenin's banner. He was Lenin's true and devoted *follower.* He made his extremely valuable contributions to *Leninist* development of the Marxist Party's . . . tenets. . . . Establishing and developing *Leninism* and relying on *Lenin's instructions (ukazniya),* Comrade Stalin developed the *tenets* of . . . industrialization. [*Digest:*12]

There are other instances where Beria states that "Comrade Stalin developed *Lenin's instructions*" (*Digest:*13) and "developed *Lenin's teaching* on the Party" (*Digest:*12), but this quotation is especially significant since Stalin is in Soviet writing almost universally credited with the decision to collectivize and industrialize the country at a rapid tempo. There are many other references to Stalin's "arming the Party with Leninism," or "defending" or "advancing" Leninism, but these are not real comparisons.

There is one statement of equality on a situation (the conduct of the Civil War) concerning which Stalin has credited himself with a role possibly higher than Lenin's, so that equality in this respect would belong to the Bolshevik image.

> During the difficult Civil War years *Lenin and Stalin* led the Party, the State, the Red Army and the country's entire defense. [*Digest:*12]

Beria even makes one statement about "the introduction of the *Leninist-Stalinist national* policy" (*Digest:*13) dealing with the one matter attributed to Stalin's own authorship prior to the middle twenties. Beria also mentions Stalin's investiture by Lenin, a theme that is rarely touched upon:

> Lenin proposed that the Central Committee of the Party elect Comrade Stalin General Secretary of the Central Committee. Comrade Stalin has been working in this high post since April 3, 1922. [*Digest:*12]

As Lenin proposed, in 1923, that the Party consider the "removal" of Stalin from this "high post," Beria's reference is unusual. . . .

Molotov also expresses the Bolshevik image of Stalin in comparison to Lenin, emphasizing his theoretical continuation rather than personal discipleship, as Beria does. Both mention the fact that after Lenin's death, Stalin headed the Communist Party. Molotov goes on, however, to state:

> Comrade Stalin upheld and developed *Lenin's theory* of the possibility of victory of socialism in one country. . . . [*Digest:*7]

> As the . . . representative of creative Marxism, Comrade Stalin has highly developed the *Leninist* principles of strategy and tactics of our party. . . . [*Digest:*10][3]

Molotov also expresses the Bolshevik image of Stalin as the successor to Lenin in his capacity as "head of the Party" and the preserver of its monolithic character, and says:

> As the great *continuer* of the *cause* of immortal Lenin, Comrade Stalin stands *at the head* of all our socialist construction. . . . [*Bolshevik:*22]

Malenkov also stresses the Bolshevik image (despite two statements of apparent equality concerning their role in the Revolution):

> Better than anyone else, Comrade Stalin profoundly *understood Lenin's* inspired *ideas* on a new-type Marxist party. [*Digest:*3]

A middle position, using both images frequently, is noticeable in the joint C.C.-Council of Ministers message, and in the article by Shvernik, entitled "Comrade Stalin—*Continuer* of the Great *Cause* of Lenin." In addition to the title of his article, Shvernik makes three weaker Bolshevik image references to Lenin and Stalin, such as the one cited below.

> From the first steps of his revolutionary struggle, Comrade Stalin was pervaded with a boundless faith in *Leninist* genius, and went on Lenin's path as the most loyal of his *pupils* and companions-in-arms. [*Bolshevik:*1]

On the other hand, he expresses the popular image four times, writing "together with Lenin, Comrade Stalin" (*Bolshevik:*91, twice), and "Lenin and Stalin" led the working class to victory (*Bolshevik:*91), and finally, in words borrowed from Mikoyan, he says: "Stalin—that is Lenin today" (*Bolshevik:*95).

Poskrebyshev (Stalin's secretary, and possibly a future member of the Politburo) also expresses a mixed attitude on this question, with three unequivocal statements of equality, three as "continuer of the cause of Lenin," and two as teacher-pupil.

Kosygin, Andreyev, and Voroshilov employ the popular image more frequently than the Bolshevik but do not compare Lenin and Stalin often. Thus Kosygin writes: "The ideas of *Lenin-Stalin* have triumphed. One-third of the population of the globe has entered firmly onto the path indicated by Lenin Stalin . . ." (*Bolshevik:*89), and later "path of socialism, indicated by *Lenin-Stalin* . . ." (*Bolshevik:*90). Kosygin even omits the name of Lenin in a passage where one might have expected to find it:

> With the name of Stalin is indissolubly connected the creation of our Communist Party and of the first Soviet socialist state in the world. . . . [*Bolshevik:*86]

Just as Andreyev's article was predominantly devoted to agricultural matters, Voroshilov's article was concerned with military affairs, more specifically the strategy and conduct of the Great Fatherland War. In addition to two references to "the Party of Lenin and Stalin" he makes only one comparison, expressing equality.

> During the years of the heroic struggle and labor [the Revolution], the Soviet people under the leadership of the Party of Bolsheviks, under the guidance of the great leaders *Lenin and Stalin,* secured a world-historical victory. [*Bolshevik:*35]

The popular image is clearly dominant, and frequent, in the articles of Mikoyan, Kaganovich, Bulganin, Khrushchev, and Shkiryatov.

Thus, Mikoyan states:

> *Stalin* not only fully mastered the entire scientific heritage of Marx, Engels and Lenin . . . [He "defended" and "brilliantly interpreted" it]; he also enriched Marxism-Leninism with a number of great discoveries, and further developed the Marxist-Leninist theory. In the words of Comrade Stalin Leninism is raised to a new, *higher* historical plane. . . .The Marxist-Leninist philosophy, which is transforming the world, has reached its *apex* in the works of Comrade Stalin. [*Digest:*19][4]

Kaganovich is even more devoted to the use of the popular image, representing Stalin as equal to (or in rare instances even superior to) Lenin. There are no clear uses of the

Bolshevik image in his article, which abounds in comparisons.

> Comrade Stalin did not *simply* defend and safeguard the Leninist theory of the possibility of the victory of socialism in one country, but on the foundation of rich experience of the struggle, he *creatively augmented* and *enriched* the theory. . . . [*Bolshevik:*59]

In one place Bulganin credits Stalin with the distinction between just and unjust wars ("as Stalin teaches . . ."), without any mention of Lenin, who first made this distinction, and until now has been generally so credited in the Soviet Union (*Bolshevik:*70).

Khrushchev also uses the popular image, with one possible exception, in all his comparisons of Lenin and Stalin. In addition to five references to "the X of Lenin and Stalin" (*X* = Party, teaching, idea, cause, and banner), he makes three statements of clear equality and one which may even attribute superiority to Stalin.

> Herein lies Comrade Stalin's tremendous and invaluable service. He is the true friend and *comrade-in-arms* of the great Lenin. [*Digest:*30]

> . . . Stalin, who *together with Lenin* created the great Bolshevist Party, our socialist state, *enriched* Marxist-Leninist theory, and *raised it* to a new, *higher* level. [*Bolshevik:*80]

Shkiryatov also expresses the extreme image most frequently, stating only three times that Stalin is continuing the "cause" or "banner" of Lenin, while using the phrase "the teaching of Lenin and Stalin" four times, and making six comparisons of Lenin and Stalin, in all of which they are clearly represented as equal.

Reviewing the treatment of this theme we see that there emerge rather distinctly a Bolshevik image and a popular image, in the treatment of the relative standing of Lenin and Stalin by Politburo members.

The "Bolshevik image" is most prominent in the articles of the top sector—Beria, Molotov, and Malenkov (in that order). It represents Stalin as the pupil of Lenin, his follower, and his continuer as Lenin's successor, who continued to implement, defend, and elaborate Leninism. He appears as the most loyal of Lenin's followers and the one who best understood his ideas. Stalin is not considered as Lenin's peer (with the single exception of Malenkov's treatment of the October Revolution).

The "popular image" of Stalin is predominant, in varying degree, in the words of all the others, especially Kaganovich, Khrushchëv, Mikoyan, Bulganin, and Shkiryatov. It represents Stalin as the equal of Lenin, also in situations where this was obviously not the case. In rare instances, Stalin even appears greater than Lenin.

Stalin: The Perfect Bolshevik Party Leader, or The Ideal Father

The Bolshevik image is employed by Beria, Malenkov, Molotov, and to a lesser degree by Shvernik and Mikoyan. Stalin appears as the great "leader" and "teacher," but by implication the Party is superior to him. He possesses a very high degree of Bolshevik virtues.

The perfect Bolshevik takes it for granted that his life is dedicated to the advancement of Communism, at whatever deprivations to himself. He regards it as improper to talk about ultimate values and personal sacrifices; attention, he feels, should be concentrated on discerning the correct line and carrying it through. The traits ascribed to Stalin by Beria, for instance, are almost all means to this end and are presented as such. A positive evaluation of a Bolshevik commends him for having made himself an effective tool in correct directions.

The popular image of Stalin, given much more profusely, does not present him as a Party leader impersonally fulfilling the moral obligation to render service to the proletariat by providing a correct policy line. It shows him as a People's Leader in the Soviet Union and in the rest of the world, bestowing boundless paternal solicitude (*zabota*) on the "simple people." The people, overwhelmed by surprise at finding such freely tendered goodness in one of their very own (*rodnoi*) on high, work harder and better for him in loving gratitude. While the aim of the Party leader is to realize Communism in the future, at the cost of current hardships, the solicitude of the Leader of the People aims at satisfying human needs now. This he does, not only by laying down over-all policy, but also by innumerable concrete actions. In all this, Stalin possesses the virtues of an ideal father (sometimes brother and friend) which his children do not strive to equal. Stalin tends to become the creator of all good things.

The use of the Bolshevik image by the top group in this respect is far from excluding the use of elements of the popular image. Nevertheless, there is a differentiation, which we shall endeavor to show.

1. One of the aspects of the Bolshevik image of Stalin is his endowment with a very high degree of Bolshevik virtues. The implication is that these distinctive virtues should be emulated by less perfect Bolsheviks and that, although the chances of attaining Stalin's degree of perfection are slight, the model is clear, and there is no predetermined limit to advance.

For example, Beria says:

> In Comrade Stalin the Soviet people saw even more clearly and distinctly the features of his great teacher, Lenin. They saw that our army and people were led into battle against a brutalized enemy by a tested leader who, like Lenin, was fearless in battle and merciless toward the enemies of the people; like Lenin, free of any semblance of panic: like Lenin, wise and bold in deciding complicated questions; like Lenin, clear and definite, just and honorable, loving his people as Lenin loved them. [*Digest:*15][5]

Molotov also stresses Stalin's Bolshevik traits in several passages, (one) outstanding example follows below.

> The works of Stalin are now appearing, containing his containing his works from 1901. It is impossible to overestimate the theoretical and political significance of this publication. Before our eyes, stage by stage, there unfolds the picture of the inspired creative work of the great Stalin, in all its diversity and spiritual wealth. Here, all the diverse practical questions of the work of the Bolshevist party and the international communist movement and, together with this, complex scientific problems of history and philosophy are treated in the light of the ideas of Marxism-Leninism. . . . [*Digest:*9]

In most cases, popular image characterizations are admixed with Bolshevik statements showing Stalin as "leader" and "teacher." Of all the statements by the top group in the popular vein, only one (by Molotov) communicates a feeling or judgment by the speaker himself; all the other instances allege judgments or feelings of the *people.*

> Comrade Stalin is rightfully considered a great and loyal friend of the freedom-loving peoples of the countries of people's democracy. . . . [*Digest:*3]

In addition to stressing his Bolshevik virtues, the Bolshevik image presents Stalin as leader in three forms: political strategist, teacher, and Party executive. We shall examine these in turn.

2. According to the Bolshevik image, Stalin's main role is to make a diagnosis and prognosis of the political situation and to derive the correct line from it. In the popular image of Stalin this is stressed much less. This aspect of the Bolshevik image is conveyed particularly by Molotov, as the examples below indicate.

> . . . [Stalin's] ability . . . to show the Party the true way and to lead it to victory. [*Digest:*11]

> In order that the anti-Hitler three-power coalition might be created during the war, it was necessary first to thwart the anti-Soviet plans of the governments of Britain, France . . . Comrade Stalin discerned in time the . . . Anglo-French intrigues . . . enabling us . . . to bring the developments of events to a point at which the governments of Britain and the U.S.A. were faced with the necessity of establishing an Anglo-Soviet-American . . . coalition. . . . [*Digest:*8]

3. Related to this in the Bolshevik image is Stalin's function in "teaching" the Party rules of organization, strategy, and tactics. This is another point less stressed in the

popular image of Stalin. But it is one of the main emphases of Malenkov (who may expect to take over this function). The following citations from his speech are but a few of many.

> Comrade Stalin *teaches* that the Bolshevist Party is strong because . . . it multiplies its ties with the broad masses of the workers . . . Comrade Stalin *teaches* that without self-criticism we cannot advance . . . Comrade Stalin *teaches* that . . . Comrade Stalin *educates* the cadres of our Party. . . . [*Digest:*4–5]

Molotov and Beria emphasize Stalin's character as the "continuer," "defender," and "developer" of Leninism more than this teaching role, but they often do refer to Stalin as "leader and teacher." (This standard phrase is also found in the popular image but less frequently and prominently.)

4. The top-level statements frequently present as the major acting force not Stalin but the Party (or, sometimes) the "Soviet Union," or the "Soviet people," while other members of the Politburo stress the personal role of Stalin by omitting references to the Party. The Party is even credited with those services most often credited to Stalin by most of the others—inspiring, mobilizing, organizing. The term "leadership of the Party" clearly refers to others besides Stalin—in fact, to the speaker himself. Thus in the following passage, Malenkov mentions the Party eight times, and Stalin only once.

> The friendship among peoples which is firmly established in our country is a great *achievement of the leadership* of the Bolshevist *Party. Only* the Bolshevist *Party* could forge the indissoluble fraternity among the peoples—the Bolshevist party which consistently carries forward the ideas of internationalism. . . . [The recent war] was a most serious one for the Bolshevist *Party itself*. The *Party* emerged from this test a great victor . . . following the instructions of Comrade Stalin, our *Party* constantly inspired the people and mobilized their efforts in the struggle against the enemy. The *Party's* organizational work united and directed. . . . Again the unsurpassed ability of the Bolshevist *Party to* mobilize the masses under the most difficult conditions was demonstrated. [*Digest:*4]

On the other hand, the image of Stalin as the People's Leader (the popular image) shows him acting directly, without using the transmission belt of the Party. Occasionally the "top group" and the "middle group" members use this image in topics intended for mass consumption:

> . . . Stalin's voice in defense of peace . . . has penetrated throughout the world. . . . *All simple and honest people responding* to his appeal group themselves into powerful columns of fighters for peace. [Voroshilov, *Digest:*19; *Bolshevik:*44]

The popular image of Stalin, as we have indicated previously, does not stop at the limits which mark *the* Bolshevik characterization described above. Indeed, *it* very rarely uses them at all, except for casual and occasional reference to the standard term "leader" and "teacher." The articles of Kaganovich, Khrushchev, Shkiryatov, Poskrebyshev, Bulganin, Kosygin, and Andreyev, in roughly that descending order, are most expressive of the popular image, in the aspects presently under review. Mikoyan, and to a lesser degree Shvernik, also use it, but there arc a number of mixed and even Bolshevik statements in their articles. On the other hand, the seven writers listed above have only four Bolshevik image statements in all their articles. Voroshilov is a special case; in his introduction and conclusion he makes a number of statements in the popular image.

1. In the popular image Stalin is characterized as the "father" of his people, who constantly helps them because of his "paternal solicitude" for them. (This is sometimes weakened to a "friend" relationship, and sometimes intimate relationship terms are not employed.) "The simple people" are grateful, loving, and industrious in return. For them Stalin is *rodnoi,* meaning "one's very own." and connoting familial intimacy.

Each of the members of the "bottom group" uses this description (to varying degrees, of course, as shall become evident). The following examples are by no means exhaustive of the instances used.

Kaganovich depicts Stalin in this manner in the following passages:

> Comrade Stalin displays *exceptional solicitude* regarding miners and the alleviation of their labor. . . . The glorious army of railway workers responds to Comrade Stalin with *warm love, devotion,* and with a growing and improving transport [system] for his *paternal warmth and solicitude*. . . . The systematic increase of wages [etc.] . . . all these are the results of the *constant solicitude and attention* of *our very own [rodnoi]* Comrade Stalin, whom the people *lovingly* call *father* and *friend.* [*Bolshevik:*60–61]

Bulganin develops a similar image:

> Comrade Stalin *always* displayed and displays up to the present time a *constant paternal solicitude* for the *bringing up* [*vyrashchivani;* used in the phrase "bringing up one's children"] of military cadres, *educating* them in the spirit of supreme fidelity to the Bolshevist Party, in the spirit of self-sacrifice in the service of the people. . . . [*Bolshevik:*67]

Khrushchev similarly states:

> Lenin and Stalin stood at the *cradle* of each Soviet republic, they guarded it from menacing dangers, *paternally* [*po-otecheski*] helped it to *grow* and become strong. . . . This is why all the peoples of our land, with the uncommon *warmth and feeling of filial love,* call the great Stalin *their very own* [*radnoi*] *father*. . . . [*Bolshevik:*81]

Andreyev, while not stressing this aspect of the extreme image, states:

> *Attentively, paternally,* daily leading and *watching over* affairs on the collective farms . . . [is] Comrade Stalin. [*Digest:*29]

The two non-Politburo members, Shkiryatov and Poskrebyshev, both use this aspect of the popular image frequently. Poskrebyshev even titled his article "*Beloved Father* and Great Teacher."

Shkiryatov writes:

> The peoples of our country grow and become stronger like one *family,* and glorify Comrade *Stalin*—*father* and *friend* of all peoples of the USSR. [*Pravda:*11]

> Stalin, our *father* and *friend,* instills in us a love for all that is *ours, native*—in science, in culture, in production, and *educates* into the Soviet people a *warm devotion* to its Motherland. . . . [*Pravda:*11]

2. As has already become evident, the popular image pictures Stalin as the People's Leader, as contrasted to the emphasis on the Party and Stalin as Party leader in the moderate view. There are several aspects to being "People's Leader," and one which has been suggested in several of the quotations already cited shows Stalin as an opponent of "bureaucracy." In his concern for the welfare of the simple people, he must overcome the indecency, selfishness, and malice of the bureaus standing between him and the people. Bulganin makes this almost explicit:

> Comrade Stalin always paid great attention to the welfare of soldiers and sailors. He was interested in food standards, the quality of uniforms, and the weight of arms carried by soldiers. Comrade Stalin frequently pointed out in his orders that concern for the soldiers' . . . welfare was the sacred duty of the commanders, that they must see to it most strictly that soldiers received all the food due under established standards, that the troops were given well-prepared warm meals in good time. . . . Due to the constant solicitude of Comrade Stalin for the suppliers of the troops our front fighters were well fed and comfortably and warmly clad. [*Digest:*28; *Bolshevik:*71]

Many other examples could be cited to demonstrate this aspect of the popular image.

The popular image of Stalin shows him, by implication, almost as a one-man Party-government-and-army apparatus. The previous quotations have pointed out this characterization of Stalin in situations where the welfare of the people required it. But this does not exhaust the range of his actions, and Kaganovich and Bulganin in particular extend Stalin's active personal role to rather extreme lengths. According to Kaganovich:

> . . . while . . . the countries of Europe, and the U.S.A., first of all, are slipping toward a crisis, here in the Soviet Union the socialist economy improves constantly. . . . We are obliged for this to the superiority of the socialist system of

> economy, and *above all to Comrade Stalin's great energy, initiative and organizing genius.* [*Digest:*25]

Bulganin concerns himself with Stalin's role during the war, where Stalin performed an apparently prodigious amount of diverse labors constantly. Already in the Civil War,

> Comrade Stalin was the creator of the most important . . . strategic: plans and the *direct leader* of the decisive battle operations. . . . At Tsaritsyn and Perm, at Petrograd and against Denikin, in the West against the Poland of Pans, and in the south against Wrangel—everywhere his iron will and military genius secured [*obespechivali*] the victory of Soviet forces. [*Bolshevik:*66]

And in the recent war,

> *All operations* of the Great Fatherland War were *planned by Comrade Stalin and executed under his guidance.* There was *not a single operation* in the working out of which he did not participate. Before finally approving a plan . . . Comrade Stalin subjected it to thorough analysis and discussion with his closest [an unusual statement] . . . Comrade Stalin *personally directed the whole course of every operation.* Each day and even several times a day *he verified the fulfillment* of his orders, *gave advice,* and *corrected the* decisions of those in command, if there was need of this. [*Bolshevik:*66]

This image of Stalin as omnipresent and competent in every matter—an image never presented by the Politburo top group—is developed to a still further extreme by Poskrebyshev:

> Attentively supervising the work of the leading *Michurinists* [the new geneticists], headed by Comrade Lysenko, Comrade Stalin gave them *daily assistance by his advice and instructions.* . . . Comrade Stalin must also be noted as a scientific innovator in specialized branches of science. . . . Among the old specialists in agriculture it was considered firmly established that the cultivation of citrus crops could not be extended on a wide scale in the region of the USSR Black Sea coast. . . . [*Digest:*34]

STALIN: PERSON OR SYMBOL?

In our material, "Stalin" often refers to more than the man, J. V. Stalin. The boundary between references to Stalin the person and, as might be said, Stalin the symbol is blurred, probably on purpose. The top group, however, is more careful than the other to distinguish between these two images, and to lay stress on Stalin the person.

One way of indicating that Stalin is being referred to as a symbol is by speaking of his "name," or actually declaring his name to be a "symbol." Thus Beria states in his introductory paragraph:

> Since the great Lenin there has been no *name* in the world so dear to the hearts of millions of working people as the *name* of the great leader, Comrade Stalin. [*Digest:*11]

And Molotov tells us that for "the world movement for peace"

> . . . the name of Stalin is its great banner. [*Digest:*9]

Malenkov also states this:

> The *name* of Comrade Stalin has long since become a *banner* of peace in the minds of the peoples of all countries. [*Digest:*3]

And Bulganin writes:

> The *name* of Stalin became for the Soviet troops the *symbol of the greatness of our nation* and its heroism. They went into battle with the slogan: "For Stalin, for the Motherland!" [*Bolshevik:*71]

Another way of differentiating between Stalin the person and Stalin the symbol is by making explicit the *personal* character of the reference. In the birthday articles, Molotov, Shvernik, and Bulganin use this mode of expression most frequently. Although many other references which do not specify that Stalin the person is meant probably do mean this, the method remains, when used by the top group, an indication of instances where Stalin's personal role is held to be highly significant. Malenkov uses a different method of achieving a similar effect. Although he refers to Stalin an average number of times (average number, 59 Malenkov's total, 60), a disproportionately large number of the references are to the effect that "Stalin teaches that . . ." or "as Stalin said," etc. Consequently, he says relatively less about other accomplishments of Stalin.

A technique used to transform "Stalin" from the person into the symbol is to employ the adjectival form of the word, "Stalinist." The Bolshevik image usually reserves the term "Stalinist" to describe the achievements of Stalin's regime rather than his personal accomplishments. The popular image is, on the whole, lax about this differentiation, and apparently allows personal and impersonal meanings to be given to "Stalinist," as well as to "Stalin."

The proportion of uses by the top group (Molotov, Beria, and Malenkov) of "Stalinist" as meaning "Stalin's" personally is only two out of a total of twenty-seven, in contrast to the very frequent use of the term in this meaning by all the others (excepting only Voroshilov's account of Stalin's role in the recent war). Very often statements are made describing "the Stalinist, Soviet path," "Soviet, Stalinist military science," and the like, inferring clearly that the term in these instances indicates merely "under the present regime" or "in a Bolshevik manner."

The relatively impersonal meaning of the adjective "Stalinist" is particularly evident in such passages as the following. Molotov, affirming that the Soviet Union has gained in strength over the last quarter of a century, says:

> This is a very great service of Comrade *Stalin and of Stalinist leadership.* [*Digest:*6]

Presumably, "Stalinist leadership" here refers to Party leaders other than Stalin, and becomes a synonym for "Party." This is shown when Kaganovich, in a rare formulation, says:

> A decisive condition for the victory of socialism was the incessant struggle of Comrade *Stalin and of the united collective Stalinist leadership* . . . for the realization of the general line of the Party. [*Bolshevik:*63]

Conclusions

Two main conclusions emerge from this study of the birthday articles:

1. Despite many individual differences among these articles and despite the variations within each of them, two major images of Stalin may be constructed, toward which each article is oriented to its particular degree. Briefly, these images are Stalin the Party Chief and Stalin the People's Leader. The Party Chief is a very great man; the People's Leader stands higher than any man. The Party Chief is characterized by Bolshevik traits; the People's Leader by constant and boundless solicitude for the welfare of all. We have referred for the sake of brevity to the first as *"the Bolshevik image,"* and to the second as *"the popular image."*

2. Three groups within the Politburo can be distinguished in terms of using these images. Malenkov, Molotov, and Beria, who presumably are the most influential members of the Politburo, stress the Bolshevik image of Stalin more than the other members, although indications of the popular image are not totally absent from their statements. Kaganovich, Bulganin, Khrushchev, Kosygin, and to a lesser degree Mikoyan and Andreyev, occupy positions near the popular image (as do Shkiryatov and Poskrebyshev). Shvernik and the joint Party-government address occupy a middle position. Voroshilov is a special case, presenting the popular image of Stalin in his introduction and peroration, but a very moderate Bolshevik image in terms of specific military operations (in contrast to Bulganin).

These two images of Stalin can now be reviewed with two questions in mind: (1) To whom is either image addressed? Is there a preferred audience for the popular image and another such audience for the Bolshevik image? (2) What political significance can be attached to the finding that the Bolshevik image is stressed by the "top group" in the Politburo, while the popular image is used most freely by the "bottom group"?

Concerning the first question, it should be remembered that all statements analyzed in this paper were published; they were not made in private. As public statements they were not primarily, or at any rate not exclusively, addressed to Stalin. It is reasonable to assume that the "masses" of the Soviet population were meant to be the consumers of the popular image, whereas the Bolshevik image was offered primarily for adoption by Communists, i.e., a small segment of the population. It is characteristic of Bolshevism, though paradoxical to Western thinking, that the symbols of nearness and intimacy ("father," "solicitude," etc.) appear most frequently in the popular image of Stalin and are stressed for that audience which is far removed from Stalin. Those closer to Stalin politically are permitted to speak of him in terms of lesser personal intimacy ("leader of the party"). This paradox results partly from the merely instrumental use in Bolshevik language of words indicating personal nearness, and partly from the Bolshevik deprecation of such nearness in political relationships. The ideal Party member does not stress any gratification he may derive from intimacy with others, much as he may use such intimacy for political ends.

For this reason it is difficult to answer the second question with certainty. It cannot be ruled out that the Politburo—or a leading group within it, or Stalin personally—decided to use both images of Stalin in the birthday statements and to adopt a certain distribution of roles among its members in presenting them. (Such a decision may have taken the form of an editorial scrutiny of each statement, in the course of which the differentiation of language was imposed.)

However, the assumption that there was a decision within the Politburo on the use of different images of Stalin does not preclude certain tentative conclusions about the status of the groups within the Politburo. The emphasis on the Bolshevik image by a few members of the Politburo and on the popular image by others not only reflects the Bolshevik evaluation of the Party as distinguished from, and superior to, the masses at large, but also indicates the relative distance of the speakers from Stalin. In the situation under review, it is a privilege for a member of the Politburo to refrain from using the crudest form of adulation, words signifying personal intimacy and emotions; that is, private, rather than political, words. Given the Bolshevik evaluation of political as against private life, the use of the Bolshevik image indicates higher political status. Hence, a planned distribution of roles in using the two images of Stalin on the occasion of his birthday would still indicate a political stratification of the Politburo, though not necessarily political antagonism within it.

Unless one were to make the somewhat absurd assumption that the roles to be performed on this occasion were distributed by lot, or the improbable assumption that they were assigned for the purpose of concealing the real stratification within the Politburo, those members who stress the Bolshevik image could be assumed to be politically closer to Stalin than those who do not.

The assumption that there had been a decision of some kind on the use of the two images would appear more plausible if either image were used by certain members of the Politburo without the admixture of elements taken from the other. As it is, the difference between the "top group" and the "bottom group" is one of *emphasis* in imagery. For this reason, we are inclined to regard the differentiation of political language discussed in this article as the result of individual choices rather than of a central decision. However, in this case we may assume that the stress—whether conscious or not—of any given Politburo member on the one or the other image of Stalin was related to his status in the Politburo in the fashion indicated above.

Notes

1. As far as is feasible, quotations are given from the translation in Volume 1, No. 52, of *The Current Digest of the Soviet Press* (hereafter cited as *Digest*). Other passages have been translated from the December 1949, No. 24 *Bolshevik.* All italics, unless otherwise indicated, are by the authors of this article.

2. A "statement" for the purposes of this table, means each incidence of an explicit idea, and may vary from a phrase to a paragraph. The examples cited in the text should clarify this point.

3. December 21, 1929, Molotov wrote more specifically that Stalin had been a "man of practice" (*praktik i organizator*) up to Lenin's death, after which he became a "theoretician." Even in 1919 Molotov has not quite suppressed his tendency to deny that Stalin was manifestly perfect from the start. He begins his speech by saying: "It is *now* particularly clear how very fortunate it was . . . that after Lenin the Communist Party of the USSR was headed by Comrade Stalin" (*Digest:*6). In the Bolshevik atmosphere of veiled language, this is bound to be understood, to some extent, as conveying: It was not *always* clear.

4. Although Molotov and Beria both praise Stalin as the theorist, they do not state explicitly (or clearly implicitly) that Stalin is as great a theorist as Lenin, to say nothing of the statement that "Marxist-Leninist philosophy has reached its apex" in Stalin's work.

5. "Loving the people" also belongs to the popular image. These occasional popular image terms in a moderate picture may be the effect of reverse seepage of esoteric propaganda into the constantly assaulted esoteric integrity of the top group.

3.4

QUANTITATIVE AND QUALITATIVE APPROACHES TO CONTENT ANALYSIS

ALEXANDER GEORGE*

Researchers have long debated the respective merits and uses of "quantitative" and "qualitative" approaches to content analysis. . . . Most writers on content analysis have made quantification a component of their definition of content analysis. In effect, therefore, they exclude the qualitative approach as being something other than content analysis.

Quantitative content analysis is, in the first instance, a statistical technique for obtaining descriptive data on content variables. Its value in this respect is that it offers the possibility of obtaining more precise, objective, and reliable observations about the frequency with which given content characteristics occur either singly or in conjunction with one another. In other words, the quantitative approach substitutes controlled observation and systematic counting for impressionistic ways of observing frequencies of occurrence.[1] The term "qualitative," on the other hand, has been used to refer to a number of different aspects of research . . . :

1. The preliminary reading of communications materials for purposes of hypothesis formation and the discovery of new relationships

   As against

   Systematic content analysis for purposes of testing hypotheses.

2. An impressionistic procedure for making observations about content characteristics

   As against

   A systematic procedure for obtaining precise, objective, and reliable data.

3. Dichotomous attributes (i.e., attributes, which can be predicated only as belonging or not belonging to an object)

*Excerpt from George, A. L. (1959). Quantitative and qualitative approaches to content analysis. In I. de Sola Pool (Ed.), *Trends in content analysis* (pp. 7–32). Urbana: University of Illinois Press.

As against

Attributes which permit exact measurement (i.e., the true quantitative variable) or rank ordering (i.e., the serial).

4. A "flexible" procedure for making content-descriptive observations, or "coding" judgments

As against

A "rigid" procedure for doing the same.

Frequency and Non-Frequency Content Indicators

While these four distinctions are important in themselves, they do not serve to differentiate between the two approaches to the analysis of communication. . . . We therefore introduce a somewhat different distinction, which focuses on the aspects of the communication content from which the analyst draws inferences regarding non-content variables.

1. Quantitative content analysis, as we here define it, is concerned with the *frequency* of occurrence of given content characteristics; that is, the investigator works with the frequency of occurrence of certain content characteristics.

2. Inferences from content to non-content variables, however, need not always be based on the frequency values of content features. The content term in an inferential hypothesis or statement of relationship may consist of the mere *presence* or *absence* of a given content characteristic or a content syndrome within a designated body of communication. It is the latter type of communication analysis, which makes use of "non-frequency" content indicators for purposed of inference, that is regarded here as the non-quantitative or non-statistical variant of content analysis.

The distinction we have introduced concerns the type of content indicator utilized for purposes of inference. Given (different uses of) . . . "quantitative" and "qualitative," it is desirable to introduce a new set of terms. We employ the term "non-frequency" to describe the type of non-quantitative, non-statistical content analysis, which uses the presence or absence of a certain content characteristic or syndrome as a content indicator in an inferential hypothesis. In contrast, a "frequency" content indicator is one in which the number of times one or more content characteristics occur is regarded as relevant for purposes of inference.

The distinction between frequency and non-frequency analysis, it should be noted, is independent of the aforementioned four dimensions to which the terms quantitative and qualitative are sometimes applied. Thus, both in frequency and non-frequency analysis (one can distinguish) between hypothesis-formation and hypothesis-testing phases of research, between impressionistic and systematic types of content description, between flexible and rigid procedures for making content-descriptive judgments.

Nor is the familiar distinction in the theory of measurement between dichotomous, serial, and quantitative *attributes* equivalent to the distinction advanced here. Thus, . . . frequency as well as non-frequency analysis may be concerned with dichotomous attributes, that is, attributes which can be predicated only as belonging or not belonging to an object. This is the case, for example, in the simple word-counts . . . deciding whether a certain word or symbol ("democracy," "Germany," "Stalin") does or does not appear in each sentence, paragraph or article. . . .

[T]he difference between the two approaches is that frequency analysis, even when it deals with dichotomous attributes, always singles out frequency distributions as a basis for making inferences. In contrast, the non-frequency approach utilizes the mere occurrence or nonoccurrence of attributes . . . for purposes of inference. Thus, for example, [from] a quantitative study, which shows a sharp decline in number of references to Stalin in *Pravda,* the frequency analyst might infer that the successors to Stalin are attempting to downgrade the former dictator or are trying to dissociate themselves from him. On the other hand, the non-frequency analyst might make a similar inference from the fact that in a public speech one of Stalin's successors pointedly failed to mention him when discussing a particular subject (e.g., credit for the Soviet victory in World War II) where mention of Stalin would formerly have been obligatory. In one case, it is the frequency distribution of attention to "Stalin" over a period of time on which the inference rests. In the other, it is the mere occurrence or nonoccurrence of the word "Stalin" on a particular occasion,* which serves as a basis for the inference. Yet, in both of these examples, the investigator deals with a dichotomous attribute . . . the presence or absence of "Stalin" in a given unit of communication.

Furthermore, the use of frequency and non-frequency methods is not determined by the fact of multiple or single occurrence of the content feature in question within the communication under examination. The fact that a content feature does occur more than once within a communication does not oblige the investigator to count its frequency. The important fact about that content feature for his inference may be merely that it occurs at all within a prescribed communication.

It should be noted, finally, that the non-frequency approach to content analysis is really an older and more conventional way of interpreting communication and drawing inferences from it than is the quantitative approach. The resemblance of the non-frequency approach to traditional methods of textual analysis, moreover, will become obvious when we consider some of the characteristics of this approach.

Some Examples of Non-Frequency Content Analysis

[Two] examples will illustrate the nature of the non-frequency approach and some of the disadvantages of relying exclusively upon frequency or quantitative content analysis. The examples are drawn from wartime propaganda analyses of German communications made by personnel of the Analysis Division, Foreign Broadcast Intelligence Service, and Federal Communications Commission (FCC).

1. [T]he FCC analyst inferred that the Nazi Propaganda Ministry was attempting to discourage the German public, albeit indirectly, from expecting a resurgence of the U-boats. This inference was also based in part upon a non-frequency content indicator. Hans Fritzsche, the leading radio commentator, had asserted the following in discussing a recent success achieved by German U-boats: ". . . we are not so naive as to indulge in speculation about the future on the basis of the fact of this victory . . ." In focusing upon this statement, the FCC analyst was not concerned with the frequency of the theme in Fritzsche's talk or in other German propaganda accounts of the same U-boat "victory," or with the question of whether it now appeared more or less frequently than in earlier propaganda on the U-boats. For his purpose, it sufficed that the content theme was present even once in the context of Fritzsche's remarks about the latest German U-boat victory.

It is interesting to speculate on what would have happened had a frequency (quantitative) approach been employed in this case. In the first place, it is problematic whether a content category could have been set up that would have precisely caught the meaning of this one phrase in Fritzsche's talk. Secondly, since the phrase (or its equivalent) appeared at best only a very few times in German propaganda at the time, the propaganda analyst, in looking over the quantitative results, might well have dismissed it as a "minor theme" or lumped it together with other items in a "miscellaneous" or "other" category. In other words, if this single phrase from Fritzsche's talk had been subsumed under a frequency indicator, it might well have lost its inferential significance.

2. The (second) example is quite similar. [Towards the end of World War II,] Mussolini had set up a Republican-Fascist government following his "liberation" by German parachutists (from his imprisonment). German propaganda gave quite a play to these events

*In the context of what is expected, a known norm.

and celebrated Mussolini's re-establishment of a pro-Axis Italian government. In looking over this propaganda, the FCC analyst noted that, after a few days, a minor theme of some sobriety was introduced into the otherwise enthusiastic publicity on Mussolini and his new government. Only a few Nazi papers carried the new message and, where it did appear, it was rather well hidden. For example, in the *Völkischer Beobachter,* September 9, 1943, the following sentence appeared: ". . . the battle is not yet won by the changes proclaimed by Mussolini, and the structural changes undertaken by him must not be regarded as a guarantee of future greatness."

The significance of this new theme to the FCC analyst lay in the fact that it appeared at all. In other words, he made use of it as a non-frequency content indicator. Had this new theme been subsumed under a general frequency-type indicator in a quantitative study, it would probably have passed unnoticed. But when singled out as a non-frequency indicator, the theme, although repeated only a few times in the total Nazi propaganda on Mussolini, provided the basis for an important inference. The FCC analyst inferred, from the appearance of the theme, that the Propaganda Ministry had decided to moderate the public's expectations regarding a resurgence of Italian fascism. Continuing the chain of inference, the FCC analyst then reasoned that such a propaganda goal must have been adopted as the result of a new, more sober estimate by Nazi leaders of the potential of Mussolini's new government. This inference was subsequently verified [by] material appearing in *The Goebbels Diaries* (Lochner, 1948).

Some Difficulties in Applying Quantitative Content Analysis for the Study of Instrumental Aspects of Communication

[I]n such fields as clinical psychiatry and propaganda analysis, content analysis is often used as a diagnostic tool for making causal interpretations about a single goal-oriented communication. In order to identify and explore some of the special problems that arise in this type of content analysis, we shall further examine the case of propaganda analysis. Other communication analyses, which operate within the framework of an instrumental model, may encounter similar problems. We will discuss the following: (1) the problem of coding irrelevant content, (2) the problem of changes in the speaker's strategy, (3) the problem of an expanding universe of relevant communication, and (4) the problem of structural characteristics of instrumental communication.*

These problems arise in part from the characteristics of propaganda communication, and in part [from] the investigator's interest in making specific inferences about some aspect of the communicator's purposive behavior. In any case, the result is that a considerable portion of the research effort must be given to discovering new hypotheses or refining old ones; systematic quantitative analysis for purposes of testing inferential hypotheses is often difficult, infeasible, or unnecessary; and, finally, non-quantitative (non-frequency) content indicators are often more appropriate and productive than quantitative (frequency) indicators.

The Problem of Coding Irrelevant Content

A variety of specific goals and strategies are usually pursued in propaganda communications. The propaganda analyst, however, may be interested in making inferences only about one or a few matters of policy interest. Accordingly, he must exercise care in considering which passages in the stream of communication are *relevant* to each of the goals or strategies of the communicator.

The difficulty of arriving at such judgments of relevance and the considerable sensitivity and discrimination, which are required for this purpose, are often reasons for not undertaking elaborate quantitative "fishing

*These issues are just as relevant today in light of the use of content analysis techniques on the Web.

expeditions" in any sizable body of propaganda communications. Not all the individual items tabulated under any given content category in such a "fishing expedition" may be relevant to the specific inference, which the analyst would like to make about the speaker's state of mind.

We are referring here obliquely to one of the important requirements of statistical content analysis, namely, that it be "systematic" in the sense that "*all* of the relevant content . . . be analyzed in terms of *all* of the relevant categories, for the problem at hand" (Berelson, 1952:17).

But the obverse of this requirement—that none of the *irrelevant* content be analyzed—is equally important and is a weighty reason for not undertaking elaborate quantitative content analyses of the "fishing expedition" variety. . . . In some cases the inclusion of irrelevant content in the analysis may be no more than a waste of manpower. But in other cases, it may rule out the possibility of making a useful inference or lead to wholly mistaken inferences. The problem may become particularly acute when the investigator, engaged in a "fishing expedition" of this sort, deliberately selects broad content categories in order to ensure large enough frequencies for purposes of subsequent statistical analysis.*

The danger of coding irrelevant content is minimized when research is designed to test clear-cut hypotheses. Hypotheses usually indicate or imply the realm of relevant content or the appropriate sample to be coded.

However, precise hypothesis formation—the assertion of a relationship between a content indicator and one or more communicator variables—is often difficult in propaganda analysis. This difficulty reflects the rudimentary state of the scientific study of communication. The lack of good hypotheses about relationships between content variables and communicator variables makes it difficult for the propaganda analyst to circumscribe the terms and categories for specific investigations.

This difficulty, of course, is by no means confined to propaganda analysis. . . . In a sober assessment of the results of their large-scale study of symbols as indices of political values, attitudes, and ideological dispositions, [Lasswell lamented]:

> . . . there is as yet no good theory of symbolic communication by which to predict how given values, attitudes, or ideologies will be expressed in manifest symbols. The extant theories tend to deal with values, attitudes, and ideologies as the ultimate units, not with the symbolic atoms of which they are composed. There is almost no theory of language that predicts the specific words one will emit in the course of expressing the contents of his thoughts. Theories in philosophy or in the sociology of knowledge sometimes enable us to predict ideas that will be expressed by persons with certain other ideas or social characteristics. But little thought has been given to predicting the specific words in which these ideas will be cloaked. The content analyst, therefore, does not know what to expect. (Lasswell, Lerner, & Pool, 1952:49)

In summary, there are relatively few theories or general hypotheses about symbolic behavior available for testing by means of rigorous quantitative content analysis. . . . [S]ome investigators, [therefore] employ quantitative content analysis for purposes of a "fishing expedition"; large quantities of content data are collected without guidance of clear-cut hypotheses in the hope of discovering, at the end of the study, new relationships and new hypotheses. Such studies tend to be time consuming, wasteful, and generally unproductive. Disappointing results with "fishing expeditions" are particularly likely when large quantities of material are processed (aided by) clerical personnel to do the coding. As a result (of being locked into a fixed coding instrument), there is insufficient opportunity to refine categories and it is usually not possible to recode the bulky material as many times as necessary in order to produce content data appropriate for testing interesting hypotheses.

---

*And thereby failing to record the distinctions that may prove critical in supporting the desired inferences.

The Problem of Changes in the Speaker's Strategy

Due to the circumstances, which have been described, the "qualitative" phase of hypothesis formation may properly receive unusual emphasis in propaganda analysis. [This is justified by] the fact that the propagandist's strategy on any single subject may change abruptly at any time. In attempting inferences about the speaker's state of mind, . . . the analyst cannot easily draw up a set of content categories, which will be appropriate for all possible shifts in the communication strategy of the speaker. [He] will hesitate to commit himself to systematic quantitative description because he fears that the speaker's strategy may change while the count is being made. If such a change is unnoticed . . ., the value of the results of the quantitative tabulation . . . may be lost. For then, such content data might well be ambiguous or inappropriate for purposes of inference.

In propaganda analysis, the instrumental use to which communication is put by the speaker is regarded as a highly unstable variable, which intervenes between various other antecedent conditions of communication (e.g., speaker's attitude and state of mind, the conditions and calculations, which have affected choice of action) and the content variable itself. In this respect, propaganda analysis has much in common with the analysis of psychotherapy protocols. Both the propaganda analyst and the psychotherapist are sensitive to the possibility that the communication intention and strategy of the speaker can change frequently during . . . a systematic count of the content features of what he says. . . . [E]xcept when there is reason to believe that the content features selected as indicators are insensitive to variations in the speaker's strategy, frequency counts may be inappropriate as a means of inferring the speaker's attitudes, state of mind, and . . . conditions that have influenced his choice of a communication strategy or goal.

In propaganda analysis, typically, the investigator is interested in inferring one or more of the following antecedent conditions of the propagandist's communication: his propaganda goals and techniques; the estimates, expectations, and policy intentions of the leadership group for whom the propagandist is speaking which have influenced the adoption of a particular propaganda strategy; the situational factors or changes which have influenced the leadership's estimates, expectations, and policy intentions and/or the propagandist's choice of communication goals and techniques.

Investigators interested in inferring elite estimates, expectations, policy intentions, and/or situational factors, which lay behind the adoption of a particular propaganda goal or strategy may employ one of two rather different methods of inference. They can attempt to find content indicators which directly reflect the component of elite behavior or the situational factor in which he is interested, or he can attempt first to infer the speaker's propaganda goal and then proceed step by step to account for the selection of that goal in terms of elite estimates, expectations, policy intentions and/or situational factors.

The first of these two methods of inference bypasses consideration of the speaker's propaganda strategy. The inferences made with this *direct method* are one-step inferences, as follows:

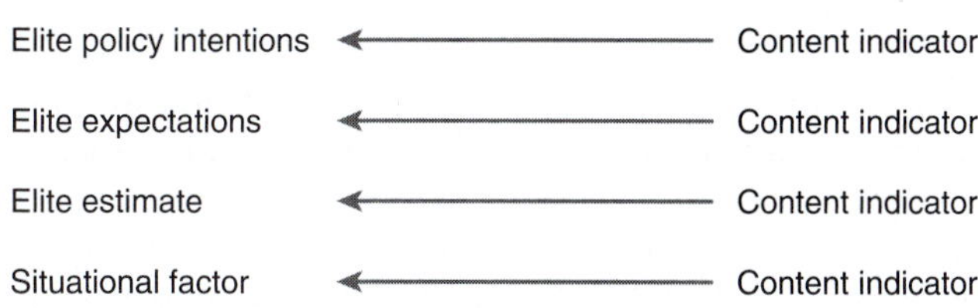

Figure 1

In contrast, the *indirect method* is comprised of an inferential chain of two or more steps, the first of which is always an inference about the speaker's goal or strategy. It may be depicted, in somewhat simplified form, as follows:

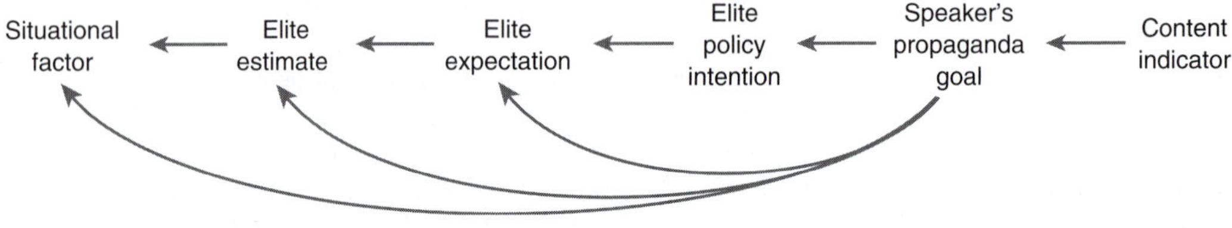

Figure 2

The direct method . . . can be successfully employed only if content features can be found which occur *regularly* and *only* when a certain type of elite policy intention, expectation, estimate, or situational factor occurs. The types of regularities or generalizations that the direct method requires as a basis for inferences, therefore, are correlations of a noncausal character. It is important to recognize that the content terms in such correlations must be insensitive to possible variations in propaganda strategy. This is necessary because propaganda strategy is an intervening and relatively unstable variable between elite policy behavior and propaganda content. The direct method is on firm ground only when it employs as content indicators features of the communication over which the propagandist does not exercise control or of whose information-giving value regarding elite policy behavior he remains unaware. Such content features are likely to be symptomatic features of a propagandist's behavior rather than part of his communication intention.[2]

The indirect method, on the other hand, attempts to utilize for purposes of inference the fact that the behavior of the propagandist in selecting communications goals and strategies constitutes an intervening set of events between elite policy behavior and the dependent variable (content of propaganda). Therefore, the investigator who employs the indirect method attempts to identify content features in the propaganda, which are sensitive to and dependent upon the speaker's strategy.

The distinction between content features that are sensitive and insensitive to variations in the speaker's strategy is useful not only in propaganda analysis, but whenever content analysis is used on instrumentally manipulated material. In such cases, obtaining good indices of attitude, value, etc., would seem to require either the avoidance of content features, which are likely to be sensitive in the first instance to variations in the speaker's communication strategy or a sophisticated awareness of that strategy.

The Problem of an Expanding Universe of Relevant Communication

Another characteristic of propaganda, which has procedural implications, is the fact that the universe of relevant communication may be expanding while [its] analyst is attempting to draw inferences from it. . . . [Under these conditions], the propaganda analyst finds himself trying to keep up with the flow of communication that has some relevance to his problem. . . . [A]s new statements on the topic are made by the source, . . . the set of alternative hypotheses under consideration and [corresponding] content categories [have to be revised]. . . .

These circumstances frequently rule out quantitative content description. A familiar prerequisite of quantitative content analysis is that the investigator knows what he is looking for before beginning to count. The propaganda analyst (who relies on quantitative accounts of communications) . . . cannot be confident that the data provided will still be adequate for purposes of inference when new statements on the topic are received from the source. For the most recent communication may throw new light on the inferential problem and, based on these new insights, the propaganda analyst may have to reread and reinterpret the earlier propaganda communications in their original form. . . .

A similar problem arises, we may note, when information about *non-content* events bearing upon the inferential problem comes to the attention of the propaganda analyst *after* he has received and analyzed the relevant propaganda communication. Such non-content events may permit the analyst retrospectively to formulate more discriminating hypotheses about the inferential significance of the propaganda. And, for this purpose, it may be necessary for him to reread and reappraise the propaganda communication in its original form, in the light of the new information available on relevant non-content events.

The Problem of Structural Characteristics of Instrumental Communication

Propaganda analysis procedures are much influenced, finally, by the necessity to take into account the structure of individual propaganda communications. Different structural types of communication are encountered in the flow of propaganda available for analysis. An article by Goebbels appearing in *Das Reich,* for example, was structurally different from a speech by Hitler; and both, certainly, were structurally different from German radio news broadcasts.

The propaganda intention of an individual communication (and its effect as well) often depends not merely on the explicit content of the individual statements or propositions therein contained but also upon the structural interrelationship of these statements within that communication.

Thus, what may be called the "whole-part" problem in content analysis has several important procedural implications. It may affect [the] choice of counting units and categories as well as the decision on the type of content indicator (frequency or non-frequency) to be employed.

Awareness of the "whole-part" problem often leads the propaganda analyst to be critical of an important implicit assumption of statistical content analyses, namely, that each individual item counted as falling under a designated content category is of equal significance for purposes of inference.[3] Similarly, the propaganda analyst is often critical of the assumption that the inferential significance of explicit propositions, themes, or statements is dependent upon the precise frequency of their occurrence. Rather, he may find explicit propositions of significance for purposes of ascertaining the strategy of the propagandist because they occur at all or because they occur in a certain relationship to each other within the communication.

This does not mean that frequency counts are useless for purposes of propaganda analysis. Frequency tabulation of words, clichés, stereotypes, and slogans may provide an indication of propaganda emphasis and techniques as well as of intentions. But such tabulations in themselves give no clue to the meaning of the content in question. They are of value, therefore, only when the investigator has prior or independent knowledge of their meaning, role, and significance in the system of language habits under study.[4]

. . . The procedure employed in ascertaining the propositional content of a propaganda communication and in weighing the structural interrelationships of parts therein undoubtedly is often less systematic than in rigorous quantitative content analysis in which coding judgments are closely prescribed. But in principle, the reliability of such content observations, too, is subject to investigation.

Some Characteristics and Special Problems of the Non-Frequency Approach

The preceding discussion has already suggested some of the characteristics of non-frequency analysis of instrumental communications. In this section, we recapitulate these characteristics briefly and single out for more extended comment the special problems to which they give rise.

Selection of Content Categories: The Search for Specific Discriminating Categories

In some quantitative investigations, the technical requirement of relatively large numbers for statistical analysis appears to exercise an important influence on the choice of content categories and on the size of the sample of raw material to be coded. Symbols and themes with low frequency of occurrence may be either ignored or grouped together under broader content categories.

The conscious selection of content categories and sample size with an eye to satisfying technical requirements of statistical analysis may be justified when the research objective is to make general inferences. But such a criterion is inappropriate when, as in propaganda analysis, the object is to make specific inferences about events at particular times and places. In the latter case, valuable opportunities for making inferences are lost. . . .

The investigator who is aware of the value of non-frequency indicators tries, rather, to formulate ever more discriminating content categories. He deliberately attempts to "narrow down" the categories and to make them relatively more specific. The fact that this results in low frequencies, in a single occurrence, or in no occurrence at all of the content feature in question is not of concern to him since he expects to employ a non-frequency indicator for purposes of inference. . . .

Emphasis on Hypothesis Formation as Against Hypothesis Testing

Perhaps more so than in most frequency analyses, the investigator who employs the non-frequency approach gives unusual attention and effort to the hypothesis-formation phase of research. There are a number of reasons for this emphasis to which we have already alluded: the search for more discriminating categories, the need to exclude irrelevant content, and, of course, the rudimentary state of knowledge and theory about the relationships between content and communicator variables.

Relative Emphasis Upon Validity as Against Reliability of Semantical Content Description

The non-frequency approach places more emphasis upon obtaining valid estimates of the speaker's intended meaning than do many versions of quantitative content analysis. Because he usually deals with relatively large frequencies, the quantitative investigator can work with somewhat lower validity requirements and can (and must) pay greater attention to reliability considerations. The inclusion of a small number of incorrect determinations of the speaker's intended meaning under a content category composed of large frequencies will probably not affect the final analysis greatly. In contrast, just because he works with low frequencies or single occurrences, the non-frequency analyst cannot afford to risk making any invalid determinations of the speaker's intended meaning.

Given the crucial importance in non-frequency analysis of validly estimating the one or few meanings, which may be of inferential significance, the investigator concentrates upon making an intensive assessment of contextual factors upon which such meanings are likely to depend. This type of assessment, however, is particularly difficult to objectify, for it requires taking into account the situational and behavioral, as well as the linguistic contexts of given words. Accordingly, the procedure for inferring the speaker's precise intended meanings cannot easily be made fully explicit. Investigators who attempt to infer intended meanings must usually settle for relatively flexible and interpretative procedures of coding content.

Each judgment of an intended meaning is a separate inference arrived at by taking into account not only dictionary meanings and rules of the language, but also all relevant aspects of the context: situational and behavioral as well as linguistic. The concern with inferring intended meaning in this manner does not distinguish the non-frequency approach from all frequency analysis. But it does serve to differentiate it radically from one variant of the quantitative approach known as "manifest" content analysis.*

. . . [I]n "manifest" content analysis the investigator estimates the meanings of words by applying a set of external criteria as to the usual, customary, or most frequent meaning of the words in question.[5] Such a judgment or estimate of meaning is not [situation] specific. . . . [Use of such criteria] increases the objectivity of the content-descriptive procedure and facilitates achieving reliability of results, but . . . may seriously prejudice the validity of results if the intended meanings . . . differ . . . from the meanings which those words ordinarily have.[6]

In coding content for its usual, or "manifest" meaning, the investigator needs to be familiar with the general rules of the language, the customary meanings of words for all users of that language, and—in some varieties of quantitative content analysis—with the usual or most frequent language habits of the communicator.

. . . [T]o make valid inference of intended meaning in each specific instance of communication, the investigator also takes into account the situational and behavioral contexts of that communication. He does so in order to determine which of the possible meanings of the words in question the speaker intends to convey in the instance at hand and the precise shading of his intended meaning. . . .

In taking into account the *behavioral* context of words, the investigator considers the instrumental aspect of the communication in its broad action setting. In order to interpret the precise meaning intended by the speaker in any individual instance he takes into account the *purpose* or *objective, which the specific communication is,* designed to achieve.

In taking into account the *situational* context of the communication being analyzed the investigator considers *who* is speaking, *to whom,* and *under what circumstances.* Clues to the speaker's intended meanings [are obtained] by considering various known characteristics of the speaker, his audience, and the nature of the speaker-audience relationship. The investigator also takes into account the time and place of the communication and related events preceding or accompanying it. He does so in the expectation that the exact intended meanings of the words employed by the speaker are shaped by (and understood by the audience with reference to) certain aspects of the setting and the stream of related events. This is particularly likely when, as in wartime propaganda, the communication being analyzed is highly situation- or event-oriented.

Such analysis of the instrumental aspect of communications in their situational contexts is not confined to non-frequency approaches, for it is by no means the case that quantitative or frequency analysis always limits itself to coding "manifest" content. In fact, the criterion of "manifest" content is not generally accepted as essential to the technique of quantitative content analysis. Cartwright (1953) explicitly rejects it, for example. Even in the area of political communication research, for which Lasswell's version of content analysis has been primarily developed, many if not most quantitative content analyses do not in practice employ the "manifest" content criterion. Rather, they often attempt to infer intended meanings and employ relatively flexible and interpretative procedures for coding content. If this is a drawback from a scientific standpoint, it is one present in many quantitative studies as well as in non-frequency analyses. The difference in this respect between frequency and non-frequency analyses, therefore, seems to be one of degree, stemming partly from the different nature of the two approaches. The non-frequency approach, by virtue of the limited number of cases with which it deals, requires that all relevant intended meanings always be

*Berelson's (1952:14–18) definition of content analysis restricts the technique to the analysis of the manifest content of communications, commonly equated with the existence of widespread agreement on what a communication means. Since agreement is also equated with reliability, Berelson concludes that only manifest content can be analyzed reliably. He thus confounds the methodological requirement of reliability with the conceptual distinction between manifest and latent content. Experts may well achieve high reliability in coding latent meanings.

estimated as validly as possible and, therefore, that full account be taken of situational and behavioral contexts.

The emphasis on validity in the non-frequency approach is accompanied by less concern with the reliability of the judgments, or inferences, being made of the speaker's intended meanings. Rarely are systematic procedures employed to ensure or to demonstrate the reliability of non-frequency content descriptions. A possible explanation for this may be suggested. Since the non-frequency analyst works with a relatively small amount of content data, which he collects himself, he tends to be less self-conscious about the reliability problem and less concerned with it than the quantitative analyst is. As a result, he is likely to overlook what the well-trained quantitative investigator knows so well and rightly emphasizes, namely, that when the procedure for obtaining content data on intended meanings is highly interpretative, it is all the more necessary to assess in some fashion the reliability of its results.

Close Relationship Between Descriptive and Inferential Procedures

Some possible circularities of procedure beleaguer the non-frequency approach to the analysis of communications content. . . . [C]ontent description is intimately intertwined with and overlaps the assessment of inferences from the contents. Inferences as to what the propagandist is trying to say and why he is trying to say it are not neatly discrete.

To illustrate, if one person addresses another as "you old rascal," the analyst who is seeking to interpret the intent validly will want to know if the addressee is an old man or an infant. If it is a baby, one infers that the intent is affectionate and simultaneously describes the content as endearment. There is a mutually interdependent set of assumptions here. One has not established the intent independently and derived the content interpretation from that nor has one established the affectionate meaning of the phrase "you old rascal" independently and derived the intent from that. The two propositions are parts of an interdependent set of inferential hypotheses.

The question arises of whether this aspect of the non-frequency approach necessarily entails the danger of analytical bias, or "circularity." That is, by not distinguishing more sharply—as in quantitative content analysis—between the descriptive and inferential phases of research, does not the investigator risk the possibility that a hypothesis formulated early in the course of his content description will determine what he subsequently "sees" and regards as significant in the communication?

The danger of circularity in this sense is indeed potentially present in the procedure described above and undoubtedly occurs in many low-grade analyses. However, the disciplined analyst guards against it in several ways. He does not read through the communication material just once, but rereads it as many times as necessary to satisfy himself that the inference favored by him is consonant with all of the relevant portions and characteristics of the original communication material. Similarly, he considers not just one inferential hypothesis when reading and rereading the original communication material, but also many alternatives to it.

He systematically weighs the evidence available for and against each of these alternative inferences. Thus, the results of his analysis, if fully explicated, state not merely 1) the favored inference and the content "evidence" for it, but also 2) alternative explanations of that content "evidence," 3) other content "evidence" which may support alternative inferences, and 4) reasons for considering one inferential hypothesis more plausible than others.

In this fashion, the disciplined analyst controls the dangers of circularity present in the overlapping of descriptive and inferential procedures. To the extent that he operates in the systematic, disciplined fashion we have outlined, the non-frequency analyst follows the accepted scientific procedure of successive approximations.

Notes

1. For a brief exposition of quantitative content analysis and some of its uses in the study of political communication, see Lasswell, Lerner, and Pool (1952). These authors' sober assessment of the difficulty of meeting various prerequisites of statistical content analysis is particularly useful.

2. On the difference between interpretation of "intent" and interpretation of "symptoms" in the analysis of communication, see Kecskemeti (1952:61–62).

3. For an explicit statement of this important (but often ignored) assumption of quantitative content analysis, see Berelson (1952:20).

4. This point is explicitly discussed in Goldstein (1942:26–27, 38–40, 150).

5. For a detailed discussion, see Lazarsfeld and Barton (1951:155–192). See also Cartwright (1953).

6. The problem of validity noted here arises only when "manifest" content is used as a rule-of-thumb substitute for intended meaning. It does not arise, or course, when the investigator is interested *only* in the usual meanings of words, as in linguistic studies or in studies of effect on a mass audience rather than of intent of the communicator. In other words, depending upon the hypotheses and questions, which are being investigated, the analyst may be interested either in "manifest" meaning or intended meaning. And, when interested in intended meaning, it can be inferred directly in each instance or employ "manifest" meaning as a rough approximation.

References

Berelson, B. (1952). *Content analysis in communication research.* Glencoe, IL: Free Press.

Cartwright, D. P. (1953). Analysis of qualitative material. In L. Festinger & D. Katz (Eds.), *Research methods in the behavioral sciences* (pp. 421–470). New York: Holt, Rinehart & Winston.

Goldstein, J. (1942). *Content analysis: A propaganda and opinion study.* Unpublished master's thesis, New School for Social Research, New York.

Kecskemeti, P. (1952). *Meaning, communication and value.* Chicago: University of Chicago Press.

Lasswell, H. D., Lerner, D., & Pool, I. de Sola. (1952). *The comparative study of symbols.* Stanford, CA: Hoover Institute Studies, Ser. C: Symbols.

Lazarsfeld, P. F., & Barton, A. H. (1951). Qualitative measurement in the social sciences: Classification, typologies and indices. In D. Lerner & H. D. Lasswell (Eds.), *The policy sciences: Recent developments in scope and method* (pp. 155–192). Stanford, CA: Stanford University Press.

Lochner, L. (Ed.). (1948). *The Goebbels diaries.* Garden City, NY: Doubleday.

3.5

Evaluative Assertion Analysis

Ole R. Holsti*

Introduction

Content analysis—which may be performed using many different techniques, depending upon the theoretical interests of the investigator—is used as a tool for research in international conflict on the premise that from . . . the decision-makers' messages, valid inference may be drawn concerning the attitudes of the speaker or writer. [A] method of content analysis must fulfill a number of requirements.

1. It must provide valid results.
2. It must provide reliable results.
3. It must provide results that are capable of quantification. A continuing study of world tension levels, for example, requires a technique that provides not only a measure of the appearance or non-appearance of certain attitudes, but also of the intensity of those attitudes.

One method meeting these requirements is "evaluative assertion analysis,"[1] a form of quantitative content analysis in which messages are translated into simple, three-element assertive format. Numerical values are then assigned to the constituent elements of each assertion, depending upon its direction and intensity.

Evaluative assertion analysis is not merely a technique for scaling previously coded data. Rather, it is an all-inclusive method of content analysis; as such, it prescribes comprehensive rules for each step from the initial preparation of the written text through the final analysis of the processed data.

This technique was designed for the study of evaluative attitudes on a "good-bad" continuum; its senior author has demonstrated elsewhere, through factor analysis of semantic differentials, that the good-bad, active-passive, and strong-weak dimensions dominate human expression (Osgood, Suci, & Tannenbaum, 1957:50–51, 72–73). The mechanics of the method,

*From Holsti, O. R. (1963). Evaluative assertion analysis. In R. C. North, O. R. Holsti, M. G. Zaninovich, & D. Zinnes (Eds.), *Content analysis: A handbook with applications for the study of international crisis* (pp. 91–102). Evanston, IL: Northwestern University Press.

however, are suitable for analysis of any dimension defined as a continuum between polar opposites. The technique is also readily adaptable for measuring categories that are defined, as in Q-Sort scaling, as a single "more-to-less" continuum. For the study of international conflict, relevant variables, in addition to those mentioned above, include: hostility-friendship, satisfaction-frustration, strength-weakness, specificity-diffuseness, and violence-nonviolence. Any dimensions chosen for analysis must, of course, be explicitly defined.

As with all kinds of content analyses, evaluative assertion analysis rests upon certain minimal premises regarding (1) the structure of messages, and (2) the operations that can be undertaken by reasonably skilled coders with an acceptable degree of reliability. These assumptions have, however, been empirically shown to be valid (Osgood, Saporta, & Nunnally, 1956:47–48).

It will suffice [here] . . . to outline very briefly the primary characteristics of this technique. A reader contemplating the use of evaluative assertion analysis should turn to the original source for a comprehensive description. The summary below will serve as an introduction to the method and as the basis for discussing its utility in research on international conflict (Osgood, 1959; Osgood et al., 1956).

Coding and Scaling

The steps for converting unedited messages into the quantified data against which hypotheses can be tested are as follows:

1. The initial step in evaluative assertion analysis is the identification and isolation of attitude objects in relation to the variables under study (Osgood et al., 1956:49). Attitude objects are symbols whose evaluative meanings vary from person to person; for example, capitalism, foreign aid, United Nations, Khrushchev. Common-meaning terms are those whose evaluative meanings vary, minimally; for example, evil, honest, benevolent. In general, terms that are capitalized are attitude objects rather than common-meaning terms.

2. After attitude objects—which might include nations, policies, ideologies, decision-makers, non-national organizations or general symbols—have been identified by the coders, they are masked with meaningless symbols. For example, the text of a Soviet note to the United States Government states that,

> In recent days, fascistic elements with the obvious connivance of the United States occupation authorities have carried out in the American sector of West Berlin a series of dangerous provocations against members of the honor guard of the Soviet forces.

After masking of attitude objects with nonsense symbols, the edited text would read as follows:

> In recent days, fascistic elements with the obvious connivance of the AX occupation authorities have carried out in the AX sector of BY a series of dangerous provocations against members of the honor guard of the CZ forces.

Note that because in the Soviet note the terms "United States" and "American" are interchangeable, both are masked with the same symbol.

3. Following these initial operations, the masked message is translated into one of two generic assertion forms:

Form *A*: Attitude Object$_1$ (A0$_1$)/verbal connector (c)/common meaning term (cm)

Form *B*: Attitude Object$_1$ (A0$_1$)/verbal connector (c)/Attitude Object$_2$ (A0$_2$)

Comprehensive guides for translation of the text have been prepared (Osgood et al., 1956:59–89), making possible the revision of the most complex sentences. Thus an editorial statement in *Jen-min jih-pao:* "The treacherous American aggressors are abetting the corrupt ruling circles of Japan," would be coded as follows:

1.	Americans	are	treacherous	(form *A*)
2.	Americans	are	aggressors	(form *A*)
3.	Americans	are abetting	Japanese ruling circles	(form *B*)
4.	Japanese ruling circles	are	corrupt	(form *A*)

The complete text is typed on a seven-column data chart (Figure 1): Values are then entered in columns 4 and 6 of the data chart. If the project involves the analysis of more than one dimension, assertions should be kept separate either by adding an additional column on the data chart in which identification of the dimension can be made, or by maintaining a separate data chart for each dimension.

1	2	3	4	5	6	7
Source	AO_1	c	Value of Column 3	cm or AO_2	Value of Column 5	Product: Columns 4 × 6

Figure 1

4. The next step is to determine the direction or valence and intensity of the attitudes, as expressed in the verbal connector and the common-meaning term. Each of these is rated for both valence (+ or –) and intensity (1, 2 or 3). The direction of the verbal connector depends upon whether the perceived relationship is associative (+) or dissociative (–). The valence of the common-meaning term is determined by whether the expressed attitude lies on the negative or the positive side—however these are defined by the researcher—of the neutral point on the dimensional scale.[2]

Intensities for the verbal connectors and common-meaning terms are also assigned according to a comprehensive set of guides. For example, most unqualified verbs or verbal phrases in the present tense are given a value of ± 3; verbs with auxiliaries are rated ± 2; and, verbs implying only a hypothetical relationship are assigned a value of ± 1. Similarly, common-meaning terms are rated 1, 2, or 3, corresponding roughly to the categories "extremely," "moderately," and "slightly." The assigned values are then entered in columns 4 and 6 of the data chart.

The values for attitude objects are first determined for all assertions in form A; only after the values for attitude objects in assertions of form A have been calculated, can the evaluation for assertions in form B be made. In the previous example, assertions 1, 2, and 4 are of type A, whereas assertion 3 (Americans / are abetting / Japanese ruling circles) is in form B. The numerical value of "Japanese ruling circles" is calculated by every assertion of type A. In assertion 4 it was stated that,

Japanese ruling circles / are / corrupt

From this and other assertions of a similar nature, ($A0_1$ / c / cm), that might appear in the text, it is possible to calculate the perceived evaluation of "Japanese ruling circles" (in this case a strongly negative one). That value is then inserted into assertion 3; thus because the Americans are closely associated ("are abetting") with the Japanese ruling circles, the value of "Americans" is a strongly negative one.

The reader may ask, "What if the text is composed entirely of assertions in form B, making it impossible to determine any values?" This can only occur in messages devoid of any adjectives or adjectival phrases. Thus, it is difficult to imagine an extensive communication in which every assertion is of the AO_1 / c / AO_2 type.

5. The scaling of an attitude object on any dimension is the sum of its evaluation in assertions of form A and form B. In each case the value is the *product* of the second (verbal connector) and third element (common meaning term [form A] or attitude object$_2$ [form B]). For example, assertion 4 above would appear as follows on the data chart (Figure 2):

1	2	3	4	5	6	7
Source	AO_1	c	Value of Column 3	cm or AO_2	Value of Column 5	Product: Columns 4 × 6
Jon-min jih-pao	Japanese ruling circles	are	+3	corrupt	–3	–9

Figure 2

The reason for multiplying the values in columns 4 and 6 is to assure the proper valence or direction of the final evaluation; thus the double negative (X is not bad) assertion will receive the same value as the double positive (X is good) assertion.

The final evaluation of each attitude object is calculated in three steps:

1. All values in column seven for assertions of type A are summed.
2. All values in column seven for assertions of type B are summed.
3. The total of the values derived in steps x and z is then divided by the modular sum of column three.

The final evaluation may he expressed algebraically as,[3]

$$\text{Evaluation } AO_1 = \frac{\sum_{i=1}^{n} c_i cm_i + \sum_{i=1}^{n} c_i (AO_2)_i}{\sum |c| cm + \sum |c| AO_2}$$

Applications of Evaluative Assertion Analysis

The results of the completed analysis may be aggregated in a variety of ways. For some projects, it might be useful to compare single documents, whereas for others the analyst may be interested in compiling totals for all documents within prescribed time periods. In other cases, it may be desirable to combine results in terms of the senders or recipients of the messages.[4] Such a decision will, of course, be dictated by the nature of the research problem.

A number of objections may be raised against evaluative assertion analysis. In the first place, the method is admittedly time consuming.[5] A second point is that the translation of the text into assertion form leads to some loss in the "flavor" of the original message.

There is some weight in both objections, but the technique has many compensating advantages. By translating all messages into assertion form, much is gained by providing a high degree of uniformity for the judges who must do the scaling. Three major sources of low reliability are (1) the ambiguity of categories, (2) confusion over the perceived roles of various attitude objects within a sentence, and (3) difficulty in assigning numerical values to complex statements. Each of these points will be considered in terms of evaluative assertion analysis.

The first problem is primarily a theoretical one and precedes the coding stage. However, a technique which reduces each sentence to its constituent elements eliminates the possibility of more than one dimension appearing in any one assertion. This may be illustrated by a typical Chinese statement during the U-2 crisis: "The Chinese people firmly support the stand of the Soviet Government in opposing United States imperialism's war provocation and its sabotage of the Summit Conference." This sentence consists of a number of attitude objects in a complex relationship. In addition, the sentence contains elements of friendship (firmly support), hostility (oppose, war provocation, sabotage), evaluation (just stand), and policy conditions (firmly support, war provocation, sabotage, opposing). The unedited text clearly poses a problem for the scaler; when coded in assertion form, which separates the various elements, the difficulties are materially reduced.

Chinese people	/	firmly support	/	Soviet Government
Soviet Government's stand	/	is	/	just
Soviet Government	/	opposes	/	the United States
United States	/	is	/	imperialistic
United States	/	provokes	/	war
United States	/	sabotaged	/	Summit Conference

A second source of difficulty with many techniques, arising usually after a sentence has been masked, is the possibility of confusing the perceived roles of the various attitude objects in any sentence. In the statement cited above, for example, there are three actors—the Chinese people, the Soviet Government, and the United States—and maintaining their perceived relationship is of crucial importance. The translation of statements into assertion form minimizes the possibility of confusion because the position of each element in the assertion is always the same. The data sheets themselves impose a high degree of uniformity, being divided into columns, which maintain that order throughout.

As stated elsewhere . . ., the essential theoretical components of any statement are (1) perceiver, (2) perceived, (3) action, and (4) target. Evaluative assertion analysis is readily adaptable to such a conceptualization:

Perceiver	=	Source
Perceived	=	Attitude Object$_1$
Action	=	Verbal Connector
Target	=	Attitude Object$_2$

In addition, there is a vital fifth element, the incorporated modifiers, which may be connected to the perceiver, perceived, or target. One of the valuable characteristics of evaluative assertion analysis is that it forces a separation, for the purposes of analysis, of "action assertions" from "evaluative assertions."[6] The importance of this point can be illustrated in the statement, "The valiant X has repelled the treacherous forces of Y." Although it includes only one perceiver (author of the statement), one perceived (X), one action (has repelled), and one target (Y), the statement creates difficulties—both for the coder who must categorize it and for the scaler who must assign it a numerical value—owing to the presence of the affective elements "valiant" and "treacherous," in addition to the action element of "has repelled." But when the sentence is translated into

1.	X	/	has repelled	/	Y	(action assertion)
2.	X	/	is	/	valiant	(evaluative assertion)
3.	Y	/	is	/	treacherous	(evaluative assertion),

much of the difficulty, both in categorization and in assigning numerical values, is resolved. Assertion 1 can then be scaled for action dimensions such as activity-passivity, specificity-diffuseness or violence-nonviolence; assertions 2 and 3 can be scaled for affective dimensions such as good-bad or hostility-friendship.

When this fifth element, the incorporated modifier, has been introduced as a separate constituent, the conversion between the theoretical framework developed in this manual and evaluative assertion analysis is complete:

Perceiver	=	Source
Perceived	=	Attitude $Object_1$
Action (or attributive verb)	=	Verbal Connector
Target	=	Attitude $Object_2$
Incorporated Modifiers	=	Common-meaning terms

A third source of low reliability—difficulty over the assignment of numerical values to complex sentences—is reduced to a minimum by allowing the scaler to focus attention first on the verbal connector and then on the common-meaning term, in each case a single word or a short phrase. When all data have been processed, it is possible to do a rapid congruity check on the finished data sheets to detect any errors (Osgood et al., 1956:98–99).

Unlike forced distribution scaling techniques, evaluative assertion analysis is amenable to comparative analysis *across* as well as *within* universes of statements. For example, a project may involve scaling all Soviet statements in the month before the U-2 incident and the month after the affair as separate bodies of data, in order to test hypotheses concerning the patterns of variables. If, however, it is also desirable to compare hostility levels between the two months, this cannot be done using any forced distribution scaling technique without further rescaling of at least samples from the combined universes, because the mean hostility level for each month is by definition identical.[7] While this additional step is by no means an insurmountable barrier, a technique which defines the value of each value category rather rigorously beforehand bypasses some of the problems of comparative analysis.

Adaptability to Computer Analysis

A final point, which may be considered, is the adaptability of evaluative assertion analysis to computer analysis. Translation into assertion form appears to be one of the methods most readily adaptable to this type of analysis.* Retrieval of relevant assertions, assignment of values, and the arithmetic computations can easily be performed by computer. Finally, the results can be aggregated in terms of the researcher's hypotheses.

Conclusion

It is almost inevitable that research into international conflict involving any extensive use of content analysis will be group research, utilizing teams of translators, coders, scalers, data recorders, programmers, analysts, and others. Because both coders and scalers are likely to be part-time and short-term employees of the research project, the rules for coding and scaling must be sufficiently comprehensive to avoid ambiguity, yet simple enough to be easily learned. For this reason, a technique of content analysis, such as evaluative assertion analysis—by imposing a high degree of uniformity on each of the various steps of data preparation and analysis—can be of great value. Moreover, research personnel can be rapidly trained. The increment of additional time required to use evaluative assertion analysis must be weighed against the degree of reliability and precision that is gained; in the end, however, the selection of a methodological tool must rest upon the nature of the research problem and the information

*See Kleinnijenhuis, de Ridder, and Rietberg (reading 7.5, this volume), who use computer aids to kernelize text in the above two and several additional types of assertions.

that the researcher seeks to obtain from the communications to be analyzed.

Notes

1. The most complete guide to this technique is Osgood et al. (1956). A briefer, and more readily accessible, summary may be found in Osgood (1959:41–54). The present brief description of the various steps in evaluative assertion analysis is derived from these sources.

2. The continuum has a middle point of zero. Any one statement, however, with an evaluative product of zero should not be coded. For example, the assertion "Kennedy is a man," has a value of zero on a friendship-hostility scale. Thus the statement is not coded.

3. This formula gives a "weighted" evaluation (see Osgood et al., 1956:92). For research of this kind described in this manual, an un-weighted evaluation (in which each assertion is given equal value), may be more desirable. In this case, the following formula may be used:

$$\text{Evaluation } AO_1 = \frac{\sum_{i=1}^{n} c_i cm_i}{3^n} + \frac{\sum_{i=1}^{n} c_i (AO_2)_i}{3^n}$$

in either case, final evaluations fall within a range of +3 to –3. The rationale for using the un-weighted evaluation formula is discussed in Appendix A of Holsti (1962).

4. Examples of the various uses of evaluative assertion analysis may be found in Holsti (1962a) and (1962b).

5. Coders are able to process completely about one page per hour. A short form of the method is described in Osgood et al. (1956:96–97). Coding speed can be increased by a factor of three without a disastrous loss of inter-coder reliability.

6. Adjectives formed from verbs or implying an object may cause some ambiguity. Consider the assertion, "X is aggressive." This is both evaluative on a number of scales (hostility, friendship, etc.) and implies action against an unspecified or general target. This point was raised by William Quandt (1962).

7. It should be noted that there are dangers inherent in the assumptions that all results are comparable. For example, even a cursory reading of Chinese Communist statements will reveal a level of affect rarely found in the more genteel diplomatic language of the nineteenth century.

References

Holsti, O. R. (1962a). *The belief system and national images: John Foster Dulles and the Soviet Union.* Ph.D. dissertation, Stanford University.

Holsti, O. R. (1962b). The belief system and national images: A case study. *Journal of Conflict Resolution 6:*245–252.

Osgood, C. F. (1959). The representational model. In I. de Sola Pool (Ed.), *Trends in content analysis* (pp. 33–88). Urbana: University of Illinois Press.

Osgood, C. F., Saporta, S., & Nunnally, J. C. (1956). Evaluative assertion analysis. *Litera 3:*47–102.

Osgood, C. F., Suci, G. J., & Tannenbaum, P. I. (1957). *The measurement of meaning.* Urbana: University of Illinois Press.

Quandt, W. (1962). The application of the General Inquirer to content analysis of diplomatic documents. *Stanford Studies in International Conflict and Integration, July.* 1.

3.6

An Ecology of Text

Memes, Competition, and Niche Behavior

Michael L. Best*

Introduction

Ideas do not exist in a vacuum. Neither does discourse, the interconnected ideas that make up conversation and texts. In this research, we investigate the pair-wise interaction between populations of ideas within discourse: Are our text populations in competition with each other? Do they mutually benefit each other? Do they prey on one another?

This work attempts to build models of *population memetics* by bringing together two disciplines: Alife** and text analysis. Through techniques of text analysis, we determine the salient co-occurring word sets, texts, and text clusters, and track their temporal dynamics. We then study the life-like properties of this human-made system by considering its behavior in terms of replicators, organisms, and species.

Richard Dawkins coined the term *meme* to describe replicating conceptual units (Dawkins, 1976). In studying the population dynamics of ideas we consider the meme to be the largest reliably replicating unit within our text corpus (Pocklington, 1996; Pocklington & Best, 1997). Through text analysis, we identify memes within a corpus and cluster together those texts, which make use of a common set of memes. These clusters describe species-like relationships among the texts.

The particular texts we study are posts to the popular USENET News (or NetNews) system. These posts form the basis of a new Alife environment, the *corporal ecology* (Best, 1996, 1997). In this ecology, texts are the organisms, the digital system defined by NetNews describes an environment, and human authors operating within some culturally defined parameters are the scarce resource.

At the core of our study sits a large text analysis software system based primarily on Latent Semantic Indexing (LSI) (Deerwester, Dumais, Furnas, Landauer, & Harshman,

---

*Best, M. L. (1997). Models for interacting populations of memes: Competition and niche behavior. *Journal of Memetics—Evolutionary Models of Information Transmission, 1.*

**Short for artificial life, the study of computer simulations of living systems and their evolution.

1990; Dumais, 1992, 1993; Furnas et al., 1988). This system reads each post and computes the frequency with which each word appears. These word counts are then used in computing a vector representation for each text. A principal component analysis is performed on this collection of vectors to discover re-occurring word sets; these are our memes. Each post is then re-represented in terms of these memes. By grouping texts, which are close to one another within this meme-space, we cluster semantically similar texts into species-like categories or *quasi-species* (Eigen, McCaskill, & Schuster, 1988).

We proceed to study the interactions between those populations that coincide temporally. For each cluster, we compute a series that represents its volume of post activity over time, for instance, how many texts of a given cluster were posted on a given day. Cross-correlations between each pair of time series are then determined. We find that some pairs have strong negative correlations and argue that these are examples of texts in competition. A number of examples of such competition are explored in depth. We argue that high competition is correlated with those text clusters that exist within a narrow ecological niche; this phenomenon is also observed in natural ecologies (Pianka, 1981).

Note that this is an unusual shift from the typical Alife environment. We are not synthesizing replicators, embodying them into agents, and observing their life-like interactions. Instead, we are studying a pre-existing artifact. Through our analysis, we *discover* replicators within organisms, and use computational techniques to observe their dynamics.

In this paper we first briefly overview the NetNews environment and describe the LSI-based text analysis system. Next, we describe the mechanism used to determine the temporal dynamics and cross-correlations given a corpus of posts. We then relate the cross-correlations to models of interacting populations. In the next section, we examine in depth a couple pairs of post clusters with strong interactions. We then describe a theory of niches within the corporal ecology and note that narrow ecological niches are correlated with significant competition. We end with our conclusions.

The NetNews Corpus

Understanding our corpus requires a basic knowledge of the NetNews system. NetNews is an electronic discussion system developed for and supported on the Internet (Kantor & Lapsley, 1986). Discussion groups have formed along subjects ranging from science to politics to literature to various hobbies. The collections of messages are organized into particular subject groups called *newsgroups.* The newsgroups themselves are organized in a tree-like hierarchy, which has general top-level categories at the root and moves to more specific topics as you progress towards the leaves. A newsgroup name is defined as the entire path from the top-level category through any subsequent refining categories down to the name of the group itself. Category and group names are delimited by the period symbol. Thus, "soc.religion" is the name of a newsgroup concerned with social issues around the world's religions and "soc.religion.hindu" is a more specific group devoted to Hinduism.

Texts sent to NetNews, the *posts,* are composed of a number of fields only a few of which are relevant here. The user creating the post is responsible for the post body (that is, the actual text of the message) as well as a subject line. The subject line is composed of a few words that describe what the post is about. NetNews software will attach a number of additional fields to posted messages including a timestamp and the user name of the person who created the post.

Posts can be either an independent message or a follow-up to a previous message. A follow-up, or "in-reply-to" message, will have special threading information in its header linking it to the previous posts to which it is a reply. This header information allows news-readers to reconstruct the discussion thread.

NetNews today has grown considerably from its beginnings in the late 70's and 80's. With over 80,000 posts arriving each day, it provides an excellent dataset for the study of cultural microevolution.

The Text Analysis Method

We analyze a corpus of posts to NetNews to distill their salient replicating unit or memes, and to cluster together posts, which make common use of those memes. We do this by employing a large system of text analysis software we have built. The techniques employed are based on the vector space model of text retrieval and Latent Semantic Indexing (LSI).

Vector Space Representation

We begin with a corpus composed of the full-text of a group of posts. We analyze the corpus and identify a high-dimensioned space, which describes the conceptual elements within the texts. For each post, we identify a point within this space, which captures it semantically. This technique is known as a vector space representation (Frakes & Baeza-Yates, 1992; Salton & Buckley, 1988). Each dimension in this space will represent a *term* from the corpus where a term is a word that occurs with some frequency (e.g., in at least three posts) but not too frequently (e.g., the word "not" is dropped from the term list). The goal is to arrive at a set of terms that semantically capture the texts within the corpus.

Given the conceptual space described by this set of terms, each post can be represented as a point within this space. We score each document according to the frequency each term occurs within its text, and assign each term/document pairing this *term weight*. The weighting we use for each term/document pair is a function of the *term frequency* (simply the number of times the term occurs in the post) and the *inverse document frequency* (IDF). Consider a corpus of m posts and a particular term, j, within a list of n terms. Then the IDF is given by,

$$IDF_j = \log\left(\left|\frac{m - m_j}{m_j}\right|\right),$$

where m_j is the number of posts across the entire corpus in which term j appears. Thus, if a term occurs in 50% or more of the texts the IDF for that term will vanish to zero. But if, for instance, a term occurs in 10% of the documents the IDF will be nearly log(10). In words, rare terms have a large IDF.

The term weight for a document, i, and term, j, is then defined by,

$$TermWeight_{ij} = w_{ij} = \log(TermFrequency_{ij}) \cdot IDF_j.$$

Each term weight, then, is a function of the inter- and intra-document term frequencies.

Each post, i, is now represented by a particular term vector, $r_i = (w_{i1}, w_{i2}, \ldots, w_{in})$. The entire collection of m term vectors, one for each post, define the *term/document matrix*, A.

This set of steps, culminating in the term/document matrix, forms the basis for much of modern text retrieval or filtering and is at the core of most Web search engines.

Latent Semantic Indexing (LSI)

LSI is a technique used to distill high-order structures from a term/document matrix, consisting of sets of terms that re-occur together through the corpus with appreciable frequency. The re-occurring term sets are discovered through a principal component method called Singular Value Decomposition (SVD). While LSI was primarily developed to improve text retrieval, we are interested in its ability to find replicating term sets, which act as memes. We will first overview the LSI technique and then discuss how it discovers memes.

LSI was originally proposed and has been extensively studied by Susan Dumais of Bell Communications Research and her colleagues (Deerwester et al., 1990; Dumais, 1992, 1993; Furnas et al., 1988). Peter Foltz investigated the use of LSI in clustering NetNews articles for information filtering (Foltz, 1990). Michael Berry and co-authors researched a variety of numerical approaches to efficiently perform SVD on large sparse matrices such as those found in text retrieval (Berry, 1992; Berry & Fierro, 1995; Berry, O'Brien, Do, Krishna, & Varadhan, 1993).

The SVD technique decomposes the term/document matrix into a left and right orthonormal matrix of eigenvectors and a diagonal matrix of eigenvalues.* The decomposition is formalized as, $A_k = U V^T$.

The term/document matrix, *A,* is approximated by a rank-*k* decomposition, A_k; in fact the SVD technique is known to produce the *best* rank-*k* approximation to a low-rank matrix (Berry, 1992).

We are interested in only the right orthonormal matrix of eigenvectors, V^T. Each row of this matrix defines a set of terms whose co-occurrences have some statistically salient re-occurrences throughout the corpus. That is, each eigenvector describes a subspace of the term vector space for which the terms are frequently found together. These *term-subspaces* describe a set of semantically significant associative patterns in the words of the underlying corpus of documents; we can think of each subspace as a *conceptual index* into the corpus (Furnas et al., 1988).

For instance, an example term-subspace generated by analyzing a collection of military posts found three words as having significant re-occurrences, and therefore replicating together with success: "harbor," "japan," and "pearl." These term-subspaces make up our replicators and are our putative memes. Memes are not single re-occurring words but are made up of *sets* of re-occurring words.

Our final text analysis step is to "compress" the original term/document matrix by multiplying it with this right orthonormal matrix of eigenvectors (in other words we perform a projection). This, in effect, produces a *term-subspace/document* matrix. Each post is represented by a collection of weights where each weight now describes the degree to which a term-subspace is expressed within its post's text.

Meme and Quasi-Species

Term-Subspace as Putative Meme

We are looking for replicators within the corpus that are subject to natural selection. Elsewhere we have argued at length as to why the term-subspace captures the requirements of a true meme because its word sets act as a unit of selection within the corpus (Best, 1996, 1997; Pocklington & Best, 1997). The strengths of this term set as a replicating unit of selection are due to it meeting the following conditions:

- it is subject to replication by copying,
- it has strong copying fidelity,
- but not perfect fidelity, it is subject to mutation,
- it has a strong covariance with replicative success (Eigen, 1992; Lewontin, 1970).

We will quickly review each of these points in turn.

SVD techniques exploit structure within the term/document matrix by locating co-occurring sets of terms. Clearly, these term sets are replicating through the corpus since that is the precise statistical phenomena the SVD analysis detects. However, it is not obvious that this replication is generally due to copying. Instances of precise copying occur when an in-reply-to thread includes elements of a previous post's text via the copying mechanism provided by the software system. Other instances of copying occur within a particular context or discussion thread when authors copy by hand words or phrases from previous posts into their new texts. More abstractly, replication occurs because certain memes are traveling outside of the NetNews environment (and thus outside of our means of analysis) and authors again act as copying agents injecting them into the corporal ecology. But, clearly, some re-occurrences are not due to copying but are a chance process where unrelated texts bring together similar words. The likelihood of such chance re-occurrences will be a function of the size and quality of our replicating unit. In summary, term-subspaces are instances of replication often due to copying.

The copying fidelity of a term-subspace is also a direct outcome of the SVD statistical

*The eigenvalue of a transformation is that value on which it converges after infinitely many applications of that transformation. The eigenvector of a transformation, here *T,* is that vector whose direction remains unchanged by that transformation.

analysis. But importantly, the copying fidelity of re-occurring term sets is not perfect across the entire corpus; the term sets will co-occur with some variation. These mutations are both changes *designed* by human authors and chance variation due to copying errors. In either case, the mutations are *random* from the vantage of selection; in other words, human authors are not able to perfectly predict the adaptive significance of their inputted variations. These mutations work "backwards" into the actual term-subspace representation for a post organism. That is, a random mutation at the post level will actually result in a random mutation in the vector subspace representation (the memotype) for the post organism. In this way, the memes as represented in the memotype are subject to mutation.

Finally, we have elsewhere shown there can be a strong covariance between the replicative success of a cluster or thread of posts and the degree to which they express certain term-subspaces (Pocklington & Best, 1997). In other words, a group of posts can increase its volume of activity over time by increasing the degree to which it expresses certain term sets within its post's text. This, then, is a covariance between the *fitness* of a population of posts and the expression of a particular *trait* as defined by a term-subspace. The demonstration of this covariance is critical to establishing that a replicator is subject to natural selection.

Quasi-Species

If the term-subspace is a reasonable model for the meme then the term-subspace vector representation of a post is a good model of the post's *memotype.* Much as a genotype describes a point within genetic sequence-space for each organism, the memotype describes a point within conceptual sequence-space. By *sequence-space,* we mean any of the search spaces defined by a replicator undergoing selection. Examples of sequence-spaces include the gene space, protein spaces under molecular evolution, and the meme space defined within a corporal ecology.

The notion of a *quasi-species* is due primarily to Manfred Eigen (Eigen, 1992; Eigen et al., 1988). He states that the "quasi-species represents a weighted distribution of mutants centered around one or several master sequences. It is the target of selection in a system of replicating individuals that replicate without co-operating with one another (RNA molecules, viruses, bacteria)" (Eigen, 1992). One organism is a *mutant* of another if it is particularly close to the other in sequence-space.

We wish to group our posts into quasi-species. This requires finding groups of memotypes that are centered together within the conceptual sequence space. To do so we employ a simple clustering algorithm, the Nearest Neighbor Algorithm (Jain & Dubes, 1988). We first normalize each post memotype to unit length; this amounts to discarding text length information and representing only the *relative* strength of each meme within a text. The clustering algorithm then considers each post memotype in turn. The current memotype is compared to each memotype, which has already been assigned to a cluster. If the closest of such vectors is not farther than a threshold distance, then the current vector is assigned to that cluster. Otherwise, the current vector is assigned to a new cluster. This continues until each and every vector is assigned to a cluster.

This process assigns each post to a quasi-species defined as those posts which are close to one another in conceptual sequence-space.

The overall aim in grouping organisms is to bring to light certain evolutionarily significant relationships. Clearly, our quasi-species clustering method is a-historical; that is, it does not directly account for descent when grouping together text organisms. The extent to which such groupings are effective when studying the relatedness of natural organisms is a matter of continued controversy as can be seen in the debates of the cladists versus evolutionary systematists versus pheneticists. While we are currently agnostic to this controversy, we do agree with an original claim of the pheneticists: the more traits are used when assessing the relatedness of individuals the more accurate are the groupings (Mettler, Gregg, & Schaffer, 1988).

We are in the happy situation of clustering based on the complete memotype for each of our organisms. The result is that under empirical verification our clusters exhibit extremely strong historical relatedness. We have found that the vast majority of texts clustered together come from the same in-reply-to thread and thus are related by descent (Best, 1997). But our clustering method has the added benefit of grouping related texts even when the in-reply-to mechanism is not used and, alternatively, breaking up texts that are within the same thread but are not semantically related. This is of value since many posters to NetNews use the in-reply-to mechanism to post unrelated texts or, alternatively, post follow-up texts without bothering to use the in-reply-to facility. Thus, we claim that our clustering mechanism, due to its access to hundreds of traits, is actually superior at grouping together both related and descendent texts then would be a simple reliance on the threading mechanism. The clustering method meets our goal of illuminating evolutionarily significant relationships.

Comparison to Natural Ecologies

We are describing phenomena within a corpus of texts in terms of population ecology and population genetics. This is not simply a metaphorical device; we believe that interacting populations of texts and their constituent memes are evolving ecologies quite exactly. However, there are clearly a number of interesting differences between genes and memes (as here operationally defined), natural organisms and texts, ecologies and corpora. Important differences include the driving forces behind mutation within the texts and the role of self-replication and lineage within the corpora. We leave to future work a more complete analysis of these differences.

Models for Interacting Populations

We now turn to studying the interaction between quasi-species of posts. We have so far only studied the pair-wise interactions between post quasi-species. Similar pair-wise interactions have been widely studied within theoretical ecology. Consider two interacting populations: one population can either have a positive effect (+) on another by increasing the other's chance for survival and reproduction, a negative effect (–) by decreasing the other population's survival chances, or a neutral (0) effect. The ecological community has assigned terms to the most prevalent forms of pair-wise interaction, in particular:

- Mutualism (+, +)
- Competition (–, –)
- Neutralism (0, 0)
- Predator/prey (+, –)

(May, 1981; Pielou, 1969).

Our goal is to study the pair-wise interactions of quasi-species within the corporal ecology with the hope of discovering some of these interaction types.

Time Series

To study how the interactions of populations affect growth rates we must define a method to measure a quasi-species' growth over time. Recall that a quasi-species describes a collection of posts, which are close to one another in sequence-space. Each of these posts has associated with it a *timestamp* identifying when that text was posted to the system; in effect, its birth time and date. (Note that a post organism has something of a zero-length life-span; it comes into existence when posted but has no clear time of death.)

A histogram of the timestamp data is created with a 24-hour bucket size. That is, for each quasi-species we count how many member texts were posted on one day, how many on the next, and so forth through the entire population of texts. The datasets currently used span on the order of two weeks and consist of thousands of posts. So, for each day a quasi-species has a volume of activity, which can range from zero to 10's of posts. This rather coarse unit, the day, has been chosen to neutralize the strong daily patterns of post activities (e.g. activity may concentrate in the afternoons and drop off late at night, different time zones will shift this behavior and thus encode geographic biases). Thus, the patterns of rise and fall in the volume of posts within a quasi-species when measured at the day level will, hopefully, reflect true changes in interest level and authorship activity rather then other external or systemic factors.

The Test Corpus

Figure 1 is a typical graph for the volume of posts within a particular quasi-species over a period of ten days. This cluster was found within a corpus of all posts sent to the soc.women newsgroup between January 8, 1997 (the far left of the graph) and January 28, 1997 (the far right). In the figure, the number of posts in a day is represented by the height of the graph. This particular cluster of texts exhibited an initial set of posts, a few days worth of silence, and then a rapid building up of activity that finally declined precipitously at the end of the dataset. The entire corpus used consisted of 1,793 posts over the same ten day period. The clustering mechanism arrived at 292 quasi-species, the largest of which contained 103 posts.

Time Series Cross-Correlation

To study the relationship between the time series of two populations of posts we use the cross-correlation function. The use of the cross-correlation to study bivariate processes, and time series in particular, is well known (Chatfield, 1989). Each time series is normalized to be of zero mean and unit standard deviation; that is, we subtract off the mean and divide by the standard deviation. In this way, the cross-correlations will not be dominated by the absolute volume of post activity within some cluster and instead will be sensitive to both large and small sized clusters.

We assume the readers are familiar with the regular covariance and correlation functions. Then the cross-correlation for two time series, *X* and *Y*, is given by

$$\rho_{xy} = \frac{\gamma_{xy}}{\sqrt{\gamma_{xx}\gamma_{yy}}}.$$

Here, $\gamma_{xy} = \mathrm{Cov}(X, Y)$ and γ_{xx} and γ_{yy} are the variance of *X* and *Y* respectively. Note this

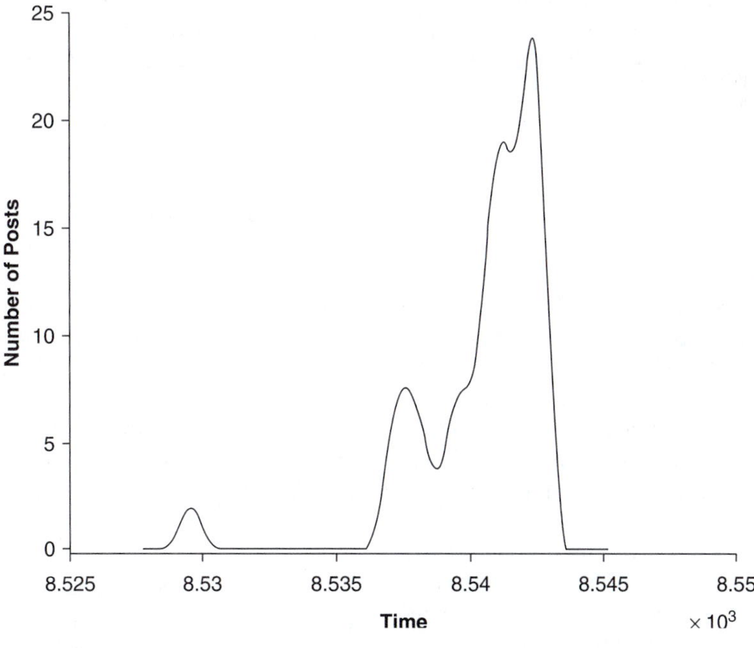

Figure 1 A typical time series of posts to quasi-species. Time axis is measured in seconds since Jan. 1 1970.

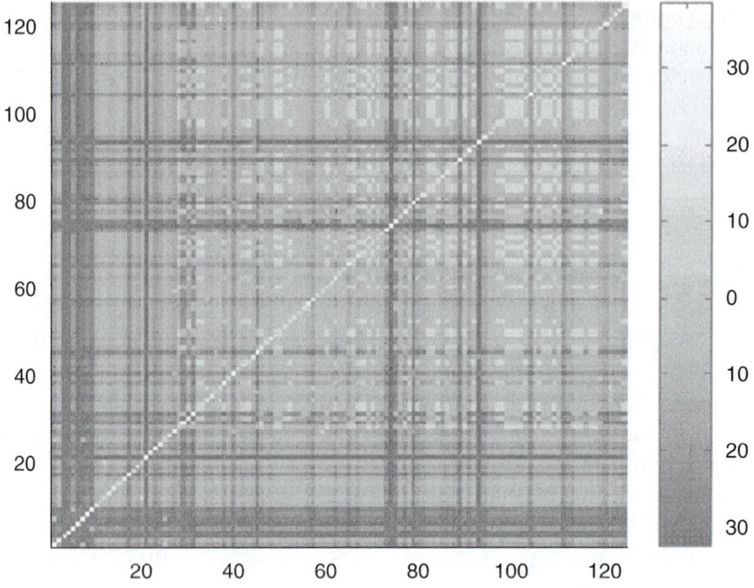

Figure 2 The Pair-Wise Time Series Cross-Correlation for 125 Largest Quasi-Species Clusters

formulation only considers the cross-correlation for a zero time lag. That is, it considers how the two time series are correlated for identically matching points in time. With a nonzero lag the cross-correlation would study cases when the two series might have correlations offset by some fixed amount of time. Since we group our time data into day-long chunks the zero-lag cross-correlation will be sensitive to covariances, which have a time offset as large as 24 hours; this builds into the time series an adequate time lag.

When the cross-correlation between two sets of data is significantly different than zero it suggests the two sets of data have some relationship between them. A positive value means an increase in one series is likely to co-occur with an increase in the other series. A negative value means an increase in one series is likely to co-occur with a decrease in the other series.

Figure 2 shows the pair-wise cross-correlations for the 125 largest quasi-species clusters within our corpus. The diagonal represents the cross-correlation between a time series and itself which, as expected, is identically one. Note that the matrix is symmetric about the diagonal. The off-diagonal values range from near one to –0.26. The mean cross-correlation is 0.3. This value is quite high, indicating that most of these post clusters are somehow positively related. We suspect this high average cross-correlation is at least partially due to external or systemic effects, which were not removed by the day-long bucket size. For instance, our analysis would be sensitive to patterns due to the Monday-Friday work week common in the West. Further, some of this correlation may be due to a high level of mutualistic interactions amongst the posts. Clearly, the ideas conveyed within the soc.women newsgroup often share similar contexts.

In our analysis, this overall high correlation does not particularly matter since we are concerned with the *relative* cross-correlation—that is, those that are the largest and those that are the smallest.

Negative Cross-Correlations: Competition Versus Predator/Prey

We have primarily studied those pairs of quasi-species with relatively strong negative

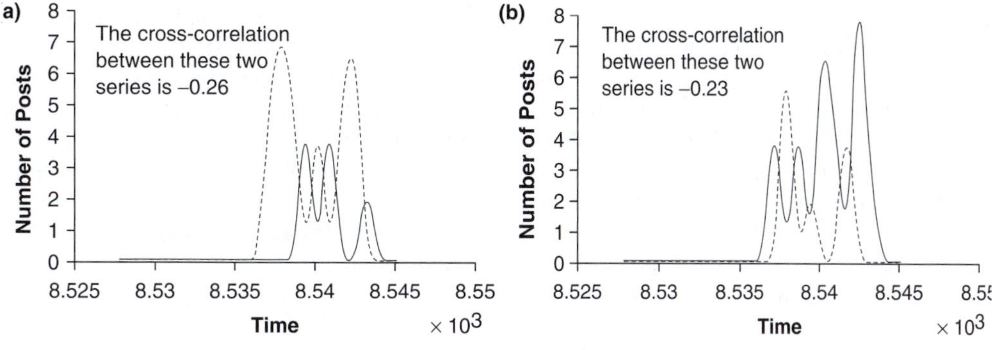

Figure 3 Volume of Activity for Two Quasi-Species

cross-correlations; to wit, those where $\rho_{xy} \leq -0.2$. Note that in all such cases (there are 42) $p < .001$, suggesting that with extremely high probability the correlations are not due to chance. Figure 3 plots two such interactions, both fairly characteristic of this population. [It] demonstrates a clear negative covariance between the two volumes of activity of the two post clusters. This negative covariance is both statistically significant and visually compelling. But what do these graphs signify and can it be interpreted within the rubric of ecological interactions?

At first glance the interactions appear to be of a predator/prey variety; they have a (+, –) relationship to them. However, competition might also produce similar interaction phenomena if the competitors are operating close to some limitation of environmental carrying capacity. In such instances, the relationship between population sizes will be a zero-sum game; when one goes up the other must come down. To be able to classify the interactions of Figure 3 we need to consider the qualitative details of these two interactions through direct study of the texts.

Recall that in the case of a predator/prey relationship, one population enjoys an increased growth rate at the *expense* of another population (e.g., one population feeds on the other). The presence of a relatively large population of predators will result in a diminished level of success for the prey (they get eaten up). Conversely, the relative absence of prey will result in diminished success for the predator (they have nothing to eat).

Now consider the case of competition. In competition, two interacting populations inhibit each other in some way, reducing each other's level of success. This often occurs when the two populations rely on the same limited resource. Unlike the predator/prey relationship where the predator requires the prey for success, with competition the two populations would just as soon avoid each other all together.

This pressure towards avoidance is the source of much ecological diversity since it propels populations to explore new and therefore competition-free niches (Pianka, 1981). An ecological *niche,* for some particular species, is simply that collection of resources the species relies on. Interspecific niche overlap occurs when two or more species share one, some, or perhaps all of their resources. When those resources are scarce, interspecific competition will result. The *width* of a niche is simply a qualitative sense of the variety and number of resources a population makes uses.

Competition and Niche Behavior

We have studied posts that make up the four quasi-species shown in Figure 3 in an attempt to qualitatively classify their interactions. The quasi-species (on the left side) of Figure 3 are made up of posts within a single thread. The subject line for these posts reads, "Men's Reproductive Rights." In general, these posts are concerned with the responsibilities and rights of men towards their unborn children. The quasi-species displayed with a dashed line in this part of the figure is centered on the use of contraceptives. It consists of a collection of posts wherein the authors debate who is most responsible, the woman or the man, when using contraception. The quasi-species with a solid line deals instead with the use of abortion and whether the father has any intrinsic rights in deciding whether or not to abort an unborn child.

[On the right side of] Figure 3, the two quasi-species are also from a single thread. The subject line here reads, "Unequal distribution of wealth?" This particular thread of discussion was rather large. In fact, there were a total of 365 posts to this thread, which our text analysis tools broke up into a number of quasi-species due to significant bifurcations of the topic. In other words, many parallel discussions occurred all within a single in-reply-to thread. The cluster of discussion shown with the solid line centered around a debate as to whether the US military was a "socialist collective." The quasi-species with the dashed line was a debate on the value of releasing the mentally ill from hospitals. Clearly, these two debates are quite dissimilar even though they span the same set of days and are posts to the same discussion thread.

The quasi-species [on the left in] Figure 3 are different but related discussions. Those [on the right] are different and not clearly related. Still, we believe that both of these sets of interactions demonstrate elements of competition. Within the texts, there is no evidence of predator memes; in fact, the memes seem entirely orthogonal to one another. However, in both examples the memes are competing for the same collection of human authors who must act as their agents if they are to propagate and succeed. This seems even more likely when we consider that all these posts are to the same newsgroup, which due to its narrow subject area supports only a limited supply of human posters. Moreover, each pair of interactions are confined to a single thread of discussion, which again has an even more limited set of potential human authors since users of the NetNews system often zero-in on particular threads they find interesting and ignore others. After inspecting most of the interactions, which demonstrated strong negative correlations, we observed no examples of predator/prey interactions but many instances, which appeared to be examples of competition.

Statistical Artifacts

We computed the cross-correlation between 125 different clusters, arriving at 15,625 different correlations. It is possible, therefore, that the cross-correlations with large negative values exist simply by chance; they represent the tail of the distribution of correlations.

However, we believe that our qualitative analysis provides strong evidence that these negative correlations are *not* artifacts but are indeed due to an interaction phenomenon between the two quasi-species. The two pairs of quasi-species described in detail above demonstrate this point. The likelihood that two quasi-species would be brought together by mere chance *and* both be from the same thread (out of 324 threads within the corpus) seems vanishingly small.

Competition

We now will test our theory that these interactions are of a competitive nature. Again, recall that competition is often caused by populations existing within the same (narrow) ecological niche. What makes up an ecological niche for a meme within NetNews? We argue that the newsgroups themselves make up spatially distributed ecological niches. Since there is relatively little interaction between newsgroups (save the phenomena of cross-posting) we would expect these niches to behave something like island ecologies—they remain relatively isolated from each other. Within a single newsgroup (which is all we have studied so far) niches might be described by threads of discussions. As previously stated, we have found that individual posters to the system tend to become involved in particular in-reply-to threads that interest them. Thus, the memes within a particular thread make use of a set of human resources, which is smaller than the entire set of potential human resources available to the newsgroup. These resources define the niche.

We theorize that cross-correlations that approach –1 in our corpus are examples of competition, and competition will be more likely between populations that are posted to the same threads and thus have overlapping niches. The most direct way to test this theory is to see if negative cross-correlations between two quasi-species correlate with the degree to which they post to the same threads. For each of the 125 × 125 pair-wise interactions we computed the number of threads each of the quasi-species pairs had in common and divided that by the total number of threads posted to by each quasi-species. For example, one quasi-species may contain posts that went to two different in-reply-to threads. Another quasi-species may have posts that span three different threads one of which is identical to a thread within the first group. So this pair of quasi-species would have posted to a total of four different groups one of which was shared. Their relative niche overlap would therefore be 0.25.

We calculated the correlation coefficient between the negative cross-correlations of Figure 2 and the percentage of thread overlap between these quasi-species pairs. We found this correlation to be –0.04. While this correlation is statistically significant ($p < .001$), it is not very pronounced. The negative sign, though, does indicate that as the level of competition increases (a negative cross-correlation) the percent of overlap of their niche also increases (a larger positive shared thread percentage).

This small correlation coefficient may be due to a small signal/noise ratio. Since most pair-wise interactions result in small correlations, the relative number of large negative correlations is quite small. The number of interactions grows with the square of the number of quasi-species. We suspect that a simpler experiment, which grows linearly with the number of quasi-species, will have a better signal/noise ratio.

We have studied the correlations between the absolute number of in-reply-to threads a quasi-species is posted to and the average degree to which the quasi-species finds itself correlated with other clusters. Our hypothesis is that the absolute number of threads a quasi-species is posted to will be related to the average degree of competition the quasi-species experiences in its interactions. Since the variety of resources used by an entity defines its niche, if a quasi-species is posted to a relatively small number of threads then it exists in a narrow ecological niche. Should there subsequently be any interspecific overlap of these narrow niches, scarcity will result in competitive encounters. We computed the correlation coefficient between the total number of threads within a quasi-species and its *average* cross-correlation value. The correlation coefficient here is 0.25. Thus, as the number of threads within a quasi-species increases (the set of available resources is widened) the average level of competition diminishes (the mean pair-wise cross-correlation also increases). This correlation is statistically significant ($p < .001$) and rather pronounced.

We further computed the correlation coefficient when the absolute number of threads was normalized by the size of the quasi-species. We might expect that the number of threads employed by a quasi-species would grow with the number of posts within that quasi-species. In other words, as a quasi-species gets larger the number of threads increases too. This might affect the analysis above such that instead of measuring niche width we were simply measuring quasi-species size. Dividing out the size amounts to computing the *average* number of threads employed by a post for a given quasi-species. When this set of values was correlated with the mean cross-correlation, we arrived at a nearly identical coefficient as above and again clear statistical significance. Thus, quasi-species size is not a major factor in level of competition.

Conclusions

We have described a set of text analysis tools, based primarily on Latent Semantic Indexing, which distill replicating memes from a corpus of text. We have trained this analysis system on a corpus of posts to NetNews. This makes up a corporal ecology where the posts are organisms, NetNews is the environment, and human authors are a scarce resource. We argue that this represents an important bridging of text analysis and the Alife research program. Further, it amounts to a novel shift for Alife research—rather than synthesizing life-like agents, we are analyzing a pre-existing environment and discovering life-like behaviors.

In results reported here, we group together posts, which make use of similar sets of memes. These groups, clouds within a conceptual sequence-space, describe quasi-species. For each quasi-species, we compute its time-wise volume of activity by histogramming its daily post levels. We then study the pair-wise interaction between quasi-species by computing the cross-correlations between their time series. In our corpus, strong negative cross-correlations signify conditions of competition between the interacting populations where the quasi-species are competing for a limited set of human authors. Furthermore, quasi-species with relatively narrow ecological niches, those that make use of a small number of in-reply-to threads, are more likely to be in competition with other quasi-species. This behavior is analogous to what is found in natural ecologies (Pianka, 1981).

Why do these quasi-species compete? Qualitative analysis of the posts, such as those described in the previous section, shows that many competing quasi-species are posts sent to the same or similar threads. Competition is over the scarce authorship resources within these specific thread niches. Over time a particular thread of discussion may bifurcate into two or more internal themes which then proceed to compete for "air-time" within the thread.

References

Berry, M. W. (1992). Large-scale sparse singular value computations. *International Journal of Supercomputer Applications 6:*13–49.

Berry, M., O'Brien, T., Do, G., Krishna, V., & Varadhan, S. (1993). *SVDPACKC (Version 1.0) User's guide.* University of Tennessee Computer Science Department Technical Report, CS-93-194.

Berry, M. W., & Fierro, R. D. (1995). *Low-rank orthogonal decompositions for information retrieval applications.* University of Tennessee Computer Science Department Technical Report, CS-95-284.

Best, M. L. (1996). *An ecology of the Net: Message morphology and evolution in NetNews.* MIT Media Laboratory, Machine Understanding Technical Report, 96-001.

Best, M. L. (1997). An ecology of text: Using text retrieval to study Alife on the net. *Journal of Artificial Life 3:*261–287.

Chatfield, C. (1989). *The analysis of time series: An introduction.* London: Chapman and Hall.

Dawkins, R. (1976). *The selfish gene.* New York: Oxford University Press.

Deerwester, S., Dumais, S. T., Furnas, G. W., Landauer, T. K., & Harshman, R. (1990). Indexing by latent semantic analysis. *Journal of the American Society for Information Science 41,*6:391–407.

Dumais, S. T. (1992). LSI meets TREC: A status report. In D. Harman (Ed.), *The First Text Retrieval Conference (TREC-1).* NIST Special Publication 500-207.

Dumais, S. T. (1993). Latent semantic indexing (LSI) and TREC-2. In D. Harman (Ed.), *The Second Text Retrieval Conference (TREC-2).* NIST Special Publication 500-215.

Eigen, M. (1992). *Steps towards life: A perspective on evolution.* Oxford: Oxford University Press.

Eigen, M. J., McCaskill, J., & Schuster, P. (1988). Molecular quasi-species. *Journal of Physical Chemistry 92,*24:6881–6891.

Foltz, P. W. (1990). Using Latent Semantic Indexing for information filtering. *Proceedings of the 5th Conference on Office Information Systems, ACM SIGOIS Bulletin, 11,*2–3: 40–47.

Frakes, W. B., & Baeza-Yates, R. (Eds.). (1992). *Information retrieval: Data structures and algorithms.* Englewood Cliffs, NJ: Prentice Hall.

Furnas, G. W., Deerwester, S., Dumais, S. T., Landauer, T. K., Harshman, R. A., Streeter, L. A., & Lochbaum, K. E. (1988). Information retrieval using a Singular Value Decomposition model of Latent Semantic Structure. *Proceedings of the 11th International Conference on Research and Development in Information Retrieval (SIGIR).* New York: Association for Computing Machinery.

Jain, A. K., & Dubes, R. C. (1988). *Algorithms for clustering data.* Englewood Cliffs, NJ: Prentice Hall.

Kantor, B., & Lapsley, P. (1986). Network news transfer protocol: A proposed standard for the stream-based transmission of news. Internet RFC-977.

Lewontin, R. C. (1970). The units of selection. *Annual Review of Ecology and Systematics 1:*1–18.

May, R. M. (Ed.). (1981). *Theoretical ecology principles and applications.* Oxford: Blackwell Scientific Publications.

Mettler, L. E., Gregg, T. G., & Schaffer, H. E. (1988). *Population genetics and evolution* (2nd ed.). Englewood Cliffs, NJ: Prentice Hall.

Pianka, E. R. (1981). Competition and niche theory. In R.M. May (Ed.), *Theoretical ecology principles and application* (pp. 167–196). Oxford: Blackwell Scientific Publications.

Pielou, E. C. (1969). *An introduction to mathematical ecology.* New York: Wiley-Interscience.

Pocklington, R. (1996). *Population genetics and cultural history,* Masters Thesis. Burnaby: Simon Fraser University.

Pocklington, R., & Best, M. L. (1997). Cultural evolution and units of selection in replicating text. *Journal of Theoretical Biology 188:*79–87.

Salton, G., & Buckley, C. (1988). Term-weighting approaches in automatic text retrieval. *Information Processing & Management 24*,5:513–523.

3.7

Identifying the Unknown Communicator in Painting, Literature and Music

William J. Paisley*

The task of identifying the author of an anonymous work has long challenged students of communication. The problem is usually posed in one of three ways:

(1) A work is attributed to a communicator well known for other works (the generic "communicator" here denotes painter, writer, composer), but it may be an imitation or forgery (e.g., the "Corelli" violin sonatas by Fritz Kreisler)

(2) A truly anonymous work is attributed by default to a well-known communicator whose own works are similar, but it may be the work of a disciple or lesser-known colleague (e.g., the "Letter to the Hebrews," long attributed to Paul)

(3) A work is attributed variously to each of two or more well-known communicators (e.g., the perennial Shakespeare-Bacon-Marlowe-Oxford wrangle)

Research directed to this problem has two goals. The practical goal is a correct attribution of the anonymous or disputed work. The theoretical goal is a better understanding of one phase of the communication process, the encoding of messages.

When authorship of a work is disputed, we may assume that historical evidence is inadequate. Therefore, clues must be sought in the text itself, usually in the style of the work. "Style," however, is a concept often embracing the ineffable qualities of a communicator's output. To focus on objective characteristics of the text, a concept such as "encoding habits" should be substituted for "style." Then the unique character of a work may be defined in terms of successive decisions made by the communicator as he chooses from his repertory of symbols (notes, words, brush strokes, etc.).

In the last quarter of the 19th century, when the connoisseur of art finally rejected

*From Paisley, W. J. (1964). Identifying the unknown communicator in painting, literature and music. *Journal of Communication 14,* 4:219–237.

dubious historical evidence and turned his attention to the encoding habits of painters as preserved in their works, he achieved a great refinement in the technique of connoisseurship. Recent successful efforts to identify the authors of anonymous literary works reveal a refinement of method in that field also. Although art connoisseurship has remained a quantitative science while literary detection has become exhaustively quantitative, nevertheless there is surprising consensus in both fields concerning those encoding habits which clearly distinguish a communicator from all other communicators with superficially similar output. This consensus is interesting insofar as it defies common sense and favors *minor* encoding habits which are inconspicuous in the work and do not carry the burden of meaning. Since the communality of the two streams of research has perhaps never been discussed, the first half of this report will summarize their shared assumptions and procedures. The second half reports the results of an extension of these procedures to the study of musical encoding habits.

The Connoisseur as Content Analyst

In 1889 the best-known connoisseur of this century, Bernard Berenson, visited Rome and discovered a new way of looking at paintings. He has left a memoir of the experience:

> A generation ago, when a beginner, I enjoyed the privilege of being guided through the Borghese Gallery by a famous connoisseur. Before the Pieta now ascribed to Ortolano I fell into raptures over the pathos of the design. My mentor . . . cut me short with, "Yes, yes, but please observe the little pebbles in the foreground. They are highly characteristic of the artist." "Observe the little pebbles" has become among *my* intimates a phrase for all the detailed, at times almost ludicrously minute, comparisons upon which so large a part of activities like mine are spent. (Kiel, 1962: 145–146)

Berenson's mentor was Giovanni Morelli, whose "scientific connoisseurship" provoked international controversy in art circles. Whereas his colleagues were content to accept the testimony of Vasari and other early historians of art, Morelli contended that paintings sufficiently identified themselves, each work signed by its creator in dozens of little details, which no two painters executed alike. Traditional criteria based on the overall style of a work were entirely misleading, he claimed, since the student in any Renaissance studio soon learned the superficial marks of his master's style.

Morelli was at heart a taxonomist, as Fig. 1 and the following excerpts illustrate:

> Look at the Raphaelesque type of ear in the children; see how round and fleshy it is; how it unites naturally with the cheek and does not appear to be merely stuck on, as in the works of so many other masters; observe the hand of the Madonna with the broad metacarpus and somewhat stiff fingers, the nails extending to the tips only. (Morelli, 1900:37)

> Among Sandro Botticelli's characteristic forms I will mention the hand, with bony fingers—not beautiful, but always full of life; the nails, which, as you perceive in the thumb here, are square with black outlines. (Morelli, 1900:35)

Such attention to minor detail brought derision from Morelli's colleagues. They did not understand his distinction between "appreciating" a work and studying a painter's encoding habits. Morelli was called "the connoisseur of fingernails." Yet the success of his method could not be ignored [he exposed scores of mislabeled Renaissance works in Italian and German galleries, 46 in the Dresden Gallery alone (Wind, 1964:29)], and connoisseurship gradually committed its future to content analysis. Bernard Berenson has summarized the assumptions of the new connoisseurship:

> Obviously, what distinguishes one artist from another are the characteristics he does not share with others. If, therefore, we isolate the precise characteristics distinguishing each artist, they must furnish a perfect test of the fitness or unfitness of the attribution of a given work to a given master. (Berenson, 1902:123–124)

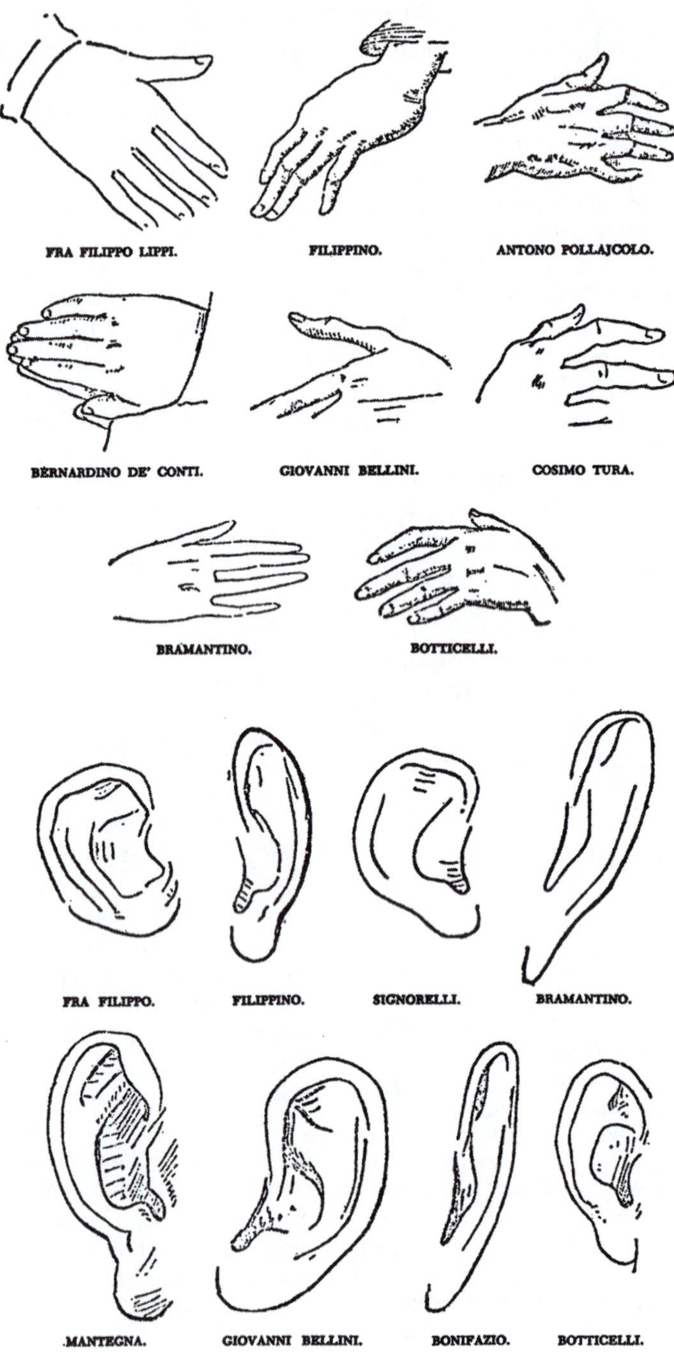

Figure 1 Hands and Ears Sketched by Giovanni Morelli to Illustrate Idiosyncrasy in the Execution of Minor Details by Renaissance Painters

SOURCE: Morelli (1900:77–78).

THE LITERARY DETECTIVE AS CONTENT ANALYST

The venerable "who was Shakespeare?" controversy provides a mirror in which the changing character of literary sleuthing can be traced. If it happened that connoisseurs of art turned to content analysis when they found historical evidence inadequate, then certainly theft colleagues in literature turned to content analysis as the only alternative to a conspiratorial view of history. That is, the modem champions of Bacon, Marlowe, the Oxford group and other contenders for the crown have admitted that history indeed appears to affirm that the playwright and the actor Shakespeare are one man, *but* history is deceitful and by clever subterfuge the plays of Bacon (or the Oxford group, or the exiled Marlowe) were performed under the name of the dull-witted and mercenary Stratfordian. Courtly discretion (they assert) led Bacon and Oxford to avoid association with the vulgar stage, while Marlowe thought it necessary to pretend that he was dead. When scholars hatch conspiracies, then content analysis of the plays themselves is clearly the only recourse.

Unfortunately, this Elizabethan imbroglio may not be solved, even by content analysis. Of all the contenders, only the least likely, Marlowe, left plays, which permit the necessary comparison of encoding habits. Mendenhall (1887) thought it legitimate to use Bacon's civil and political essays as a corpus for comparison, but no modem scholar would insist that a communicator's encoding habits must remain constant between works as topically and structurally remote as the essays and the plays. If a striking consistency had been found between essays and plays in Mendenhall's analysis of word-length frequencies, then Bacon's claim would have been strengthened. The inconsistencies actually found are evidence of nothing.

If content analysis is not likely soon to disclose who Shakespeare was, nevertheless other applications of the technique in authorship identification have been successful. Moreover, over time the focus of these efforts has shifted steadily from major to minor encoding habits. Three representative efforts will be discussed in chronological order:

(1) Yule's study of Gerson, à Kempis, Macaulay and others.

George Udny Yule contributed a great deal more to the study of literary vocabulary than can be acknowledged here, but at least his study of the *Imitatio Christi* must be described. Because the *Imitatio* had been ascribed both to Gerson and to Thomas à Kempis, Yule first compiled a large sample of undisputed works by each man. Then in the *Imitatio,* he chose words, chiefly nouns, which seemed to be favored by the unknown author. Finally, he tabulated frequencies of occurrence for these words not only in the *Imitatio* but also in the two comparison samples. When the *Imitatio* distributions were arrayed beside those of Gerson and Thomas à Kempis, it could not be doubted that à Kempis was the author.

Yule's perseverance in this most tedious research was remarkable, but his concentration on *major* encoding habits may have increased his labor while reducing the sensitivity of his measure. Thus use of the noun "prayer" involves a major encoding (in this context major encoding habits are those that carry the burden of meaning), while use of the article "the" involves a minor encoding habit. Unlike the ubiquitous "the," "prayer" is a relatively rare word; large samples of text must be scanned to obtain minimum stable frequencies. Moreover, because "prayer" is topic-constrained (found in texts with a religious topic), texts on different topics *by the same author* may yield anomalous frequencies of "prayer."

In his comparison of three essays ("Milton," "John Hampden," "Frederick the Great"), Yule (1944:122) shows—perhaps inadvertently—the effect of topic differences on major encoding habits. The most common nouns in each essay are (in descending order):

Milton	*Hampton*	*Frederick*
Man	King	King
Poet	parliament	man
Character	man	army
Poetry	house	war
Mind	time	time
Time	commons	year
Work	people	prince
People	member	part
Liberty	year	power
Power	party	day

Although all three essays are biographies of public figures by the highly idiosyncratic Macaulay, these lists lack authorship communality. Sixteen words are found in one list only; four words in two lists; only two words in all three lists. Of all literary encoding habits, the use of nouns is perhaps most constrained by topic differences.

In the course of this research Yule himself considered, and decided against, the study of minor encoding habits:

> Would it be of service to include other words (in addition to nouns, adjectives, and verbs)? If so, should it be *all* other words or should there be some specified exceptions, such as say the definite article in English, or auxiliary verbs? My impression is that the inclusion of all words without exception would be a mistake; that the inclusion of a and the and is and the like, each with a very large number of occurrences in any author, would merely tend to obscure differences, and it would be best to limit data to what are in some sense "significant words." (Yule, 1944:280)

Two recent studies indicate that Yule's bias against "insignificant words" was unjustified.

(2) Ellegard: the "Junius" letters.

Ellegard (1962) incorporated many of Yule's procedures in his investigation of the authorship of the "Junius" letters (published over that pseudonym between 1769 and 1772 in the London Public Advertiser). Alert, however, to the noun-counting trap, which cost Yule so much labor, Ellegard limited his own selection of words to abstract nouns, adjectives, adverbs and prepositional constructions. Without explaining his strategy in these terms, Ellegard nonetheless rejected Yule's focus on major encoding habits.

There are five steps in Ellegard's procedure:

(i) The disputed text is scanned for words that are conspicuously frequent. These are "plus words" for that text

(ii) A large body of contemporary writing is scanned for words which are conspicuously absent in the disputed text. These are "minus words" for that text

(iii) When lists of "plus words" and "minus words" have been compiled, all texts are scanned again and exact frequencies of occurrence are recorded. These counts may show that some words are not as "plus" or as "minus" as had been supposed, and the list may have to be revised

(iv) All likely authors of the disputed text are sampled. Their texts are counted for frequencies of "plus" and "minus" words

(v) That author whose word-profile most nearly resembles that of the pseudonymous author is the probable choice, provided that other candidates' profiles are significantly dissimilar (i.e., their counts regularly fall outside the confidence limits established for the many samples of disputed text)

This painstaking procedure permitted Ellegard to conclude that Sir Philip Francis, historically regarded as the author of the "Junius" letters, is a best choice on statistical grounds also.

(3) Mosteller and Wallace: the Federalist papers.

In 1963, about 80 years after Morelli observed the stable idiosyncrasy or minor encoding habits in painting, Mosteller and Wallace reported the same phenomenon in literature. Morelli ignored major encoding habits because he assumed that any competent forger could fool him at that level. In their study of twelve disputed Federalist papers, Mosteller and Wallace chose to ignore major encoding habits for two reasons: (i) the two authors in question, James Madison and Alexander Hamilton, conformed their writings to the intricate and formal rhetoric of the time—hence superficial differences cannot be found; (ii) the disputed Federalist papers discuss a wide range of topics—hence authorship differences and topic differences may be confounded in the case of semantically significant words.

Mosteller and Wallace define their focus in these terms:

> As we implied in discussing the word war, the words we want to use are noncontextual ones, words whose rate of use is nearly invariant under change of topic. For this reason, the little filler words, called function words, are especially attractive for discrimination purposes. (1963:280)

Within the class of function worth (as distinguished from content words, cf. Fries, 1952) there is great variation in frequency of occurrence. After they had tested each function word for low variance within an author's works and high variance between the works of the two authors, Mosteller and Wallace divided their list of words into sets according to frequency. They found that the highest-frequency set (consisting of the words *to, there, on, of, by, an* and *also*) discriminated as powerfully as the three lower-frequency sets taken together. Remarkably, the preposition upon proved to be a reliable discriminator by itself, since Hamilton used it five times more often than Madison.

Calculating odds from these discriminations, Mosteller and Wallace were able to attribute all the disputed papers to Madison. The least distinctive paper gives Madison 80 to 1 odds; the next weakest gives him 800 to 1 odds; thereafter the odds become astronomical.

In summary, Mosteller and Wallace relied on the "insignificant" words which Yule thought too ubiquitous to distinguish between authors. As a result they achieved discrimination (when the two sets of known papers are compared) with median odds *of 3 million to 1.*

A Working Definition of "Minor Encoding Habits"

The distinction between major and minor encoding habits has been viewed from two perspectives, which may now be combined. Morelli and Berenson introduced four defining criteria:

(1) The detail to be studied should not be prominent; else imitators will appropriate it

(2) It should be executed mechanically (i.e., with little feedback for self-criticism); else the communicator may consciously vary it for effect

(3) Its use should not be dictated wholly by convention (e.g., the halo in Renaissance paintings)

(4) It should not be so rare that examples cannot be found in each disputed work

To this list, Mosteller and Wallace would add:

(5) The detail should remain constant in frequency whatever the topic of the work; else topic difference will confound authorship differences

But their quantitative procedure requires a restatement of other criteria:

(2a) Use of the detail should exhibit low variance within a communicator's works

(3a) Use of the detail should exhibit low variance within a communicator's works

(4a) Frequency of occurrence should be high relative to the sampling error

These criteria have helped to identify unknown communicators in painting and literature. It would be desirable to report their relevance to the study of authorship differences in music, the third leg of the triangle of "artistic" communication, but that research has yet to be done. The findings reported below concern only one of many aspects of musical communication, which invite investigation.

Identifying the Communicator in Music

In the encoding process called musical composition, certain variables can assume many states and therefore require successive choices on the part of the communicator. Among these are: (1) tempo, (2) dynamics, (3) harmony, (4) instrumentation, (5) pitch. Each variable implies a set of encoding habits, major or minor, and each may prove to discriminate reliably between composers. However, it is within the scope of the present study to consider only the variable of pitch, of note-to-note pitch transitions in the themes of selected composers. This variable has been chosen for two reasons: (1) changes in pitch are easily coded for processing by computer; (2) some research involving tonal transitions has already been reported.

Previous studies of tonal transitions have been guided either by information theory or by the probability model of stochastic processes. The measures employed in the information-theory studies are those of uncertainty and constraint, each composer or sample of works described by two or three parameters only (cf. Youngblood, 1958). The stochastic process studies (cf. Brooks et al., 1957) yields matrices of transitional probabilities over 1, 2, 3 . . . n steps, a rich mine of information about the composer's encoding habits.

Unfortunately, no study reports testable data on differences between composers. Lacking replication within the works of each composer, variance terms necessary for testing the inter composer difference cannot be computed. This is not to be construed as a defect in method, of course, since the investigators were not seeking to test such differences. They sought single best estimates for each composer (or for each sample of melodies) either of uncertainty or of the probability of a given transition, and these estimates they obtained.

Therefore, this study focuses on a variable that, although not entirely unresearched, varies in yet-undetermined patterns between and within composers' works.

Problem

Bernard Berenson said that connoisseurship "proceeds, as scientific research always does, by the isolation of the characteristics of the known and theft confrontation with the unknown" (Berenson, 1902:124). This study seeks to isolate, in the themes of five composers (Bach, Haydn, Mozart, Beethoven, Brahms), those minor encoding habits, which identify each man. Then, given the characteristics of the known, four "unknown" samples are tested to determine whether they may be accepted or rejected as the work of any of the five composers. Since the four test samples are actually of known authorship (Handel, Mozart, Beethoven, Mendelssohn), the validity of the discrimination technique may be assessed. Yet the rigor of the test is preserved by setting aside the "unknown" samples and leaving them unanalyzed until the discriminating characteristics of the five composers have been established.

Procedure. The collection of hundreds of compositions, the transcription of sections from them and the transposition of these sections to a common tonality for comparison are a task, which only a team of well-financed investigators could undertake. Fortunately, for the fate of the present modest study, a source was found in which this work has already been done. Barlow and Morgenstern (1948) have indexed about 10,000 themes from the works of dozens of composers after transposing each theme from its original tonality to the keys of C major and C minor. Since each theme is represented in the index as a sequence of letters (e.g., E F B C F# F#—the first theme of Beethoven's First Symphony), it is a relatively simple task to keypunch and then code the samples of themes for computer processing.

The major composers named above were chosen for this study because Barlow and Morgenstern have indexed particularly large reactions of their themes. Altogether, 2,240 themes were sampled systematically from this source. Because the index consists only of those opening notes of each theme, which clearly identify it, only the first six notes from each theme (the minimum entry in the index) could be keypunched. This is a waste of data in those frequent instances in which it takes as many as 12 notes to identify a theme, but sampling consistency is the more important consideration. The entire data of this study therefore consist of 13,340 notes, divided as follows: Bach, 1,920; Handel, 960; Haydn,

1,920; Mozart, 2,880; Beethoven, 2,880; Mendelssohn, 960; Brahms, 1,920.

The samples from Handel and Mendelssohn (160 themes each) were set aside as "unknowns." Random samples of 160 themes from Mozart and Beethoven were also set aside for later testing. The remaining 320 themes from each of the five comparison composers were randomly divided into half-samples of 16 themes in order to permit the estimation of variance within the works of each composer.

A first step in the computer processing (performed on the Stanford University 70901) was the recoding of letters as numbers. For this purpose a twelve-tone scale is a more efficient model than a diatonic scale, and the letters received the following values: C, 1; C# and Db, 2; D, 3; D# and Eb, 4; E, 5; F, 6; F4 and Gb, 7, G, 8, G and Ab, 9, A, 10, A# and Bb, 11, B, 12. In a later analysis the twelve categories were reduced to five: the tonic (1), the third (5), the fifth (8), all other diatonic tones (3,6,10,12) and all chromatic tones (2,4,1,9,11). This collapsing yields more equal proportions in each category by taking account of the do—mi—sol trimodality of this music.

Results: First Analysis

It was decided to look first at the simplest transitions and subsequently, if necessary, to study also the more complex ones. Greatest idiosyncrasy is found in greatest complexity, of course, since no two composers have ever assembled even a hundred notes in quite the same sequence, but idiosyncrasy found in complexity is not generalizable to other works by the same man—as other composers do not repeat the sequence, neither does he.

If two-note transitions are classified in terms of the identities of the first and second notes, 144 (12 × 12) categories result. As the number of original categories is reduced by collapsing (say from 12 to 5), then the number of joint classifications diminishes in proportion to the square of the number of categories, to 25. There is great economy in reducing all pitch encoding decisions to 25, but even greater simplicity may be achieved by sacrificing pitch identities and considering only the size of the interval separating the first and second notes. Since two notes can be separated by no more than six semitones (e.g., the distance from C to fl in either direction), the number of categories needed is only seven (from 0 to 6 semitones). Thus, the 800 2-note transitions in each 160-theme sample may be coded just seven ways.

Table 1 shows the tabulation of "jumps" (so called to avoid the term "interval," which suggests vertical harmony rather than horizontal motion) for the ten samples of the five composers.

Table 1 Frequency With Which The Five Composers "Jump" From 0 to 6 Semi-Tones in Each of Their 160-Theme Samples

Number of Semi-Tones "Jumped" in Each Transition	*Bach*		*Haydn*		*Mozart*		*Beethoven*		*Brahms*	
	1	*2*	*1*	*2*	*1*	*2*	*1*	*2*	*1*	*2*
0	60	86	141	150	163	164	147	136	76	100
1	200	199	175	177	172	168	159	182	193	211
2	264	269	229	196	203	191	216	222	235	225
3	90	80	98	106	100	99	96	99	113	112
4	72	62	75	69	71	76	81	70	73	52
5	113	103	82	100	86	101	98	89	104	93
6	2	2	1	3	6	2	4	3	7	8

NOTE: Number of 2-note transitions in each sample is 800.

Since pitch identities have been lost, category 0 represents such transitions as C-C, C#-C#, D-D, etc. Category 2, the modal category in all ten samples, represents such whole-tone (two semitone) transitions as C-D, C#-D#, D-E, D#-F, etc. Three facts are immediately apparent in Table 1: (1) composers agree roughly in the frequency with which they use each "jump," (2) there is error variance between the two samples of each composer, (3) yet the two samples of each composer tend to vary less around their own mean than around the ten-sample mean. This last fact is a test of the discriminatory power of these simple categories in both the known and the "unknown" samples.

The appropriate statistic is the chi-square goodness-of-fit test.[1] Theoretical frequencies are defined as the means for each composer's two samples of the six categories (six rather than seven, with 5 and 6 aggregated, because the theoretical frequencies for category 6 by itself would be insufficient for chi-square). Table 2 reports chi-squares obtained for the original samples and also for the "unknown" samples. Values entered on the major diagonal are in effect error terms—chi-squares of the extent to which each composer deviates from his own mean. With 5 degrees of freedom, chi-squares of 11.1, 15.1 and 20.5 have probabilities of .05, .01, and .001, respectively. Thus in the matrix of known samples Bach and Brahms each reject, and are rejected by, all composers except himself. This pattern persists in the group of "unknown" samples, the probability being extremely small that either Bach or Brahms could have written any of the four.

Unfortunately, Haydn, Mozart and Beethoven cannot be distinguished on the basis of "jumps." Discrimination of the three classical composers is not only weak; it is anomalous in that Haydn accepts Beethoven's known samples with less error than his own. Therefore, the "jumps" analysis separates Bath and Brahms from the group and establishes that neither could have written the "unknown" samples, but the three contemporaries cannot be found to differ in this encoding habit.

Second Analysis

The next simplest classification of two-note transitions has already been described: 25 joint classes based on the tonic, the third, the fifth, all other diatonic tones and all chromatic tones. Accordingly, the ten known samples were processed again on the computer to provide the frequency distributions reported in Table 3. The patterns observed in Table 1 reappear in this table: error variance within a composer's works, but less variance around each two-sample mean than around the ten-sample mean.

The tables have other affinities. In Table 1 it was seen that Mozart was the composer most likely to repeat a note (i.e., make a

Table 2 Goodness-of-Fit Chi-Squares Obtained When the Mean "Jump" Frequencies for Each Composer Are Taken as Expected Frequencies and the 14 Sets of Sample Means Are Taken as Observed Frequencies

Source of Expected Frequencies	*Known Samples*[a]					*Unknown Samples*[b]			
	Bach	*Haydn*	*Mozart*	*Beethoven*	*Brahms*	*1*	*2*	*3*	*4*
Bach	3.2	94.6	139.7	83.2	21.8	78.1	164.2	49.9	89.5
Haydn	61.3	2.8	4.5	2.7	35.5	6.2	8.5	10.2	4.2
Mozart	85.9	6.5	0.6	7.2	53.7	11.4	4.2	21.2	9.4
Beethoven	54.8	3.7	6.3	1.7	35.3	3.3	13.6	6.6	3.6
Brahms	18.4	48.9	79.3	45.2	4.1	48.2	90.0	27.5	51.0

a. Each entry in these cells is derived from the mean for the two samples of each composer.
b. The four "unknown" composers are Handel, Mozart, Beethoven and Mendelssohn.

0-semitone "jump"). In Table 3 it is Mozart who most often uses the repetitions transitions (tonic—tonic, third—third, fifth—fifth). In Table 1 Bach and Brahms were highest in 1-semitone "jumps," which in ten out of twelve eases involve chromatic tones (E-F and B-C being the only 1-semitone intervals in the diatonic scale of C major). Therefore, it is not surprising that Bach and Brahms lead the group in all chromatic transitions in Table 3. Other examples may be found in which the tables mutually support the patterns of encoding habits found in each.

Table 3 Frequency of 25 Types of Two-Note Transitions in Each of the Ten 160-Theme Samples From the Five Composers

	Bach		*Haydn*		*Mozart*		*Beethoven*		*Brahms*	
From-To	*1*	*2*	*1*	*2*	*1*	*2*	*1*	*2*	*1*	*2*
Tonic to tonic	9	23	46	63	64	74	34	33	19	17
Tonic to third	23	19	24	28	31	41	22	22	11	12
Tonic to fifth	47	37	23	31	25	35	22	24	25	19
Tonic to other diatonic	88	101	80	93	69	70	97	81	62	79
Tonic to all chromatic	24	20	11	8	12	14	10	16	32	21
Third to tonic	9	14	26	21	15	21	25	17	10	17
Third to third	6	11	20	17	29	18	23	42	18	26
Third to fifth	15	15	11	28	22	26	17	17	25	19
Third to other diatonic	50	44	80	53	69	63	52	54	63	46
Fifth to tonic	52	52	36	53	45	40	44	40	40	30
Fifth to third	14	23	30	31	32	35	27	18	23	21
Fifth to fifth	31	28	48	55	51	59	58	38	16	36
Fifth to other diatonic	65	59	50	56	50	52	54	57	57	61
Fifth to all chromatic	33	34	9	13	19	18	14	27	41	41
Other diatonic to tonic	52	63	62	69	49	59	63	65	56	48
Other diatonic to third	36	29	54	44	43	44	40	45	43	42
Other diatonic to fifth	51	51	48	32	42	33	49	39	41	35
Other diatonic to other diatonic	37	48	77	64	76	35	86	75	47	67
Other diatonic to all chromatic	56	38	19	9	13	14	17	19	44	36
All chromatic to fifth	25	28	8	12	21	19	6	23	35	41
All chromatic to other diatonic	51	42	22	12	16	17	20	22	53	33
All chromatic to all chromatic	8	15	9	5	3	7	10	9	23	25
[a]All chromatic to tonic and third [a]Third to all chromatic	21	6	7	3	4	6	10	17	16	27

a. Aggregated to provide sufficient expected frequencies for chi-square analysis.

Table 4 Goodness-of-Fit Chi-Squares Obtained When the Mean Transitional Frequencies for Each Composer Are Taken as Expected Frequencies and the 14 Sets of Sample Means Are Taken as Observed Frequencies

Source of Expected Frequencies	*Known Samples*[a]					*Unknown Samples*[b]			
	Bach	*Haydn*	*Mozart*	*Beethoven*	*Brahms*	*1*	*2*	*3*	*4*
Bach	16.2	295.3	376.7	229.4	110.7	157.9	414.6	181.9	148.6
Haydn	355.5	20.0	51.9	82.5	468.2	116.3	55.5	78.8	236.5
Mozart	324.3	51.2	14.3	100.3	386.0	127.2	24.2	65.9	180.6
Beethoven	201.3	65.6	103.0	17.3	214.1	91.1	114.6	36.5	102.7
Brahms	94.9	278.7	351.1	155.0	17.4	195.4	343.1	122.8	143.0

a. Each entry in these cells is derived from the mean for the two samples of each composer.
b. The four "unknown" composers are Handel, Mozart, Beethoven and Mendelssohn.

Table 4 reports chi-squares obtained when the goodness-of-fit test is applied to means computed from the data of Table 3.

Since there are 23 means for each composer (3 of the 25 classes having been aggregated to provide sufficient frequencies), the resulting chi-squares must be evaluated with 22 degrees of freedom. The .05, .01 and .001 probability values of chi-square are 33.9, 403 and 483, respectively.

Unlike Table 2, Table 4 shows sharp discrimination in the matrix of known samples. The chi-squares on the major diagonal, again measures of inter-sample error, give each composer at least 50–50 odds that he actually wrote his own works, while the remaining chi-squares in this matrix give odds exceeding 1,000 to 1 that each composer did not write the known samples of the other four composers. As before, Bach and Brahms are separated from the other composers by extremely high chi-squares, but even the Haydn-Beethoven distinction is sharply drawn. The weakest discrimination, between Haydn and Mozart, easily meets a 1,000–1 criterion of rejection.

With the assurance that this set of encoding habits actually does discriminate, the four "unknown" samples may be tested again. Chi-squares resulting from this phase of the analysis show immediately that *none* of the five composers could have written samples 1 and 4. Nor, if a .001 criterion is established, could Bach, Haydn or Brahms have written *any* of the four. Nor could Beethoven have written sample 2, nor Mozart sample 3. But sample 2 could easily represent a chance deviation from Mozart's mean frequencies, while sample 3 suggests a more outlying but quite possible deviation from Beethoven's mean frequencies. Foreknowledge of the authorship of samples 2 and 3 may dispose the investigator to attribute them to Mozart and Beethoven, but it seems that the chi-squares also speak for themselves.

Summary of the Analyses

It was decided to begin with the simplest classifications of encoding habits and to seek the least complex behavior, which would prove to be reliably idiosyncratic. Whereas it had been expected that analyses would be required of 3-note, 4-note and perhaps even higher-order transitions, a classification of 2-note transitions into only 25 categories satisfied a stringent discrimination criterion and led to the proper disposition of the "unknown" samples.

Discussion

As a contribution to communication research, this study scarcely ranks with the precedent studies reviewed above. In the first place, it lacks their research problem—an unknown communicator to identify. Secondly, modest amounts of data are involved. Thirdly, computer processing eliminates most of the tallying and testing which attained awesome proportions in Yule's work.

Yet, acknowledging these differences, this study seems to close the triangle of "artistic" communication by establishing that composers too have their minor encoding habits—analogs of the writer's prepositions and the painter's fingernails. Although only the variable of pitch was studied, it seems safe to infer that composers also differ at this microanalytic level in their use of rhythms, harmonies, etc.

Indeed, converging evidence now suggests that all human communicative behavior exhibits two types of idiosyncrasy deserving study. The first is the obvious idiosyncrasy of complex constructions. That is, no two men could independently encode *Paradise Lost* or even three stanzas from it. Even the single sentence "Him the Almighty Power/Hurled headlong flaming from the eternal sky/With hideous ruin and combustion down/To bottomless perdition, there to dwell/In adamantine chains and penal fire/Who durst defy the Omnipotent to arms" would keep the fabled chimpanzees at their typewriters for centuries. The second type of idiosyncrasy is that of minor encoding habits, which lie at an opposite pole from complex constructions on the continua of deliberation and self-consciousness. For instance, whether he was aware of his proclivity or not, Fra Filippo liked to render an earlobe as circular while Bonifazio preferred an elongated ellipse (see Fig. 1). Mozart liked to repeat a tone in consecutive notes while Bach preferred to move up or down a semitone. If asked, could these communicators state why they had chosen certain patterns and not others?

It is tempting to link such behaviors to unconscious determinants and thus escape responsibility for explaining them. But the behaviors under consideration here (e.g., the use of prepositions) are as devoid of affect as human activity can be, and motivation for unconscious determination is therefore lacking. It would be absurd to argue that Hamilton felt impelled to use upon or that Madison felt impelled to censor his use of it.

A more satisfactory perspective is that of learning theory. Having at some time, somehow, been reinforced for using upon, Hamilton continued to use it more frequently than did his contemporary Madison, who may or may not have been reinforced for avoiding it. We cannot yet infer what the relevant reinforcements might have been, but we may certainly infer that selective reinforcement was involved and that behavior was "shaped" to this end.

Common sense supports the assertion that trivial details are subject to random variation while significant details are frozen in the mold of the communicator's intention. Evidence now suggests, however, that no detail is so trivial that it does not vary systematically within and between communicators' works. Many studies, most recently this one, have asked *how?* Perhaps the next will ask *why?*

Note

1. Chi-square provides an estimate of the probability that a given set of departures from theoretical frequencies could have occurred by chance. Unlike tests based on the standard error of the mean (t test, analysis of variance), chi-square requires no assumptions of normality and variance homogeneity and is therefore applicable in situations (such as this) in which each mean is computed from only two values and in which information about the sampling distribution is unavailable.

References

Painting

Berenson, B. (1902). *The study and criticism of Italian art.* London: G. Bell and Sons.

Kiel, H. (Ed.). (1962). *The Bernard Berenson treasury.* New York: Simon and Schuster.

Morelli, G. (1900). *Italian painters* (Vol. 1, C. J. Ffoulkes, Trans.). London: John Murray.

Wind, E. (1964). Critique of connoisseurship. *Art News 63:*26–29, 52–55.

Literature

Ellegard, A. (1962). *A statistical method for determining authorship.* Goteborg, Sweden: Elanders Boktryckeri Aktiebolag.

Fries, C. (1952). *The structure of English.* Ann Arbor: University of Michigan Press.

Mendenhall, T. C. (1887). The characteristic curve of composition. *Science 9,* 214:237–246.

Mosteller, F., & Wallace, D. L. (1963). Inference in an authorship problem. *Journal of the American Statistical Association 58:* 275–309.

Yule, G. U. (1944). *The statistical study of literary vocabulary.* Cambridge, England: Cambridge University Press.

Music

Barlow, H., & Morgenstern, S. (1948). *A dictionary of musical themes.* New York: Crown.

Brooks, F. P., Jr., et al. (1957). *An experiment in musical composition.* I.R.E. Trans. Elec. Computers, EC-0:175.

Youngblood, J. E. (1958). Style as information. *Journal of Music Theory 2:*24.

3.8

Wheels of Time and the Interdependence of Value Change in America

J. Zvi Namenwirth*

. . . It is my contention that the history of value change is neither progressive nor regressive, but basically cyclical. I shall therefore try to demonstrate the plausibility of this assertion; relate cycles of change in a variety of values, thereby delineating the underlying structure of the cyclical findings, or "The Wheel of Time"; attempt to interpret the meaning of the wheel; and then conclude with a speculation about its possible causes.

Values: Concept and Assessment

The definition and assessment of value change determine to some extent the findings, and an explication is therefore in order. For this exposition, the distinction between goods and values is basic. Goods are the available resources of a society at any one time. These resources are not restricted to material commodities, but also include such things as friendship, recognition, health, or power. Values are goal states, or conceptions about the *desirable* level of goods. Lasswell's conceptions have structured this understanding, and he asserts that eight categories will exhaustively classify both goods and values. In his schema, there are four deference values (power, rectitude, respect, and affection) and four welfare values (wealth, well-being, enlightenment, and skill) (Lasswell & Kaplan, 1950:55).

To assess changes in value priorities over time, American Republican and Democratic party platforms from 1844 through 1964 were content analyzed, using procedures described by Stone, Dunphy, Smith, and Ogilvie (1966).[1] The use of content analysis is predicated by two assumptions: (1) The differential occurrence of a content category is an indication of the differential concern with the value

*From pages 649–664, 671–677, and 680–683, with the permission of the editors of *The Journal of Interdisciplinary History* and The MIT Press, Cambridge, Massachusetts.

classified by that category; and (2) the relative value concern which is thus measured is an appropriate measure of the relative priority of that value in the total value schema of each and all documents. The content analysis, then, produces a profile of frequency changes in reference to seventy-three categories.[2] What are these categories?

About 95% of the words which occur in party platforms were entered in a dictionary, and these words were defined by one or more of the seventy-three categories. Many of these are really subcategories of the Lasswell Value categories. When possible, a distinction was made between categories (and, therefore, words) which indicate a substantive

Table 1 Classification of the Value Dictionary

I. Deference Values	***Substantive Values***	***Value Transactions***
1. Power	other	Arena
	authoritative power	indulgence
	cooperation solidarity	deprivation
	conflict	scope value indicator
	doctrine	general participant
		authoritative participant
2. Rectitude	ethics	indulgence
	religious	deprivation
		scope value indicator
3. Respect	other	indulgence
		deprivation
4. Affection	other	deprivation
		participant
II. Welfare Values	***Substantive Values***	***Value Transactions***
1. Wealth	other	transaction
		participants
2. Well-being	somatic	indulgence
	psychic	deprivation
3. Enlightenment	other	indulgence
		deprivation
		scope indicator
4. Skill	aesthetics	participants
	other	

III. General Value Transaction Indicators

1. transaction indulgence
2. transaction deprivation
3. transaction
4. scope indicators
5. base indicators
6. arena
7. participant
8. nations
9. self
10. audience
11. others
12. selves

IV. Anomie

1. anomie

V. Sentiments

1. positive affect
2. negative affect
3. not
4. sure
5. if

VI. Space-Time Dimension

1. space-time

VII. Residual Categories

1. n-type word
2. undefinable
3. undefined

value concern and categories which indicate a concern with some value transaction whereby the actor (participant) gains (indulgences) or loses (deprivations) in a particular value environment (arenas, countries, etc.). Also, some categories indicate whether the values and the considerations are intrinsic for the participant (scope values) or instrumental (base values). If a subclassification were not feasible, words were classified in a residual category (other). For some words it is unclear what the particular value reference is; they are classified as general value unspecific indicators.

Three residual categories deserve further explanation: *n-type* words are high frequency words with little semantic information, such as articles and conjunctions. The category *undefinable* contains words that have no value implications whatsoever. The category *undefined* includes words with ambiguous value implications, which will change from context to context.

Armed with this instrument and using computers, the full text of the platforms was matched with the dictionary (or word classifications) and this matching produced the noted frequency profiles. Even if one were to agree that these frequencies may indicate changing value preferences in party platforms, the reader may well question the relevance of such data. Why bother with party platforms?[3]

The choice of party platforms to assess magnitude and direction of changing values in American society seems justified for the following reasons: (1) The two-party system in the United States is competitive in most states of the Union, i.e., the parties compete in the same electoral market for the sympathies of various interests. The planks therefore contain the platform committee's best guesses about policies and values that will maximize the party's appeal to the electorate, and, in order to survive, parties must guess their voters' preferences correctly more often than not. Consequently, the content of party platforms is especially suitable for the study of values of the whole society. (2) Party platforms not only reflect predominant values, but they also create or modify value orientations by their presentation and the ensuing public disputes during election campaigns. (3) Parties and party platforms are features of many other societies so that their examination allows for future cross-national comparisons.

Data and Cycles

Basic data of this investigation are as follows: For each Democratic and Republican platform and for each campaign from 1844 to 1964 (or thirty-one campaigns), there are seventy-three observations, one observation for each category (or variable). Each observation is the frequency of that category in the particular platform. This frequency is then expressed as a percentage of words in that category of all words in the document, since this manipulation controls for the fact that campaign documents are of varying lengths. A plot of the thirty-one observations for the category "wealth-total" (a summary measure of all wealth subcategories) over the years 1844–1964 indicates that the concern with wealth varies a good deal from campaign to campaign.

Figure 1 illustrates . . . that in general the concern with *wealth* is low in the 1840s and 1850s; it increases over the next eighty years, to decrease again after 1932. This long-term cyclical tendency is estimated by a sine curve (the dotted line . . .). As will be noted, the actual observations do not lie on the dotted line. . . . If we plot the deviations from the dotted line (residuals) over time (see Figure 2, which represents these deviations for the Democratic platform), then we note a secondary cyclical trend which in the nature of the case has a more limited swing (or amplitude) and a shorter time span. This secondary cycle is also described by a sine curve which varies about the first one, and these secondary curves are represented by the drawn line in Figure 1. In conclusion, two cyclical trends seem to describe, if not operate on, changing concern with *wealth* in American platforms. . . . [S]imilar cycles tend to operate in most other value categories as well. How did I arrive at the latter conclusion?

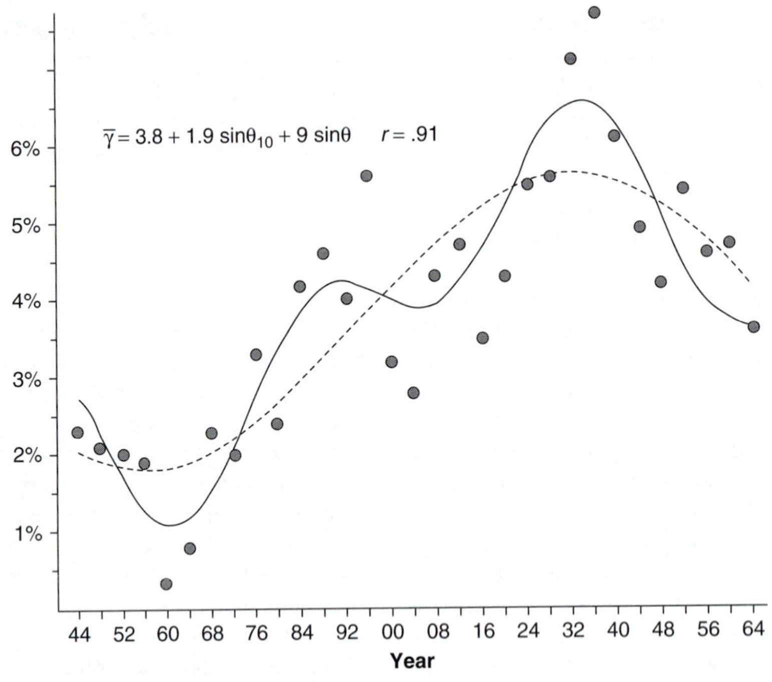

Figure 1 Two Superimposed Sine Curves Fitting Percent Concern With References to Wealth (Wealth Total) in Democratic Party Platforms, 1844–1964

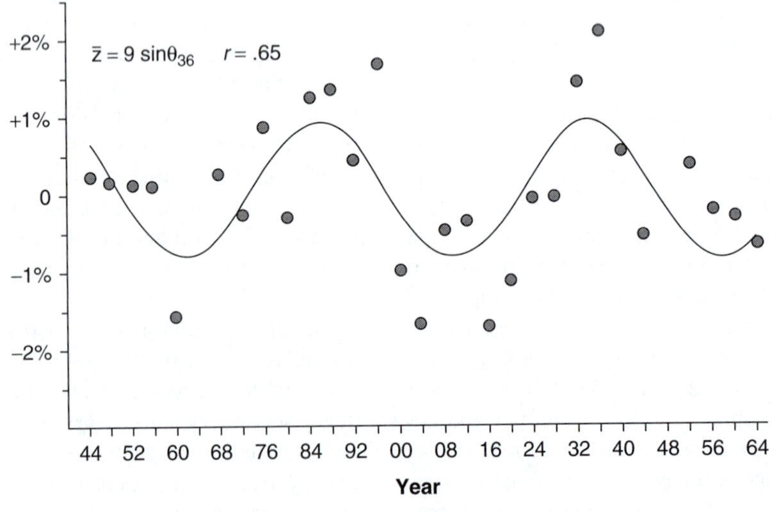

Figure 2 Short-Term Sine Curve Fitting Deviations From Long-Term Cycle Describing References to Wealth in Democratic Party Platforms, 1844–1964

Plots of the data revealed provisional outlines of a curve in each category and therefore the amplitude, wavelength, and year of maximum (or minimum) of each of these curves. These first estimates were subsequently tested and adjusted by an iterative computer program. A particular sine curve is considered an acceptable estimate of the underlying cyclical trend if it correlates with the data at r = .45 or better (Namenwirth & Ploch, 1968; Porter & Johnson, 1961). This conservative decision rule is not wholly arbitrary since it provided a unique solution only in these cases. In a similar manner, if a short-term cycle correlated .40 with the data, I accepted the existence of a secondary curve. Of the forty-two categories, about 80% displayed some type of cycle.

To state that sine curves approximate a good part of value change is not just to say that value changes display fluctuations, but that they display fluctuations of a particular kind. First, values fluctuate around an average level of concern, which is constant over time. Second, the magnitude of these fluctuations (or amplitude) is also constant over time. Third, the time span of each wavelength is constant, as well. In the case of the primary curve, the data, therefore, suggest static equilibrium. In the case of the secondary curve, the findings suggest a moving equilibrium, since the curve varies about an average level, which itself, is subject to constant change i.e., the primary curve.

In this manner, one can conceive of all value concerns and their changes as consisting of long-term curves, short-term curves, and detrended fluctuations. These three component parts have their own causes and dynamics.

The Fit of Long-Term Value Cycles

Table 2 presents all of the content categories which fit a longer-term sine curve and four characteristics of each curve: (a) the party, i.e. Democratic or Republican; (b) wave length (or time span) in number of years; (c) the peak (or year when the curve is at its maximum); (d) r^2, a measure of goodness of fit. The table indicates that in the long run, concern with the category *others* in the Republican platform, for instance, is at its height in the year 1808, and that this will again be the case in the year 2040 (i.e., 1808 + 232). The long-term cycle explains about 64% of the variance in changing references to the category. In other words, the curve fairly well describes the varying usage of this concept over time, since the variance explained would equal 100% if it were to describe the variation perfectly, and zero percent if it were not to describe this variation at all. Even so, there was no party platform in 1808, and the statement about the platform in 2040 is only a projection into the future. The estimation of long-term change in value concerns is therefore often based on extrapolation.

In the Republican platforms, about three-fifths of the content categories, and more than seven-tenths of the categories in the Democratic platforms, were estimated by the long-term sine curve. Approximately one-fourth of the categories did not fit a long-term sine curve in either the Democratic or Republican Party platforms.

Unfortunately, the fifty-five long-term sine curves do not all have the same wavelength, and this complicates their interpretation. Although the modal wavelength is 152 years, the shortest cycle runs 104 years, while the longest lasts 232 years—or more than twice as long. Table 3 presents the specifics.

The Structural Interdependence of Long-Term Value Change

The internal relationships among the long-term sine curves are presented by a circle. To the right are the sine curves, which peak in subsequent years; to the left, are the curves, which peaked in previous years. The whole circle represents a 152-year sequence of peaking and dropping concerns with a variety of values. For instance, while long-term concern with the category *wealth* peaks around 1932, long-term concern with the categories *affection, respect,*

Table 2 Selected Characteristics of 55 Long-Term Sine Curves

Content Category & Party[a]	*Peak*	*Wave Length (in Years)*	r^2
1. *Others*	1808	232	0.64
2. Undefined	1816	184	0.46
3. Rectitude Scope Indicator	1820	232	0.37
4. *Rectitude Scope Indicator*	1860	168	0.43
5. *Respect Indulgence*	1864	168	0.46
6. Rectitude Total	1864	152	0.40
7. Affection Total	1864	152	0.30
8. *Respect Total*	1868	152	0.49
9. *Rectitude Total*	1868	136	0.45
10. *Affection Total*	1872	120	0.38
11. Respect Total	1872	152	0.21
12. Respect Indulgence	1880	136	0.32
13. Power Authoritative Participant	1880	184	0.28
14. Power Participant	1884	136	0.22
15. Power Authoritative	1888	168	0.35
16. *Power Authoritative Participant*	1896	152	0.18
17. Positive Affect	1924	152	0.62
18. *Wealth Participant*	1928	136	0.58
19. *Skill Total*	1928	184	0.53
20. Wealth Transaction	1928	184	0.34
21. *Nations*	1928	184	0.24
22. *Wealth Total*	1932	152	0.73
23. *Wealth Other*	1932	152	0.73
24. Wealth Other	1932	152	0.69
25. Wealth Total	1932	152	0.69
26. *Skill Other*	1932	184	0.51
27. Wealth Participant	1932	136	0.46
28. Wealth Transaction	1936	152	0.32
29. *Transaction Indulgence*	1940	184	0.54
30. skill Total	1944	152	0.67
31. Selves	1944	168	0.65
32. Selves	1944	184	0.30
33. Skill Other	1948	152	0.69
34. *Well-being Total*	1948	136	0.34
35. Transaction	1948	168	0.26
36. *Transaction*	1948	184	0.25
37. Well-being Total	1952	136	0.68
38. *Well-being Somatic*	1952	152	0.32
39. Well-being Somatic	1956	152	0.74
40. *Base Indicator*	1956	168	0.70
41. Transaction Indulgence	1956	184	0.65

a. *Italics = Republican Party Platforms*; otherwise, Democratic Platforms.

Table 3 Distribution of Long-Term Sine Curves by Wave Length

Wave Lengths (in years)	*N*
104 years	1
120 years	1
136 years	7
152 years	20
168 years	9
184 years	11
200 years	1
232 years	5

and *rectitude* peak half a cycle earlier or later (76 years), i.e., where concern with *wealth* is at its peak, preoccupation with *affection* and *respect* is at a low. In addition, an increasing concern with wealth over time leads to a fixed decrease in concern with *respect,* and *vice versa.* An understanding of these dynamics requires a description of the sequence of peaking value concerns around the wheel of time.

Around 1856, concern with the categories *others, affection-total, rectitude-total,* and *respect-total,* and several of their subcategories, is at a maximum. The category *others* contains all references to the third person plural pronoun (they, their, their's, themselves). In

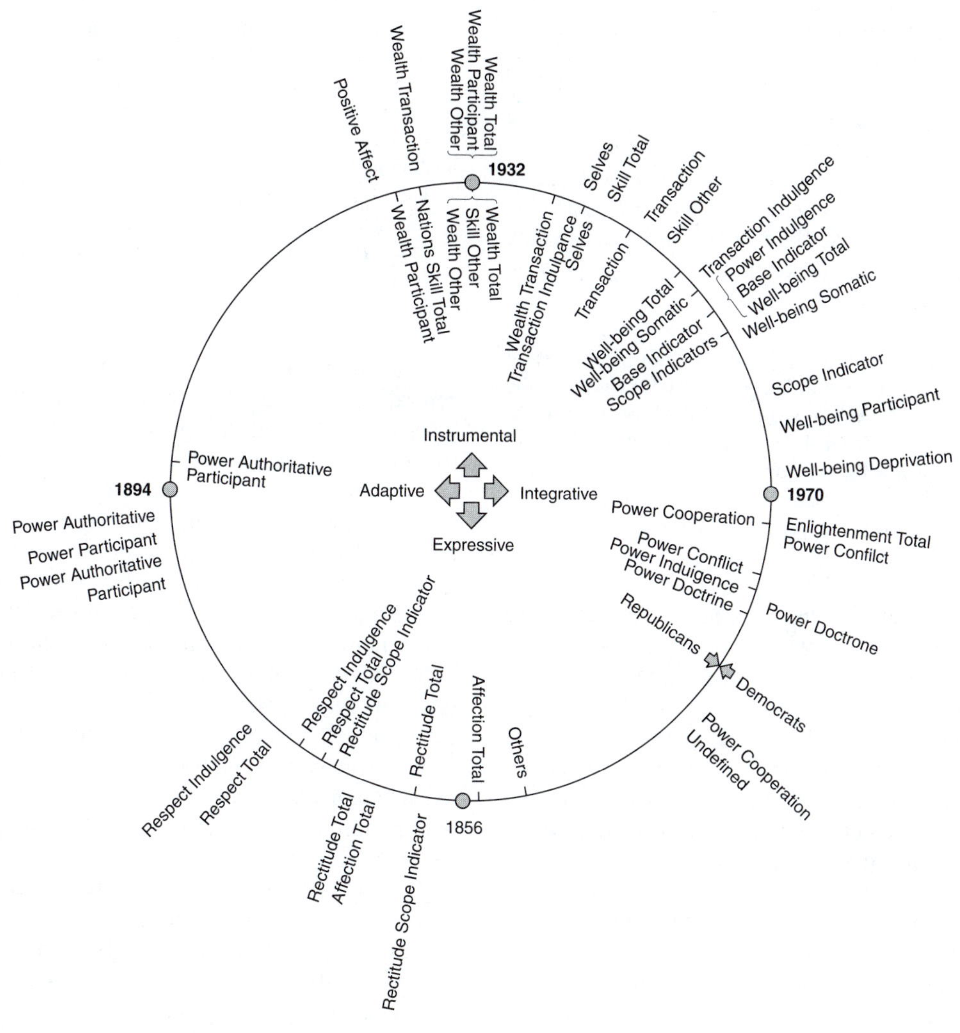

Figure 3 The Internal Structure of Long-Term Value Changes (Cycle Lengths Set at 152 Years, Variable Origins)

Party platforms, such references often stand for a concern with the "other" party, but more often with people in general, and their wishes and qualities. A frequent usage of this category invokes a distinction between leadership and the masses, the "they" and all of those without a name, and it therefore indicates an elitist orientation to social reality and the political order.

The category affection contains references to love and friendship in general, and in party platforms, such references often indicate an association between devotion to family life and loyal patriotism. For instance;

> Resolved that, with our Republican Fathers [affection-participant], we hold it to be a self-evident truth, that all men are endowed with the inalienable right to life, liberty, and the pursuit of happiness. . . . (Porter & Johnson, 1961:27)

In party platforms, the category *respect* includes the words honor, equality, and inequality. The category *rectitude* contains recurrent words like ought and must, which suggest a call for natural duty and principles. To illustrate:

> We recognize the equality [*respect-others*] of all men before the law and hold that it is the duty [*rectitude-scope-indicator*] of the government in its dealings with the people to mete out equal and exact justice [*rectitude-ethics*] to all, of whatever nativity, race, color or persuasion, religion [*rectitude-religious*] or politics. (Porter & Johnson, 1961:41)

Slavery was the preponderant issue in these years. Policy preferences on this score divided the parties and changed over time—the Democrats favored slavery and its extension into the territories, the Republicans opposed the latter. However, our findings pertain to similarities, not differences, between the two parties, and the mutual concern with *rectitude* indicates that whatever the nature of substantive policy differences, there was a great and similar concern with the justification of policy preferences. In addition, at that time the terms of justification were largely rectitudinal.

In the 1890s, concern with *rectitude, respect,* and *affection* declined while concern with *power-authoritative participant* and *power-authoritative* was at a peak. These categories contain many words, but most frequent are references to the federal government and the constitution. At first sight, it seems as if the political issues remained the same, i.e., the relationship between the states and the federal government. However, the justification of policy preferences changed from ethical to legal grounds, from substantive to formal justice, from traditional to legal. To illustrate:

> During all these years the Democratic party has resisted the tendency of selfish interest to the centralization of governmental [*power-authoritative*] power, and steadfastly maintained the integrity of the dual scheme of government [*power-authoritative participant*] established by the founders of this republic of republics. Under its guidance and teachings the great principle of local self-government has found its best expression in the maintenance of the right of the states and in its assertion of the necessity of confining the general government [*power-authoritative participant*] to the exercise of the powers granted by the constitution [*power-authoritative*] of the United States. (Porter & Johnson, 1961:97)

On further inquest, one notes that the central issue is no longer the relationship between federal and state government, but the role of the federal government in the creation and maintenance of the economic infrastructure of an industrial society. The parties are in conflict about this role in regard to tariffs, transportation, politics (domestic as well as international, i.e., a canal through the isthmus), homesteading, banking and monetary policy, antitrust legislation, immigration, and taxation. Yet, the essential conclusion remains the same. Divergent policy preferences may appear from party to party and from campaign to campaign, and the justification of the divergent preferences is in terms of very identical legalistic constructs.

By 1932, the role of the federal government is much less disputed. The party program does not elaborate on justification, but simply states its preferences in regard to economic policy. The peaking concern with *wealth* and its subcategories indicates this finding. Thus, one reads in the Democratic platform:

> We favor the maintenance of national credit [*wealth-other*] by a federal budget [*wealth-other*] annually balanced based on accurate executive estimates within revenues [*wealth-other*], raised by a system of taxation [*wealth-other*], levied on the principle of ability to pay [*wealth-transaction*]. We advocate a sound currency [*wealth-other*] to be preserved at all hazards and an international monetary [*wealth-other*] conference called on the invitation of our government to consider the rehabilitation of silver [*wealth-other*] and related questions. (Porter & Johnson, 1961:331)

And the Republican platform states:

> Generally in economic [*wealth-other*] matters we pledge the Republican Party: 1. to maintain unimpaired the national credit [*wealth-other*]. 2. To defend and preserve a sound currency [*wealth-other*] and an honest dollar [*wealth-other*]. 3. To stand steadfastly by the principle of a balanced budget [*wealth-other*]. . . . (Porter & Johnson, 1961:350)

First, there is a near total absence of justification of policy preferences. Second, a preoccupation with the material and technological (*skill*) well-being of the nation is a characteristic for the platforms at this time. This is further confirmed by the frequent references to the category *selves.* In party platforms, the use of we, us, ourselves, etc., often reveals a denial of status differentiation, either within the party or within the nation as a whole.

Typical for platforms in the 1950s and 1960s is an orientation toward the future rather than the past. This is revealed by maximum preoccupation with the category *transaction.*

> We shall [*transaction*] insist [*transaction*] on businesslike and efficient administration of all foreign aid . . . We shall [*transaction*] erect [*transaction*] our foreign policy on the basis of friendly firmness. . . . We shall [*transaction*] pursue [*transaction*] a consistent foreign policy. . . . We shall [*transaction*] protect the future. . . . (Porter & Johnson, 1961:453)

Frequent references to *base* and *scope indicators* with words such as plan, strategy, future, project, and development, point in the same direction. In this framework, there is also maximum concern with health and *well-being* in general.

Projecting the findings into the future, the major concerns of the 1970s will be again of a different order. Since the 1930s, society as a whole was the object of concern; in the 1970s, the major preoccupation will be with conflicting groups and individuals. Frequent words in the subcategory *power-cooperation* are agreement, coalition, compromise, cooperative, organization, solidarity, unity, and, in the subcategory *power-conflict,* agitation, anarchy, breakdown, disagreement, disunity, fight, hostility, rebellion, resistance, and revolution. Seemingly, problems of the distribution of power and other social resources will be the major value issue at that time.

The Fit of the Short-Term Value Cycles

Table 4 presents all of the categories that fit a short-term since curve. According to this table, Republican concern with the category *well-being*-total tended to be at its height in 1908, as it did in 1868 and 1948. The short-term sine curve explains 26% of the residual variance in the category over time. The shorter-term cycle is therefore only a tendency in the data, which often explains but a limited part of the total amount of value change. In addition, the estimation of the cycles is based in part on extrapolation.

As was done with the long-term cycles, the wavelengths of the shorter-term cycles were set at the modal length of forty-eight years and peaks transformed accordingly. In this case, the wavelength of the transformed sine curve is considerably less than the period under observation, and, therefore, each point on the circle represents a set of peaks, which are forty-eight years apart. For instance, the top of the circle (in Figure 4) represents the years 1884, 1932, and 1980.

Table 4 Selected Characteristics of Short-Term Sine Curves

Content Category and Party[a]	*Peak*	*Wave Length (in years)*	r^2	*% Total*[b] *Variance*
1. *Well-being Total*	1908	40	0.26	0.17
2. *Arena*	1908	68	0.22	—
3. *Respect Total*	1908	36	0.19	0.1
4. Respect Total	1910	32	0.22	0.18
5. *Others*	1912	68	0.23	0.08
6. Enlightenment Total	1916	52	0.21	0.15
7. Power Indulgence	1916	44	0.2	0.11
8. Scope Indicator	1916	32	0.17	0.03
9. Undefined	1920	80	0.3	0.16
10. Power *Authoritative Participant*	1920	52	0.23	0.19
11. *Undefinable*	1920	32	0.2	—
12. *Power Scope Indicator*	1926	32	0.3	—
13. *Power Indulgence*	1926	32	0.17	0.13
14. Well-being Participant	1928	32	0.25	0.14
15. Wealth Transaction	1928	48	0.17	0.13
16. Power Participant	1928	48	0.12	0.09
17. *Power Arena*	1932	40	0.24	—
18. Wealth Other	1934	48	0.43	0.13
19. Wealth Total	1934	48	0.43	0.13
20. *Rectitude Total*	1934	68	0.35	0.19
21. *Wealth Total*	1936	48	0.26	0.07
22. *Wealth Other*	1936	48	0.24	0.06
23. *Wealth Transaction*	1936	48	0.2	0.15
24. *Power Cooperation*	1936	64	0.18	0.15
25. Power Conflict	1938	36	0.25	0.19
26. Power Cooperation	1940	40	0.33	0.18
27. *Power Other*	1940	64	0.3	—
28. Wealth Participant	1940	48	0.21	0.11
29. Rectitude Scope Indicator	1942	48	0.24	0.15
30. *Undefined*	1944	20	0.21	—
31. *Transaction*	1944	44	0.17	0.13
32. *Selves*	1946	48	0.27	0.19
33. Affection Total	1946	52	0.23	0.16
34. Positive Affect	1946	44	0.17	0.06
35. Power Scope Indicator	1948	64	0.23	—

a. *Italics = Republican Party Platforms;* Otherwise, Democratic Platforms.

b. Where blank, curve fitted to raw data.

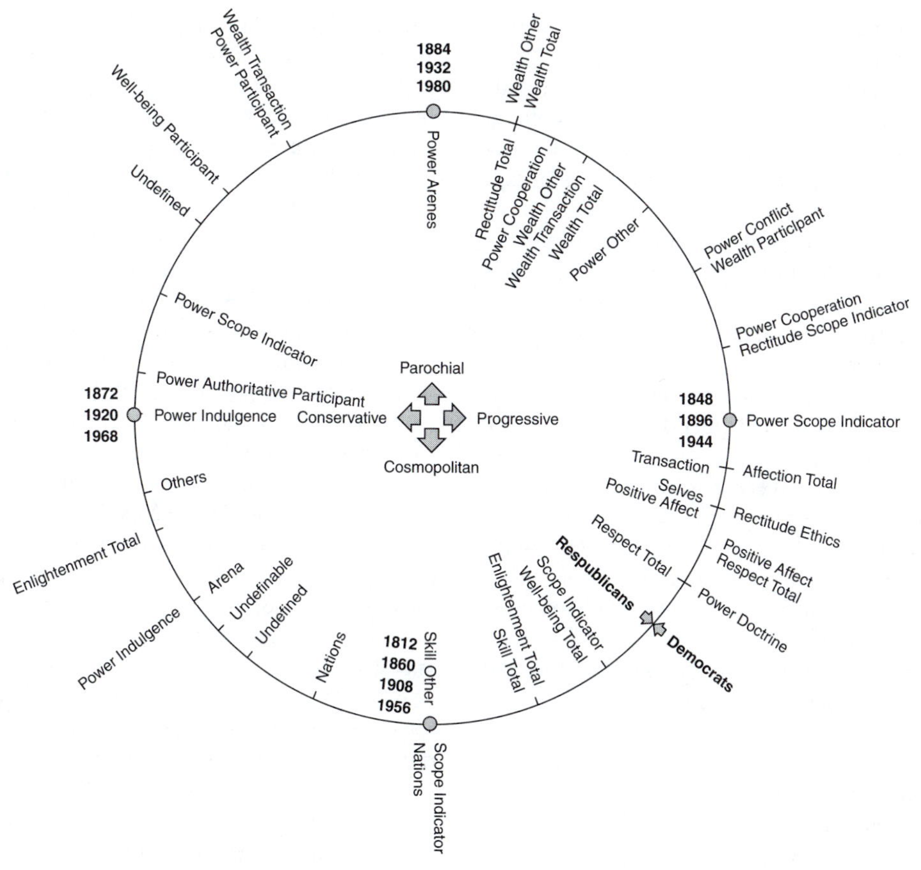

Figure 4 The Internal Structure of Short-Term Value Changes (Cycle Length Set at 48 Years, Variable Origins)

An Explanation of Short-Term Cyclical Value Changes

The reader will have noted that the early 1890s and the years around 1932 represent periods of sustained depression and business contraction in the American and world economy. In addition, twenty-five to thirty years earlier or later were periods of sustained economic growth (Burns & Mitchell, 1946:429; Fellner, 1956:43–54; Gordon, 1952:235–243). In short, there appears a rather striking fit between the short-term wheel of time and a particular economic cycle. What is the latter cycle?

Economists distinguish between various cyclical fluctuations in business activity: seasonal fluctuations, the business cycle, the long wave, and the secular trend (Fellner, 1956). The long wave, even though disputed by some economists, is said to vary, extending and contracting over a period of fifty to sixty years. How does the latter process relate to value articulations?

During long-wave economic deterioration, the nation turns inward, gradually relinquishing international ventures and then obligations, becoming more and more parochial in its orientations. This parochialism is first conservative, probably stressing discipline, the tightening of belts, the necessity of temporary unemployment as well as charity to overcome the economic decline. Usually, this goes together with growing indifference, if not hostility, toward foreign claims and conditions as the outside world will be seen as competitive, fickle, a cause of troubles, and an object of scapegoating. With the ongoing but diminishing calamity, the mood will change from conservative to progressive. Increasingly, belt tightening and charity will be seen as palliatives. A growing demand will arise for a change in collective arrangements and structural intervention. Whether cause or effect, the ensuing structural change seems to work since prosperity returns. With increasing surplus, attention turns again to the world scene; value articulations become more cosmopolitan, at first in a progressive vein. Progressive intervention works at home; therefore, it needs to be exported in the fulfillment of America's ethos and liberal designs. At any rate, money is there in growing abundance. However, once the expansion turns its peak and contraction sets in, the cosmopolitan impulse turns from progressive to conservative, from national mission to national interest, from, for instance, Marshall Plan to Green Berets. One may well speculate that with Vietnamization and the Nixon Doctrine, the parochial phase is on the rise again.

The relationship between long-wave economic contraction and expansion, and a shift in basic understandings regarding the nature of morality and criteria of worth, are equally systematic. Briefly, the shift from conflict to consensus and *vice versa* commences at the beginnings of the period of sustained debacle and prosperity, while the shift from particularistic to universalistic and *vice versa* begins at the onsets of sustained growth and contraction.[4]

Conclusions

A content analysis of American party platforms produced results, which seem to fit a variety of trends in a great many different value categories. In addition to a long-term trend of about 148 years, one can often discern short-term trends of about forty-eight years. The latter represent variations in value concern over and above long-term trend variations. In combination, the short- and long-term cycles describe (or explain) a good part of the variation in value concerns.

The wheels of time summarize the internal structure of both types of value cycles. Sequentially, the varying value concerns of the long wheel of time are explained in terms of four fundamental functional problems of any society. Accordingly, the solution of one problem always takes precedence over the solution of the next one until all four problems—adaptive, instrumental, integrative, and expressive—have been articulated to the fullest and the progression commences anew.

The sequential articulations of the short wheel of time—parochial, progressive, cosmopolitan, and conservative—are most likely produced by a dynamics that differs from the long-term functional mechanisms, and the "long wave" periodic contraction and expansion of the national economy seems, for the moment, the most plausible explanation.

Long- and short-term dynamics are not equally important in the determination of value change. On the average, long-term cycles describe about three times as much of the variance in value change as do short-term cycles. The larger part of changing value articulations in platforms is therefore attributed to the dynamics of social problem-solving rather than to social structural changes. Yet, the theory is not purely functional, since it is suggested that economic mechanisms are operating beyond and above the functional dynamics.

In the exposition, it is assumed that the time span and magnitude of value change are constant for all times. This seems an unwarranted assumption. Indeed, if the "long wave" explains the shorter-term wheel of time, then the sine curve may well be too constrictive a model of value change. Even though the "long wave" is a recurrent and rhythmically alternative cycle, the magnitude and wavelength of these cycles seem to vary in history. If this is the case for the cause, so it must be for the consequences, and thus the sequence of political philosophies must be of varying duration. One would like to believe that changes in duration and amplitudes are themselves a simple function of time and therefore gradual and continuous, but the world of value transformations may not submit itself so readily to this persistent search for elegance and order.

Quantitative procedures, such as content analysis and curve fitting, suggest to the uninitiated reader an exactness and precision which are far greater than the results of more customary procedures of historical analysis. This practitioner is under no such illusions. I forewarned the reader about the approximate nature of estimates and the speculative character of subsequent interpretations and explanations. Their correctness cannot be established in one experiment, and judgments on that score must await future examinations of different historical sources using different procedures of analysis.

Notes

1. In 1844, 1848, and 1852, there were no Republican platforms since the Republican Party did not exist prior to 1856. For the first three campaigns, I used the Whig platforms because the Whigs are in many respects the precursors of the Republican Party.

2. Thirty-one categories were eliminated from the analysis because of low frequencies or poor distribution. For a discussion of all of the categories, see Namenwirth and Weber, 1987.

3. The study of party platforms has other uses besides the assessment of value changes. See Benson, L. (1961). *The concept of Jacksonian democracy: New York as a test case* (Princeton, N.J: Princeton University Press), p. 216, and Klingberg, F. L. (1952). The historical alternations of moods in American foreign policy. *World Politics,* IV:239–274.

4. For a general discussion of the relationship between economic cycles and political if not philosophical thought, see Pareto, V. (1935). *The mind and society.* New York: Harcourt & Brace, paragraph 2387.

References

Burns, A. F., & Mitchell, W. C. (1946). *Measuring business cycles.* New York: National Bureau of Economic Research.

Fellner, W. J. (1956). *Trends and cycles in economic activity: An introduction to problems of economic growth.* New York: Holt.

Gordon, R. A. (1952). *Business fluctuations.* New York: Harper.

Lasswell, H. D., & Kaplan, A. (1950). *Power and society: A framework for political inquiry.* New Haven, CT: Yale University Press.

Namenwirth, J. Z., & Ploch, D. R. (1968). *Structural and contingent value changes in American political party platforms.* Unpublished master's thesis, Yale University, New Haven, CT.

Namenwirth, J. Z., & Weber, R. P. (1987). *Dynamics of culture.* Boston: Allen and Unwin.

Porter, K. H., & Johnson, D. B. (1961). *National party platforms, 1840–1960.* Urbana: University of Illinois Press.

Stone, P. J., Dunphy, D. C., Smith, M. S., & Ogilvie, D. M. (Eds.). (1966). *The General Inquirer: A computer approach to content analysis.* Cambridge, MA: M.I.T. Press.

3.9

Inferring the Readability of Text

Klaus Krippendorff

We tend to attribute readability to written text. The 2000 *Oxford English Dictionary* defines it as "the quality of, or capacity for being read with pleasure or interest, considered as measured by certain assessable features as ease of comprehension, attractiveness of subject and style." This definition backgrounds the obvious—that it requires a reader for texts to be readable, in fact, for texts to be texts. Readability, like literacy, is a cultural phenomenon, and efforts to infer readability from text serve various social institutions, in effect creating functional differentiations of individuals' ability. Readability research provides content analysts with an interesting case study of how analytical constructs are constructed and applied.

Inferring Readability From Texts: A Brief History

Educational research pioneered efforts to measure readability in the 1920s. Readability became an issue in deciding on reading material appropriate for schoolchildren on different levels. In the 1930s, readability research expanded to adults, serving the emerging needs of industry, government, and the military to evaluate magazines and books for their publishability, as well as technical communications, training manuals, and forms for their reliable use in processes of an administrative nature. Now, leading word-processing software features readability measures, intended to aid good writing.

The guiding idea of readability research is to find an index of readability that is general, not content specific. This is why traditional content analysts have not participated in its development. However, what students of readability and content analysts have in common is the effort of making reliable and valid inferences from text to a chosen context, as well as the need to connect the two empirical domains by means of what content analysts call analytical constructs. The whole history of readability research is one of gradually refining definitions of readability so that it can be inferred from measurable textual attributes and of improving the underlying analytical constructs.

Early readability studies looked into vocabularies—cataloging words with which students on various grade levels would be familiar (Thorndike, 1921) and could be expected to cause few reading problems. In the 1930s, readability researchers began to employ statistical correlations between numerous measurable attributes of texts and judgments of the difficulty of reading these texts. Regression equations were used to identify predictors of readability from which computationally efficient formulas could be constructed. For schoolchildren, a series of test lessons, developed by McCall and Crabbs (1925), still published, increasingly became the standard criterion against which most readability measures were tested. For adults, researchers used the opinions of library users, the popularity of publications, and multiple-choice comprehension tests. Adults showed more diversity than did children owing to the influence of different interests, backgrounds, levels of education, and occupation, rendering a common formula more difficult.

In 1934, Rudolph Flesch, probably the most cited readability researcher, proposed a simple three-factor formula, which correlated .74 with McCall-Crabbs test scores (Klare, 1963:56ff). His procedure:

Systematically select samples of 100 words throughout the material to be rated

Compute average sentence length in words (x_s)

Count the number of affixes (x_m)

Count the number of personal references (x_h)

Average the results and insert in the formula:

$$.1338x_s + .0645x_m - .0659x_h - .7502.$$

The resulting index brought most of the measured texts between 1 (easiest) and 7 (most difficult). Adding the constant 4.2498 instead of .7502 gave the reading grade placement at which 75% comprehension could be observed. His formula acknowledged earlier findings that long sentences are difficult but added the intuition that abstractions, indicated by affixes, add to this difficulty while personal references subtract from it.

An interesting controversy led Flesch to modifications of his formula. According to Klare (1963:58), the statistician S. S. Stevens, known for his distinctions of four levels of measurement, and Geraldine Stone (1947) applied the Flesch formula to psychology textbooks used at Harvard University and found the difficulty of William James's *Psychology* to be overestimated and Koffka's *Principles of Gestalt Psychology* to be underestimated according to student judgment. Following this controversy, Flesch (1948) separated readability into two kinds: reading ease and human interest. Because of the laborious nature of counting affixes, in his new reading ease formula, the count of affixes was replaced by a count of the number of syllables per 100 words. Flesch's reading ease (see below) continued to correlate highly with the McCall-Crabbs criterion, .7047, whereas human interest was .4306. Counting syllables has been the most common feature of most readability measures ever since. Flesch did not abandon his earlier insight that reading ease had much to do with using abstractions and developed a measure of the level of abstraction (Flesch, 1950) of words in a text. This could be used as such but also as a readability measure because it correlated .72 with the criterion, a slight increase over the .7047 for the reading ease measure.

The 50 years following Flesch's and his predecessors' proposals were filled with readability studies. Some 40 formulas have been proposed, tried out, abandoned, or refined—not all of them tested by empirical evidence (DuBay, 2004). But the analytical constructs evolved very little.

Currently Popular Analytical Constructs

Flesch Reading Ease (Flesch, 1948)

This formula has now withstood the test of time. It calls for selecting any 100-word sample from a text, counting

ASL = the average sentence length = total number of words/total number of sentences

ASW = the average number of syllables per word

and computing

206.835 – 1.015 ASL – 84.6 ASW.

The resulting score ranges from 0 to 100 and suggests that fifth graders can read texts at score 90 to 100, eighth to ninth graders at 60 to 70, and college graduates at 0 to 30. According to Wikipedia, *Readers Digest* magazine scores about 65, *Time* magazine about 52, and *Harvard Law Review* below 30. Microsoft Word computes this score after using its spell checker. This chapter scores 29.9.

Flesch-Kincaid Grade Level

This formula translates the components of Flesch's reading ease into a score that reflects grade levels of education, making it easier for teachers, parents, and librarians to recommend appropriate reading materials, including books, to students. It too calls on counting:

ASL = the average sentence length = total number of words/total number of sentences

ASW = the average number of syllables per word

but computing this index:

0.39 ASL + 11.8 ASW – 15.59.

Its score corresponds to the grade level at which an average student would be able to read the measured text. Microsoft Word produces this automatically as well. This chapter scores 12.6, which would suggest a level below college.

Passive Sentence Readability

Microsoft Word also computes the proportion of passive to all sentences of a document. It ranges from 0 (supposedly easiest) to 1 (supposedly most difficult) and is based on the contention that passive sentences weaken the direction of the verb and can confuse the meaning of a sentence, even when grammatically correct. A reference for this index could not be found, nor evidence of its validity. Since it has become available, it is being discussed. Writers insist that one cannot do entirely without passive constructions, suggesting that 25% would still be readable. In this chapter, 9% of sentences are passive.

Dale and Chall Formula (Dale & Chall, 1948)

These researchers sought to improve on Flesch's AWS, replacing it by a count of difficult words, defined as not occurring on a carefully researched list of 3,000 easy words. Forty years later, Dale and O'Rourke (1981) revised this list. They recommend taking several 100-word samples from different parts of a text, for books every 10th page, counting

PDW = the proportion of words not on the list of 3,000 easy words = number of difficult word/total number of words

ASL = the average sentence length = total number of words/total number of sentences

and computing

0.1579 PDW + 0.4996 ASL + 3.6365.

Its score, designed to indicate the grade level, consistently correlated .70 with the McCall-Crabbs criterion.

SMOG (Simple Measure of Gobbledygook) (McLaughlin, 1969)

SMOG scores too indicate reading levels, defined as the level at which readers can understand 90% to 100% of the information in a text. It calls for counting

NS = the number of sentences involved—at least 30: 10 consecutive sentences selected near the beginning of a text, 10 in the middle, and 10 near the end. In long sentences with colons or semicolons followed by a list, count each part of the list, together with the beginning phrase of the sentence, is an individual sentence.

NP = the number of polysyllable words in these sentences (i.e., words with three or more syllables, even if the same word appears more than once). Count words with hyphens as one. Read numbers aloud to determine the number of syllables it takes to verbalize them. Take abbreviations as the whole word they represent.

and computing

$$1.0430\sqrt{\mathrm{NP}\left(\frac{30}{NS}\right)}+3.1291.$$

Fry Readability Formula (Fry, 1977)

Fry's approach surely is most user-friendly. It requires randomly selecting three passages of exactly 100 words, beginning with a sentence, counting

X = the number of sentences in the 100 words, estimating the last sentence to the nearest 1/10th

Y = the number of syllables in the 100 words

and finding the grade level in the intersection of the X and Y coordinates in the following graph.

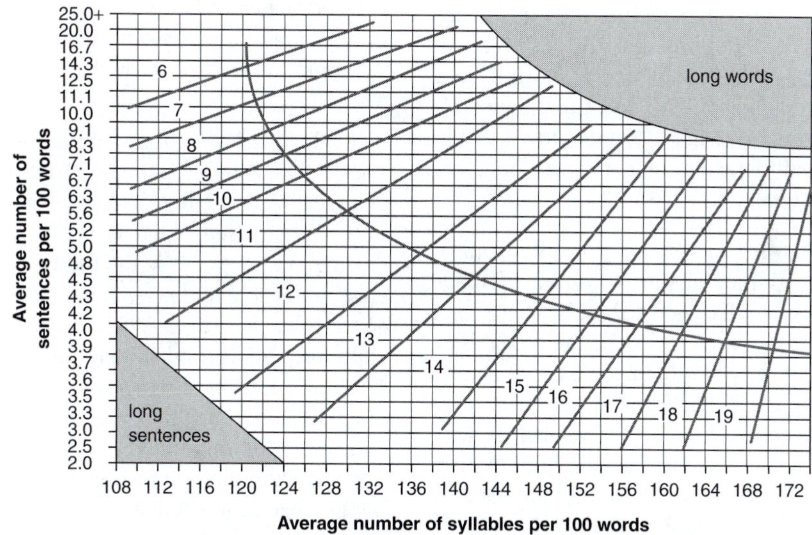

Figure 1 Fry Graph for Estimating Reading Ages (in Years)

FORCAST Readability Formula (Caylor, Sticht, Fox, & Ford, 1973; see DuBay, 2004, p. 51)

The use of this formula is even simpler than Fry's. It was developed to evaluate reading requirements in the U.S. Army, applied to military reading matters, especially technical instructions, and tested with members of the Army in various occupational roles. It asks to count

N_1SW = the number of one-syllable words in a passage of exactly 150 words

and compute

$$20 - N_1SW/10.$$

This surprisingly simple formula was found to correlate .98 with Flesch's formula, .98 with Dahl-Chall's, and .77 with graded military reading matter. It had the advantage of working within a relatively homogeneous adult population of military recruits and service personnel. DuBay (2004:52) reports on a similar research project for the U.S. Navy.

Structural Problems of the Paths Taken

Over 80 years of efforts by a growing community of researchers to improve the validity of the construct underlying these formulae, multiple regression equations, have reached a ceiling. Correlations with readability criteria seem to stay below .80. One can identify six reasons for this ceiling. They can serve as a warning to content analysts who seek to develop similar computational constructs for making inferences from text:

• *Surface measures.* Sentence lengths, numbers of syllables in words, short words, difficult words, and so on are easily countable but pertain only to epiphenomena of reading and writing. Long words, for example, are not difficult as such, but because they tend to be used less often, they naturally include more unfamiliar words than short words do. There are multisyllable words most English readers have no problems with, like *television,* and monosyllable words, like *hod,** that may well bring reading to a halt. Counts attend to the rarely noted surface of texts that readers typically penetrate.

• *Typography.* Webster's dictionary includes legibility in the definition of readability, originally good handwriting. As graphic artists know too well, the readability of printed matter is influenced by font styles, sizes, colors, and background, as well as by the organization of text (hierarchical organization of headlines, bullets, and highlighting devices) and layouts, including the use of illustrations and graphs, known to add to interest and comprehension.

• *Narrative structures.* Counts cannot capture the organization of the counted words, propositions, sentences, or paragraphs into larger compositions. Narratives, arguments, syllogisms, coherence, and the development of plots that writers consider crucial for making complex ideas clear escape context-free counting of units of text.

• *Readers' choices.* Readers of technical instructions, even of large newspapers, rarely feel bound to work through a text linearly, from its beginning to its end. They typically navigate through textual matter, selecting what supports the construction of their own mental narratives along the way. Hypertext documents support nonlinearities explicitly.

• *Discursive competencies.* Students, during their formal education, constitute a population that is relatively easy to differentiate into grades, but adults develop unequal competencies and approach texts situationally. Discourse communities distinguish themselves by their members' interests, use of specialized vocabularies, customary patterns of reasoning, and prior knowledge of relevant subject matter. What is readable in one community may be incomprehensible in another. A single formula cannot do justice to this diversity.

• *Cultural dynamics.* Familiarity with vocabularies and grammatical constructions changes with reading experiences and over time. When used, what is difficult today is destined to be less so in the future. The difference in vocabulary between young people and older folks is not merely developmental, as supposed by formulae that predict reading grades. It signals a dynamics of culture and language use to which reading and writing contribute, literature and poetry in particular. For one example, in pre-Elizabethan English, the average sentence length was 50 words. In Elizabethan English, it was 45 words. In Victorian English, it was 29 words (Sherman, 1893, cited in DuBay, 2004). Currently, average sentence length is down to 20. As readability shifts, ways to infer it must do as well. Culture-free formulae cannot.

Writers and teachers associations have considered it a danger and resisted equating the components of readability formulae with guidelines for good writing. Indeed, if writers were rewarded by achieving high readability scores, and only that, they could easily produce meaningless strings of monosyllable words. This possibility suggests that the above formulae address only one epiphenomenon of reading and writing, not the heart

*A tray with a pole handle that is borne over one's shoulder for carrying loads, typically mortar or bricks. Hods are most likely familiar to masons.

of it. Inferred readability is unlike actual readability. Readability has to do with how readers understand texts and whether their writers can put themselves in the place of readers and make sense of their texts: together. For writers, readability formulae can at best serve as a warning that something may have to be addressed.

Measuring the Readability of Texts: The Cloze Procedure

The above formulae are analytical constructs, derived from multiple regressions of textual attributes on a criterion variable. They are used predictively, to infer not the readability of texts but various measures of it. Prediction takes place in advance of a text being read—other than by their authors. This inference implicitly assumes that the analytical construct underlying these formulae could model and represents readers in some respect. As shown above, this representation is shallow indeed.

Taylor (1953) developed a test that overcomes most of the above-mentioned shortcomings. It relies on an ability of readers that is most closely aligned with comprehension: their ability to anticipate and make sense of words from their context of use. Osgood (1959:78–88) introduced Taylor's "Cloze procedure" to the community of content analysts. The procedure is simple enough. From a text:

> *Replace,* say, every fifth word by a blank that readers can fill in. Texts with at least 50 blanks make the procedure quite reliable.
>
> *Count* the number of correct guesses of the deleted word—correct in form (no synonyms), number, person, tense, voice, and mode. Ignore differences in spelling.
>
> The *proportion* of correct guesses is the Cloze score.

Cloze scores correlate highly with the multiple-choice answers by readers and can be considered a substitute for subjective judgments of reading difficulty.

Guessing the correct words from their context of use enables readers to employ most of the abilities that the above formulae must ignore: the information provided by typography, grammar, narrative structures, readers' discursive competencies, author-reader commonalities, and changes in culture—readers are always from the present and can be chosen from the population of interest.

Scores below .35 indicate frustration, .35 to .50 assisted reading, instructional, and .50 to .60 unassisted reading (DuBay, 2004:27). The Cloze procedure does not infer readability from textual attributes; it measures the redundancy needed for reading comprehension. It relies on real people rather than regression equations. Inferences are inductive (from a sample to a population of texts + readers), not abductive (from text to the human ability to read it).

Lessons for the Content Analyst

For content analysts, the lessons from the history of readability research are as follows:

- It is important to be clear about the research questions to be answered and what is to be inferred, and to develop and empirically validate analytical constructs before applying them inferentially.

- To allow validity to accumulate. It pays to consider the categories and analytical constructs of previous research before inventing new categories whose validity is uncertain.

- Most analytical constructs have structural limitations. They reach ceilings in their ability to answer research questions, in their accuracy of the inferences they enable. Going beyond these ceilings requires structural innovations in the analytical constructs used to bridge the gap between text and what is to be inferred from it.

- Using the intellectual capabilities of readers, coders, and observers may introduce problems of reliability but can greatly enhance validity in the end.

REFERENCES

Caylor, J. S., Sticht, T. G., Fox, L. C., & Ford, J. P. (1973). *Methodologies for determining reading requirements of military occupational specialties* (Technical Report No. 73-5). Alexandra, VA: Human Resources Research Organization.

Dale, E., & Chall, J. S. (1948). A formula for predicting readability. *Educational Research Bulletin 27:*1–29, 37–54.

Dale, E., & O'Rourke, J. (1981). *The living world vocabulary: A national vocabulary inventory.* Chicago: World Book-Childcraft International.

DuBay, W. H. (2004). *The principles of readability.* Costa Mesa, CA: Impact Information. Retrieved October 25, 2006, from www.impact-information.com/impactinfo/readability02.pdf

Flesch, R. F. (1934). Estimating the comprehension difficulty of magazine articles. *Journal of General Psychology 28:*63–80.

Flesch, R. F. (1948). A new readability yardstick. *Journal of Applied Psychology 32:*221–233.

Flesch, R. F. (1950). Measuring the level of abstraction. *Journal of Applied Psychology 34:*384–390.

Fry, E. B. (1977). Fry's readability graph: Clarification, validity, and extension to level 17. *Journal of Reading 24:*242–252.

Klare, G. R. (1963). *The measurement of readability.* Ames: Iowa State University Press.

McCall, W. A., & Crabbs, L. M. (1925). *Standard test lessons in reading: Teacher's manual for all books.* New York: Bureau of Publications, Teachers College, Columbia University.

McLaughlin, G. (1969). SMOG grading: A new readability formula. *Journal of Reading 12:*639–646.

Osgood, C. E. (1959). The representational model and relevant research methods. In I. de Sola Pool (Ed.), *Trends in content analysis* (pp. 33–88). Urbana: University of Illinois Press.

Sherman, A. L. (1893). *Analytics of literature: A manual for the objective study of English prose and poetry.* Boston: Ginn & Co.

Stevens, S. S., & Stone, G. (1947). Psychological writing, easy at hand. *American Psychologist 2:*230–235.

Taylor, W. L. (1953). Cloze procedure: A new tool for measuring readability. *Journalism Quarterly 30:*415–433.

Thorndike, E. L. (1921). *The teacher's word book.* New York: Bureau of Publications, Teachers College, Columbia University.

PART 4

CODERS AND CODING

Content analysis, more than any other research method, is inextricably tied to human intellectual abilities. Even with a sample of texts available for examination, an analytical construct in place, and a system of relevant categories defined, texts must be read and translated into the terms of an analysis. There is the hope that computers will eventually "read" textual data without human involvement. Yet no matter how powerful the computer, it is impossible for any machine to "read" or interpret texts the way literate adults do. The General Inquirer, the first widely used computer system developed to code texts, needs a researcher to construct a dictionary so that the program "knows" what to categorize and how. It produces a leftover list of words whose relevance also needs to be determined by the analyst. Similarly, CATPAC requires the identification of words relevant to a research question. While a "trained" computer is extremely helpful, familiarity with the text and its context is indispensable. The most successful computer-aided content analyses rely on software for what computers do efficiently and resort to coding by literate humans for those areas where computers fail. In this section, we provide articles that conceptualize what coders can do best, offer insights for coder training, give advice on the development of coding instructions, and make suggestions on how to decide whether human coders or computers might be a better way.

Kathleen MacQueen, a researcher with the U.S. Centers for Disease Control and Prevention, used content analysis to study interview data in order to learn about individual health habits. Unlike many content analysts, she employs coders at physically different locations, making reliability a serious challenge. In her article, she describes the coding process, what the coders' job should be, and how they may best be instructed to work reliably, contributing comparable data to larger projects. Her article provides the clearest guidance for collaborative codebook development we could find, including valuable recommendations for how categories should be defined in human coders' terms.

Using transcripts of conversations among coders, Tony Hak and Ton Bernts explore how coders resolve the difficulties they encounter when coding instructions seem to be ambiguous, incomplete, or inapplicable. While the assessment of reliability needs independently working coders, conversations among them are informative for researchers to improve their coding instructions. However, Hak and Bernts also found that the pressure to reach intercoder agreement encourages coders to develop coding conventions that may not end up in the communicable coding instructions. They make clear that agreement measures cannot distinguish between the replicability of written coding instructions and ad hoc group processes, which they aptly call coder socialization. Socialization inflates intercoder agreement measures beyond the reliability they are designed to indicate.

Are computers, which are reliable by design, a better tool for coding textual matter? Gilbert Shapiro's article explores this question and firmly decides in favor of using human coders as translators of complex texts into the terms that a computer may then be able to analyze and summarize.

Brigitte Nacos compares the results of her own manual content analyses of news reports with her collaborators' use of computer coding of the same texts and comes to an assessment that is more favorable than Shapiro's. One of the coauthors of this article, David Fan, had developed a method of "successive filtration" for directional content during which coding decisions are made sequentially, using one criterion at a time, which also involves eliminating irrelevant text. Nacos et al. report that there were nontrivial differences in the results of the two methods, but the time saved by computer coding made these differences tolerable. One can conclude from this article that the success of coding by human coders and/or machines depends on the nature of the text, the availability of applicable computational resources, and the research questions pursued.

Joseph Cappella and collaborators provide an outstanding example of formulating coding instructions for a content analysis of the risks inferred from reported relationships between genetic information and health. Formulating reliable instructions is an art that can be appreciated only when one has tried and failed. The authors' coding instructions start with an admirably clear definition of the units of analysis in terms of the search terms from several search engines and some qualitative criteria that units must satisfy to be included. Then they describe the variables to be coded. Because the researchers were interested in very subtle differences, including in some ordinal scales, the categories of these variables necessitated very careful specifications of what each meant. We include only the part on framing. Incidentally, all variables yielded alpha reliabilities of 0.75 and above.

4.1

CODEBOOK DEVELOPMENT FOR TEAM-BASED QUALITATIVE ANALYSIS

KATHLEEN M. MACQUEEN, ELEANOR MCLELLAN, KELLY KAY, AND BOBBY MILSTEIN*

This paper describes (1) how a structured codebook provides a stable frame for the dynamic analysis of textual data; (2) how specific codebook features can improve inter-coder agreement among multiple researchers; and (3) the value of team-based codebook development and coding.

ORIGINS OF THE CODEBOOK FORMAT

Our codebook format evolved over the course of several years and a variety of projects. The conceptual origins took shape in 1993 during work on the Centers for Disease Control (CDC)–funded Prevention of HIV in Women and Infants Project (WIDP), which generated approximately 600 transcribed semi-structured interviews. One research question pursued was whether women's narratives about their own heterosexual behavior could help us understand general processes of change in condom-use behavior (Milstein, Lockaby, Fogarty, Cohen, & Cotton, 1998). The researchers decided to use the processes of change (POC) constructs from the Transtheoretical Model (DiClemente & Prochaska, 1985; Prochaska, 1984) as a framework for the text analysis. However, the validity of the POC constructs for condom-use behavior was unknown, and a credible and rigorous text coding strategy was needed to establish their applicability and relevance for this context.

To do this, the analysts had to synthesize all that was known about each POC construct, define what it was, what it was not, and, most importantly, learn how to recognize one in natural language. Several years earlier,

*From MacQueen, K. M., McLellan, E., Kay, K., & Milstein, B. (1998). Codebook development for team-based qualitative analysis. *Cultural Anthropology Methods 10*, 2:31–36.

O'Connell (1989) had confronted a similar problem while examining POCs in transcripts of psychotherapy sessions. Recognizing that "coding processes of change often requires that the coder infer from the statement and its context what the intention of the speaker was," O'Connell (1989:106) developed a coding manual that included a section for each code titled "Differentiating (blank) from Other Processes." Milstein and colleagues used O'Connell's "differentiation" section in a modified format in their analysis of condom behavior change narratives. They conceptualized the "differentiation" component as "exclusion criteria," which complemented the standard code definitions (which then became known as "inclusion criteria").

To facilitate on-line coding with the software program Tally (Bowyer, 1991; Trotter, 1993), components were added for the code mnemonic and a brief definition, as well as illustrative examples. Thus, the final version of the analysis codebook contained five parts: the code mnemonic, a brief definition, a full definition of inclusion criteria, a full definition of exclusion criteria to explain how the code differed from others, and example passages that illustrated how the code concept might appear in natural language. During the code application phase, information in each of these sections was supplemented and clarified (often with citations and detailed descriptions of earlier work), but the basic structure of the codebook guidelines remained stable.

A similar codebook format was used in an analysis of brief open-ended responses to a question about perceived exposure to HIV, which was included in a standardized survey of 1,950 gay and bisexual men enrolled in the CDC Collaborative HIV Seroincidence Study (MacQueen et al., 1996). For this project we needed a codebook that would facilitate coder recognition of discrete events and specific behaviors as well as the ability to distinguish statements of fact (e.g., a partner who was known to be HIV-seropositive) from statements of perception (e.g., a partner who was thought to be uninfected). More recently, we have used the structured codebook format as a key element in data management and analysis for Project LinCS: Linking Communities and Scientists, a multi-site study with over 300 transcribed in-depth interviews (MacQueen & Trotter, 1997). Thus far, we have developed seven distinct codebooks to guide and structure our use of the extensive Project LinCS database. In addition, our codebook format has been incorporated into in-house software applications for qualitative data management and analysis such as CDC EZ-Text (Carey, Wenzel, Reilly, Sheridan, & Steinberg, 1998).

Codebook Structure

The codebook structure has evolved to include six basic components: the code; a brief definition; a full definition; guidelines for when to use the code; guidelines for when not to use the code; and examples. Table 1 illustrates how the components were operationalized for a code we developed as part of an analysis of emic representations of "community" (Blanchard, 1997).

Though the structure is simple and stable, the process of building the codebook is complex and dynamic. We have found that a relational database management program such as Access® (Microsoft Corporation) is conceptually well suited for both maintaining the structure and supporting the process. In a relational database, the basic unit is the *relation,* which is generally conceptualized as a table with rows of "observations" (in our case, the codes) and columns of "attributes" (the definitional parameters for the codes). The rows and columns look like a standard quantitative data set, and the format provides all of the flexibility and automated processing typically associated with quantitative data management. However, unlike many database management systems that are specifically designed for quantitative data, the cells in a table or relation in Access can contain unlimited amounts of text. This feature makes it possible to work with the codebook as a qualitative database.

There are practical advantages to using a database management program for codebook development. First, it facilitates a systematic approach by providing a template that

Table 1 Example of a Codebook Entry

Code:	MARGIN
Brief Definition:	Marginalized community members
Full Definition:	Community groups that are negatively perceived as socially and/or physically outside the larger community structure. In marginalized groups, boundaries are imposed by others to keep "unfavorable" groups from participating in or interacting with the mainstream community groups.
When to Use:	Apply this code to all references to groups of individuals that the larger community has marginalized. These individuals or groups may be referred to as outcasts, extremists, radicals, or explicitly described as peripherals, strangers, outsiders, ostracized, bizarre, etc.
When Not to Use:	Do not use this code for reference to community groups institutionalized for health or criminal reasons (see INSTIT) or for groups that have voluntarily placed themselves on the outer boundaries of community life (see SELFMAR).
Example:	"Then you got the outcasts—drug dealers, junkies, prostitutes."

prompts for key components. Second, it facilitates the production of multiple versions of the codebook, for example, a simple listing of the codes with brief definitions for quick reference and a full version with all components for detailed reference and comparison of coding guidelines. Third, it is easy to revise the codebook and then print only the modified codes and their definitions (rather than the whole codebook). Fourth, use of a date field makes it easy to generate reports that list coding guidelines that were changed after a particular date. Fifth, the codebook can be output in a wide variety of formats including ASCII text files, spreadsheets, and other database formats. Some of these formats may then be imported directly into qualitative analysis programs such as Tally, NUD*IST (Qualitative Solutions & Research), and ATLAS/ti (Scientific Software. Development). Sixth, the fact that the codebook can be detached from other parts of the analytic database means it can easily be modified, copied, and replaced.

Last, but not least, a codebook expressed as a relation or table in a relational database can, in turn, be linked to other codebook tables. This allows the analyst to define directional links between sets of codes and add new dimensions to the relationships among codes. For example, hierarchical relationships can be defined such that a single code in one table is linked to a series of related codes in another table (a "one-to-many" relationship). Hierarchical relationships can be used to create families of codes (Muhr, 1994) that can be aggregated, reviewed and analyzed at increasingly general levels. Thus, the scale of analysis can be easily and systematically modified. Alternatively, a set of codes in one table may have multiple links to those in other tables, forming a "many-to-many" relationship. In this case, the code relationships can be summarized as a network. Both hierarchical and network linkages can be portrayed graphically.

In our approach, the codebook functions as a frame or boundary that the analyst constructs in order to systematically map the informational terrain of the text. The codebook may or may not reflect "natural" boundaries for the terrain, but it always reflects the analyst's implicit or explicit research questions. It forces the analyst to place his or her assumptions and biases in plain view. The codes, in turn, function like coordinates on the map frame; when applied to the text, they link features in the text (e.g., words, sentences, and dialog) to the analyst's constructs. The adequacy of answers to research questions can then be assessed in terms of the sensitivity and specificity of the codes, the richness of the text, and the validity and reliability of the links established among them. From this perspective, the central challenge of systematic qualitative analysis lies within the coding process.

The Coding Process

As Bernard (1994:193) points out, a code can be used as an encryption, indexing, or measurement device; we focus on using index codes to tag text for retrieval and measurement codes to assign values to text such as the frequency, amount, or presence/absence of information (Bernard, 1994; Bernard & Ryan, 1998; Seidel & Kelle, 1995). In both cases, the code adds information to the text (rather than reducing the text) through a process of interpretation that simultaneously breaks the text down into meaningful chunks or segments. Thus, the coding process must include explicit guidelines for defining the boundaries of the text associated with a particular code. How the text is segmented is influenced by the data collection strategy and the way that strategy structures the resulting text. Data collection strategies generally fall along a continuum from minimally structured (e.g., transcribed interviews) to maximally structured (e.g., brief responses to open-ended survey questions).

With large databases comprised of in-depth transcribed interviews, we find it useful to begin by coding text according to the specific research questions used to frame the interview; we label this type of index coding as Stage 1 or *structural coding.* The purpose of this step is to facilitate subsequent analysis by identifying all of the text associated with a particular elicitation or research question. The code inclusion criteria can include linguistic cues that signal the coder to apply structural codes to text that is out of sequence with the original interview structure. This is important for situations where respondents spontaneously return to earlier topics or make a cognitive leap to a topic that the interviewer intended to cover later. With regard to segmenting the text for structural coding, we find it useful to include within each segment the full elicitation from the interviewer and the full response from the participant, including all dialogs between the interviewer and participant that flow from the elicitation. This preserves both the flow of the interview and the full context of the discussion on a particular topic.

Structural coding generally results in the identification of large segments of text on broad topics; these segments can then form the basis for an in-depth analysis within or across topics. We have found that code definitions that incorporate substantial references to professional jargon (i.e., etic codes) tend to encourage the use of coders' preconceptions in the analysis, making it difficult to distinguish the text (or "voice") of the respondent from that of the analyst or researcher. In contrast to structural coding, we therefore attempt to use respondents' own terms and semantics to guide the construction of codes and their definitions for in-depth analysis (i.e., emic codes). In addition, the use of linguistic cues to assist coders in correctly applying codes to text tends to reduce the potential for misinterpretation and omission of relevant information.

For example, in one of our projects we created three socioeconomic class status codes (poor, middle class, and rich) to measure the salience of socioeconomic class for the way individuals perceived the structure of their community. This was based on an etic or "objective" viewpoint. However, these codes did not capture the more subjective viewpoint of the participants, who often described the financial status of others relative to their own, e.g., richer, poorer, "those with more money." The etic codes and definitions also led the coders to make implicit assumptions about education, employment, access to resources, and basic living conditions that were not always supported in the text. We therefore eliminated the etic codes with their implicit assumptions about social conditions and used a single code to capture all references to income levels and socioeconomic class, with additional codes to capture explicit references to homelessness and employment status.

Text segmentation during in-depth analysis is less straightforward than during structural coding. A coded segment could be as simple as a text marker or tag placed over a word or phrase, with the boundaries of the segment free floating; in this case, the segment can be continuously redefined during analysis to include only the word, a set number of lines above and below the word, or the full text document. Alternatively, rules for bounding segments can be established a priori, e.g., through use of textual units such as sentences or grammatical guidelines such as requiring the inclusion of subject references.

With brief responses to open-ended questions on standardized surveys there is generally little need to develop structural codes because the data are pre-structured by question and participant. Here the goal is to code the text in such a way that the information can be combined meaningfully with a quantitative database. The codes are used primarily to signal the presence or absence of particular pieces of information. The open-ended responses can then be summarized in a 0/1 matrix where the rows are labeled with participant identification numbers and the columns with the codes; the cells are filled with either a "0" (to indicate that the information was not present) or a "1" (to indicate that it was present). For example, Table 2 presents a matrix for a hypothetical group of responses to a question concerning how persons think they may have been exposed to HIV. It would also be possible to attach values to the codes, for example, the MULTPARTS code could be valued to reflect the total number of partners that a person reported (provided that information is available from the data).

In order to facilitate quantitative analysis of open-ended responses it is generally advisable to limit the total number of codes to be used. However, this can easily be done by collapsing code categories together through data transformations performed on the matrix. The final code categories can be built into the coding process through the use of hierarchical codes and code families. Such a strategy is preferable to limiting the content of the codebook a priori only to find that the resulting codes are too crude to permit a meaningful analysis.

Between the examples discussed above (transcribed interviews and open-ended survey questions) lies a range of other possibilities. For example, rather than record and transcribe interviews verbatim, researchers may take notes and then organize their notes according to specific research topics. Although the elicitation is relatively unstructured, the resulting text is highly structured and presegmented by research topic. Another possibility would be the collection of open-ended responses on a single question across multiple waves of structured interviews with the same individuals. The responses from each wave could be compiled into a single textual response for each individual that permits segmentation by recurrent themes as well as by interview wave.

Table 2 Examples of Coded Responses From a Structured Survey Question "How Do You Think You Were Exposed to HIV?"

		Codes				
ID	*Response*	*ANON*	*MULTPARTS*	*ANAL*	*EJAC*	*PERCEV+*
101	"Had anal sex with a guy I think was infected and he ejaculated."	0	0	1	1	1
102	"Had a lot of partners, some of them I don't know. I'm worried about HIV in ejaculate."	1	1	0	1	0
103	"Been exposed to ejaculate from 2 or 3 different partners."	0	1	0	1	0

The analysis of other types of text such as field notes, diaries, and newsletters each presents their own challenges and possibilities. The issues of data collection and text segmentation as elements in the coding process are complicated and deserve further systematic exploration.

Refining the Codebook

Before coding an entire data set, we systematically evaluate the utility of the codes and the coders' ability to apply the codes in a consistent manner. The steps in this process begin with the development of an initial code list derived from etic concepts, emic themes, or both (Figure 1). Usually, one or two team members take a lead role in developing the list, which is then reviewed by the full research team (Figure 1). Once there is agreement on the scope and level of detail for the items in the list, the team leaders begin the process of codebook development. Definitions are proposed and reviewed by the team, with an emphasis on achieving clarity and explicit guidance for code application.

When the team is comfortable with the code definitions, two or more coders are then given the task of independently coding the same sample of text. The results of their coding are then compared for consistency of text segmentation and code application. If the results are acceptable and consistent, the coding continues with periodic checks for continued inter-coder agreement. If the results are unacceptable and inconsistent, the inconsistencies are reviewed by the coders and team leader(s).

The codebook is reviewed to determine whether the inconsistencies are due to coder error, e.g., misunderstanding of terminology or guidelines. We view these as training errors and they are generally handled by the coders and team leader(s). Other inconsistencies are due to problems with the code definitions, e.g., overlapping or ambiguous inclusion criteria that make it difficult to distinguish between two codes. These types of problems are generally discussed by the whole team, as they have implications for the interpretation of the text. Once the problems are identified and the codebook clarified, all previously coded text is reviewed and, if necessary, recoded so that it is consistent with the revised definitions. Intercoder agreement is again checked, to ensure that the new guidelines have resolved the problem. This iterative coding process continues until all text has been satisfactorily coded.

There are a variety of ways that inter-coder agreement can be assessed. For transcribed interviews, we generally prefer a detailed segment-by-segment review that includes assessments of consistency in defining the beginning and end of segments as well as the application of codes within segments. All inconsistencies are noted, discussed, and resolved. When only a sub-sample of the text is coded by multiple coders, this strategy may not capture all coding errors. In particular, it is prone toward the loss of pertinent text, that is, text that is not captured by any code. Erroneously captured text, in contrast, is more likely to be spotted during the course of either coding checks or subsequent analysis.

We also use kappa to statistically assess the level of inter-coder agreement.* This approach is useful for identifying coder error, as long as the error is not due to systematic mistraining of all coders. It is also helpful for identifying poorly defined codes, which tend to be applied erratically.

Some Practical Suggestions

We have learned eight practical lessons from our experience with team-based codebook development and application.

1. Assign primary responsibility to one person for creating, updating, and revising a given codebook. This will ensure that the codebook is consistent, and it will minimize ambiguities due to differences in vocabulary and writing styles. Require all members of the coding team to clear all coding questions and clarifications with the codebook editor. Make certain that the codebook editor has the basic competence for the task.

*For a critique of this statistic, see reading 6.2, this volume.

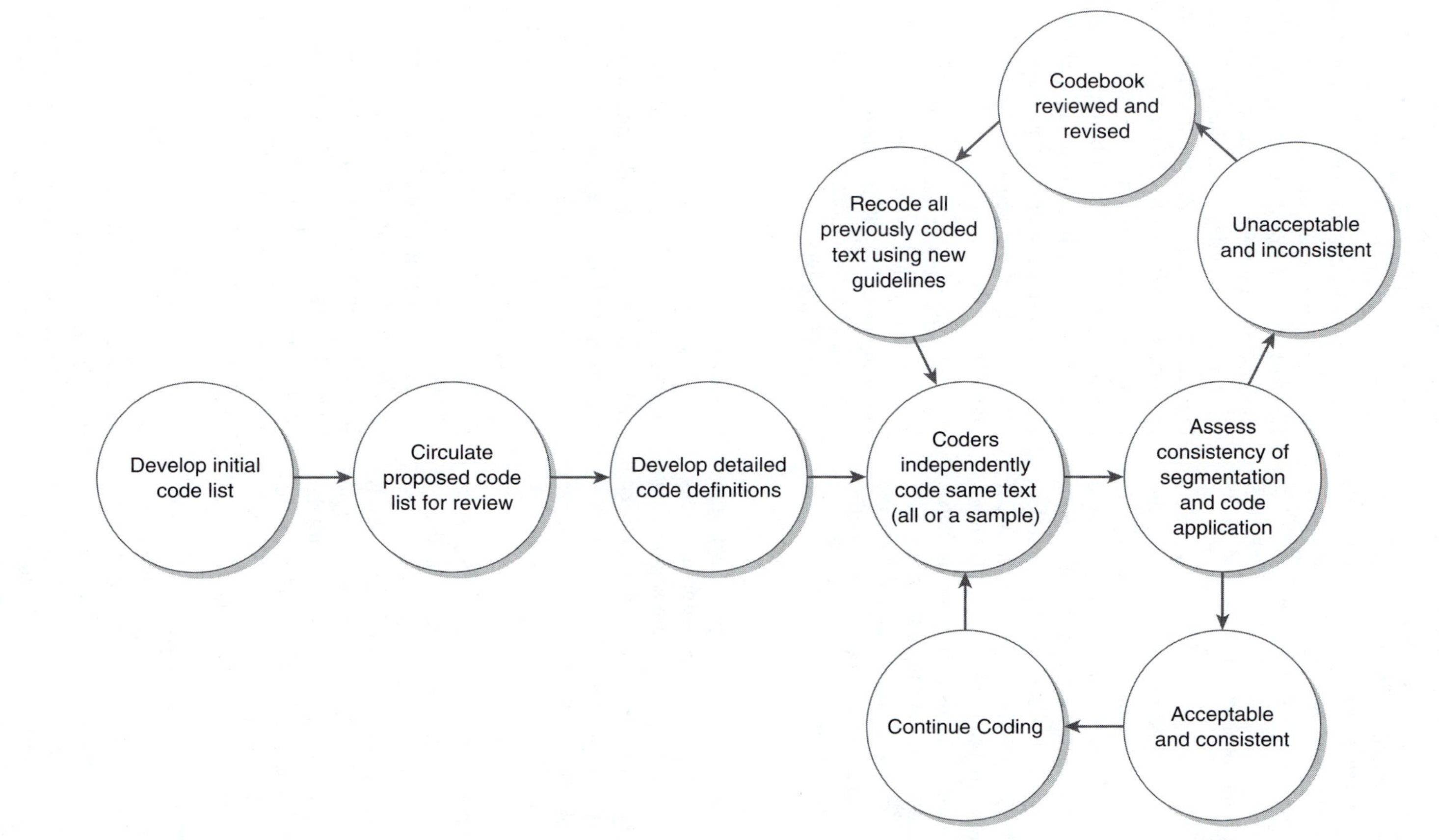

Figure 1 Testing and Refining the Codebook

2. Schedule regular meetings where the coding team reviews each code and definition in the codebook. It is easy for a coder to develop a set of implicit rules without realizing that the codebook no longer reflects his or her actual coding process; in addition, this evolving process mayor may not be shared by other members of the coding team. Without regular review sessions, the codebook can quickly become obsolete and useless as an analytic tool.

3. Establish a coding process that consciously seeks to enhance inter-coder agreement. One way to do this is to create a codebook that someone can learn to use within few hours. For the most part, coders can only handle 30–40 codes at one time. If the codebook contains more than 40 codes, the coding process needs to be done in stages. Separate the codebook into three or four related components or domains and have the coders apply one set of codes to the entire data set before moving on to the next set.

4. Develop a written plan for segmenting text at the same time the codebook is being developed. Segmenting complex text into smaller natural units, such as a line or a sentence, may be helpful. If you are segmenting less than a sentence, it may be better to utilize a word-based content analysis strategy than a codebook strategy. Of course, the word-based strategy can evolve into codebook development.

5. Establish inter-coder agreement measures early in the process of codebook development. Decide a priori how much variability you are willing to permit with regard to both segmentation and code application, and how you will assess that variability. Make sure the coding team understands and agrees with the criteria, and that coding will not be considered final until those criteria are met.

6. When defining codes, do not assume that anything is obvious; always state specifically what the code should and should not capture. This includes defining common abbreviations and "shorthand" references that may occur in the text. Include all such information in the full definition of the code and explanations for its use. Things that seem obvious to coders at a certain place and time can be totally obscure in another.

7. Don't clutter the codebook with deadwood: throw out codes that do not work, and rework definitions for codes that are problematic. Some codes may capture the specificity of a single response rather than general patterns and themes. It is best to eliminate these types of codes from the codebook or expand their usage. A single generic code (e.g., UNIQUE) can be designed to capture all unique responses on a given topic. The codebook should be a distillation, not an historical document. If maintaining a history of the codebook development process is relevant, then develop a separate strategy for that purpose.

8. Finally, accept the fact that text will need to be recoded as the codebook is refined. Recoding should not be viewed as a step back; it is always indicative of forward movement in the analysis.

Conclusion

The interdisciplinary team-based approach to qualitative analysis at CDC has provided us with both the incentive and the resources to develop explicit guidelines for and documentation of our methods. For coding, this has led to the generation of a basic structure for organizing codebooks that is also flexible enough to meet the needs of a variety of coding situations. When combined with an informed discussion of the coding process, the use of a flexible yet standard structure facilitates coder training. It also enhances the analyst's ability to transfer skills from one project to another, regardless of variability in the particular software tools used.

References

Bernard, H. R. (1994). *Research methods in anthropology: Qualitative and quantitative approaches* (2nd ed.). Walnut Creek, CA: AltaMira Press.

Bernard, H. R., & Ryan, G. (1998). Qualitative and quantitative methods of text analysis. In H. R. Bernard (Ed.), *Handbook of research methods in cultural anthropology.* Walnut Creek, CA: AltaMira Press.

Blanchard, L. (1997, November). *How do you define community? Perspectives of community members.* Paper presented at the American Anthropological Association Annual Meeting, Washington, DC.

Bowyer, J. W. (1991). *Tally: A text analysis tool for the liberal arts.* Dubuque, IA: William C. Brown Publishers.

Carey, J. W., Wenzel, P. H., Reilly, C., Sheridan, J., & Steinberg, J. M. (1998). CDC EZ-Text: Software for collection, management, and analysis of semi-structured qualitative data sets. *Cultural Anthropological Methods 10,*1:14–20.

DiClemente, C. C., & Prochaska, J. O. (1985). Processes and stages of self-change: Coping and competence in smoking behavior change. In S. Schiffinan & T.A. Wills (Eds.), *Coping and substance abuse* (pp. 319–343). New York: Academic Press.

MacQueen, K. M., Kay, K. L., Bartholow, B. N., et al. (1996, July). *The relationship between perceived exposure to HIV and actual risk in a cohort of gay and bisexual men.* Poster presentation at the XI International Conference on AIDS, Vancouver, Canada.

MacQueen, K. M., & Trotter, R. T. (1997, November). *Project LinCS: A multisite ethnographic design for public health research.* Paper presented at the American Anthropological Association Annual Meeting, Washington DC.

Milstein, B., Lockaby, T., Fogarty, L., Cohen, A., & Cotton, D. (1998). Women's processes of behavior change for condom use. *Journal of Health Psychology 3,*3:349–368.

Muhr, T. (1994). *ATLAS-ti—computer aided text interpretation & theory building: Release 1.1E. User's Manual* (2nd ed.). Berlin: Thomas Muhr.

O'Connell, D. (1989). *Development of a change process coding system.* Ph.D. dissertation, University of Rhode Island, Kingston.

Prochaska, J. O. (1984). *Systems of psychotherapy: A transtheoretical analysis* (2nd ed.). Homewood, IL: Dorsey Press.

Seidel, J., & Kelle, U. (1995). Different functions of coding in the analysis of textual data. In U. Kelle (Ed.), *Computer-aided qualitative data analysis: Theory, methods, and practice* (pp. 52–61). Thousand Oaks, CA: Sage Publications.

Trotter, R. T. (1993). Review of TALLY 3.0. *Cultural Anthropological Methods 5,* 2:10–12.

4.2

Coder Training

Explicit Instruction and Implicit Socialization?

Tony Hak and Ton Bernts*

Introduction

Coder training is a standard procedure in sociology, in particular when a method of content analysis is used. Although methodological studies and textbooks on methods provide instructions regarding coder training, there is no *empirical* evidence of what coder training consists of in practice. This, we think, is the corollary of another gap in our empirical knowledge of sociological practice, namely coding itself. Little is known of coding problems encountered and solved in everyday sociological practice. The literature describes coder training primarily as a procedure for improving the study's inter-coder reliability by means of theoretical instruction and practical advice. It is doubtful, however, whether these instructions provide the basis for the actual practice of coder training. This doubt arises from the scarce empirical literature on the coding process (Cicourel, 1964; Garfinkel, 1967; Katz & Sharrock, 1976; Rehbein & Mazeland, 1991) which suggests that coding decisions are very complex interpretive activities that can be learned only to a limited degree through training. Although it seems reasonable to suppose that some knowledge about the coding process must be available to the trainer before training can be provided, in fact this knowledge does not exist. Coding is, in the words of Rehbein and Mazeland (1991:166), "a very specific form of linguistic action of which almost nothing is known. Often it will be practiced intuitively. It is, thus, a complex blind spot in the analysis of scientific communication." It is the substantive focus of this paper to describe coding and coder training as 'a specific form of linguistic action.'

Describing some fundamental features of coding practices leads directly to a criticism of how coding and coder training are dealt with in textbooks on methods and in sociological practice. Lack of systematic knowledge

*From Hak, T., & Bernts, T. (1996). Coder training: Theoretical training or practical socialization? *Qualitative Sociology 19*, 2:235–257.

of coding problems and how these are solved relates intrinsically to a lack of knowledge of how the quality of the coded data can be assessed and improved. The effectiveness of coder training as a means to improve the inter-coder reliability is usually considered a result of (successfully) communicating the coding scheme to coders. In this paper we present fragments of a transcript of a coder training that demonstrate that inter-coder reliability improves not only (or even not primarily) through communicating the coding instructions to coders (*theoretical training*) but also by *socializing* coders into practical rules which are not part of the coding instructions and hence are not warranted by them. This finding suggests that, in practice, coding decisions are less well-controlled than generally assumed in research reports. This is the methodological focus of this paper.

The problem for coding and for coder training is summarized by Mishler (1986:4):

> Because meaning is contextually grounded, inherently and irremediably, coding depends on the competence of coders as ordinary language users. Their task is to determine the 'meaning' of an isolated response to an isolated question, that is, to code a response that has been stripped of its natural social context.

Having noted that there is considerable individual variation in frames of reference, values, and levels of understanding, Mishler states that

> . . . the actual work of coding cannot be done reliably until coders build up a set of shared assumptions, specific to the study, that allow them to implement the code in a mutually consistent way. The development of such a coder's subculture is the most significant by-product of training and periodic reliability checks of coders. Often these assumptions are ad hoc, reflect coders' everyday understandings and competences as language users, and tend to remain tacit in the research process (1986:4).

It is this coder's subculture, usually remaining tacit in the research process, which we want to discover and describe in the case study presented here.

The Quality of Coded Data

The quality of assigned codes—for answers to open-ended questions in our case; see below—depends on two values: validity and (inter-coder) reliability. The *validity* of the coding process is the degree to which the theoretically relevant features of the answers are represented in the codes. The quality of the relation between the answers and the codes, however, cannot be discovered in a way that is independent of coding itself. It is precisely the aim of coding to establish whether, and how, a theoretically relevant feature is observable in the answer. This means that the validity of the coding process and of the resulting codes cannot be determined in an independent way. Validity is a matter of *argumentation.*[1,*]

In contrast to validity, (inter-coder) reliability can be assessed easily, without any reference to the substance of the coding process. It is possible to assess unequivocally whether a coding of an answer is identical to another coding of the same answer, whether done at another time by the same coder or at the same time by another coder. Inter-coder reliability can, thus, be established and discussed without any reference to actual features of the coding process. Reliability is a matter of *computation.***

---

*In their endnote, the authors include statistical correlations with other variables (see also readings 4.1 and 5.4, this volume) as a form of argumentation. A more direct criterion for the validity of recorded, categorized, or transcribed textual data is "semantic validity." See Krippendorff, K. (2004:323–330). *Content analysis: An introduction to its methodology* (2nd ed.). Thousand Oaks, CA: Sage.

**It is important not to confuse the measurable *intercoder agreement* with *reliability.* Reliability is inferred from agreement, not observed as such. The reliability of interest in content analysis is reproducibility, which is the *raison d'être* for using multiple coders. To infer the reproducibility of the explicit coding instructions elsewhere, coders must be demonstrably replaceable and work independently of each other and under diverse conditions, often at different locations, having gone through a specific (repeatable) course of training and following the same instructions (see reading 6.2, this volume).

Usually the validity of the coding process is considered dependent on the quality of the coding *instructions,* i.e. on the quality of the researcher's argumentation, whereas inter-coder reliability is considered dependent on coders' *application* of these instructions. According to the literature, . . . reliability can be improved by . . . coding in pairs of coders, developing more detailed instructions, selecting professional coders (e.g., the researcher's colleagues or graduate students) and, last but not least, coder training. It is remarkable, however, that this literature gives hardly any instruction about the way a coder training must be organized in order to have the required effect.[2] When the inter-coder reliability* has been improved through coder training, this result is usually interpreted as an effect of the improved quality of the study's concepts and their operationalization, *and* of the coders' improved understanding of the meaning of the concepts. This improvement is considered as the result of *theoretical* training resulting in a more consistent interpretation of the coding instructions. This is, to give only one example, the presupposition of the following remark in a textbook: "any discrepancies will indicate an imperfect communication of your coding scheme to your coders" (Babbie, 1989:360).

Two comments can be made here. First, the literature does not recognize sources of coding discrepancies other than coders' inability to interpret the instructions adequately. It thus, presupposes that it is possible, even necessary, that the researcher can make the coding instructions sufficiently transparent for allowing an unequivocal coding of each answer. This presupposition, however, neglects the fact that coders not only must interpret the coding instructions but the answers as well. Second, although this is less obvious, it is assumed that the absence of discrepancies in codes (i.e., when inter-coder reliability is high) guarantees that the assigned codes are warranted by the coding instructions. The fact that two coders assign the same code is assumed to be a sufficient guarantee that the researcher himself, coding the same answer according to his instructions, would have chosen that same code. Having the same coding result is thus considered as evidence of theoretical soundness. In this way inter-coder reliability functions implicitly as a measure of validity: when the coding *instructions are valid* (that is, when the instructions are theoretically warranted) and when the coding process produces *reliable codes,* it is assumed that these reliable codes are the result of a *valid application* of the instructions.

It is, however, quite possible that a high degree of inter-coder reliability is the result of a training artifact in Muskens' (1980:124–126) sense: "Artifacts are outcomes of those practices, inherent to a variety of distinct levels of a research design and its execution, which lead to distortions in the data, and thus to unmonitored conclusions about reality. . . ."

The possibility, hypothesized by Muskens, that the ultimate agreement between coders . . . is an *artifact* and yields *invalid data,* forms our methodological focus for the following empirical case study of what coder training in practice consists. Our question is whether in this case inter-coder reliability is improved by theoretical instruction only (which is the received wisdom of textbooks though it has not been studied empirically), and whether this is done in a way that is theoretically sound. . . . Our research question therefore, is: *Does coder training consist only of training in the correct application of the coding instructions (theoretical training) or also of coders' socialization into practical rules, which are not warranted, by the coding instructions?*

Method of This Study

In the course of a study of opinions on equity in health care (Bernts, 1991) the authors assisted in the coding of answers to an open-ended question. Bernts' study consisted of a survey of a representative sample of Dutch households. Respondents were asked to

*Evidently, here as well as in the following, the authors accept intercoder *agreement* as the criterion for successful coder training, not reliability—see previous footnote. We invite the reader to read "intercoder agreement" when the authors speak of "reliability."

answer a series of (closed-ended) questions on preferences regarding sanctions in health care (e.g., differential treatment of smokers and non-smokers) and attitudes to health, health risks and health care. . . . One of the attitudes assessed was the *definition of health,* a variable that was conceived as an indication of the *demand* side of health care. It was expected that definitions of health as a means to personal creativity (*expressive* definitions) would be correlated with a low degree of risk-solidarity in health care (e.g., by differentiating health insurance premiums according to lifestyle), whereas *instrumental* definitions of health (as a means to being able to do one's work) would be connected with high risk-solidarity.

The respondents' definitions of health were [obtained] . . . by an open-ended question derived from a French study (d'Houtaud, 1978). The (Dutch) question was a translation of its English version: "What is, according to you, the best definition of health?" (d'Houtaud & Field, 1984:34). It was expected that the answers could be coded unequivocally as either belonging to the class of expressive definitions of health or to the class of instrumental definitions. However, an initial attempt by Bernts to categorize answers as either 'expressive' or 'instrumental' failed, mainly because many answers appeared to consist of multiple parts whose sense could differ in terms of expressivity and instrumentality. Therefore, he developed a multidimensional coding scheme (see Appendix) in which definitions of health are considered as answers to three questions:

— how does one perceive health? (CRITERION)[3]

— how does one get or maintain health? (MEANS)

— what is the value or the aim of health? (VALUE)

A respondent's statement may entail an answer to all three questions, but often it answers only one or two of them. Within the broad category of CRITERION, Bernts distinguishes three aspects: SIGN (is the definition positive, negative, or both?), POINT OF VIEW (is it subjective or objective?), DOMAIN (is it physical, or more than that?).

It is important to note that these categories and their classes have a direct relation to the theory on 'instrumental' and 'expressive' definitions of health, which is explicitly discussed by the researcher in a note to the instructions (see at the bottom of the Appendix): "A 'positive' SIGN, a 'mental' DOMAIN, a 'subjective' POINT OF VIEW, a 'harmonious' MEANS and a 'growth' VALUE are taken as indicative of an *expressive* definition of health. A 'negative' SIGN, a 'physical' DOMAIN, an 'objective' POINT OF VIEW, a 'preventive' MEANS and a 'work' VALUE are taken as indicative of an *instrumental* definition of health."

The training procedure was as follows. The researcher first gave the coders the instructions with no formal introduction: The researcher and two coders then coded about 40 (out of 800) answers in order to test their ability to use the coding instructions. It appeared that many answers were assigned different codes. This presented sufficient reason for the researcher to organize a meeting in which these differences were discussed. In that meeting, the coding instructions were explained and additional coding rules were formulated. A second coding of the same answers, however, resulted again in many differences between coders. In a second meeting, even more detailed instructions were formulated. This resulted eventually in a sufficiently high inter-coder reliability (more than 95% identical codes between pairs of coders, over all 800 answers). The process described, consisting of two rounds of coding each followed by a meeting in which coding decisions and coding instructions were discussed, has all the features that, according to the literature, are characteristic for coder training. Therefore, an analysis of these two meetings (which both were tape recorded and transcribed for analysis) can illuminate the practice of coder training.

We are interested, first, in how coding discrepancies are discussed and how agreement is sought and achieved. Second, we are interested in whether achieved agreement (on the correct coding of a specific answer) affects how other answers will be coded, either because the agreement entails a clarification or a specification of the coding instructions (theoretical training) or because it implies the application of rather informal rules (practical socialization). Our starting-point is that the purpose of this coder training was to improve the inter-coder reliability and that this was achieved. Our effort then is to determine how this was achieved and whether the way it was achieved had effects pertinent to the theory that underlies the coding instructions.

STRATEGIES IN CODER TRAINING

Our assumption that only matters of inter-coder reliability (and not matters of theoretical soundness) would be discussed in the coder training was confirmed in the transcript. When the three coders had coded an answer in the same way, the code itself was never a matter of discussion. Extract 1 gives some examples.[4]

Extract 1

Researcher:	uh 2502 . . . is a . . . 3
Coder l:	yes
Coder 2:	that's what I have too
Researcher:	2511 is a 4
Coder 1:	yes
Researcher:	2522 is a 2 of MEANS
Coder 1 & 2:	yes
Researcher:	3041 is a 3
Coder 2:	yes
Coder 1:	yes

This extract shows that the quality of a code is not a matter of discussion when coders agree on what the correct code is. Coders only check whether they agree; they do not check, at least not explicitly, whether the agreed code is warranted by the coding instructions. In our transcript we do not find any exception to this rule that there is discussion between coders only in those cases in which at least one coder had coded differently. This documents our assumption that an apparently reliable code is considered to be theoretically correct.

The Interpretation of Answers

There is a necessary preliminary stage in the coding process, which is not covered by the coding instructions, a stage in which an answer's 'sense' or a respondent's 'intention' is to be assessed. A coder's reading of an answer's sense cannot be controlled, because it is dependent on the coder's (non-professional) lifeworld. Interpretive problems in this stage cannot be solved by consulting the coding instructions, nor for that matter by the theory underlying the instructions. When the coders encounter a discrepancy in their coding of an answer, the first question attended to is how the difference can be explained. This implies that the coders must give accounts for the codes they have given. These accounts will be discussed, and that discussion will eventually lead to an agreement between coders on the correct reading of the answer's sense. There is, however, no coder *training* in a strict sense. In these cases, there is neither a specification of the instructions nor a formulation of rules for future cases. The reason is that there is no other useful device available than members' everyday methods of making sense, which hardly can be influenced by instruction.

An example is presented in Extract 2. The answer discussed here is "Not going to the doctor too often, determining yourself what is good and . . . what isn't," and the problem is that the coders do not agree on what this answer *means*. The Researcher and Coder 2 interpret the answer as a description of a MEANS to improve and maintain health: Coder 1, in contrast, refers to everyday talk in which 'going to the doctor' is seen as a CRITERION of 'having complaints.' In the discussion, the researcher accounts for his code by referring to everyday talk as well: "For instance there is the saying 'if you go to the doctor too often they talk you into all sorts of disorders' isn't it?" In his interpretation, 'not going to the doctor too often' is not a manifestation of the absence of complaints (a CRITERION) but rather of a MEANS to maintain health. Thus, both refer to everyday talk in order to account for their interpretation of the answer:

Extract 2

Researcher:	this is a 1 of MEANS; harmony with the environment
Coder 1:	I have something quite different.
Researcher:	yes, what is your code?
Coder 1:	I had a . . . uh . . . CRITERION because I consider 'not going to

	the doctor too often' as absence of complaints and 'determining yourself what is good and what isn't' I consider as uuh vitality so that is VALUE 1.
Researcher:	well I think that it is dubious . . . I think that it is both a CRITERION and a MEANS because for instance there is the saying 'if you go to the doctor too often they talk you into all sorts of disorders,' isn't it
Coder 1:	yes but . . . 'determining yourself what is good and what isn't' . . . you read it, as not allowing the doctor to determine what happens
Researcher:	precisely.
Coder 1:	yes, yes . . . oh yes then then I do not consider it as a CRITERION any more no . . . no then I consider it a MEANS indeed yes . . . yes I agree completely on that . . . then it becomes clearly something different from 'not going to the doctor too often'
Researcher:	yes, so it is a MEANS . . . yes?
Coder 1:	Yes.

Eventually, the researcher's interpretation is accepted by Coder 1. The reason is not that there is a better fit between the researcher's quote ("They talk you into all sorts of disorders") and the answer 'not going to the doctor too often' than between the coder's quote and the answer. The superiority of the researcher's proposal is that it allows for assigning only one code to the answer (Coder 1: "Yes but . . . 'determining yourself what is good and what isn't' . . . you read it as not allowing the doctor to determine what happens.").

This extract, thus, shows how an initial difference of interpretation has been resolved. The means used to establish agreement consisted of (a) paraphrasing the answer in such a way that both parts of the answer could be read as versions of one underlying pattern ("Doctors talk you into all sorts of disorders") and (b) claiming that the underlying pattern can be attributed to respondents ("There is a saying . . ."). It must be emphasized that analytically this disagreement and its solution have no relation whatever to the coding instructions. Although the problem can only arise because of the requirement to make a distinction between two kinds of definitions of health, MEANS and CRITERION, the problem is not one of the application of these categories. The problem is rather one of determining the sense of an answer, which is independent of the coding process proper. This explains why the presented discussion resulted neither in a specification of the coding instructions nor in a formulation of rules for future cases. The problem is, thus, considered restricted to that particular answer only, and hence as unique.

This confirms Garfinkel's (1967:19–20)* observation that coders must *ad hoc* in order to determine an answer's sense. *Ad hocing* consists of finding an (*ad hoc*) rule that in one way or another can account for the decision made. Because that rule cannot be found in the coding instructions, it is the coder who must provide it. In the example above, the coding decision is accounted for by invoking the *ad hoc* rule that an answer is coherent and consistent and that, therefore, one code for the answer is preferable to two codes, one for each of the two parts of the answer. This is the only reason why the paraphrase "If you go to the doctor too often they talk you into all sorts of disorders," is preferred. It is clear, however, that the application of this economy rule is neither part of the coding instructions nor can be grounded in the respondent's intentions.

It goes without saying that the problem that an answer's sense is indeterminate is partly due to the fact that answers (in this study) have been isolated from the context in which they were given, i.e. the setting in which the respondent has answered the questionnaire. That the coders are conscious of the absence of the natural context is apparent from the fact that coders sometimes explicitly mention that answers could have been interpreted more easily if more information had been available about the respondent.

An example is the discussion in Extract 3 about the interpretation of the answer "Feeling well and being able to move easily." It is discussed whether 'being able to move

---

*See reading 2.1, this volume, on ad hocing.

easily' is only a CRITERION ('being able to move well' as a manifestation of good health) or a VALUE ('being able to move well' as an aim for which one needs good health) as well. In this discussion, it is mentioned that knowing the respondent's age would have been of help in determining the sense of the answer. Similarly, to the previous example, the problem is solved by choosing the alternative by which the complete answer can be covered by one code, although the researcher considers this a low quality solution. He would have preferred a solution in which the respondent's age had been decisive.

Extract 3

Researcher: this is a CRITERION . . . 'feeling well and being able to move easily.'

Coder 1: yes . . . I have put also a VALUE 1 . . . look . . . similar to 'hard work' isn't it? . . . and so here 'to move' . . . we have decided that hard work that if . . . if the category VALUE can be used too. . .

Researcher: shall I . . . shall I just look what is the respondent's age «laughing»? If he is 75, then it probably must be a CRITERION

Coder 2: «laughing loudly»

Coder 1: I consider it a CRITERION . . . but I think . . . the point is . . . is it a requirement to use the category VALUE?

Researcher: Yes I see, but if it is a CRITERION, 'being able to move easily,' then it becomes clear . . . so it is meant explicitly . . . as uh that one is able to rise from a chair easily and the like

Coder 2: «still laughing»

Coder 1: oh yeah yeah, you mean yeah

Researcher: 'being able to move easily' . . . it may mean . . . I am still able to walk to the cupboard without too much pain

Coder 1: yes

Researcher: or does the respondent mean moving easily . . . in social relations . . . so it is necessary to know whether the respondent is 25 . . . such a person would probably mean another thing than a person of 65.

Coder 1: I do agree that strictly speaking it is not uh . . .VALUE . . . it is an addition to the CRITERION.

Researcher: I too, I think that it is meant that way

Coder 1: Yes.

Researcher: Let's make a joke; let's look what is his age. . .

Coder 1: yes . . . I agree . . . but don't do that . . . then you introduce circular reasoning . . . then you will find later on that a CRITERION is mentioned more often by the elderly. Yes, that is only because you have coded it that way.

In the examples given, the researcher does not attempt to instruct the coders about how to determine the sense of answers. The obvious reason is that there is no other useful device available than members' everyday methods of making sense, which hardly can be influenced by the researcher in a coder training. In these examples, therefore, there is no coder *training* in a strict sense. The only thing achieved, besides an agreement on the coding of these answers, is that it is demonstrated that an economy rule can be used in order to improve inter-coder reliability. Decisions in these kinds of cases can be influenced neither by instructions nor by training. Because different readings of the same answer are equally defensible, there is no way out of *ad hocing.*

Theoretical Training

The coding process consists of two different stages. After the stage in which an answer's sense is determined (see *The Interpretation of Answers* above), this sense has to be connected to a coding category. Whereas the everyday interpretive means used in the first stage cannot be influenced (let alone be improved) by instructions, the procedures used in this second stage are open to training. In the extracts presented below it is shown how the discussion functions as 'training.' The theory underlying the coding instructions is explained and the coding instructions themselves are specified. Because these specifications are the joint product of the coders, it is likely that they will be applied in a more or less consistent way by different coders. This results in an improvement of inter-coder reliability. The specifications are correct to the degree that the researcher relates the specifications to his theory. Thus, the application of coding instructions to the 'sense' of answers can be 'trained' and this can be done in a way that does not damage, but instead can enhance, the quality of the coding process. Take the following example. We have seen in Extract 2 how the researcher and coder 1 agreed on interpreting the answer "Not going to the doctor too much" as the expression of a MEANS to maintain health. But, which of the codes within the category MEANS has to be chosen now? Extract 4, which is the continuation of Extract 2, shows how the coders find a solution to this problem. The coding instructions provide for three kinds of MEANS, 'harmony with the environment,' 'prevention/hygiene' and 'other means.' Coder 2 denies that; the advice to avoid doctors fits in the category 'harmony with the environment.' He proposes the category 'other means' instead. Coder 1, in contrast, attempts to support the researcher's interpretation by finding a way of connecting the answer with the category 'harmony': "With harmony is meant that the environment is adapted to the health aim as well." But he admits immediately "there is no environment here." The researcher takes this as an occasion for explaining what the coding instructions mean: "Adapting the environment is a kind of autonomy . . . it is sort of meant that way." He gives an example of autonomy (having less work) which he apparently considers to be an example of adapting the environment and hence of 'harmony with the environment.' Coder 2, however, denies the applicability of this reasoning because he reads the answer "Not going to the doctor too often" as merely 'criticizing' doctors. In his view 'harmony with the environment' presupposes rather 'positive' aspects such as 'having contact with people' and 'a stroll in the country.' He admits that both 'self-determination' and 'harmony' have a positive value, but this does not imply that self-determination can be considered a form of harmony.

Extract 4

Coder 2: but what kind of MEANS? In that case, I would choose 'other means' uh . . .

Coder 1: yes but you can also uh for instance interpret it . . . as safeguarding autonomy and then it may be something more of . . . with harmony is meant that the environment is adapted to the health aim as well . . . yes that's here . . . but strictly speaking there is no environment here, is there?

Coder 2: no I choose 'other means' . . . it is merely 'other means' . . . it is a kind of criticizing the medical class yes

Researcher: Well adapting the environment is a kind of autonomy, isn't it? You are right, it is sort of meant that way.

Coder 1: yeah, yeah, uh

Coder 2: yes but I do not see harmony with the environment

Researcher: and that one says as well for instance I would like to have less work or . . . I understand . . . that you . . .

Coder 2: but harmony with the environment can only be concluded from rather positive . . . things such as uh having contact with people or things like that . . . maintaining health . . . by uuuh a stroll in the country or things like that? . . . rather than by criticizing doctors?

Coder 1: Yes but self-determination is of course a very positive value.

Coder 2: Yes but does this necessarily mean harmony or even harmony with the environment . . . self-determination?

Researcher: well it uh, it uh, it uh the definition is difficult indeed.

Coder 2: look he is determined . . . It is a determined person that that is clear.

This example shows that, even when the 'sense' of an answer has been established (see *Interpretation of Answers,* above), there is still the problem of how this sense can be related to the abstract categories of the coding instructions. The solution of this problem depends on the successful interplay of two procedures, a bottom-up procedure in which the answer can be shown to be a member of a larger class of statements and a top-down procedure in which the coding categories must be specified in terms of more concrete subcategories. In Extract 4, Coder 2 uses the bottom-up procedure. This results in more general categories such as 'criticizing doctors' and 'a determined person.' In contrast, Coder 1 attempts to find specifications of the coding category in order to reach a point at which the answer can be read as one of its possible specifications. Both fail because they cannot find a way to connect the bottom-up generalizations ('criticizing,' 'self-determination' and 'determined person') to the top-down specifications (such as 'adaptation of the environment').

After an extensive discussion (which is not presented here) about the correct interpretation of the code 'harmony with the environment,' Coder 1 formulates an interpretation that eventually allows them to find a solution:

Extract 5

Coder 1:	prevention and hygiene is functional and this is everything with a rather intrinsic value.
Researcher:	Yes.
Coder 2:	I like that word, intrinsic value.
Researcher:	OK.
Coder 1:	It may be stated in a negative form as well . . . not doing exaggerated exercises
Researcher:	Yes, you see also that that . . . bipolar structure . . . the fact is that I want to have it in a sense because uh . . .
Coder 2:	if you take this formulation I will agree . . . intrinsic value and uh autonomy and that kind of things

This discussion is eventually concluded with the agreement that 'harmony with the environment' must be read as 'intrinsic value' (as opposed to 'functional' or 'instrumental'). Both the agreement on the coding of this answer and the general agreement on the correct reading of the category 'harmony with the environment' have been achieved by the introduction of the one word 'intrinsic.' Its achievement is having bridged the distance between the words 'harmony' and 'determined person' in a way that appears to be acceptable to Coder 2. This solution is even more than acceptable to the researcher because it accentuates an underlying structure of the coding instructions: "That bipolar structure . . . the fact is that I want to have it in a sense." Although it is not formulated explicitly, the researcher's satisfaction certainly derives from the bipolar structure of his research question in which only two types of definitions of health figure: 'expressive' and 'instrumental.'

There is an interesting difference between how the agreement between the coders was achieved in this discussion about the appropriateness of a coding category and how it was achieved in the discussion about the answer's sense. We have seen that the problem of determining the answer's sense was treated as a unique problem of which the solution had no bearing on other cases. The discussion about the interpretation of the coding category 'harmony with the environment,' in contrast, has resulted in a specification that can be used in other cases. The chance that this category will be applied by coders in a more or less consistent way will be increased, which results in an improved inter-coder reliability. Moreover, because the researcher had an active part in the discussion, in which he explicitly referred to the underlying theory the fit between this interpretation and the researcher's theory and intentions is safeguarded.[5]

Practical Socialization

In this section, we discuss other rules of applying coding instructions, which are aimed at improving inter-coder reliability. We refer to rules that are developed in the course of the coder training, but are not grounded in the coding instructions. By applying these kinds of rules, agreement on coding decisions can be achieved without grounding them in a specific interpretation of the theory. Because these rules are not a part of the coding instructions proper, their use is usually not accounted for in the research report. Typically, these rules specify how an answer can be coded by taking only its form (rather than its 'sense') into account. These kinds of rules short-circuit the problems discussed in the previous sections. If the answer's form is the only relevant criterion for the code it will receive, it is not necessary any more to determine the answer's sense or to connect this sense to a coding category interpretatively.

It is clear that this manner of non-interpretative coding improves inter-coder reliability. Because, however, coders are not machines, they often cannot resist reinterpreting these rules. Thus, in applying these rules coders will appear to be *ad-hocing* again. In Extract 6 the application of the rule that the presence of the phrase 'be(ing) able to' is a sufficient condition for coding the answer as a VALUE is discussed. This discussion started with a disagreement on whether this rule should be applied to the answer "Feeling fine in one's body and being able to do normal exercise." In Extract 6, Coder 1 extends this discussion to the coding of the answer "Feeling well and being able to move easily" (discussed also in Extract 3 above).

Extract 6

Researcher: I think that . . . If the word 'being able to' occurs in the answer we can almost always choose VALUE if it is possible . . . uh . . . to read the answer in that way

Coder 1: thus, in that case we don't take CRITERION

Researcher: yes . . . yes only 'feeling fine in one's body' is the CRITERION. . .

Coder 1: then the same would apply to 'feeling well and being able to move easily'

Researcher: uh yes 'being able to move easily' . . . it was ambiguous . . . yes . . . does it mean moving socially or really . . . I mean uh . . . physical movement . . . being able to move knees and legs and the like

Coder 1: yes, I think . . . I agree that one can read it as moving socially but it is also very difficult to consider it not a CRITERION

Researcher: yes I would say moving easily is . . . being able to move is an experience as well

This extract documents two cases in which the coders hesitate to apply the rule that 'being able to' must be coded as a VALUE because it conflicts with another (more informal) rule, namely the economy rule that two codes for one answer must be avoided. Applying the economy rule would result in not coding the answer as a VALUE. Instead, the code CRITERION would be chosen in both instances. In order to account for this kind of decision an additional rule was formulated in the subsequent discussion. "The phrase 'being able to' will be coded as a VALUE, unless it can be argued convincingly that it is not a VALUE, e.g. when 'being able to move easily' must be seen as an expansion of 'feeling well.'" Although its formulation ('argued convincingly') suggests that the quality of the code prevails, in practice this rule boils down to merely giving priority to one formalism (the economy rule) rather than another (the standard code for 'being able to').

Extract 7 documents a similar discussion about the correct coding of "feeling well." It is clear that it must be coded as CRITERION but the question is what kind of CRITERION, 'subjective' or 'objective' or both? The justification of the rule that well-being must be coded as 'objective' is questioned because it is seen as counter-intuitive. The result of the discussion is that the rule is maintained and even has received a validation: "We must assume that 'feeling' is not at stake here."[6]

Extract 7

Coder 1: you say it is an experience too and hence subjective . . . but in the instructions, you cite well-being as an example of objective

Coder 2: is well-being uh uh . . . I have coded it as subjective all the time.

Researcher: yes . . . mental and physical well-being . . . I think it is the formulation of a kind of norm . . . is it a mere subjective experience and hence a subjective criterion or is it a . . . a definition that is applied socially . . . someone is healthy if he feels well (zich welbevindt) . . . it is not very clear how well-being can be determined . . . but yes uh

Coder 1: Yes, but I cannot see a difference with uh being able to move . . . then

Coder 2: I made a mistake . . . I have coded well-being as subjective all the time . . . it was not clear for me

Researcher: wait a moment . . . 'a state of mental and physical well-being' that's a typical . . . is it subjective? . . . I would choose objective uh . . . an objective criterion . . . because this criterion applies to others as well whereas . . . 'I like the feeling' . . . that's yes . . . yeah . . .

Coder 2: you consider mental and physical well-being as objective?

Researcher: yes it is 'being' isn't it . . . being well

Coder 2: yes okay

Researcher: yes or do you think that it. . .

Coder 1: no I think in this case uh uh . . . literally it says 'feeling' (bevinden) but that's only . . . we must assume that 'feeling' is not at stake here

Researcher: yes, uh it's a decision . . . we could make three categories but then . . . we have only few cases . . . at a certain point we must . . . let's attempt to make a kind of dichotomy . . . I have chosen to consider well-being . . . to locate it on the more objective uh side.

In a similar way the coders discussed the rule "Apply the category 'body' if, and only if, the 'body' or a synonym is mentioned explicitly." According to one of the coders, it is 'clear' that many answers refer to the body even if the body is not mentioned explicitly. According to the researcher, however, "[I]t is interesting to look at explicit statements, because otherwise you can read the body in any answer. By looking at whether it is mentioned explicitly we can differentiate the answers." This is another case in which an *a posteriori* validation is provided for a practical rule, which is introduced only in order to improve inter-coder reliability by avoiding the interpretation of answers. The application of this rule implies that a new research question is introduced: "It is interesting to look at who mentions the body explicitly." It cannot be denied that this might be an interesting research question. The problem here is that this was not a research question at the beginning of the coder training. The original research question referred to 'expressive' and 'instrumental' definitions of health. The researcher fails to clarify how the coding of the *explicit* mentioning of the body relates to the concept of health definition that he wanted to measure with this open-ended question in the first place.

Characteristic of practical rules as discussed in this section is that they are formulated by the researcher and that Coders 1 and 2 only discuss problems, which arise in their application, in particular, when these rules are seen intuitively as invalid. The researcher then 'saves' the rules by accounting for their theoretical justifiability. The result is that coders 'understand' why they can apply the rules, even if these might be seen as invalid. This allows a rigid and uniform application, which explains why they are effective means to improve inter-coder reliability.

Summarizing this section, we have seen that practical rules are formulated in order to solve the problem that coders can neither be instructed nor trained in reliably determining the sense of answers. The solution consists of instructing coders in such a way that they be able to code mechanically according to the form of the answers. The practical rules in question are explained and justified to coders by the researcher (by claiming, for instance, that a certain categorization is 'interesting') but not to the readers of the research report who are led to *believe* that the yielded data are the results of an unproblematic, direct, and therefore valid, application of the coding instructions. In other words, we have discovered a training artifact.[7]

Conclusions

Our question was: *Does coder training consist only of training in the correct application of the coding instructions (theoretical training) or also of coders' socialization into practical rules, which are not warranted, by the coding instructions?*

We can conclude that in answering this question we must make a distinction between two types of coding problems, a distinction which is notably absent in the literature. There are problems in interpreting an answer (determining its 'sense' or the respondent's intention) on the one hand, and problems of interpreting the coding instructions on the other hand. These two types are not only different analytically, but are treated quite differently in coder training as well. The typical solution of the second type of problem (regarding the interpretation of the coding instructions) is theoretical training, i.e. the specification of the instructions and the socialization of coders into its theoretical logic. The first type of problem, however, cannot be solved in this way. The reading of respondents' intentions in answers is an everyday competence that has no direct relation to professional views and instructions. Differences in interpretations of answers can only be superseded by active dialogic search for a common ground in specific cases, not by general instruction. Such differences can only be prevented by rules that permit coders to neglect the answers' sense, i.e., by rules that refer to the form (e.g. the presence of certain expressions) only. Because, however, those informal rules cannot be grounded in the coding instructions, they have a negative effect on the codings' validity.

Apparently, this is a fundamental and general feature of professional classificatory work. For the particular case of sociological coding, this distinction is—as far as we know—only made by Rehbein and Mazeland (1991:167). They refer to two kinds of data: "interpretations of utterances which are grounded in coder's everyday knowledge and the subsequent categorization in accordance with the coding system."

The answer to our question, thus, is that both strategies (theoretical training and practical socialization) inevitably must be applied in coder training in order to achieve an improvement of inter-coder reliability. It cannot be excluded that a high degree of inter-coder reliability is achieved by informal rules that are not accounted for in the research report. Our findings, therefore, give further ground to Muskens' (1980:126) suggestion that satisfying results of a coder training in terms of inter-coder reliability can be due to a training artifact. However, because we have studied only one case of coder training (consisting of two sessions), we cannot generalize this finding to all instances of coder training.

What are the implications of our conclusion? The most important implication is that researchers must document each decision rule that is developed in the course of a coder training (or, for that matter, in any form of instructing coders) and in the course of the coding process. This means that coded data can never be considered as 'given' but instead must be seen and treated as 'produced.'

The implication for editors of professional journals is that they must not accept papers for publication in which information on coding consists merely of a discussion of the coding instructions and a presentation of measures of reliability. In research reports it must be shown also how specific coding problems have been solved and what kind of practical rules have been applied.

Our findings allow us also to formulate the relation between quantitative and qualitative research in another way than is usually done by sociologists who are mainly involved in quantitative research. They tend to see qualitative methodology as an approach that may be combined with quantitative methodology (e.g., in an exploratory phase of the research, or as another method of measurement in triangulation, or in the development of an instrument) but that, at any rate, is quite distinct and separate from the quantitative approach. Our findings suggest that the quality of coded data in a quantitative approach can only be known and safeguarded (and communicated to readers) through a qualitative assessment of the coding practices (or, for that matter, of the interview practices and of the way respondents, or interviewers, select the pre-coded options in a questionnaire) that have produced these specific data. It appears, thus, that quantitative research is intrinsically dependent on qualitative decisions in the coding process. This implies that good quantitative research must scrutinize and explore its application of qualitative methods. It must, in fact, acknowledge its dependency on these methods (Rehbein & Mazeland, 1991). At the same time this provides us a definition of (good) qualitative research. Whereas in quantitative research only the validity of the researcher's guidelines (e.g., the validity of the coding instructions in relation to their underlying theory) is discussed, not their application in practice, in qualitative research the quality and the theoretical status of each datum are assessed carefully.*

———***———

*Another implication of this research is that socialization during coder training (and during coding as well) introduces an unmonitored artifact into the data-making process. As the effect of socialization escapes agreement measures, usually spuriously inflates them, this makes it difficult to infer reliability (reproducibility) from intercoder agreement measures. For coded data to be trustworthy, the socialization process must be replicable as well.

APPENDIX

Coding Instructions *(Translated from Dutch)*

Definitions of health can be considered answers to three questions:

— how does one perceive health? (CRITERION)
— how does one get or maintain health? (MEANS)
— what is the value or the aim of health? (VALUE)

A respondent may answer all three questions in one statement, but often answers only one of them.

CRITERION: three aspects can be distinguished: SIGN, is the definition positive, negative (not ill; no physical complaints) or both? POINT OF VIEW, is it subjective (experience) or objective (being, having, well-being)? DOMAIN, is it physical, or more than that?

	Codes:
SIGN	1. positive 2. negative 3. both
POINT OF VIEW	1. subjective 2. objective 3. both
DOMAIN	1. physical 2. physical and mental 3. undetermined

MEANS: 'harmony' means that one adjusts the environment to the health aims (adaptation of the environment), whereas 'prevention' rather represents adjusting oneself to the requirements of health (assimilation to the environment). *Codes:*

1. harmony with the environment
2 prevention/hygiene
3. other means

VALUE: 'vitality' refers to health as subservient to individual aims (among others), whereas 'work' refers to the aim of adequately adapting oneself to societal requirements. *Codes:*

1. vitality/growth
2. work/functioning
3. other value

Comment: A 'positive' SIGN, a 'mental' DOMAIN, a 'subjective' POINT OF VIEW, a 'harmonious' MEANS and a 'vitality/growth' VALUE are taken as indicative of an *expressive* definition of health. A 'negative' SIGN, a 'physical' DOMAIN, an 'objective' POINT OF VIEW, a preventive/hygiene' MEANS and a 'work/functioning' VALUE are taken as indicative of an *instrumental* definition of health.

Notes

1. This applies also to cases in which the construct validity of a measurement is established by means of a statistical correlation with other variables, because this procedure depends on the argumentative plausibility of the expected correlation.

2. An exception is mentioned by Sonquist and Dunkelberg (1977:88). These authors recommend, among other means, "In a group, the coders and the research staff should go over each (interview), discussing procedures for dealing with different data structures and the concepts underlying the procedures and decision rules."

3. Throughout this article, both in the transcripts and in the body of our text, we will use capitals when we refer to the categories of the coding Instructions: CRITERION, SIGN, POINT OF VIEW, DOMAIN, MEANS, and VALUE.

4. The extracts presented are translations of edited versions of the (Dutch) transcripts. Because we are not interested in an analysis of the conversation itself, but only use the fragments for a discussion of some aspects of coder training, many details of the transcripts (such as hesitations, repetitions and interruptions) are not relevant for the purpose at hand. The coding instructions to which the coders refer in their talk are presented in the Appendix.

5. We are tempted to suggest that the researcher's efforts to control the fit between his theory and the specification of the category 'harmony with the environment' (in terms of 'intrinsic value') have resulted in a valid interpretation of the coding instructions. As stated above, however, validity cannot be measured, and is a matter of argumentation. Our claim in this case is that the specification of the instructions that has emerged in the coder training can convincingly be explained by the researcher to his audience.

6. In order to understand this discussion it is necessary to know that in Dutch the expression 'welbevinden,' a rather formal word which literally means 'feeling well', has almost the same sense as the English 'well-being.' The expression's literal meaning opens the possibility to question the degree to which 'well-being' (welbevinden) is a 'feeling,' and hence 'subjective,' as well.

7. Note that the researcher could have reported that and why the rule "Apply the category 'body' if, and only if, the 'body' or a synonym is mentioned explicitly" was developed. This, however, would have imposed upon him the onus of explaining how this rule fits his theoretical distinction of expressive and instrumental attitudes to health (which would have been a rather difficult task).

References

Babbie, E. (1989). *The practice of social research* (5th ed.). Belmont, CA: Wadsworth.

Bernts, T. (1991). *Leven zonder zorg.* Lisse: Swets Zeitlinger.

Cicourel, A. (1964). *Method and measurement in sociology.* New York: The Free Press.

Garfinkel, H. (1967). *Studies in ethnomethodology.* Englewood Cliffs, NJ: Prentice Hall.

d'Houtaud, A. (1978). L'image de la santé dans une population lorraine: approche psychosociale des repréentations de la santé. Rev. *Epiélm. et Santé Publ. 26:*299–320.

d'Houtaud, A., & Field, M. (1984). The image of health: Variations in perception by social class in a French population. *Sociology of Health and Illness 6:*30–60.

Katz, B. A., & Sharrock, W. W. (1976). Eine Darstellung des Kodierens. In E. Weingarten, F. Sack, & J. Schenkein (Eds.), *Etnomethodologie. Beiträge zu einer Soziologie des Alltagshandelns* (pp. 244–271). Frankfurt/Main: Suhrcamp.

Mishler, E. O. (1986). *Research interviewing.* Cambridge, MA: Harvard University Press.

Muskens, O. (1980). *Frames of meaning: Are they measurable?* Ph.D. thesis, Katholieke Universiteit Nijmegen.

Rehbein, J., & Mazeland, H. (1991). Kodierentscheidungen. In D. Flader (Ed.), *Verbale Interaktion* (pp. 166–221). Stuttgart: Metzlersche Verlagsbuchhandlung.

Sonquist, J., & Dunkelberg, W. (1977). *Survey and opinion research.* Englewood Cliffs, NJ: Prentice Hall.

4.3

The Future of Coders

Human Judgments in a World of Sophisticated Software

Gilbert Shapiro*

Since the introduction of computers, there have been prodigious efforts to eliminate human judgments entirely from such fields as language translation, information retrieval, and content analysis, not always with much success. Researchers point to two advantages to purely machine procedures: they are more cost effective, and are more (indeed, they are completely) reliable. But these advantages are purchased at the cost of *validity*, a price many, if not most researchers find too high. . . . We seem to face a dilemma: human coders are expensive and of questionable reliability, but they provide us with the opportunity to freely specify the meanings in the text we seek to categorize, while available machine procedures, though efficient and reliable, require that we restrict our research to particular theoretical orientations or accept farfetched and bizarre interpretations of text as indicative of the variables we are truly interested in. In this chapter, I will discuss new methods of using coders as human instruments along with computers in a two-stage procedure that shows promise of avoiding the worst penalties of pure machine analysis as well as the pre-computer use of coders.

As a historical sociologist, I find it impossible to begin a discussion of the future of coders without a look at their past. During the heroic age of content analysis (that is, before computers), coders were, of course, all we had. In the tradition of Lasswell (Lasswell, Leites, & Associates, 1949), they were used to count symbols; in the tradition of Murray (1938) and McClelland (1961; McClelland, Atkinson, Clark, & Lowell, 1953), to identify needs and themes in communications. Most clearly, in the latter case, coders were regarded as surrogate scientists. Surely, if Murray or McClelland had an infinite amount

*From Shapiro, G. (1997). The future of coders: Human judgments in a world of sophisticated software. In C .W. Roberts (Ed.), *Text analysis for the social sciences: Methods for drawing statistical inferences from texts and transcripts* (pp. 225–238). Mahwah, NJ: Lawrence Erlbaum.

of time and patience they would prefer to read all the documents themselves and make their own professional judgments of the presence of needs or themes. The coder was an unfortunate economic necessity, a second choice, and a source of error. For this reason, extensive efforts were made by the researchers to control the coder's judgments, or to convince themselves and their colleagues that they had done so, by the development of definitions of code categories that were to have the scientific status of operational definitions. The objective was to develop a coding manual so detailed and specific as to effectively eliminate the influence of human judgment in the coding process. For the same reason, it was important to keep the coding categories simple so that the instructions could, in effect, be performed by clerks, despite the inherent complexity of any translation of theoretical hypotheses into language expectations. The human content coders, conceived as surrogate scientists, were tolerable only if they followed the detailed rules of observation laid down by the researcher. On a number of occasions, McClelland claimed that his written instructions to coders constitute operational specifications defining his categories: "Ideally, the judge simply 'points to' an identifiable phrase and classifies it according to a scoring definition as belonging in a category, just as he might classify a movement of a rat as a 'right turn' or a certain visual image under the microscope as a 'red blood corpuscle'" (McClelland et al., 1953:32).

When we examine the coder instructions themselves, however, we find this claim far from justified. The coder is provided only with general guides and illustrative examples. The coder gets nothing resembling the exact conditions (which must be language specifications) under which he or she is supposed to isolate some portion of text and classify it in a given category. For example, in scoring for the need for achievement, one is supposed to seek indicators of "competition with a standard of excellence," which is defined as follows:

> One of the characters in the story is engaged in some competitive activity (other than pure cases of aggression) where winning or doing as well or as better than others is actually stated as the primary concern. Wanting to win an essay contest, or an apprentice wanting to show the master that he, too, can fix the machine, are typical examples. (McClelland et al., 1953:181)

What . . . is a "competitive activity (other than pure cases of aggression)?" And how do we decide when a particular concern is "primary"? Any of the other instructions to coders could be cited to illustrate the same point. They all provide a very incomplete form of guidance to the coder, who must exercise his or her capacity for complex, intuitive, semantic judgments in assigning text to categories. He or she certainly does not merely follow explicit rules. The analogy between the judgment that some text indicates a "pure case of aggression" and the judgment that a rat turned to the right is nothing short of ludicrous.

Two Approaches to Computational Content Analysis

Two very different models of computerized content analysis are available: special purpose programs using the tools of artificial intelligence to [address] the complexities of natural syntax and general purpose systems of computerized content analysis, with little or no use of artificial intelligence methods and much less elaborate attention to the complexities of syntax and context. [T]he application of artificial intelligence to content analysis is in its infancy, so that, although I look at the kinds of content analyses to which it has been successfully applied, any estimate of its ultimate potential would be premature (van Cuilenberg, Kleinnijenhuis, & de Ridder, 1988).

The most important and the most widely applied general purpose computerized system for content analysis is the General Inquirer (Stone, Dunphy, Smith, & Ogilvie, 1966). This system moved the art far beyond the mere counting of individual words in a heroic effort to capture at least some of the subtleties and complexities of natural language. It retrieves sentences (or, with the aid of hand-coding, clauses) on the basis of the presence of Boolean functions of words listed in a dictionary (i.e., a list of words or phrases associated with theoretical concepts of interest). The system provides for multiple complex forms of analysis. The researcher can specify the order in which these various elements occur in the sentence. Idioms—word sequences with a distinct aggregate meaning—can be treated as if they were single words. Provision is made for preliminary hand coding to distinguish homographs. Computer routines eliminate such word endings as the plural "s" and the past tense "ed." A given sentence may be retrieved or counted if the previous sentence meets specified conditions.

Representational Versus Instrumental Analysis

The methodological problems for content analysis posed by the occasional presence of deception in human communications initially gave rise to a distinction by Mahl (1959) between representational and instrumental uses of language by the source of the communications studied, and to corresponding modes of content analysis.* . . . Osgood (1959), . . . however, uses the term *representational model* in a somewhat different way, to stand not for the guileless expression of the communicator's views but for the attempt on the part of the analyst to represent the structure of thought found in the communication, rather than some other characteristic of the source or audience. Although Osgood's derivation of the model from the vocabulary of behavioral psychology is rather intricate, his summary is simple enough: "This, of course, is merely a more formal way of saying that words 'express' the ideas of the speaker and 'signify' ideas for the hearer" (p. 39).** The distinction between analyses that are representational in this sense and those that are instrumental is crucial to an understanding of the strengths and limitations of the computerized content analysis methods hitherto available.

As conventionally understood, the normal role of the source of a communication is to express views, beliefs, attitudes, values or ideas that are held, whereas the normal role of the receiver of a communication is to discover precisely what meanings are intended by the source. This latter task is also what a representational content analysis seeks to do. Those who approach the language behavior of the source instrumentally, as so many symptoms from which unconscious or unacknowledged characteristics are to be inferred, are engaged in so different an enterprise that they will have little use for the kinds of models or research tools that are necessary for the proper comprehension of the message that was intended. Those whose conception of their role is representational will not be satisfied with the solutions found by those with instrumental orientations. In particular, those who seek seriously to meet the requirements of operational specificity by the development of coding rules that can be translated into computer programs invariably work with an instrumental orientation to text.

To what extent does the General Inquirer in fact liberate us from the unreliability and expense of human coders? Its dictionaries are supposed, in principle, to derive from theories (Stone et al., 1966:139). The insistence that dictionary construction ought to be based upon theory seems clearly based upon a model

---

*George (see reading 3.4, this volume) addresses the requirements to analyze these two kinds of communication. He distinguishes between direct (or one-step) and indirect (or multistep) inferences from text. Inferences from psychiatric interviews, political negotiations, and propaganda, clearly having instrumental intents, require much more knowledge (assumptions and theory) than an analysis of concepts mentioned in texts, which Shapiro calls representational. Interestingly, Mahl (1959), who analyzes psychiatric interviews, bypasses the analytical complications posed by their underlying instrumentality by applying a direct method on aspects of speech not under the control of patients.

**Osgood considers the task of inferring psychological states a representational method, and his effort is driven by theory, for example, association psychology (see reading 3.1, this volume). Shapiro is right to say that this aim is not commensurate with what a source intends to convey or is talking about.

of content analysis in which words are objects that are observed by the scientist much as flowers are observed by botanists. However, as Stone et al. (1966:9–10) have acknowledged, "Unfortunately, although our social scientific theories may lead us to the concepts we wish to study, we lack an adequate theory of language to direct us in finding the alternative signs that express a particular concept. In a situation where something is to be said, there is no theory to tell us what words will be used to say it." This modesty of the founder is not always reflected in his followers: Goldhamer (1969:343) described the Inquirer dictionaries not just as deriving from theory, but as operationalizing a theory in fact.

The judges engaged in constructing a dictionary are described as drawing "upon their collective experience as language users in deciding which meaning should be regarded as most common and which tags should be chosen to make the best representation of . . . meaning" (Stone et al., 1966:154). The elimination of subjective, intuitive judgments of meaning from content analysis, then, has been very incomplete in the General Inquirer. The difference between the work of the general inquirers and the coding normally performed by traditional human coders is not that the former eliminate intuitive judgments of meaning but rather that in constructing a dictionary they render them wholesale. In a study of the Icarus complex, an obsession with flight, for example, the attribution of Icaran tendencies based on the use of a word, such as *leap,* is performed collectively, in the process of dictionary construction, for all authors using the word in all contexts. There are of course advantages—economy, for one—in such a procedure, but there are also disadvantages, of the sort the transformational linguists alert us to: The coder dealing individually with documents can judge the same words quite differently, depending upon their contexts. One can leap to a conclusion, during leap year.[1]

The most impressive special-purpose computerized content analysis system mobilizing the techniques of artificial intelligence is in the work of Louis Gottschalk, Robert Bechtel, and associates (1982, 1989, 1993). [T]he objectives of Gottschalk are clearly instrumental in character. He aims at the measurement of psychological states and traits, such as anxiety, hostility, social alienation, hope, and cognitive impairment—characteristics of the person not at all intrinsic to the intended meaning of the communications analyzed. Evidence of the validity of these measures is impressive. The achievements to date of this group surely demonstrate the importance of further research on other applications of artificial intelligence methods to the study of text. One limitation must be noted: Thus far, every field of study has required new and extremely costly program development, which tends to cancel the advantages of economy in the elimination of human coders.

Coding Versus Scaling*

It appears that representational content analysis continues to require the use of human coders. In the computer era, however, the coder can be conceptualized in an entirely new way and consequently can be assigned an entirely different role in the research process. If a coder is viewed not as a surrogate scientist but as a research instrument, we need not struggle with the impossible problem of explicating the full complexities of the natural language rules governing the assignment of text to a code category. The coder is then subject to the requirements that govern all instruments: the measurable criteria of reliability and validity. Like many other scientific instruments, a coder can be a black box; the researcher may have no idea of the language rules, the internal circuitry that governs the coder's behavior, but if the coder provides reliable and valid outputs for known inputs,

*Shapiro's distinction between coding and scaling chimes with Krippendorff's distinction between two tasks of content analysis: recording text into analyzable terms, a data language, and the use of analytical constructs of the chosen context of the analyzed text to support the desired inferences. Scaling is just one analytical operation. See Krippendorff, K. (2004). *Content analysis: An introduction to its methodology,* (2nd ed.). Thousand Oaks, CA: Sage.

he or she is a useful instrument of research. In this view, the manual of instructions given to coders is not a collection of operational definitions but merely one of many tools used in the training of the coders, a process that is understood as the fashioning of the instrument.

This conceptualization of the coder as an instrument is particularly appropriate to a new division of labor between the coder and the analyst and between the human and the machine that has already been instituted in some pioneering work. The kinds of coding systems that are constructed, the definition of the coder's function in the research process, and the coder's training and evaluation are profoundly affected by the coder's new association with computer processing. In this approach, the tasks that were generally performed by human coders before the advent of the computer are now broken down into two steps. One, conveniently called coding, is the peculiar province of the coders, for which they are particularly qualified and for which they have been specifically recruited and trained. The other, called scaling, is performed later by an analyst, a scientist, or scholar, who may or may not be the originator of the study, equipped with an electronic computer along with the required computer programs. The coder's task, in this division of labor, is no longer to interpret the text within a conceptual framework provided by the researcher in order to judge its status on each of the theoretical variables that enter into the research design. The coder is charged with a more modest duty: an act of translation, ideally a many-to-one transformation from the natural language of the document to the artificial language of the code . . . [In this view, coders] are assigned the tasks that can be effectively performed by virtue of their competence in the natural language rather than (as formerly) tasks of theoretical interpretation that were always more properly the province of the director of the research or other professional scholars.

Coders clearly are regarded as instruments recording what they, as competent language users, understand as the contents of newspapers and other accounts of events in such work as that of Tilly (1981, 1986), Franzosi (1987), and Olzak (1989). It is also the basic methodology of a study of the grievances of the French Revolution—a study that I review here to illustrate the principles of a two-step content analysis, using the coder as a research instrument, with a division of labor between coder and analyst (Markoff, Shapiro, & Weltman, 1974; Shapiro & Markoff, 1998).

An Illustration

The *cahiers de doléances* are well-known lists of grievances drawn up during the Convocation of the Estates-General in 1789 and frequently used by historians in less than systematic fashion over the past two centuries. More than 40,000 eligible individuals, status groups, corporations, and territorial entities, including craft guilds, rural parishes, towns, and *bailliages* (local judicial districts) drafted and approved lists of grievances or demands to serve, roughly speaking, as mandates for the delegates to the national convocation of the Estates-General in Versailles in May. The *cahiers* vary significantly in their length, their tone, the range of subjects covered, their mode of expression, as well as actual opinions.

Any quantitative study of such a mass of documentation must depend heavily upon a coding scheme. Ours utilizes a human coder as an intermediary between the text and a computer. In the construction of the code, our objective was to translate every grievance in the documents into a language that is convenient for computer analysis. We attempted to capture as much as possible of the concrete meaning (as distinguished from the analytical significance) of the text in its coded representation.

The code for a given demand consists of a designation of the subject of the grievance (ordinarily an institution or problem area, such as the church's finances, or the salt tax) and a code for the predicate, which consists of the action (for example, the abolition or reform of the subject) and an optional object, which is sometimes required to complete the meaning of the demand. Finally, there might be qualifications, for which there are codes for conventional remarks[2] as well as a provision for free text recording.[3]

The action codes are usually simple, common verbs of the sort to be found in grievances and demands in many historical situations. Some are relatively precise, such as "reestablish," "abolish," "maintain," "equalize," or "simplify," whereas others must be extremely vague if they are to capture faithfully the diffuse character of some of the texts. For example, we have a code for the demand that somebody merely "do something about" the subject. The optional object code usually is required when some particular aspect of the subject is the concern of the demand. For example, "Abolish venality of office in the judiciary" would be coded with the code for "venality" as the object, along with that for "judiciary" as subject and "abolish" as action.

The code for the subject of the grievance, its institutional or problem area, is somewhat more complex: It is organized as a four-level hierarchy. I illustrate the hierarchical principle by showing those sections of the code that are required to encode the demand that the *gabelle* (i.e., the salt tax) be standardized (i.e., subject to the same rate and administrative rules throughout the country). The full code reads: G TA IN GA ST, meaning Government, Taxation, Indirect Taxes, Gabelle, Standardize. To begin with, the Level 1 category of "Government" is chosen from a list of major institutional categories of 18th-century France:

0 MISCELLANEOUS[4]

1 GENERAL

C CONSTITUTION

E ECONOMY

G GOVERNMENT

J JUDICIARY

R RELIGION

S STRATIFICATION SYSTEM

"Government" is broken down into the following Level 2 codes:

G 0 GOVERNMENT, MISCELLANEOUS

G 1 GOVERNMENT, GENERAL

GAA ADMINISTRATIVE AGENCIES

G FI GOVERNMENT, FINANCES

G KI THE KING

G MI MILITARY

G RL REGIONAL AND LOCAL GOVERNMENT

G TA GOVERNMENT, TAXATION

G TA, taxation, is then divided at Level 3 into categories as follows:

G TA 0 GOVERNMENT, TAXATION, MISCELLANEOUS

G TA 1 GOVERNMENT, TAXATION, GENERAL

G TA AD TAX ADVANTAGES

G TA DA DIRECT TAX AGENCIES

G TA DI EXISTING DIRECT TAXES

G TA IA INDIRECT TAX AGENCIES

G TA IN EXISTING INDIRECT TAXES

G TA NT NEW TAXES

G TA TA TAX ADMINISTRATION

Finally, G TA IN, Indirect Taxes, is divided into the following relatively concrete Level 4 coding categories:

G TA IN 0 EXISTING INDIRECT TAXES, MISCELLANEOUS

G TA IN 1 EXISTING INDIRECT TAXES, GENERAL

G TA IN A1 AIDES

G TA IN CD CENTIEME DENIER ACCESOIRES

G TA IN CU CUIR, TAXES ON LEATHER

G TA IN DC DROITS DE CONTROLE

G TA IN DD DROITS DOMINIAUX

G TA IN DF DROITS SURE LA FABRICATION

G TA IN DJ DROITS JOINTS AUX AIDES

G TA IN ES DROITS D'ENTRÉE ET DE SORTIE

G TA IN FE FER

G TA IN GA	GABELLE
G TA IN HU	HUILES
G TA IN IN	INSINTUATION
G TA IN OC	OCTROIS DES VILLES
G TA IN OF	CENTIEME DENIER DES OFFICES

A major advantage of this kind of hierarchical organization is that it facilitates the analysis of grievances at multiple levels. We can study, for example, the frequencies of grievances on the specific subject of the *gabelle* or, just as easily, on the more general category of indirect taxes, or on taxes in general, or even demands relative to government, whether they have to do with taxes or not. The analyst, however, is not restricted to the use of the hierarchy in constructing scales comprising Boolean functions of the codes. If an analyst wishes to study grievances related to impositions of financial burdens upon peasants, for example, he or she can retrieve or count the demands relative to taxation along with those on the subject of the ecclesiastical tithe and seigneurial dues.[5]

The coder's role is to read the text and translate it into this artificial language. It is important to note the fabulous variety of expressions by which the natural language may communicate the same essential meaning. For example, the demand for the standardization of the *gabelle* might be expressed as follows:

- The *gabelle* should be standardized.
- The salt tax should be made equal throughout the realm.
- It is unfair that the tax on salt should be higher in some provinces than in others.
- We are obliged to pay indirect impositions on salt from which other communities in the nation are excused, and this is unacceptable.
- Our community is in a condition of great distress, due to the unfair discrimination it suffers at the hands of the tax collectors. They extract from us many taxes, including the *gabelle,* which exceed the requirements imposed upon other regions.
- The burden of an obligatory payment to the government for the salt required to sustain our life and that of our animals is particularly distressing because others in France are excused from all or part of that obligation.

This list could go on endlessly. Although no computer program can reduce such a variety of surface structures to the single meaning represented by our code,[6] it is demonstrably possible for a competent human user of the natural language (such as the reader) to do so. This is a job for coders. The question of the historical or theoretical significance of such a demand is to be decided by the analyst at the second stage of the two-step process. For example, the grievance may be regarded as one of many on the subject of the particular tax or some broader class of taxes, or it might be regarded as one of many indicators of a demand for homogenization of national institutions or a manifestation of an abstract commitment to the principle of *égalité.*

This new division of labor between coder and analyst implies the use of concrete, inductive codes rather than abstract, theoretical codes. The coder supplies the analyst with a dataset holding, in the ideal, the same concrete meanings to be found in the original documents but in a language that can be readily manipulated by the researcher (given the appropriate computer programs) to measure the theoretical variables of interest. Such a code must necessarily have a vast number of categories. The richness of the code results from the desire to capture the concrete meaning of the original document. The mastery of such a large code is substantially facilitated by its organization in a hierarchical structure, and, in this era of inexpensive desktop computers, the code can be provided on a screen in a series of hierarchical menus, relieving the coder and the analyst of the requirement of memorizing a large system or frequently referring to a paper code manual.

Once coding is complete, researchers or other analysts are able, by means of computer programs, to create scales or scores that reflect the conditions in the documents that they interpret as representing the concepts they wish to measure. Technically speaking, a good scaling program permits complete freedom to specify any Boolean function of the coded data, whose satisfaction would lead the computer to take a specified action. Most commonly, the computer is asked to retrieve or identify the records that satisfy the function, to change those records in some way, or to add a constant to a counter in order to find the frequency of the condition in some set of records. In the process of scaling, retrieval is particularly useful when the researcher is in doubt regarding the appropriate theoretical interpretation of some class of grievances (such as demands that are somehow qualified). Doubts tend to disappear when the decision is led by a retrieval of particular cases.

It would clearly be impossible to tell the computer what to do with every possible code combination. Although, for any given problem, most of the code combinations can be ignored, the richness of the vocabulary does, nevertheless, frequently impose a heavy burden on the researcher who seeks to include within the scaling instructions every grievance that is actually relevant to his or her interests. This burden is the other side of the coin, the price paid for the advantages of a concrete code and the division of labor this method offers. Giving code a mnemonic character and organizing it in a hierarchy substantially reduce this burden. Another device for reducing the burden of scaling is the establishment of pre-scales, classifications of code categories that are of general utility (such as positive and negative actions). Interactive microcomputer programs can appreciably reduce the work and the error in scale construction. Following the semantic structure of the coding unit, the various coding options can be displayed, and choices can be reduced to the click of a mouse button. Scaling problems (such as the exclusion of demands with some recorded qualifying conditions) that might otherwise be overlooked can be automatically raised for review.

Two Concluding Comments

First, it is of great importance that such a procedure produces a data file, the coders' output, which is no more committed to one theoretical orientation, hypothesis, or intellectual interest than was the original set of documents. For historical studies, this is particularly important because it enables multiple researchers to explore the data from different perspectives and with different theoretical orientations.

Second, the question of whether representational analyses can, in principle, be performed by digital computers (or some other machines) in the distant future is an entertainment. . . [W]orking researchers engage in science, not science fiction, and to do such science requires, for the foreseeable future, the use of coders as human instruments.

Notes

1. Furthermore, the enormous expense of dictionary construction at least significantly reduces the advantage of efficiency in pure machine methods over the use of human coders, unless dictionaries are reused. Such reuse presumes that later research is in the same language with similar documents and research objectives. There is a serious danger here that materials and research problems will be chosen that fit these requirements, particularly by researchers such as graduate students with limited access to research resources.

2. Codes include COND, meaning the demand is conditional, the exact conditions recorded in the free text field; ALT, the action demanded is one alternative among others; LO, the demand is focused on the local community rather than the province (PV) or the nation (NA).

3. If the rarely used negated actions are counted, the code has 91 standard actions, 1,227 institutional subjects, 76 standard objects, and 45 conventional remarks code categories. Because there are frequently demanded actions that are relevant only for particular subjects, the standard actions are supplemented by 286 special action codes.

4. In any position of the hierarchy, or even in the action or object fields, a "0" or miscellaneous code refers to a grievance that does not fit any of the categories provided. In the present instance, the first hierarchical level, it would mean a grievance neither constitutional nor economic nor governmental, nor referring to the judiciary, religion or stratification. A "1" is very different: It refers to a general grievance, which falls under all or (at least, diffusely) most of the categories provided.

5. This facility, of course, assumes the availability of highly flexible computer programs for use in analysis, which is not a trivial consideration.

6. Note that the idea of a tax on salt is not necessarily expressed by any single term or even one of a small number of terms, and, for the programmer, the idea of standardization is even more elusive.

REFERENCES

Franzosi, R. (1989). From words to numbers: A generalized and linguistics-based coding procedure for collecting event-data from newspapers. In C. Clogg (Ed.), *Sociological methodology, 1989* (pp. 263–298). Oxford: Basil Blackwell.

Franzosi, R. (1987). The press as a source of socio-historical data: Issues in the methodology from newspapers. *Historical Methods 20:*5–16.

Goldhamer, D. H. (1969). Toward a more general inquirer: Convergence of structure and context of meaning. In G. Gerbner, O. R. Holsti, K. Krippendorff, W. J. Paisley, & P. J. Stone (Eds.), *The analysis of communication content: Developments in scientific theories and computer techniques* (pp. 343–354). New York: Wiley.

Gottschalk, L. A., & Bechtel, R. (1982). The measurement of anxiety through the computer analysis of verbal samples. *Comprehensive Psychiatry 23:*364–369.

Gottschalk, L. A., & Bechtel, R. (1989). Artificial intelligence and the computerization of the content analysis of natural language. *Artificial Intelligence in Medicine 1:*131–137.

Gottschalk, L. A., & Bechtel, R. (1993). *Psychologic and neuropsychiatric assessment applying the Gottschalk-Gleser content analysis method to verbal sample analysis using the Gottschalk-Bechtel computer scoring system.* Palo Alto, CA: Mind Garden.

Lasswell, H. D., Leites, N., & Associates. (1949). *Language of politics: Studies in quantitative semantics.* New York: George W. Stewart.

Mahl, G. F. (1959). Exploring emotional states by content analysis. In I. de Sola Pool (Ed.), *Trends in content analysis* (pp. 89–130). Urbana: University of Illinois Press.

Markoff, J., Shapiro, G., & Weltman, S. (1974). Toward the integration of content analysis and general methodology. In D. R. Heise (Ed.), *Sociological methodology, 1975* (pp. 1–58). San Francisco: Jossey-Bass.

McClelland, C. A. (1961). *The achieving society.* New York: Van Nostrand.

McClelland, C. A., Atkinson, J. W., Clark, R. A., & Lowell, E. L. (1953). *The achievement motive.* New York: Appleton-Century-Crofts.

Murray, H. A. (1938). *Explorations in personality.* New York: Oxford University Press.

Olzak, S. (1989). Labor unrest, immigration and ethnic conflict in urban America, 1880–1914. *American Journal of Sociology 94:*1303–1333.

Osgood, C. K. (1959). The representational model and relevant research methods. In I. de Sola Pool (Ed.), *Trends in content analysis* (pp. 33–88). Urbana: University of Illinois Press.

Shapiro, G., & Markoff, J. (1998). *Revolutionary demands: A content analysis of the Cahiers de Doléances of 1789.* Stanford, CA: Stanford University Press.

Stone, P. J., Dunphy, D. C., Smith, M. S., & Ogilvie, D. M. (Eds.). (1966). *The General Inquirer: A computer approach to content analysis.* Cambridge, MA: MIT Press.

Tilly, C. (1981). *As sociology meets history.* New York: Academic Press.

Tilly, C. (1986). *The contentious French.* Cambridge, MA: Harvard University Press.

van Cuilenberg, J., Kleinnijenhuis, J., & de Ridder, J. (1988). Artificial intelligence and content analysis. *Quality and Quantity 22,*1:65–97.

4.4

COMPARING HUMAN CODING AND A COMPUTER-ASSISTED METHOD

BRIGITTE L. NACOS, ROBERT Y. SHAPIRO, JOHN T. YOUNG, DAVID P. FAN, TORSTEN KJELLSTRAND, AND CRAIG MCCAA*

Although this is the age of computers, most content analyses of the text of media reports are still done by human coders. Clearly, the coding of large volumes of text is a very labor intensive, time consuming, tiresome, and costly task, and this fact limits how much text researchers can examine. If computers could be programmed to help do sophisticated coding with the degree of reliability expected of human coders, social scientific analyses of large amounts of text could be done in a fraction of the time and at significantly lower costs than is currently the case.

This report describes our research comparing the results of content analyses of news coverage done by human coders with the results from a computer-assisted method of coding. While the performance of the computer program was not completely satisfactory, its successes and pitfalls encourage us to conclude that large-scale computer-assisted content analyses can make significant contributions to social science research.

Our research involved a somewhat unusual collaboration—unusual at least compared with current social science norms and styles of research—between Shapiro, Nacos, and Young at Columbia University and Fan, Kjellstrand, and McCaa at the University of Minnesota. . . . Nacos had coded . . . a large and exhaustive number of newspaper stories for a comprehensive study of press coverage during national political crises (Nacos, 1990). The availability of her data sets assembled through human coding offered an opportunity to compare them with content data that could be collected through machine-assisted coding of the same material. The Minnesota researchers were eager to test the reliability of computer-assisted content analysis for use in the social behavioral sciences.

While their Columbia colleagues, all of whom had done hundreds of hours of often complex coding (Page, Shapiro, & Dempsey, 1987; Shapiro & Young, 1988) were interested in the prospect of leaving the painstaking and

*From Nacos, B. L., Shapiro, R. Y., Young, J. T., Fan, D. P., Kjellstrand, T., & McCaa, C. (1991). Content analysis of news reports: Comparing human coding and a computer-assisted method. *Communication 12:*111–128.

tedious scoring step of future coding to computers, Shapiro, Nacos, and Young recognized the speed and mechanical consistency of computer-assisted content coding, but given their knowledge of content analysis and their more substantive interests, they were somewhat skeptical as to the reliability and validity of such coding.

Computer-Assisted Content Analysis Methods

Computer programs designed to content analyze text are not a new development. The General Inquirer program (Stone, Dunphy, Smith, & Ogilvie, 1969), one of the original programs of this kind, categorizes and counts words, as do related ones such as MCCA (McTavish & Pirro, 1984) and DICTION (Hart, 1984). As new words are read into the computer, they are counted into one of approximately 100 different word categories. The MCCA program, for example, distinguishes between categories like "good," "bad," "happy," "dislike," and so forth, while DICTION defines categories related to speaking styles such as "aggressiveness," "inspiration," and the like (Hart, 1985). An important feature of modern General Inquirer type programs is their procedure for differentiating between words that can be either verbs or nouns (for example, "house"). As dictionaries increase in size, the differentiation procedures for assigning dictionary words to appropriate categories become progressively unmanageable. As a result, the dictionaries of these programs typically include only the most common words.

The General Inquirer and programs using similar methods seem ideal for certain content analyses such as examining the characteristics of speeches. The MCCA program, for example, may score repeatedly words in the "good" or "bad" category and thereby suggest that a speaker is judgmental. However, this kind of coding does not reveal what particular judgment a speaker has made. Thus, these types of programs are not suited to scoring the positions taken by news sources, such as "pro" or "con" attitudes toward a particular policy or political figure. To accomplish this task, programs must be able to analyze relationships between words.

Recently, the corporate sector has begun to utilize "automated message handlers"—computer programs that sift through large volumes of wire service and other media text in order to extract those articles which contain information useful to a particular firm and/or individuals in the user company. The new systems are able to extract specific information "through a primitive ability to understand language" (e.g., Pollock, 1989).

Artificial intelligence researchers, too, have developed methods to analyze text. One of these methods links words or concepts into complex interrelated networks (Sager, 1985), before rules are established to specify the relationships among a great number of words or categories. Because human language is quite complicated, these kinds of network content analysis programs have been developed only for small samples of specialized, carefully selected text. While their applicability is limited, these programs are helpful in providing valuable insights into the structure of language (Hicks, Rush, & Strong, 1985).

Artificial intelligence researchers have also devised other kinds of text analysis programs that identify relationships among ideas within a narrative. One of these discerns the logical structure within text as the researcher enters a sequence of events into a computer file (Heise, 1988). Since this program can only analyze one narrative at a time, it is suitable for qualitative rather than quantitative analysis.

As this brief summary of computer-assisted methods shows, researchers have to determine the objectives of a text analysis before choosing an existing computer program or writing one of their own. Different computer programs have different objectives. Some find and count predefined categories of words. Artificial intelligence programs can be useful when the objective is to explore the structure of the language or ideas in a particular text. But for other purposes, researchers may need programs that can help analyze large volumes of text and take the context of words into account.

THE COMPUTER METHOD OF SUCCESSIVE FILTRATIONS

To meet the needs of researchers who seek to determine the directional content of messages conveyed by the media toward particular attitude objects (e.g., public figures, political issues), Fan developed a computer program that categorizes and counts words and also extracts the context of words in large volumes of text. Recognizing that it is easier to design and implement several simple steps than a single complex procedure, this program departs from others by processing text through a series of different stages leading up to a final coding or scoring run.

In the case of news reports, which we examine here, it is most convenient to retrieve stories from an electronic database, but any text can be analyzed after conversion into machine-readable form. For example, in a study of news coverage of aid to the Nicaragua Contras, the researcher could start out by retrieving articles that appeared in major newspapers or on the wire services. In a study of coverage of aid to the Contras (Fan, 1988; McAvoy, Fan, & Freeman, 1988) the computer program was instructed to search for stories containing the words "Contra" within twenty-five words of "aid," "budget," "expenditure," "spend," "fund," "funds," or "funding." Should such a search yield thousands of stories, the researchers could decide to retrieve only a random sample.

Following this retrieval, the text is then "filtered" through the program one or several times, so that only paragraphs remain which are relevant to the issue or other matter under study. This makes use of filtering rules, which the researcher must develop, program, and then test and refine, using a representative subset of the retrieved paragraphs. In the Contra aid study, for example, one story contained text concerning a farm bill that had been passed by Congress on the same day a Contra aid bill was up for consideration; but since there was no other text related to Contra support, the filtration step removed the irrelevant passages.

Finally, the program scores remaining paragraphs according, for example, to positions expressed in support of, or in opposition to, a specific government policy. To determine such "pro" and "con" scores, however, the coder first must create a dictionary of words associated with key concepts in the text in relation to the issue positions that are to be scored. Rules are then established to define the meaning of the text by using criteria for the distance between, and the sequence of, words associated with the concept categories.

In the Contra study one of the simple rules for scoring "opposed to Contra aid" concerned words in the following categories and situated in the following order: "not," "approve," and "aid" (the "not" concepts category contained words like "no," "not," and "never." The category for "aid" included words like "fund" and "money"). For scoring positions "approving Contra aid," the dictionary included words like "increase" and "favor" (see McAvoy et al., 1988). Thus, with machine coding as well as with human coding, much thought has to be put into coding and determining subtle decision rules.

Paragraphs can be scored as containing one viewpoint (e.g., for or against Contra aid) or expressing two different viewpoints (e.g., one source expressing support for, another source expressing opposition to, Contra aid). In the second example, the total paragraph score of 1.0 is divided in two scores of .5 each, one half paragraph for each viewpoint. If a paragraph does not contain a "pro" or a "con" viewpoint, it is simply not scored.

COMPARING THE COMPUTER PROGRAM WITH HUMAN CODING

The objective of our project was to examine the reliability and validity of quantitative content analysis facilitated by computer coding. This involved two levels of analysis: comparing aggregate measures of content over time based on computer-assisted versus human coding, and comparing computer versus human coding of the same pieces of text. The latter examines coding reliability directly, while the former is of primary substantive interest in studying over time the causes and consequences of media content. The aggregated data allow some of the (presumably random) errors in opposite directions in the coding of the individual pieces of text to offset each other.

The data assembled and coded by Nacos (1990) concerned various aspects of news reporting during national crises (the Cuban Missile Crisis, 1962; the Dominican Republic invasion, 1965; the Detroit riot, 1967; the Three Mile Island nuclear accident, 1979; the attempt to assassinate President Reagan, 1981; and the Grenada invasion, 1983). Nacos content-analyzed all relevant news items in the first parts or sections of three newspapers: the *New York Times,* the *Washington Post,* and the *Chicago Tribune,* with the exception of letters-to-the-editor and Op-Ed page pieces. Her focus was on aggregate content over time—the messages and number of lines attributed to news sources such as the president, White House staffers, other members of the administration, members of Congress, etc. Adapting a method developed by Page et al. (1987), Nacos categorized the messages from each type of source toward the crisis-related presidential policy as either supportive/probably supportive, neutral/ambiguous, or against/probably against. For example, during the acute phase of the Grenada invasion, it was reported that Senator Malcolm Wallop said, "We are seeing an increasing level of Soviet adventuring all over the world" (Coffey & Rawley, 1983:10). This was coded as fitting the supportive/probably supportive category. Senator Daniel Patrick Moynihan labeled the invasion as "an act of war" (Balz & Edsall, 1983). His remark was counted in the against/probably against category. House Speaker Thomas O'Neill's comment, "Now is not the time . . . to be critical of our government when Marines and Rangers are in action down there" (Balz & Edsall, 1983), was coded as neutral/ambiguous.

To compare over time the coding of the directional thrust of such messages in the aggregate, we selected two of the above crises, the Three Mile Island nuclear accident and the Grenada invasion, for which complete data were already assembled and coded by a human coder. To compare coding methods, we needed to use the computer-assisted method to analyze the same news reports Nacos had coded. Our choices were limited, because only news stories concerning the three most recent crises were available from electronic databases in computer readable form. We selected one crisis that had occurred during the term of President Jimmy Carter (Three Mile Island) and one from Ronald Reagan's presidency (the Grenada invasion). In neither case was the news coverage of the *Chicago Tribune* available, but the full text of the Three Mile Island coverage in the *Washington Post* (not the *New York Times*) and the coverage of the Grenada invasion in both the *Times* and the *Post* were retrievable from the Nexis database.

Turning to the analysis at the level of individual paragraphs of text, as described below, two coders at Columbia analyzed a sizeable set of news stories, which had been scored separately by computer at Minnesota. This analysis focused on support versus opposition to increases in U.S. defense spending.

The Capabilities of the New Computer Method

The effective capability of the computer-assisted method was demonstrated in the aggregate-level comparison of the Grenada invasion coverage in the *New York Times* and in the *Washington Post.* While less striking, the content analysis of the same paragraphs by both computer-assisted and human coding showed considerable reliability between human and machine, although the former won.

In the Grenada invasion case, the computer analysis started out by searching the Nexis database for stories in both the *Times* and the *Post* concerning the developments, which began January 1, 1983, leading up to the Grenada invasion in the fall of 1983, the event itself, and the aftermath of the intervention extending through November 25, 1983. A total of 1,174 stories were found which contained the search word "Grenada." The text within fifty words of this search word was retrieved from 1,000 randomly selected stories, a total of 539 *New York Times* articles and 458 *Washington Post* pieces.

The first filtration step had two purposes: It excluded all paragraphs that mentioned

"Grenada Avenue" and therefore had absolutely no relevance to U.S.-Grenada relations, and it kept paragraphs that mentioned words or phrases referring to the U.S. (for example, "White House," "administration," or "Reagan") or to troop policy ("forces," "invade," "marines," etc.).

Because Nacos had restricted her analysis to the first sections of the newspapers, which generally contained the complete Grenada coverage (with the exception of specialized articles in the business, travel, book review, or Sunday news summary sections), only the relevant news items appearing in the first sections of the *Post* and *Times* were retained in an early filtration step. Also, relevant articles appearing on the Op-Ed pages were filtered out, because they had not been included in the hand-coded material.

After the filtration steps described above, the remaining paragraphs were machine-scored in terms of containing material that expressed positions either for or against the relevant presidential or administration policies toward Grenada. Critical for this scoring step was the establishment of a dictionary with key categories of words. For example, the category "BadGuys" contained words like "Cuba" and "Cubans"; the category "ProAction" included words like "rescue/rescued" and "liberators/liberated"; the category "FavorWord" was made up by words such as "moral," "legitimate," and "hailed," etc. The scoring of pro and con positions was determined by 34 rules that had been established, tested, and refined by working with a sample of paragraphs. For example, a "ProAction" word like "liberated" or "rescued" within 30 spaces of "Grenada" was scored as favoring the relevant presidential policy; a word fitting the "ConAction" category, for instance, "antiwar" or "protest" within 30 spaces of an "InvasionWord" such as "invade" or "invasion," was scored as opposing President Reagan's Grenada policy.

While the human-coded data contained three positions (for/probably for, neutral/ambiguous, and against/probably against), the computer scored only pro versus con positions—either a score of 1.0 per paragraph or, if both positions were expressed, a split score for each position. Consequently, in the interest of comparability, we dropped the lines that were hand-coded neutral/ambiguous from our statistical comparison of the two coding methods. We then added up each day's total number of lines, which were hand-coded as favorable and then each day's machine-coded favorable paragraphs. The Pearson correlation coefficient (r) for the over-time relationship between each day's human and machine coded favorable scores was .90 ($p < .0.5$). The ratio of human coded lines to machine coded paragraphs was approximately 25 to 1 (24.79 to 1 as estimated by a bivariate regression coefficient). This same procedure was repeated for the text coded as opposed to the U.S. invasion of Grenada. Here the time series correlation between the machine coded oppose scores and the human coded oppose scores was .89 ($p < .05$), and the ratio of lines to paragraphs was 19.21 to 1. These correlations clearly indicate that in this case the traditional method of content coding and the faster and more efficient computer-assisted method had a high level of [correlation]* over time in their pattern of "favor" and "oppose" scores.[1]

In the Grenada case, we compared the content of messages over time, which masks possible discrepancies in story-by-story or paragraph-by-paragraph codings. How much discrepancy might we expect at that level? A separate comparison of the coding results on a paragraph-by-paragraph basis was required to assess this, since the computer program scored paragraphs. These coding comparisons were done for news reports relating to defense spending during Jimmy Carter's and part of Ronald Reagan's presidency. For an earlier project, Fan and his colleagues had used the new computer-assisted method to examine how the issues surrounding U.S. defense spending had been covered from January 1977 to April 1986 (see Fan, 1988).

In searching for AP dispatches related to defense spending in the Nexis database, the

*The authors said "agreement," which cannot be measured by a correlation coefficient; see reading 6.2 in this volume.

investigators used three search concepts which referred to American defense, and spending and thereby assured that the text concerned U.S. defense spending and not that of another country. The concept "America," for example, included terms like "United States," "House," "Senate," etc. For the retrieval of relevant AP dispatches the requirement was that an article had to contain at least one word from each of the three search concepts, for instance, U.S., defense, and spending. From the pool of stories that fulfilled this condition, text within fifty words of any of the three search concepts was retrieved.

In a second filtration step, entire dispatches were discarded in order to get rid of articles, which contained the required concept words but were still not relevant. For example, dispatches reporting about American aid for defense spending in another country or referring to topics such as the Environmental Defense Fund were weeded out.

Finally, after a dictionary and rules were established, the remaining text was analyzed for three positions concerning defense spending: either favoring more, the same, or less funding in the defense sector. The criterion was that a "defense word" be in close proximity to "modifier words" which revealed preference for either of the three attitudes concerning defense spending.

In this defense spending case, the computer program, Nacos, and Young separately coded the same text. From the 58 stories on defense spending the two coders examined a total of 531 paragraphs on which some scoring decision had to be reached. Nacos and Young agreed on the coding of 499 paragraphs. This . . . agreement . . . might, in part, be explained by the . . . researchers' experience. More importantly, one of the four decisions to be reached was whether the paragraph was to be coded at all as favoring more, less, or the same amount of defense spending; that is, whether the paragraph was minimally relevant to U.S. defense spending and whether it could be placed into one of these categories. This task is sufficiently straightforward that we would expect a high frequency of inter-coder agreement. Nacos and the computer program agreed on 83% of these decisions, and Young and the program agreed on 81% of the cases.*

Once this relatively simple initial decision was made, each coder then assigned the paragraph to one of the three substantive categories. (The reliability of Nacos and Young's coding was $\alpha_{ordinal} = 0.896$,** between Young and the computer, $\alpha_{ordinal} = 0.565$. While the computer and Nacos agreed less often, $\alpha_{ordinal} = 0.387$), . . . when Nacos coded a paragraph as favoring less defense spending, the computer did likewise.

When interpreted together with the computer method's effective filtration of relevant text we consider this reliability to be minimally adequate for purposes of aggregating large numbers of these scores in order to track changes in media content over time. . . . [B]ecause aggregation helps eliminate random error, the lower reliability (of coding paragraphs) is not inconsistent with higher correlation found at the aggregate level over time, although it suggests that less reliable coding might cause serious problems even after aggregation, especially if the numbers of relevant news stories scored and aggregated are small.

Some Unsatisfactory Results

In contrast to the Grenada case, the second aggregate level comparison was clearly a failure, but one that demonstrated the pitfalls and limitations in the use of the computer program—most of them obvious enough to be avoided. This part of our analysis examined the coverage of the Three Mile Island accident and, more specifically, the positions of

*Percent agreement—other than 100%—is not particularly indicative of reliability; see reading 6.2, this volume.

**Alpha reliabilities for the authors' ordinal data were calculated by the editors. The authors had used Pearson's *r*, Gamma, and Somers's *D*, which are coefficients of association, not of agreement. See reading 6.2, this volume.

news sources concerning President Carter's nuclear power policies and his handling of the most serious nuclear power plant accident up to that date. Again, the computer analysis began by searching the Nexis database for stories that appeared in the *Washington Post* between January 1 and May 31, 1979. A total of 245 news items were found that mentioned the key words "Three Mile Island" or TMI. Text within fifty words of those two key words for all 245 stories was retrieved.

In the first filtration step, all paragraphs referring to relevant administration policies concerning the Three Mile Island emergency as well as nuclear power in general were kept and irrelevant paragraphs discarded. The second filtration phase extracted text, which appeared in the first part of the *Post* from articles published in other sections. Only the news items published in the first section of the newspaper (with the exception of pieces on the Op-Ed page) were kept. A third step filtered out material that concerned foreign protest actions against nuclear power plants that referred to the Three Mile Island incident but were directed against foreign governments and not against the U.S.

In scoring the remaining paragraphs in the final step of the computer analysis, the goal was to identify positions that expressed support or opposition toward the relevant president policies and actions. As the method of successive filtrations requires, a comprehensive dictionary had to be established. For example, the category "Carter" included words like "Carter" and "White House"; the category "Support" contained "defend," "support," and similar terms; the category "Opposition" listed "doubt," "accuse," "blame," etc. To enable the computer to score the "for" and "against" positions of the text, the researchers chose a total of 36 rules. One rule, for example, established that a word in the "Carter" category within 25 spaces ahead or behind a "Support" word, represented a position supportive of the presidential policy under discussion. On the other hand, a "Carter" word within 30 spaces ahead of a tem fitting the "Negate" category containing words like "defeat," "fall," "lack," etc. was scored as a position opposing the relevant presidential policy. If a paragraph contained text that expressed both a supportive and an oppositional attitude, the score of 1.0 was divided between the two positions.

In the Three Mile Island case as with Grenada we added up the "favorable" paragraphs of lines from the relevant stories that appeared each day during the most intense period of activity, from March 29th, 1979 to May 22nd, 1979. This yielded 41 time points with which to examine scoring reliability. We again computed a Pearson's correlation (r) between the computer program's scores and Nacos' result, and then repeated this process for the "opposed" paragraphs and lines. In the case of the lines/paragraphs coded as opposed to Carter's policy, there was a correlation of .67. While this correlation is lower than for Grenada, it might be considered minimally acceptable for aggregate data. However, when we compare the lines and paragraphs coded as favorable to Carter's policy, the correlation drops to a small and discouraging .33. We thought that we may have picked up unusually severe error, because many (16) of the 41 cases were composed of very few paragraphs (≤ 5). Therefore we aggregated the 41 days into three-day periods (except the last period which was two days) which gave us 14 time points. The new correlation for the opposed scores was a higher $r = .76$, but the correlation for the scores favorable to Carter only increased slightly to .35. The latter estimate is clearly unacceptable, especially given that the additional aggregation should have eliminated more random error.

The results of this last comparison are nevertheless informative and useful. In particular, they alert researchers to important concerns during the research design stage in projects of this nature and to several characteristics of this particular case that contributed greatly to unsatisfactory findings. Also, the results of this comparison seem to point to some limitations of the computer program and the need for further refinements. Specifically, our . . . comparison . . . made us aware of several conceptual or research-specific problems and others concerning the computer program itself.

How to Deal With Problems

First, in both the Three Mile Island and the Grenada invasion study, Nacos had coded four distinct time periods; a pre-crisis, an acute crisis, a lingering crisis, and a post-crisis phase. While in the Grenada case, the basic presidential policy remained fairly constant (prior to the invasion President Reagan had claimed that the island was in the process of becoming a beachhead for Communism; later on he justified the intervention with the necessity to rescue Americans from the island and to help other Caribbean countries liberate Grenada from Communism), the presidential policy priorities in the Three Mile Island accident case were more complex and changed over time. For example, during the short acute crisis phase the issue was not—as it was before and after this period—President Carter's support of "safe" nuclear energy but, rather, the handling of the nuclear threat in Pennsylvania by Carter and his stand-in crisis management team at the accident site. Unlike the hand-coded material, the machine-coded text was coded with one set of rules. Using a single set of rules affected the results of our Three Mile Island comparison much more than those in the Grenada invasion case because, as was mentioned, the Reagan administration policy toward Grenada was fairly constant and clear-cut in the four crisis phases.*

Second, Nacos had examined the relevant daily newspaper coverage as it appeared on microfilm and had extracted the number of column lines published per source and the positions taken concerning the particular presidential policy. The computer-assisted analysis, on the other hand, had to rely on the version of the text provided by Nexis and scored its paragraphs for pro and con positions. There are great differences in the length of paragraphs in the two newspapers used for this comparative study. In the *Post,* for example, paragraphs ranged from two or three to well over twenty column lines. This can result in rather significant scoring differences. For example, an article may contain four short paragraphs, totaling twenty lines, expressing opposition to a particular policy issue and two long paragraphs of perhaps forty lines expressing support for the policy. In the paragraph scoring, this would produce a 4–2 score opposing the policy, whereas the line scoring would yield a 40–20 or 2–1 advantage in support of the policy. Since Nacos had finished her project well before we began our collaboration, we had to settle for the line versus paragraph comparison. While the paragraph versus line problem was encountered in both cases, it affected the Three Mile Island comparison to a much greater extent, because the amount of text analyzed was significantly less than in the Grenada invasion case. Our judgment is that the paragraph versus line discrepancies are likely to balance out as larger volumes of text are examined.

Third, there was no in-person or phone contact between Nacos, who had coded the media text for both the Grenada Invasion and the Three Mile Island accident, and Kjellstrand and McCaa who wrote the dictionaries and rules for the computer analysis. Although Nacos had provided the researchers at Minnesota with written coding objectives, we are certain that personal discussions, as they are common among coders working on the same project, would have helped to clarify the scoring objectives much more fully.** This lack of communication among coders also negatively affected our paragraph-by-paragraph comparisons on the defense spending issue. With hindsight, we are convinced that the researchers who establish the text analysis objectives must be closely involved in all steps of the successive filtration method, especially in the establishment of the search words, the dictionaries, and the rules as well as in the testing of the rules by scoring sample paragraphs. In this respect, again, the Three Mile Island study was affected to a much greater extent than the Grenada case because of the changing coding objectives concerning the nuclear accident as explained above.

---

*In other words, frequency accounts are permeation measures. Therefore, systematic variations in the counted phenomenon necessarily escape such accounts.

**See reading 5.5, this volume.

Fourth, since the Grenada invasion was covered more extensively and over a longer time period than the accident at Three Mile Island and related policies, and because the Grenada comparisons included the coverage of both the *New York Times* and the *Washington Post,* whereas the Three Mile Island accident comparison included only the *Washington Post,* there was a significant difference in the quantity of text that was analyzed. In the Grenada study, approximately 1,000 items were examined, in contrast to about 250 in the Three Mile Island case. The new computer-assisted method more accurately captures the trend, in reported "pro" and "con" positions on particular policy issues when large samples of text are examined, and less accurately when small amounts of text are coded (McAvoy et al., 1988).

Fifth, the computer method retrieved relevant text from the Nexis database within fifty words of search words (for example, "Three Mile Island" and "TMI" in the case under discussion). This seems to be a satisfactory method in projects that are interested in capturing the important trends in media coverage for a great many kinds of issues (Fan, 1988; McAvoy et al., 1988) and that analyze large amounts of text. However, for more complex studies of media coverage which require accurate content scores and corresponding measures of amounts of content for different policy positions, and which concern relatively small numbers of news items, the retrieval of the complete text of all stories related to a particular topic would prevent the loss of relevant text. For example, in the aftermath of the Three Mile Island accident, when President Carter had reaffirmed his support for more nuclear power plants, opponents of this energy source staged protest demonstrations in Washington. At one point, the president met some protesters. While "Three Mile Island" or "TMI" might have been mentioned in one or two paragraphs of the news coverage, these terms were not mentioned in most paragraphs of the long articles reporting about the events in the capital. Accordingly, much of the text was neither retrieved nor scored, even though it covered Carter's position toward nuclear power. It is conceivable that the retrieval method using the fifty-word requirement is sufficient if a large enough sample of text is analyzed. This would explain the satisfactory results in the Grenada invasion comparison and the unsatisfactory correlation between manual and computer-assisted coding in the Three Mile Island case.

Sixth, it seems that human coders are more inclined to recognize the meaning of text in the context of an entire article, or at least a few paragraphs, while the computer scoring treats each paragraph separately. We observed this contextual shortcoming of the computer program not only in the Three Mile Island case but also in the Grenada invasion study. In the latter, for example, an article about a speech by Fidel Castro extensively quoted the Cuban leader characterizing U.S. claims about the Cuban role in Grenada as lies. Several of these alleged lies were detailed in a number of paragraphs. Each of the paragraphs contained an American justification for having invaded the island and thus contained words that were identified by the computer as messages expressing support for President Reagan's Grenada policy. But since all of this was part of Castro's accusations against the United States, it had to be scored as *against* Reagan's Grenada position. Although the computer method does, in theory, permit thoughts in one paragraph to be transferred to later ones, there was no attempt to use such transfers, since it was not initially apparent that they were needed.

Conclusion

Our analysis has convinced us that the use of computer-assisted methods offers very promising possibilities for quantitative media research. The method involving successive filtrations of text, which we have described here, is an important step in this direction, even though we have observed that computer-assisted content analysis not only has great advantages but also has certain weaknesses that must be dealt with.

The predominant reason for preferring computer-assisted methods to human coding is the speed and consistency with which the former can code (once the coding rules are programmed) large volumes of text, especially when the goal is to obtain aggregated measures of content. For human coders alone, this would be a very labor intensive, time consuming, tiresome, and costly task. Moreover, human coding will be accurate or error-prone depending on the ability of coders to concentrate throughout extensive coding sessions.

The limitations that we found in the computer-assisted method are not trivial. While scoring or coding text, the computer follows programmed rules and does not recognize ambiguities or problems as an attentive human coder would, in particular when instructions are not sufficiently precise; when text does not seem to fit into prescribed categories; or when a mechanical paragraph-by-paragraph coding does not make sense in the context of several preceding paragraphs.

Demonstrating the impact of the news media may indeed be comparable to hunting particles of dust in a sunbeam, but with the possibilities of computer-assisted text analysis, media researchers have a far greater chance of succeeding in these efforts, and of doing so at a much quicker pace than before.

Note

1. It is revealing that when we tried to compute a single "net" daily score for each method by subtracting the unfavorable daily scores, the correlation dropped to a small .28. This suggests that error can readily occur in computing such net scores unless care is taken, as is observed below in the case of Three Mile Island, to find all relevant text, going beyond the computer program's 50 word limit. To date, statistical models that have been examined using this computer program have avoided using net/difference scores on theoretical grounds (Fan, 1988, cited in Page et al., 1987).

References

Balz, D., & Edsall, T. E. (1983, October 26). Gap rallies around Reagan; Democrats divided on Grenada. *The Washington Post,* p. A8.

Coffey, R., & Rawley, S. (1983, October 26). Why U.S. acts. *Chicago Tribune,* pp. 1, 19.

Fan, D. P. (1988). *Predictions of public opinion from the mass media.* Westport, CT.: Greenwood Press.

Hart, R. P. (1984). *Verbal style and the presidency: A computer-based analysis.* New York: Academic Press.

Hart, R. P. (1985). Systematic analysis of political discourse. Development of DICTION. In K. R. Sanders, L. L. Kaid, & D. Nimmo (Eds.), *Political communication yearbook, 1984.* Carbondale, IL: Southern Illinois University.

Heise, D. R. (1988). Computer analysis of cultural structures. *Social Science Computer Review 6,*1:183–196.

Hicks, C. E., Rush, J. E., & Strong, S. M. (1985). Content analysis. In E. D. Dym (Ed.), *Subject and information analysis* (pp. 57–109). New York: Marcel Dekker.

McAvoy, G. E., Fan, D. P., & Freeman, J. R. (1988, September). *Gauging the effects of the media on public opinion: Content analysis using the method of successive filtrations.* Paper presented at the annual meeting of the American Political Science Association, Washington, DC.

McTavish, D. G., & Pirro, E. B. (1984, April). *Cultural content analysis.* Paper presented at the Pacific Sociological Association Meetings, Seattle, WA.

Nacos, B. L. (1990). *The press, presidents, and crises.* New York: Columbia University Press.

Page, B. I., Shapiro, R. Y., & Dempsey, G. R. (1987). What moves public opinion? *American Political Science Review 81:*23–43.

Pollock, A. (1989, June 7). Computers that read and analyze. *The New York Times,* pp. D1, D6.

Sager, N. (1985). Natural language analysis and processing. In E. D. Dym (Ed.), *Subject and information analysis* (pp. 154–168). New York: Marcel Dekker.

Shapiro, R. Y., & Young, J. T. (1988, September–October). Le vote des televisions. *Le Journal des Elections, No. 4.*

Stone, P. J., Dunphy, D. C., Smith, M. S., & Ogilvie, D. M. (Eds.). (1969). *The General Inquirer: A computer approach to content analysis.* Cambridge, MA: MIT Press.

4.5

Coding Instructions

An Example

Joseph N. Cappella, Danielle J. Mittermaier, Judith Weiner, Lee Humphreys, Tiara Falcone, and Mario Giorno*

Editors' Note: This is an excerpt from the codebook for a content analysis of 964 articles from twenty U.S. newspapers with the highest readership and four major national news broadcast stations. The content analysis sought to infer genetic risks of cancer and other diseases from how news stories were framed. The actual codebook is 40 pages long. It defines several simple variables but had to become very detailed to achieve adequate reliability for theoretically motivated variables that can be expressed variously. We are including a portion that illustrates the level of specificity necessary to retrieve and identify relevant news stories with the help of search engines and code them.

Section A—Searching for Articles on the Computer

1. Search Engines

To perform our search, we use three search engines—NEXIS.COM, FACTIVA, and NEWSBANK. Nexis.com is available at http://www.nexis.com (username and password will be supplied to you). FACTIVA and NEWSBANK are both available on the University's library web page. The media sources that we use are the four major broadcast channels (ABC, NBC, CBS, and CNN), the Associated Press, and the top 20 newspapers in circulation (as of July 2004). We cannot access all of these sources through one search engine, so you will need to search each media outlet through the engine it is associated with, as detailed below.

*This codebook was developed as part of *The Effects of Public Information in Cancer* project conducted in 2006 at the Center for Excellence in Cancer Communication Research at the University of Pennsylvania's Annenberg School for Communication and funded by the National Cancer Institute, grant number 5P50CA095856. The study is accessible at http://ceccr.asc.upenn.edu/primary/Framing_Genetic_Risk.asp, including the original codebook.

a. NEXIS.COM*

Sampled Media

Newspapers:

- *New York Times*
- *Associated Press*
- *USA Today*
- *Los Angeles Times*
- *Washington Post*
  (. . .)
- *The San Diego Union-Tribune*
- *Chicago Tribune*
- *Dallas Morning News*
- *The Arizona Republic*
- *Philadelphia Inquirer*

Broadcast:

- *ABC News Transcripts*
- *CBS News Transcripts*
- *NBC News Transcripts*
- *CNN News Transcripts*

Search Terms for NEXIS.COM:

(NOCAPS (gene) OR genetic! OR DNA OR genome) AND NOT (modified OR corn OR rape OR murder OR lewinsky OR crime OR crops)

2. Dates of the Sample

The articles sampled for the content analysis will be dated from January 1, 1997–December 31, 2007. We will concentrate on six month intervals at a time (January 1997–June 1997; July 1997–December 1997; January 1998–June 1998; and so on through December 2007). The appropriate dates for your assigned time period should be entered into the search engine to limit the time frame of the articles being sampled.

3. Number of Articles to Sample

For each six-month period, **150 articles** will be randomly sampled from the above sources (100 from print sources, 50 from broadcast sources). For specific and detailed information regarding the sampling strategy, please refer to the *Content Analysis Sampling Protocol.*[**]

Section B—Coding for Articles Inclusion or Exclusion

1. Should an article be included in our sample?

For an article to be included in our sample ***there must be at least one sentence in the article that expresses a gene-outcome relationship***. For example, does the sentence discuss how genes influence behavior, disease susceptibility, or mental abilities? The outcome must be a *specific* disease, behavior, mental or physical characteristic, or result (for details of what constitutes a sentence expressing a gene-outcome relation, see **Section E**).

*The original codebook includes similar instructions for the FACTIVA and NEWSBANK search engines.

**Refers to specific sampling instructions, not included in these coding instructions.

- Sentence <u>must be a statement</u>, not be in the form of a question.
- Sentence <u>must be real</u>, not a hypothetical statement.
- Sentence <u>must express a gene-outcome relationship in humans</u> (not plants or animals)

2. Identifying Framing Sentences:

Words or phrases that represent <GENE>:

Gene, gene mutation, genetic variant, genetic, genetically programmed, genetic role, genetic component, genetic basis, genetic disorder, genetic disease, genetic predisposition, genetic causes, genetic link, genetic makeup, a specific name of gene like BRCA1 or CYP1B1, DNA, genome, human genetic programming, biogenic forces, genetic marker.

Words that should NOT be coded as representing <GENE>:

Protein, enzyme, chromosome, gene therapy, genetic test, cancer, amino acids, molecule, cell, condition, heredity, inherited, family history, biological, tumor, stem cell, virus, mutation, variant.

You must be able to answer YES to all of the following questions for the sentence to be considered a framing sentence (examples below for each condition):

a. Does the sentence explicitly mention genes and genes in humans?

b. Does the sentence have an identifiable outcome?

c. Does the sentence have a specific outcome?

d. Does the sentence have a verbal link between the outcome and gene?

e. Is the gene affecting something in the sentence?

a. Does the sentence explicitly mention genes and genes in humans?

Do not include sentences that are NOT about genes or genes in humans, such as:

- "Sickle cell anemia also increases a person's vulnerability to infections."
- "Gene Identified in Worm May Offer a Key to the Aging Process."
- "Before her daughter did anything drastic, the 63-year-old Atlanta resident wanted to discover whether some kind of hereditary abnormality linked to cancer ran in their family."

b. Does the sentence have an identifiable outcome?

Do not include sentences that do NOT have an identifiable outcome, such as:

- "They discovered that 44% had a genetic alteration called loss of imprinting, meaning a gene is abnormally turned off or on."
- "Among black girls, the relationship is less clear-cut, he said, and some researchers believe that genetic factors may be more influential among African Americans."

c. Does the sentence have a specific outcome?

Do not include sentences that do NOT have a <u>specified</u> outcome (disease, condition, illness, and prognosis are too vague when used alone in a sentence—cancer & tumor okay), such as:

- "The study will look for genetic links to the major diseases as well as examine the influence of personal health habits."
- "Specific foods or eating patterns may alter the activity of our individual genes, making at-risk people more, or less, susceptible to illness."

d. Does the sentence have a verbal link between the outcome and gene?

Do not include sentences in which the gene-outcome relationship is expressed in an adjective-noun form, such as:

- "Others may be extra radiosensitive too, including people who carry the <u>breast cancer genes</u> called BRCA1 and BRCA2." *In this case, "breast cancer gene" should not be read as "the gene that causes breast cancer."*

- "That committee has just recommended that some people whose blood has not been used before—those with a genetic disease called hemochromatosis—should now be considered donors."

e. Is the gene affecting something in the sentence?

Do not include sentences that do not express specific gene-outcome relationship in one sentence (from first word to ending punctuation), such as:

- "It is well known in medicine that even tiny genetic differences between populations can have powerful health consequences. The Pima Indians have one of the highest rates of diabetes in the world."
- "Whether ADHD occurs because of a mother's worrying is not clear, said Dr. David Feinberg, a child psychiatrist at UCLA. It could be a combination of things, including genetics and maternal smoking."

Do not include sentences which claim that genetics do NOT affect something.

- "A study of twins provides the strongest evidence yet that environmental factors, not genetics, cause Parkinson's disease in people over age 50."
- "Those who have the low-performing gene but are not exposed to maltreatment were not at higher risk, the researchers found."

Section C—Identifying Information in Article

ID#:	Identification number of newspaper article/story
Coder Initials:	Initials of the coder who is coding the article
Coding Date:	Date that the coding is taking place
Source:	Identification of the news source (e.g., *NYTimes* or *NBC*)
Title:	Identification of the article's title (do not put the title in quotation marks unless that is how it appears in the title when it is retrieved)
Reporter:	Identification of the story's reporter (if no reporter, identify anchor or wire service, like AP Press)
Location:	– For print—Where in the newspaper the article appeared (ex. Late Edition - Final, Section F; Column 1; Health & Fitness; COMMENTARY; Page 5) – For broadcast—The show on which the story aired (ex. World News Tonight with Peter Jennings)
Time:	For broadcast, the time that the show aired on television. There is NO coding of time for print articles
Date:	When the story was published or aired (Month / Day / Year)
Length:	Number of words in the article or transcript

Section D—General Coding Structure

This section is designed to provide the general format and order that you will be using to code. For more details about how to code for each category, please see the section(s) that elaborate on each category, starting with Section E. . . .

There are four categories for which you will be coding:

1. Framing sentences (every article must have at least one to be coded)*
2. Credibility (may not be present in every article)
3. Exemplars (may not be present in every article)
4. Efficacy (may not be present in every article)

1. Framing Sentences

✓ Must code 4 items for each framing sentence
✓ Code up to 5 framing sentences per article

- **Complexity:** The degree of conditionality expressed in the sentence involving genetic and/or environmental factors

  0 = No conditions
  1 = Complex condition
  2 = Contingent condition

- **Framing:** Framing verb in the sentence that expresses a relationship between genetics in humans and a specific outcome:

  1 (Probabilistic) —— through —— (Deterministic) 5.
  Please note: If the sentence was pre-determined to be complex or contingent, the framing of the sentence *must* be of some degree of probability. Also, if the sentence involves a person *with* the gene, the sentence *must* be some degree of probability

- **Location:** Where in the article the sentence appears

  1 = Title
  2 = First Paragraph
  3 = Elsewhere in the article

- **Outcome:** For the identified sentence, specify the particular outcome related to the gene's effect in humans

  See **List of Outcomes** below

2. Credibility statements

✓ Must code for 2 items if credibility statements are present
✓ Code up to 2 credibility statements per article

- **Position of Credibility:** Determine whether the credibility is a supporting or opposing statement about the genetic claim or study

  1 = Statement(s) supports the genetic claim or study
  2 = Statement(s) supports and opposes the genetic claim or study
  3 = Statement(s) opposes genetic claim or study

- **Credibility Location:** Where the credibility statement appears in the article

  1 = Title
  2 = First Paragraph
  3 = Elsewhere in the article

3. Exemplars

✓ Must code for 7 items if exemplar is present
✓ Code up to 3 exemplars per article

- **Exemplar Location:** Where in the article the exemplar is first mentioned

  1 = Title
  2 = First Paragraph
  3 = Elsewhere in the article.

---

*For space considerations, we have included only the coding instructions for Framing. The original instructions include equally specific instructions for coding Credibility, Exemplars, Efficacy and Location.

- **Exemplar Quote:** Presence or absence of a quotation from a person or persons in the exemplar

  0 = Absence
  1 = Presence

- **Exemplar Vividness:** Code for the presence or absence of personal and/or emotional details:

  0 = Absence of both personal and emotional details
  1 = Presence of either personal OR emotional details
  2 = Presence of both personal AND emotional details

- **Exemplar Illustration—Framing:** Code for whether or not the stated gene-outcome relationship is alluded to in some way in the exemplar. The person or family does not have to be the gene carriers.

  0 = Exemplar does NOT allude to the stated relationship
  1 = Exemplar DOES allude to the stated relationship

- **Exemplar Illustration—Relationship:** Code for whether or not the stated gene-outcome relationship is explicitly mentioned in the exemplar:

  0 = The person has the gene/gene mutation/family history but fails to manifest the outcome
  1 = The person has the gene/gene mutation/family history but the outcome is yet undetermined
  2 = The person has the gene/gene mutation/family history and manifests the outcome (condition, behavior, disease, etc.)

- **Additional Exemplar:** Code for the presence or absence of more than three exemplars

  0 = Absence
  1 = Presence

- **Children:** Code for the presence or absence of children as the focus of the exemplar

  0 = Absence
  1 = Presence

4. Efficacy

✓ Must code for 2 items (presence and location) for each type of efficacy present in the overall article (coding only for presence, not for number of occurrences).

- **Efficacy:** Presence or absence of response (specific, practical suggestions) and/or personal (motivational) efficacy statements in an article:

  0 = Absence of both Personal AND Response Efficacy
  1 = Presence of Personal Efficacy
  2 = Presence of Response Efficacy
  3 = Presence of both Personal AND Response Efficacy

Proceed with the following question, if you coded for the presence of personal efficacy sentences above—1 or 3

- **Personal Efficacy:** Is there at least one instance of personal efficacy?

  0 = No
  1 = Yes

- **Personal Efficacy Location:** Where does the presence of personal efficacy appear?

  1 = Within an exemplar
  2 = Elsewhere in the article
  3 = Statements of personal efficacy located both within an exemplar AND elsewhere in the article

Proceed with the following question, if you coded for the presence of response efficacy sentences above—2 or 3

- **Response Efficacy:** Is there at least one sentence that is an example of response efficacy?
  - 0 = No
  - 1 = Yes
- **Response Efficacy Location:** Where the presence of the response efficacy statement(s) appears:
  - 1 = Within an exemplar
  - 2 = Elsewhere in the article
  - 3 = Statements of response efficacy located both within an exemplar AND elsewhere in the article

Proceed with the following question, ONLY if you coded for the presence of response efficacy located WITHIN the exemplar above—1

- **Response Efficacy Failure:** The response efficacy adopted by the person or family in the exemplar has failed to thwart the outcome's effects
  - 0 = approach was successful
  - 1 = approach failed

Section E—Coding Framing Sentences

For each article, identify and code up to five (5) sentences that express a gene-outcome relationship (framing sentence). *There may be grammatical variations of this relationship, but a* ***verb*** *must always be present linking gene and outcome (see below).* Both active (example A) and passive (example B) sentences are valid.

A <gene> <verb> <outcome>	Genes can cause depression
B <outcome> <verb> <gene>	Depression can be caused by genes
C <verb> <gene> <outcome>	The causal impact of genes on depression is significant

1. Complexity

For each identified framing sentence, code the complexity or conditionality of the relationship between genetics and the outcome, ranging from no conditions (0) to contingent condition (2). Use the examples . . . to help determine the complexity of each sentence.

No Condition		**Complex Condition**		**Contingent Condition**
This gene affects X		This gene *AND other factors*, affects X		This gene *in this environment* affects X
0	—	1	—	2

(0) No condition: These sentences express the relationship between the gene and outcome without involving any other social, behavioral or environmental factors or conditions.

(1) Complex condition: These sentences express the relationship between the gene and other social, behavioral or environmental factors affecting the outcome. The complex condition is one where the gene and other factors both affect the outcome.

(2) Contingent condition: These sentences express the relationship between the gene and outcome as dependent upon another social, behavioral or environmental factor. Think of the contingent condition as an "if . . . then" statement—a prerequisite condition must exist for the statement to be true (e.g., being a smoker, pregnant, menopausal, sedentary lifestyle, alcoholic, etc.).

Examples of (0) NO Conditionality:

- "Officials at both companies said the gene probably is only one of several genes responsible for various forms of osteoarthritis."
- "Asthma has a strong genetic component."

Examples of (1) COMPLEX Conditionality:

- "Because family members share a proportion of their genes and, often, their environment, it is possible that the large number of cancer cases seen in these families may be partly due to other genetic or environmental factors.
- "Studies of twins suggest that whether a person exercises regularly or slacks off is influenced in roughly equal parts by genetics, social environment and physical environment, said Rod Dishman, co-director of the exercise psychology laboratory at the University of Georgia."

Examples of (2) CONTINGENT Conditionality:

- "Obesity and lack of physical exercise during adolescence increase a woman's risk of breast cancer if she is a carrier of a BRCA1 or BRCA2 gene mutation . . ."
- "Children who grow up in homes that are psychologically, physically or sexually abusive were found to have a nine-fold increased risk of becoming anti-social as adults if they had a low-performing version of the MAOA gene rather than a normal version."

2. Framing

Code the identified sentence(s) using one of the 5 different types of framing listed below (ranging from probabilistic to deterministic). Use key words and examples (pages 15–20) to help determine how each sentence is framed.

Note: If the sentence was pre-determined to be complex or contingent, it can only be coded as a 1 (probabilistic) or a 2 (slightly probabilistic) below.

Note: If the sentence is about a person with the gene, it can only be coded as a 1 (probabilistic) or a 2 (slightly probabilistic)

Probabilistic		Slightly Probabilistic		Probabilistic & Deterministic in the Same Sentence		Slightly Deterministic		Deterministic
1	—	2	—	3	—	4	—	5

The verbs reported below have been divided into four categories based on judgments of their perceived intended meaning (verbs in normal font) as well as based on Judi Weiner's Q-Sort study (verbs in *italics*). These lists are to be used as guideposts to help coders make decisions about a sentence's framing category. They are neither fixed nor exhaustive, and they may change—even by a considerable degree—according to the article's context. The list has also been alphabetized for ease of use (see **Alphabetized List of Verbs** below).

When deciding whether a sentence is probabilistic or slightly probabilistic, pay attention to any language intensifiers that might be present, such as "highly", "strongly" or "significantly." If they accompany the verb, code the sentence as a 2, rather than a 1. The same decision must be made when there are language mitigators, such as "in part" or "usually"—present in a deterministic sentence. In this case, the sentence is to be coded as a 4 versus a 5.

(1) **Probabilistic Key Words:** *appears to predict, as a possible cause, can affect, can lead to, can lead to the development of, could play a role,* fosters, influences, is involved in, is related to, *may account for, may be implicated, may be involved in, may cause, may play a role, might affect,* plays a role, probably has, *risk of developing,* seems to, *seems to help create,* suggesting, susceptibility, *tends to be, that might control, thought to affect,* underlie, vulnerable.

(2) **Slightly Probabilistic Key Words:** any sentence that involves a specific number or percentage (ex. Genes cause cancer in 60% of the cases), affects the chances, *affects the risk of developing, associated with, can cause,* can cause a high risk, *can determine, can make a big difference,* caused in part, component, determined in part, *elevated*

risk, greater risk for, helps to, helps to determine, *higher risk of developing, increases a person's chance of, increases risk, increases susceptibility, increases the chances of developing, linked to hereditary predisposition,* occurs more frequently in, *predict, shown to increase the risk of,* strong likelihood, *that causes a predisposition towards, that helps determine, that plays a role in determining.*

(4) **Slightly Deterministic Key Words:** accounts for, affects, can be caused, can give rise to, *connected to, decreases risk, has been linked to a high risk, has been traced, increased the risk of,* is important, *linked to, lowers the risk of,* may be blamed for, mostly determined, *predisposes, reduce the risk of, responsible for susceptibility to, sharply increases the risk of, strongly suggests, that contribute to, that determines the risk of developing,* thought to be caused, *which affects.*

(5) **Deterministic Key Words:** *are tied to,* brought about, *causes, determined by, due to,* has produced, *have identified, it is a major cause of, it's an absolute guarantee, lead to, leads to the development of,* makes, *plays an essential role, plays an important role, powerfully predisposes,* programmed, *responsible for, results from, stem from, strongly determines.*

Please see (below) an **Alphabetized List of Verbs** in columns (better for reference while coding.

Examples of verb phrases and their framing

Verb Phrase "causes"	**Framing**
cause	deterministic
is a major cause of	deterministic
can be caused	slightly deterministic
thought to be caused	slightly deterministic
caused in part	slightly probabilistic
can cause a high risk	slightly probabilistic
that causes a predisposition towards developing	slightly probabilistic
can cause	slightly probabilistic
as a possible cause	probabilistic
may cause	probabilistic

Verb Phrase "plays a role"	**Framing**
plays an important role	deterministic
plays an essential role	deterministic
that plays a role in determining	slightly probabilistic
plays a role	probabilistic
could play a role	probabilistic
may play a role	probabilistic

Verb Phrase "leads to"	**Framing**
lead to	deterministic
leads to the development of	deterministic
can lead to	probabilistic
can lead to the development of	probabilistic

Verb Phrase "affects risk"	Framing
that determines the risk of developing	slightly deterministic
sharply increases the risk of	slightly deterministic
decreases risk	slightly deterministic
lowers the risk of	slightly deterministic
reduce the risk of	slightly deterministic
increased the risk of	slightly deterministic
has been linked to a high risk	slightly deterministic
can cause a high risk	slightly probabilistic
shown to increase the risk of	slightly probabilistic
elevated risk	slightly probabilistic
increases risk	slightly probabilistic
greater risk for	probabilistic
higher risk of developing	probabilistic
affects the risk of developing	probabilistic
risk of developing	probabilistic

Examples of (1) PROBABILISTIC Framing:

- "Changes, called alterations or mutations, in certain genes make some women more susceptible to developing breast and other types of cancer."
- "Scientists have identified a faulty gene that appears to make some families prone to developing prostate cancer."
- Scientists have identified a gene that may help explain why some people become depressed in response to the stresses of life and others skate by relatively unscathed."

Examples of (2) SLIGHTLY PROBABILISTIC Framing:

- "The likelihood that breast and/or ovarian cancer is associated with BRCA1 or BRCA2 is highest in families with a history of multiples cases of breast cancer, cases of both breast and ovarian cancer, one or more family members with two primary cancers (original tumors at different sites), or an Ashkenazi Jewish background."
- "About 5 to 10% of colorectal cancers are caused by known gene mutations."
- "29% of heart attack victims carried the gene."
  (. . .)
- "Now some research scientists at the Washington University Medical School in St. Louis say they've identified a gene that appears to be linked to both alcoholism and depression."
- ". . . has found a variant gene that doubles the risk of heart attack and stroke among Icelanders who carry it."

If the framing sentence contains a percentage or number, it is coded as being slightly probabilistic (2), independently from the verb's degree of determinism or probabilism. This supersedes all other factors about the sentence (including if the subject of the sentence is the person carrying the gene).

- "In 35 families with the highest genetic risk, sisters and daughters who smoked had more than doubled the risk of developing breast cancer than the nonsmokers."— this would be coded as a (2)

Examples of (3) PROBABILISTIC and DETERMINISTIC Framing in same sentence:

- "Certain inherited DNA changes can cause a high risk of developing certain cancers and are responsible for cancers that run in some families."
- "Inheriting two bad copies of the gene, one from the mother and one from the father, causes a brain and immune system problem linked with an increased risk of breast cancer."

Examples of (4) SLIGHTLY DETERMINISTIC Framing:

- "Common diseases like cancer and diabetes are thought to be caused by many variant genes acting in concert."
- "Breast cancer is sometimes caused by inherited gene mutations."
- "There is often a genetic predisposition for addiction."

Examples of (5) DETERMINISTIC Framing:

- "Every cancer is caused by changes in DNA, whether it is a change inherited at birth or a change caused by something that happens later in life."
- "In the mid 1990s, scientists identified mutations in genes now called BRCA1 and BRCA2 that are the major cause of the hereditary form of the disease."
- "The gene, which comes in two forms, or alleles, can either protect people from depression or make them more vulnerable, researchers report today in the journal Science."

In addition, please note that there are instances when the framing sentence varies from the linear gene-outcome structure and is still included in our sample. This happens when the subject of the sentence is the person carrying the gene, and not the gene itself. While the relationship between the gene and the outcome is relatively clear in these sentences, it is not expressed as strongly as it would be in a sentence where the gene is the subject. Therefore, these sentences have some degree of probability and will be coded as probabilistic, unless there is a word intensifier to make it slightly probabilistic.

Examples of sentences where the subject is the gene's carrier:

- "A woman with BRCA1 or BRCA2 alteration is more likely to develop breast or ovarian cancer than is a woman without an alteration."
- "This study suggests men with a particular gene variant have an increased risk of prostate cancer."
- "Although most women with BRCA mutations develop breast cancer, some don't and these women would not benefit from the surgery."
- "If you have an inherited changed gene from either parent, you are at an increased risk for breast cancer."

3. Location

The location of the framing sentence refers to where it appears in the article.

1 = Title
2 = First Paragraph
3 = Elsewhere in the article

4. Outcomes

For each of the identified framing sentences, specify the particular outcome that is being expressed by the gene. Isolate the sentence when deciding an outcome. Choose all that apply.

Note*: When coding on CAS, always choose a category from the "outcome" field. If you can not identify the outcome specifically, choose one of the "other" options, which are available in each category of outcomes. There is also a variety of "other" categories in the "Miscellaneous" category. Do not leave the field blank.*

See **List of Outcomes** below.

List of Outcomes to code Section D; 1. Framing, and Section E; 4. Outcomes

Disease

Cancer

1. Bladder cancer
2. Brain cancer
3. Breast cancer
4. Cervical cancer
5. Colon cancer
6. Colorectal cancer
7. Endometrial cancer
8. Head and Neck cancer
9. Leukemia
10. Lung cancer
11. Melanoma
12. Non-Hodgkins Lymphoma
13. Ovarian cancer
14. Prostate cancer
15. Rectal cancer
16. Testicular cancer
17. Uterine Cancer
18. Unspecified cancer
19. Skin Cancer
20. Resistance/Prevention of Cancer

21. – 49. OPEN FOR NOW

50. Other cancer

Non-Cancer

51. Obesity
52. Overweight
53. Heart Conditions (heart attack, heart disease, coronary artery disease)
54. Type 1 Diabetes (juvenile onset)
55. Type 2 Diabetes (adult onset)
56. Alzheimer's Disease
57. Alopecia
58. Anemia
59. Asthma
60. Cystic Fibrosis
61. Allergies
62. Hemophilia
63. Disease of Hormonal Imbalance
64. Kidney Disease
65. Lou Gehrig's Disease
66. Meningitis
67. Muscular Dystrophy
68. Parkinson's Disease
69. Stroke
70. Vision Problems
71. Unspecified Tumor
72. Deafness
73. Migraines
74. High cholesterol
75. Resistance/Prevention to Non-Cancer Disease

76. – 79. OPEN FOR NOW

80. Other non-cancer

Psychiatric Conditions

81. Anxiety
82. Delirium, dementia, amnesic
83. Schizophrenia
84. Panic Disorder
85. Mood disorders
86. Somatoform Disorders
87. Dissociative Disorders
88. Sexual Disorders
89. Eating Disorders
90. Sleep Disorders
91. Factitious Disorders (hypochondria)
92. Impulse Control Disorders
93. Personality Disorders
94. Autism
95. Depression
96. Mental Retardation
97. Tourette's Syndrome
98. Substance Abuse
99. Drug Addiction
100. Alcoholism
101. Addiction
102. Manic-Depressive Disorder (bi-polar)
103. Downs Syndrome
104. Attention Disorders (ADD, ADHD)
105. Suicide
106. Resistance/ Prevention to Psychiatric

107. – 112. OPEN FOR NOW

113. Other Mental Disorder

Behavior

114. Athletic performance
115. Homosexuality
116. Sexual Experimentation
117. Thrill Seeking
118. Appetite
119. Personality

120. – 129. OPEN FOR NOW

130. Other behavior

Tobacco

131. Smoking
132. Tobacco Use
133. Tobacco Dependence
134. Nicotine Dependence
135. Nicotine Addiction
136. Smoking Cessation

137. – 147. OPEN FOR NOW

148. Other Tobacco

Physical Characteristics

149. Height
150. Weight (not obesity)

151. – 161. OPEN FOR NOW

162. Other Physical Characteristic

Other

163. Longevity
164. Intelligence
165. Unspecified cellular activity
166. Life cycles (menopause, puberty)
167. Cognitive functions (visual, spatial, speech)

168. – 199.OPEN FOR NOW

200. Other miscellaneous

Alphabetized List of Verbs indicating degrees of probability and determinism to code Section E; 2. Framing

(1) Probabilistic	**(2) Slightly Probabilistic**	. . .	(4) **Slightly Deterministic**	**(5) Deterministic**
*Appears to predict**	Affects the chances		Accounts for	*Causes*
As a possible cause	*Affects the risk of developing*		Affects	*Determined by*
Can affect	*Associated with*		Can be caused	*Due to*
Can lead to	*Can cause*		Can give rise to	Has produced
Can lead to the development	*Can cause a high risk*		*Connected to*	*Have identified*
Could play a role	*Can determine*		*Contribute to*	*It is a major cause of*
Fosters	*Can make a big difference*		*Decreases risk*	*It's an absolute guarantee*
Influences	*Caused in part*		*Determines the risk of developing*	*Lead to*
Involved in	*Causes predisposition towards developing*		*Has been linked to a high risk*	*Leads to the development of*
May account for	Component		*Has been traced*	Makes
May be implicated	Determined in part		*Increased the risk of*	*Plays an essential role*
May be involved in	*Elevated risk*		Is important	*Plays an important role*
May cause	*Greater risk for*		*Linked to*	*Powerfully predisposes*
May play a role	*Help determine*		*Lowers the risk of*	Programmed
Might affect	*Higher risk of developing*		May be blamed for	*Responsible for*
Plays a role	*Increases a person's chance of*		Mostly determined	*Results from*
Probably has	*Increases risk*		*Predisposes*	*Stem from*
Related to	*Increases susceptibility*		*Reduce the risk of*	*Strongly determines*
Risk of developing	*Increases the chances of developing*		*Responsible for susceptibility to*	*Tied to*
Seems to	*Linked to heredity predisposition*		*Sharply increases the risk of*	
Seems to help create	Occurs more frequently in		*Strongly suggests*	
Suggesting	*Predict*		Thought to be caused	
Susceptibility	*Shown to increase the risk of*		Which affects	
Tends to be	Strong likelihood			
That might control	*That plays a role in determining*			
Thought to affect				
Underlie				
Vulnerable to				

*The words in italics have been categorized by empirical tests while the non-italicized words are categorized on the basis of their semantic character only.

PART 5

CATEGORIES AND DATA LANGUAGES

Content analysis has been applied to a great variety of texts, images, and sound. Categories and systems of variables—data languages, for short—are intended to render the diversities of texts analyzable* while preserving the meanings that are relevant to a research question. There have been calls to standardize categories across large empirical domains. Some standardization has been achieved when using formal analytical methods, evaluative assertion analysis,** or the LIWC-computer system.*** Most content analyses, however, do not ask the same research questions, sometimes even of the same texts, making standardization difficult. This section offers examples of alternative ways to develop application-specific categories.

Elihu Katz and colleagues analyzed petitions to a government agency for the reasons that petitioners gave in the hope to persuade the authority. The article describes the researchers' close analysis of the grammar of these requests and persuasive devices used by the letter writers. They found six dimensions by which the petitions varied, leading to 45 empirical types. The article is exemplary for grounding categories empirically—leaving theory-motivated inferences for a subsequent step.

Developing categories can become more involved when they are meant to inform a dictionary for the computer analysis of texts. David Bengston and Zhi Xu provide a step-by-step account of their effort to construct categories that fit their research question: How do stakeholders in the national forests value them and nature? The process they describe starts from only one preconception—how values function in texts—but moves to explore the diverse manifestations of values held by three stakeholder groups: forest professionals, environmentalists, and the general public. Bengston and Xu's process is instructive and generalizable to many applications.

If Katz et al., Bengston and Xu, and Kracauer derive their categories from the nature of available texts, Harold Lasswell, political scientist and early communication theorist, brings his own conceptions to the text. These two approaches to category formation are called emic and etic, respectively. The article we include here consists of the bulk of Lasswell's proposal for a "world attention survey," tracing what is going on in the world through the leading newspapers, similar to what Tenney**** had proposed to study in the United States. The categories Laswell outlines

*See reading 4.3, this volume.

**See reading 3.5 and reading 7.5, this volume.

***See reading 7.7, this volume.

****See reading 1.4, this volume.

in this article exemplify the systematicity of theoretical conceptions. It is noteworthy that these categories were the precursors to Lasswell's eight value categories, used by Namenwirth,* among others, and incorporated in the General Inquirer dictionary. His proposal grew roots at the beginning of the cold war in the form of a well-financed study at Stanford University.**

In their article, psychiatric researchers Linda Viney and Peter Caputi argue for the use of content analysis scales in counseling research and present a set of criteria for constructing content analysis scales that satisfy the psychometric requirements of reliability and validity.

Milton Hakel's short survey on "How Often Is Often?" reminds us of the need to be clear about the meaning of verbally defined scale points or categories and, when uncertain, to carefully test their meanings. The adjectives that Hakel studied show superficial resemblances but actually stem from vastly different semantic domains: high and low frequencies, more or less general, expected or rare, and so on. Mixing semantic domains in systems of categories is a common source of unreliability and signals subsequent inabilities to interpret one's data.

Public health researcher Karen Frost and her colleagues used content categories for which comparable population statistics were available. By comparing the causes of death in news stories to public health data, she is able to support an interesting claim: News stories exaggerate the lethality of relatively rare health problems while downplaying the truly serious threats to public health such as smoking or poor nutrition. What scares us the most is not necessarily what poses the most danger to our health.

Violence in the mass media is a perennial target for media critics and government regulators. Defining violence and coding for it, however, are complicated and can touch institutional interests and ideologies, as seen in the Gerbner-Blank debate.*** Anu Mustonen and Lea Pulkkinen here describe in admirable detail how that complex construct, media violence, needs to be dimensionalized and broken down into unambiguously codable categories.

Lyle Shannon studied violence in an often-neglected medium: comics. Shannon, however, was interested in inferring the political philosophy of the comic artist from the ways *Little Orphan Annie* villains were treated in the storylines. The article also exemplifies a more qualitative approach to category use. Instead of coding text by checking categories and later counting the frequencies of these categories, Shannon entered descriptive accounts into the categories he devised, thus preserving many meanings of the original data. This facilitates the narration of findings that are closer to the analyzed texts.

Randi Sims applied content analysis to a rather unusual data set: test bank questions in management education. She asked whether gender biases are woven into such tests, intended to be objective and neutral, and could demonstrate that they were imbued with far from subtle sexist messages. With a similar intent, Kelly Chappell applied content analysis categories to video games, used successfully to teach such a gender-neutral subject as mathematics to children. Here too, the research demonstrated prevailing gender biases. And in a straightforward content analysis of music videos, Richard Baxter and his colleagues explored levels of perhaps the only thing on television that concerns parents as much as violence: sex.

---

*See reading 3.8, this volume.

**Lasswell, H. D., Learner, D., & Pool, I. de Sola. (1952). *Comparative study of symbols.* Stanford, CA: Stanford University Press.

***See reading 6.6, this volume.

5.1

Petitions and Prayers

An Analysis of Persuasive Appeals

Elihu Katz, Michael Gurevitch,
Brenda Danet, and Tsiyona Peled*

A social worker in a development town told us of two clients who came to her office with identical requests. One was a new immigrant from North Africa, who made his request and said, "If I don't get what I've asked for, I'll blow up the office!" The second client, an equally new immigrant from Eastern Europe, sat down and calmly put his request, following which he leaned toward the social worker and said confidentially, "Actually, I have a friend in your head office in Jerusalem to whom I could have taken my request. But I thought," he continued, "that it would be good for *you* if I channeled my request through your office."

From the point of view of the theory of bureaucracy, both of these are illegitimate appeals. The only legitimate appeal, in fact, is one to the laws or the organization. Yet, though they both may be "illegal," the two appeals represent very different kinds of deviations, and reflect different conceptions of the workings of bureaucracy. The first client sees the official as the locus of power and decision-making in the organization and assigns to himself enough power to disrupt the system or at least to deprive the official. The second client perceives the hierarchical nature of bureaucratic authority and implicitly offers the official a positive reward rather than a negative one, which is to come not from the client himself but from the official's superior.

Development of the Scheme

In attempting to devise a content-analytic scheme that would catch some of these differences, we began with a formula based on the idea that a persuasive appeal must consist of some motivating mechanism in which the promise of reward or the threat of deprivation plays a central role. This led to the development of a four-faceted formula in which one

*From Katz, E., Gurevitch, M., Danet, B., & Peled, T. (1969). Petitions and prayers: A method for the content analysis of persuasive appeals. *Social Forces 47:*447–463.

actor (*X*) rewards or deprives another (*Y*) of some resource. In terms of this formula, the first of the two above-mentioned clients says, "I/will deprive/you/of (let's say) health or life," and the second says, "He/will reward/you/with status." Table 1 presents the scheme as designed for a study of letters of appeal to the Israel Customs Authorities.

Note the range of *X's* and *Y's* in *facets 1* and *4* of this table: To these were added two modifiers (*facets 2* and *5*), which describe the roles played by *X* and *Y*. Thus, "I/as a person/will deprive/you/as officials," and "He/as hierarchical authority/will reward/you/as an official." Note also that *X* and *Y* do not necessarily refer to client and official but may refer to any pronoun, which might feature in the appeal, including impersonal pronouns. For example, "They/circumstances in my country of origin/deprive/them/my family/of health." The roles in *facets 2* and *5* are classified into four large groupings, according to whether they are associated with the bureaucracy or not, and according to whether they are personal or impersonal.

Development of *facet 3,* the verb, was rather more complicated. We began with "will reward" and "will deprive," but very soon discovered that appeals are often couched in terms of the past or the present as well as the future. "Grant my request, because I have rewarded you," is a typical appeal to what Gouldner (1960) calls the norm of reciprocity. This distinction between future and past (or present) tends to coincide with conditional and unconditional appeals ("If you grant my request, I will reward . . . ," *vs.* "I have rewarded . . ."), although the offer of future reward or deprivation need not necessarily be conditional. That is, a client may say, "I will reward you," hoping that the promise will make an impression but not making the offer contingent on the official's action.

A second discovery was that conditional appeals—that is, those which are contingent on the official's actions—may involve any X or *Y*, as in "If you don't grant my request, it/the illness/will deprive/her/my wife/of health," or as in the case of a business relationship, "If you grant my request, I/ as a client (customer) or another organization/will deprive/it/the other organization (your competitor)/of cooperation (my business)."

The most important modification of the scheme occurred when we realized that the verbs "reward" and "deprive" were not adequate to the task we set ourselves. The rhetoric of appeals is not limited to the language of direct exchange; we had to make provision for the verb "to owe" which ushers in the entire normative realm. An example of appeals based on the verb "to owe" is: "Grant my request because it/the State/owes/me/as a new immigrant/this service."

We had, in other words, simply "rediscovered" in this very specific context the two bases of social control, which are operant in society—personal influence or direct surveillance on the one hand, and commonly held internalized social norms on the other. In the first case it is the manipulation of rewards and punishments by significant others in the immediate environment, which influences individuals to conform to pressures brought to bear on them. In the second, presumably, it is the individual's response to a felt moral (and/or legal) obligation, which leads to conformity, and not the ability of others to reward or deprive him of valued resources. Consequently, in order to make our scheme maximally applicable, we incorporated the verb "to owe." The two major types of appeals are, then, appeals to an individual's profit, and appeals to his obligation to some norm.[1]

Facet 6 refers to the resources, which are exchanged or made salient in persuasive appeals. Following Longabaugh (1963), who has developed an empirical method to analyze social interaction as an exchange process, we define a resource as simply, "anything one wants." The list of resources in Table 1 is derived from the data with which we worked and is *ad hoc,* although we have made several attempts to structure it theoretically and it appears to be quite general. Two classifications of dimensions, which appeal to us in particular, are (1) a "symbolic-material" dimension, and (2) a "personal-relational" dimension. Thus, happiness may be classified as "personal-symbolic," health or money are "personal-material," status and esteem are

Table 1 The Coding Scheme

"Grant my request because . . ."		
X—the Source *(facet 1)*	**Role of X** *(facet 2)*	**Verb** *(facet 3)*
I (we) You (singular, plural) We (including official) He, They It, they (impersonal)	**Group I: Bureaucratic-personal roles** Official/client of the Customs Official/client of other organization Hierarchical authority in Customs Hierarchical authority in other organization Legal status: new immigrant/citizen/tourist **Group II: Bureaucratic-impersonal roles** The Customs regulations Other organization, its regulations Israeli law, government, State of Israel Other law or government The press **Group III: Non-bureaucratic-personal roles** Newcomer/veteran in Israel The enemy, Gentiles, other people Ethnic group, pressure group, political party Relative or friend of X Relative or friend of someone other than X widow, orphan, bereaved parent Human being, a person Occupational role, a professional Jew(s), Jewish nation, State of Israel Public personalities, celebrities, leaders Sick person, patient, disabled, aged person **Group IV: Non-bureaucratic-impersonal roles** Profession, occupation, working conditions Conditions in Israel, in foreign countries An item, the goods (about which appeal is made) Fate, objective circumstances, God A principle, a general norm	**Group I** ***A. If you grant the request*** Will reward Will not deprive Will not reward Will deprive ***B. If you don't grant the request*** Will reward Will not deprive Will not reward Will deprive **Group II** Rewards rewarded, will reward Doesn't/didn't/won't deprive Doesn't/didn't/won't reward Deprives, deprived, will deprive **Group III** Owes, is obliged to . . . Doesn't oblige, doesn't require Doesn't owe, is not obliged to Obliges, requires

(Continued)

Table 1 (Continued)

"Grant my request because . . ."		
Y—the Recipient *(facet 4)*	**Role of Y** *(facet 5)*	**Resources** *(facet 6)*
	Group I: Bureaucratic-personal roles	Health, life, years
Me (us)	Official/client of the Customs	Happiness, peace of mind
You (singular, plural)	Official/client of other organization	Occupation (income), source of income
Us (including official)	Hierarchical authority in Customs	Material goods, money
Him, them	Hierarchical authority in other organization	Voluntary services or behavior; favor, mercy, understanding, help, forgiveness, idealism, sacrifice
It, them (impersonal)	Legal status: new immigrant/citizen/tourist	Obligatory services or behavior appropriate to a formal role: information, conformity, cooperation, attention
	Group II: Bureaucratic-impersonal roles	Rights, justice
	The Customs regulations	Esteem, gratitude, thanks, trust, hope
	Other organization, its regulations	Status, raise in job status, authority
	Israeli law, government; State of Israel	Convenience, comfort, standard of living
	Other law or government	
	The press	
	Group III: Non-bureaucratic-personal roles	
	Newcomer/veteran in Israel	
	The enemy, Gentiles, other people	
	Ethnic group, pressure group, political party	
	Relative or friend of X	
	Relative or friend of someone other than X, widow, orphan, bereaved parent	
	Human being, a person	
	Occupational role, a professional	
	Jew(s), Jewish nation, State of Israel	
	Public personalities, celebrities, leaders	
	Sick person, patient, disabled, aged person	
	Group IV: Non-bureaucratic-impersonal roles	
	Profession, occupation, working conditions	
	Conditions in Israel, in foreign countries	
	An item, the goods (about which appeal is made)	
	Fate, objective circumstances, God	
	A principle, a general norm	

"relational-symbolic," service and cooperation are "relational-material."

We are, of course, by no means the first to attempt to classify the various kinds of resources or values seen as desirable by individuals or society. Our list is somewhat similar to a typology of values proposed by White (1947) some time ago.

Another typology is that of von Mering (1961), though his comprehensive "grammar of values" focuses on values as "anything about which one can make a value judgment" rather than more specifically on "anything one wants."

Taken together, then, the scheme is a six-faceted sentence in terms of which we think we can classify any "persuasive reason" at all, with minor modifications of the roles and resources, which figure in particular situations. Grammatically, the scheme divides appeals into the subject, verb, direct and indirect objects of a sentence, plus two roles to identify the pronouns mentioned as subject and indirect object.

In developing the scheme, we encountered two related problems. First, we had to decide what exactly constitutes a persuasive appeal. Petitioners often make statements like "I am sick" or "I am a new immigrant." Are these statements to be understood and coded as persuasive appeals or are they merely statements of neutral information with no intent to influence the official? Our inclination, throughout, was to assume that all but the most rudimentary information was introduced to bolster the request.

The second problem has to do with the translation of appeals into the language of the scheme. Obviously, petitioners do not usually speak in neat six-faceted sentences. Whenever the language of the appeal did correspond to the categories of the scheme—about 25 percent of all appeals were "explicit" in this sense—the appeal could be coded directly. In doing so, we made a choice in favor of "representational" as opposed to "instrumental" coding, in the sense that we preferred to code the rhetoric of the appeal rather than the motive implicit in it (Pool, 1959:206–212). Take the example, "I was injured by a car." This might mean "You/the official/owe/me/a sick person/consideration," but it was coded "It/fate/deprived/me/as human being/of/health." Many appeals, however, are not as readily codable as representational statements. "I am a new immigrant," for example, cannot easily be coded until its instrumental meaning is agreed upon. It might mean, "I have suffered hardship and therefore deserve consideration," or "The state owes me certain rights as a new immigrant," or "I am rewarding you by my coming here, therefore you ought to help me in getting settled." In such cases, there was no choice but (1) for coders to confer and agree on the most appropriate meaning for the statement, and (2) to code the statement rather more in terms of its instrumental than its representational meaning. Thus, "I am a new immigrant," is coded consistently as "It/the Customs/owes/me/as a client/rights," except where the context made some other meaning more appropriate. The central directive in the coding of appeals was to preserve as much as possible of what was explicitly said, to avoid interpreting the instrumental meaning, or motivating mechanism. Inclusion of statements like "I am a new immigrant" shows, however, that this was not always possible. To give some index of the extent to which coders made inferences—whether at the level of representational or instrumental meaning—we therefore coded with regard to each facet whether it was explicitly stated by the appellant or whether the coder made a judgment.

Application of the Scheme: Some Examples

To illustrate how the scheme may be applied, as well as to give the flavor of the kind of material with which we are working, we now present several more extended (but not necessarily representative) quotations from letters to the Israel Customs Authorities, sampled from the years 1959 and 1962. One man wrote as follows: "Two of my sons are studying at the University. If I have to pay the duty (on a car), they will have to leave the University and our nation will be deprived of their services." We translated this as two separate appeals: (1) "If you don't grant my request, you/as an official/will deprive/them/my sons/of status." (2) "If you don't grant my request, you/as an official/will deprive/us/the nation of (their) service." Another client, a Chicagoan, offered a rare inducement: "I am in touch with some 20 families in Chicago who are considering the possibility of migration to Israel, and if my petition is successful it will certainly influence them." We render this as, "If you grant my request, they/as new (potential) immigrants/will reward/us/the nation, with a voluntary service, a sacrifice."

An even more colorful example is drawn from the letter of a man who is suspected by the Customs Authorities of importing 14 ladies' slips in order to sell them (all goods imported by individuals must be for personal use only). Claiming that the slips are for his daughters, he writes as follows: "Please consider the situation of my daughters so that I can marry them off as befits them. The hope of three girls lies in Haifa port. . . . Ask your wife how many slips she has in her wardrobe. . . . Are 14 slips so many for three who are about to be married?" The coders recorded the following three appeals: (1) "If you grant my request (let me have the slips duty-free), I/their father/will reward/them/my daughters/with happiness." (2) "If you grant the request, you/the official/will reward/them/my daughters/with hope." (3) "They/the slips/will not reward/them/my daughters/with (too high) a standard of living, luxury."

Coder Reliability

The problem of coder reliability, always important in social research, was particularly crucial in the case of the rather, subtle kind of content analysis we wished to carry out. Our procedure was as follows: Each letter was broken down into discrete units of persuasive appeals and the various appeals coded by two individuals working independently. Then the pairs of coders met over each letter and came to an agreement as to the number of appeals to be coded and the precise coding for each appeal.

Three tests of coder reliability were carried out. The first was done at the beginning of the coding period and two others at later stages. The coding of the letters chosen for the tests was performed by the entire group of coders as individuals, working independently. Thus, if anything, the tests overstate discrepancy, since the regular coding was done in teams of two.

One kind of check was to determine the extent of coder agreement on the *number* of appeals in three test letters. Table 2 shows the modal number of appeals extracted, as well as the range, for each of the three tests.

Table 2 Reliability in Dividing Letters Into Coding Units (Appeals)

	Modal Number of Appeals in Test Letters	*The Range*
Test 1	16	12–19
Test 2	5	7–11
Test 3	14	11–19

Second, the reliability of the coding of content of appeals was checked for each of the facets separately, over all the appeals of each test letter. The degree of reliability here is expressed as percent of modal ("correct") decisions out of total coder decisions, and is shown in Table 3. In general, reliability was quite good, despite variation from one *facet* to another.

A Typology of Appeals

We have come to classify appeals in five distinct categories. We divide appeals to profit into three basic types. First are *appeals to reciprocity,* in both positive and negative forms (inducements and threats, respectively). This type of appeal is best illustrated by "If you grant the request, I will reward you" (or "I will deprive you"). Second, there are appeals based on *pure persuasion,* as in "You will reward you (yourself)." Third, we include a category for appeals to altruism, for example, "If you grant the request, you will

Table 3 Reliability of Fact Coding of Appeals in the Three Tests (by Percent)

	X	*Role-of-X*	*Verb*	*Y*	*Role-of-Y*	*Resource*
Test 1	77.6	65.8	76.1	81.7	62.6	71.7
Test 2	77.2	81.8	86.3	95.4	95.4	77.2
Test 3	82.5	80.0	71.3	95.0	81.2	81.2

reward me." Interestingly, all these types of appeals require knowledge of at least three *facets (1, 3, 4)* for classification, but only the Signal "owe" (or "obliges") is needed for appeals to norms.

As for appeals to norms, we further divide this group into two types, which seem quite different. One basic type of normative appeal attempts to awaken in the other the obligation to comply with the directives of the norm of reciprocity. That is, "You owe it to me now because I have done favors for you in the past." The obligation here is confined to the relations of the two parties involved. In contrast, there are appeals to impersonal obligations of the other, which are independent of past interaction between the two parties involved. Thus, we distinguish between *appeals to the norm of reciprocity* on the one hand, and *appeals to impersonal norms,* on the other. These categories are, to some extent, similar to those of most writers who have concerned themselves with the bases of power and influence in interpersonal relations. In an analysis of the concept of influence, Parsons (1963), for example, has suggested a typology of "ways of getting results." Thus, in "situational" influence attempts, one person seeks to influence another to comply with his wishes by either offering a positive reward ("inducement") or threatening to change some aspect of the other's situation to his detriment ("deterrence"). Combined, these categories correspond to our *appeals to reciprocity.* In "intentional" attempts, a person may influence another by suggesting the ways in which the other will reward himself by complying (positive), or if he does not comply, will punish himself in some sense by violating a commitment he has already made (negative). The first of these categories, obviously, corresponds to our category of *persuasion.* The second, called "activation of normative commitments," seems to incorporate *both* our normative categories.

A more recent paper by Raven (1965), extending earlier work with French and others (1960), presents a strikingly similar analysis of types of influence and their underlying dimensions, and although a recent review article by Cartwright (1964) concludes that no universally accepted set of categories of interpersonal power has been established, the paper goes on to describe three bases of power very similar to those suggested by Parsons, Raven, and others: (1) control over the other's rewards and costs; (2) control over information available to the others; (3) use of the other's willingness to accept (one's) authority. These three types of power form the bases for our appeals to reciprocity, persuasion, and appeals to impersonal norms. These is also a considerable overlap between our categories and those used by Rosenberg and Pearlin (1962), Kelman (1961), Etzioni (1965), and Marwell and Schmitt (1967), though none of these authors focus exclusively on strictly verbal strategies of persuasion.

Some Theoretical Considerations

A. The Problem of Altruism: From Rhetoric to Motivation

With the exception of the paper by Marwell and Schmitt (1967), none of those reviewed above has dealt with the topic of altruism in interpersonal relations, probably on the assumption that to ask for a favor or to plead extenuating circumstances is a sign of weakness rather than of power, and therefore is not likely to be an important basis for motivating another person to comply with one's wishes. In our own study of letters to the Customs, we were confronted with statements like "I lost all my possessions when I left Romania," or "We need a car because my wife is ill and it's too far to walk to the bus stop." Such statements turned up again and again. Intuitively, this type of appeal is oriented to the target's altruism. Now, both common sense and experimental evidence tell us that appeals to altruism are often effective. Studies by Leonard Berkowitz and his associates (1965), and by John Schopler (1966) and his colleagues (1965), have focused precisely on the determinants of the effectiveness of altruistic appeals. Schopler and Bateson (1965) were able to show that the greater the dependence of a person making an altruistic appeal, the greater the compliance of the more powerful ones (Schopler & Bateson, 1965).

These researchers explain the effectiveness of altruistic appeals by the concept of "norm of social responsibility," by which they mean that the appeal awakens in the target person a feeling of obligation to help the appellant.[2] Thus, they might argue that one must translate "I am needy" into "You/owe/me/an obligatory service," or "You are obliged to help needy people," thus appealing, in our terms, to an impersonal norm. This is an extension of the view of Thibaut and Kelley (1959) that one important function of norms is to protect the rights of the weak—power lies not in the person's ability to control the outcomes of the other, but in the norm itself.[3]

Even if we accept the notion that altruism is really normative in character, there is the general problem of the nature of conformity to norms. Some might hold, as Ladd (1957: 292–297) does, that conformity to norms is ultimately motivated by egoistic self-interest, and that altruism and egoism are entirely compatible. Others, however, might want to postulate an elementary, "purely" altruistic motive, refusing to accept the premise that all social behavior is ultimately motivated by self-interest, or even by obligation to reciprocate. To make things still more difficult, there seems to be a component of reciprocity in altruism: one pays with deference when one portrays oneself as needy before a superordinate. Further evidence that reciprocity and altruism may have something in common comes from Marwell and Schmitt's (1967) factor-analysis of the dimensions of compliance-gaining strategies, in which their strategies of debt (i.e., activation of the norm of reciprocity: "You owe me compliance because of past favors") and altruism ("I need your compliance very badly, so do it for me") had high loadings on a common factor (Marwell & Schmitt, 1967). Finally, it is not enough for the observer to have his own theory of motivation—he must know those of the appellant and the target as well.[4] Since we have no information on the perceptions of appellants as they wrote their letters, we do not feel justified in classifying appeals to altruism in any of the other types, and we have therefore made a separate category for them.

B. Appeals to Norms—Two Types or One?

Since all appeals to norms ultimately say: "You owe it to me," one might argue that they should form one category, as Parsons has suggested. It seems to us, however, that the norm of reciprocity works quite differently from other norms. In their normative categories Parsons, Raven and Etzioni, among others, have in mind appeals to *legitimate authority.* Now, legitimate authority, as Weber (1964) has defined it, implies *suspension of one's own judgment,* and acceptance of the other's right to give a directive. This is true of all of the three types of legitimate authority described by Weber. Appeals to the laws of the Customs Authorities, in our own case, are clearly appeals to Weber's rational-legal authority. The norm of reciprocity, on the other hand, seems to us to be more closely related to the principles of elementary social exchange. Blau (1964) and Gouldner (1960) have shown how normative considerations emerge out of "primitive" exchange situations. One conforms to the norm of reciprocity because it is *worthwhile* and secondarily because of the obligation to comply. The clients of the Customs Authorities often say such things as "I filled out all the forms on time," which we translate as "I rewarded the Customs with cooperation," and interpret as "Therefore you owe me something in return." Thus we can, in our own research, further distinguish between appeals to the norm of reciprocity where the two parties concerned are the Customs and the client, or appeals whose frame of reference is broader and not relevant to the bureaucratic role-relationships involved, as in "I sacrificed a great deal in order to come and live in the Jewish state" ("I rewarded the State with a favor, sacrifice").

The work of Marwell and Schmitt (1967) provides some support for our decision to divide appeals to norms into two groups. Their factor analysis of compliance-gaining strategies resulted in five factors, two of which they tentatively label "activation of impersonal commitments" and "activation of personal commitments." The first of these is defined by such strategies as Moral "Appeal" ("You are immoral if you do not comply"), "Self-Feeling," both positive and negative ("You will feel better about yourself if you comply"), "Altercasting," both positive and negative ("A person with 'good' qualities would comply") and "Esteem," positive and negative ("People you value will think better of you if you comply"). All of these either focus on the obligation to comply to an impersonal norm or to the state of one's conscience if one does or does not comply.

As mentioned above, the fifth factor in the Marwell and Schmitt (1967) study is defined partially by the two strategies of debt ("You owe me compliance because of past favors") and altruism ("I need your compliance very badly, so do it for me"). While the labeling of this factor is problematic, the fact the debt was not important in any of the other factors reinforces our view that appeals to the norm of reciprocity should be treated separately.[5]

The Problem of Data Reduction

It is apparent from Table 1 that the data generated by the coding scheme can be very complex. As the scheme was designed for the Customs study, there are no less than 2,500,000 possible theoretical types! In fact, there were some 2,600 different empirical types in the nearly 10,000 appeals collected from the letters of 800 different clients of the Customs Authorities. As a first step to simplify the procedure of data reduction, we decided to work only with the appeals in letters written by clients themselves, thus omitting for the time being all letters written by various "go-betweens" writing on a client's behalf. This left a total of 7,423 appeals.

By inspecting the distribution of the data in various cross-tabulations of the facets, we were able to collapse closely related categories and to reduce the number of different empirical profiles to 45.[6] Decisions as to which categories might be combined were made almost totally on an empirical basis. These 45 types, in the language of the scheme, appear in Table 4.

At this point theoretical considerations were introduced and the 45 profiles regrouped into 17 subtypes, or "motive types," as we have come to call them. Table 5 lists these 17 motive types, now with a name which points to why they should motivate the other to comply. An example in the original language of the client is given for each of the 17, and in addition, we show how we collapse the 17 in terms of the basic five-part typology of persuasive appeals presented under the heading "A Typology of Appeals." Note that in the Customs data neither appeals to reciprocity nor those to pure persuasion were frequent enough to merit separate categories in the final analysis. Threats were virtually absent and the only positive inducements offered are a ritual "thank you" coded as "I will reward you (or the Customs) with thanks" (profile 15 in Table 4) and a promise to cooperate with the Customs in the future (profile 11 in Table 4). These have been grouped with appeals to the norm of reciprocity for purposes of analysis of the data.

Uses of the Scheme I: Bureaucracy and the Public

Little research has been done on the general topic of official-client relations, and consequently even less on problems of persuasion

Table 4 Appeals to the Israel Customs Authorities: 45 Empirical Types

1. "You owe me cooperation." (41)
2. "The Customs owes me rights." (399)
3. "The Customs rewards me with rights." (110)
4. "The Customs rewarded him with rights." (60)
5. "Fate rewards me with status." (46)
6. "My organization rewards me with status." (75)
7. "My fate obliges me to have the goods." (308)
8. "I owe my family a living." (92)
9. "I rewarded the Customs with cooperation." (683)
10. "I rewarded you with cooperation." (52)
11. "I will reward the Customs with cooperation." (52)
12. "The Customs rewarded me with cooperation." (104)
13. "Another official rewarded me with cooperation." (47)
14. "You owe me esteem (trust)." (107)
15. "I will reward you with thanks." (146)
16. "I reward you with thanks." (358)
17. "I rewarded us Jews with a favor." (120)
18. "You will reward me with cooperation." (43)
19. "You will reward me with rights." (42)
20. "You will deprive me of goods." (90)
21. "The Customs deprives me of goods." (165)
22. "Another official deprived me of goods." (74)
23. "The Customs deprived me of cooperation." (99)
24. "Another official deprived me of cooperation." (99)
25. "The Customs deprived me of rights." (95)
26. "Another official deprived me of rights." (66)
27. "The Customs deprived me of happiness." (70)
28. "I deprived myself of rights." (71)
29. "I deprived myself of goods." (61)
30. "Fate deprived me of cooperation." (158)
31. "My fate obliges you (to give me) cooperation." (58)
32. "Fate deprived me of rights." (103)
33. "Fate deprived me of health." (170)
34. "Fate deprived me of happiness." (112)
35. "Fate deprived me of income." (119)
36. "Fate deprived me of comfort." (165)
37. "Fate deprived me of goods, money." (569)
38. "You will reward me with a favor." (86)
39. "My organization rewards me with a favor." (41)
40. "Fate rewards me with goods, money." (SO)
41. "Fate rewards me with income." (54)
42. "Fate rewards me with comfort." (54)
43. "I reward myself with goods, money." (113)
44. "My friend, relative rewards me with goods, money." (182)
45. "My friend, relative rewards me with a favor." (51)

Table 5 Seventeen Motive-Types in Appeals to the Israel Customs Authorities and the Re-grouping According to the General Typology of Persuasive Appeals

APPEALS TO IMPERSONAL NORMS

1. *Appeal to Explicit Rational-Legal Norm (1,2)*[a]
   ("I am a new immigrant.")
2. *Implicit Variants of the Appeal to* a *Rational-Legal Norm (3,4)*
   ("I understand that new immigrants are granted certain rights.")
3. *Appeal for Show of Deference (5,6)*
   ("I have a high-level job in the Ministry of Education.")
4. *Appeal for Support of Job Obligation (7)*
   ("I need the car for my work.")
5. *Appeal for Support of Family Obligation (8)*
   ("I have a wife and five children to support.")

APPEALS TO THE NORM OF RECIPROCITY

6. *Customs-specific Appeal to Norm of Reciprocity (9,10,11)*
   ("I filled out all the required forms on time.")
7. *Variant A of Customs-specific Appeal to Norm of Reciprocity—"Good Faith" (12,13)*
   ("You haven't given me any trouble till now, so why have you changed?")
8. *Variant B of Customs-specific Appeal to Norm of Reciprocity—"Notarized Declaration" (14)*
   ("I sent you a notarized declaration, so you should trust me.")
9. *Thank you—Norm of Reciprocity (15,16)*
   ("Thank you very much for considering this matter.")
10. *Appeal to Norm of Reciprocity to Fellow Jew (17)*
   ("I sacrificed a great deal in order to come and live in the Jewish State.")

APPEALS TO ALTRUISM

11. *Explicit Appeal to Official's Altruism for "Bureaucratic" Resource (18,19,20)*[b]
   ("If you don't grant this request, you will deprive me of my rights.")
12. *Appeal to Customs for Compensation because of Deprivation of "Bureaucratic" Resources—Customs' Fault (21–27)*
   ("The official in the Tel Aviv office refused my request without justification.")
13. *Implicit Appeal to Extend Client's "Credit"—"Bureaucratic" Resource (28,29)*
   ("When I came to the country I didn't take advantage of my rights.")
14. *Appeal for Compensation because of Deprivation of "Bureaucratic" Resource, Extenuating Circumstances (30,31,32)*
   ("I couldn't come to the office to fill out the form on time because I was sick.")
15. *Appeal for Consideration or Compensation because of Deprivation, Non-bureaucratic Resource (33–37)*
   ("I'm a sick man.")
16. *Explicit Appeal for* a *Favor (38)*
   ("Granting my request will help me a great deal.")
17. *Appeal for Support of Client's Good Luck (39–45)*
   ("My uncle is willing to send me the money for the car, though I can't afford the taxes on it.")

a. The numbers in parentheses refer to the profile types listed in Table 4, and thus show which types have been grouped together.

b. "Bureaucratic" resources are "cooperation-obligatory behavior," "rights," "authority." Also, "goods" are defined as "bureaucratic" if the subject of the sentence is The Customs, as in profile 21.

in this area. One study is that of Rosenberg and Pearlin (1962), who asked members of the staff of a mental hospital to choose the strategies they would use in getting a patient to change his sleeping habits. Results showed that staff members overwhelmingly preferred and said they actually used the strategy of *persuasion* ("You will reward yourself in some way"). Use of *legitimate authority* (appeals to an impersonal norm, in our terms) was related to amount of time on the job. Newcomers preferred more personal methods, while old-timers said they would rely more on legitimate authority. In addition, there was some interesting variation in choice of strategies or appeals by the status or rank of personnel. Their findings seem to confirm the notion that norms protect or are used by the weak.[7] This hypothesis was directly tested by Schmitt (1964) in a study of determinants of appeals to a "moral obligation."

In our own studies of bureaucracy and the public, we are relating analysis of appeals to such variables as personal attributes of clients, type of organizations, and extent of exposure to Israeli bureaucracy over time. The pilot study of our project produced some suggestive findings in each of these respects. There we asked a group of 116 respondents to tell what appeals they would use to influence officials in four hypothetical situations to grant four kinds of requests. The three main findings of that study were as follows. (1) Respondents of non-Western origin were more likely to appeal to the altruism of the official, while those of Western origin were higher on appeals to norms, suggesting that non-Westerners lack the proper "bureaucratic socialization" and deal with bureaucracy in ways more appropriate to personal relationships. (2) The type of appeals varied with the type of organization. Appeals to altruism were highest in the situation of a person attempting to convince a policeman not to give him a traffic ticket, suggesting that clients are weakest in organizations where the beneficiary is the public-at-large. Appeals to norms were highest in a mutual-benefit organization (prime beneficiary the member) i.e. a factory worker appealed to his union representative to argue his case for a raise before the management. (3) Old-timers of both Western and non-Western origin were more alike in their appeals than the two groups of newcomers. This quite reasonably suggested a kind of leveling effect over time: former differences in attitudes and behavior are being smoothed out. However, the evidence for the precise effects of experience with Israeli bureaucracy, i.e., whether clients become more or less normative over time, was ambiguous.

Preliminary results from our study of persuasive appeals to the Israel Customs Authorities appear promising. For example, we hypothesized that persons of relatively higher socioeconomic status and background are more likely to appeal to the Customs in the language of bureaucracy, i.e., to invoke impersonal norms. Table 6 shows a clear relationship between a client's occupation and the type of appeal he uses. Appeals to impersonal norms are highest for professionals and salaried bureaucrats and lowest for farmers and skilled and unskilled workers. Appeals to the altruism of the official or the organization are *inversely* related to occupation: professionals are lowest, and farmers and workers are highest. Note also that for *all* groups altruistic appeals are the most frequent.

Two other uses of the scheme to study appeals can be suggested. First, types of appeals could be related to characteristics of the target—in this case, of the official. Are officials of various kinds addressed differently? Are high status officials more likely to yield to an altruistic or otherwise inappropriate appeal than lower-status bureaucrats? Again, one might compare the appeals which clients (or officials, as in the case of the nurses in Rosenberg and Pearlin's study) say they would use, with those they actually do use. . . .

Conclusions

In this article, we have introduced in some detail a method, which we have developed for the content analysis of persuasive appeals. While the scheme was mainly designed for studies of bureaucracy and the public, we think it should be applicable to any situation

Table 6 Appeals to the Israel Customs Authorities by Client's Occupational Status %

	Type of Appeal			
Occupation	*Impersonal Norms*	*Norm of Reciprocity*	*Altruism*	*% & n*
Professionals	25.7	28.8	45.4	99.9 (1,734)
Salaried bureaucrats	23.5	29.8	46.7	100.0 (634)
Merchants	16.9	29.6	53.5	100.0 (355)
Transportation, communication, technical workers	15.0	23.9	61.1	100.0 (633)
Farmers, skilled, unskilled laborers	11.4	23.2	65.4	100.0 (367)

where one person makes a request of another, and offers "reasons" or appeals, as we have called them, in support of his request. In addition to summarizing some of the possible uses of the scheme in our initial area of interest, official-client relations, we have tried to suggest ways in which it might be applicable to such diverse fields as politics, advertising, socialization studies, and the comparative study of religions. One virtue of this scheme, therefore, is in pointing up the commonality of the structure of persuasive appeals in such disparate fields. Another is in its ability to take account of a larger number of the component elements of appeals than have heretofore been identified in content analyses of this sort. Most important, of course, is that it makes feasible the exploration of the interrelations among these components. The ultimate test of the value of the scheme, therefore, lies in the extent to which patterns of such interrelations emerge and are found to be meaningfully associated with the conditions and consequences of their use.

Notes

1. For an interesting and unusual kind of support for our argument that the verb is the "heart" of persuasive appeals, see Abelson and Kanouse (1966). Summing up results of studies of conditions under which individuals are likely to accept or reject verbal generalizations, they conclude that the verb of a sentence is the most important element: "*Verbs trigger subroutines.* That is, we postulate that incoming assertions are processed by individuals with a variety of packages of subjectively logical steps, and that the choice among these packages is made primarily on the basis of the type of action encoded in the verb of the incoming assertion" (pp. 196–197). A comprehensive discussion of the interrelations between principles of exchange or profit and normative aspects of social life can be found in Blau (1964).

2. The concept was first used in Berkowitz and Daniels (1965).

3. Schmitt (1964) expresses essentially the same view in a study of the determinants of the appeal to a norm, or moral obligation, as he puts it. Contemporary social scientists are, in fact, expressing a view, which goes back at least as far as Nietzsche's (1956) *The Genealogy of Morals.*

4. Ideally, one should be able to distinguish "pure" altruism from situations where one does a favor for another and is able to expect reciprocation some time in the future. Giving a man a dime for a cup of coffee, when you know you will never see the man again, might be construed as "pure" altruism, though some would argue that the reward is the good feeling one gets.

5. Marwell and Schmitt (1967) admit that the various strategies which have high loadings in the fifth factor do not have a visibly common characteristic. They argue that altruism and debt, at least, have in common the appeal to the system of rights and obligations characterizing a personal

relationship. One can, however, ask a perfect stranger for a favor. On the other hand, as we have suggested above, there may be an element of reciprocity in asking someone, even a stranger, for a favor.

6. A residual category of deviant types is not shown in Table 4. This category contained about 20 percent of the 7,423 appeals. Since deviant cases were found to be randomly distributed throughout the sample, and since their total proportion was relatively low, they were omitted from all further analysis.

7. High-status nurses preferred the technique of benevolent manipulation or indirect influence, to direct verbal or other behavioral methods, while the lowest-ranking group, nursing assistants, was highest on appeals alluding to their legitimate authority to give the patient an order.

References

Abelson, R. P., & Kanouse, D. E. (1966). Subjective acceptance of verbal generalizations. In S. Feldman (Ed.), *Cognitive consistency* (pp. 171–197). New York: Academic Press.

Berkowitz, L., & Daniels L. R. (1965). Responsibility and dependency. *Journal of Abnormal and Social Psychology 2:*247–254.

Blau, P. M. (1964). *Exchange and power in social life.* New York: John Wiley & Sons.

Cartwright, D. (1964). Influence, leadership, control. In J. G. March (Ed.), *Handbook of organizations* (pp. 1–47). Chicago: Rand McNally.

Etzioni, A. (1965). Organizational control structure. In J. G. March (Ed.), *Handbook of organizations* (pp. 650–677). Chicago: Rand McNally.

French, J. R. P., & Raven, B. (1960). The bases of social power. In D. Cartwright & A. Zander (Eds.), *Group dynamics: Research and theory* (pp. 607–623). Evanston, IL: Row, Peterson & Co.

Gouldner, A. W. (1960). The norm of reciprocity: A preliminary statement. *American Sociological Review 25:*161–178.

Kelman, H. C. (1961). Processes of opinion change. *Public Opinion Quarterly 25:*57–78.

Nietzsche, F. (1956). *The genealogy of morals.* New York: Doubleday.

Ladd, J. (1957). *The-structure of a moral code.* Cambridge, MA: Harvard University. Press.

Longabaugh, R. (1963). A category system for coding interpersonal behavior as social exchange. *Sociometry 26:*319–344.

Marwell, G., & Schmitt D. R. (1967). The dimensions of compliance-gaining behavior: An empirical analysis. *Sociometry 30:*350–364.

Parsons, T. (1963). On the concept of influence. *Public Opinion Quarterly 27:*37–62.

Pool, I. de Sola (Ed.). (1959). *Trends in content analysis.* Urbana: University of Illinois Press.

Raven, B. H. (1965). Social influence and power. In I. D. Stein & M. Fishbein (Eds.), *Current studies in social psychology* (pp. 371–382). New York: Holt, Rinehart & Winston.

Rosenberg, M., & Pearlin, L. I. (1962). Power orientations in the mental hospital. *Human Relations 15:*335–350.

Schmitt, D. R. (1964). The invocation of moral obligation. *Sociometry 27:*299–310.

Schopler, J. (1966). Interpersonal power. In L. Berkowitz (Ed.), *Advances in experimental social psychology* (Vol. 2). New York: Academic Press.

Schopler, J., & Bateson, N. (1965). The power of dependence. *Journal of Personality and Social Psychology 2:*247–254.

Thibaut, J. W., & Kelley, H. H. (1959). *The social psychology of groups.* New York: John Wiley & Sons.

von Mering, O. (1961). *A grammar of human values.* Pittsburgh, PA: University of Pittsburgh Press.

Weber, M. (1964). The types of authority and imperative coordination. In *The theory of social and economic organization* (pp. 324–363). New York: The Free Press.

White, R. K. (1947). Black boy: A value analysis. *Journal of Abnormal and Social Psychology 42:*440–461.

5.2

Changing National Forest Values

David N. Bengston and Zhi Xu*

The evolution of forest values is currently being widely discussed and debated in the forestry community. It is often claimed that a fundamental shift in forest values has taken place in recent decades. For example, historian Samuel Hays (1988:550) suggested, "New values have emerged about what the forest in America is and what role it ought to play in modem society." Shands (1991) stated that managing the national forests in ways that are responsive to changing public values is the core problem faced by the USDA Forest Service. Gordon (1993) argued that a shift in public values is part of the explanation for the declining influence of the multiple-use sustained-yield paradigm of forest management. It is increasingly recognized that the values people hold about forest ecosystems are an important part of the social underpinning of ecosystem management, the emerging forest management paradigm. Grumbine (1994:34) went further, arguing that "Ecosystem management is an early stage in a fundamental reframing of how humans value nature." Thus, ecosystem management can be viewed as a response to changing values or as a driving force that is creating value change. In either case, values play a critical role in identifying ecosystem management goals, setting the context for decision-making, and guiding our choices.

Forest values are defined here as relatively enduring conceptions of "the good" related to forests and forest ecosystems. Value in this sense is sometimes referred to as an ideal or a held value. A more systematic understanding of recent changes in forest values is needed to develop resource management approaches that are responsive to changing forest values and to anticipate the future evolution of forest values. Several recent studies have analyzed forest and related value systems at a particular point in time (e.g., Holler, 1990; Steel, Ust, & Shindler, 1994; Vining & Ebreo, 1991). But there has been little research on how forest values—or environmental values in general—have changed over time. This is

*From Bengston, D. N., & Xu, Z. (1995). *Changing natural forest values: A content analysis* (Research Paper NC 323). St. Paul, MN: U.S. Department of Agriculture, Forest Service, North Carolina Forest Experimental Station.

due in part to the limited number of approaches available to analyze the evolution of abstract constructs such as values. . . .

In this study, we used computer-coded content analysis to empirically analyze the evolution of forest values in the United States from 1982 through 1993. We developed a classification system that identifies four broad categories of forest values: economic/utilitarian, life-support, aesthetic, and moral/spiritual values (Bengston, 1994). A content analysis procedure was developed to identify expressions of these values related to public forests in databases of text representing the views of three groups: the general public, forestry professionals, and mainstream environmentalists. The value system of each group was quantitatively summarized, and changes in value systems—i.e. changes in the relative frequency of expression of forest values—were tracked over time. Our main working hypotheses in this study were that 1) forest value systems have shifted over the study period, and 2) significant differences exist between the forest value systems of the three groups. In a concluding section, we discuss the implications of this study for ecosystem management.

Methodology

The basic idea of content analysis is that the large numbers of words contained in a piece of text are classified into content categories of interest. This requires the development of a coding scheme—a system for classifying text designed to achieve the objectives of a particular study. The coding scheme is the heart of any content analysis. The first step in developing a coding scheme is to define the content categories, which in this study are the four types of forest value described above. Therefore, our objective was to produce a set of reliable and valid indicators of the expression of our four broad categories of forest value.

A second step in developing a coding scheme is to define the basic unit of text to be classified. Individual words and phrases, sentences, paragraphs, and whole texts may be used as the unit of text for analysis. Choice of an appropriate unit of text depends on the specific research questions of interest. For certain purposes, large units of text are quite appropriate. But Weber (1990) noted that it is often difficult to achieve high reliability when coding large units of text. In this study, we have chosen to use individual words and phrases as the basic unit of text to be classified. This approach is most appropriate given the interweaving of forest values. For example, the sentence, "The production of goods and services is essential, but it does not preclude maintaining the natural beauty of forests" expresses both economic/utilitarian value (as indicated by the phrase "goods and services") and aesthetic value (as indicated by the word "beauty"). By classifying individual words and phrases rather than larger units of text, our content analysis procedure can account for multiple expressions of forest values within a given unit of text.

The third step is to develop lists of words and phrases—"dictionaries" in the nomenclature of content analysis—associated with each of the content categories. These words and phrases serve as indicators of the concepts of interest. Forest values are abstract concepts not capable of being directly observed. The dictionaries enable us to indirectly observe and quantify expressions of forest values. Development of the forest value dictionaries involved an iterative process.[1] Initial dictionaries were developed for each value category by examining forestry related texts that clearly express a particular type of value. Texts that emphasize a particular value are common in forestry. Classic examples include the writings of Gifford Pinchot, which tend to emphasize the economic/utilitarian value of forests, in striking contrast to the writings of John Muir, which frequently and strongly express aesthetic value. Articles by forest economists, traditional foresters, and others focusing on the economic or utilitarian value of forests were examined to identify an initial list of words and phrases expressing economic/utilitarian value. Similarly, the writings of forest ecologists and others focusing on ecological functions and values were examined to identify words expressing life support value; the writings of landscape architects, aestheticians, environmental philosophers, and others were examined to identify indicators of aesthetic value; and the writings of environmental philosophers, environmental psychologists, Native Americans and others were examined to identify indicators of moral or spiritual value. Almost 80 documents were examined to develop the initial forest value dictionaries.

The initial value dictionaries were then sent to subject matter specialists for review and refinement. A landscape architect, who conducts research on the aesthetic value of forests, reviewed the initial aesthetic value dictionary, an environmental psychologist, involved in research on the spiritual value of forests, reviewed the moral/spiritual value dictionary, and so on. The subject matter specialists were asked to comment on the dictionaries and suggest additional words and phrases that express forest values within their area of expertise.

The next step—examining the use of the words and phrases in our databases of text—was crucial in refining the value dictionaries and ensuring their validity. Weber (1990:15) noted, "A content analysis variable is valid to the extent that it measures the construct the investigator intends it to measure." Using three databases of text on the national forests, we examined computer-generated key-word-in-context (KWIC) lists to determine which of the words and phrases contained in the draft value dictionaries were accurate indicators of the expression of the four values. Table 1 illustrates KWIC records for selected words from each of the value categories. Words and phrases found to be used ambiguously or incorrectly for this study were dropped from the dictionaries. For example, the word "spirit" was originally included in the moral/spiritual value dictionary, but we found it was used as an expression of the moral or spiritual value of forests only about 16 percent of the time. We also found phrases such as "a spirit of compromise" and "a cooperative spirit." which do not express the moral/spiritual value of forests. The word "spirit" was therefore dropped from the moral/spiritual value dictionary. We could cite many other examples of words and phrases that were dropped because they were found to be inaccurate indicators of the expression of particular values.

The process of refining the dictionaries by applying them to a large sample of text, assessing the accuracy of coding in context, and revising the dictionaries as needed was repeated until a satisfactory level of validity was achieved. We defined a "satisfactory level" as correct usage 80 percent of the time or more. A final validity check of each of the four dictionaries on a representative, random sample of text from each of the three databases revealed that the dictionaries accurately captured expressions of value with a minimum of 80 percent accuracy, and most of the words and phrases contained in the dictionaries were valid value indicators 90 to 95 percent of the time.

In addition to concerns about validity in content analysis, the reliability or consistency of text classification is a concern when multiple human coders are used. Despite a well-conceived set of coding rules and careful training of human coders, people inevitably introduce variability in how they interpret and apply category definitions or other coding rules. In this study, we used computer coding to avoid problems with coder reliability—the computer always applies the coding rules consistently.

Table 2 shows the final forest value dictionaries. Words and phrases in the economic/utilitarian value category include participants or actors that fill various roles related to utilitarian values (e.g., logger, tree farmer), various objects of utilitarian value (e.g., goods and services, raw materials), ends or goals related to utilitarian value (e.g., economic development, economic growth), and various means to achieve these ends (e.g., exports, intensive management).

The life support value dictionary shown in Table 2B includes both the specialized language of ecologists and many words used by non-ecologists to describe various ecological functions and to express life support value. Included are actors that fill roles related to life

Table 1 Key-Word-in-Context Records Illustrating the Expression of Each Value

Economic/Utility Value Expressions	*Aesthetic Value Expressions*
. . . at least some insulation of the plan from legal challenges in order to quickly get more **timber** moving through the pipeline in **economically** depressed communities.	Of all the leafless trees, I think the most beautiful against the winter sky is the little flowering dogwood with its **graceful** horizontal limbs that reach skyward at their tips and form a fine lace pattern
A third reason for concern about the decay of biodiversity is purely **economic.**	. . . **spectacular** areas of natural **beauty** — national parks, forests and historic sites. . . .
Intensive management must be increased to meet our projected population increases which will bring about a 75 percent increase in **timber** demand in the next three decades.	Finally, and most **gloriously**, trees: More than 130 flowering trees and fourteen native conifers, as many total species as are to be found in all of Europe
Life Support Value Expressions	***Moral/Spiritual Value Expressions***
It is a subsidy for which Americans pay dearly. An obvious cost is in the **degradation** of streams and the rich terrestrial ecosystems that border them.	At one time, the chestnut occupied a **cherished**, seemingly unshakable place in the landscape
Like any other timber cut, salvage sales punch roads into hitherto roadless areas, compact and erode soil, wound **watersheds,** and **fragment** forests.	It is fresh and new-looking, a dark slash through the forest, a **desecration**, as out of place among these old trees as. . . .
The values of southern forested wetlands to society relate to each of the three major wetland functions—**habitat**, hydrology, and biogeochemical cycling.	First and foremost, my forester must have a land ethic. They must feel the same bond to the land that they feel for one close to them.

NOTE: Abridged from the original.

support values (e.g., restoration ecologist, landscape ecologist), various ecosystem functions (e.g., carbon storage. soil stabilization, water purification), ends or goals related to life support value and indicators of the achievement of these goals (e.g., biodiversity, ecosystem health, keystone species), and various indicators of problems with environmental functions and loss or degradation of life support value (e.g., acid rain, erosion, degradation, fragmentation, unraveling). Creighton (1983:153) noted that one of the strategies for communicating values is prediction of dire consequences of a certain course of action: "The kind of consequence they fear will reflect their values. The man from the Chamber of Commerce will predict a loss of jobs, while the preservationist will predict a total disruption of the ecosystem." Our experience developing forest value dictionaries confirms Creighton's observation: Words expressing negative, undesirable consequences were outstanding value indicators.

Table 2C, our aesthetic value dictionary, includes words such as "ugly," which expresses aesthetic value by calling attention to a loss or lack of aesthetic value, as in the phrase "clear-cuts are ugly scars on the land." This word list should pick up both personal reflections on the aesthetic value of forests as well as expressions of aesthetic value found in the research literature on forest aesthetics. Our aesthetic value dictionary is based on fairly traditional notions of forest aesthetics, but it does reflect the wide range of senses, intellectual powers, and emotions involved in the perception and appreciation of aesthetic beauty, not just visual perception (e.g., words like emotive, fragrant, musical, orchestral, poetic, savor).

Table 2 Value Dictionaries

A: Economic/Utilitarian Value Dictionary

benefits of timber
bid price
commercial
commodity, commodities
crops of tree, tree crop
dollars in timber
earning, earnings
economic, economical
economically
economic analysis
economic development
economic effect
economic growth
economic impact
economic sense
economy, economies
exports, exporter
exporting
exploited
firewood
forest product
goods and services
grazing fee
harvest level
harvest timber
harvest tree
harvesting timber
harvesting trees
harvesting of timber
harvesting of trees
timber harvest
tree harvest
housing market
industrial forest
industrial forestry
industrial land
industrial interests
intensive culture
intensive forest management
intensive forestry
intensive management
intensively managed
log price
log export
lumber price
limber product
market price
market value
market system
non-market, nonmarket
monetary
monetizing
monetization
plantation
processed timber
profits, profitable
rangeland
raw log, raw materials
scarcity
stumpage
supply and demand
supply-demand
timber harvest
timber-dependent
timber export
timber industry
timber job
timber loss
timber management
timber operation
timber plantation
timber-producing
timber production
timber sale
timber shortage
shortage of timber
timber supply
timber supplies
supply of timber
timber value
timberland
tree farmer
tree farming
tree plantation
utilization
utilize, utilized
underutilized
wage
willing to pay
willing-to-pay
willingness to pay
willingness-to-pay
workforce

B: Life-Support Value Dictionary

absorb air pollutants
absorption of pollutants
air purifier
air purity
air purifying
air and water
air quality
assimilative capacity
waste assimilation
aquatic life
aquatic zone
breakdown of pollutants
acid drainage
acid precipitation
acid rain
biodiversity
bio-diversity
biotic diversity
ecosystem diversity
genetic diversity
landscape diversity
species diversity
structural diversity
biological diversity
biological health
biological integrity
biological legacy
biological legacies
biological processes
biological systems
biological wealth
biosphere, biospheric
biota, biotic
binding of soil
soil-binding
buffer strip, buffer zone
carbon cycle
carbon dioxide
carbon fixation
carbon sequestration
carbon sink
carbon storage
CO_2 fixation
CO_2 sequestration
CO_2 sink
CO_2 storage
climate amelioration
climate ameliorate
climate ameliorating
climate buffer
degrade, degradation
degrading
detritus
downstream habitat
ecological
ecological benefits
ecological communities
ecological community
ecological diversity
ecological functions
ecological health
ecological integrity
ecological processes
ecological restoration
ecological services
ecological values
ecologically valuable
ecologically complex

(Continued)

Table 2 (Continued)

B: Life-Support Value Dictionary (Continued)

ecosystem diversity	erosion	landscape ecologist	self-sustaining
ecosystem complexity	eutrophication	life-support	siltation
ecosystem functions	exotic species	life-supporting	species abundance
ecosystem functioning	extinct species	life supporting	species loss
ecosystem health	extinction	life-sustaining	species-poor
healthy ecosystem	endemic species	life sustaining	species-richness
ecosystem integrity	endangered species	life-cycle	soil conservation
ecosystem maintenance	filtration	life cycle	soil erosion
ecosystem processes	flood control	material cycling	soil formation
ecosystem resilience	controlling flooding	mycorrhizae	soil movement
ecosystem restoration	flood mitigating	mycorrhizal	soil nutrients
ecosystem services	flood mitigation	nature's services	soil structure
ecosystem structure	storm abatement	nitrogen cycle	generation of soil
ecosystem sustainability	food chain	nitrogen cycling	topsoil loss
ecosystem values	food level	fixation of nitrogen	unstable soil
energy value	food web	nitrogen-fixing	solar energy
energy capture	forest health	nitrogen-fixation	solar equivalents
energy cycling	fragment	nutrient cycle	solar radiation
energy exchange	fragmentation	nutrient-cycling	streamside buffers
energy flow	fragmented	nutrient export	stream sedimentation
flow of energy	fragmenting global change	nutrient uptake	threatened species
energy flux	global climate	old growth corridor	trophic activity
energy transfer	global warming	ozone depletion	trophic flow
environmental cost	greenhouse effect	ozone hole	trophic functioning
environmental concern	greenhouse gases	ozone layer	trophic interactions
environmental degradation	groundwater	stratospheric ozone	trophic level
environmental function	ground water	pollution	trophic organization
environmental health	ground-water	oxygen production	trophic specialization
environmental impact	groundwater contamination	production of oxygen	trophic structure
environmental processes	habitat	photosynthesis	trophic transfer
environmental quality	habitat protection	radiation balance	trophic web
environmental restoration	habitat loss	radiation flux	unraveling
environmental services	habitat fragmentation	restoration ecologist	water cycle
environmental toxin	wildlife habitat	restoration ecology	water-purification
environmental value	fish habitat	restored	water-purifier
environmentally beneficial	homeostasis	ecosystem	water-quality
environmentally sensitive	homeostatic	riparian	water purification
environmentally sustainable	hydrologic cycle	riparian area	water purifier
erode, eroded	hydrological cycle	riparian boundary	water quality
erodible, eroding,	indicator species	riparian communities	watershed
	integrity of ecosystem	riparian system	watershed stabilization
	jeopardized species	riparian zone	watershed stabilizer
	keystone species	revegetate	wetland restoration
	landscape ecology	self-maintenance	valuable wetland
		self maintenance	wildlife habitat
		self-replicating	wildlife population
		self-sustaining	wildlife support

C: Aesthetic Value Dictionary

adorn, adorned
aesthetic
aesthetically
affective
artistic
artist, artist's
awe, awesome
awe-inspiring
beauteous
beautiful
beautifully
beauty
natural beauty
breathtaking
breathtakingly
captivate, captivating
charming
dazzling
delight
delights
delightful
delighted
ecstasy, ecstatic
elegant, elegance
emotive
enthrall, enthralling
evoke
evocative
evocatively
evocation exhilarate
exhilarated
exhilarating
exhilaration expansive
exquisite
exquisiteness
fragrance
fragrant
glory, glories
glorify, glorious
graceful
grandeur
harmony
harmonious
heart-stopping
hue
landscape architecture
landscape architect
lavish
lovely
lush
luxuriant
magnificence
magnificent
majestic, majesty
marvelous
musical
natural setting
noble
orchestral
ornate
ornament
ornamented panorama
panoramic
poetry, poems
pristine
rapture, rapturous
resplendent
restorative
rustic
savor, savored
savory
scenery
scenic, scenically
scenic beauty
scenic value
sensibility
sensibilities
sensory
sensual, sensually
sensualness
sensuous
sensuously
sensuousness stately
stateliness
spectacular
splendor
splendorous
splendorous
stunning
stunningly
stupendous
sublime
sublimely
sublimeness
sublimity
sumptuous
sumptuousness
superb
symphony
symphonic
towering
ugly
unspoiled
untrammeled
vast expanse
vast wilderness
visceral
vista, vistas
visual
visual quality
visual resources
woodland realm

D: Moral/Spiritual Value Dictionary

ancient forest
ancient tree
anthropocentric
nonanthropocentric
bio-centric
cathedral
cathedrals
cherish
cherished
cherishing
consecrate
consecrated
consecration
desecrate
desecration
dignity
divine, divinity
duties and obligations
ecocentric
eden, edenic
environmental ethics
exalted
exaltation
exaltedness
exaltedly
future generations
good steward
heritage
holier, holy, holiness
immortal, immortality
inherent value
intrinsic value
inspiration
inspirational
inspire
inspired
inspiring
irreplaceable
land ethic
legacy
meditate
meditation
meditative
morals
morality
mythic
mythical
mythological
mythology
national treasure
natural treasure
normative
paradise
posterity
profaned, profaning
religion, religious
revered
reverence
reverential
reverently
rights and duties
sacred
sacredness
sanctity
sanctuary
sanctuaries
sanctum
shrine, enshrine
spiritual
stewardship
tabernacle
transcendence
transcendent
transcendental
transcending
venerate
venerable

NOTE: Abridged from the original.

The final moral/spiritual value dictionary is shown in Table 2D. This dictionary contains words and phrases found to be good indicators of the expression of the moral and spiritual value of forests, such as the following: biocentric, cherish, future generations, heritage, irreplaceable, land ethic, revered, sacred, and venerate. Although moral value and spiritual value are usually expressed in distinctive language, we combined them into a single category because they are closely related values and they are expressed relatively infrequently in the text we analyzed. This dictionary also includes words such as "desecrate" and "profaned," which indicate a loss or abuse of spiritual value.

It should be noted that the four value dictionaries do not each contain the same number of words and phrases. The life support value dictionary is the largest due to the inclusion of technical terms describing ecological functions and services, and the moral/spiritual value dictionary is the smallest. In developing these dictionaries, we found that their relative size has little impact on their ability to capture the bulk of the expressions of forest value contained in text because many of the words and phrases, while accurate indicators of the expression of values, are used infrequently. The results of our analysis would not change significantly if we limited each dictionary to the ten most frequently used words and phrases expressing a particular value. Therefore, we have focused on the quality of the words and phrases contained in each of our value dictionaries rather than on the quantity.

In the course of developing our four value dictionaries, we quickly discovered that the words and phrases in the economic dictionary were good indicators of the expression of economic/utilitarian value for forestry professionals and the public or news media, but they were poor indicators when applied to environmentalists. We found that in the environmental literature, economic/utilitarian words and phrases were usually cast in a negative or skeptical light; environmentalists frequently use economic words and phrases while expressing concern about the harmful environmental impacts of economic activities, rather than in positive expressions of economic/utilitarian value. For example, we found many phrases such as "destructive logging practices," in which the word "destructive" appearing in close proximity to the word "logging" clearly indicates the perceived negative consequences of an economic activity. To handle simple cases such as this example, it would be possible to develop a set of transition rules as part of a content analysis procedure, which describe how two ideas in the text, represented by individual words or word groups, are combined to give a third idea. For example, the use of words such as "abuse," "devastating," "indiscriminate," "misuse," and "ravaged" in close proximity to certain economic words would be counted as expressions of negative economic value.

We developed a set of transition rules to capture negative expressions of economic/utilitarian value, but found that negative expressions of this value were much more subtle in most instances and could not be captured by a simple set of rules. The complexity and nuances of the language exceeded the ability of our transition rules to capture more than a small portion of the negative or skeptical expressions of economic/utilitarian value. For example, the phrase ". . . harvest levels are higher than what is sustainable on a long-term basis" (Watson, 1990:25) expresses concern about an economic activity rather than positively expressing economic value. But no word of phrase within this phrase indicating this attitude of concern can be generalized to a large body of text.

To account for the negative expressions of economic/utilitarian value in the environmental literature, we conducted a human-coded content analysis on a representative random sample of our database. This involved examining the text in which economic/utilitarian words and phrases were used and coding it into two categories: positive and negative expressions. . . . We found that the use of words and phrases from our economic/utilitarian dictionary was associated with positive value only 25 percent of the time in the environmental literature, and the remainder of the uses was clearly negative or skeptical. This percentage was found to be stable over the time period covered by our data and was used as a correction factor to adjust the computer-coded counts of expressions of economic/utilitarian value in the environmental literature.

We also found many qualified expressions of economic/utilitarian value in the environmental literature, i.e., expressions of economic value that were positive but which clearly ranked economic value below other values, such as the following example: "While the forests can and should help serve the immediate commodity needs of American citizens, this should not be allowed to compromise those priceless assets which are becoming increasingly unique to the national forests—and are no less real than our economic demands for lumber and paper, oil and iron" (The Wilderness Society 1983:33,38). Qualified but positive expressions of economic value such as this were coded as positive expressions.

Once the value dictionaries and coding rules were finalized, expressions of forest values were measured by applying them to databases of text, i.e., using the InfTrend software;[2] we searched our databases for the words and phrases contained in the four dictionaries. Each use of one of the words or phrases that was found counted as one expression of the particular value. For example, the sentence "Of all the leafless trees, I think the most *beautiful* against the winter sky is the little flowering dogwood with its *graceful* horizontal limbs that reach skyward at their tips and form a fine lace pattern" (Borland, 1984:5) would be counted as two expressions of aesthetic value because of the use of the words "beautiful" and "graceful," which are included in our aesthetic value dictionary. The sentence "At one time, the chestnut occupied a *cherished* seemingly unshakable place in the landscape" (Toner, 1985:27) would be counted as one expression of moral/spiritual value due to the presence of the word "cherished." which is included in our moral/spiritual dictionary. The value expressions were then aggregated by each type of value, database, and year to develop time trends.

Data

We developed databases of text on the national forests for three populations of interest: 1) the general public, 2) forestry professionals and 3) environmentalists. The content of newspaper articles was used as a proxy for the expression of public forest values. Kellert, in his landmark study of wildlife values and attitudes, argued that newspaper articles ". . . can be relatively good indicators of generally held views and interests" (Kellert, 1985:20). Others have argued that, rather than reflecting the attitudes and values of their readers, the news media shape the opinions and attitudes of the public (Fan, 1988). We argue that there is some truth to each of these positions—the news media both reflect and shape public values to some degree—and therefore the news media may serve as a rough proxy for the values of the public. It is important to recognize that the use of news media text to identify expressions of national forest values for the public is a proxy and not a direct measure. Therefore, the value trends for this group should be interpreted more cautiously than trends for the other two groups.[3]

News media stories were obtained from the NEXIS electronic database, which contains the full texts of a large number of major and minor newspapers from all regions of the United States and a large number of national regional and state news services. Stories included in our database were located using the search command "national forest." For the period 1982 to 1993, NEXIS was found to contain more than 15,000 stories that included the phrase "national forest." and out of this total population, we randomly retrieved 2,000 stories for inclusion in our database.

To minimize the inclusion of irrelevant text, the retrievals did not include the full text of stories. Only text within 100 words of the phrase "national forest"—50 words on either side—was downloaded. This greatly reduces the amount of irrelevant text that would have been retrieved from stories that mention the national forests only in passing and helps ensure that the measured expressions of value are linked to national forests as opposed to other types of owners or land. Experience with many electronic text retrievals from news media sources on a wide range of topics has shown that text outside of a 50- to 100-word window around the search words is often not relevant to the topic of interest.[4] The public/news media database consists of 5.5 megabytes of text.

The values of forestry professionals were represented in a second database consisting of two components: 1) the complete text of keynote and general session papers presented at the Society of American Foresters National Conventions from 1982 through 1993, and 2) the complete text of articles in the *Journal of Forestry* that dealt specifically with national forests over the same period. This database was constructed by using an optical scanner to enter the text of the papers and articles. The database representing the views of forestry professionals consists of 415 articles and 6.7 megabytes of text.

Similarly, a database to represent the values of mainstream environmentalists was constructed by scanning in the complete text of articles dealing with the national forests from magazines published by three major forest-related environmental groups: the National Wildlife Federation's magazine *National Wildlife,* the Sierra Club's *Sierra,* and the Wilderness Society's *Wilderness.* The National Wildlife Federation was the largest U.S. forest-related environmental organization in 1993 with 6,200,000 members (Hendee & Pitstick, 1994). The Sierra Club and the Wilderness Society were also among the largest forest-related environmental groups in 1993, with 650,000 and 310,000 members, respectively. Taken together, text from the magazines published by these three groups should contain a good cross-section of expressions of the values held by mainstream environmentalists about the national forests. This database contains the full text of 238 articles and 3.1 megabytes of text.

Results

A generalized logit model was used to test hypotheses concerning differences in forest value systems between the three groups and to test for a shift in forest value systems over time. . . . To mention just one example of the latter, the trends in relative frequency of life support value are almost a mirror image of the economic/utilitarian trends. The trends for environmentalists and forestry professionals are upward and fairly dramatic. The public/news media group seems to be lagging behind the other groups, with no discernible trend until the upturn in the expression of life support value in the early 1990's. . . .

To facilitate comparison between groups in recent years, Figure 1 summarizes the forest value system of each of the three groups for the last four years of our data (1990–93). This figure shows the average relative frequency of expression of each value, to portray only the current value system of each group. Economic/utilitarian value clearly still dominates the forest value systems of forestry professionals and the public/news media, accounting for more than half of the value expressions in recent years. Environmentalists place much less emphasis on the economic/utilitarian value of the national forests. Expressions of life support value clearly dominate the value system of environmentalists, and life support value is a strong second for the other groups. Life support value accounts for about 40 percent of total value expressions in recent years for forestry professionals and about 30 percent for the public/news media.

The aesthetic value of the national forests is expressed least often relative to the other values among forestry professionals and significantly more often in the news media and environmental literature in recent years. Finally, Figure 1 reveals that moral/spiritual value plays a significantly larger role in the current value system of environmentalists than for the other groups, and it plays the smallest role in the value system of forestry professionals.

Discussion

The trends revealed in this study suggest that a gradual shift has been occurring in the structure of national forest values in the United States since the early 1980's, at least among forestry professionals and mainstream environmentalists. Given our definition of forest values as relatively enduring conceptions of what is good or desirable about forests and forest ecosystems, we would expect gradual change. If this analysis had found dramatic shifts in forest values over this short span of time, it would be reasonable to conclude that we were measuring something other than values, such as attitudes or opinions, which tend to be more variable. Value systems are relatively stable and change slowly. But, as our results suggest, even gradual shifts in the relative importance of values may eventually result in a significant reordering of priorities among values. . . .

The decline in the relative frequency of expression of economic/utilitarian value and concomitant increase in life support value among forestry professionals and environmentalists are the most striking aspects of the shift in national forest values revealed by our analysis. The shift away from economic/utilitarian value is especially noteworthy for forestry professionals, because the philosophical base of traditional forestry is utilitarianism and the forestry profession has been heavily influenced by economic concepts of value (Kennedy, 1985; McQuillan, 1993). Thus, the decline in economic/utilitarian value suggests a fundamental change in the culture of forestry professionals. . . .

Finally, our finding that the life support value of the national forests plays a prominent and growing role in the value systems of forestry professionals, environmentalists and, in recent years, the public/news media suggests that this concept of what is good about forests is now widely recognized and appreciated. The importance of life support value that we found tends to confirm environmental historian Donald Worster's observation about the influence of ecology on our culture: "So influential has their branch of science become that our time might well be called the 'Age of Ecology'" (Worster, 1994:xiii). The increase in the expression of life support value that we observed suggests that ecosystem management—often characterized as being based on ecological principles and placing greater emphasis on ecological values than traditional forest management—may indeed be an idea whose time has come.

Notes

1. The iterative process we used is similar to what David Fan . . . [calls] successive filtrations. [He] explained the method as follows: "From biochemistry, I learned that the study of complicated materials frequently benefits from a series of

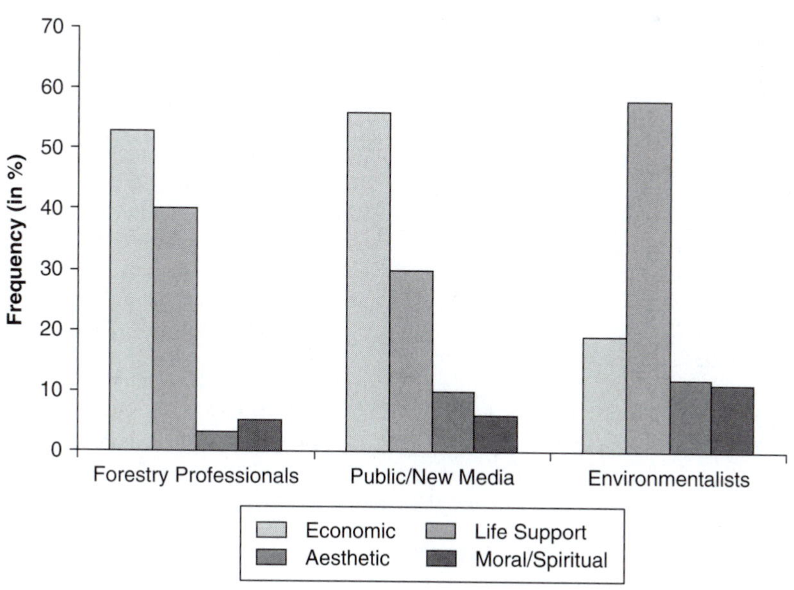

Figure 1 Forest Value Systems by Group, 1900–1993

purification steps, each one removing extraneous components to yield progressively more homogeneous preparations enriched in relevant materials. This logic led to the strategy of successive 'filtrations' during the text analyses" (Fan, 1988:xvii) [Editors' note: See also reading 7.6, this volume].

2. The computer software to generate the KWIC lists and carry out the actual content analysis was InfoTrend, developed by Prof. David Fan, Department of Genetics and Cell Biology, University of Minnesota.

3. Strictly speaking, the databases of text for forestry professionals and environmentalists are also indirect reflections of the values of these groups, because the included texts are the outcome of editorial decisions by people in leadership positions rather than a random sample of the populations of interest.

4. Personal communication, David Fan, University of Minnesota, February 15, 1994.

References

Bengston, D. N. (1994). The nature of value and the value of nature. In *Foresters together: meeting tomorrow's challenges: Proceedings of the 1993 Society of American Foresters national convention* (pp. 57–62). November 1993, Indianapolis, IN: SAF Publ. 94–01. Bethesda. MD, Society of American Foresters.

Borland, H. (1984). A tree in winter. *National Wildlife 22,*1:4–5.

Creighton, J. L. (1983). The use of values: Public participation and the planning process. In G. A. Daneki, M. W. Garcia, & J. Delli Prisol (Eds.), *Public involvement and social impact assessment* (pp. 143–61). Boulder, CO: Westview Press.

Fan, D. P. (1988). *Predictions of public opinion from the mass media: Computer content analysis and mathematical modeling.* New York: Greenwood Press.

Gordon, J. C. (1993). *The new face of forestry: Exploring a discontinuity and the need for a vision.* 1993 Distinguished Pinchot Lecture. Milford, PA: Grey Towers Press.

Grumbine, R. E. (1994). What is ecosystem management? *Conservation Biology 8,*1:27–38.

Hays, S. P. (1988). The new environmental forest. *University of Colorado Law Review 59:*517–550.

Hendee, J. C., & Pitstick, R. C. (1994). Growth and change in US forest-related environmental groups. *Journal of Forestry 92,*6:24–31.

Holler, J. I. (1990). *Valuing wildlife: A Minnesota perspective.* Master's thesis, University of Minnesota, St. Paul.

Kellert, S. R. (1985). Historical trends in perceptions and uses of animals in 20th century America. *Environmental Review 9,*1:19–33.

Kennedy, J. J. (1985). Conceiving forest management as providing for current and future social value. *Forest Ecology and Management 13,* 4:121–132.

McQuillan, A. G. (1993). Cabbages and kings: The ethics and aesthetics of new forestry. *Environmental Values 2,* 3:191–221.

Shands, W. E. (1991). Beyond multiple use: Managing national forests for distinctive values. *American Forests 94,* 3–4:14–15, 56–57.

Steel, B. S., Ust, P., & Shindler, B. (1994). Conflicting values about federal forests: A comparison of national and Oregon publics. *Society and Natural Resources 7,* 2:137–154.

Toner, M. (1985). Is this the chestnut's last stand? *National Wildlife 23,*6:24–27.

Vining, J., & Ebreo, A. (1991). Are you thinking what I think you are? A study of actual and estimated goal priorities and decision preferences of resource managers, environmentalists, and the public. *Society and Natural Resource 4,* 2:177–196.

Watson, J. (1990). The last stand for old growth? *National Wildlife 28,* 1:24–25.

Weber, R. P. (1990). *Basic content analysis* (2nd ed.). Thousand Oaks, CA: Sage.

The Wilderness Society. (1983). Toward the twenty-first century: A Wilderness Society agenda for the national forests. *Wilderness 47,* 161:32–38.

Worster, D. (1994). *Nature's economy: A history of ecological ideas* (2nd ed.). New York: Cambridge University Press.

5.3

The World Attention Survey

Harold D. Lasswell*

We gain insight into the lives of others when we know what they read, see and hear. This is one of the chief purposes to be served by any systematic survey of public attention. One general, though far from universal, human attribute is the tendency to over-estimate the amount of attention given to the self by other persons. Everything concerning the precious ego is so intimate and immediate that it is difficult to accept a realistic picture of what other people are thinking and feeling about us. We know this is true in our person-to-person relationships. It is equally true when we think of ourselves as Americans in contrast to Germans, British, or Russians.

. . . [A] World Attention Survey [can] . . . correct any tendency to over-estimate the amount of attention given [to a symbol]. . . . [Moreover, it] is useful in correcting any false ideas about the [attention paid, for example, to the United States by charting whether it] is favorably or unfavorably presented to foreign peoples. The *Excelsior,* an important paper in Mexico City, was publishing news relatively unfavorable to the United States in the autumn of 1939. Since that time, the presentation of this country has been more favorable, or more balanced.

Public Attention

The stream of public attention is related to policy. This is particularly true in totalitarian countries, where the press and other agencies of mass communication are under strict discipline. [Figure 1] shows something about totalitarian press strategy. The summer of 1939 was a period of active negotiation between Germany and the Soviet Union. The amount of attention paid to Germany in the influential Russian newspaper *Pravda* remained steady during the summer. Not so the references to Russia in the *Völkischer Beobachter.* Here we see less and less attention paid to the Soviet Union, previously a target of bitter hostility. This indicated that Germany was clearing the path for a sudden change in diplomatic orientation, as was learned when the pact was announced.

---

*From Lasswell, H. (1941). The world attention survey. *Public Opinion Quarterly 5,* 3:456–462.

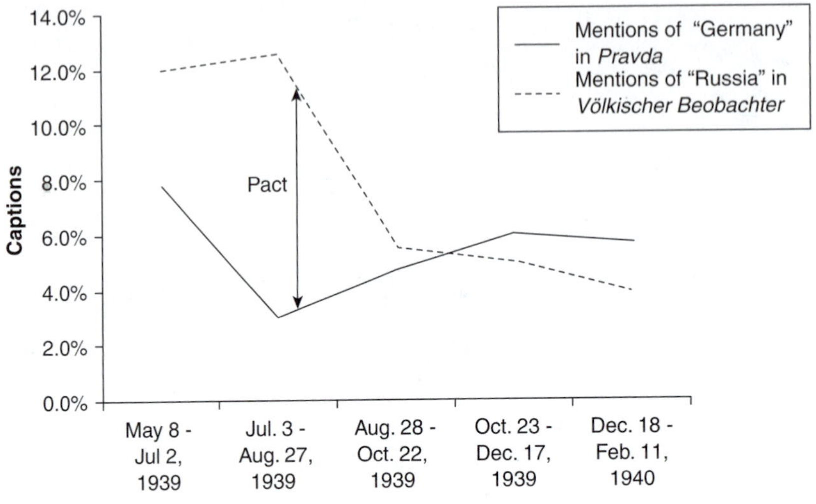

Figure 1 Comparing Coverage in *Pravda* and *Völkischer Beobachter*

Bridging Opinion and Action

The survey of world attention is able to supply us with data about many of the missing links in the process of political and social development. For a great many years scientific students of politics have been concerned about the connection between "material" and "ideological" factors. The propagandists of Marxism have contended for the primacy of the material over the ideological. Many anti-Marxists have indignantly rejected the primacy of the material and asserted the power of ideas in shaping society. It has been difficult to discuss these questions objectively for lack of data about ideological changes through time. Part of the deficiency is to be attributed to inadequate technique; but this limitation is in process of being superseded. The symbols that come to the focus of attention can be objectively described, and their changes can be presented in convenient graphical form.

The attention survey is needed to supplement our knowledge of opinion and of material shifts in the environment. Between "opinion" and "material" change lie important intermediate events; namely, the focusing of public attention. People cannot respond to an environment that is not brought to their notice. Hence, we must describe the fluctuating focus of collective attention if we are to trace the connection between environment and response.*

Scope and Technique

It is impossible to rely upon any single channel of communication if we are concerned with the total focus of attention. The charts in this article depict certain changes in the press. A total survey would supplement them with data about other publications and about the contents of radio, newsreel and other agencies of mass communication. It should not be forgotten that the mass agencies themselves account for but a fraction of the daily span of attention. After all, most of the hours of the day are given over to other activities than reading newspapers, listening to broadcasts or looking at motion pictures.

Technique of Analysis

. . . The general purpose of the technique is to describe the field of attention, to show the relative prominence of selected symbols, like the names of leaders, nations, policies, institutions.

*See Lasswell (1935) for a statement of the scientific importance of the focus of attention.

One index of prominence is appearance in a news caption; the charts show the percentage of total captions (words) containing significant symbols. Where captions are missing, or de-emphasized (as on the editorial page), the number of inches (or words) is taken.

In the interest of objectivity papers are described according to a code that is applied by workers who have learned how to use it. Coders are given regular tests to verify the comparability of their results. When the problem is to count the frequency of occurrence of explicit unit symbols—like "Germany"—the reliability is, of course, very high (99% agreement).

Value of Symbols

Since we are not only interested in the frequency of occurrence of specific symbols, but in the plus or minus character of the presentation, additional rules are laid down for coders. A *plus* presentation of a symbol puts it in a favorable light (an "indulgence"); a *minus* presentation puts it in an unfavorable setting (a "deprivation"). A symbol is presented favorably when shown as strong, or in conformity with a normative standard (or morality, legality, or divinity, for example). Properly applied, the reliability of plus and minus coding is high.

It may be of general interest to publish some of the distinctions that have proved of value in content analysis. The following kinds of "indulgence" and "deprivation" may be distinguished:

1. *Indulgence*

2. *Positive Indulgence Realized*

The gain is realized when the environment has already treated the object of reference indulgently: "British Win Battle."

3. *Negative Indulgence Realized*

Sometimes the gain is in the form of avoided loss: "British Evacuate Dunkirk Successfully."

4. *Positive Indulgence Promised*

Gains may be promised for the future, or presented as bound to occur in the future: "British Victory Sure."

5. *Negative Indulgence Promised*

Avoided losses may be promised for the future, or shown as certain: "British Squadron Will Escape Destruction."

6. *Deprivation*

7. *Positive Deprivation Realized*

Losses may already be sustained by an object of reference: "London Bombed Severely."

8. *Negative Deprivation Realized*

Gains may have been blocked in the past: "British Plans Thwarted."

9. *Positive Deprivation Threatened*

The losses may be referred to the future: "Britain Will Lose."

10. *Negative Deprivation Threatened*

Also blocked gains may be deferred to the future: "British Advance Will Be Blocked."

A representative—certainly not an exhaustive—list of standards is the following:

1. Expediency: (strength) describes the position of the object or reference in regard to such values as safety, power, goods, respect (power and respect are sub-categories of deference.).

1a. Safety: Refers to physical integrity of persons, groups or things. "British Lives Lost;" "British Pilots Rescued;" "King Escapes Bombs;" "Air Minister Dies in Plane Collision."

1ab. Efficiency (Safety): Efficiency refers to level of performance of a function: "Health of Evacuated Children Improves" (biological efficiency); "Resistance to Diphtheria in Deep Bomb Shelters Decreases."

1b. Power: In the most general sense, power is control over important decisions. It is measured according to the means of decision-making—fighting, diplomacy, voting, for example. "Germans Break Through at Sedan," "German Peace Offer Rebuffed," "Labour Gains in By-Election," "Court Revokes License of Communist Periodical."

1bb. Efficiency (Power): "Superiority of New Anti-Aircraft Devices," "Clever Axis Gain," "Prime Minister Splits Opponents and Wins Vote of Confidence."

1c. Goods: This term refers to volume and distribution of goods and services: "Food Reserves Doubled," "South American Market Preserved."

1cb. Efficiency (Goods): "War Plants 80 Per-Cent Efficient," "Highly Skilled German Opticians."

1d. Respect: "British Prestige Suffers," "British Respect German Airmen," "Carol Booed as He Leaves Roumania; Speaks Contemptuously of Italian Army."

1db. Efficiency (Respect): "Ribbentrop Received With Great Pomp," "Exquisite Courtesy of Chinese Diplomats Extolled."

2. *Morality*

2a. Truth/Falsehood: "German Lies are Bolder," utilizes a moral standard, the obligation to refrain from the deliberate dissemination of falsehood. "BBC Sticks to the Truth."

2b. Mercy/Atrocity: "German Atrocities Multiply"—the term "atrocity" makes use of a moral standard to justify acts, the obligation to refrain from inflicting unnecessary cruelty in the conduct of war. "Germans Rescue British Sailors."

2c. Heroism/Cowardice: The obligation to act courageously; "Risks Life to Rescue Comrade," "Soldier Deserts Wounded Comrade."

2d. Loyalty-Disloyalty: The obligation to serve a common purpose; "All Sections of Population Patriotic," "Fifth Column Active in Norway."

3. *Propriety:* The obligation to learn a conventional code; "Germans Are a Crude and Barbarous People," "His Manners Are Perfect." If a code is deliberately violated, we have an example of disrespect (1).

4. *Divinity:* The standard is an obligation to abide by the Will of God; "God Is on Our Side," "God Will Punish Our Enemies."

5. *Legality:* The standard is the obligation to abide by law; "Japanese Government Violates International Law," "Court Upholds International Law."

6. *Beauty:* The standard is aesthetic; "Beautiful Equipment Designed by United States of America," "Hideous German Art on Display."

7. *Consistency:* The standards are logical relationships among proposition; "Hitler Contradicts Self," "Churchill States Logical Case."

8. *Probability:* Probability of a statement with no imputation of deliberate falsification; "Einstein's Theory Is Confirmed."

9. *Euphoria/Dysphoria:* The standard is agreeable or disagreeable subjective states; "Terror Grips Brussels," (terror is dysphoric); "Festive Spirit in Rome," (festive spirit is euphoric). "Hate" is dysphoric unless explicity qualified; "Glorious Hate Sung by Poet."

10. *Omnibus:* Statements fusing many standards, "The Unspeakable Hun."

Reference

Lasswell, H. D. (1935). *World politics and personal insecurity.* New York: McGraw Hill.

5.4

CONSTRUCTING CONTENT ANALYSIS SCALES IN COUNSELING RESEARCH

LINDA L. VINEY AND PETER CAPUTI*

Counselors who conduct research need to have available to them a variety of assessment devices, the scores for which are reliable and valid. Qualitative tools can be helpful to these researchers when meanings of verbal communications are important (Elliott, 1999). Quantitative tools are equally important, however, and content analysis scales to assess psychological states can provide meanings together with rigorous, scaled measurement. Winter (1992) has recommended content analysis scales to counseling researchers. Gottschalk, who in the 1960s in the United States developed the first content analysis scales to assess counseling processes in verbal communications, still uses them for this purpose (Gottschalk, 1996).

In this article, we define content analysis and content analysis scales, as well as provide the nine steps necessary to develop such scales. The types of verbal communications to which the scales can be applied are also considered, with a discussion of the limitations of the scales. We . . . review the psychometrics of their scores. Their roles in counseling research are considered, that is, in assessing clients and counselors, in outcome and prediction, as well as process research. . . .

Recent research . . . used content analysis to (among other purposes) identify the words chosen by music therapists as they worked with clients (Wolfe, O'Connell, & Epps, 1998) and to better understand the processes in counseling sessions (Richards & Lonborg, 1996). Content analysis has also been used to describe the emotional reactions of clients to traumatic experiences (Murray & Segal, 1994) and to determine whether psychoanalytic concepts are used by the Malan counselors (de Wolf, 1993).

---

*From Viney, L. L., & Caputi, P. (2005). Assessment in action: Using the Origin and Pawn, Positive Affect, CASPM and Cognitive Anxiety content analysis scales in counseling research. *Measurement and Evaluation in Counseling and Development 38:*115–126.

What Is a Content Analysis Scale?

How does a content analysis scale applied to verbal communications differ from content analysis of those communications? The scale meets the same criteria. However, this tool also provides a continuously scaled quantitative summary of a series of qualitative content analyses. The scale results in normally distributed scores amenable to complex statistical analyses, such as analysis of variance and regression. This tool, the content analysis scale, is best understood through a description of its construction. There are nine steps involved in this process before reliability and validity can be established. We provide a description of the development of a content analysis scale, including these steps. We have chosen the Origin and Pawn Scales (Westbrook & Viney, 1980) for this purpose.

1. *Describe the psychological state to be assessed and define all its dimensions.* The Origin and Pawn Scales grew out of the conceptual work of De Charms (1968). De Charms chose the term *origin* to describe the state in which people see their actions as primarily determined by themselves and the term *pawn* for the state in which people believe themselves to have no choice of action. His concepts are similar to that of Rotter's (1966) *locus of control.* The Origin and Pawn Scales were devised to avoid the unidimensionality of questionnaires that measure these states.

2. *Define the unit of content to be analyzed.* The next step was to select the clause as the unit of measurement for a verbal communication. We followed Gottschalk, Winget, and Gleser (1969) in this decision, because the clause, as parsed as a group of words with a finite verb (Gore et al., 1981), focuses on action in meaning.

3. *Describe the content of the verbal communications or the cues from which the psychological state is to be inferred.* De Charms's (1968) accounts of differences in the perception of action, together with readings of a range of samples of verbalizations, led us to select five types of verbal content from which origin- and pawn-like experiences were to be inferred.

4. *Add, if appropriate, any cues used to demonstrate the intensity of the psychological state.*

5. *Apply the differential scoring weights to these cues.* These two steps are not taken if the intensity of the state is not considered to vary, as for the Origin and Pawn Scales. The Cognitive Anxiety Scale is the only scale included in our discussion for which Steps 4 and 5 are followed.

6. *Because participants will give communications of different lengths, include a scaling or correction factor, taking into account the number of words in the verbal communication.* When time sampling is used, this step is important because of the differing opportunities participants have to express the content they intend and the differing number of words they might choose in each case. We used, with all of these scales, the Gottschalk-Gleser Correction Factor (*CF;* Gottschalk et al., 1969), that is, the number of words in the scored communication, divided into 100, $CF = 100/N$.

7. *Derive* a *total score or, in the case of multidimensional concepts,* a *set of subscores.* This step followed Gottschalk and Gleser (Gottschalk et al., 1969) again in calculating the Total Scores: Total Raw Score (f) × CF plus $CF/2$. Adding $CF/2$ is useful with communications that have little of the sought content to score because by spreading the scores, it discriminates between them. This procedure does not appear to distort, in the final score, the amount of the content assessed (again see Gottchalk et al., 1969).

8. *Examine the distributions of scores for each scale and transform, when necessary, for greater normality.* The penultimate step that examined the distributions of these scores led to a square root being used for normality.

The calculation of the final, Total Score

$$= \sqrt{(f \times CF) + CF/2}$$

9. *Collect normative data from specified samples.* Normative data for the Origin and Pawn Scales were available from 524 participants: street youth (97), psychology students (47), successful students (33), external students (48), relocated women (25), childbearing women (200), relatives of emergency patients (30), people with quadriplegia (15), and people with psychiatric disorders (29).

Types of Communications to Which the Content Analysis Scales Can Be Applied

Data collection and data analysis are two separate phases of the process of measurement. Content analysis scales provide a form of data analysis. These scales can be applied to verbal communications that have been spoken or written, spontaneous or planned, public or private. They can also be applied to counseling transcripts (Viney, 1994) or to suicide notes (Gottschalk & Gleser, 1961). Units of communication can be sampled in two ways: by the number of words (e.g., 500-word samples of communications from clients, counselors, or both in counseling transcripts) or by duration (e.g., 5-minute samples of verbal communications). The instructions to participants for providing communication samples, which can be useful for outcome research, can vary from the highly structured to much less structured, depending on the purpose of the research. The instructions need to be sufficiently open-ended so that participants have a wide range of meanings they can choose to use. An example of such instructions is:

> I'd like you to talk to me for a few minutes about your life at the moment—the good things and the bad—what it is like for you. Once you have started, I shall be here listening to you, but I would rather not reply to any questions you may have until the 5-minute period is over. Do you have any questions you would like to ask now, before we start? (Viney, Rudd, Grenyer, & Tych, 1995:7)

Responses to such instructions are usually transcribed from tape recordings for analysis, but participants can also reply by e-mail.

Limitations of the Content Analysis Scales

All content analysis scales are limited in at least six ways. First, they are based purely on verbal cues and ignore extra-verbal cues, such as "ums" and sighs; they deal exclusively with conscious, verbalized experiences. Second, they can be developed only if the psychological state to be measured is clearly conceptualized so that criteria and scoring examples can be devised. Third, they should not be applied to verbal communications from people who cannot adequately express themselves in the language being used. Translations of the five content analysis scales we are discussing have been made. The usual criterion of back translation, for example into Mandarin Chinese in the Peoples' Republic of China, has been applied successfully (Wang & Viney, 1996, 1997), but there are still likely to be problems of communication. Fourth, the scale scores from the Chinese translations show none of the normative differences we have observed for some other content analysis scales in English-speaking countries, such as the United States, Britain, and Australia; they cannot be assumed to tap into concepts and experiences represented in the languages of other cultures. Fifth, in their application, the content analysis scales can be time-consuming. Sixth, they can require extra resources for the training of judges.

The Psychometrics of the Content Analysis Scales

Reliability

Reliabilities are most important, especially *inter-judge* reliability, examining the agreement between, in these cases, two independent users of the scales. . . .

Evidence for the internal consistency of these scale scores is also only useful for certain scales. Scales that are independent can then be used together in the same multivariate analyses of variance. However, with these scales, it is also helpful to know that pairs of these scale scores show inter-correlations (e.g., Trust with Mistrust, Autonomy with Constraint, and so on; Viney & Tych, 1985).

The other form of reliability to be reported here is *stability* of scores over time. This reliability is only useful for some types of concepts, and so it is applicable only for certain types of psychotherapy research. For example, the Origin Scale scores, assessing potentially variable psychological states, show low stability (.22; Westbrook & Viney, 1980). Whereas, for its companion, the Pawn Scale scores, the high degree of stability (.51) is impressive, as is that for the Cognitive Anxiety Scale (.63; Murphy & Davidshofer, 2001; Viney & Westbrook, 1976). These stabilities differ appropriately according to the intervals between testing.

Validity

Validity becomes evident in networks of correlations with extreme variables. The Origin Scale scores are independent of gender and age, but are related to occupational status, higher scorers having higher status (.12). They are also related to scores on other positively toned measures (Positive Affect, .21 to .43; and Sociality, .25 to .50; Westbrook & Viney, 1980). . . . They also discriminate people who are in controllable situations from those who are not in controllable situations (Westbrook & Viney, 1980), youth workers from their clients (Viney, 1981), and those who face their own death in a psychologically healthy way from those who have a less healthy approach to death (Viney, Walker, Robertson, Pincombe, & Ewan, 1994). The validity of the Pawn Scale scores is similar, as it should be, to that for its partner, the Origin Scale.

Discussion

Content analysis scales are of value to counselors who are researchers because they allow responses that preserve the intended meanings expressed by the study participants while their scaling makes possible complex statistical analyses of their data. In the following paragraphs, we summarize examples of scale score findings that are of particular interest to researchers; the first two focusing on clients, representing dependent variables.

First, there are those findings related to the psychological functioning of clients. Content analysis scales can differentiate one group of clients from another, for example, needy youth from their youth workers, people who stutter from people who speak fluently, ill people from those who are not ill, and those not in controllable situations from those in controllable situations.

Second, these scale scores can be responsive to counseling of both individual and group types and with personal construct and psychodynamic approaches to counseling. For example, the scale scores for people who were ill showed immediate improvement after these individuals had received counseling sessions, with the increase being maintained at follow-up 12 months later.

Third, the scales, with their meaning-based measurement, can also be used to assess the psychological functioning of counselors. One existing study dealt directly with verbal reports from counselors. Three other studies have dealt with nurses. The first, in 1983, examined differences in professionally trained and non-professionally-trained telephone counselors. The predictions that the non-professionally-trained counselors would report their clients to be less helpless, more powerful, and with more positive feelings than would the professionally trained counselors were supported. The second study showed the impact on nurses who worked in nursing homes of an intervention to give these nurses a greater sense of power in their work with residents. The same Origin and Pawn Scales identified nurses who were more concerned about causing pain to their patients and, together with the scale measuring Positive Affect, distinguished palliative care nurses from nurses specializing in burns (Grenyer, Viney, & Luborsky, 1996; Nagy, 1998).

Conclusions

Content analysis of free verbal communications overcomes many of the problems that are involved in asking participants to describe their states. Content analysis scales, in turn, make possible an approach that reduces intrusiveness and demands characteristics for both clients and counselors, while giving clients opportunities to deal with what is important to them. The scales are preferable to standardized tests and questionnaires, which can be seen as assessing the meanings of the test creators rather than the meanings of the participants who respond to them (Child, 1976; Wallerstein, 1986). Future research with content analysis scales should confront the questions that have become increasingly more crucial: Who benefits from counseling and who makes a good counselor? In both outcome and process research, the advantages of the content analysis scales have withstood thorough scrutiny.

References

Child, I. (1976). *Humanistic psychology and the research tradition.* New York: Wiley.

De Charms, R. (1968). *Personal causation.* New York: Academic Press.

de Wolf, T. (1993). How psychoanalytic are the Malan therapies? A study of the process in short-term time-limited psychoanalytic psychotherapy. In H. Groen-Prakken (Ed.), *The Dutch annals of psychoanalysis* (pp. 281–288). Amsterdam, Netherlands: Swets & Zetlinger.

Elliott, R. (1999). Editor's introduction to a special issue on qualitative psychotherapy research: Themes and descriptions. *Psychotherapy Research 9:*251–257.

Gore, P. B., et al. (Eds.). (1981). *Webster's third new international dictionary.* Springfield, MA: Merriam Webster.

Gottschalk, L. A. (1996). *The content analysis of verbal behavior: New findings and clinical applications.* Hillsdale, NJ: Erlbaum.

Gottschalk, L. A., & Gleser, G. C. (1961). An analysis of suicide notes. *British Journal of Medical Psychology 30:*195–204.

Gottschalk, L. A., Winget, C., & Gleser, G. C. (1969). *Manual of instructions for the Gottschalk-Gleser content analysis scales.* Berkeley: University of California Press.

Grenyer, B., Viney, L. L., & Luborsky, L. (1996, August). *Changes in psychosocial maturity levels in therapy for depression over the course of psychotherapy.* Paper presented at the 29th annual meeting of the Society for Psychotherapy Research, Florida.

Murphy, K. R., & Davidshofer, C. O. (2001). *Psychological testing: Principles and applications.* Upper Saddle River, NJ: Prentice-Hall International.

Murray, E. J., & Segal, D. L. (1994). Emotional and social processing in vocal and written expression of feelings about traumatic experiences. *Journal of Traumatic Stress 7:*391–401.

Nagy, S. (1998). A comparison of the effects of patients, pain on nurses working in bums and neonatal intensive care unit. *Journal of Advanced Nursing 27:*335–340.

Richards, P., & Lonborg, S. D. (1996). Development of a method for studying thematic content of psychotherapy sessions. *Journal of Consulting and Clinical Psychology 64:*701–711.

Rotter, J. B. (1966). Generalized expectancies for internal versus external control of reinforcement. *Psychological Monographs 80:*1–28.

Viney, L. L. (1981). An evaluation of an Australian youthwork program. *Youth and Society 14:*447–454.

Viney, L. L. (1994). Sequences of emotion expressed by clients and acknowledged by therapists. *British Journal of Clinical Psychology 33:*469–381.

Viney, L. L., Rudd, M., Grenyer, B., & Tych, A. M. (1995). *Content analysis scales of psychosocial maturity: A scoring manual.* Wollongong, Australia: University of Wollongong.

Viney, L. L., & Tych, A. M. (1985). Content analysis scales to measure psychosocial maturity in the elderly. *Journal of Personality Assessment 49:*311–317.

Viney, L. L., Walker, B. M., Robertson, L., Pincombe, J., & Ewan, C. (1994). Dying in palliative care units and in hospital: The quality of life of terminal cancer patients. *Journal of Consulting and Clinical Psychology 40:*157–165.

Viney, L. L., & Westbrook, M. T. (1976). Cognitive anxiety: A method of content analysis for verbal samples. *Journal of Personality Assessment 40:*140–150.

Wallerstein, R. S. (1986). Psychoanalysis as a science: A response to the new challenges. *Psychoanalytic Quarterly 32:*415–451.

Wang, W., & Viney, L. L. (1996). A cross-cultural comparison of Eriksonian psychosocial development: Chinese and Australian children. *School Psychology International 17:*33–48.

Wang, W., & Viney, L. L. (1997). The psychosocial development of children and adolescents in the People's Republic of China: An Eriksonian approach. *International Journal of Psychology 32:*139–153.

Westbrook, M. T., & Viney, L. L. (1980). Perceptions of self as origin and pawn measured by content analysis scales. *Journal of Personality Assessment 44:*157–166.

Winter, D. A. (1992). *Using personal construct psychology in clinical settings.* London: Routledge.

Wolfe, D. E., O'Connell, A. S., & Epps, K. S. (1998). A content analysis of therapists' verbalizations during group music therapy. *Music Therapy Perspectives 16:*13–20.

5.5

How Often Is Often?

Milton Hakel*

Is "almost never" almost always never? Which is more frequent: "frequently" or "often"? And anyway, how often is "often"? We use frequency words imprecisely. Worst of all, it is difficult to say just how imprecisely.

Frequency words are frequently ambiguous. Sometimes (occasionally?) we need to be reminded of that ambiguity. Thus, 100 students from an introductory psychology course at the University of Minnesota complete the following questionnaire (Simpson, 1944):

Table 1 "What Do These Words Mean to You?"

1.	almost never	11.	often
2.	always	12.	once in awhile
3.	about as often as not	13.	rarely
4.	frequently	14.	rather often
5.	generally	15.	seldom
6.	hardly ever	16.	sometimes
7.	never	17.	usually
8.	not often	18.	usually not
9.	now and then	19.	very seldom
10.	occasionally	20.	very often

SOURCE: Simpson, R. H. (1944). The specific meanings of certain terms indicating different degrees of frequency. *Quarterly Journal of Speech 30:*328–330. Reprinted with permission from Taylor & Francis Ltd., http://informaworld.com.

[Table 1 lists] a group of words that we use to indicate differing degrees of "oftenness" with which events tend to happen. Obviously, some of the words mean different things to different people. We wish to determine what each word means to you.

For instance, if "almost never" indicated to you that a thing would happen about ten times out of a hundred, you should mark in the space before the expression "10." If it means about one time out of 100 to you, you should put "1" in the space before the expression. Simply indicate how many times out of 100 you think the word indicates an act has happened or is likely to happen.

All responses were tabulated, and the results are shown in Table 2: some precise data about imprecision.

Variability is rampant. Someone's "rarely" is someone else's "hardly ever." "Often" and "rather often" have the same medians. "Rather" is rather meaningless. "Very seldom" is very seldom less than "seldom."

Simpson (1944) obtained similar results. How similar? The correlation between the rank orders of the medians is .99. The correlation between the rank orders of the quartile ranges is .78. We are exceedingly stable about being exceedingly imprecise.

*Hakel, M. D. (1968). How often is often? *American Psychologist 23:*533–534.

Table 2 Medians, Quartiles and Quartile Ranges for 20 Frequency Words

Word	*Median*	Q_1	Q_2	QR[a]
Always	100	98	100	2
Very often	87	81	92	11
Usually	79	73	83	15
Often	74	69	82	13
Rather often	74	65	79	14
Frequently	72	68	75	7
Generally	72	60	84	24
About as often as not	50	50	50	0
Now and then	34	22	39	17
Sometimes	29	21	45	24
Occasionally	28	21	38	17
Once in awhile	22	14	30	16
Usually not	16	9	20	11
Not often	16	9	24	15
Seldom	9	7	15	7
Hardly ever	8	4	12	8
Very seldom	7	4	10	6
Rarely	5	3	10	7
Almost never	2	1	5	4
Never	0	0	0	0

a. $Q_2 - Q_1$.

In view of the magnificent imprecision of frequency words, it is amazing we can communicate at all. Do you know what I mean?

Reference

Simpson, R. H. (1944). The specific meanings of certain terms indicating different degrees of frequency. *Quarterly Journal of Speech 30:*328–330.

5.6

RELATIVE RISK IN THE NEWS MEDIA

A Quantification of Misrepresentation

KAREN FROST, ERICA FRANK, AND EDWARD MAIBACH*

INTRODUCTION

Although the news media's representation of health risk information is often lamented, the extent to which the media distort the causes of mortality has never been adequately quantified. The American public depends on news media for reliable health information (Gellert, Higgins, Lowery, & Maxwell, 1994; Nelkin, 1985; Singer & Endreny, 1987). Previous studies, however, indicate that the public has a skewed perception of relative mortality rates (Fischhoff, 1985; Lichtenstein, Slovic, Fischhoff, Layman, & Combs, 1978; Slovic, 1987). Biases such as the overestimation of infrequent causes of mortality and the underestimation of frequent causes may be, in part, attributable to the media's misrepresentation of mortality (Lichtenstein et al., 1978).

The print news media exert an agenda-setting function in that issues reported in the media are more likely to be seen as important and meritorious of public discourse (Jones, Beniger, & Westoff, 1980; McCombs & Shaw, 1972; Meyer, 1990, Wallack & Dorfman, 1992; Weiner, 1986). Amount of copy space is an important indicator of perceived newsworthiness** (McCombs & Shaw, 1972).***

A limited number of previous studies have investigated disproportionate reporting of

*From Frost, K., Frank, E., & Maibach, E. (1997). Relative risk in the news media: A quantification of misrepresentation. *American Journal of Public Health 87*:842–845.

**The amount of newsprint devoted to an issue can be interpreted as indicating its newsworthiness. Although there is little doubt that the mass media set the agenda of public discussion, newsworthiness, however, is often conflated—incorrectly—with relevance or importance to the public and others. Misperceptions of reality, truths, are another matter. Lack of correlation between the volume of coverage of mortality and statistics of the causes of death may have many reasonable explanations, for example, a lack of public health initiatives, impossibility of prevention, or simply dramatic accidents.

***See reading 2.7, this volume.

mortality; however, they either failed to quantify the disproportion (Singer & Endreny, 1987), used extremely limited samples (Combs & Slovic, 1979), or are outdated (Combs & Slovic, 1979). The current study employed content analysis to compare representations of mortality in national print media with actual mortality and risk factors for mortality in 1990.

Methods

The *World Almanac and Book of Facts 1992* (Hoffman, 1991) was used to determine the 1990 circulation figures for periodicals in the following categories: weekly news magazines; general interest women's magazines; general interest monthly magazines; and daily newspapers (Hoffman, 1991:311–313). The publication with the widest circulation in its category was selected to represent that category. The following publications were selected: *Time* (weekly news magazine, circulation 4,094,935); *Family Circle* (general interest women's magazine, circulation 5,431,779); *Readers Digest* (general interest monthly magazine, circulation 16,264,547); and *USA Today* (daily newspaper, circulation 1,347,450). A random sample of 12 issues of each periodical from 1990 (except for *Readers Digest,* of which all issues were used) was selected for analysis.

Each of the periodicals was coded for mortality-related text (measured square centimeters) based on definitions of the nine leading risk factors for death (McGinnis & Foege, 1993) and the 11 leading causes of death in 1990 (National Center for Health Statistics, 1993). Only text involving mortality of Americans was eligible for coding. Advertisements (including classifieds), photographs, obituaries, fiction, and text about war were excluded. All other text, including relevant photograph captions, tables of contents, and magazine covers, was considered eligible. Causes of mortality were coded in all instances where they were mentioned. The sentence in which the mortality cause appeared was considered the least measurable unit; for example, when an article contained only one sentence referring to a cause of mortality, that sentence alone was measured for analysis. To be coded as a discussion of a risk factor, text must have clearly stated that the mortality was due explicitly to a risk factor or must have implied or stated the potential for mortality at some time in the future due to the effects of the risk factor.

When necessary, selections were coded under more than one heading. For example, text regarding an instance of lung cancer stated to have been caused by smoking cigarettes was classified as an issue involving both malignant neoplasms and tobacco. When a cause of or risk factor for mortality appeared in a title, both the title and the accompanying text were measured in full; this was likewise the case when a title included the word "death" or some variation thereof, as in "Twenty Confirmed Dead in Accident," or "Lethal Injections Claim Lives of Two." Titles were otherwise not coded, and full articles were otherwise dissected for relevant passages. A single investigator iteratively coded all of the content; as protocol modifications were made, all previously coded material was re-coded. For every cause of and risk factor for death, a risk ratio was calculated to compare the proportion of actual deaths attributable to the cause with the proportion of copy accorded to the cause.

Results

There were substantial disparities between actual causes of death and the amount of coverage given those causes in the print media. For most causes of and risk factors for death, there was a substantial disproportion between the amount of text devoted to the cause and the actual number of deaths attributable to the cause (Figures 1 and 2).

Most underrepresented by the news media were tobacco use (which received 23% of expected copy), cerebrovascular disease (31%), and heart disease (33%). Illicit use of drugs (1740%), motor vehicles (1280%), toxic agents (1070%), and homicide (733%) were most over-represented.

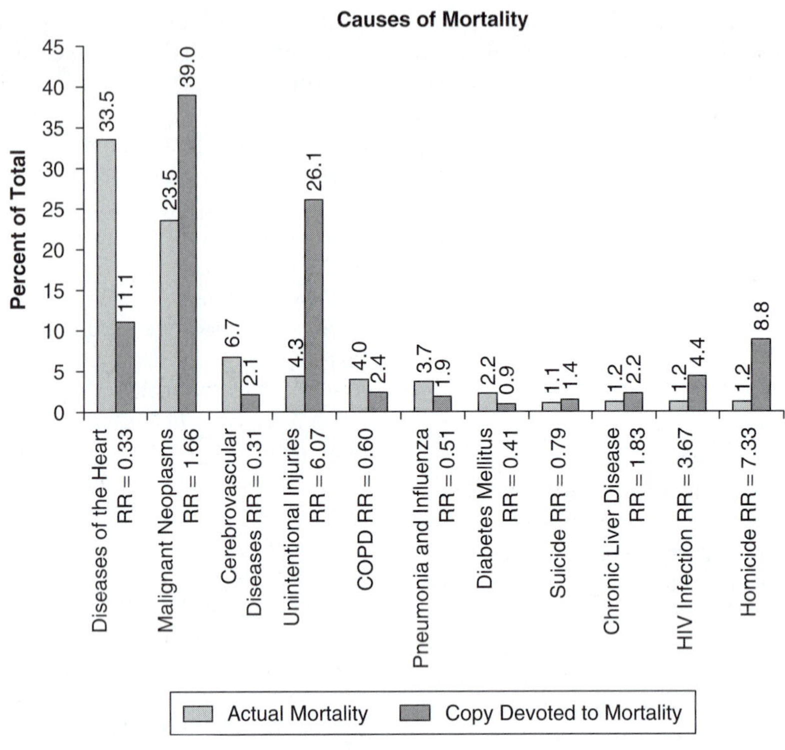

Figure 1 Percentages of Actual Mortality vs. Copy Devoted to Mortality in Print Media, by Cause of Death, 1990

SOURCE: Actual mortality percentages are from the National Center for Health Statistics.

NOTE: COPD = chronic obstructive pulmonary disease, RR = Relative Risk.

Conclusions

The amount of print media devoted to certain causes of mortality is impressively disproportionate to the actual number of deaths attributable to those causes. While a few risk factors (alcohol, firearms, diet, and sexual behavior) and one cause of mortality (suicide) were reported at a frequency proportionate to their occurrence, the 11th-ranked cause of death, homicide, received virtually the same amount of news media coverage as heart disease, the top-ranked cause. Similarly, the lowest-ranking risk factor for mortality, use of illicit drugs, and the number-2 risk factor, diet and activity patterns, received nearly equal news media coverage. This study is the first to quantify the extremely disproportionate representations of mortality causes and risk factors in the national print media.

News media over- and under-emphasize certain causes of death for a variety of reasons, including competition for viewers and commercial interests (Meyer, 1990). This pattern has been particularly well documented in the case of the leading risk factor for death, tobacco use, where the relative lack of news coverage has been attributed to the influence that tobacco companies, with their enormous advertising budgets, have over media organizations (Warner, Goldenhar, & McLaughlin, 1992). News reporting is also driven by rarity, novelty, commercial viability, and drama more than by concerns about relative risk (Adams, 1992). Yet the unusual, novel, lucrative, or dramatic report must be placed in a broader context to help the reader better interpret the story's implications.

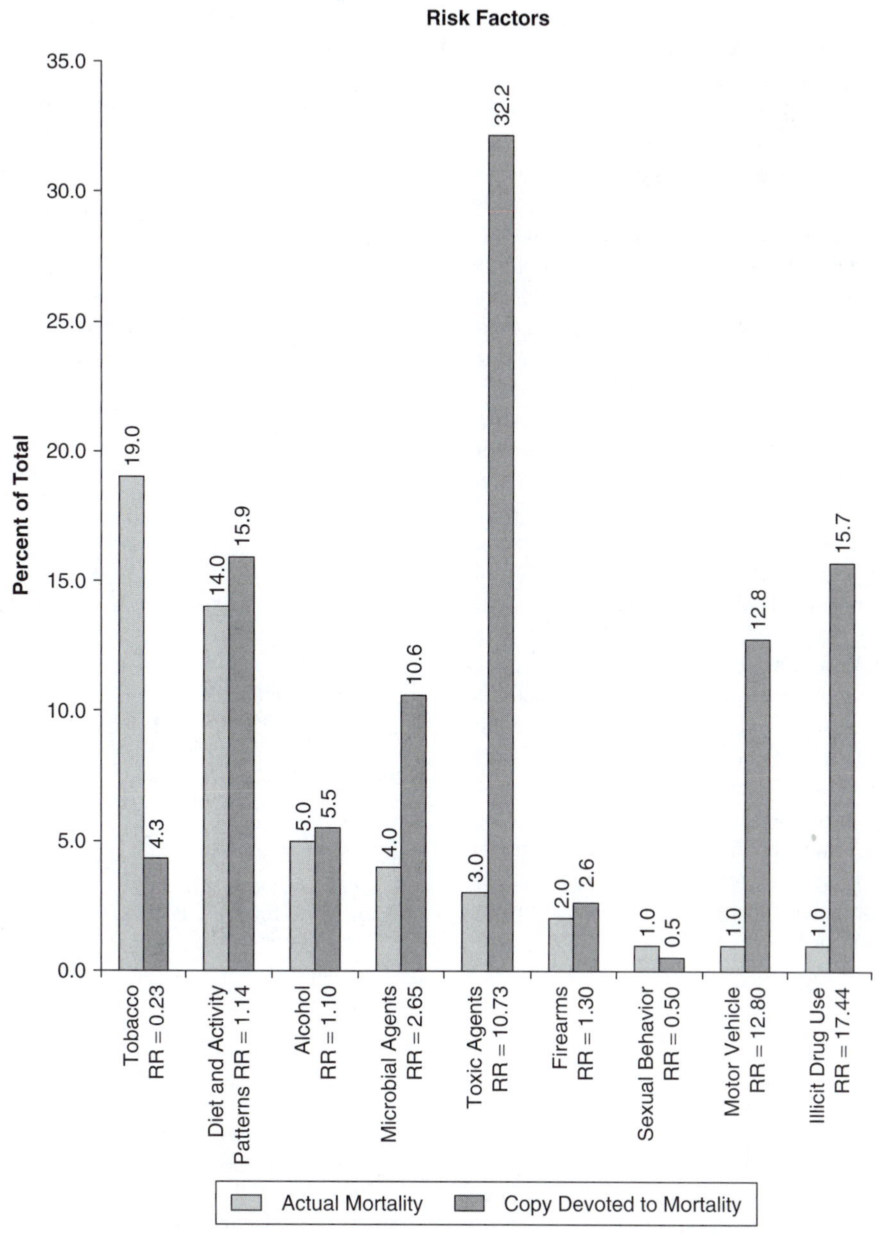

Figure 2 Percentages of Actual Risk Factor–Related Mortality vs. Copy Devoted to Risk Factor–Related Mortality in Print News Media, by Risk Factor, 1990

SOURCE: Actual risk factor–related mortality percentages are from McGinnis & Foege (1993).

Studies of cognition indicate that people judge the frequency or probability of an occurrence by the ease with which they can retrieve relevant instances from memory or imagination (Tversky & Kahneman, 1974). This bias of cognition is referred to as the availability heuristic. The media's overemphasis on certain causes of death helps distort public risk perception by making these causes more available and thus more easily retrieved

(Lichtenstein et al., 1978; Tversky & Kahneman, 1974; Warner et al., 1992). The print news media's distorted representations of mortality likely skew the public's perceptions of risk through a second cognitive mechanism as well. Studies of risk perception indicate that threats that are perceived to be externally imposed loom larger than self-imposed threats (Slovic, 1987). Thus, not only do the news media emphasize relatively rarer causes of and risk factors for death, but those causes emphasized are those that are instinctively overestimated (Frank, 1989).

These data quantify the extent to which modern journalistic practices distort the portrayal of the leading causes of death and their risk factors. Merely quantifying these pervasive and widely discussed reporting biases is unlikely to affect the output of the journalistic process. Rather, we believe that the primary value of such quantification is to persuade health professionals to aggressively and proactively work with the news media to produce a more balanced agenda and to counteract the effects of journalistic practices that distort accurate presentations of relative risk. Health professionals must focus the attention of the news media and the public on the health issues of greatest concern so that the most prevalent health risks receive appropriate attention.

References

Adams, W. E. (1992). The role of media relations in risk communication. *Public Relations Quarterly 37:*28–32.

Combs, B., & Slovic, P. (1979). Newspaper coverage of causes of death. *Journalism Quarterly 56:*837–843.

Fischhoff, B. (1985). Managing risk perception. *Issues in Science & Technology 2:*83–96.

Frank, E. (1989). Not everything causes cancer. *Journal of the American Medical Association 262:*1429.

Gellert, G. A., Higgins, K. Y., Lowery, R. I., & Maxwell, R. M. (1994). A national survey of public health officers' interactions with the media. *Journal of the American Medical Association 271:*1285–1289.

Hoffman, M. S. (Ed.). (1991). *The world almanac and book of facts 1992.* New York: Pharos Books.

Jones, E. F., Beniger, J. R., & Westoff, C. F. (1980). Pill and IUD discontinuation in the United States 1970–1975: The influence of the media. *Family Planning Perspectives 12:*293–300.

Lichtenstein, S., Slovic, P., Fischhoff, B., Layman, M., & Combs, B. (1978). Judged frequency of lethal events. *Journal of Experimental Psychology: Human Learning & Memory 4:*551–581.

McCombs, M. E., & Shaw, D. L. (1972). The agenda-setting function of mass media. *Public Opinion Quarterly 36:*176–187.

McGinnis, J. M., & Foege, W. H. (1993). Actual causes of death in the United States. *Journal of the American Medical Association 270:*2207–2212.

Meyer, P. (1990). News media responsiveness to public health. In E. Atkin & L. Wallack (Eds.), *Mass communication and public health* (pp. 52–59). Thousand Oaks, CA: Sage.

National Center for Health Statistics. (1993). Advance report of final mortality statistics, 1990. *Monthly Vital Statistics Report*: 41,45.

Nelkin, D. (1985). Managing biomedical news. *Social Resources 52:*625–646.

Singer, E., & Endreny, P. (1987). Reporting hazards: Their benefits and costs. *Journal of Communication 37:*10–26.

Slovic, P. (1987). Perception of risk. *Science 236:*280–285.

Tversky, A., & Kahneman, D. (1974). Judgment under uncertainty: Heuristics and biases. *Science 185:*1124–1131.

Wallack, L., & Dorfman, L. (1992). Television news, hegemony, and health. *American Journal of Public Health 82:*125–126.

Warner, K. E., Goldenhar, L. M., & McLaughlin, C. G. (1992). Cigarette advertising and magazine coverage of the hazards of smoking. *New England Journal of Medicine 326:*305–309.

Weiner, S. L. (1986). Tampons and toxic shock syndrome: consumer protection or public confusion? In H. M. Sapolsky (Ed.), *Consuming fears* (pp. 141–158). New York: Basic Books.

5.7

TELEVISION VIOLENCE

A Coding Scheme

ANU MUSTONEN AND LEA PULKKINEN*

We define TV violence as actions causing or designed to cause harm to oneself, or to another person, physically or psychologically, including implicit threats, nonverbal behavior, and outbursts of anger directed towards animals, and inanimate objects. Portrayals of the mere victims of violence were also included in the definition, if the connection between violent behavior and a victim's injuries was reliably cued. Antisocial activities with no aggressive connotations, such as deceit and theft; or mere negative affective or hostile reactions unaccompanied by physical injury or damage, were excluded from the analysis as well as verbal reports of violence.

Definitions and scales of psychological violence were formulated utilizing Greenberg (1980), and Yudofsky, Silver, Jackson, Endicott, and Williams (1986) ideas. Psychological harm was understood as assaulting another person's self by noxious symbolic messages (e.g., by verbal insults, threatening, scorning gestures, forcing, or pressuring). Verbal and nonverbal modes of aggression were further classified.

The wide definition of violence applied here did not interfere with the comparability of our study and with other content analyses (of TV violence).** Rather, separate coding of varying forms of violence enabled the breakdown of certain forms and thus promoted comparability between our findings and those of other studies applying a variety of definitions. In addition, because it covered programs of every type, this study made possible the comparisons between different studies focusing on only selected TV genres.

---

*From Mustonen, A., & Pulkkinen, L. (1997). Television violence: A development of a coding scheme. *Journal of Broadcasting & Electronic Media 41:*168–189.

**The original paper reviews many content analyses of TV violence. It is noteworthy that the authors are cognizant of the need to refine previously used coding schemes, where possible, to retain comparability of findings.

Amount of Violence

In measurement of the frequency of TV violence, we employed a basic unit identical to that used by Gerbner et al. (Gerbner, Gross, Signorielli, Morgan, & Jackson-Beeck, 1979; Gerbner, Gross, Morgan, & Signorielli, 1980) since 1967 and Cumberbatch, Lee, Hardy, and Jones (1987). Hence, the basic unit of our analysis was a violent act, which referred to a coherent, uninterrupted sequence of violent actions (one or several) involving the same agents in the same roles. The conservative basic unit was selected in order to promote the comparability and reliability of the coding. Because the duration of TV programs varies considerably, we assessed the frequency of TV effective and attractive violence on the basis of the number of violent acts per hour, standardized for the length of each program. This rate is preferred to the rate of violent acts per program in most of the previous TV studies of violence.

Intensity of Violence

Based on the findings (reviewed in the original article) and our own viewer interview, we defined intensity of TV violence as the degree to which violence is obtrusive, or able to arouse and frighten viewers. We interpreted intensity of TV violence from several viewpoints: seriousness, realism (fictionality), and the mode of dramatization (clarity and vividness).

Attractiveness of Violence

Attractive violence referred to attitudinal, or moral features of TV violence, which we coded separately from the intensity of violence. We defined attractiveness of violence as depictions in which violence is seen as a justified, glamorized, and effective behavior model. Attractive scenes usually romanticize aggressive action, and minimize the portrayal of the negative consequences of violence.

Methods

Sample

The new coding scheme was applied to analyze a program sample of the Finnish network television. The program sample consisted of 259 programs (153 hours) of all genres presented during one week in November 1991, on the three TV channels of the Finnish Broadcasting Company (FBC). The analysis included all programming of six randomly selected days per a channel. The FBC provides public service broadcasting (see Slade & Barchak, 1989) and sells broadcasting time to commercial companies. Therefore, about 20 percent of the programs were of commercial production. Two programs out of three were of Finnish origin, one out of five was produced in other European countries, and one out of ten in the United States. Few programs came from South America, Australia,

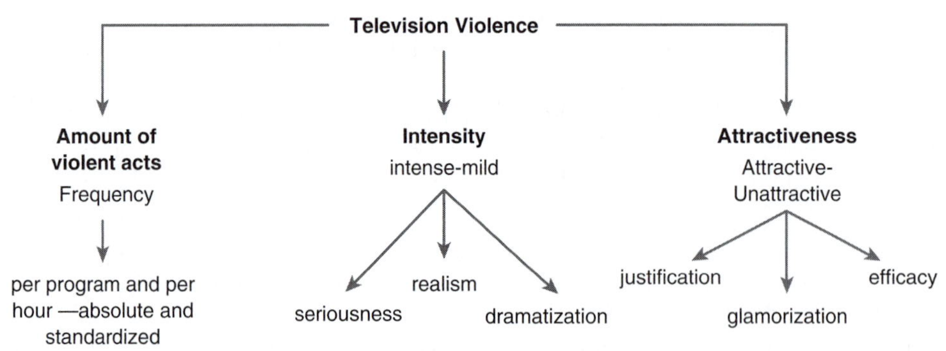

Figure 1 The Themes of the Analysis of Television Violence

or Asia. The imported programs seen on the Finnish TV are not dubbed, but translated into Finnish in textual form. No seasonal programs, sports games, or acute international crises characterized the programming of the sample. The war in former Yugoslavia dominated the news themes.

The Coding Scheme

The final coding scheme was a result from pilot content analysis process during which we identified the elements of TV violence, which were theoretically valid and reliably codable in terms of general TV conventions. Because the TV world is not a replica of the real world, all the elements relevant to real world violence did not appear as relevant in TV violence. We found that information of some aspects concerning the motivation of violence (e.g., first strike vs. retaliatory motivation; masochistic or (offensive) altruistic motivation) was casually, or genre-specific represented by TV narration. Some of the relevant topics proved not to be reliably measurable because their interpretations were culture-specific, or because they required special expertise on the part of the coders (e.g., legal vs. illegal violence), or because they were a matter of taste (gratuitous violence; surprising vs. anticipated violence). Furthermore, identifying the principal and minor characters, as well as punishment of violence, proved to be problematic, particularly in the case of non-fictional material. We decided to exclude these unclear themes from the scheme, as well as the themes whose intercoder agreement in our pilot analysis was not sufficient (Mustonen, 1991).

Our final coding scheme involved two levels. General program level information (ten items, see Appendix) included background data of every program such as the program genre, country of production, channel, TV company, broadcasting time, popularity, and duration of a program which themes can be coded before viewing the sample. Additionally, the number of violent acts identified in the program was added to program level coding after viewing each videotaped program.

At the level of a violent act, each violent act of a program was coded separately during the viewing of the programs. When a violent act was identified, the viewing was interrupted, and the scene was viewed again. The act was then coded for 13 variables concerning modes and intensity of the violence, and for another 13 variables concerning attractiveness of violence (Appendix).

Classification of certain variables to either intensity or attractiveness was not totally unambiguous. The themes were subsumed based on the more relevant properties. Generally, if a variable contained an attitudinal/moral dimension, we saw it as an element of attractiveness. For instance, justification of violence was seen as an element of the intensity (called brutality in Mustonen & Pulkkinen, 1993) of violence in the earlier phase of our study. However, our preliminary analysis showed that it is semantically nearer to the attitudinal dimension and thus it needs to be subsumed under attractiveness. Similarly, the realism (fictionality) of violence can be seen bearing elements of both intensity and attractiveness. Because we had observed both attractively depicted realistic violence and unattractively portrayed violence in cartoons, we did not see realism to present a factor determining attractiveness, but rather, an element of intensity. Our coding scheme includes also a suggestive method of summing up the information on both of the basic themes (i.e., intensity and attractiveness). The more accurate operationalizations of the intensity and attractiveness ratings are elaborated below.

Intensity of Violence

The intensity of violence was measured using several variables concerning seriousness, realism, and mode of dramatization (Appendix). First, the modes of physical and psychological violence were coded separately to enable comparisons to be made between the present study and other studies, which have ignored psychological damage. The seriousness of violence was estimated as the degree to which the violence was realized (i.e., whether the violent act portrayed the actual insulting or killing) out of the attempts to hurt or kill. Additionally, the seriousness of the consequences of violence was assessed ranging from the complete escape to the death of the victim.

Violent acts occurring in psychologically realistic (i.e., believable or familiar settings) were seen as more intense than those portrayed in psychologically distant or fantasy settings). The nearer the temporal and cultural setting, the more threatening and intense the portrayal appears to viewers. We measured psychological realism as the cultural, linguistic, and temporal distance between the program context and the life contexts of the Finnish audience. Additionally, realism was evaluated as a function of the degree of fictionality of the films, ranging from fantasy to complete authenticity.

The more detailed and exciting the method of dramatization, the more intense it appears to the viewers. Thus, dramatization was coded for the duration of the act in seconds, for the atmosphere, and for the clarity and vividness of the depiction. As for the ratings of atmosphere, humorous aggression referred to caricatured, funny depictions, in which antisocial acts were portrayed as hilarious or in which quite neutral scenes were presented in an ambiguous context (serious violence accompanied with background laughter). Frightening or horrific violence was most typically characterized by anticipation, accompanied by threatening visual and audible climaxing effects. The vividness of violence was judged on a scale running from scant to very graphic and detailed portrayals.

In order to summarize the information described above, the coding system also included a summative three category rating of the intensity of TV violence. Only the three elements seen as the most crucial—severe consequences, non-fictionality, and graphic presentation—were considered in the rating. Thus, the category of intense violence (rated 3) referred to scenes, which contained highest ratings in at least two of these themes. Most typically intense violence referred to threatening portrayals of killing, or attempts to kill. Violent portrayals were evaluated as intermediate (rated 2), if they were neither intense nor mild, or if serious violence was moderated by symbolic context, or scant presentation. Conversely, a rating of intermediate violence could apply to relatively non-serious, but realistic acts, the violence of which was exaggerated by detailed or frightening portrayals. Mild violence (rated 1) referred to fantastic or scant portrayals of unharmful aggression, or even to severe, or realistic acts, which were hinted at, but not explicitly portrayed. An act of mild violence was supposed to contain lowest ratings in at least two of the three elements of intensity.

Attractiveness of Violence

Attractive violence was defined as portrayals in which violence is seen as a justified, glamorized, and effective (profitable) model of behavior (Appendix). *Justified violence* was defined as externally (see Potter & Ware, 1987) and reactively (see Pulkkinen, 1996) motivated violence between equal partners, whereas internally and proactively motivated violence between unbalanced partners was seen as unjustified. In the coding, intentional and unintentional violence (e.g., violent acts performed in an unconscious state) were firstly separated, and intentional violence was divided into internally (personal interest) and externally (role-bound violence) motivated forms. For further semantic analyses, reactively and proactively motivated violence were distinguished. Since, for instance, Lagerspetz, Bjorkqvist, Bjorkqvist, and Lundman (1988) have shown that altruistic motives for aggression are interpreted as more justified than selfish motives, reactive/ altruistic violence was separated from reactive/ selfish violence. Proactive violence was divided into instrumental and angry (expressive) forms (see Buss, 1988). In addition, spontaneous (impulsive) aggression was distinguished from planned acts of violence. Finally, the gender and age of the characters involved were classified in order to evaluate the power relationships between the partners. Violence between characters who are unequal (a male hurting a female, or an adult violating a child/elderly person) is seen as less justified than violence between equal partners (e.g., Gunter, 1985).

The *glamorization of aggression* was conceptualized as the degree to which formal features are used to portray violence as heroic and romanticized action. Violence appears more glamorized if the aggressors are seen as heroes, rather than villains. Violence of "bad guys" towards "good guys" is generally approved less readily (Gunter, 1985; Van der Voort, 1985). Furthermore, the dramatization of violent action accompanied by various audiovisual TV effects, such as slow-downs, replays, and musical effects, was seen as an element of glamorization.

The way in which effective, or profitable violence is seen is strongly moderated by the way in which the producer depicts the victims of violence. Thus, efficacy ratings were measures of the way in which producers had manipulated the portrayal of the consequences of violence. Ignoring the consequences of violence represents an effective strategy for increasing the attractiveness of violence. If a violent act seemingly has no negative effects, it is readily interpreted as profitable and effective.

Depictions of the *gratification* derived from violence were also considered as an element of its *efficacy.* If the aggressor completely achieves the desired ends by violent means, his/her behavior was interpreted as more effective and attractive than the unsuccessful use of violence. In the interpretation of the gratification the type of violence has to be considered: gratification of angry aggression (pain, discomfort of the victim) differs from gratification of instrumental aggression (material reward, or dominating, see Buss, 1988).

Attractiveness of violence (Appendix) was also rated on a summative three-point scale. As the equivalent summative variable of the intensity of violence, also this scale consisted of three basic themes which we saw as the most relevant: justification (reactive motivation), glamorization (aggressor as a hero), and efficacy of violence (consequences are ignored). If a violent act earned highest ratings in at least two of these elements, it fulfilled the criterion of attractive violence (rated 3). Unattractive perspective (rated 1) characterized acts, which were rated with the lowest ratings in at least two of the three critical variables. Typically, unattractive violent scenes emphasized the consequences of violence more than violent action. Portrayals in which violence was presented as neutral or unclear, or in which the elements of glamorization, justification, and efficacy were rated un-homogeneously, formed the intermediate category (rated 2).

Some genre specific qualitative information was needed to complete the final coding. For sports programs, for instance, commentators' glorified style (see Sullivan, 1991) was seen as a crucial determinant of attractiveness, together with detailed replays of violent acts. As for the dramatic films, we paid attention to the type of humor: overtly ironic portrayals of violence were usually interpreted as unattractive, whereas funny and permissively humorous depictions were evaluated as attractive violence.

Intercoder Reliability of the Coding Scheme

In order to test the reliability of the coding we double-coded sufficient programs to yield a sample of 9% of the total violent acts included in the program sample ($N = 259$) of our final analysis. The coders (students of psychology) were first given an introductory course in the psychology of aggression, and to the concepts and definition applied in our analysis. To test the intercoder agreement of the definition of TV violence, all test coders were asked to identify the violent acts seen in a sub-sample representing programs of different genres (new, documentaries, cartoons, dramatic fictions, music programs). Of all acts identified as violent by any of the coders, 83% were seen as violent by all the coders.

In order to compute the Scott's pi reliability coefficients (see Krippendorff, 1980) for the 26 variables concerning intensity and attractiveness of violence, each test coder analyzed her own sub-sample of the programs (one-third of the test material). For the pairwise calculations, the test coder's ratings were compared to the equivalent ratings of the main coder. For Likert scales*—which were mainly 5-point scales—a deviation of one point was accepted.

*Scott's π is applicable for nominal data only. Likert scales have an ordinal metric. Applying π to them is insufficient. A nominal statistic can over- or underestimate their reliability—see reading 6.2, this volume.

The reliabilities varied between .65 (motivation of violence) and .95 (the age of the aggressor; fictionality of the program). The modes of physical and psychological violence, and the seriousness of the consequences of violence were among the variables with lower reliabilities (approximately .70), whereas the variables concerning cultural and temporal program context, and the demography of the characters involved were more reliably codable (Scott pi's of approximately the .90 level). For the variables concerning the intensity of violence, the average Scott's pi was .82, and .74 for the variables concerning the attractiveness of violence. For the summative coding of the intensity and attractiveness of violence, the reliabilities were .87, and .81, respectively.*

Results

Overall Rates

The rate of violence was calculated in three different ways: as a rate per program, as a rate per hour, and as a rate per hour standardized for the length of the show. In the program sample, there were seen 1.51 violent acts per a program and 2.55 violent acts per broadcasting hour, when all programs and all types of violence were considered. Thus, the rate of violence was slightly higher than the rate of 1.98 acts per hour found in the BBC programs. In the British study (Cumberbatch et al., 1987), verbal threats represented the only modes of psychological violence, which were included. When violence was standardized for the length of the show, the average rate of violent acts/hour in a program was 3.43. This is very similar to the average rate of violence (3.46) found in our preliminary study (Mustonen & Pulkkinen, 1993). Following Gerbner's methodology in which only physical violence in dramatic prime time setting is considered, the average rate of violence was 5.66 acts per hour. This represents just the rates of around 5–6 reported by researchers following the methodology by Gerbner in most countries (Cumberbatch, Jones, & Lee, 1988).

Elements of the Intensity of TV Violence

Seriousness of TV Violence

Physical violence, or the combination of physical and psychological modes of violence, dominated psychological violence. Only one in ten violent acts represented threats, while 90% of acts depicted aggressive attacks. In accordance with the findings of Cumberbatch et al. (1987), both extremes of the consequences (escape and death) were most frequent. Moderate and severe injuries together formed only 11% of violent acts (see Appendix). The most frequent modes of violence included shooting, scuffle or hitting. Extremely shocking and unusual forms of violence like slashing, suicides, or sexual violence, did not appear.

Realism

Violence took place mainly in fictional and psychologically distant settings rather than in realistic contexts. Violent acts in non-fiction, or in psychologically proximal Finnish contexts were more untypical. As for temporal proximity, present time appeared more frequently than distant—historical or future—settings.

Dramatization

Different means of audiovisual dramatization, as well as changes in tempo and music, generally accompanied violent acts. However, time devoted to each violent act was quite short. The majority of all violent acts lasted less than 30 seconds. Violent acts were typically characterized by a quarrelsome or exciting atmosphere. In 39% of the violent acts, violent action was depicted in a graphic, or a very graphic way.

Elements of the Attractiveness of TV Violence

Justification

The elements of justification of violence were diversely represented. As for the motivation of violence, intentional, proactive, and internally motivated violence dominated the violent portrayals, which refer to typically

*For an argument against reporting averages of reliability coefficients, see Krippendorff (reading 6.2, this volume).

unjustified violence. On the other hand, because violence occurred mainly between adult males, violence between unequal or unbalanced partners (i.e., unjustified violence) was rarely observed.

Glamorization

There were more moderately presented portrayals of violence than glamorized ones. In fact, less than half of the violent programs provided viewers with clear personifications of good and evil. Typically, heroes were more likely to be victims than aggressors were. On the contrary, villains acted more likely as aggressors than as victims of violence. One in three violent acts was presented with glamorizing audiovisual effects, such as replays, slowing ups, or climaxing music effects.

Efficacy

Violence was more often portrayed as a profitable than as an unprofitable behavior model. The desired ends were achieved at least partially by violent means in every second violent act. Similarly, in every second violent act the consequences of violence were presented only as hints or ignored which may also contribute to the overall evaluations of the efficacy of violence.

Combination of Intense and Attractive TV Violence

The summative three category ratings of intensity and attractiveness also supported our assumption that TV violence does not exist as a uniform entity. Overall, two thirds of violent acts were evaluated as mild whereas less than one tenth as intense. In general, unattractive depictions, which showed the consequences of violence, were observed more frequently (28%) than attractive (16%) presentations. In 56% of violent acts, the elements of attractiveness were inhomogeneously represented. Correlation analysis (Pearson) showed intensity and attractiveness to form independent elements of TV violence ($r = -.011$; n.s.). Neither was there a relation between the intensity and frequency of violence of a program ($r = .025$; n.s.). Attractiveness of violence in a program correlated, however, with the frequency of violence in a program ($r = .337$; $p < .0001$).

In order to analyze portrayals of violence both in terms of their intensity, and of their attractiveness, violent acts were cross-tabulated according to their summative ratings for both of these variables (Table 1). The most typical group of violent acts combined portrayals of mild and intermediately attractive (neutral) violence ($\chi^2(8) = 3.47$, n.s.). If only the extreme groups of intensity and attractiveness were considered, scenes of mild and unattractive violence dominated other extreme groups. The combination of intense and attractive violence represented the most infrequent type of TV violence.

Discussion

Measuring the Content of TV Violence

The coding scheme established in our study outlined ways of producing more exhaustive and valid analyses of the nature of TV violence, and of the messages it conveys. In agreement with most contemporary analysts (e.g., Potter & Ware, 1987; Williams, Zabrack, & Lesley, 1982), we considered all overt physical and psychological modes of

Table 1 Violent Acts Groups According to the Intensity and Attractiveness of TV Violence

	Intensity		
Attractiveness	*Mild*	*Intermediate*	*Intense*
Unattractive	62 (16%)	34 (9%)	11 (3%)
Intermediate/Neutral	145 (37%)	59 (15%)	16 (4%)
Attractive	35 (9%)	22 (6%)	6 (1%)

human aggression in our definition. Like Kunkel et al. (1995) and Potter and Ware (1987), we went on to analyze the context of violent portrayals and to link the content analysis categories to the research evidence documenting the viewer reactions to TV violence. Following Cumberbatch et al. (1987), we designed an analytical scheme, which would be applicable to TV violence across all genres of network television.

Our analysis differed from previous analyses in the more detailed descriptions of the intensity (seriousness, realism, dramatization) of filmed violence in different contexts. To accomplish our semantic analysis we turned our attention also towards the elements of attractiveness of violence, which referred to violence portrayed as a justified, glamorized, and effective type of behavior. Therefore, along the lines with the previous Scandinavian communication studies (see Rosengren, 1981), our study basically dealt with the objectivity and rationality of communications. Our analysis showed that intensity and attractiveness are independent elements of filmed violence and they can be utilized in extending the contextual analysis of TV violence. It is possible to utilize the themes of our coding system selectively depending on the purpose of the study. Certain items can be relevant for several purposes. For instance, the variables concerning the gender, age, and character of the persons involved in violence can be utilized in analyzing the demography of the TV violence, or in examining the power relationships of the aggressors and victims. Besides analyzing several sub-categories of intensity and attractiveness, we suggested summative categorization, which combines information obtained on different elements.

Regardless of some stereotypes, TV violence cannot be seen as a homogenous entity. Rather, we observed much stylistic and semantic variation in the portrayals. Generally, the elements of intensity and attractiveness of violence were diverse, allowing plenty of room for the viewers to interpret the messages conveyed by violent acts. Finnish network TV as a whole was mainly characterized by a combination of mild and neutrally, or unattractively presented violence, rather than by a combination of intense and attractive depictions of violence. In the TV discourse, developmentally earlier, primitive modes of aggression, such as physical attacks (see Buss, 1988) appeared more often than the later, more sublimated forms of aggression, such as threat, or psychological aggression, which are typical modes of aggression in the real world. This may reflect general TV conventions, which prefer physical action and dramatic events to the static, dramaturgically unattractive everyday affairs. On the other hand, the most extreme modes such as slashing, suicides, or sexual violence were not presented in the programs.

The moderate nature of violence on Finnish TV is probably due to the parliamentary controls governing the Finnish TV companies. However, the control system does not seem to influence the frequency of TV violence: amounts of violence in the prime time fiction in Finland proved to be very similar to the rates of TV violence reported in international studies. Because TV programs are universal mass media products with relatively uniform genres, our analytical scheme can be utilized in future comparative content analyses focusing on the nature of violence in different TV cultures.

Identifying Harmful and Harmless TV Violence

Based on a mere content analysis we cannot locate "harmful" violence. Therefore, our analysis was not constrained by any fixed presuppositions of effects of TV violence on the viewers. Rather, all possible modes of filmed violence were covered, even though in some of them the scenes are capable of promoting prosocial behavior, as well as antisocial models. The cutting back process of TV companies can be more efficient if we know which types of television violence are more and which less harmful (Belson, 1978). Future research concerning the influence of TV violence will benefit from our classification of certain elements of violence, whether the focus is on affective, cognitive, or behavioral effects of TV violence.

Appendix: The Coding Scheme of TV Violence

Program Information & Amount of Violence

1. The number of the program
2. The name of the program
3. The program genre
4. The country of origin
5. The date of the production
6. The broadcasting channel
7. The TV company
8. The day of broadcasting
9. The hour of broadcasting
10. The duration of the program
11. The amount of violent acts in the program

Intensity of Violence

	%
12. Mode of violence:	
1 = physical	61
2 = psychological	15
3 = physical and psychological	24
13. Mode of physical violence	
0 = no physical violence	15
1 = shooting	24
2 = threatening or forcing with guns	5
3 = fist-fighting, pushing, striking	14
5 = strangling	1
6 = poisoning	0.5
7 = slashing	3
8 = sexual violence	0.5
9 = kidnapping/tying up/arresting	9
10 = damaging property	5
11 = other	14
14. Mode of verbal aggression	
0 = no verbal aggression	58
1 = angry talk	12
2 = mild personal hurt	16
3 = verbal threat or humiliating	10
4 = serious threatening "I'll kill you!"	4
15. Mode of nonverbal psychological aggression	
0 = no nonverbal aggression	36
1 = forcing, subjection, pressuring	31
2 = threatening, intimidation	7
3 = violating one's human rights	10
4 = irony, scorning gestures	3
5 = other	1

	%
16. Seriousness: realization of violence	
0 = cannot code	13
1 = playful aggression	1
2 = threatening/hostile gesturing	4
3 = trying to insult	6
4 = insulting	45
5 = trying to kill	18
6 = killing/suicide	13
17. Seriousness: the consequences of violence	
0 = portrayed not at all	18
1 = no harm	28
2 = only material harm	11
3 = mild harm or injuries	20
4 = moderate injuries (medical care needed)	7
5 = severe injuries (hospital care needed)	4
6 = death	13
18. Realism: cultural distance	
1 = Finnish/Swedish language and culture	12
2 = Finnish/'Swedish language, foreign culture	14
3 = foreign culture and language	59
4 = fantasy (scifi, cartoons)	15
19. Realism: temporal distance	10
0 = cannot code	10
1 = modern (the 90's)	53
2 = near past (from the 50's-90's)	8
3 = near history (1900–1950)	20
4 = earlier than 19th century	8
5 = future	1
20. Realism: fictionality	
1 = a cartoon/animated program	13
3 = unrealistic fiction (caricatured and fantasy characters involved)	21
4 = realistic fiction	47
5 = authentic	19
21. Dramatization: duration of the act	
1 = 1–5 seconds	29
2 = 6–15 seconds	28
3 = 16–30 seconds	25
4 = 30–60 seconds	9
5 = more than 60 sec.	9
22. Dramatization: atmosphere	
1 = humorous, comic	15
2 = neutral or unclear	14
3 = quarrelsome	37
4 = exciting, adventurous	21
5 = frightening, threatening, horrific	14

(Continued)

Appendix (Continued)

Intensity of Violence (cont.) %

23. Dramatization: clarity and vividness
    - 0 = cannot code 4
    - 1 = very scant/unclear depiction 4
    - 2 = quite scant/unclear depiction 20
    - 3 = moderate depiction 33
    - 4 = quite detailed and graphic depiction 34
    - 5 = very detailed, graphic depiction 5

24. Intensity of violence (a summative rating)
    - 1 = mild 62
    - 2 = moderate 30
    - 3 = brutal 8

Attractiveness of Violence %

25. Justification: intentionality
    - 0 = cannot code 3
    - 1 = intentional, internally motivated 73
    - 2 = intentional, externally motivated (e.g., in the role of a police) 22
    - 3 = unintentional, unconscious 2

26. Justification: motivation of violence
    - 1 = cannot code 8
    - 2 = defensive, altruistic 3
    - 3 = defensive, self-preservation 2
    - 4 = both offensive and defensive 15
    - 5 = offensive, instrumental 41
    - 6 = offensive, angry (reactive-expressive) 31

27. Justification: planned violence
    - 0 = cannot code 5
    - 1 = spontaneously produced violence 57
    - 2 = planned, systematic violence 38

28. Justification: the sex of the aggressor
    - 0 = cannot code/fantasy character 17
    - 1 = a male 41
    - 2 = a female 10
    - 3 = a group of males 23
    - 4 = a group of females 0
    - 5 = a mixed group 9

29. Justification: the age of the aggressor
    - 0 = cannot code 15
    - 1 = child, 0–13 yrs. 9
    - 2 = young, 13–20-yrs. 2
    - 3 = adult, 20–60-yrs. 61
    - 4 = adult, 60 or older 6
    - 5 = people of several age groups 7

30. Justification: the sex of the victim %
    - 0 = cannot code/fantasy character 14
    - 1 = a male 41
    - 2 = a female 10
    - 3 = a group of males 9
    - 4 = a group of females 1
    - 5 = a mixed group 19
    - 6 = an animal 2
    - 7 = unanimated objects 4

31. Justification: the age of the victim
    - 0 = cannot code 18
    - 1 = a child, 0–13 yrs. 12
    - 2 = a young person, 13–20 yrs. 1
    - 3 = an adult, 20–60 yrs. 49
    - 4 = an adult, 60 or older 5
    - 5 = people of several age groups 15

32. Glamorization: nature of the aggressor
    - 0 = cannot code 5
    - 1 = a villain, "a baddy" 29
    - 2 = neutral, ordinary 49
    - 3 = a hero, "a goody" 16

33. Glamorization: nature of the victim
    - 0 = cannot code 9
    - 1 = a villain, "a baddy" 9
    - 2 = neutral, ordinary 57
    - 3 = a hero, "a goody" 25

34. Glamorization: audiovisual effects
    - 1 = no audiovisual glamorization 17
    - 2 = some audiovisual glamorization 22
    - 3 = moderate audiovisual glamorization 28
    - 4 = much audiovisual glamorization 26
    - 5 = very much audiovisual glamorization 7

35. Efficacy: ignoring the consequences of violence
    - 0 = no consequences to be depicted 2
    - 1 = suffering specially emphasized 1
    - 2 = quite a lot of portrayals of suffering 11
    - 3 = consequences partially depicted 38
    - 4 = the consequences depicted as hints 38
    - 5 = no depictions of the consequences 10

36. Efficacy: achieving the desired ends/gratification by violent means
    - 0 = cannot code 23
    - 1 = not at all/no gratification 10
    - 2 = only a little 14
    - 3 = partially 21
    - 4 = quite well 19
    - 5 = completely 13

37. Attractiveness of violence (a summative rating)
    - 1 = unattractive 16
    - 2 = moderate, neutral 56
    - 3 = attractive 28

References

Belson, W. A. (1978). *Television violence and the adolescent boy.* Westemead: Saxon House.

Buss, A. H. (1988). *Personality: Evolutionary heritage and human distinctiveness.* Hillsdale, NJ: Erlbaum.

Cumberbatch, G., Lee, M., Hardy, G., & Jones, I. (1987). *The portrayal of violence on British television.* London: British Broadcasting Corporation.

Cumberbatch, G., Jones, I., & Lee, M. (1988). Measuring violence on television. *Current Psychology: Research & Reviews 7,*1:10–25.

Gerbner, G., Gross, L., Signorielli, N., Morgan, M., & Jackson-Beeck, M. (1979). The demonstration of power: Violence profile No.I. *Journal of Communication 29:*177–196.

Gerbner, G., Gross, L., Morgan, M., & Signorielli, N. (1980). The "mainstreaming" of America: Violence profile No. II. *Journal of Communication 30:*10–29.

Greenberg, B. S. (1980). *Life on television: Content analyses of U.S. drama.* Norwood, NJ: Ablex.

Gunter, B. (1985). *Dimensions of television violence.* Aldershot: Gower Publishing Company Limited.

Krippendorff, K. (1980). *Content analysis: An introduction to its methodology.* Thousand Oaks, CA: Sage.*

Kunkel, D., Wilson, B., Donnerstein, E., Linz, D., Smith, S., Gray, T., Blumenthal, E., & Potter, J. (1995). Measuring television violence: The importance of context. *Journal of Broadcasting & Electronic Media 39:*284–291.

Lagerspetz, K. M., Bjorkqvist, K., Bjorkqvist, H., & Lundman, H. (1988). Moral approval of aggression and sex role identity in officer trainees: Conscientious objectors to military service, and in a female reference group. *Aggressive Behavior 14,*5:303–313.

Mustonen, A. (1991). *Aggressio Suomen Televisiossa* [Aggression on Finnish Television]. Oy Yleisradio Ab. Tutkimus-ja kehitysosasto. Tutkimusraportti 9. Helsinki: Hakapaino Oy.

Mustonen, A., & Pulkkinen, L. (1993). Aggression in television programs in Finland. *Aggressive Behavior 19:*175–183.

Potter, W. J., & Ware, W. (1987). An analysis of the contexts of antisocial acts on prime-time television. *Communication Research 14:*664–686.

Pulkkinen, L. (1996). Offensive and defensive aggression in humans: A longitudinal perspective. *Aggressive Behavior 13,*4:197–212.

Rosengren, K. E. (1981). *Advances in content analysis.* Thousand Oaks, CA: Sage.

Slade, J. W., & Barchak, L. J. (1989). Public broadcasting in Finland: Inventing a national television programming policy. *Journal of Broadcasting & Electronic Media 33:*355–373.

Sullivan, D. B. (1991). Commentary and viewer perception of player hostility: Adding punch to televised sports. *Journal of Broadcasting & Electronic Media 35:*487–504.

Van der Voort, T. H. A. (1986). *Television violence: A child's eye view.* Amsterdam: Elsevier.

Williams, T. M., Zabrack, M. L., & Lesley, A. J. (1982). The portrayal of aggression on North American television. *Journal of Applied Social Psychology 12:*360–380.

Yudofsky, S. C., Silver, J. M., Jackson, W., Endicott, J., & Williams, D. (1986). The overt aggression scale for the objective rating of verbal and physical aggression. *American Journal of Psychiatry 143,* 1:35–39.

*Krippendorff, K. (2004). *Content analysis: An introduction to its methodology* (2nd ed.). Thousand Oaks, CA: Sage.

5.8

The Opinions of Little Orphan Annie and Her Friends

Lyle W. Shannon*

Public speculation and a number of earlier articles on the effects of reading comic cartoon strips directed the author's attention to the problem of determining the social idealism expressed in such cartoon strips as Little Orphan Annie, Dick Tracy, Li'l Abner, Joe Palooka, Terry and the Pirates and others.[1] It has been said that Joseph Patterson guided his comics as cunningly as his anti-Roosevelt campaigns. "By design or not, they all seem to be in harmony with the editorial views of the cartoonist's bosses, Capt. Joseph Patterson and Col. Robert McCormick" (*Newsweek,* 1945: 67–68). It is the purpose of this article to present a detailed analysis of Little Orphan Annie, a strip, which has, unlike many others, a record of more adult than child readers. . . .[2]

Methodology

The Sunday comic section of Little Orphan Annie was collected for the period from April 18, 1948, through July 2, 1950, a period of some 116 weeks. Six sections were lost and were unobtainable from library files. It is believed, however, that the missing sections were not atypical of the cartoon as their loss on certain weeks was merely a chance affair.

In this analysis, we shall define an *appearance* as the inclusion of a comic character in the cartoon section on the particular date referred to. The character may appear in the section one or more times on a particular date but we shall count an appearance on this date as *one* appearance regardless of the number of times that the artist shows the character. Thus, a character could have a maximum *appearance* of 110. The same approach has been used in measuring the relative importance of various goals in life suggested by Annie or her friends. Methods of reaching life's goals have likewise been enumerated in order to obtain some idea of the means most frequently suggested by Annie or her friends.

*From Shannon, L. (1954). Little Orphan Annie and her friends. *Public Opinion Quarterly 18,* 2:169–179.

Approved and condemned symbols are treated in the same fashion.

Each week's cartoon section of Little Orphan Annie was carefully read by two persons who answered the following questions in writing as they proceeded from week to week.

1. Which villains are pursuing Annie; which persons are in opposition to her?
2. What is the occupation, overt and covert, of the persons mentioned above?
3. Which opponents are killed or injured, how and by whom?
4. Who are Annie's friends?
5. What is the occupation, overt and covert, of the persons mentioned above?
6. Which friends of Annie are killed or injured, how and by whom?
7. What goals in life are approved by Annie and her friends?
8. What means or methods for reaching these goals are suggested by Annie and her friends?
9. What symbols are approved by Annie and her friends?
10. What symbols are condemned by Annie and her friends?

The author likewise read the entire series of Little Orphan Annie and collated the answer sheets of the other readers, thus arriving at a third set of answers, which represented a consensus of three persons' answers to the questions listed above. These answers were further summarized in certain categories and will be presented later in the article.

Observation of the Data

But let us see what adventures Annie has had for this period of 110 weeks. It should not be too surprising to most readers to find that 39 weeks were spent in conflict with foreign agents whose identities were thinly disguised and presumably Russian with names such as Ivan Ichalotski, Andrei and Alex. For another period of 15 weeks, Annie had numerous encounters with a gang of young hoodlums working the protection racket. Thus 50 percent of Annie's time was devoted to conflict with specific persons and to definite causes, namely preservation of capitalism in the struggle against Communism and aid to small, honest, decent businessmen having difficulty with young hoodlums engaged in the protection racket.

The other 50 percent of Annie's time was devoted to helping the poor and unfortunate with money, which she obtained either from the sale of her store or the vast treasure which she discovered with the aid of a magic whistle. As a result of her find, Annie undertook construction of an entire community for orphans to live in and run in their own way. This project collapsed, however, when government men inadvertently toppled a mountain over the entrance to the treasure cave in their effort to retrieve and impound the treasure until the law was determined and taxes were computed.

The setting in which Annie's adventures took place changed from time to time and the people with whom she lived during this period of 110 weeks are listed below in chronological order:

27 weeks: Patrick and Mrs. Puddle, wealthy millionaire who immigrated to U.S. as a boy and became a great steel mill owner (mansion)

29 weeks: Jeb and Flossie Jitters, poor n'er do well farmers, happily married but without children (farm)

15 weeks: Rocky and Lena, rugged rolling-stone and girl whose wife-beating husband had left her (barge)

16 weeks: Mr. and Mrs. Dan Drift and eight children, unemployed husband and sick, pregnant mother (small house)

13 weeks: Daddy Warbucks, wealthy industrialist who uses his fortunes to battle enemy countries in his own way (estate)

10 weeks: On the road

The above data indicate that Annie has an amazing ability to rub elbows with people in extreme walks of life, but it is rather noticeable that she has never lived with coal-miners, steel-workers, punch-press operators or laboring people in general. Annie's associates tend to be either the great captains of industry or the poor and unfortunate who lack initiative or are unwilling to work for a living. The latter usually benefit from their contact with the ambitious and always energetic Orphan Annie. Her poor associates are not the great masses of people whose daily labors barely keep them above the subsistence level, but instead are the poor whose personal disorganization clearly has no connection with the disorganization which exists in our economic system. Thus we see that Annie is concerned with the unfortunate, but the causes of their poverty are carefully shown to be of a non-social nature. This will be evident in more detail as we proceed. An examination of Table 1 reveals the nature of Annie's opponents and the methods used in combating them. Table 2 describes Annie's friends.

Annie's opponents are polished off with a clock-like regularity. Foreign spies and their radical American counterparts are far and away the wiliest opponents Annie meets; their numbers are overwhelming as contrasted to other opponents, such as hoodlums, young and old. In almost every instance the criminals in this comic strip are the dirty-collar type of offender; the white-collar criminal is seldom seen. The etiology of crime as presented in this strip has all the authoritarianism of Ivan's pronouncements on the class struggle, and less accuracy. The causes of juvenile delinquency are likewise stated with the finality of holy writ.

We have already noted the frequent appearance of the needy, but we may also observe that many of Annie's associations are with millionaire leaders of industry. Professional and middle class people appear as frequently as the wealthy but most interesting is the appearance of tough guys, largely in the employ of Daddy Warbucks, the benevolent millionaire. Small business men appear often, but not as frequently as people in the categories already mentioned.

Many of Annie's opponents are removed from the scene by the Pied Piper-like schemes of Annie's friend Kansk while others disappear under the magic cloak of Punjab, the giant Oriental. Annie's opponents are not always removed with such convenience; others are drowned, shot, hanged or their necks are broken. Some of Annie's adversaries receive rather bad beatings and others are merely frightened away in one manner or another. Annie is quite willing to use force when necessary.

Actually, Little Orphan Annie presents a picture of the world about us as many see it, one in which the hard-working captains of industry struggle against a vicious and uncompromising underground in order to protect capitalism, earn large profits and thus assume their social responsibilities, i.e., be charitable to the needy. A much fuller elaboration of this may be found in Max Weber, *The Protestant Ethic.*

Annie's Life Goals

Let us consider the goals in life approved by Orphan Annie and her friends and the methods which are proposed for their attainment. The goals suggested in Little Orphan Annie do not appear to be greatly divergent from the goals which people in our own society have. Their similarity to Weber's *Protestant Ethic* has already been noted. Making a large amount of money was mentioned as a goal six times; doing charitable works appeared seven times. We are told on three different occasions that the country should be kept free from the slavery of foreign lands. Being a law-abiding citizen is mentioned with the same frequency. At other times we are told that one should marry the rich and beautiful daughter of the boss, have a happy marriage, have a large happy family and bring up one's children to be good citizens. Money is both a means and an end in Annie's life. The methods suggested for reaching goals place considerable emphasis on the forceful techniques so eloquently condemned in the larger society. The use of force of one kind or another was mentioned nine times; hard work was mentioned five times; and wealth was mentioned on three other occasions. Annie's methodology is that of the Rockefellers, Carnegies and other captains of industry of the Nineteenth Century. How much of it is the methodology of mid-century government today is debatable. The most forceful

Table 1 Frequency and Type of Annie's Opponents

Number of Appearances	*Annie's Opponents*	*Who They Are & What Happens to Them*
9	Axel	Head of foreign spy ring, sent away on ship by Kansk
7	Max	Handyman & chauffeur, member of spy ring, sent away on ship by Kansk
6	Ivan Ichalotski	Foreign agent, sent home in box by Warbucks
4	Peter Petard & Pola Petard	Run second-hand store, member of Axel's spy ring, sent away on ship by Kansk
3	Andrei	Foreign spy with Axel, pushed into sewer by Annie
1	Axel's messenger	Foreign spy, neck broken by Kansk
1	Michail	Scientist, gives secrets to foreign agent, sent away by Punjab
1	Unnamed foreign agent	Gets secrets from scientist, sent away by Punjab
1	Three foreign agents	Pursuing Warbucks, stumble into quicksand and Annie misleads them
0	Agent disguised as crewman	Pursuing Warbucks, shot by other crew members
0	Unnamed "party" member	Leaving country, killed by Peter Petard
0	Unknown member of Ivan's gang	Pursuing Warbucks, sent away by Punjab
0	Unnamed foreign agent	Pursuing Warbucks, killed by Asp
6	Mrs. Puddle	Wife of millionaire, sympathetic to radicals
3	Little Monster and gang	In the protection racket, beat up and reformed by Big Monster
2	Snozz	Member of Little Monster's gang, sent to reformatory
2	Goldtooth and gang	In the protection racket, beat up by Annie's gang
2	Big Monster and gang	Older hoods, racketeers, four killed by Big Monster
1	Dotty the Dip	Mother of Snozz, a fence and former thief
1	Blackjacker #1	Held by Mrs. Jot, hit on head with rock by Annie
1	Blackjacker #2	Hit Annie over head for money, hit on head with cane by Mr. Puddle
1	Armed robbers #1 & #2	After Annie's money in safe, fell into river through Annie's trap door
1	Two tough guys	After treasure in cave, scared away by python of Gypsy Belle
1	Ex-convict	After treasure in cave, killed by the hoodlum
1	Three hoodlums	After treasure in cave, 2 killed by the ex-convict
1	Stranger	From SE Asia after treasure, killed by Punjab
0	Three gangsters	After treasure in cave, apparently killed by Punjab
3	Cap'n Krok	Wife-beating husband of Lena; muscles in on barge business, falls into own trap and drowns in bay
2	Prissy Putsch	Housewife, reformer campaigning against comics, etc.
2	Two government agents & soldiers	Attempt to impound treasure
2	Angry people of the village	Anxious to receive some of Annie's treasure and then angry when it is lost

Table 2 Frequency and Type of Annie's Friends

Number of Appearances	*Annie's Friends*	*Who They Are & What Happens to Them*
19	Daddy Warbucks	Millionaire industrialist
6	Patrick Puddle	Millionaire steel man (killed in an airplane crash)
5	Mrs. MacBond	Former hasher come rich on oil wells
15	Doc Croaker	Doctor who gave up practice because of drink and now returns in a pinch and reforms
5	Mr. Locust	Annie's lawyer
4	Kurt Kolly	Small town sheriff
2	Two uniformed police	Sympathetic policemen who arrest Rocky
2	Mr. Starr	Plainclothes policeman who enjoys seeing Annie's gang beat up "Clipper" Gang
1	Jerry	Truck driver who gives Annie a ride
13	Punjab	Giant Oriental assistant to Warbucks
11	Rocky	Rolling-stone tough-guy, leader of wharf rats
11	The Asp	Tough-guy Asiatic assistant to Warbucks
7	Gypsy Belle	Tough old witch living alone in forest
5	Funjab	Small nephew of Punjab
4	Kansk	Counter espionage agent from Eastern Europe
4	Seeress Kahn Kahn	Hypnotist from Middle East
4	Big Monster	Reformed gangster
1	Little Monster	Reformed son of Big Monster
4	Mr. Mustard	Small business man with general store
4	Business and Junior Grade Gang	Small business people on Annie's street organized to oppose protection rackets with force
2	Mr. Jolt	Ran store for Annie
1	Mr. Wire	Bought store from Annie
32	Melissa	Orphan child
12	Mrs. Drift	Sick, pregnant mother of 8 children
12	Drift children	8, later increased to 11
11	Dan Drift	Unemployed father
9	Lena	Farmer's daughter married to wife-beating husband
6	Jeb Jitters	Poor n'er do well farmer
5	Flossie Jitters	Jeb's loving wife
3	Mrs. Jot	Elderly domestic servant in wealthy home
3	Aunt Ivy	Wife of Uncle George, business ruined by Dan Drift
0	Jack Sack	Janitor friend of Dan Drift
1	Irene	Daughter of Big Monster
246 = Total appearances of friends of Annie		

speeches of Oliver Warbucks could well have come from the mouths of prominent leaders in either of the two major political parties. The greatest divergence from today's ideology would probably occur in Warbucks' emphasis on doing things in his own way rather than appealing to the law. Other means of attaining goals mentioned are: thinking fast, outguessing the other boys, outtalking the other boys, using all the angles, taking chances, accepting poverty, providence, magic, and hope.

While a rather crude attempt to quantify goals and methods of reaching them has been made, there is considerable room for improvement and this aspect of the analysis should be treated as a first approximation rather than any final estimate of the relative importance of values stressed in Little Orphan Annie. The list of symbols approved or condemned by Annie and her friends is another aspect of the analysis in which our method of quantification cannot be considered too reliable but in which the results are suggestive enough to be included in this preliminary paper.

Orphans are approved five times and work is approved four times. Other symbols mentioned favorably are: honest merchants, smart business men, little business men, people with class whether they are rich or poor, honest-to-goodness people and the Horatio Alger type. In addition, Little Orphan Annie approves of honesty, brains, going straight, decency and fair dealing, curiosity, love of countrymen, Santa Claus, Providence, school, peace, prosperity and equal opportunity.

On six occasions Annie vigorously condemns lazy, mean people who are unwilling to work. She refers to them as lazy, whining failures who sneer at success. Stupid radicals who do not know how well off they are, who follow the party line like sheep and who sell out their friends and country are criticized four different times. On eleven occasions Annie condemns slave labor camps; truth treatments; fake confessions; the five year plan; those who would make everybody equal to the lowest village idiot; and makes other similar references to conditions in the Soviet Union. Hitler and book-burning are condemned three times. Braggarts and fatheads are mentioned six times. Annie also disapproves of parents who do not take care of their children, the "bleeding hearts" who spend too much time worrying about the troubles of other people, the belief that wealth is a sin, people unwilling to pay the price for peace, and those who become too concerned with great causes and crackpot schemes.

Here again we see that the symbols approved or condemned are very similar to the symbols approved or condemned by the upper and middle classes in the United States. It is difficult to show the extent to which Gray leans in approving one set of symbols and totally ignoring others which are approved by a large section of the population, albeit by persons on a lower socio-economic level than many of the characters in Little Orphan Annie. The experience gained in our analysis of Little Orphan Annie suggests a larger project in which more refined techniques could be used in an analysis and comparison of the content of several comic strips.

Notes

1. The entire issue of the *Journal of Educational Sociology,* December 1944, was devoted to a discussion of comic cartoon strips. A few but very inadequate articles have appeared on the effect of cartoon strips. The best empirical study to date is (Wolf & Fiske, 1949). Also see Muhlen (1948), Bender and Lourie (1941), and Hadsel (1941).

2. Harper, M., Jr., and Epes Harper, V. M. *4500 Newspaper pictures and their significance for advertisers,* McCann-Erickson Advertising Agency. *The Daily Oklahoman* reports for every 100 adult readers, Little Orphan Annie has 95 child readers as compared with Dick Tracy who has 161 child readers.

References

Bender, L., & Lourie, R. S. (1941). The effect of comic books on the ideology of children. *The American Journal of Orthopsychiatry 11:*540–550.

Hadsel, F. L. (1941). Propaganda in the funnies. *Current History 1:*365–368.

Muhlen, N. (1948). Comic books and other horrors. *Commentary 7:*80–87.

Wolf, K. M., & Fiske, M. (1949). The children talk about comics. In P. F. Lazarsfeld & F. N. Stanton (Eds.), *Communications research 1948–1949* (pp. 3–50). New York: Harper & Bros.

5.9

GENDER EQUITY IN MANAGEMENT EDUCATION

Inferences From Test Bank Questions

RANDI L. SIMS*

The Sapir-Whorf theory suggests that the language that we use may reflect or shape our thoughts (Whorf, 1956; as cited in Merritt & Kok, 1995). Research suggests that sexist language supports and encourages sexist thinking and action (Cronin & Jreisat, 1995; Gastil, 1990; McMinn, Williams, & McMinn, 1994). For example, Gastil (1990) concluded that the use of *he* as a generic pronoun is not generic, but clearly biases the reader toward imagining a male person. "Most agree that passages using sexist language affect the way a reader interprets the passage" (McMinn, Lindsay, Hannum, & Troyer, 1990:390). Thus, the study suggests that sexist language and a bias toward male managerial examples will support and encourage negative stereotypes against women as managers.

Pirri, Eaton, and Durkin (1995) proposed that the knowledge of a person's gender is enough to invoke preconceived stereotypes about expected performance. McGlashan, Wright, and McCormick's (1995) study found that negative stereotypes against women as managers led to lowered performance evaluations by the respondents, even when there were no actual performance differences between male and female managers. A number of other researchers (Hartman, Griffeth, Crino, & Harris, 1991; Maurer & Taylor, 1994; Shore, 1992) have demonstrated similar findings. "Research on occupational stereotypes confirms that images of jobs are actually images of people who hold those jobs" (Glick, Wilk, & Perreault, 1995:565). For example, undergraduate students were found to be significantly influenced against career choices that were described using sex-biased language (Benoit & Shell, 1985). Thus, it is suggested that when management students read predominantly

*From Sims, R. L. (1997). Gender equity in management education: A content analysis of test bank questions. *Journal of Education for Business 72,* 5:283–287. Reprinted with permission of the Helen Dwight Reid Educational Foundation. Published by Helref Publications, 1319 Eighteenth St., NW, Washington, DC 20036-1802.

about male managers, stereotypes that all managers should be male are reinforced. Given the implications of the use of sexist and biased language within management education, in this study we evaluate the content of management test bank questions for sexist language and gender equity.

METHOD

Sample

All the test questions contained in the test banks for 17 management books were included in the sample.

Procedure

. . . A content analysis was conducted for each question in the test banks. Test bank questions referring to a person included hypothetical situations and references to popularly known entrepreneurs or managers. Management theorists or historical figures known for their contributions in the development of the management field were not included in the analysis. Questions were evaluated for gender role in the question and name. To test for reliability of the evaluation, one test bank was evaluated by two independent raters (one male and one female) and the results compared.

Measures

Gender: Each person referred to in the test question was evaluated for gender and by name and/or pronoun and was counted only once, no matter how often the single question repeated reference to the person.

Role: The role the person played in the test question was measured as one of three categories: The first category included managers, supervisors or owners; the second, employees or subordinates; the third, co-workers, students or any other role that would fall outside the first two categories.

Name: The way the person was referred to in the question was categorized as either "first name only," Mr. or Ms, Mrs., or Miss, or "other," which included he or she only, and full name. Each person was categorized for name only once per question. For example, if a person was called both Mr. Jones and John, the classification was given to Mr. because the first name classification was given only when the first name was used exclusively.

RESULTS

The first book contained 2,662 test items. Most books contained over 1,500 items to be evaluated. All but the first test bank were evaluated by only one researcher.

The results indicate that for all 17 tests combined, males were referred to significantly more often (frequency = 1,803) than females (frequency = 1,003). Based on a Z test of proportion, the findings indicate that males are referred to 64% of the time ($Z = 15.45$; $p < .01$). Evaluation of each test independently showed results indicating that males were referred to significantly more often ($p < .05$) than females in 15 of the 17 test banks reviewed. The test banks that did not portray males significantly more often than females were the VanFleet and Peterson book (males were portrayed 53% of the time; $Z = 0.65$) and the Dubrin book (males were portrayed 44% of the time; $Z = -0.36$). For the test banks that portrayed males significantly more often, the percentage of questions using males in the examples ranged from a low of 60% ($Z = 3.46$, $p < .01$) for the Lewis, Goodman, and Fandt test to a high of 79% ($Z = 4.88$, $p < .01$) for the Plunkett and Anner test.

In addition to the percentage of test items that referred to males, the role the person played in the test item was also evaluated for gender equity. The test items that referred to a managerial role were classified as either a male or a female manager. In Table 1, I provide a breakdown of frequencies, percentages, and tests of proportions of managerial role by gender and test bank. Using a Z test of proportion, I found that managers were males 68% of the time ($Z = 15.67$; $p < .01$). When evaluating the tests independently, I found that males were used significantly more often ($p < .05$) as managerial examples than were females in 14 of the 17 books. Females were not portrayed significantly more often as

Table 1 Gender Equity by Test Bank: Frequencies and Tests of Proportion

Book Author and Publisher	Gender: Male	Gender: Female	% Male	Z-Score
Bedeian, A.G. (1993). *Management* (3rd Ed.) Dryden Press. Test bank author: Foegen, G.	53	15	78	5.57††
Bounds, G. M., Dobbins, G. H., & Fowler, O. S. (1995) *Management: A Total Quality Perspective*. (1st Ed.), South-Western. Test bank author: Hastings, B.	112	44	72	6.12††
Certo, S. C. (1994). *Modern Management: Diversity, Quality, Ethics, and the Global Environment* (6th Ed.) Allyn & Bacon. Test bank author: Kemper, R.	60	19	76	5.41††
Daft, R. L. (1995). *Understanding Management* (1st Ed.) Dryden Press. Test bank authors: Vincent, W. E. & Murphy, D.	93	59	61	2.78†
Dessler, G. (1995). *Managing Organizations in an Era of Change* (1st Ed.). Dryden Press. Test bank authors: Clinebell, S. & Peluchette, J.	53	18	75	4.86††
Donnelly, J. H., Gibson, J. L. & Ivacevich, J. M. (1995). *Fundamentals of Management* (9th Ed.) Irwin. Test bank authors: Kroot, I. B. & Gorski, B. A.	81	27	75	6.00††
Dubrin, A. J. (1994) *Essentials of Management* (3rd Ed.). South-Western. Test bank author: Dubrin, A. J.	2	2	50	0
Dubrin, A. J. & Ireland, R. D. (1993) *Management and Organization* (2nd Ed.). South-Western. Test bank authors: Dubrin, A. J. & Ireland, R. D.	9	3	75	2.00††
Gatewood, R. D., Taylor, R. R. & Ferrell, O. C. (1995). *Management: Comprehension, Analysis and Application* (1st Ed.). Irwin. Test bank author: Gardiner, G.	73	12	86	9.57††
Griffin, R. W. (1993). *Management* (4th Ed.). Houghton Mifflin. Test bank author: Kacmar, K. M.	48	35	58	1.48
Hellriegel, D. & Slocum, J. W. (1992). *Management* (6th Ed.). Addison & Wesley. Test bank authors: Fischthal, E. & Fischthal, S.	206	106	66	5.97††
Kreitner, R. (1995). *Management* (6th Ed.). Houghton Mifflin. Test bank author: Kreitner, R.	35	14	71	3.24††
Lewis, P. S., Goodman, S. H. & Fandt, P. M. (1995) *Management: Challenges in the 21st Century* (1st Ed.). West. Test bank author: Young, N.	89	56	61	2.72†
Plunkett, W. R. & Attner, R. F. (1994). *Introduction to Management* (5th Ed.). Wadsworth Publishing. Test bank author: Herrik, R.	19	3	86	4.87††
Robbins, S. P. (1994). *Management* (4th Ed.). Prentice Hall. Test bank author: Schrantz, D.	33	16	67	2.06
Stoner, J. A. F., Freeman, R. E. & Gilbert, D. Jr. (1995). *Management* (6th Ed.). Prentice Hall. Test bank author: Quirk, T. J.	129	67	66	4.73††
VanFleet, D. D. & Peterson, T. O. (1994). *Contemporary Management* (3rd Ed.). Houghton Mifflin. Test bank author: Wagner, F.	31	28	53	0.46
Total	**1126**	**524**	**68**	**15.67††**

NOTE: Total number of male managers referred to. Total number of female managers referred to.

† $p < .05$.

†† $p < .01$.

managers in any of the books. The tests that were not found to be biased toward males as managerial examples were the Dubrin, the Griffin, and the VanFleet and Peterson books.

The name used to refer to the managers was also evaluated by gender. A *Z*-test of independent proportion indicated that male managers were referred to by their first name 29% of the time and female managers were referred to by their first name 42% of the time ($Z = -5.22$; $p < .01$). When I evaluated the tests independently, I found that in 11 of them female managers were referred to by their first name only more often than male managers were referred to by their first name only. For example, the Dessler test referred to female managers by their first name 72% of the time, whereas male managers were referred to by their first name 49% of the time. *Z*-tests of independent proportions were not calculated for each test because of the rather small subgroups (11 of the 17 tests have fewer than 30 female managers referred to).

Discussion

The results of this study demonstrate that the test banks for management books are not written in an unbiased and non-sexist manner. These results actually support other research studies that have demonstrated that gender stereotypes continue to exist within the business and educational environments (Bergen & Williams, 1991; Cooper & Lewis, 1995; Norris & Wylie, 1995; Scheidt, 1994; Street, Kimmel, & Kromrey, 1995; Ware & Cooper-Studebaker, 1989). "There still appears to be a need for education to eliminate outworn stereotypes about women and men" (Street et al., 1995:199). However, because of legislation and greater societal awareness of the problem of gender bias, current forms may be more subtle than in the past (Shore, 1992).

University faculty are often seen as role models for students (Street et al., 1995). In fact, Cronin and Jreisat (1995) found that students who were given nonsexist instructions were less likely to use sexist language than students who were given sexist instructions or no instructions at all. Unlike the way they view most textbooks, students often view exams as written by their own instructor. Thus, through our exams, we have the opportunity to model nonsexist, nonbiased writing for our students. "Identifying and correcting sexist language is an important part of any educational program that attempts to move students beyond sexist stereotypes" (McMinn et al., 1994:742).

The sample size of management test banks used in this study appears to adequately represent the population of management test banks. We do not know, however, if the evaluation of management test banks is representative of other subject areas within management. Future research could determine if other management area test books are similarly biased.

References

Benoit, S. S., & Shell, W. (1985). Can sex biased communication affect business students' career decision? *Delta Pi Epsilon Journal 28:*123–129.

Bergen, D. J., & Williams, J. E. (1991). Sex stereotypes in the United States revisited: 1972–1988. *Sex Roles 24:*413–423.

Cooper, C. L., & Lewis, S. (1995). Working together: Men and women in organizations. *Leadership & Organizational Development Journal 16,*5:29–31.

Cronin, C., & Jreisat, S. (1995). Effects of modeling on the use of nonsexist language among high school freshpersons and seniors. *Sex Roles 33:*819–830.

Gastil, J. (1990). Generic pronouns and sexist language: The oxymoronic character of masculine generics. *Sex Roles 23:*629–643.

Glick, P., Wilk, K., & Perreault, M. (1995). Images of occupations: Components of gender and status in occupational stereotypes. *Sex Roles 32:*565–582.

Hartman, S. J., Griffeth, R. W., Crino, M. D., & Harris, O. J. (1991). Gender-based influences: The promotion recommendation. *Sex Roles 25:*285–300.

Maurer, T. J., & Taylor, M. A. (1994). Is sex by itself enough? An exploration of gender bias issues in performance appraisal. *Organizational Behavior and Human Decision Processes 60:*231–251.

McGlashan, K. E., Wright, P. M., & McCormick, B. (1995). Preferential selection and stereotypes: Effects on evaluation of female leader performance, subordinate goal commitment, and task performance. *Sex Roles 33:*669–686.

McMinn, M. R., Lindsay, S. E., Hannum, L. E., & Troyer, P. K. (1990). Does sexist language reflect personal characteristics? *Sex Roles 23:*389–396.

McMinn, M. R., Williams, P. E., & McMinn, L. C. (1994). Assessing recognition of sexist language: Development and use of the gender specific language scale. *Sex Roles 31:*741–755.

Merritt, R. D., & Kok, C. J. (1995). Attribution of gender to a gender-unspecified individual: An evaluation of the people = male hypothesis. *Sex Roles 33:*145–157.

Norris, J. M., & Wylie, A. M. (1995). Gender stereotyping of the managerial role among students in Canada and the United States. *Group & Organizational Management 20,*2:167–182.

Pirri, C., Eaton, E., & Durkin, K. (1995). Australian professional women's evaluations of male and female written products. *Sex Roles 32:*691–697.

Scheidt, S. D. (1994). Great expectations: Challenges for women as mental health administrators. *Journal of Mental Health Administration 21,*4:419–429.

Shore, T. H. (1992). Subtle gender bias in the assessment of managerial potential. *Sex Roles 27:*499–515.

Street, S., Kimmel, E. B., & Kromrey, J. D. (1995). Revisiting university student gender role perceptions. *Sex Roles 33:*183–201.

Ware, R., & Cooper-Studebaker, J. J. (1989). Attitudes toward women as managers with regard to sex, education, work, and marital status. *Psychological Reports 65,*1:347–350.

5.10

Mathematics Computer Software Characteristics and Gender

Kelly K. Chappell*

Many studies have argued that preschool children's attitudes toward computers are more similar than different (Sherman, Divine, & Johnson, 1985; Williams & Ogletree, 1991). Unfortunately, by high school, females tend to have developed more negative attitudes toward computers than males (Collis, 1985; Fetler, 1985). The way in which many children were first introduced to computers may have fostered gender differences. A review of the literature suggests that girls' negative attitudes have been exacerbated by gender role socialization coupled with a bias in computer software. Educational software programs, often modeled after video games, have been accused of serving as a gateway to technology for boys, but not for girls, as they reinforce the societal programming that males have received but conflict with the societal programming that females have received (Braun, Goupil, Giroux, & Chagnon, 1986). Past studies have found that females dislike the typical video game format (Dolan, 1994). This dislike is disturbing since frequent video game use by girls has been positively correlated to achievement, improved attitudes, and motivation in computer related areas (Gibb, Bailey, Lornbirth, & Wilson, 1993). Thus, it is crucial that educators begin to consider the aspects of video games and the educational software modeled after video games, which distract from girls' attitudes and interest in using the software.

From this literature review, a trend emerged. Several studies that claimed to introduce gender-neutral computer materials prior to attitude assessment manifested similar attitudes toward computers across gender groups (Forsyth & Lancy, 1989; Johnson & Swoope, 1987). Whereas, when studies claimed to introduce girls to "male biased"

*From Chappell, K. K. (1996). Mathematics computer software characteristics with possible gender-specific impact: A content analysis. *Journal of Educational Computing Research 15,* 1:25–35.

computer materials, interest decreased and attitudes became more negative (Dolan, 1994; Johnson & Swoope, 1987). Thus, evidence indicates that girls' attitudes toward using video games and educational software were strongly influenced by the format of the computer software.

Overwhelmingly, the literature suggests that violence, competition, and the underrepresentation of female characters have been the main factors negatively affecting girls' attitudes and interests in using computer software (Biraimah, 1993; Braun et al., 1986; Fisher, 1984; Johnson & Swoope, 1987). However, no empirical evidence exists which systematically considers the impact of each of these factors on girls' attitudes. This study presumes that these three elements may affect girls' attitudes and, thus, warrant attention. Therefore, this study will analyze, via a content analysis, the role these three elements play in recently published mathematics software programs.

Ultimately, it is important to systematically discern whether these elements influence the attitudes of girls toward computers. However, it is first important for educators to determine if these elements prevail in the software currently being purchased by schools. Especially, do these elements, previously identified in educational software, continue to pervade the more recently purchased educational software programs? This exploratory analysis seeks to uncover whether or not these aspects prevail in current software.

This study considers mathematics software specifically. Although content analyses of software have been conducted, many are based on the assumption that certain elements, such as competition and violence, are masculine and, thus, of more interest to males than to females. It is questionable whether these assumptions are valid or faulty overgeneralizations. Thus, the terms *masculine* and *feminine* are reserved. Finally, the software is analyzed as a function of grade level. According to the literature, the attitudes toward computers that girls exhibit depend largely on grade level. Recall, preschool children's attitudes toward computers were more similar than different. Unfortunately, by high school, females tend to have developed more negative attitudes toward computers than males. Therefore, it is reasonable to question whether the elements contained in the software programs designed for preschoolers differ from the elements contained in the software programs designed for high school use.

Methodology

Software

This study analyzes seventeen educational software programs designed for use in the mathematics classroom as a function of grade level, the representation of gender, competition, and violence. Each program was listed on the Educational Resources' top-ten topseller list for either the 1993–1994 school year or the 1994–1995 school year. Educational Resources' primary clients are school districts, schools, teachers and administrators in both the United States and Canada. Educational Resources is the leading distributor of software to schools in North America. Therefore, these top-selling products are a real reflection of the software purchased for use in classrooms.

Design

This study analyzes latest developments in mathematics software (1990–1994) including interactive CD-ROMs and videodiscs. Each software program is evaluated on the basis of gender representation, violence, and competition. This content analysis is strictly exploratory and descriptive. The percent of male characters and voices portrayed and the percent of female characters and voices portrayed are reported for each software program. A violence percentage is reported for each software program. Both a competition against the program percentage and a competition against a peer percentage are reported for each program. A mean percentage of each variable is recorded for each grade level. The variable definitions and calculation procedures are described in the following sections.

Variables

Violence is defined as actions which cause (or intend to cause) injury, damage, destruction or devastation to another being or object.

Competition against a Peer involves any situation in which two persons are striving for the same goal (prize, high score, end result etc.) but only one person can win by achieving this goal. If the student's performance in an activity affects or determines whether the outcome will be a win or defeat, this activity is considered to contain competition.

Competition against the Program involves any situation in which the player will either win by achieving the desired end or be defeated by the program. If the student's performance in an activity influences or determines whether the outcome will be a win or defeat, this activity is considered to contain competition.

Gender Representation: A character's sex is only reported if it could be accurately determined by either appearance or voice. Therefore, non-gendered characteristics with no voice are not reported.

Procedures

Violence: The seventeen software programs are each composed of one or more distinct activities. The percent of violence in a particular program = (the number of the program's activities containing violence ÷ the total number of activities in the program) × 100.

Competition Against a Peer: The percent of competition against a peer = (the number of activities containing competition against a peer ÷ the total number of activities in the program) × 100.

Competition Against the Program: The percent of competition against the program = (the number of activities containing competition against the program ÷ the total number of activities in the program) × 100.

Gender Representation: The percent of female characters = (the number of characters determined to be female ÷ the number characters to which a gender could be attached) × 100. Likewise, the percentage of male characters in the program = (the number of characters determined to be male ÷ the number of characters to which a gender could be attached) × 100.

Mean Percentages: Each mean percentage serves to describe (in a single number) the overall level of the variable present at a particular grade level. For instance, the mean violence percentage for a particular grade is the mean of the individual violence percentages of the programs designed for that grade. Three programs are designed for twelfth grade use with individual violence percentages of 100 percent, 50 percent, and 0 percent. Thus, the mean violence percentage for the twelfth grade is [(100 + 50 + 0)/3] percent = 50 percent.

Educational Level Means: Each educational level mean percentage serves to describe (in a single number) the overall level of the variable present at a particular educational level (i.e., preschool, elementary school, middle school and high school). Elementary school is considered to include kindergarten through fifth grade. Middle school is considered to include sixth through eighth grade. High school is considered to include ninth through twelfth grade. For instance, the mean violence percentage for high school is the mean of the violence percentages of the programs designed for use in at least one of the high school grade levels. In calculating the mean violence percentage for each educational level, the violence percentages are differentially weighted by the number of grades for which the corresponding program is appropriate. The violence percentage of a program designed for ninth through twelfth grade use is weighted by four, whereas a violence percentage of a program designed only for ninth grade is weighted by one.

Results and Discussion

Results

A violence percentage, a competition against program percentage, and a competition against peer percentage are reported for each software program (arranged by grade level appropriateness) in Table 1. The percent of female characters and voices portrayed and the percent of male characters and voices portrayed are also reported for each software title in Table 1. When the data in Table 1 are reviewed from a quantitative perspective, patterns of gender imbalance emerge. Of the 112 characters to which a gender could be attached, twenty-eight (or 25%) are female and eighty-four (or 75%) are male.

A mean violence percentage, which serves to describe the overall violence level of a particular grade, is reported for each grade level in Table 2. The results indicate that the mean percentages of violence increase across grade level. The programs designed for preschool use contain a mean violence percentage of 4.2 percent. In contrast, the programs designed for high school use contain a mean violence percentage of 46.2 percent (see Figure 1).

The results in Table 2 further indicate that the mean percentages of competition against the program increase across grade level. Of the programs designed for preschool use, none requires the student to compete against the program. The programs designed for high school use contain a mean competition against the program percentage of 53.8 percent (see Figure 1).

The results in Table 2 indicate that the mean competition against a peer percentages increase across grade level. Of the programs designed for preschool use, none requires the student to compete against a peer. The

Table 1 Characteristics of Each Software Program Arranged by Grade-Level Appropriateness

Title of Software	*Violence*		*Competition Against Program*		*Competition Against Peer*		*Female Characters*		*Male Characters*	
Millie's Math House	0%	(0/6)	0%	(0/6)	0%	(0/6)	41.7%	(5/12)	58.3%	(7/12)
Kidsmath	12.5%	(1/8)	0%	(0/8)	0%	(0/8)	all characters non-gendered			
Thinkin' Things 1	0%	(0/6)	0%	(0/6)	0%	(0/6)	38.1%	(8/21)	61.9%	(13/21)
Treasure MathStorm	43%	(3/7)	100%	(7/7)	0%	(0/7)	27.3%	(3/11)	72.7%	(8/11)
Stickybear's Math	0%	(0/12)	50%	(6/12)	50%	(6/12)	50%	(2/4)	50%	(2/4)
Number Maze	0%	(0/1)	0%	(0/1)	0%	(0/1)	0%	(0/9)	100%	(9/9)
Countdown	0%	(0/3)	0%	(0/3)	100%	(3/3)	100%	(1/1)	0%	(0/1)
Coin Critters	10%	(1/10)	10%	(0/10)	0%	(0/10)	20%	(1/5)	80%	(4/5)
Turbo Math Facts	80%	(4/5)	100%	(5/5)	0%	(0/5)	0%	(0/2)	100%	(2/2)
Math Blaster Plus	50%	(2/4	50%	(2/4)	25%	(1/4)	0%	(0/2)	100%	(2/2)
Math Blaster 1	75%	(3/4)	100%	(4/4)	0%	(0/4)	25%	(1/4)	75%	(3/4)
Math Workshop	0%	(0/7)	28.6%	(2/7)	28.6%	(2/7)	16.7%	(5/30)	83.3%	(25/30)
Math Blaster 2	50%	(2/4)	100%	(4/4)	0%	(0/4)	25%	(1/4)	75%	(3/4)
Tesselmania	0%	(0/1)	100%	(0/1)	0%	(0/1)	no characters			
Cruncher, The	0%	(0/3)	0%	(0/3)	0%	(0/3)	25%	(1/4)	75%	(3/4)
Number Munchers	100%	(1/1)	100%	(1/1)	100%	(1/1)	all characters non-gendered			
AlgeBlaster 3	50%	(2/4)	75%	(3/4)	0%	(0/4))	0%	(0/3)	100%	(3/3)

Table 2 Mean Percentages by Grade Level

Grade Level	*Number of Programs*[a]	*Mean Violence*	*Mean Competition Against Program (%)*	*Mean Competition Against Peer (%)*	*Mean % Female Representation*
Pre K	3 (2)	4.2	0	0	39.9
K	9 (8)	11.4	21	19.8	33.3
1	12 (11)	22.5	36.6	17	29
2	12 (11)	22.5	36.6	17	29
3	15 (12)	28.0	42.6	20.2	27.3
4	13 (11)	28.1	41.4	23.4	27.3
5	12 (10)	30.4	44.9	25.3	26.2
6	11 (9)	33.2	44.4	23.1	23.5
7	6 (4)	33.3	50.6	21.4	16.7
8	6 (4)	33.3	50.6	21.4	16.7
9	4 (2)	37.5	43.8	25	12.5
10	3 (2)	50	58.3	33.3	12.5
11	3 (2)	50	58.3	33.3	12.5
12	3 (2)	50	58.3	33.3	12.5

a. The number of data points (number of programs) upon which each mean percentage is based is uneven across grade levels. It is important to consider that the preschool and ninth through twelfth grade means are based on relatively few data points, as only a few of the top-selling software programs are designed for use in these grades. The numbers in parentheses indicate the number of data points upon which each mean percentage of female characters is based.

programs designed for high school use contain a mean competition against a peer percentage of 30.8 percent (see Figure 1).

In contrast, the mean percentages of female characters portrayed decrease with grade level (see Table 2). The mean percentage of female characters and voices portrayed in the programs designed for preschool use is 39.9 percent. The mean percentage of female characters and voices portrayed in the programs designed for high school use is 12.5 percent (see Figure 1). The software programs that contain no characters or only non-gendered characters were not included in the calculations.

The orderliness of the means can be misleading.[1] If the entire data set is taken into account, the trends of increasing violence and competition and decreasing representation of female characters and voices are more unclear. The systematic trends in the means of each element across grade level and educational level pale in comparison to the wide spread of percentages for each variable within each grade level and educational level. For each variable, the within grade variability and within educational level variability are quite high. Within each grade level, with the exception of preschool, there is a wide range of violence, competition, and female representation levels from which to choose. Students have access to programs containing no violence, no competition, and no female characters and voices. However, they also have access to programs containing considerable violence, competition, and female characters and voices.

In fact, each software program services multiple grade levels. To some extent, the elementary school students have access to the same programs as high-schoolers. With the

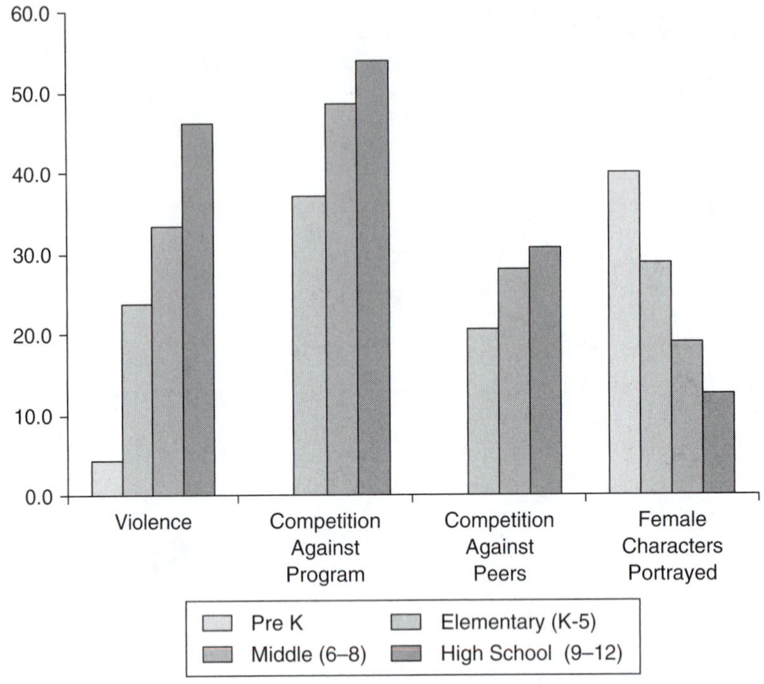

Figure 1 Educational Level Mean Percentages

exception of preschoolers, younger kids are not being spared violence and competition and the older kids are not being fed only violence and competition.

Discussion

Do violence, competition, and the under-representation of female characters considered to prevail in 1980's educational software pervade these more recent educational software programs? In regards to these top-selling programs, the answer is yes. However, the results do not indicate that all of these top-selling programs are characterized by violence, competition, and an under-representation of female characters and voices. Given any one of these three elements, sellers exist which are completely void of the element and top-sellers exist which are loaded with the element.

The software programs analyzed in this study were not randomly selected from the general pool of existing software programs. Therefore, the results that emerged from this content analysis cannot and should not be generalized to other software programs. The study should be replicated, analyzing different educational software programs.

We can garner several important trends as they exist among these 17 best-selling programs. First, the top-selling programs designed for preschools contain considerably less violence and competition than the top-selling programs designed for use in high schools. Second, a gender imbalance, favoring males, pervades the majority of these seventeen software programs. However, the software programs designed for preschool use contain higher percentages of female characters and voices than the programs designed for high school use.

As the literature underscores, preschool children's attitudes toward computers are more similar than different. Unfortunately, by high school, females tend to have developed more negative attitudes toward computers than males. At this point, it would be far too simplistic to conclude that it is the increase in violence and competition and the decrease in female representation that cause girls' attitudes and interest to plummet. Instead, it seems that these variables' relationships to girls' attitudes toward computers warrant further investigation.

Violence, competition, and the under-representation of female characters certainly continue to prevail in current software. The trends across grade level found in respect to these variables warrant further exploration. Educators need to identify the exact elements of computer software that are discouraging (or encouraging) to girls. Only then can we design more effective and relevant instructional software programs that engage a broader range of students.

Note

1. A number of different analyses were considered. Since each software program services multiple grade levels, the independence assumption required for analyses (such as linear regression) was violated. Reporting the means seems to be the most straightforward way to present the data.

References

Biraimah, K. (1993). The non-neutrality of educational computer software. *Computers Education 20,*4:283–290.

Braun, C. M., Goupil, G., Giroux, J., & Chagnon, Y. (1986). Adolescents and microcomputers: Sex differences, proxemics, and task and stimulus variables. *The Journal of Psychology 120,*6:529–542.

Collis, B. (1985). Sex-related differences in attitudes toward computers: Implications for counselors. *The School Counselor 33,* 2:120–130.

Dolan, C. (1994). Off course. *The Wall Street Journal,* pp. R16–R17, June 27, 1994.

Fetler, M. (1985). Sex differences on the California Statewide Assessment of Computer Literacy. *Sex Roles 13,* 3–4:181–191.

Fisher, G. (1984). Access to computers. *The Computing Teacher 11,* 8:24–27.

Forsyth, A. S., & Laney, D. F. (1989). Girls and microcomputers: A hopeful finding regarding software. *Computing in the Schools 6,* 3–4:31–59.

Gibb, C. D., Bailey, J. R., Lornbirth, T. T., & Wilson, W. P. (1993). Personality differences between high and low electronic video game users. *Journal of Psychology 144:*159–165.

Johnson, C. S., & Swoope, K. F. (1987). Boys' and girls' interest in using computers: Implications for the classroom. *Arithmetic Teacher 35,* 1:14–16.

Sherman, J., Divine, K., & Johnson, B. (1985). An analysis of computer software preferences of preschool children. *Educational Technology 25:*39–41.

Williams, S. W., & Ogletree, S. M. (1991). Preschool children's computer interest and competence: Effect of sex and gender role. *Early Childhood Research Quarterly 7:*135–143.

5.11

A Content Analysis of Music Videos

Richard L. Baxter, Cynthia De Riemer, Ann Landini, Larry Leslie, and Michael W. Singletary*

The music video, as shown on Music Television (MTV), is a contemporary hybrid of rock music and film imagery. This study analyzed a sample of 62 MTV music videos in 23 content categories. Of the content categories studied, frequent occurrences were found in visual abstraction, sex, dance, violence, and crime. MTV sexual and violent content is characterized by innuendo and suggestiveness, perhaps reflecting MTV's adolescent audience appeal.

De Fleur and Ball-Rokeach (1982) have argued that exposure to mass media content indirectly affects behavior by shaping cultural norms. Research studies, often centered on the sexual and violent content of television, have investigated the relationship between mass media content and cultural norms. For example, the cultural indicators group (Gerbner & Gross, 1976; Gerbner, Gross, Morgan, & Signorielli, 1980)** has found that televised violence may cultivate perceptions of mistrust, apprehension, danger, and a "mean world." In addition, analyses of the sexual content of television (Fernandez-Collado, Greenberg, Korzenny, & Atkin, 1978; Franzblau, Sprafkin, & Rubinstein, 1977) have revealed that physical intimacy appeared most often in less sensuous forms. Kissing, embracing, and nonaggressive touching dominated the screen, while sexual behaviors such as rape and intercourse were almost never seen but often suggested. Others have studied television as a form. Wright and Huston (1983:841) proposed that the visual and auditory representation possible with television was a potent means of communication and "could induce active cognitive processing," especially for the young.

Little attention, though, has been given to the form and content of Music Television (MTV), which began in 1981. MTV airs video clips of recording artists performing their current popular music hits. The staple of MTV

*From Baxter, R. L., De Riemer, C., Landini, A. L., Leslie, L., & Singletary, M. W. (1985). A content analysis of music videos. *Journal of Broadcasting & Electronic Media* 29, 3:333–340.

**See reading 6.6, this volume, for a related discussion.

content is the music video, which consumes 80% of programming time (Foti, 1981). MTV does not represent the only programming service, which airs music videos. Music videos also appear on USA Cable's *Nightflight,* and on HBO's *Jukebox,* among other services. However, MTV often obtains the exclusive right to show a particular video first.

Critics have charged that MTV stresses sex and violence and makes rock music impersonal by removing the individual "pictures in our minds" generated by the music (Levy, 1983). In exploring both the format and the content of MTV music videos, Gehr (1983:39) proposed that MTV might alter the relationship between the audience and the musicians in live performances and might change how audiences hear records and radio. Gehr believed the music video separates music from visual content, resulting in ". . . discontinuity and disjunction. Gestures, actions, and intentions are nearly always divorced from systematic content."

The content of music videos may be significant from another standpoint. Larson and Kubey (1983) found that both watching television and listening to music (as separate activities) could deeply involve adolescents. Even greater emotional involvement was reported when listening to music. The music video combines elements of both music and television in a nontraditional format. Considering that 85% of the MTV audience is estimated to be between the ages of 14 and 34 (Zimmerman, 1984), the music video has potential for contributing to the cultural norms of a relatively impressionable audience.

Given the lack of systematic content analysis of music videos, the research questions focused on how specific areas of content can be quantified. The following questions guided the research effort: (a) What are the major categories of content that emerge from the observation of music videos and can these categories be analyzed systematically? (b) Do specific content categories, such as those centered on sex and violence, appear with great frequency in music videos? (c) Do music videos focus on bizarre, unconventional representations? Is androgyny present in portrayals of video characters? (d) Do symbols dealing with government, politics, and American culture and lifestyles appear with discernible frequency?*

Method

Although previous analyses of television content are available, their coding instruments used could not be applied readily to music videos. Thus, there was a need to develop a coding form for collecting the data. The development of the coding instrument was guided by the desire to gain an exhaustive overview of music video content and not to focus on one or two areas of possible content, such as sex or violence.

A search of the literature revealed anecdotal data relating to the content of rock music and music videos. For instance, Peatman (1954) and Horton (1957) found lyrics dealt primarily with love, sex, and romance. Gehr (1983) suggested that MTV content centered on themes such as liberty, growing up, death, and fear of the loss of freedom. These suggested themes were grouped into content categories. To examine the relationship of these derived categories to actual music video content, a purposive sample of primetime MTV programming was examined, comparing content suggested by the literature with actual music video content. As a result, the content categories were expanded and each category (with two exceptions) was defined by a short descriptor and by a listing of possible actions or behaviors, which could occur in that category. Defining categories by major properties was suggested by Krippendorff (1980) as a means of assuring exhaustiveness.

This preliminary coding instrument was pre-tested, resulting in the addition and refinement of categories. The final coding form included an "other" choice for each category so that coders could add observed elements

*Research questions are answered by the nature of the data, here: What is the content of MTV in a chosen set of categories? How bizarre are they (relative to everyday life)? Which symbols of democracy, politics . . . are presented? What is their frequency distribution? The author's questions mix research questions with those concerning an analyst's competence: Can I analyze these categories reliably? Are frequencies discernible?

that the researchers had overlooked. Twenty-three content categories were identified.

A random sample of 62 videos was drawn from the music videos aired on MTV during the week of April 28–May 4, 1984. One hour from each of the seven days was recorded. The hour for each day was determined by using a table of random numbers; military time equivalents were used for the hour designates. Videos in the sample were coded only once.

The unit of analysis was the individual music video of approximately 3 minutes in duration. The length and complexity of the coding instrument influenced the researchers' decision to instruct the coders not to indicate multiple references of content in the same music video. The researchers were interested in the number of videos containing at least one reference to a content category and not in the number of times the same element appeared in a particular video.

Coders were undergraduate students trained in the use of the coding form. Each coder viewed each video twice. During the first viewing, the video was stopped every 30 seconds to allow coding of all content categories to that point. For the second viewing, the video was played nonstop and coders were allowed to make any appropriate changes on the coding form. The videos were viewed by the coders without sound, because the researchers were interested in the visual, rather than audio, content elements of the videos.

To test inter-coder reliability, 21 coders recoded randomly selected videos, which had already been analyzed by original coders. Coder and re-coder results were analyzed using Scott's pi for nominal scale coding (Scott, 1955).* A .82 reliability coefficient was obtained.

Results

A total of 62 videos were analyzed for occurrences in 23 content categories. Table 1 contains frequencies of the leading seven content categories with descriptive behaviors and/or actions for each category included. The researchers' decision not to code multiple occurrences of actions or behaviors in the content categories must be considered in interpreting these results.

Discussion

The physical structure of the music videos studied reveals that producers rely heavily on special camera techniques, film imagery, and special effects in creating music videos. The intent may be to dazzle the eye and thus hold the attention of the largely adolescent audience. Music videos also allow the performer to dominate the action and showcasing the artist may be a prime concern.

Against the backdrop of visual structure, what other content categories appear in music videos? Consistent with Levy's (1983) observation, MTV videos stressed sexual content. However, like other studies of televised sexual content, music video sexual content was understated, relying on innuendo through clothing, suggestiveness, and light physical contact rather than more overt behaviors.

Thus, music video sexual content may have a decidedly adolescent orientation, suited to its audience; fantasy exceeds experience and sexual expression centers primarily on attracting the opposite sex. Sexual behavior, as portrayed in music videos, may reflect actual or desired adolescent courtship behavior, or the expression of attraction impulses. This issue is beyond the scope of this study. The study's results indicate, however, that sexually oriented, suggestive behavior is portrayed frequently in music videos. Questions regarding the impact of this portrayal on adolescent socialization, peer relationships, and modeling are raised.

The frequency of instances of violence and crime content also merits further attention. Frequent content elements in the violence and crime category also exhibited understated characteristics. The most frequently coded content elements were physical aggression, not the use of weapons, murder, or sexual violence. Violent action in music videos often stopped short of the fruition of the violent act.

Besides the question of *what* is on MTV, there is the question of *who* is on MTV. White, adult males, appearing in 96% of the

---

*See reading 6.1, this volume.

Table 1 Frequencies of Actions/Behaviors in Seven Leading Music Videos Content Categories

Category	*Action/Behavior*	*Percentages*
Visual Abstraction	Unusual camera techniques, i.e., use of convex lens, unconventional camera angles, rapid film cuts between scenes or video segments	48
	Special lighting—varying colors and techniques	48
	Fog	32
	Superimposition imagery—filming technique which inserts persons, objects or places onto the ongoing action of the music video although the superimposed subjects are not physically part of the action	27
	Costuming—use of clothing to portray characterizations beyond those associated with contemporary garb, cavemen, 18th-century aristocrats	19
	Use of fire and flames	18
	Distortions	16
Sex	Provocative clothing	31
	Embrace or other physical contact	31
	Dance movements of sexually suggestive nature	27
	Non-dance movements of sexually suggestive nature	21
	Date or courtship (male-female)	15
	Kissing	11
	Male chasing female or vice versa	11
	Use of musical instrument in sexually suggestive manner	8
	Sadomasochism	5
	Date or courtship (homosexual or lesbian)	2
	Sexual bondage	2
Dance	Group dancing—spontaneous or natural	36
	Group dancing—choreographed	16
	Couple dancing	13
	Individual or group doing jazz	10
	Individual or group doing ballet	3
	Individual or group doing tap	3
	Individual or group doing break-dancing	2
Violence and Crime	Physical aggression against people	26
	Physical aggression against objects	16
	Dance movements imitating violence	15
	Destructiveness	15
	Use of weapons (chains, guns, knives, axes, hammers, etc.)	11
	Physical aggression against self	8
	Chase	7
	Murder	3
	Victimless crime	2
Celebration	Activities which stimulate a happy or joyful reaction in participants	21
	Audience at rock concert	16
	Social gatherings or party scene with light, happy setting	18
Friendship	Togetherness of nonsexual variety (male-female)	24
	Camaraderie—pals, girlfriends, clubs, or social groups	24
	Companionship in settings such as home, school, work, etc., where one person provides company for another	13
Isolation	Physical separation from others in indoor setting	32
	Physical separation from others in outdoor setting	12
	Desertion by loved one	5

NOTE: $n = 62$. Frequency is the percentage of videos in the sample that contained at least one occurrence of an action or behavior from that content category.

videos studied, were most represented on these MTV videos. This may reflect the dominance of this group in the rock music industry. The race most depicted in this study was Caucasian (by a 2 to 1 ratio), but other races including Black, Oriental, Hispanic, and Native American were present.

At this time, most persons, from the uninitiated to the MTV fan, have little knowledge about the possible impact of music videos. Studies like the one reported here may do much to replace myth and anecdotal observation and form the basis for future empirical analysis.

References

De Fleur, M. L., & Ball-Rokeach, S. J. (1982). *Theories of mass communication* (4th ed.). New York: Longman.

Fernandez-Collado, C. F., Greenberg, B. S., Korzenny, F., & Atkin, C. K. (1978). Sexual intimacy and drug use in TV series. *Journal of Communication 28,* 3:30–37.

Foti, L. (1981, August 29). Punk to classics. *Billboard,* 4.

Franzblau, S., Sprafkin, J. N., & Rubinstein, E. A. (1977). Sex on TV: A content analysis. *Journal of Communication, 27,* 2:164–170.

Gehr, R. (1983). The MTV aesthetic. *Film Comment 19,* 4:37–40.

Gerbner, G., & Gross, L. (1976). Living with television: The violence profile. *Journal of Communication 26,* 2:173–199.

Gerbner, G., Gross, L., Morgan, M., & Signorielli, N. (1980). The "mainstreaming" of America: Violence profile no. 11. *Journal of Communication 30,* 3:10–29.

Horton, D. (1957). The dialogue of courtship in popular songs. *American Journal of Sociology 62:*569–578.

Krippendorff, K. (1980). *Content analysis: An introduction to its methodology.* Thousand Oaks, CA: Sage.*

Larson, R., & Kubey, R. (1983). Television and music: Contrasting media in adolescent life. *Youth and Society 15:*13–31.

Levy, S. (1983, December 8). Ad nauseum: How MTV sells out rock and roll. *Rolling Stone,* 30.

Peatman, J. G. (1944). Radio and popular music. In P. F. Lazarsfeld & F. N. Stanton (Eds.), *Radio research 1942–43* (pp. 335–393). New York: Duell, Sloan & Pearce.

Scott, W. A. (1955). Reliability of content analysis: The case of nominal scale coding. *Public Opinion Quarterly 19:*321–325.

Wright, J. C., & Huston, A. C. (1983). A matter of form: Potentials of television for young viewers. *American Psychologist 38:*835–843.

Zimmerman, D. (1984, March 29). Rock video's free ride may be ending. *USA Today,* D1–2.

*Krippendorff, K. (2004). *Content analysis: An introduction to its methodology* (2nd ed.). Thousand Oaks, CA: Sage.

PART 6

RELIABILITY AND VALIDITY

Readers know that writing can be unclear, confusing, and ambiguous. Different people may interpret texts differently, and their meanings may change over time or with different contexts. Because content analysts use texts as data, they have to justify their analyses in the face of these uncertainties.

The two most important criteria for a sound content analysis are *reliability* and *validity,* to which one might add *social relevance.* Content analysts need to be clear about what these criteria intend to ensure, use appropriate measures, and satisfy acceptable standards. Content analysts often experience trade-offs among these criteria, but the criteria do not go away. For example, computer users are eager to point out that reliability is no longer their issue—computers are deterministic machines that compute the same results from the same data. However, the perfect reliability of computational approaches to content analysis is often offset by the lack of their validity and social relevance, which needs to be addressed as well.

We start with the original article by William Scott, who, in 1955, proposed what came to be one of the most widely used reliability coefficients: Scott's π (pi). His statistic is easy to compute, not affected by the number of categories available for coding, and corrected for chance agreement. π is limited, however, to two coders, basic nominal data, and large sample sizes. However, unlike other coefficients, π has withstood the test of time.

When to use Scott's π is part of Klaus Krippendorff's comprehensive discussion of what reliability means and the properties of agreement coefficients from which the reliability of data can be inferred. In content analysis, reliability essentially means replicability of the research process in general and of coding in particular. However, agreement measures can also be used to evaluate the qualities of coders, locate unreliabilities in coding instructions under development, and assess the appropriateness of categories to the nature of the coded texts. The most important motivation to assess reliability is the assurance it provides to content analysts that their results have at least the *potential* to be valid—without guaranteeing that validity.

Validity, by contrast, is the degree to which research results are supported by *evidence* external to the analysis. For content analysts, validation presents a dilemma: The virtue of content analysis lies in its unobtrusiveness—texts can be analyzed in the absence of their sources—and its ability to infer something unobserved at the time (for example, the distribution of power in the Kremlin under Stalin* or the network of an author's associations**).

---

*See reading 3.3, this volume.

**See readings 1.6 and 3.1, this volume.

What motivates a content analysis is the very absence of direct evidence for the phenomena of interest.*

Given this dilemma, Irving Janis, who worked in Lasswell's propaganda analysis unit during World War II and later became a well-known social psychologist, examines ways of validating content analyses *indirectly,* suggesting "productivity" as an alternative criterion. While his discussion is rooted in the semiotics of his time, he had an early grasp of the difficult problem of validation wherever meanings are involved and suggested a solution to testing the validity of content analyses.

Scott Poole and Joseph Folger offer finer and more recent differentiations of the kind of validity issues that content analysts face when studying social interaction. They build on Bales's groundbreaking work.**

Milton Stewart, a former journalist and early champion for civil rights, is represented here by a content analysis of early African American newspapers. Stewart's nuanced analysis of how "importance" can be indicated in the press addresses validity issues that are often ignored today.

The pioneering work of George Gerbner and his cultural indicators team with respect to television violence in the 1960s and 1970s attracted much public attention. At that time, there were only three major television networks; viewers had far fewer programs from which to choose, and programming was discussed in terms of its pro- and antisocial consequences. In this context, the frequency of violence on TV became a key concern for the U.S. Congress and various advocacy groups, parents and teachers included. The social relevance of their research was evident in how key players responded. Not surprisingly, Gerbner's television violence measure became the target of self-serving attacks by network executives, using scientific arguments but conveniently ignoring the larger social-cultural context from which Gerbner et al. argued. One of the key contentions was the definition of violence, which affected the networks' ratings. In the public exchange that we include here, one can see the importance of the transparency of scientific research to be publicly examined. We invite our readers to consider whether comic violence or dramatic re-creations of natural disasters should be considered violent.***

---

*For an exception, see reading 7.1, this volume. Ogilvie, Stone, and Shneidman describe the use of genuine suicide letters and simulated ones side-by-side in order to develop an analytical construct in the form of a generalizable discriminant function.

**See reading 2.5, this volume.

***See reading 5.7, this volume.

6.1

Scott's π (Pi)

Reliability for Nominal Scale Coding

William A. Scott*

This article suggests an improved method of reporting the extent of inter-observer agreement in assigning overt or verbal behavioral items to a set of categories. It was developed specifically for standard survey research coding operations, but it can be used in a wide variety of research situations to measure the reliability of classifying a large number of responses into nominal scale categories. The requirements are that the categories be mutually exclusive and that observations be duplicated on a random sample of the total set of responses being studied.

The Survey Research Coding Procedure

In standard interview survey procedures, a respondent's answer to "open-ended" questions is recorded verbatim by the interviewer. The first major step in the analysis process then becomes one of "coding" all of the thousands or more different responses to each question into a relatively small number of categories, which can be meaningfully and conveniently related to other responses. This is usually done by a staff of coders, and the interviews are distributed among them by a procedure that approximates randomization.

To improve the accuracy of content analysis and get some measure of the extent of inter-coder agreement on each of the dimensions, a random sample of the interviews is assigned for "check-coding." A second coder makes an independent analysis of the entire interview, and the two persons discuss their differences, to arrive at the "best" judgment in every case of disagreement. A record of differences is kept, and this constitutes the basis of a report on the overall coding reliability for the entire set of interviews.

It is apparent that the ambiguity of the dimension and the skill of the analyst are reflected in the total number of differences obtained for any given dimension. Two skilled

*From Scott, W. A. (1955). Reliability of content analysis: The case of nominal scale coding. *Public Opinion Quarterly 19*,3:321–325.

clinicians could be expected to show a higher proportion of agreements than average coders (college students) in assigning protocols to categories descriptive of personality types. Moreover, anyone could presumably code dimensions such as "sex" or "race" more reliably than attitudinal responses, which ordinarily require a certain amount of judgment in determining the proper category. It would seem that these "ambiguity" and "skill" factors are legitimate components of the total measure of coding error. Certain extraneous factors should be excluded, however, and this is not done by present methods of reporting the extent of inter-observer agreement.

Conventional Methods

One commonly used "reliability" index is simply P_o or the percentage of judgments on which coders agree, out of the total number of judgments. Unfortunately, this measure is biased in favor of dimensions with a small number of categories. By chance alone, one would expect better agreement on a two-category than a five-category scale.

To correct for this bias, Bennett, Alpert, and Goldstein (1954) have used an index of consistency, *S*, which takes into account the number of categories in the dimensions.

$$S = \frac{k}{k-1}\left(P_o - \frac{1}{k}\right),$$

where P_o is the observed percentage agreement between two independent coders and *k* is the number of categories. As the number of categories increases, *S* increases for a fixed P_o. And herein lies a spurious effect. Given a two-category sex dimension and a P_o of 60%, the *S* calculated from this equation would be 0.20. But a whimsical researcher might add two more categories, "hermaphrodite" and "indeterminant," thereby increasing *S* to 0.47, though the two additional categories are not used at all. *S* is based on the assumption that all *k* categories in the dimensions have equal probability of use (1/*k*) by both coders. This is an unwarranted assumption for most behavioral and attitudinal research. Even though *k* categories may be available to the observers, the phenomena being coded are likely to be distributed unevenly, and in many cases will cluster heavily in only two or three of them. To the extent that the distribution over categories varies from a rectangular one, *S* would appear to be an unsatisfactory measure coding reliability.

A Suggested Index of Inter-Coder Agreement

Pi(π), the index of inter-coder agreement to be reported here, corrects for the number of categories in the code, and the frequency with which each is used. In the practical coding situation, it varies form 0.00* to 1.00, regardless of the number of categories in the dimension and is thus comparable with the "percentage agreement" figure.

For certain data indices are already available. When the coding dimensions are composed of equal-interval scales, a Pearson product-moment correlation coefficient** is appropriate for reporting inter-coding reliability. If the phenomena are ordered along a dimension of unknown intervals, a rank-difference correlation gives an adequate measure of the extent of agreement between coders. Frequently, the coding dimensions used in survey and observational research are composed of nominal scales, where categories are not ordered along a dimension of "more-or-less" of some attribute. For such cases π is suggested.

$$\pi = \frac{P_o - P_e}{1 - P_e}$$

where P_o (observed percent agreement) represents the percentage of judgments on which the two analysts agree when coding the same data independently; and P_e is the percent

*Note, mathematically, π can be less than zero. It is negative when coders systematically disagree, e.g., when they communicate with each other to avoid using the same categories, a possibility that would be incompatible with the requirement that coders work independently when generating reliability data.

**This would be the intraclass correlation coefficient r_{ii}.

agreement to be expected based on chance. π is the ratio of the actual difference between obtained and chance agreement to the maximum difference between obtained and chance agreement. It can be roughly interpreted as the extent to which the coding reliability exceeds chance.*

Calculation of Expected Percent Agreement

The percentage agreement, which could be expected by chance, depends on not only on the number of categories in the dimension but also on the frequency with which each of them is used by coders. Minimum chance agreement (or "maximum uncertainty") occurs when all categories are used (by both coders) with equal frequency. Any deviation from a rectangular distribution of frequencies across categories will increase the "expected percent agreement." In general, the total probability of chance agreement equals the sum of the probabilities of agreement on each of the categories taken individually (since the categories are mutually exclusive).

In survey data, the distribution of coded responses to a particular question can be obtained easily for the entire set of interviews. . . . As an illustration we may consider the following distribution of responses to the question: "What sorts of problems are your friends and neighbors most concerned about these days?"

Nature of Problem	**Percent of all Responses**
Economic problems	60%
International problems	5
Political problems	10
Local problems	20
Personal problems	3
Not ascertained	2

Although the observed percentage agreement P_o is calculated on only a part of the total set of interviews, and individual coders will actually vary somewhat in their distributions of responses over the set of categories, it is convenient to assume that the distribution for the entire set of interviews represents the most probable (and hence "true" in the long-run probability sense) distribution for any individual coder. (This assumption is not a necessary one; P_e can be calculated from the actual distribution of each pair of coders. . . .)

The expected percent agreement P_e for the dimension is the sum of the squared proportions over all categories (since the categories are mutually exclusive, and the two coders' probabilities of using any one of the categories are assumed equal).

$$P_e = \sum_{i=1}^{k} p_i^2,$$

where k is the total number of categories and p_i is the proportion of the entire sample which falls in the ith category.

In the present example, $P_e = (.60)^2 + (.05)^2 + (.10)^2 + (.20)^2 + (.03)^2 + (.02)^2 = .41$. If the pair of coders had agreed on P_o of 80% of their judgments, the index of the inter-coder agreement would be:

$$\pi = \frac{0.80 - .41}{1 - .41} = 0.66$$

Reference

Bennett, E. M., Alpert, R., & Goldstein, A. C. (1954). Communications through limited response questioning. *Public Opinion Quarterly 18, 3*:303–308.

*Scott's π is that special case of Krippendorff's α for nominal data (as distinct from data with ordinal, interval, and ratio metric), two coders (as opposed to many, including missing data), and large sample sizes. See Krippendorff, K. (2004:221–250). *Content analysis: An introduction to its methodology* (2nd ed.). Thousand Oaks, CA: Sage. We reproduce Scott's original proposal here not only for historical reasons but because it explains the coefficient in simple terms and describes an easily hand-calculable coefficient for situations most commonly encountered in content analyses. For comparing π with other coefficients, see reading 6.2, this volume. For computing α, see A. F. Hayes and Krippendorff, K. (2007). "Answering the Call for a Standard Reliability Measure for Coding Data." *Communication Methods and Measures 1*,1:77–89 and http://www.asc.upenn.edu/usr/krippendorff/dogs.html (accessed 2008.3.3).

6.2

Testing the Reliability of Content Analysis Data

What Is Involved and Why

Klaus Krippendorff*

What Is Reliability?

In the most general terms, reliability is the extent to which data can be trusted to represent the phenomena of interest rather than spurious ones. Sources of unreliability are many. Measuring instruments may malfunction, be influenced by irrelevant circumstances of their use, or misread. Content analysts may disagree on the readings of a text. Coding instructions may not be clear. The definitions of categories may be ambiguous or do not seem applicable to what they are supposed to describe. Coders may get tired, become inattentive to important details, or are diversely prejudiced. Unreliable data can lead researchers to mistaken conclusions about the phenomena of their interest.

Especially where humans observe, read, analyze, describe, or code phenomena of interest, researchers need to assure themselves that the data that emerge from that process are trustworthy. Those interested in the results of empirical research expect assurances that the data that led to them were not biased. Moreover, as a requirement of publication, respectable journals demand evidence that the data underlying published findings are reliable indeed.

In the social sciences, two compatible concepts of reliability are in use.

- From the perspective of *measurement theory*, which models itself by how mechanical measuring instruments function, reliability means that a method of generating data is free of influences by circumstances that are extraneous to processes of observation, description, or measurement. Here, reliability tests provide researchers the assurance that their data are not the result of spurious causes.

*Expanded "recommendations" from Krippendorff, K. (2004). Reliability in content analysis: Some common misconceptions and recommendations. *Human Communication Research 30,*3:411–433.

- From the perspective of *interpretation theory,* reliability means that the members of a scientific community agree on talking about the same phenomena, that their data are about something agreeably real, not fictional. Measurement theory ensures the same, albeit implicitly. Unlike measurement theory, however, interpretation theory acknowledges that researchers may have diverse backgrounds, interests, and theoretical perspectives, which lead them to interpret data differently. Plausible differences in interpretations are not considered evidence of unreliability. But when data are taken as evidence of phenomena that are independent of a researcher's involvement—for example, historical events, mass media effects, or statistical facts—unreliability becomes manifest in the inability to triangulate diverse claims, ultimately in irreconcilable differences among researchers as to what their data mean. Data that lead one researcher to regard them as evidence for "A" and another as evidence for "not A"—without explanations for why they see them that way—erode an interpretive community's trust in them.

Both conceptions of reliability involve demonstrating agreement, in the first instance, among the results of independently working measuring instruments, researchers, readers, or coders who convert the same set of phenomena into data and, in the second instance, consistency among independent researchers' claims concerning what their data mean.

What is Important When Testing Reliability?

Reliability of either kind is established by demonstrating agreement among data-making efforts by different means—measuring instruments, observers, or coders—or triangulation of several researchers' claims concerning what given data suggest. Following are five conceptual issues that content analysts need to consider when testing or evaluating reliability:

Reproducible Coding Instructions

The key to reliable content analyses is *reproducible coding instructions.* All phenomena afford multiple interpretations. Texts typically support alternative interpretations or readings. Content analysts, however, tend to be interested in only a few, not all. When several coders are employed in generating comparable data, especially large volumes and/or over some time, they need to focus their attention on what is to be studied. Coding instructions are intended to do just this. They must delineate the phenomena of interest and define the recording units to be described in analyzable terms, the categories relevant to the research project, and their organization into a system of separate variables—also called a data language.

Obviously, coding instructions must be understandable to those who are asked to apply them. However, in content analysis, they serve three purposes: (a) They operationalize or spell out the procedures for coders to connect their observations or readings to the formal terms of an intended analysis. (b) After data were generated accordingly, they provide researchers with the ability to link each individual datum and the whole data set to the raw or no-longer-present phenomena of interest. And (c), they serve as the medium of communication, enabling other researchers to reproduce the data-making effort or add to existing data. In content analysis, reliability tests establish the reproducibility of the coding instructions elsewhere, at different times, employing different coders who work under diverse conditions, none of which should influence the data that these coding instructions are intended to generate.

The importance of good coding instructions cannot be underestimated. Typically, their development undergoes several iterations: initial formulation; application on a small sample of data; tests of their reliability on all variables; interviews with coders to access the conceptions that cause disagreements; reformulation, making the instruction more specific and coder-friendly; and so on until the instructions are reliable. Coders may also need training. For data making to be reproducible elsewhere, training schedules and manuals need to be communicable together with the coding instructions.

Appropriate Reliability Data

Content analysts are well advised not to confuse the *universe of phenomena* of their ultimate research interest; the *sample* selected for studying these phenomena, the data to be analyzed in place of that universe; and the *reliability data* generated to assess the reliability of the sample of data.

Reliability data may be visualized as a coder-by-units table containing the categories of any one variable (Krippendorff, 2004:221ff). Its recording units—the set of distinct phenomena that coders are instructed to categorize, scale, or describe—must be representative of the data whose reliability is in question (not necessarily of the larger population of phenomena of ultimate interest). In addition, the coders, at least two but ideally many, must be typical if not representative of the population of potential coders whose qualifications content analysts need to stipulate.* Finally, the entries in the cells of a reliability data table must be independent of each other in two ways. (a) Coders must work separately (they may not consult each other on how they judge given units), and (b) recording units must be distinct, judged and described independent of each other, and hence countable.

Testing the reliability of coding instructions before using them to generate the data for a research project is essential. However, an initial test, even when performed on a sample of the units in the data, is not necessarily generalizable to all the data to be analyzed. The performance of coders may diverge over time, what the categories mean for them may drift, and new coders may enter the process. Reliability data—the sample used to measure agreement—must be representative of and sampled throughout the process of generating the data, especially of a larger project. Some researchers avoid the uncertainty of inferring the reliability of their data from the agreement found in a subset of them by duplicating the coding of all data and calculating the reliability for the whole set. Where this is too costly, the minimum size of the reliability data may be determined by a table found in Krippendorff (2004:240). Since reproducibility demands that coders be interchangeable, a variable number of coders may be employed in the process, coding different sets of recording units—provided there is enough duplication for inferring the reliability of the data in question.

An Agreement Measure With Valid Reliability Interpretations

Content analysts need to employ a suitable statistic, an *agreement coefficient,* one that is capable of measuring the agreements among the values or categories used to describe the given set of recording units. Such a coefficient must yield values on *a scale with at least two points of meaningful reliability interpretations:* (a) *perfect agreement* among all coders and on each recording unit, without exceptions, usually set to 1 and indicative of perfect reliability, and (b) *chance agreement*—the complete absence of correlation between the categories used by all coders and the set of units recorded—usually set to zero and interpreted as the total absence of reliability. Agreement coefficients suitable for assessing reliability must register *all* conceivable sources of unreliability, including the proclivity of coders to interpret the given categories differently. The values they yield must also be comparable across different variables, with unequal numbers of categories and different levels of measurement (metrics).

While limited to two coders, large sample sizes and nominal data, Scott's (1955) π (pi)** satisfies these conditions, and so does its

---

*In academic research, students are often recruited as coders. Students constitute an easily specifiable population, differing mainly in academic specialization, language competencies, carefulness, and specialized training for the job of coding. Content analysts also make use of experts—psychiatrists for coding therapeutic discourse, nurses for coding medical practices, or specially trained coders. The choice of coders can affect the validity of the measured reliability. For example acquaintances of the content analyst may well yield higher reliability but are unlikely to be found elsewhere. The choice of coders should be limited by the requirement that they be interchangeable and, hence, available elsewhere to reproduce the data-making process.

**See reading 6.1, this volume.

generalization to many coders, Siegel and Castellan's (1988:284-291) K. Krippendorff's (2004: 211–243) α (alpha) goes beyond π and K by handling any number of coders; nominal, ordinal, interval, ratio, and other metrics; and in addition, missing data and small sample sizes. It also generalizes several other coefficients known for their reliability interpretations in specialized situations, including π (Hayes & Krippendorff, 2007).

Some content analysts have used statistics other than the two recommended here. In light of the foregoing, it is important to understand what they measure and where they fail. To start, there are the familiar correlation or association coefficients—for example, Pearson's product moment correlation, chi-square tests, and Cronbach's (1951) alpha—and there are agreement coefficients. Correlation or association coefficients measure 1.000 when the categories provided by two coders are perfectly predictable from each other (e.g., in the case of interval data, when they occupy any regression line between two coders as variables). Predictability has little to do with agreement, however. Agreement coefficients, by contrast, measure 1.000 when all categories match without exception (e.g., they occupy the 45-degree regression line exactly). Only measures of agreement can indicate when data are perfectly reliable; *correlation and association statistics cannot, which makes them inappropriate for assessing the reliability of data.*

Regarding the zero point of the scale that agreement coefficients define, one can again distinguish two broad classes of coefficients, raw or percent agreement, including Osgood's (1959:44) and Holsti's (1969:140) measures, and chance-corrected agreement measures. Percent agreement is zero when the categories used by coders never match. Statistically, 0% agreement is almost as unexpected as 100% agreement. It signals a condition explicitly excluded by the definition of reliability data, the condition of coders communicating with each other and agreeing to disagree in effect. This condition can hardly occur when coders work separately and apply the same coding instruction to the same units of analysis. It follows that 0% agreement has no meaningful reliability interpretation. On the percent agreement scale, chance agreement occupies no definite point either. It can occupy any point between close to 0% and close to 100% and becomes progressively more difficult to achieve the more categories are available for coding.* Thus, *percent agreement cannot indicate whether reliability is high or low.* The convenience of its calculation, often cited as its advantage, does not compensate for the meaninglessness of its scale.

Chance-corrected agreement coefficients with meaningful reliability interpretations should indicate not only when reliability is perfect but also when it is absent. Reliability can be regarded as absent when units of analysis are coded blindly, for example, by throwing dice rather than responding to their properties. When reliability is absent, the coders' use of categories bears no relation to the phenomena to be categorized, leaving researchers clueless as to what their data mean. However, here, too, two concepts of chance must be distinguished.**

First, Benini's (1901) β (beta) and Cohen's (1960) κ (kappa) define chance as the statistical independence of two coders' use of categories—just as correlation and association statistics do. Under this condition, the categories used by one coder are not predictable from those used by the other, regardless of the coders' proclivity to use categories differently.

*For example, when coding with two categories, chance agreement can be anywhere between 50% and nearly 100%. When coding with 10 categories, chance agreement ranges between 10% and nearly 100%. Thus, 99% agreement could signal perfectly chance or almost reliable data. One would not know.

**Scott (1955), also reproduced in reading 6.1, discusses and discounts a third concept of chance, invoked by Bennett, Alpert, and Goldstein (1954). Realizing that the difficulties of achieving agreements increase with the number of categories available for coding, these authors propose a coefficient S to account for this number. Their conception of chance is a function neither of the distribution of categories found in the data, nor of the statistical independence of coders, but of the number of categories chosen by the researcher. The latter is arbitrary and enables the researcher to manipulate the value of S—as Scott makes clear.

Second, Scott's π and Krippendorff's-α, by contrast, treat coders interchangeably and define chance as the statistical independence of the phenomena—the set of recording units under consideration—and the categories collectively used to describe them. In other words, whereas the zero point of β and κ represents a relationship between two coders, the zero point of π and α represents a relationship between the data and the phenomena in place of which the data are meant to stand. By not responding to individual differences in coders' proclivity of using the given categories, β and κ fail to account for disagreements due to this proclivity. This has the effect of deluding researchers about the reliability of their data by yielding higher agreement measures when coders *disagree* on the distribution of categories in the data and lower measures when they *agree!* Popularity of κ notwithstanding, *Cohen's kappa is simply unsuitable as a measure of the reliability of data.*

Finally, how do π and α differ? Scott corrected the above-mentioned flaws of percent agreement by entering the percent agreement expected by chance into his definition of π—just as β and κ do, but with an inappropriate concept of chance. As chance-corrected percent agreement measures, β, κ, and π are all confined to the conditions under which percent agreement can be calculated, that is, two coders, nominal data, and large sample sizes. Krippendorff's α is not a mere correction of percent agreement. While α includes π as a special case, α measures disagreements instead and is, hence, not so limited. As already stated, it is applicable to any number of coders, acknowledges metrics other than nominal, accounts for missing data, and is sensitive to small sample sizes.

In assessing agreement, it is also important to match the metric of the data, their level of measurement, and what the agreement coefficient is designed to measure. For example, if π or the α for nominal data were applied to data whose values are ordered, the information in their ordering would be ignored. Disagreement among the neighboring values of an interval scale would be given the same weight as disagreements between values that are far apart, and hence an agreement coefficient designed for nominal metrics would be an invalid indicator of the reliability of ordered data. The same is true when using an agreement coefficient designed for metrics more powerful than the data at hand. For example, when the α for interval data is applied to nominal variables, whose categories happen to numbered, the amount of agreement measured depends on the arbitrary numbering and therefore cannot serve as a valid measure of reliability. A frequent mistake is to apply interval coefficients to ordinal data—not just in reliability assessments.

The foregoing evaluation of statistical indices is to caution against the uninformed application of so-called reliability measures. There is software that offers its users several such statistics without revealing what they measure and where they fail, encouraging the disingenuous practice of computing all of them and reporting those whose numerical results show their data in the most favorable light. Before accepting claims that a statistic measures the reliability of data, content analysts should critically examine its mathematical structure for conformity to the above stated requirements.

A Minimum Acceptable Level of Reliability

An acceptable level of agreement below which data have to be rejected as too unreliable must be chosen. Except for perfect agreement on all recording units, there is no magical number. The choice of a cutoff point should reflect the potential costs of drawing invalid conclusions from unreliable data. When human lives hang on the results of a content analysis, whether they inform a legal decision, lead to the use of a drug with dangerous side effects, or tip the scale from peace to war, decision criteria have to be set far higher than when a content analysis is intended to support mere scholarly explorations. To ensure that the data under consideration are at least similarly interpretable by researchers, starting with the coders employed in generating the data, it is customary to require $\alpha \geq .800$. Only where tentative conclusions are deemed acceptable may an $\alpha \geq .667$ suffice (Krippendorff, 2004: 241).*

Ideally, the cutoff point should be justified by examining the effects of unreliable data on the validity and seriousness of the conclusions drawn from them.

To ensure that reliability data are large enough to provide the needed assurance, the confidence intervals of the agreement measure should be consulted. Testing the null hypothesis—that agreement is *not* due to chance—is insufficient. Reliable data should be very far from chance, but not significantly deviate from perfect agreement. Therefore, the probability q that agreement could be below the required minimum provides a statistical decision criterion analog to traditional significance tests (Krippendorff, 2004:238).

Testing the Appropriate Distinctions

Unless data are perfectly reliable, each *distinction that matters should be tested for its reliability.* Most agreement coefficients, including π and α, provide one measure for each variable of a larger data set and treat all values of that variable alike by averaging their disagreements. Depending on what a research needs to show, assessing the reliability of larger data sets variable by variable may not always be sufficient.

- When researchers intend to correlate content analysis variables with each other or with other variables, obtaining separate agreements for each variable is appropriate, mainly because these variables are then analyzed whole as well.** Content analysts may use their data differently, however, and then need to tailor the agreement measures to ascertain the reliabilities that matter to how their data are put to use.

- When some distinctions are unimportant and subsequently ignored for analytical reasons—for example, by lumping several categories into one—reliability should be tested not on the original but on the transformed data, as the latter are closer to what is being analyzed or inferred and needs to be reliable as such.

- When individual categories matter—for example, when their frequencies are being compared—the reliability of these comparisons (i.e., each category against all others lumped into one) should be evaluated for each category.

- When a system of several variables is intended to support a conclusion—for example, when these data enter a regression equation or multivariate analysis in which variables work together and matter alike—the smallest agreement measured among them should be taken as an index of the reliability of the whole system. This rule might seem overly conservative. However, it conforms to the recommendation to drop all variables from further considerations that do not meet the minimum acceptable level of reliability.

- For the same reasons, the averaging of several agreement measures, while tempting, can be seriously misleading. Averaging would allow the high reliabilities of easily coded clerical variables to hide the typically lower reliabilities of the more difficult to code variables of analytical importance and unwittingly mislead researchers into believing their data are reliable when they are not. Average agreement coefficients of separately used variables should not be obtained or reported and cannot serve as a decision criterion.

As already suggested, pre-testing the reliability of coding instructions before settling on their use is helpful, while testing the reliability of the whole data-making process is decisive. However, after data are obtained, it is

*These standards are suggested for π and α. For other agreement measures different cutoff points may apply. In choosing a cutoff point, one should realize that for nominal data, $\alpha = 0.8$ means that 80% of the units recorded are perfectly reliable, while 20% are the results of chance. Not all research projects can afford such margins of error.

**In measures of association, correlation, analyses of variance, and so on, deviations from expectations are averaged. This is mathematically compatible with averaging the above-chance agreements associated with the values of a variable, as in π and α. The agreement measured by π and α therefore is a good index of the reliability of subsequently analyzed whole variables.

not impossible to improve their reliability by removing from them the distinctions that are found unreliable, for example, joining categories that are easily confused, transforming scale values with large systematic errors, or ignoring variables in subsequent analyses that do not meet acceptable reliability standards. Yet, resolving apparent disagreements by majority rule among three or more coders, employing expert judges to decide on coder disagreements, or similar means does not provide evidence of added reliability. Such practices may well make researchers feel more confident about their data, but without duplication of this very process and obtaining the agreements or disagreements observed between them, only the agreement measure that was last measured is interpretable as a valid index of the reliability of the analyzed data and needs to be reported as such (Krippendorff, 2004:219).

Relations to Validity

Finally, reliability must not be confused with validity. *Validity* is the attribute of propositions—measurements, research results, or theories—that are corroborated by independently obtained evidence. Content analyses can be validated, for example, when the reality constructions of the authors (sources) of analyzed texts concur with the findings, the effects on their readers (audiences) are as predicted, or the indices computed from them correlate with what the analysts claim they signify. *Reliability,* by contrast, is the attribute of data to stand in place of phenomena that are distinct, unambiguous, and real—what they are cannot be divorced from how they are described. In short, validity concerns truth; reliability concerns trust.

Since an analysis of reliable data may well be mistaken, *reliability cannot guarantee validity.* Inasmuch as unreliable data contain spurious variation and errors in the process of their creation, their analysis has the potential of leading to invalid conclusions. In fact, for nominal data, $(1 - \alpha)$ is the proportion of data that is unrelated to the phenomena that gave rise to them. This suggests being cautious about conclusions drawn from unreliable data. *Unreliability can limit validity.*

Within the proportion $(1 - \alpha)$, one can distinguish two kinds of disagreements, systematic and random (Krippendorff, 2008). Systematic disagreements, or spurious structures in the data, can be explained, for example, in terms of diverse coder prejudices toward the phenomena as described, ambiguities of particular terms in the coding instructions, or statistical associations among coders who should have been working independently. Systematic disagreements tend to encourage Type I errors, i.e., increasing the likelihood of rejecting a null hypothesis when it should have been accepted. Random disagreements, by contrast, introduce random variation into the data that cannot be explained and tend to encourage Type II errors, i.e., increasing the likelihood of accepting a null hypothesis when it would have been rejected in the absence of random disagreements.

Without the availability of validating evidence, reliability is the best safeguard against the likelihood of invalid research results.

For calculating α, consult Krippendorff (2004:211–256) or http://www.asc.upenn.edu/usr/krippendorff/dogs.html (accessed 2008.3.3).

References

Bennett, E. M., Alpert, R., & Goldstein, A. C. (1954). Communications through limited response questioning. *Public Opinion Quarterly 18, 3*:303–308.

Benini, R. (1901). *Principii di Demographia.* Firenze: G. Barbera. No. 29 of Manuali Barbera di Scienze Giuridiche Sociali e Politiche.

Cohen, J. (1960). A coefficient of agreement for nominal scales. *Educational and Psychological Measurement 20:*37–46.

Cronbach, L. J. (1951). Coefficient alpha and the internal structure of tests. *Psychometrica 16:*297–334.

Hayes, A. F., & Krippendorff, K. (2007). Answering the call for a standard reliability measure for coding data. *Communication Methods and Measures 1,* 1:77–89.

Holsti, O. R. (1969). *Content analysis for the social sciences and humanities.* Reading, MA: Addison-Wesley.

Krippendorff, K. (2004). *Content analysis: An introduction to its methodology* (2nd ed.). Thousand Oaks, CA: Sage.

Krippendorff, K. (2008 in press). Systematic and random disagreement and the reliability of nominal data. *Communication Methods and Measures.*

Osgood, C. E. (1959). The representational model and relevant research methods. In I. de Sola Pool (Ed.), *Trends in content analysis* (pp. 33–88). Urbana: University of Illinois Press.

Scott, W. A. (1955). Reliability of content analysis: The case of nominal scale coding. *Public Opinion Quarterly 19:*321–325.

Siegel, S., & Castellan, N. J. (1988). *Nonparametric statistics for the behavioral sciences* (2nd ed.). Boston: McGraw-Hill.

6.3

THE PROBLEM OF VALIDATING CONTENT ANALYSIS

IRVING JANIS*

INTRODUCTION

Any analytic technique, whether it be a means of measuring visual acuity, manual dexterity, "verbal" intelligence, political attitudes or references of a particular type in a communication, is of dubious value until it can be shown that the results obtained by using it describe what they purport to describe. This is the problem of *validation.*

In non-technical language, a measuring instrument is said to have *validity* if it measures what it purports to measure; it is said to have *reliability* if it gives the same results consistently (Janis, Fadner, & Janowitz, 1943).

The validity of a measuring device is usually studied by comparing the results or measures obtained from it with those obtained by another device, the validity of which is already established for measuring the same characteristic. If such a measuring device of established validity is not available, and this is often the case, the problem of establishing validity becomes difficult. In cases of direct measures, validity is self-evident. In fact, we call those measures direct, which unquestionably measure precisely what we intend them to.

SOURCES OF ERRORS IN CONTENT-ANALYSIS PROCEDURES

The main purpose of this paper is to consider the means by which evidence may be obtained to demonstrate that content analysis techniques do in fact describe what they purport to describe. In the case of sign-vehicle analysis* there is little difficulty with respect to validation, because such techniques provide a *direct* measure of physical occurrences. The analyst's operations involve simple perceptual discriminations: determining the presence or absence of a given physical configuration and counting the number, which are present. Hence, no special validation procedures are necessary. Of course, the reliability

*From Janis, I. L. (1965). The problem of validating content analysis. In H. D. Lasswell, N. Leites, & Associates (Eds.), *Language of politics* (pp. 55–82). Cambridge: MIT Press.

**The author uses semiotic terminology throughout this discussion. By sign-vehicles, the author refers to mere character strings, including words, which are distinguished by being same or different, without regard to their meanings.

of the analyst should be checked, in order to preclude the possibility that he has misunderstood or misapplied the rules of the analysis. This is the only condition necessary, to warrant the conclusion that a sign-vehicle analysis measures what it purports to measure: the frequency of occurrence of a given sign-vehicle or of a given set of sign-vehicles.

The problem of validating semantical content analysis,* on the other hand, is an extremely difficult one. In designation analysis, attribution analysis and assertion analysis, the operations require judgments of meaning—an extremely complex and variable type of human response. In estimating the meaning that would be attributed to the sign-vehicles, either by a given audience or by a given communicator, the analyst's judgments are guided to a large extent by the rules of the content analysis. We may expect that such estimates can be made with a fair degree of accuracy for communications which employ everyday discourse, inasmuch as there is a high degree of constant and generally accepted signification for the signs of a language. Nevertheless it is inevitable that borderline cases will arise for which the meaning is not clear-cut, and for which the content analysis rules do not provide a ready answer.

This is especially true when one is classifying characterizors in carrying out an assertions analysis. A typical characterizor category, for example, is "attributions of dishonesty." Consider a statement of the following type: "Political leader X denied that he was negotiating a military alliance, whereas in fact he was doing so." To some people who read this sentence, the words may signify that X was dishonest—he lied to the public. To others the words may signify that X was merely being guided by political expediency. There may be disagreement among audience-members as to what this sentence asserts about X, in terms of dishonesty. Obviously, then, if one classified this sentence one way or the other, it could not be said that this classification would represent the signification which the sentence has for the *entire* audience; one would not even be sure as to which signification this sentence has for the majority of the audience. Moreover, different audiences might show characteristic differences as to what these particular words mean in terms of the moral standard of honesty-dishonesty.

Let us suppose that the content analyst, because he is aware that such borderline cases may arise, sets up a special rule: Assertions to the effect that there is a discrepancy between what is said about one's actions and what is actually done, are to be classified as attributions of dishonesty. In this case, the content analyst would have little difficulty in making a decision, and incidentally there would be high reliability among analysts, because the rule requires that this sentence be classified as an attribution of dishonesty. But following this rule would give an erroneous result in this case if the sentence signifies "expediency" rather than "dishonesty" to the audience.

From the discussion of this example, it is seen that there are two main potential sources of error in estimating the significations attributed to signs by an audience:

1. The particular terms may be ambiguous for the audience; several different meanings may be attributed to the signs by different audience members.

2. Different audiences may attribute different meanings to the signs. If the content analysis results are correlated with certain responses of a particular audience, the meanings attributed to the contents by that particular audience may be different from those which the content analyst estimated.

Because content-analysis results attempt to describe meanings attributed to signs by the

*In earlier work (Janis, 1943), the author defines semantical content analysis as a classification of sign-vehicles (recording units) in terms of their significations (meanings). He distinguishes:

(a) *designations,* that is, references to objects (persons, things, groups, or concepts);

(b) *attributions,* that is, characterizations (e.g., dishonesty) regardless of where they are applied;

(c) *assertions,* that is, themes involving how particular objects are characterized (e.g., a dishonest foreign policy).

audience as a whole (or by the overwhelming majority of audience members) difficulties of the first type are unavoidable. If the signs have two different meanings for equally large sections of the audience, either way in which the signs are classified will be incorrect.

In order to minimize such errors, it appears best to weight in some appropriate way assertions that have this sort of ambiguity. In cases where the classification scheme is dichotomous and the hypothesis under investigation deals with the ratio between the two categories (e.g., honesty vs. dishonesty), classifying as neutral an assertion for which the audience's signification responses* are estimated as split into the two dichotomous categories would appear to be the simplest solution. We might consider this as excluding a fractional occurrence of an assertion from both categories.

In cases like the above example (dishonesty vs. expediency), where only one of the categories is under investigation (dishonesty), not counting a partial occurrence of an assertion in this category is not balanced by not counting the alternative category. Nevertheless, one might still decide to classify such ambiguous assertions as *neutral,* because it would be a more serious error to give them equal weight as clear-cut assertions. Moreover, if an approximately equal number of ambiguous cases arise for those categories that are to be compared, the omission of fractional occurrences is balanced and has little effect. This is one of the grounds for the frequent exclusion of the use of rules, which require taking account of *implicit* assertions in content analysis, because implicit meanings have a high degree of ambiguity. By requiring the analyst to restrict his categories to occurrences of explicit references (manifest meanings), errors of commission are avoided; but some errors of omission are inevitable.

If it appears that errors of omission will not be of negligible frequency, the content analyst can attempt to set up numerical weights to be assigned to assertions, which are estimated to be ambiguous. These weights would be fractional values, if unambiguous assertions are counted as unity.

Another possibility—especially if the content analyst is aware of a high probability of many intra-audience differences in their signification responses to the same assertions—is to narrow down the audience whose significations he is attempting to describe, so that signification responses will be more homogeneous.

The second source of errors, inter-audience differences, is much more likely to occur but, fortunately, is easier to handle. Social scientists are often aware of characteristic differences in meaning which words have for different social groups. Signification differentials are known to occur for various national, ethnic, regional, occupational and income groups. These differences have not been systemically elaborated, nor is it likely that they will be formulated in the near future, in view of the tedious detail, which would be necessary. But content-analysts can recruit personnel (coders) who are aware of these differences and able to carry out the content-analysis procedures. Obviously, in order to minimize errors arising from the peculiarities of the signification responses of any particular audience, content analysts should at least formulate the purpose of their experiments (including the) *audience* they are considering. Once the audience is defined, the content analyst is unlikely to overlook gross peculiarities in the signification responses of that audience.

The above discussion of errors in estimating signification responses of sign-interpreters is concerned only with those content-analysis experiments, which relate content characteristics to pragmatical reactions of the audience. For those experiments that relate intentions or other characteristics of the *communicator* to the content characteristics of his communications, the content analyst is concerned with

*The semiotic term *signification response* may be translated as "reading," here, how an audience "reads" a text. In psycholinguistic mediation theory, signification responses are an individual's internal responses to a sign-vehicle, which may or may not cause a behavioral or pragmatic response to that sign-vehicle.

estimating the meanings attributed to the signs by the *communicator,* i.e., the semantical meanings which the communicator is attempting to convey. Sources of error in this case are similar; the sign-classification procedures may require taking into account certain details of the personal history of the communicator, in order to take care of eccentric, personalized meanings.

From this discussion, it is clear that there are many sources of errors, which affect validity. The extent to which a content analysis technique provides results which describe the frequency of occurrence of *all* the signs that belong to each class of signs set up in the classification scheme—excluding those which do not belong to the given class—depends on the frequency with which errors occur. *Systematic errors* may arise because of procedural rules that may entail faulty classification. *Spurious errors,* which are attributable to unknown differences in significations or to the observational standpoint of the content analyst, may arise because of incorrect judgments of signification responses. The latter type of error is probably even more frequent. One of the chief advantages of precise and detailed definitions of the content analysis categories is the reduction of spurious errors of judgment. Of course, the spurious errors may simply be replaced by systematic errors, but the latter type is more easily eliminated, as will be seen in the discussion below.

. . . . [T]he results of any particular content analysis may be open to question on the grounds that so many systematic and/or spurious errors have been made as to give false frequencies. How does one know whether these errors have occurred sufficiently rarely so that the content-analysis results describe what they purport to describe?

It is necessary to discover some procedure by means of which the validity of a semantical content analysis can be tested. Without such a validation procedure it is impossible to give a rational justification for the operations of semantical content analysis. It would be necessary to rely solely upon the *opinion* of the content analysts themselves that semantical content-analysis techniques estimate signification responses correctly. Thus, when a content analysis reports that a given publication contains 25 references which characterize German foreign policy as dishonest, we would be forced to accept or reject this frequency on the basis of our *a priori* faith in the analyst and in his procedures; we would have no means of knowing, a) whether each of the 25 references would in fact be interpreted in that way by a given audience, or b) whether the 25 references were in fact the only references in the publication which would be interpreted in that way. If there were errors of the first sort, the frequency reported (25 references) would be too high; if there were errors of the second sort, the frequency reported would be too low. The purpose of a method of validation is to provide evidence that both sorts of errors occur infrequently.

Productivity and the Problem of Validation

One possible way to [solve] the problem of validation would be to reduce semantical content analysis to sign-vehicle analysis. This would be a matter of replacing the rules that define the specific kinds of references, which are to be counted as falling into a given category with rules, which specify sets of sign-vehicles. If this could be done, then designations analysis, attributions analysis and assertions analysis would no longer require the analyst to take account of meanings; such analyses would be sign-vehicle analysis and, accordingly, would constitute direct measures of the frequency of occurrence of a set of sign-vehicles. Thus, validation procedures would be unnecessary.

The main difficulty lies in the fact that the semantical signification of a given sign depends upon the linguistic *context.* The reduction would require not merely the listing of all sign-vehicles, which elicit more or less equivalent significations, but also the listing of the sign-vehicles, which make up every possible context in which those sign-vehicles occur. For example, there are thousands of arrangements of sign-vehicles, which provide linguistic contexts for the explicit characterization of dishonesty. The magnitude of the task is so great that it is highly improbable that such a reduction will ever be carried out, particularly for any assertions-analysis technique.*

It is useful at this point to examine the concept of *productivity* as applied to content analysis. To say that a content analysis technique has a high degree of productivity is to say that the categories of the particular classification system occur as variables in many true empirical propositions. Productivity is a major component of what is vaguely referred to as "scientific significance." It provides an answer to the question that is so often raised whenever a new research technique is presented "So what?"

A content-analysis procedure is productive insofar as the results it yields are found to be correlated with other variables. Whenever there is a substantial correlation between two variables, one variable may be regarded as *an indicator* of the other, because it is possible to predict, within known limits of error, the value of the second variable from the first. We may say, then, that a technique is productive to the extent that the results it provides serve as *indicators* of other variables.** Thus, a content-analysis technique would be highly productive if its results served as indicators of such variables as a) intentions of the communicator to produce favorable attitudes toward a foreign country, b) periods of severe frustration for the political organization with which the communicators are affiliated, c) "unconscious" guilt feelings on the part of the speaker, d) changes in attitudes toward democratic practices on the part of an audience, and (e) feelings of insecurity about the future on the part of the audience, etc.

Yet, too few content analysis studies have been made to permit empirical statements about the relative productivity of the various types of content analysis procedures. One may predict, based on existing knowledge about communicative processes, that sign-vehicle analysis will prove to have a low degree of productivity.[1]

Designations analysis may be expected to be more productive than sign-vehicle analysis but nevertheless restricted. In a sense, designations analysis amounts to describing the "exposure-attention" of a communication—that is, the subject matters which are brought to the focus of attention of the audience. We may expect designations analysis to be productive in the study of phenomena related to attention, interests, taboos, preferences with respect to subject matter, and the like. Therefore, designations analysis will probably be productive only in establishing "key symbols" as indicators of relatively non-persistent, peripheral types of behavior, e.g., correlations with retention rather than with changes in attitude.

Attributions analysis, since it does not provide information about the subject matters to which characterizations are applied, will probably have low productivity, as far as political analysis is concerned. On the other hand, it may be productive in the study of certain aspects of character structure, particularly of deviant-personality types. Evidence of pessimism-optimism, generalized aggressiveness, preferred standards (e.g., use of religious standards as against efficiency in evaluating objects), etc. may be obtained by an attributions analysis of an individual's communications. By indicating which characterizations are most frequently used, attributions analysis should prove useful in determining how an individual perceives his environment.

Assertions analysis will probably be found to be the most productive type of content analysis, inasmuch as the "thematic content" corresponds most nearly to the overall signification of a communication. Thus, the signification-*gestalt* for a magazine article—the answer which most people would give when asked what the article has to say—is in terms of how certain objects are characterized (e.g., "the article says that the war will be over within a year"). The assertions found in a communication are the primary content

---

*This is the path taken by computational content analysis, the *General Inquirer* (see reading 7.1, this volume, for example). It exhibits the very threats to semantic validity that the author describes.

**Today we call this form of validity "correlative." See Krippendorff, K. (2004:320ff). *Content analysis: An introduction to its methodology* (2nd ed.). Thousand Oaks, CA: Sage.

indicators of the intentions and motives of the communicator. Similarly, the effects that a communication produces on an audience are primarily due to the assertions content. We may expect, therefore, many correlations between the results of assertions analysis and pragmatical responses, which are of major political and psychological significance.

Content categories are unlikely to be productive unless they contain homogeneous significations. The grounds for this proposition, which is based on existing knowledge about the communicative process, will be discussed below. This proposition may be formulated as two criteria to be applied in setting up the rules for any content analysis: 1) All sign-vehicles or groups of sign-vehicles which are classified into the same category refer to the same thing; 2) all sign-vehicles or groups of sign-vehicles which are excluded from a given category, do not refer to the same thing as do the sign vehicles which are included. In the case of a designations analysis, for example, these criteria would be satisfied if: a) each term that, according to the rules, is classified as referring to Germany actually does so, and b) no term which is not classified as referring to Germany actually does so. If the first criterion is violated, errors of *commission* are made; if the second criterion is violated, errors of *omission* are made.

A Method of Indirect Validation

. . . As far as I know, there are no techniques available for the *direct* measurement of signification response. There are a number of possible ways in which signification responses might be determined, for example, by means of a questionnaire which requires each subject to indicate the (semantical) category which is most appropriate for given sign-vehicles. If such a technique were available, it would be possible to make a *direct* test of the validity of content analysis procedures by presenting a representative sample of the contents to a representative sample of the audience or communicator.

. . . [I]n view of the enormous difficulties involved in obtaining an unambiguous delineation of the semantical meanings which occur spontaneously when words are perceived, [w]e are impelled, therefore, to look for some *indirect* method of validating content analysis procedures.

It appears to me that the same principle, which is used in testing definitions in everyday life, may be applied as the basis of indirect validation of content analysis procedures. In our day-to-day experience with language, one is rarely aware of the process by which we come to accept a given signification response as the appropriate one for a given sign-vehicle. The meaning of a word is inferred from the wide varieties of behaviors, which accompany the use of the word. One infers what is taken account of by the mediation of a sign-vehicle on the basis of the behavioral context in which the sign-vehicle occurs.

When we define a term we specify what is taken into account when that term is perceived by some group of sign-users. Such definitions may be regarded as hypotheses that are to be tested by observing the behavior of those who use the sign. If we find that the stimuli which elicit the use of the term and the responses of those who perceive the term are consistent with our hypothetical definition of that term, we accept that definition as correct. This description of the definitional process, as it operates in everyday life, may be applied to the procedures of semantical content analysis.

Sign-vehicles are classified into different semantical categories on the basis of explicit or implicit definitions. When a sign-vehicle is perceived, it is often possible to observe some particular change in the behavior of the perceiver. These observable modifications in behavior (pragmatical responses) imply an intermediate subjective event, a signification response. Accordingly, the communicative process may be schematized as follows: the communicator's observable reactions to the situation (pragmatical responses of the communicator) → certain signification responses which he attempts to convey to others → production of particular sign-vehicles → particular signification responses of the audience → observable reactions to the signification responses (pragmatical responses of the audience).

The pragmatical responses of the communicator, which lead to the production of sign-vehicles, may be regarded as the behavioral *causes* of the communication; the responses of the audience may be regarded as the *effects* of the communication. When similar pragmatical responses are found to be associated with a given sign-vehicle on different occasions, it is assumed that the same signification response to the sign-vehicle has occurred. When different sign-vehicles, in different linguistic contexts, are associated with the same pragmatical responses, the different sign-vehicles are regarded as equivalent (synonymous).

The basic assumption, which is used in determining meanings, is that relationships among various observable aspects of the communicative process are mediated by signification responses. Different signification responses tend to have different behavioral causes and effects; similar signification responses tend to have similar causes and effects. This is the basis for the two criteria for productivity discussed in the preceding section. Unless the content analyst groups together those sign-vehicles, which have common significations, he or she will not be likely to discover relationships between content characteristics and pragmatical responses. On the other hand, if many relationships are found, it is highly improbable that the content analysis procedures are incorrect in estimating signification responses. On the basis of this view of the communicative process, it appears to me that an indirect method for the validation of semantical content analysis procedures may be derived. This method consists of *inferring validity from productivity.*

If one is able to show that a content analysis procedure provides results, which are correlated with many types of pragmatical responses of sign-interpreters, then it may be concluded that the content analysis procedures correctly describe the signification responses of those sign-interpreters. This inference is made based on an assumption derived from the procedures, which are used in determining meanings in everyday life: Unless the signs have the significations assigned to them by the content analyst, relationships between the classifications frequencies and the responses of the sign-interpreters would not be found. Offhand, this may sound like a rather tenuous assumption. First, there is the possibility of spurious correlations. But this offers little difficulty if we recognize that a single correlation provides but a low degree of probability that the content analysis procedure is valid; that the more correlations yielded by the procedure, the higher the probability that it is valid. Secondly, one might argue that a correlation—if it is not spurious—shows only that the sign-vehicles have *some* meaning for the sign-interpreters, but there is no basis for assuming that correlations show that the sign-vehicles have the particular meaning which the content analysis imputes to them.

This argument may be broken down into two questions: 1) How do we know that the sign-vehicles, which are grouped together, have a common signification for the sign-interpreters? 2) Even if we do know that the content analysis procedures group together sign-vehicles which have a common signification, how do we know that the common signification is correctly specified by the content analyst?

The first question may be answered by considering that the number of possible groupings of sign vehicles is unlimited. Why should a particular grouping of sign-vehicles be found to co-vary with many of the sign-interpreters' pragmatical responses, unless it is because there is a relationship between *significations* and *pragmatical responses?* If such a relationship exists, then it is likely that there is something common to the significations, because not all significations co-vary with those pragmatical responses. Again, the higher the degree of productivity, the higher the probability that each category of the content analysis is a functional class. That is to say, high productivity indicates that the sign-vehicles, which are grouped together, elicit significations that have some characteristic in common, and that those sign-vehicles whose significations do not have the common characteristic are excluded.

The second question is concerned with naming the common characteristic of the significations of the sign-vehicles which are grouped together. This problem is not an important one, because so long as it is established that the content analysis categories are functional classes of signs, the classes may be designated by their entire definition as stated in the procedural rules of the content analysis. In general, there is no need to resort to this.

There is usually no reason for questioning the ability of the content analyst to name correctly the common characteristic of the significations of the sign-vehicles, which fall into the same category. After all, the content analyst knows, when setting up content analysis categories, what characteristics of the significations he or she wants to separate. If the resulting classification scheme is reliable and has proved to be productive, it would be most unlikely that the meaning of the words being classified was misinterpreted.

The assumption therefore appears to me defensible that correlations between content characteristics and pragmatical responses of sign-interpreters imply correct estimation of the signification responses of sign-interpreters. In general, then, the following principle of validation is proposed: *The larger the number of relationships established by use of a content analysis technique, the higher the probability that the procedures estimate signification responses correctly and hence the higher the degree of validity. . . .*

Summary

The problem of validating semantical content analysis is an extremely serious one, because the operations require judgments of *meanings,* which are attributed to the sign-vehicles in a communication by a given audience or by a given communicator. Such judgments may be in error, because the procedural rules may entail faulty classification (systematic errors), or because the content analyst may make incorrect judgments of signification responses in those cases which are not explicitly covered by the rules (*spurious errors*). Without a validation procedure, it would be necessary to accept or reject content analysis results solely upon the basis of *a priori* faith in the analyst and the procedures. The purpose of a method of validation is to provide evidence that systematic and spurious errors occur infrequently.

Since there is no available method for testing directly the significations responses to sign-vehicles, an indirect validation procedure is proposed—namely, inferring validity from productivity. The following principle of validation appears to be defensible: The larger the number of relationships established by use of a content analysis technique, the higher the probability that the procedure estimates signification responses correctly and hence the higher the degree of validity. This indirect method of validation is based on the procedures used for the determination of the meaning of words in everyday life.

The use of this indirect method of validation entails certain consequences for the design of content analysis research. These may be summarized in the form of technological principles:

1. The classification rules should be as explicit as possible.
2. Content analysis procedures—classification rules, rating scales for the purpose of weighting, indices, etc.—can be systematically improved by selecting those which provide the largest correlations between content characteristics and other (pragmatical) variables.
3. Every application of a content analysis technique should put some evidence of validity by showing some relationships between content characteristics and other variables.
4. Content analysis should not be used to disconfirm hypotheses; improbable hypotheses should be ignored.
5. In choosing hypotheses to test by the use of content analysis, the decision should be in favor of those, which most closely approximate the following type of relationship: a quantitative co-variation between a content characteristic and a pragmatical response which is directly mediated by the communication.

Note

1. Grey, Kaplan and Lasswell (1949) refer to "rigid" as against "flexible" procedures in distinguishing between what I have called "sign-vehicle" and "semantical content analysis." [T]heir remarks . . . imply the criterion of productivity: "In general a recurring problem of content analysis is the proper balance to be struck between reliability and significance. We can be completely reliable about the frequency of occurrence of any selected word, but this may be of very trivial importance."

References

Grey, A., Kaplan, D., & Lasswell, H. D. (1949). Recording and context units—Four ways of coding editorial content. In H. D. Lasswell & N. Leites et al. (Eds.), *Language of politics* (pp. 113–126). Cambridge, MA: MIT Press.

Janis, I. L. (1943). Meaning and the study of symbolic behavior. *Psychiatry 6:*425–439.

Janis, I. L., Fadner, R. H., & Janowitz, M. (1943). The reliability of a content analysis technique. *Public Opinion Quarterly 7:*293–296.

6.4

Modes of Observation and the Validation of Interaction Analysis Schemes

M. Scott Poole and Joseph P. Folger*

From a number of different perspectives, the argument has been advanced that researchers should concern themselves with the meanings and functions of communicative acts in human interaction (Cappella, 1977; Fisher, Drecksel, & Werbel, 1979; Lamb, Suomi, & Stephensen, 1979). In pursuit of this goal, interaction analysis procedures have been employed to classify utterances based on categories and theoretical criteria specified prior to observation (for example, see Bales, 1950;** Fisher, 1970; Mabry, 1975; Rogers & Farace, 1975). These schemes are valuable research tools because they yield data that are amenable to powerful statistical and analytical techniques and they encourage systematic analysis of the observer's assumptions prior to data collection.

A central problem in utilizing coding schemes, however, is that of ensuring their validity. A coding system is essentially a translation device that allows investigators to place utterances into theoretical categories. Unless this translation is valid, any conclusions investigators draw are, at best, useless and, at worst, misleading. Surprisingly, little attention has been given to the validation issues surrounding the development and use of interaction analysis schemes. These coding procedures are susceptible to the type of criticism that Ruzicka, Palisi, and Berven (1979:41) level in their recent review of problems in small group research:

> Instrumentation in small group research has been inadequate. Loosely tied to theoretical foundations, themselves often suspect, instruments are of questionable validity. . . .

Although there are no simple solutions to the knotty problems surrounding validation,

*From Poole, M. S., & Folger, J. P. (1981). Modes of observation and the validation of interaction analysis schemes. *Small Group Behavior 12,*4:477–493.

**See reading 2.5, this volume.

we feel that the key to the validation question lies in a closer examination of the observational modes available to a researcher when translating utterance types into theoretical categories. In constructing interaction coding schemes, researchers begin with a set of theoretical constructs and attempt to identify the utterance types that embody the constructs in human interaction. The descriptions of the utterance types are an empirical translation of the theoretically meaningful categories. Besides delineating the utterance categories, however, the researcher chooses a *mode of observation that determines the evidence he or she will use to claim that the utterances occur in the interaction.* The mode of observation does not affect the definition of the coding categories, but it does define what status the categories will hold in the researcher's theory. The mode of observation reflects what the researcher feels is important for explaining social interaction and it delimits the claims a researcher can make with the coded data.

For example, Mabry (1975) developed a coding instrument for assessing content themes in group interaction. The scheme is based on Parsons' systems theory of social action and encodes eight types of symbolic action. One type of symbolic action, particularism, alludes to the individualization of responses and evaluation of actors (Mabry, 1975:291). In defining an utterance category for this construct, Mabry (1975:293) says that particularistic themes are those in which members take "direct account of one another's presence in the situation." He includes "direct supportive or non-supportive, statements, eye and body contact shifts that single out each member from the others and talking about individual contributions" as acts which embody the construct.

In using this utterance category, Mabry relies upon an outside observer's perspective to conclude that an interactant has taken direct account of another's presence. It is an outside observer who will say that a statement or body movement in an interaction is a particularistic behavior. Another researcher interested in coding the particularism construct might identify those behaviors that "take direct account of another's presence" but would rely solely upon the interpretation of each individual in the interaction to claim that a particularistic behavior has occurred. In employing the categories, Mabry has opted for a certain mode of observation that specifies the type of information he will accept as evidence for the occurrence of the utterance categories. His results are summarized from an outside observer's perspective and he makes no claims about the interpretations of the interactants in the task-oriented small groups he studied.

Our objective is to clarify the bases of validity for interaction analysis schemes by proposing that (a) a researcher chooses a mode of observation when translating utterance types into theoretically meaningful categories; (b) there are at least three possible modes of observation that a researcher can adopt; and (c) each mode of observation requires different procedures for validation.

Modes of Observation for the Study of Interaction

There are three modes of observation that an investigator could employ in studying interaction.[1] Each mode focuses on a different aspect of social experience: Experience may be observed from an outsider's view of what is *experienced,* or in terms of the social process of *experiencing,* or from the viewpoint of the *experiencer.* These three modes differ in the kinds of operationalizations they imply. In choosing an observational mode, the researcher becomes committed to a particular way of viewing interaction and to a particular set of methodological assumptions. In this section, we will discuss each of the three modes in terms of its theoretical and methodological assumptions. In the next section, we will consider how one would go about validating category systems for the analysis of interaction in the three modes.[2]

The Experienced Mode

The investigator who chooses the *experienced m*ode chooses to study interaction from the viewpoint of an external observer. The test of a theory in the experienced mode is whether relationships among observable variables defined by the investigator do, in fact, hold as the investigator's theory specifies. The external observer is assumed to have direct access to the variables that figure most importantly in explaining and understanding interaction. Subjects' perceptions do not enter into theories couched in the experienced mode. Variables are operationalized solely in terms of measurement operations, which can be performed by the external observer.

In this view, categories for coding interaction represent different types of external stimuli which participants in an interaction experience. No assumptions are made regarding how the subjects perceive statements that fall into the categories; instead, theories in the experienced mode are concerned solely with explaining interaction in terms of categories as they are specified by the observer and the observer's theory.

The Experiencing Mode

The researcher working within the *experiencing* mode of observation assumes that the key to understanding and explaining interaction lies in characterizing the socially constructed reality that participants in an interaction share. Here the test of a theory depends not only upon whether the hypothesized relationship among theoretical constructs hold, but also upon whether the key variables of the theory are in fact part of the socially defined reality of the interaction. The researcher has access to central variables insofar as he or she can identify the socially determined meaning of the utterance. In the experiencing mode of inquiry, the researcher attempts to get at what is common to the participants in the interaction when translating theoretical constructs into utterance categories. In this mode, the researcher does not attempt to describe subjects' individual perceptions of the interaction but looks only for what is common to the participants.

Within this perspective, categories for coding interaction represent the consensually validated meanings of the utterances to the participants in the interaction or to the population of language users from which the participants are drawn. In the terminology of Cushman and Whiting (1972), the categories of an interaction coding scheme represent various standardized usages. Of course, the investigator still chooses the categories he or she uses based on theoretical inclinations. The important point here is that the experimenter views the set of categories as having a socially defined and culturally shared meaning for all subjects.

The Experiencer Mode

For the researcher who chooses the *experiencer* mode, interaction is best understood and explained in terms of the interpretations of each individual who participated in the interaction. The test of a theory in the experiencer mode is whether the hypothesized relationships among variables, which refer to the subject's point of view, do, in fact, hold as the investigator's theory specifies. The researcher has access to the variables that are central in understanding or explaining interaction only insofar as he or she can grasp the unique interpretations of each participant in the interaction. In the experiencer perspective, the investigator wants to encode a subject's individual frame of reference. Utterances are identified based on subjects' interpretations of the interaction. Ideally, the investigator can achieve an understanding of each participant's point of view and explain the interaction by examining individual viewpoints.

There are, then, three modes of observation that a researcher can adopt when translating theoretical constructs into utterance categories. The experienc*ed* view takes interaction as a product of observable messages and situational effects on the interactors. The experienc*ing* mode is concerned with the common interpretive scheme that the participants in the interaction develop or bring with them, and focuses on relational variables, consensually defined by the participants, as determinants of the course of interaction. The experienc*er* view takes interaction as a product of individual interpretations of others' utterances. It is concerned with the unique interpretive schemes used by each participant in the interaction. Each mode implies different methodological approaches to the study of interaction and each dictates a different set of conditions for validation of the instruments used to code interaction. In the next section, we will consider how one might validate a coding scheme in each of the three perspectives.

Theory and Method of Validation

In their classic piece on the construction of coding categories, Lazarsfeld and Barton (1969) argue that the purpose of coding schemes is to allow the researcher to systematically and rationally reduce the complex set of attributes that characterizes a phenomenon to a simpler set of attributes that is more tractable. In Lazarsfeld and Barton's view, a coding scheme is valid if its reduction of a complex set of attributes does not distort the phenomenon, that is, if it meets two conditions: (1) The set of classificatory dimensions built into the coding schemes must capture the phenomenon adequately for the researcher's purposes; and (2) the coding scheme must not confound or distort dimensions of the phenomenon which are important to explaining or understanding it. For coding interaction, the traditional validity question, "Does the test measure what it is supposed to measure?" becomes "Does this coding scheme give us an adequate, undistorted picture of what is happening in the interaction?" To be valid, a coding scheme does not have to embody every important variable that operates in the interaction being studied. It does, however, have to code accurately those aspects of interaction it is designed to code.

In this section, we will consider theory and methods of validation for each of the three perspectives. This discussion assumes that there is no established criterion, such as a personality test, that can be used as a standard for judging the adequacy of the system. For this reason, neither predictive validity nor concurrent validity, which are criterion-oriented types of validity, are considered. Because the vast majority of interaction coding systems have no identifiable criterion, we do not consider this omission to be a serious one. We also assume that the coding system in question possesses an acceptable level of inter-rater reliability, a necessary although not a sufficient condition for validity.*

Validation in the Experienced Mode

In the experienced mode, validity may be defined as accurate correspondence between coding categories and the theoretical domain specified by the researcher. Categories are valid to the extent that they encode the theoretical constructs they are intended to encode. In the experienced mode categories are chosen and accepted as part of an analytical scheme if they map a particular theoretical domain effectively. In his study of phases of group development, for example, Fisher (1970) recommends dropping two categories and adding several others in order to improve the usefulness of his decision-proposal coding scheme. He makes these recommendations because his study of several decision-making groups indicates that certain categories were seldom used and that the addition of certain others might improve the resolving power of the scheme. He bases his revisions on the assumption that categories should fit the interaction as seen by the observer (and as the observer's theory of interaction specifies). Thus, Fisher is attempting to improve the mapping of decision-making interaction that his category scheme provides by improving the ability of the observer to discriminate among theoretically interesting interaction behaviors.

There are two types of validity necessary and sufficient for a coding scheme to be adequate in the experienced perspective: face validity and construct validity. Face . . . validity concerns judgments about the coding scheme after it has been constructed. In the

*See reading 6.2 in this volume and Chapter 11 in Krippendorff, K. (2004). *Content analysis: An introduction to its methodology* (2nd ed.). Thousand Oaks, CA: Sage.

experienced approach to interaction, a coding scheme possesses face validity when it seems to the investigator and other knowledgeable observers to satisfy the following conditions: (a) the coding scheme accurately embodies the assumptions of the investigator's theory; and (b) the coding scheme is logically consistent and its categories are clearly defined.[3] Face validity is a necessary condition for validation of category schemes. It is a sufficient condition, however, only if we are willing to assume that the observer's theory needs no revisions and that the coding categories operationalize their corresponding theoretical terms precisely.

A somewhat more systematic way of validating a coding scheme is to assess its construct validity. Construct validity was explicated by Cronbach and Meehl (1955) and is appropriate when there is no adequate criterion for assessing a measure (that is, where there is no standard test or objective against which the measure can be compared). The rationale and method for construct validity may be summarized as follows:

> A construct derives its meaning from the theory in which it occurs. The theory can be expressed as a network of propositions and associations among variables. When some of the statements in the network lead to predicted relations among observables, the measure corresponding to the constructs in question may be validated by ascertaining whether it relates to these observables as the theory specifies. The construct may be related to the observable directly or through intermediate statements in the network. If the construction question (as tapped by the measure) shows the relationships to the other observables that are predicted by the theoretical network, this is positive evidence for the validity of the measure. If the predicted relation fails to occur, the fault may lie either in the proposed interpretation of the measure or in the theoretical network. If the network is altered, the measure must be revalidated with a new set of data. If the researcher is confident of the theoretical network, then the measure is invalid. (Cronbach & Meehl, 1955:300)

In assessing the construct validity of a scheme, one would first identify a number of input and output variables that should relate to interaction as coded by the scheme.[4] If the relationships that are predicted by the observer's theory do, in fact, hold, then there is evidence for the construct validity of the scheme. Research reviews are a major means of assessing construct validity. Often better is a systematic validity study in which a coded sequence of interaction is related to a number of input and output variables incorporated into a single research design. A careful validity study circumvents many of the problems of reviewing and synthesizing past research since it guarantees uniform experimental or observational conditions. Face validity and construct validity, taken together, provide a necessary and sufficient set of conditions for validating a coding scheme in the experienced perspective. Ascertaining face validity provides a logical determination of how well the coding categories correspond to the theoretical domain they are designed to encode. Ascertaining construct validity provides an *empirical* determination of how well the coding categories map the theoretical domain in the context of the observer's theory as a whole.

Validation in the Experiencing Mode

A researcher working within the experiencing mode studies interaction in terms of socially shared meanings. The researcher is concerned with the perceptions and interpretations of the participants in the interaction insofar as they are based on a common, socially shared set of meanings or interpretive rules. Therefore, in the experiencing mode, the validity of a coding system depends not only upon the correspondence between the coding categories and the researcher's theoretical domain, but also upon the correspondence between the meanings ascribed to utterances by the coding scheme and the meanings which are commonly ascribed to the utterances by the interactors (or by the population of language users to which the interactors belong). A necessary and sufficient set of conditions for a coding scheme to be adequate in the experiencing perspective is formed by three types of validity—face validity, construct validity, and what we will call *representational* validity.[5,*] The first two forms of validity are similar to the forms required for a valid coding scheme in the experienced perspective, although they will be interpreted somewhat differently by researchers committed to the experiencing viewpoint. In this mode, as in the experienced mode, face validity concerns judgments about the coding scheme after it has been developed. Just as in the experienced mode, the face validity of a coding scheme depends upon whether it accurately embodies the investigator's theory and whether it is consistent and clearly defined. However, the nature of the category scheme is conceived differently in the experiencing perspective. Here, theoretical terms and the categories that embody them represent meanings or interpretive rules common to all members of the population from which the interactors are drawn, rather than a set of labels, which are imposed by the researcher on observable interaction. In assessing face validity, the investigator approaches other knowledgeable observers not only as theorists, but also as fellow language users who are capable of doing more than simply indicating whether the categories fit the theory. Assessing face validity in the experiencing mode involves interpretive understanding of the coding categories: Knowledgeable observers, in light of the investigator's theory, evaluate his or her coding scheme in terms of its meaning to them as native language users. Thus, face validity involves both assessing the fit of the category scheme to the theoretical domain it is designed to tap *and* judging whether the category scheme is meaningful to the body of language users it will be used to study. Both of these determinations must be made if face validity is to provide an adequate logical evaluation of the worth of the coding system. In both the experiencing and the experienced modes of inquiry, construct validity is concerned with empirical evaluation of how well the coding scheme encodes the theoretical domain it is designed to encode. The main divergence in the theory of construct validity for the two perspectives stems from the difference in status accorded to constructs by the two views. In the experiencing mode, constructs represent shared, socially defined meanings. Constructs in the experienced mode are defined and explicated solely by the researcher. This theoretical divergence, however, makes little difference in the procedures used to assess construct validity. The procedures outlined for the experienced mode are also applicable to the experiencing perspective.

Taking the experiencing approach to interaction requires that the investigator consider another type of information relevant to the validation of coding schemes. In addition to determining whether the coding scheme is a good operationalization of certain terms in a theoretical network, the researcher must determine whether the category scheme describes the socially defined "reality" of the interaction situation. The researcher must provide information establishing that the theoretical domain specified by the researcher and the category system which operationalizes it are, in fact, meaningful *vis-à-vis* the socially defined interaction situation. A category scheme, which is adequate in terms of this last criterion, possesses *representational validity.*

Folger and Sillars (1980) argue, for example, that the relational scheme developed by Rogers and Farace (1975) to code the dominant and submissive functions of utterances should be built in such a way that the meanings assigned to utterances by the researcher are in agreement with the *shared meanings* of interactors. Folger and Sillars note that one might have a perfectly acceptable theoretical justification for labeling a certain utterance type (such as a question) as a "dominant" move, but, unless it can be shown that everyday language users classify the statement as a dominance bid, a researcher cannot claim that the coded data accurately

*These authors' "representational validity" is called "semantic validity" by Krippendorff (2004:323–330), op. cit., "the degree to which the analytical categories of texts correspond to the meanings these texts have for particular readers or the role they play within a chosen context."

portray the *shared* meanings that an interaction has for its participants. Without testing the dominant and submissive functions assigned to the interaction categories by the coding scheme authors, the classifications are not acceptable as valid categories in the experiencing perspective. Folger and Sillars attempt to establish the representational validity of the Rogers and Farace scheme by determining (a) whether there is consensus regarding the meaning of categories among individuals drawn from the group of language users the scheme is designed to code, and (b) whether the consensus, if one exists, matches the meanings assigned to the categories by the relational scheme (that is, do everyday interactants see questions as dominant acts as the coding scheme authors have assumed in the construction of the instrument?).

In summary, then, three types of validity—face validity, construct validity, and representational validity—make up a necessary and sufficient set of conditions for validity in the experiencing mode. Face validity provides a logical evaluation of the coding scheme; construct validity and representational validity provide an empirical evaluation of the scheme using the two types of empirical information available to the investigator for checking the coding system.

Validation in the Experiencer Mode

The experiencer mode studies interaction in terms of the perceptions and interpretations of each individual in the interaction. The researcher is concerned with the relationship between the individual's cognitive process and interaction. For this reason, in the experiencer mode of inquiry, the validity of a coding system depends upon two factors: (a) correspondence between coding categories and the researcher's theoretical domain and (b) correspondence between the meanings assigned to utterances by the categories and the meaning of those utterances to the specific individual under study. The second factor requires that the researcher consider information concerning whether his or her theoretical domain and the category scheme which encodes it are an accurate representation of the individual's interpretive scheme. Thus, three types of validity are germane to experiencer coding systems—face validity, construct validity, and what we shall *callidiographic* validity.[6]

Theory and method of assessing face validity in this mode are similar to that discussed under face validity in the experiencing mode, with a shift in perspective by the judges. Rather than attempting to assess how well a coding system maps a common body of meanings, knowledgeable observers judge how adaptable the categories are to the individual cognitive schemes people use to interpret interaction. In the experiencer perspective, face validity involves both assessing the fit of the category scheme to its theoretical domain and judging whether the category scheme is capable of (or can be adapted to) accurately classifying utterances as the individual does. Both determinations must be made in an adequate, *logical* evaluation of an experiencer coding system.

Construct validity in the experiencer perspective differs from construct validity in the other two perspectives only in the theoretical status held by the constructs. Experiencer constructs refer to individualized cognitive processes, which always contain elements idiosyncratic to each person. The procedures used for construct validation of experiencer coding systems are identical to those used in the other two approaches.

Since the experiencer perspective focuses on individual perceptions of interaction, the investigator must consider how well the classification of utterances by the coding system corresponds to the meanings of the utterances to the individual. An adequate experiencer coding system should have idiographic validity; that is, it should be able to classify utterances according to the meanings they hold for each individual in the interaction. In developing coding procedures in this mode, the researcher may start with a broad set of theoretical categories of interest, determine whether these categories have adequate face and construct validity, and then rely on the interactants themselves to place the utterances into the categories which best fit *their* interpretation of the interaction. Fanshel and Moss's (1972) work on the analysis of therapeutic counseling sessions and Hawes's (1972) use of the stimulated recall technique for constructing coding systems demonstrate possible approaches to the development of interaction coding schemes in the experiencer mode. Hawes has described the general objectives of the stimulated recall technique as follows:

> We are trying to determine if the conceptual rationale we are developing has any pragmatic, empiric, or logic linkage to that used by the social actors who are engaging in the conversation. By moving from the descriptions of what people say their talk is doing, we ask them to go the next step and sort their different types of utterances. The third step is to have the subjects give names to the categories of utterance types and describe the common denominators of the different categories. Thus, a coding system is developed—a system based on social actors' conception of the pragmatics of talk. (Hawes, 1976:2)

While these suggested procedures are promising, there are several unexplored problems that stem from a reliance on self-reports for the interpretations of utterances in interaction. Nisbett and Wilson (1977), for example, have argued that individuals often cannot accurately report on their cognitive processes. Even if self-report data can be proved valid, however, subjects must reduce their own perceptions to a common code system in communicating their internal states to the researcher. This translation may smooth over idiosyncratic elements of the subject's experience and render accurate assessment of idiographic validity problematic. The stringent requirements for establishing the validity of a coding scheme in this mode demand that methods for systematically validating experiencer interpretations be developed.

Conclusion

It has not been our objective in this article to "cubbyhole" existing researchers or to advocate any particular approach to the study of interaction. Rather, this article is an attempt to clarify the epistemological basis of interaction analysis by exploring the modes of observation researchers adopt when using interaction coding schemes and outlining the validation requirements these options entail.

Notes

1. This typology was adapted from McKeon (1969). The authors are indebted to Donald P. Cushman of SUNY-Albany for his interpretation and elaboration of McKeon's paper. Robert Craig of the University of Illinois–Chicago Circle has done an excellent explication of this typology in an unpublished paper entitled "Theories of Communication."

2. Note that these approaches are, to some extent, ideal types. Some researchers will meld two approaches and few will explicitly set forth the assumptions of an approach in their work.

3. In this account of face validity, we draw heavily on Lazarsfeld and Barton's (1969) criteria for the construction of qualitative measures. We differ with them in one respect, however; we do not wish to restrict ourselves only to coding systems with mutually exclusive and exhaustive categories. Referring to Lazarsfeld and Barton leads us to systematize the process of face or content validation to a greater extent than other authors have. Nunnally (1967), for example, is not at all clear on specific criteria for face validity or content validity. In the construction of coding systems, issues concerning the logic of the system are crucial; thus, face validity becomes a more important requirement in the validation of coding systems than it is in test construction. Tudor (1976) would argue that face validity also concerns the process by which the coding scheme is constructed. He contends that the social scientist's method of abstraction from social life must be made clear before the status of his or her theoretical terms and the coding scheme that embodies these terms can be evaluated.

4. An argument that Hewes (1978) has advanced suggests that procedures such as Cronbach and Meehl's confound theory testing and validation. He argues that construct validation should be done by locating multiple measures of a construct and relating these measures to all one-step links in the propositional network. If the multiple measures all relate to the measures of one-step-removed constructs in the same way, then the construct is validated. If there is inconsistency, then either the theory or the measure must be changed. Hewes's procedure differs from that of Cronbach and Meehl in that he only allows construct

validation through one-step links, while Cronbach and Meehl do not specify such a limitation.

5. Technically, representational validity is a form of construct validation. Our use of the representational label is meant to emphasize the type of information needed to establish the validity of coding schemes, which invoke an experiencing mode of observation.

6. Like representational validity, idiographic validity is a construct validation procedure. The term *idiographic* is used to stress the type of information needed to establish validity in the experiencer mode.

References

Bales, R. F. (1950). *Interaction process analysis.* Cambridge, MA: Addison-Wesley.

Cappella, J. N. (1977). Research methodology in communication: research review and commentary. In B. Rueben (Ed.), *Communication yearbook 1* (pp. 37–53). New Brunswick, NJ: Transaction.

Cronbach, L. J., & Meehl, P. (1955). Construct validity in psychological tests. *Psychiatric Bulletin 52:*281–302.

Cushman, D. P., & Whiting, G. (1972). An approach to communication theory: Toward consensus on rules. *Journal of Communication 22:*217–238.

Fanshel, D., & Moss, F. (1972). *Playback: A marriage in jeopardy examined.* New York: Columbia University Press.

Fisher, B. A. (1970). Decision emergence: Phases in group decision making. *Speech Monographs 37:*53–66.

Fisher, B. A., Drecksel, G., & Werbel, W. (1979). Social information processing analysis (SIPA): Coding ongoing human communication. *Small Group Behavior 10:*3–21.

Folger, J., & Sillars, A. (1980). Relational coding and perceptions of dominance. In B. Morse & L. Phelps (Eds.), *Interpersonal communication: A relational perspective* (pp. 322–333). Minneapolis, MN: Burgess.

Hawes, L. (1972). Development and application of an interview coding system. *Central States Speech Journal 23:*92–99.

Hawes, L. (1976, April). *Critique of Division II papers, interpersonal communication.* Presented at the annual conference of the International Communication Association, Portland, Oregon.

Hewes, D. (1978, April). *Small group interaction process: A critique of four papers.* Paper presented at the annual conference of the International Communication Association, Chicago.

Lamb, M., Suomi, S., & Stephensen, G. (1979). *Social interaction analysis.* Madison, WI: University of Wisconsin Press.

Lazarsfeld, P. F., & Barton, A. (1969). Qualitative measurement: A codification of techniques for social science. In L. I. Krimerman (Ed.), *The nature and scope of social science: A critical anthology* (pp. 514–549). New York: Appleton Century-Crofts.

Mabry, E. A. (1975). An instrument for assessing content themes in group interaction. *Speech Monographs 42:*291–297.

McKeon, R. (1969). Gibson Winter's "elements of a social ethic": A review. *Journal of Religion 49:*77–84.

Nisbett, R., & Wilson, T. (1977). Telling more than we can know: Verbal reports on mental processes. *Psychological Review 84:*231–259.

Nunnally, J. C. (1967). *Psychometric theory.* New York: McGraw-Hill.

Rogers, L. E., & Farace, M. (1975). Relational communication analysis: New measurement procedures. *Human Communication Research 1:*222–259.

Ruzicka, M. A., Palisi, A., & Berven, N. L. (1979). Use of Cattell's three panel model: Remedying problems in small group research. *Small Group Behavior 10:*40–48.

Tudor, A. (1976). Misunderstanding everyday life. *The Sociological Review 24:*479–503.

6.5

IMPORTANCE IN CONTENT ANALYSIS

A Validity Problem

MILTON D. STEWART*

One of the mainsprings of the developing science of content analysis is its concern with symbols that are assumed to have the greatest significance for politics. Studies of content, as a rule, attempt to report the relative attention and the direction given these symbols at some time in some channel. As a gauge of the attention that symbols command, almost universal reliance has been placed on a single dimension of content: frequency. In this sort of analysis, all the units discerned are equated. Differences in the degree of emphasis by semantic or physical devices are ignored, so that every item counts as "I" compared with every other item. Such qualifications as have been made for other functions of importance have been limited to sample selection, as in the decision to analyze only the part of a newspaper's contents contained in headlines on the front page.

This does not permit comparison between this most prominent content and that in the rest of the paper. Moreover, it makes the assumption that, within the front-page headlines, one needs to count only the occurrences of symbols or symbol-groups to measure their relative importance.

It is the validity of this reliance on frequency, with no reference to other pragmatic or semantic functions of importance, that we shall experimentally test.

Some clarification of the problem can come from a consideration of the needs that content analysis results must serve. Primarily, information about changes in the importance of politically crucial symbols is used as a basis for estimating what is being brought to the attention of the various channel audiences. Two further, and much mooted, steps are the drawing of inferences from content distributions back to the communicator and his

*From Stewart, M. (1943). Importance in content analysis: A validity problem. *Journalism Quarterly 20*,4:286–293.

intentions, and forward to the audience and its probable response. Admittedly, content analysis by itself cannot supply any complete answer on either matter. The intentions of communicating persons or groups may be hypothesized from the symbols they produce. Further illumination may come from data about their other activities. But a reasonable degree of finality demands reference to their own statements about the techniques to be used to achieve a given objective. The same kinds of qualification hold for the use of content analysis results for the prediction of response to symbols. The precise impact of what is communicated is the subject matter of another field—opinion research.

Neither of these secondary functions is essential to content analysis. Simple statements about what people are being exposed to in the most important channels at various times are (or should be) of sufficient importance to public and private policy makers and social scientists to justify the work. Nonetheless, based on generalizations that vary in their trustworthiness, assumptions *are* made about intent and response from content data. But whichever of the three uses is made of the results of a content analysis, the problem of justifying the use of frequency as a measure of importance remains. For the frequency with which a symbol occurs is only one indication of the anxiousness of the communicator that it be stressed, of the strength it has as opposed to the other symbols in the channel, and of how large it will loom in the minds of the audience.

Variations in the importance of a symbol may be said to be due to stress or non-stress. But it makes a great deal of difference if the 57 references to Japan in a week's issues of a German daily are all in colored, streamer headlines, editorial leaders or stick-long, agate type items at the bottom of back pages. One possible way of summarizing why some symbols are more "important" than others is to say that:

Importance is a function of

I. Physical characteristics of a content universe
   A. Frequency of symbol occurrence
   B. Channel prominence devices (see below)
II. Semantic characteristics of a content universe
   A. Assertions of importance
      1. In language ("This Italian purge is the most important since Mussolini came to power")
      2. In punctuation (exclamations points, underlining)
   B. Intensity of symbols ("Nazis Crushed in Greatest Setback" as opposed to "German Drive Slowed")

It is the end product of all these factors operating in combination in which we are ultimately interested. At present, however, it is certainly beyond us to assess correctly the role that each element plays. Instead, we shall limit ourselves to the "physical characteristics" to learn whether one of them, frequency, provides an adequate measure of all of them. If the distribution of a content universe taken by the frequency with which its component parts occur is the same as that taken in accordance with channel prominence devices, the latter need not be considered in reporting physical importance.

The channels of communication are finite. There is only a limited amount of space in a newspaper, a limited amount of time on a radio program, a limited amount of each in a newsreel.* The content universe from which symbols are taken is theoretically also finite, although for practical purposes, much less limited. In the selection of symbols to be communicated some conscious choice is made; in the arrangement of a content-mass, alternatives in the use of space and time to stress or suppress any part of it are fewer and demand at least as much choice. A multitude of technical emphasis or de-emphasis possibilities are available. To fully define "channel prominence devices,"

*Internet space may seem "infinite," yet a home page, where editorial decisions are made, is limited in what can be included to grab a user's attention.

it is necessary, once again, to consider the purposes of study.

If the problem is one of determining what actions an élite plans based on its communications, it is necessary to ask, "What will it do when it wants to stress something?" To examine the performance of American newspapers, one must know what city room practices are, how editors think they can call attention to something. If, on the other hand, predictions of audience response are to be essayed, what is needed is readership of listenership data telling what devices *actually* increase the possibility that some part of the content will get across to the public. Until precise data of these sorts are accumulated, it is possible only to suggest the most important factors, but not their relationship to one another. A preliminary list would include, for the major channels, the following:

A. Newspaper (news articles)
   1. Space occupied
      a. Length (column inches)
      b. Column width of text and headlines
   2. Page location
   3. Placement on page
      a. From outside columns in
      a. From top to bottom
   4. Size of headline type
   5. Type-face
      a. Style
      b. Roman, bold-face, italics, capitals, etc.
   6. Number of lines in headlines, banks, decks, cross-lines
   7. Use of accompanying maps, pictures, cartoons, others
   8. Use of color
   9. Use of leads to space text-lines
   10. Use of boxes around stories or leads

B. Radio Broadcasts
   1. Length of time devoted
   2. Order of parts
   3. Intonation in speakers' voices
   4. Sound effects
   5. Music

C. Films*
   1. Length of time
   2. Order of parts
   3. Captions, types, sizes, etc
   4. Technicolor
   5. Special camera effects
   6. Intonation in speakers' voices
   7. Sound effects
   8. Music

It is clear that these are the relevant prominence variables; it is far less clear how some of them function. For experimental purposes, therefore, the number of prominence measures tested along with the total frequency were limited to four characteristics of press content about which assumptions can safely be made: (1) Length: the longer a story, the more important it tends to be. (2) Column width of headline: the wider the headline, the more important the story. (3) Placement on the page: the top of the page is more important than the middle or the bottom. (4) Page location: page one is more important than pages two and three. Just as importance may be said to vary with frequency, so it may be said to vary with each of these. If the symbol types that are most frequent were also most prominent in terms of these four factors, then in our test case it would have been sufficient simply to count them. Otherwise, the count must be qualified for prominence devices.

More than 4,000 articles appearing on the first three pages of ten[1] Negro** weekly newspapers over a four-month period were analyzed for this test. The general purpose of the analysis was to determine what this sample of the Negro press (probably the most important channel in the Negro community) was presenting to its readers as news about the relations between America's twelve-million Negroes and the rest of the country. Basically the problem was one of participation. Was the

---

*Here, regarding the concept of "prominence," Stewart recommends work by S. Kracauer. See reading 2.6, this volume.

**While outdated, this was not, at the time, a disrespectful reference to African Americans. We keep Stewart's language in place in keeping with the tone of the original article.

stress on news about increases or blockages in Negro participation in the total community? How much relative attention was given to the protests of Negro leaders, groups and organizations—their demands for further participation? To answer these questions an "attitude" or "direction" code was set up. Subject preoccupations—the armed forces, the economy, general race relations and so on—were handled in a separate category system.

In addition to analyzing each article for direction and subject, its prominence according to the four devices mentioned was noted. Five length groups were set up to measure the number of column inches occupied by each story from the top of its headline to the final cut-off rule. Four groups of headline column widths were also used. Location of articles on pages 1–3 was marked, as was their placement in the top, middle or bottom thirds of a page. It was thus possible first to study the distribution, according to direction and subject of *all* the articles, and then to compare with the total picture only those stories in the *most* prominent group of each of the four device categories: those stories located on page one; those at the tops of the pages; those that were twenty inches or more in length; and those whose headlines spanned eight columns. This comparison was repeated for direction and subject, making eight pairs of distributions in all (Tables 1 and 2).

Two kinds of information come from testing the most prominent groups and the total group for significant difference. First, we can tell whether it is valid to report on a content mass in terms of the frequency with which the parts occur. If there is a difference greater than might be due to chance, it is *less* valid to do so than if there is no such difference. The existence of a difference means that, taken by another measure, the importance of the symbols or symbol-groups is other than that which they have by frequency. No difference means that it is unnecessary to do more than distribute all the articles by the number that fall in each category, since this estimates importance identically with the prominence device tests.

A second, and here incidental, kind of information is the adequacy of the most prominent group in each device category as a sample of the total contents. Here if there is no difference, let us say, between the total distribution and that of the articles that are longest, it would suffice for a content analysis to rely only on the longest ones. This information is enhanced by the sizes of our sample. About half the items occurred on page one, about one fourth at the tops of the pages, and less than one-tenth were 20 inches long or had headlines eight columns wide. Roughly, then, we may say we are using a contracting analytical frame moving from the total sample to its most prominent part.

Table 1 Attitude of All Articles Compared With Attitude of Most Prominent According to Four Channel Devices

Category	*Pages 1–3*		*Page 1 Only*		*Top of Page*		*≥ 20 Inches*		*8 Column Heads*	
Fact/more participation	1362	32%	672	32%	328	31%	137	35%	97	32%
Demand/more participation	661	15%	348	17%	179	17%	90	23%	70	23%
Fact/less participation	664	16%	403	19%	217	20%	101	25%	79	26%
Demand/less participation	6	—	3	—	1	—	1	—	1	—
Neutral	473	11%	209	10%	112	11%	23	6%	29	9%
Irrelevant	1127	26%	462	22%	224	21%	43	11%	31	10%
Totals	**4287**		**2094**		**1060**		**394**		**306**	

Table 2 Subjects of All Articles Compared With Subjects of the Most Prominent According to Four Channel Devices

Category	*All Articles Pages 1–3*		*Page One*		*Top of Page*		*≥ 20 Inches*		*8 Column Heads*	
Negroes in the armed forces	664	15%	364	17%	162	15%	80	20%	50	16%
Negroes and economic life	500	12%	251	12%	153	14%	67	17%	53	17%
Negroes and civil liberties	401	9%	258	12%	118	11%	46	12%	41	13%
General race relations	394	9%	215	19%	109	10%	55	14%	36	12%
Negroes in civilian war work	192	5%	72	4%	41	4%	10	2%	8	3%
Negroes in crime	175	4%	80	4%	53	5%	9	2%	16	5%
Negroes in other countries	149	4%	81	4%	40	4%	27	7%	18	6%
Other Negro-White fields[a]	618	14%	279	13%	150	14%	50	13%	43	14%
Negro-Negro Affairs	903	21%	395	19%	166	16%	34	9%	26	9%
Irrelevant	297	7%	102	5%	69	7%	16	4%	16	5%
Totals	**4293**		**2097**		**1061**		**395**		**307**	

a. Each less than 4% of all articles.

A. Attitude

The six attitude categories* set up were:

1) FM: a factual report of more or maintained Negro participation in the war or the total community
2) DM: a report of demands for more Negro participation
3) FL: A factual report of lessened or blocked Negro participation
4) DL: a report of demands for diminished Negro participation
5) N: a report of Negro-total community relations with no direction
6) O: an item irrelevant to the relations between Negroes and the larger community.

The distributions in the five samples described above are shown in Table 1. Each "prominent" category when tested against the total sample breakdown differed significantly

*Modern researchers usually use the word *attitude* as a social-psychological term, but here Stewart is using it to describe story tone, whether objective/factual (F) or opinionated/editorial (D), regarding either increased integration and equality (M) or less integration and equality (L).

(χ^2 test). Inspection immediately shows that there is not much difference between that part of the sample taken from the front page and that taken from the tops of the three pages. They form a similar pair, as do those based on the twenty-inch and longer stories, and those with eight column headlines.

Factual stories about Negro gains form a relatively constant proportion of the diminishing samples. The next or "protest" category shows a gradual but definite rise. As the sample becomes restricted to those parts of the paper presumably most important in the minds of editors and readers, the proportion of reports of symbolic activity demanding a greater share of the society's benefits for Negroes goes up.

The same increase is apparent in the next category, which contains accounts of rejection by the larger community of the Negro subgroup. Here, too, the more prominent the part of the paper, the greater the role of reports of deprivation. Reports of demands for the rejection of Negroes are so small as to be insignificant. Neutral stories remain fairly constant, dropping off only slightly.

The items showing the greatest consistent change are those that are irrelevant to race relations. Although they constitute a little more than a fourth of the total group, they fall off until they are only one-tenth of the most refined sample.

To summarize the differences, we might reduce the five relevant categories to three, combining demands for more participation with facts about blocked participation, and the neutral with the irrelevant items. This yields a rough imbalance ratio of satisfaction: dissatisfaction: neutrality. Or indulgence: deprivation: neutrality. The various samples break down as follows:

In general, stories carrying indulgent fact are as important in terms of prominence devices as they are in terms of frequency. Protest and deprivation stories are stressed more in the most prominent parts of the paper than in the rest of it. And neutral and irrelevant items are much less prominent than their frequency of occurrence would lead one to suspect.

B. Subject

The basic distinction made in the classification of articles by subjects was between those dealing with the Negro sub-community, those dealing with its relations with the total group and those not concerned with either. In the original analysis (see tables), eighteen subject categories were set up. Because eight of them were each less than 4% of the total, they are combined in Table 2 into a single "Other Negro-White Fields" category.

The four chief inter-racial subjects are Negroes in the armed forces, in economic life, their civil liberties and race relations in general. Aside from these, only the Negro-Negro and irrelevant categories are of interest. So far as the inter-racial areas are concerned, those that are the biggest by number are also the most important in terms of prominence. As a group, they increase (45%, 51%, 50%, 63%, 58%) at the expense of the Negro-Negro category, which is less and less important as the sample is limited to the most stressed parts. If all the Negro-Total Community items are lumped, and then compared with the Negro-Negro category and the Irrelevant category, we may set up an in-balance series like the one for attitude:

Table 3 "Attitude" (Story Tone) in Percent

	Fact/More	*Fact/Less or Demand/More*	*Neutral*	
Total sample	32	31	37	(4293)
Page one of sample	32	36	32	(2097)
Top of page sample	31	37	32	(1061)
≥ 20 inches sample	35	48	17	(395)
8-column heads sample	32	49	19	(307)

Table 4 Subject in Percent

	Negro/Total Community (Inter-Group Relations)	*Negro/Negro (Within the Community)*	*Irrelevant*	
Total sample	72	21	7	(4293)
Page one of sample	76	19	5	(2097)
Top of page sample	77	16	7	(1061)
≥ 20 inches sample	87	9	4	(395)
8-column heads sample	86	9	5	(307)

The differences between the total group distribution and the four most prominent group distributions are all significant for subject as well as for attitude (χ^2 test). So far as the news columns of the Negro press go, stories dealing with the relations of the minority to the rest of the community are given greater prominence than those dealing with its "internal" affairs. And the inter-racial subjects most frequently dealt with are most often stressed in other ways.

We have been getting information about two matters: the contents of the Negro press, and the adequacy of frequency as a measure of importance.

So far as the first is concerned, the most important finding is that stories reporting discontent and deprivation are stressed more in terms of prominence than their frequency would suggest. Stories dealing with achieved acceptances form the same proportion of leading stories that they do of others, and neutral or irrelevant items are played down. In terms of subject-matter, "ethnocentric" news is relegated to the lesser parts of the first three pages. Those inter-racial subject classes, on the other hand, that are most frequent also show the greatest increase in moving from the total sample to its most important parts.

So far as content analysis procedures go, the raw frequency figures in this case present a strikingly different picture of the Negro press, news subject and attitude stressess from that given after reference to prominence devices. These same differences, however, between the total group and its most prominent parts indicate that the latter would make an inadequate sample of the former. This case, then, makes clear the invalidity of reliance on frequency data for analysis of physical importance. The most useful and valid analysis, it would appear, is one that makes use of as large a number of cases as can be handled, and then qualifies for stress by channel devices.[2]

Notes

1. The sample included: California *Eagle,* Chicago *Defender,* Detroit *Tribune,* New York *Amsterdam Star News,* Philadelphia *Tribune,* Pittsburgh *Courier,* Washington *Afro-American,* Dallas *Express, Oklahoma* City *Black Dispatch,* and Tampa *Tribune:* all issues of these papers published between October 1, 1942 and February 1, 1943. Although there were several single category deviates, the group consistency was sufficient so that the generalizations hold for all the papers.

2. The general conclusion that limiting the sample to the most prominent parts of the paper will cut down the neutral content sharply is borne out by another experiment. Using six daily, general circulation newspapers published in July and August, 1942, all front page headlines were coded for reference to four nations (cf. Lasswell, 1941) [see also reading 5.3, this volume]. The headlines coded were broken down by *size of type* into three prominence classes. Not only was the most prominent group significantly different from the others, but it contained a higher proportion of favorable-unfavorable (as against neutral) content.

Reference

Lasswell, H. D. (1941). The world attention survey. *Public Opinion Quarterly 3:*456–462.

6.6

The Gerbner Violence Profile

*A Public Debate in Four Parts**

(1) The Gerbner Violence Profile

David M. Blank**

Each year for almost a decade George Gerbner and his associates at the Annenberg School of Communication have produced a report on depictions of violence on network television, titled the Violence Profile.[1] The current Violence Profile #8, reporting on fall 1976 television network programming, incorporates three distinct areas of study. The first is the well-known Violence Index; the second deals with so-called Risk Ratios; and the third is Gerbner's Cultivation Index. In this analysis, we deal with the first two areas of study.

With regard to the Violence Index, our review indicates that the Index itself is not a measure of the amount of violence on network television, that it may, and in fact often does, change over time in different directions from the changes in the amount of television violence and that it is, in substance, an arbitrarily weighted set of arbitrarily chosen measures of aspects of violence on television, whose meaning is totally unclear. It cannot be used as a measure of the trend of televised violence over the years, or as an indicator of whether that violence is increasing or decreasing.

Gerbner's count of violent incidents, which is only one component of the overall Violence Index, has numerous and fatal deficiencies. It includes kinds of dramatic incidents, which should not be included: comic violence, accidents, and natural disasters. It counts as multiple acts of violence, single incidents that should be counted as single incidents. And most importantly, it rests on a single week's sample at a time in the television industry's history when programs are constantly changing and when there are no longer any typical weeks.

The Risk Ratio analysis is equally defective. Instead of directly measuring relative risks among various population segments, Gerbner devised indirect measures which do not reflect the differences in actual risk among differing population segments nor, in

*The articles in this reading are four parts of an extended discussion, which are best read together.

**From Blank, D. M. (1977). The Gerbner Violence Profile. *Journal of Broadcasting 21*:273–279.

all likelihood, do they correspond at all to viewers' perceptions. Simpler and more direct measurements of risks often show a totally different relationship among social groups from the Gerbner measures.

The Violence Index

The Gerbner Violence Index is deficient in a number of important ways and is, in fact, very misleading. First, the Violence Index itself is not, and does not purport to be, a measure of the amount of violence on television, although that is the way it is generally interpreted. The Violence Index is the sum of a number of measures, only one of which is Gerbner's count of violence. Another measure included in the Index, for example, is the proportion of leading characters engaged in violence. Because the Violence Index is composed of a number of factors in addition to the violence count itself, it is quite conceivable that the Violence Index could show a rise in a given year at the same time that Gerbner's own count of the amount of violence goes down.

That, in fact, is exactly what happened in the family viewing hour on CBS in the fall of 1976. Gerbner's Violence Profile #8 states "CBS . . . lifted its two-season lid on 'family viewing time' violence in 1976." In fact, the number of incidents of violence on CBS in the family viewing hour actually declined in 1976, according to the same Gerbner report. In the fall of 1975, according to Gerbner (Table 1), family viewing hour programs on CBS contained 20 incidents of violence; CBS family viewing hour programs in the fall of 1976, again according to Gerbner, contained only 11 incidents of violence![2] So the Violence Index is a measure which simply does not tell anyone whether violence on network programming is increasing or decreasing.

Other components of the Violence Index include measures of the proportion of programs that week containing any violence, of the rate of violence per program and per hour, and of the proportion of all leading characters involved in killings. These measures are combined by the use of a set of arbitrary weights. Indeed, the index is composed of so many varied and incomparable elements which are combined in such an arbitrary fashion that it is difficult to know what it means.[3]

Bruce Owen of the Office of Telecommunications Policy, in a staff research paper which addressed the meaning and validity of the Gerbner Index, stated that: "This exercise [i.e., combining and arbitrarily weighting the various components of the Violence Index] involves adding apples and oranges . . . One is always free to add apples and oranges if one wishes, but it isn't at all clear what the result means, and some people may take it seriously" (Owen, 1972). Unfortunately, many people have taken Gerbner's Violence Index seriously.

When Gerbner's violence count itself is examined, a variety of deficiencies are apparent. Violence is counted presumably to measure the number of incidents depicted on network television, which might conceivably make potentially wayward youths wayward. On this view, Gerbner includes a number of kinds of dramatic action, which clearly ought not to be included in a count of violence. Thus, he includes comic violence (e.g., a custard pie in the face on an "I Love Lucy" program), and injuries caused by accidents or acts of nature (e.g., injuries occurring in earthquakes or hurricanes). None of these, we think, are included in what reasonable citizens would consider to be potentially harmful dramatic forms.

A second difference in definition is related to a very complex set of social hypotheses that Gerbner superimposes upon his violence counts. Because Gerbner's hypotheses relate to the power relationships among individuals (men vs. women, whites vs. nonwhites, etc.), he counts as new violent actions, a period of violence in which a new person enters the action. Thus, if two men are fighting in a restaurant, and one of them knocks down a waiter while trying to escape, Gerbner would count this as two separate episodes of violence. Since we do not believe that the count of violence should be distorted by extraneous social theories, we feel that the proper count is the number of violent incidents themselves, not affected by changes in the participants of the action.

The result of these differences between the Gerbner measure of violence, and what we consider to be the more rational measure that we use, is that Gerbner's count results in a much higher number than is valid and may often move in an opposite direction than to that indicated by the count one would get on a more reasonable basis.

A final deficiency of the Gerbner violence count is the size of the sample Gerbner uses. Since its inception, the Gerbner effort has measured violence during one week a year. In the last two seasons, he has added a second week in the spring, purportedly to verify the results of the fall count, but he does not use this week in his year-to-year comparisons of the magnitude of violence.

From the beginning of our monitoring, we felt that there was too much change between fall and spring network schedules to permit reliance on a single week's results. So we always measured two weeks a year, one in the initial network season and one in the so-called second network season. Several years ago, as the network schedules became increasingly variable from week to week, with series being cancelled and new series being brought on board all through the year and with mini-series becoming a new programming category, we decided to review the statistical basis of our count. As a result of this review, we concluded that one could no longer make statistically valid comments about the level of violence on network television without a much larger sample of weeks. Accordingly, in the fall of 1975 we began to monitor 13 weeks a season and have continued that practice.

We have measured violence on the television networks for 13 weeks in each of two years; based on these data we have learned that estimates of current year-to-year changes in television violence, based on single-week samples, are normally subject to too much random error to be valid. For we have found in the 1976–77 season that the range in the weekly number of incidents of violence on individual television networks is on the order of 2½ or 3 to 1; that is, the week with the highest number of incidents of violence on any network was 2½ or 3 times the number with the lowest number of incidents. Accordingly, we do not believe, for statistical reasons, that one can accept the Gerbner violence counts even if we waive the deficiencies of his definitions.

The Risk Ratio

Since 1969, Gerbner has made much of a statistic to which he variously refers as the "Victimization Ratio," the "Risk Ratio," the "Violence Victim Ratio," and which will here simply be called "RR." This statistic is obtained by noting, in reference to specific population subgroups, the number of such characters in "principal roles"[4] who are depicted as "violents" (aggressors), the number who are depicted as victims, and dividing the larger number by the smaller. If victims exceed violents, the figure is preceded by a minus sign; if violents exceed victims, by a plus sign.

Gerbner considers that these RR's "provide a calculus of life's chances for different groups of people in the world of television drama" (p. 8). He occasionally modifies this description in an important manner by stating that the RR's are indices of "risks of victimization (relative to the ability to inflict violence)" (p. 8). As the terms "Victimization Ratio" and "Risk Ratio" suggest, he is primarily interested in the groups with minus sign RR's—i.e., those in which victims exceed violents. He considers the RR's indexes, or at least clues, to "conceptions of social reality that television viewing cultivates in the minds of viewers" (p. 8) regarding "the structure of power. In "Highlights of TV Violence Profile #8" he notes especially the high negative RR's of women, children, old women, unmarried women, and various other groups. Explicitly or implicitly, Gerbner regards the RR's as either distortions of social reality or perpetuations of existing stereotypes, regards negative RR's as reason to believe that viewers regard such groups as relatively powerless, and believes that viewers themselves become fearful of becoming victims of violence.

At least two important questions arise regarding the meaning of the RR and its presumed effects. First, the RR is not a measure of simple risk, in reference to which the number of "violents" is irrelevant. If, as Gerbner's tables show, 243 of 697 women (34.9 percent) in "principal roles" across 10 sample weeks since 1969 were depicted as "victims," what matters whether the number depicted as "violents" is, as he indicates, 184, or whether it is 284 or 26? The "risk" is the same. (Comparative risks are further discussed below.)

The RR is also not a measure of "victimization (relative to the ability to inflict violence)," since the *ability* to do so is not normally a theme of television drama. The fact that 513 of the 697 women were not portrayed as inflicting violence is not an indication of their inability to do so. What the RR actually measures is victimization relative to the *commission* of violence. The implications of such an index are somewhat difficult to conceive.

Second, it is very difficult to believe that viewers would become aware, consciously or unconsciously, of the differential RR's—i.e., the relative proportions of different groups, which are depicted as violents or victims, and the differences between groups in this regard. It is not at all difficult to believe, however, that viewers would become to one or another degree aware of something much simpler and more easily statistically stated, namely, that certain groups are more often victims than others (or more often violent than others, or more often involved in violence, one way or another, than others).

Maintaining the emphasis on risk, the more telling statistics would seem to be the simple number of persons in that group who are depicted as victims, or, for somewhat greater refinement, the percentage so depicted (the number of victims divided by the total number of persons in that group who are depicted at all). These are, to the best of our knowledge, the measures used in calculating risks of contracting given diseases, the likelihood of being in an automobile accident, and other "risk" statistics.

When Gerbner's tables are examined in terms of these simpler statistics, what emerges is often a very different picture from the RR. Briefly, it is frequently found that a group with a *higher* RR than other groups is both numerically and proportionately *less* often depicted either as involved in violence at all or as victims.

By way of example, women have a higher RR (–1.32) than do men (–1.20). The simpler statistics (Gerbner's Table 44) reveal that Gerbner observed 2,328 male characters, of whom 1,604 (68.9 percent) were involved in violence and 1,400 (60.1 percent) depicted as victims. In comparison, 697 females were observed, of whom 311 (44.6 percent) were involved in violence and 243 (34.9 percent) depicted as victims. Of what is the viewer more likely to become aware: the complex fact that female victims outnumbered female violents to a greater degree than male victims outnumbered male violents, or the simpler facts that, both in terms of absolute numbers and proportionately, women were less often than men involved in violence at all, and far less often than men depicted as victims? This same sort of situation applies to various other groups, which Gerbner notes as having high RR's.

In summary, the RR is not a measure of *risk* as such, and the simpler and more telling statistics often reveal that groups with *higher* RR's than others are in fact *less often* than the others depicted as victims, both numerically and proportionately to their depiction.

Notes

1. We are aware that the authorship of current Violence Profiles is credited to a number of people in addition to George Gerbner. However, for ease of reference and because Gerbner is normally the spokesman for the group, we refer to the various materials produced by the group as if they were prepared by Gerbner alone.

2. All page and table references herein relate to Violence Profile #8.

3. The formula for the Gerbner Violence index is:

$$100\frac{P_v}{P} + 2\frac{R}{P} + 2\frac{R}{H} + 100\frac{N_v + N_k}{N}$$

where, P_v is the number of programs containing any violence; P is the number of programs; R is the number of violent episodes; H is the number of hours of programming; N_v the number of leading characters involved in violence; N_k the number of leading characters involved in killing or death; and N, the number of leading characters.

4. On p. 14 of his Violence Profile #8, Gerbner states that "The findings summarized in this report include the analysis of major characters only." He defines "major characters" as those in "principal roles essential to the story," whereas "minor characters (subjected to a less detailed analysis) are all other speaking roles." It is therefore here assumed that the RR applies only to "major characters."

Reference

Owen, B. M. (1972). *Measuring violence on television: The Gerbner Index.* OTP Staff Research Paper, OTS-SP-7.

(2) "The Gerbner Violence Profile" *An Analysis of the CBS Report*

The Cultural Indicators Research Team*

The CBS report deals with two of three areas of the annual Violence Profile. It discusses the Violence Index and the Risk Ratios showing relative levels of victimization. . . .

Organized in logical order, the CBS report focuses on four main criticisms:

1. The Violence Index is deficient because (a) it defines violence too broadly and (b) it is composed of "an arbitrarily weighted set of arbitrarily chosen measures of violence on television, whose meaning is totally unclear."

2. The Violence Index employs faulty units of analysis because "It counts as multiple acts of violence, single incidents which should be counted as single incidents."

3. A single week's sample is inadequate for representing an entire television season.

4. "The Risk Ratio analysis is equally defective" because it measures relative rather than absolute victimization which "in all likelihood" does not correspond "to viewers' perceptions."

Each of these claims rests on erroneous—if convenient—assumptions and results in highly misleading conclusions. We shall analyze them in turn.

The Index

CBS claims that the Violence Index is deficient because "It includes kinds of dramatic incidents which should not be included—comic violence, accidents, natural disasters." The report suggests the unlikely example of a "pie in the face," and amplifies its conception of what *should* be included: violence "which might conceivably make potentially wayward youths wayward" and violence "in what reasonable citizens would consider to be potentially harmful dramatic forms."

*From Gerbner, G., et al. (1977). "The Gerbner Violence Profile"—An analysis of the CBS Report. *Journal of Broadcasting 21:*280–286. The Cultural Indicators Research Team was composed of George Gerbner, Larry Gross, Michael F. Eeley, Marilyn Jackson-Beeck, Suzanne Jeffries-Fox, and Nancy Signorielli.

The fact is that our analysis of television content as reported in the Violence Index does not presume effects—useful or harmful. The reporting of trends in the Gross National Product, the Employment Index, or in weather conditions cannot depend on the presumed effects of the facts being reported, be they good, bad, indifferent, or mixed. CBS confuses communications *content* with the scientific study of communications *effects* and thus ignores our study of television viewers. Yet only by studying the conceptions and behaviors of the public, rather than speculating about "wayward youths" or what seems "potentially harmful," can one determine the actual consequence of exposure to any form of violence.

CBS would also prefer to discount all violence in a comic context, which is especially frequent in children's programming. But CBS recently published, "They Learn While They Laugh," a public relations booklet extolling the educational virtues of its children's programming, including cartoons. The weight of scientific evidence, including the recent Rand Corporation research summaries compiled by George Comstock, indicates that a comic context is a highly effective form of conveying serious lessons. If CBS wants to maintain that comedy teaches only what they wish for it to teach, the burden of proof lies with them.

Overall, the Violence Index for fall 1976 shows that violence occurs at the average rate of nearly 10 incidents per program hour. Yet CBS—and other industry spokesmen—typically attack these findings by the supposedly disarming example of the "pie in the face." First, we do not think there has been "a pie in the face" in one of our samples of TV drama in a long time.

Second, the Violence Index rules specifically exclude any non-credible comic gesture or verbal abuse. We classify as violence only the credible indication or actual infliction of overt physical pain, hurt, or killing. Thus, if a pie in the face does that—which depends on the actual incident—it is violence and should be so recorded.

The contention that "serious" violence is only what "reasonable citizens would consider harmful" is equally specious. It again confuses communication content with the assessment of effects. For example, we know from independent studies of the physical environment and of foods and pharmaceuticals that citizens are not necessarily aware of the full range of consequences of many of our industrial activities and products, including the products of the television industry. That is why independent research is needed. That is why the scientific diagnosis of a complex cultural industrial phenomenon—such as television—cannot be left to conventional wisdom, and even less to rationalizations by the corporate interests involved.

CBS also argues for the exclusion from the definition of TV violence dramatic incidents portraying "accidents," and "acts of nature." But there are no "accidents" in fiction. The author invents (or the producer inserts) dramatic disasters and "acts of nature" for a purpose. The pattern of violent victimization through such inventions may be a significant and telling part of television violence. It is hardly accidental that certain types of characters are accident-prone or disaster-prone in the world of television. Such TV content patterns may have significant effects on some viewers' conceptions of life and of their own risks in life. These patterns are, therefore, important to report if one is concerned with the full range of potentially significant consequences.

Another objection raised by CBS is that the Violence Index includes a set of measures rather than only a single indicator, and that different measures may move in different directions. The CBS report also cites an OTP Staff paper by Bruce M. Owen as complaining that the Index "involves adding apples and oranges." CBS could just as easily criticize any set of comprehensive indicators such as the GNP, labor statistics, or the weather report.

As pointed out in our response to the Owen paper (dated July 13, 1972, and also distributed through OTP but not cited by CBS), the usefulness of any index is precisely that it combines measures of different aspects of a complex phenomenon. One *must* add apples and oranges if one wants to know about *fruit*.

The Violence Index reports all its components separately as well as in combination. That has made it possible for any user of the

Violence Index, including CBS, to observe the movement of each component, and to weight each as they see fit.

The CBS report correctly notes that the absolute number of violent incidents in CBS family hour programs declined in 1976, while other components of the Index showed an increase. CBS fails to discuss the nature of these other measures. It also ignores the reasons for including them in the Index. Mr. Schneider's letter further confuses the issue by claiming that the Index rose "apparently because we had the 'wrong people' involved in the action."

The *kind* of people involved had nothing to do with it. As Table 31 of Violence Profile No. 8 (to which the CBS report refers) clearly shows, 23.1 percent of *all* leading CBS family hour characters were involved in violence in 1975, compared to 31.8 percent in 1976. Even more important, violence was more broadly distributed in 1976 CBS family hour programming, making it more difficult for viewers to avoid (or have their children avoid) violence during family viewing time. While in the 1975 sample only 27.3 percent of CBS family hour programs contained violence, in the 1976 sample, 62.5 percent contained violence. So, although the number of violent acts was reduced in 1976, the percent of leading characters involved in violence increased and violence was found in many more programs. Much as we empathize with the CBS attempt to get credit for partial effort, we cannot agree that such contrary evidence should be covered up or omitted from the Index.

Units of Analysis

The CBS complaint about counting multiple acts of violence when single acts should be counted is unfounded. In the tradition of such research since the first studies of the 1950's, our coding instructions specify that a violent act is "a scene of some violence confined to the same agents. Even if the scene is interrupted by a flashback, etc., as long as it continues in 'real time' it is the same act. However, if new agent(s) enter the scene it becomes another act."

The CBS coding instructions define a violent act as "One sustained, dramatically continuous event involving violence, with essentially the same group of participants and with no major interruption in continuity." The two definitions are similar except for the ambiguous CBS qualification of "essentially." As the criteria for determining the "essential" set of agents are not specified, the CBS rule permits the arbitrary and subjective manipulation of the unit of violence. Such ambiguity not only tends to reduce the reliability of the measure but also gives the coder employed by CBS the opportunity to stretch the rule on which all other measures depend. For example, under the CBS rule it would be possible to ignore shifting participation in a long series of violent scenes, possibly involving an entire program, as not "essential" and thus to code the whole program as a single violent incident. Such a defective measure cannot be accepted as the basis for the sole standard of network performance.

Sampling

CBS asserts that "Dr. Gerbner only measures one week of television, which can lead to statistical errors of horrendous proportion." Elsewhere the report states that CBS research found wide variability in its own count of violent incidents.

Plausible as that claim seems, in fact it reflects the limitations, instabilities, and ambiguities of the CBS definition. Our own interest in assessing the representativeness of the one-week sample led to an initial analysis in 1969, to repeated spring-season test samplings in 1975 and 1976 and to an analysis of six additional weeks of fall 1976 programming. These studies indicate that while a larger sample may increase precision, given our operational definitions and multi-dimensional measures that are sensitive to a variety of significant aspects of TV violence, the one-week sample yields remarkably stable results with high cost-efficiency.

With respect to the number of violent actions per program (the measure of most concern to CBS) our six-week analysis found the same rank-order of the three networks no matter which week was chosen, except for one instance when ABC and CBS were tied (see Table 1).

CBS claims it found that the week with the highest number of incidents on any network had 2.5 to 3 times the number of incidents of the lowest week. We found in our six-week test that this multiple was 1.98 to one for CBS; for the others, it was even less: 1.29 to one for NBC, 1.23 to one for ABC.

The explanation for the discrepancy between our results and those of CBS lies more in differences of methodology than of sampling. CBS limits its observation of violence to those acts its coders presume to be intentionally harmful and excludes the majority of violent presentations they judge to be "comedic" or "accidental." These arbitrary limitations involve much subjective speculation and introduce variability and instability leading to gross statistical aberrations.

Sharply reducing both the number and potential reliability of observations, and then limiting the analysis to a single unstable measure, do indeed lead to "statistical errors of horrendous proportion." These are the errors that our broadly-based and precisely operationalized methods are designed to overcome.

Risk Ratios

The Violence Index reports absolute as well as relative risks. It makes clear, for example, that women are less likely to get involved in violence on television than men do. But it also finds that, when involved, relatively more women than men end up as victims.

Table 1 Analysis of CBS (Cultural Indicators) Analysis of Six Weeks of Fall 1976 Programming

	Test Sample Week						
	1	*2*	*3*	*4*	*5*	*F76*[a]	*Total*
Total							
No. of programs	58	58	57	58	61	61	353
No. of violent acts	345	342	365	365	341	342	2,100
Rate (acts per program)	5.9	5.9	6.4	6.3	5.6	5.6	5.9
ABC							
No. of programs	20	20	19	19	20	19	117
No. of violent acts	114	107	112	132	116	110	691
Rate (acts per program)	5.7	5.4	5.9	6.9	5.8	5.8	5.9
Network rank	2	2	1.5	2	2	2	2
CBS							
No. of programs	22	21	22	21	21	24	131
No. of violent acts	90	91	130	97	66	84	558
Rate (acts per program)	4.1	4.3	5.9	4.6	3.1	3.5	4.3
Network rank	1	1	1.5	1	1	1	1
NBC							
No. of programs	16	17	16	18	20	18	105
No. of violent acts	141	144	123	136	159	148	851
Rate (acts per program)	8.8	8.5	7.7	7.6	8	8.2	8.1
Network rank	3	3	3	3	3	3	3

a. Fall 1976 week reported in Violence Profile No. 8.

CBS claims that relative victimization (i.e. victimization compared to the commission of violence across different social types) is difficult to grasp, and is, therefore, a "meaningless statistic."

We must repeat that the validity of a TV content indicator does not depend on viewers' conscious understanding of its meaning. Our Cultivation Analysis shows that exposure to violence-laden television drama cultivates a sense of exaggerated fear and mistrust in the minds of heavy viewers. Young women—with an especially unfavorable Risk Ratio—are particularly affected, despite the fact that in absolute terms they are not as likely to get involved in violence as are the men. What CBS terms a "meaningless statistic" turns out to be potentially important in its consequences.

Our analysis of the CBS report and methodology confirms the judgment of social scientists, legislators, and the general public that only a scientifically tested, independent, and comprehensive set of indicators, measuring both TV content and effects, can be the basis for judging network performance. Our experience indicates that the Violence Index and Profile provide such a set of indicators. For independent confirmation, we recommend the findings of an international panel of distinguished industry-affiliated and academic social scientists to "conceptualize and give scientific context to the research required for the development of a multi-dimensional profile of violence in television programming." The recommendations, published in the Annual Report for 1974–75 of the Social Science Research Council (pages 67–72), provide broad scientific support for the general direction and methodology of the Violence Index and Profile and offer advice, which is directly opposed to the CBS methodology. A detailed study comparing the Violence Index and Profile with CBS methods will be published in the near future, providing further documentation.

(3) Final Comments on the Violence Profile

David M. Blank*

The Violence Index

The Gerbner response to our evaluation of the Violence Index touches on four areas of our disagreement: Gerbner's overly-broad definition of violence, the arbitrary weighting of the components of the Gerbner Index, the definition of a violent incident in terms of the persons involved rather than the continuity of the incident itself, and the statistically deficient use of a single week's sample. We discuss each of these questions in turn.

Comic Violence

By far the most attention is paid to our view that comic and accidental violence, and violence resulting from acts of nature, ought not to be included in any measure of the amount

*From Blank, D. (1977). Final comments on the Violence Profile. *Journal of Broadcasting 21*:287–296. This article reproduces the key sections of the original CBS response.

of violence. We continue to believe that this is the correct position.

To support his stand, Gerbner makes four points. First, his measure is neutral—it "does not presume effects useful or harmful." He justifies this view by analogizing with the reporting of trends in the Gross National Product on the employment index or in weather conditions. But this is nonsense. In all of these areas, what is reported is, in fact, reported because the devisers of these measures, after much discussion within their respective professions, have concluded that their measures report on phenomena, which are of consequence to society. The inclusion in weather reports of a wind-chill factor or a sunburn index, or the proposals for changes in the employment index or exclusion from the GNP measure of financial transactions, all result from closely-reasoned efforts to measure phenomena which are of social or physical consequence.

For Gerbner and his colleagues to say that they don't know what forms of violence are important and, therefore, they will, by default, include anything that anyone might conceivably include simply avoids the basic question of where the boundary line should be drawn, and why.

Second, Gerbner refers to our work at CBS on the significant amount of transmission of social messages in selected Saturday morning children's television programs, a research program in which we have invested much time and resources and of which we are very proud. He attacks our exclusion of comic violence on the basis that our research demonstrated that children can receive pro-social messages in a comic context. He ignores the fact that these programs were designed to convey and reinforce messages of a socially acceptable, socially reinforced nature. It is a long and unsupported jump to the assumption that children are picking up hidden messages of violence from comic routines.

Third, Gerbner suggests that we have exaggerated the irrationality of the inclusion of comic violence by giving "a pie in the face" as an example of the kind of comic act he would include but which most others, would not. Gerbner says he does not think there has been "a pie in the face" in one of their samples of television drama in a long time. Since Gerbner refuses to identify the weeks he has chosen as samples, we cannot completely determine the accuracy of this comment. But, we have found many incidents of innocuous "violence" in prime-time television during the current and prior seasons that we know from our dealings with the Gerbner group, would be counted as acts of violence. For example, Ted Baxter on the "Mary Tyler Moore" show did push a pie into someone's face, and this would count as violent; when Phyllis' grandmother, in a fit of pique, kicked someone in the ankle, this was also a violent act by Gerbner's standards and when Charlie Brown once again missed a placekick in a dramatic fall because Lucy pulled the ball away, this is also considered violent.

Fourth, the reply comments on our view that serious violence is that violence which reasonable citizens consider harmful: Gerbner views this as a specious view and argues again that this "confuses communications content with the assessment of effects." But surely, neither Gerbner nor anyone else would measure all aspects of content. Only those aspects of content which are meaningful in some sense or other should be measured or else the researcher is simply wasting time and money. And someone *must* decide what is meaningful. In our view, comic and accidental violence is simply not meaningful in the context in which the debate over television violence is being conducted.

Accidents

Gerbner then turns to our view that accidents and acts of nature ought not to be included in the definition of violence. His defense of their inclusion in the Violence Index is that "there are no 'accidents' in fiction. The author invents (or the producer inserts) dramatic disaster and 'acts of nature' for a purpose." But this is sheer sophistry. It is equivalent to saying that Greek tragedy does not really portray the inexorable inevitability of fate because the dramatist could have chosen to have written the play differently!

In truth, the point here is not what is in the author's mind but what is in the dramatic vehicle, and we continue to believe that, because accidents and acts of nature do not involve interpersonal violence, their inclusion is inappropriate for any violence count that attempts to measure dramatic incidents that might engender violence in the real world.

The Calculation of the Index

We turn now to a discussion of our second major area of objection to the Violence Index, namely, (a) that it is not, and does not purport to be, a simple measure of violence, and (b) that it is in fact an arbitrarily weighted sum of arbitrarily chosen programming characteristics; this weighted sum has some undefined relationship to violence.

The first problem is that while the Index, as we have earlier pointed out, includes measures other than the number of acts of violence, it is generally treated by others as if that alone is what is being described. Gerbner states that the "Violence Index reports all its components separately as well as in combination. That has made it possible for any user of the Violence Index, including CBS, to observe the movement of each component, and to weigh each as they see fit." But that is disingenuity at its worst. For years, in Gerbner's own discussion of violence, in his testimony at hearings, and in his reports, little reference was made to any other measure than his Violence Index.

Thus, in his most recent Violence Profile No. 8 issued in March 1977 and covering the 1976–77 season, Gerbner devotes only six lines of text to any discussion of data for the components of the Violence Index and then only for the aggregate of all programs and all networks. All the detailed commentary on individual networks and day parts are based only on the total Violence Index itself. While the 43 appendix tables in Violence Profile No. 8 do give all the components of the Violence Index, who is going to probe those more abstruse measures if Gerbner himself normally does not? The answer is essentially no one. Indeed, in all the public and professional discussion of the Violence Profile, we can think of only one or two occasions other than our comments in which *anyone* has had recourse to the components of the Index.

A current example of the confusion created by use of the Violence Index is Gerbner's assertion, in Violence Profile No. 8, that "CBS, leader in the 'family viewing' concept, lifted its two-season lid on family viewing time violence . . ." We had earlier pointed out that Gerbner's own figures, using his definition of violence, showed a *decline* in the *number* of incidents of violence from 20 per week to 11 per week between 1975 and 1976. That scarcely appears to be lifting the lid on violence.

But Gerbner now defends his statement primarily by arguing that the proportion of programs containing violence increased, consequently raising the level of the Violence Index. This makes sense, according to Gerbner, because "violence was more broadly distributed in 1976 CBS family hour programming, making it more difficult for viewers to avoid (or have their children avoid) violence during family viewing time." But what are the family viewing-time programs that suddenly became so violent? Aside from "Sixty Minutes" and variety programs (both of which Gerbner excludes from his count), the following eight programs constituted the family viewing programs during the fall of 1976: "Rhoda," "Phyllis," "Good Times," "Ball Four," "The Waltons," "The Jeffersons," "Doc," and "Spencer's Pilots." Which of these programs did parents need to have their children avoid because of violence? The unreality of the definition of Gerbner's definition of violence and of the peculiar and arbitrary form of the Violence Index should be apparent.

More fundamentally, the question remains as to what basis in research or logic Gerbner has for the particular set of numbers and weights he uses for the development of his Violence Index. Whence does he derive support for his view that the proportion of leading characters involved in violence has any meaning in terms of the effect of television violence on viewers? Why not minor characters as well? And why is that proportion precisely equal, in terms of importance to the

Index, and presumably in effect on the audience, to the proportion of programs containing violence, and only one-half as important as the rate of violent incidents per hour? Is Gerbner sure this ratio should not be one-third? Or one-fifth?

The truth is that the components of the Violence Index have been chosen by Gerbner without convincing scientific proof of their relevance, and the weights used in their combination have been arbitrarily chosen by Gerbner without any scientific support for their relative importance. So the weighted combination of these components—the Index itself—can vary over time with no one being able to identify a valid meaning for such movements.

It was precisely the arbitrariness of the entire construct that was challenged by Bruce Owen of the Office of Telecommunications Policy and it is the same arbitrariness which leads us to reject the Index as a measure of anything.[1] It is true that "one *must* add apples and oranges if one wants to know about *fruit,*" just as one must add rabbits and elephants if one wants to know about animals. But does one rabbit equal one elephant? Whether one rabbit equals one elephant is of fundamental importance in determining whether the summing of rabbits and elephants in a certain fashion to measure some characteristic of animals is valid or not.

When the Consumer Price Index, which does combine apples and oranges, is reported to have risen, some components have gone up in price and some have gone down. But the Bureau of Labor Statistics can validly report that the aggregate of the various components went up because it has used a weighting process in which the weights have been derived from experience in the real world, i.e., the distribution of the actual market basket of goods and services purchased by the families covered by the survey.

Where does Gerbner get his weights from? What evidence does he have that his weights are superior to some other set of weights? For example, assume that the rate of violence per hour and rate of violence per program, two of Gerbner's Index components, were given a weight of 90-percent, rather than the modest weight they are actually given. Under these circumstances, Gerbner on the basis of his own data would have had to say that CBS reduced the amount of violence in the family hour between 1975 and 1976, instead of saying that "CBS lifted the lid on violence." And nowhere in the many pages written by the Gerbner group on their monitoring results is there any discussion of why one system of weighting is better than another.

Units of Analysis

Gerbner discusses our criticism that his definition of a violent incident requires the participation of "the same agents." Our definition is less restrictive and focuses in practice on the unity of a dramatic incident, rather than the identification of the agents involved.

Gerbner severely criticizes our definition as "ambiguous" and as one that permits arbitrary and subjective manipulation of the unit of violence. He goes on to state that, "such ambiguity not only tends to reduce the reliability of the measure but also gives the coder employed by CBS the opportunity to stretch the rule on which all other measures depend."

However, as Gerbner is well aware, "reliability" in content analysis is a measurable dimension, rather than an offhand assessment based upon one's view of whether a definition reads well. Neither Gerbner's monitors nor ours can be handed a definition and set to work without further explanation through training and example. That is true of our definition, and it is equally true of the Gerbner definition. . . .

We have applied measures of reliability to the CBS monitoring and very high levels of agreement among coders have, in fact, been established. The basic measure—intraclass correlations—has consistently exceeded 0.90. Since reliability is very high, the operating definitions used by CBS are clearly effective, efficient, and unambiguous. This information has been published.

We continue to believe that the unit of count should be defined by the dramatic incident, not by the participation of particular characters. The emphasis on changing participants in Gerbner's procedures is a result of abstract considerations, related to his interest in power relationships (about which we have more to say below) and not intrinsic to any evaluation of the extent of violence. One could more validly propose that each blow or shot fired is a single act of violence than that a change in participants denotes a new act of violence.

Finally, Gerbner asserts that under the CBS definition it is conceivable that a whole program might be coded as a single violent incident. This, of course, could occur just as well under his definition, as for example, if there were a prolonged kidnapping sequence covering essentially an entire program without any change in participants. But, more to the point, we have tallied and published data showing the average duration of violent episodes as calculated by our monitoring system. During the current season, length of incidents of violence was only 1.4 minutes.

Sampling

Finally, we turn to questions of sampling error and of statistical significance. We had earlier pointed out the increasing statistical dangers of choosing a single sample week a year, as the television network schedules became more complex and as programming became more irregular. We indicated that the substantial variation in the amount of violence from week to week makes year-to-year comparisons drawn from single-week samples highly suspect. We showed this large variation in our monitoring data.

Gerbner says he has now tested his procedures over an additional five weeks. And he concludes that he has found more stability than we did and that "the one-week samples yields remarkably stable results with high cost efficiency." Indeed, he charges that our evidence of instability stems from the "limitation, instabilities and ambiguities" of our definition.

Several comments are in order on this view. First, we have already indicated that our results are highly reliable, measured in terms of inter-coder agreement, and, therefore, there simply is no problem with our definition—it is not ambiguous or unstable.

Second, Gerbner may be satisfied with the statistical results of his extended sampling but we are not. Thus, for the CBS Television Network, the variance shown by the Gerbner extended sample is so large[2] that, by standard statistical measure, *no* year-to-year change in the number of acts of prime-time violence so fulsomely reported by Gerbner in the years since 1967 has been statistically significant! To put it another way, for CBS the year-to-year change in the number of incidents of violence, as defined and measured by Gerbner, between years that Gerbner has reported has been far smaller than the inherent variability in the underlying Gerbner data. It has been so much smaller that, by generally accepted scientific standards, Gerbner should have said throughout this entire period that he couldn't identify any significant change in the number of acts of prime-time violence on CBS. This, of course, is vastly different from what he has actually said.

But in addition, in reviewing the Gerbner statistical data we were reminded of an aspect of the Gerbner technique which raises serious questions about the entire relationship between the Gerbner sample and the universe of network programming from which the sample is drawn. Gerbner indicates that, in his one-week sample, "when and if an episode of a regularly scheduled program is preempted by some special offering during the selected week, the next available episode of that series is videotaped." It is perhaps understandable why Gerbner chose this approach when he began his monitoring a decade ago. During a period when most programs broadcast were episodes of regularly-scheduled series, preempted only occasionally by clearly defined specials, it might have been reasonable for Gerbner, desiring to choose a "representative" week, to replace "specials" by the regular programs they preempted. But television network programming has changed enormously in the last decade. Variation in scheduling has become the standard, rather than the unusual. During this last season, and even more during the upcoming season, it is almost impossible to define what is a "regularly-scheduled" program and what is a "special." Is a series of specials such as NBC's "Big Event" a regularly-scheduled program? What about a program such as "Roots," which appeared with varying episode lengths on eight consecutive nights? How do we deal with hour programs which occasionally appear in two-hour form? Or with mini-series in episodes which vary in length? We don't know where we would draw the line, and Gerbner never discusses the criteria by which he makes these decisions.

The arbitrariness of this technique is surely apparent. Further, the elimination, in whatever degree Gerbner happens to decide, of non-regular programming from the Gerbner Index leaves out of network programming a large and increasing fraction of actual programs broadcast. The only procedure that appropriately reflects television entertainment programming as it in fact appears on one's television set is the procedure CBS follows, namely, the inclusion of all prime-time entertainment programs actually broadcast during a sample week and the inclusion of enough sample weeks to achieve statistical reliability. Whatever Gerbner is measuring these days, it is *not* the total array of current entertainment offerings by the television networks.

Risk Ratios

For some years, Gerbner has defined the purpose for which he measures his Risk Ratios. He has traditionally argued that television has become the tool by which society "demonstrates an invidious (but socially functional) sense of risk and power . . ."

Television is considered by Gerbner to be a primary method by which society conveys to its underclasses that their role in life is subservient to that of the rest of society. Among those groups defined as "underclasses" by the Gerbner Risk Ratios are women and nonwhites. Accordingly, if one believed in this view of society and of television, one would expect women and nonwhites to have been taught their proper roles in society and to behave appropriately.

However, about a decade after this hypothesis was first propounded, Gerbner himself states (in Violence Profile No. 7), that "we do not yet know whether it [the pattern of relative victimization] . . . cultivates a corresponding hierarchy of fear and aggression"!

Indeed, one can make a more positive statement. No one in his right mind would seriously suggest that, after 30 years of television, women and nonwhites are meeker and less aggressive in defending their rights than they used to be. But for Gerbner's view of society and television to have any meaning, this is exactly what should have happened.

The truth is that this hypothesis about the effects of dramatic portrayals on television has no support in fact. The Risk Ratio measure itself probably does not measure significant characteristics of television drama in the minds of viewers. Neither society nor television has the kind of monolithic value system that Gerbner presupposes. And there simply is no evidence that the artificial view of society and television that Gerbner has constructed has its counterpart in the real world. . . .

Summary

In this document, and in our preceding comments, we have examined the Gerbner Violence Profile and its components. We have concluded that the Violence Index does not measure the amount of violence on prime-time television nor is there objective support for the particular elements combined in that Index or the weights, which are used to combine them. Even the violence counts themselves are based on overly-broad definitions of violence and on overly-narrow samples. . . .

These days many studies are being undertaken of one aspect or another of television program content and its effect on viewers; numerous hypotheses are being put forward about the effect of television on society. We do not feel it incumbent on us to comment on or respond to every such study or hypothesis. If the Violence Profile had been simply one among the many studies, we would not have expended as much effort in reviewing its validity as we have. But, in fact, the Violence Profile has been in a unique position and played a unique role. Dr. Gerbner and his group have been supported in their work in this area by federal government funds for the last decade. The Profile itself has been put forward as an all-encompassing model of the way in which depictions of violence on television affect our society. And many people concerned with this issue have treated the Profile and its conclusions as if they were of demonstrated scientific validity and, therefore, had major social implications. . . .

Notes

1. The Social Science Research Council Committee on Television and Social Behavior, in their report on "A Profile of Televised Violence" (July 1975), said that: "Initially, the aggregation of the components should be avoided and should not be undertaken without prior research into the technical problems involved, the understanding of the profile by its users, the consequences for the intended functions of the violence profile, etc." More generally, we do not consider this report either the rigorous review of the Violence Profile or the endorsement of the Profile that Gerbner does.

2. During the six Gerbner sample weeks, the acts of violence on CBS prime-time programming, as reported by Gerbner, numbered: 90, 91, 130, 97, 66, and 84.

(4) One More Time

An Analysis of the CBS "Final Comments on the Violence Profile"

George Gerbner, Larry Gross, Marilyn Jackson-Beeck, Suzanne Jeffries-Fox, and Nancy Signorielli*

Symmetry more than substance compels us to pursue a dialogue that threatens to make the lively subject of television violence bog down in tedium. But behind the contentions and technicalities over a mixed bag of issues, we perceive a deeper structure shaping and straining this colloquy. As our (we hope) final contribution in this context, we shall try to elaborate what that constraint might be, and what it suggests for the future of research relevant to television program policy.

CBS persists in claiming that "comic and accidental violence, and violence resulting from acts of nature, ought not be included in any measure of the amount of violence." Our previous analysis clearly indicates that there are no real "accidents" or "acts of nature" in fiction. They are simply ways of presenting violence and victimization. We have also noted that comic content is a highly effective form of conveying serious lessons. Finally, we have indicated that idle threats, comic gestures, verbal abuse, or any non-credible suggestions of violence are not included in our definition. Also, our findings are reported separately for comic programs so that any careful reader can assess their independent contributions to the total pattern. So why this insistence on excluding comic and "accidental" violence?

Of course, the more inclusive the count the higher the number CBS considers damaging. But there is also another clue in the CBS attempt to determine what violence is "meaningful." Previously, that attempt led CBS to suggest that the criterion of "meaningfulness" is "that violence which reasonable citizens consider harmful." But why? Why not that which reasonable citizens consider *helpful?* Is that less meaningful? Our research does not find it so. But it may be less troublesome from the point of view of corporate policy, and therefore, less "meaningful" from a strictly policy-oriented point of view.

*From Gerbner, G., Gross, L., Jackson-Beeck, M., Jeffries-Fox, S., & Signorelli, N. (1977). One more time: An analysis of the CBS "Final comments on the Violence Profile." *Journal of Broadcasting 21:*299–303.

That point of view becomes even more sharply defined in the new CBS criterion of meaningfulness, now offered as an argument for exclusion: "In our view, comic and accidental violence is simply not meaningful in the context in which the debate over television violence is conducted." Our research has shown that context to be relatively uninformed of a variety of significant lessons to be derived from exposure to television violence. We believe that a scientific effort to discover all socially important effects of television violence, rather than to take the terms of the popular debate at face value, would serve both the public and CBS better than its rigid defense of corporate policy in the face of often unwarranted criticism.

Apparently, CBS researchers also believe that comic and accidental violence may be significant, even if they continue to exclude it from the "overall count." There is a discrepancy between what Vice President Blank writes and what the CBS Office of Social Research reports.

The May 1977 CBS Monitoring Report states (on pages 15–16) that the CBS definition (modeled on and very similar to ours) "included accidents or acts of nature which occurred in a violent context as, for example, a person being killed in an automobile accident while escaping from a crime." In another passage, the CBS report notes (page 6, footnote) that "In this season's tabulations, episodes of dramatic violence that occur in situation comedies were included in the totals for the 'other programs' category . . . We continue to exclude comic violence from our overall count."

It seems, therefore, that the need for the exclusion does not come from research considerations but from pressures for a "better bottom line." What is most at stake here is the area of children's programming, particularly cartoons, which contain the most frequent (and stereotyped) violence. We cannot agree that such a critical area should be exempt from accounting and scrutiny.

The CBS discussion of the "neutrality" of our content measures is puzzling. We said that measures of content should not *presume* effects. Rather, content measures facilitate the effective investigation of effects. Ecologists measure the amount of certain chemicals in the air or water (as we do in the symbolic environment) in order to ascertain their presence and then to test—rather than to presume—their effects on people. So the "boundary line" should be drawn not in accepting the popular presumption of ill-defined effects but in the clear and unambiguous observation of the element (in this case of violence) in any context. Only such observation can lead to the investigation of the behavioral and conceptual correlates of exposure to strictly defined violence. Proceeding in that way, our research indeed found several very meaningful correlates of exposure, some of which may be quite helpful to some groups.

The underlying problem again may be that CBS is constrained by the nature of critical public discussion, which often jumps to unwarranted conclusions. One such conclusion is that the major or only "meaningful" effect of exposure to television violence is the instigation of aggression. That presumption forces on CBS the task of corporate defense, even at the risk of distorting the research issue.

In the course of accepting rather than attempting to transform the terms of the popular debate about TV violence, CBS gets into even more hot water. CBS prides itself on its own research on a few children's programs demonstrating "that children can receive pro-social messages in a comic context." CBS claims that we "ignore the fact that these programs were designed to convey and reinforce messages of a socially acceptable, socially reinforced nature." Well, last fall's overall CBS weekend daytime fare hit a five-year record of 19.2 violent episodes per hour (up from 14.2 the year before). Does CBS mean to suggest that all these other programs were *designed* to be socially unacceptable and destructive? Its defense against simplistic criticism puts CBS in that box. CBS sinks even deeper when it contends that our measures of the abundance of gross and explicit violence in children's programs constitute "a long and unsupported jump to the assumption that children are picking up hidden messages of violence from comic routines!"

Similar problems plague the CBS discussion of the Violence Index itself. Vice President Blank as an economist can see the validity of multidimensional measures of GNP or unemployment. These and other measures he approves "result from closely-reasoned efforts to measure phenomena which are of social or physical consequences." But similar efforts to establish Cultural Indicators (of which the Violence Index is a current example) are dismissed as "nonsense." Why?

The closest we can get to a cogent reason is that the weighting of the components going into the Index is "arbitrary" and that we have not given sufficient attention to the individual components, even though we have included them in our reports.

What are these weightings and components? The Violence Index is composed of 1) the percent of programs containing any violence, plus 2) the rate of violent episodes per program, plus 3) the rate of violent episodes per hour, plus 4) the percent of major characters involved in any violence, plus 5) the percent of major characters involved in any killing. Each of these measures has a specifically defined meaning and function in our analysis. The *only* "weighting" is that we double two rates (2 and 3) in order to raise the low numerical values of these ratios to the level of importance that we believe the concepts of the frequency and program saturation of violent incidents deserve when combined with the other numbers which, being percentages, typically have much higher numerical value. No one is forced to agree with or follow that simple assumption. The individual components for all years are included in our reports and are available for any combination.

The bulk of the Violence Index and Profile is a set of 71 Tables. Thousands of Profiles have been distributed. The composite Violence Index combines the components by means of the formula explained above. Violence Profile No. 8 specifically states (on page 21) that the individual "measures of violence are based on analysts' observations. They are provided in all tabulations and should be used as basic indicators of trends. However, for ease of illustration and comparison, they are combined to form summary scores and an index. These are not statistical findings in themselves, and should not be treated as such. Rather they serve as convenient illustrators of the basic findings and to facilitate gross comparisons."

It is true that most public discussion revolves around the composite Index. Similarly, the broadcast industry refers to overall Nielsen or Arbitron ratings, although these are composed of demographic and other separate—and sometimes conflicting—components. We believe that there is a general validity to the overall Index, and that consistently applied, it does show meaningful trends in performance. As CBS knows best, the detailed tabulations do not get on network news or into newspaper headlines. We disseminate complete information; it is up to the media to do their homework and use such Violence Index components or combinations of components as they see fit.

CBS reflects some irritation with the perhaps less than felicitous phrasing in our 1977 Report that "CBS, leader in the 'family viewing' concept, lifted its two-season lid on family viewing time violence . . ." Let us look at the individual components of the "family hour" Index for 1973, 74, 75, and 76.

Percent of fall season CBS family hour programs containing any violence: 50, 50, 27, 63. Percent of hours containing violence: 60, 56, 31, 60. Rate of violent episodes per program: 4.4, 3.1, 1.8, 1.4. Rate of violent episodes per hour: 5.9, 3.9, 3.1, 2.2. Percent of leading characters involved in any violence: 43, 29, 23, 32. Percent of leading characters involved in killing: 13, 7, 0, 0. It is clear as we report, that while the number and rate of "family hour" violent incidents declined, and killing by or of leading characters was eliminated, the percent of programs with violence and characters involved in some violence has increased, making the overall "family hour" Index 127 in 1973, 100 in 1974, 60 in 1975, and 101 in 1976. *(The corresponding Index numbers for all CBS drama were 174, 174, 154 and 181.)* The factors that determine these movements are clearly not our measures but network policy and its application by the network's department of Standards and Practices. If next season's program mix shows a policy of replacing the "lid" on more or all aspects of violence, we shall be pleased to report it.

The CBS list of family hour programs and the rhetorical question "Which of these programs did parents need to have their children avoid because of violence?" continue the persistent misreading of the issue and of our reports. Nothing we report suggests that parents have children avoid specific programs. The Violence Index and Profile measure aggregate programming policy and its consequences. These are cumulative over the years, do not stem from single programs, and involve a variety of lessons of different potential value for different groups. Reducing violence to a mechanical and one-dimensional issue only reinforces the superficiality of the popular debate.

The CBS discussion of units of analysis and sampling adds little of substance to what we have discussed before. Our units, defined according to participation of the same characters, are easier to code, yield more information—and more but briefer incidents—than those of CBS. They further help to place the violence in a social context. That is something CBS and other networks have long demanded, but refuse to do themselves. The investigation of such context is highly indicative of a variety of potential lessons to be derived from TV violence. But it is not a prime subject of popular criticism and is therefore of little corporate interest.

The variability of year-to-year incidents of violence has been equally large in both our and the CBS samples (cf. the 1977 CBS report, page 4). That is why we (unlike CBS) use the much more broadly-based Index which combines several measures, and discuss upward or downward trends over the years, rather than statistical differences from one year to another. In fact, until the sharp and surprising rise in violence last year, our reports tended to emphasize the *lack* of significant change, despite repeated network promises and protestations.

The rationale for focusing on regularly scheduled dramatic programs should be obvious. Our study is designed to investigate the representative and repetitive patterns of programming, and not the occasional or exceptional "specials." It is not at all difficult to define what is a "special"; the networks promote them heavily and usually announce that "the regularly scheduled program will return next week." However, *any dramatic production* such as "Roots" or a mini-series would be included in our analysis if it fell within our sample week. If and when the actual variability of the week-to-week programming pattern justifies enlarging the sample to obtain representative results, we shall do so. At the present time that is far from the case. Behind the revolving door of formats and titles, there is a persistent stability of basic content elements and social patterns portrayed in the programs.

This brings us to the last point of some substance. CBS claims that our findings would suggest that "women and nonwhites are meeker and less aggressive in defending their rights than they used to be." That is careless reading and tendentious reporting of what we actually found. We say nothing about what women and minorities do because that is not what we study. We study the pattern of television violence and find that it places a higher burden of relative victimization upon women, nonwhites, and other minority groups such as children and the elderly than upon the white male majority. We also find that heavy viewing of television, with other factors kept constant, is related to a sense of exaggerated danger and mistrust. An independent study by Dr. Nicholas Zill of the Foundation for Child Development has since come to the same conclusion for children. Of course this does not mean that television alone determines human behavior. What it indicates is that violence-laden television drama cultivates an unequal sense of vulnerability within a conventionally stereotyped power and value structure. Both the growing militancy of some groups and the growing resistance to change of others, as well as the increasing fear of most, take place in that cultural environment. Television is an important contributor to these trends.

We are in the process of expanding and diversifying our monitoring and cultivation studies. We are developing additional indicators of family life, aging, health and medicine, and other key issues regularly presented in television programming. What we have profited from this and other exchanges will thus be put to use in our continuing studies.

Only an independent effort can afford to let the chips fall where they may. In the long run, that is the best protection for the public and also for the TV industry. As broadcasting policy develops in new directions, we will report the facts, as we have in the past. Independent scientific research is the best defense against uninformed or unwarranted public criticism and the best guide to policies that reflect careful consideration of all important social consequences.

PART 7

COMPUTER-AIDED CONTENT ANALYSIS

Since the data of interest to content analysts can be massive, computers offer an extraordinarily powerful tool for identifying, sorting, and counting strings of characters, for example, words and propositions. What computers cannot do, however, is tell us what they mean. It is the content analyst who needs to tell a computer how people read text, or use available computational tools in view of this ability, and check out the validity of the computations. This section presents several computer aids—not so much for their data requirements but for their analytical constructs implicit in their algorithms.

This section does not include software reviews or instructions. Software changes too quickly. For instance, the popular qualitative data analysis (QDA) software ATLAS.ti and NUD•IST have had several offspring, some not adopting their parents' names. They do share, however, in enabling their users to manually associate codes or labels with chunks of text, whole images, and video or sound recordings; to search these codes for patterns; and to construct classifications of these codes related to conceptual models that are to be tested for whether they underlie the data. Interested users will need to explore for themselves which QDA software is best suited to answer their research questions.

More generally, we encourage researchers interested in using available content analysis software to read its descriptions critically and attend to not only their user-friendliness and computational capacities but also to whether and what evidence is provided for the validity and relevance of their results. Much too often, software is promoted with tempting claims that turn out to be shallow after significant investment of time.

We start this section with an article by Daniel Ogilvie and associates, who describe the General Inquirer, the first fully implemented computer program for content analysis. The General Inquirer relies on a user-definable dictionary that tags relevant character strings in texts and offers various accounts of these tags and of the tagged text for subsequent examination by the analysts. Here, Ogilvie and colleagues were interested in discriminating between genuine and simulated suicide notes. The analytical construct they developed took the form of a discriminant function, effectively representing the difference between the two kinds of note writers' letters.

Michael Palmquist and colleagues apply a map extraction program, developed by Kathleen Carley, for constructing the cognitive maps of writers from manually coded texts. The analytical

---

*See reading 3.1, this volume.

construct is a semantic network, derived from an artificial intelligence model of human cognition. The researchers demonstrate their method by means of science fiction narratives that contained robots. The software requires manually translating a text into relational statements containing two concepts from a selected set, here including robots, and what relates them. From such a semantic network, the program can answer questions about what is said about each of these concepts. Applied to robots, Palmquist et al. found that their early depictions were negative and fearful, but by the late 20th century, robots became more sympathetic characters with more human features.

Based on the co-occurrences of selected words—not of concepts, as in Osgood's contingency analysis*—Marya Doerfel and George Barnett describe what a software package called CATPAC is capable of doing with texts. The virtue of this software is that it does not require manual coding or tagging by a dictionary. It automatically removes syntactical features and function words from text and allows researchers to identify key words from which to proceed. All word co-occurrences within a specifiable distance from each other give rise to clusters and multidimensional representations. Doerfel and Barnett demonstrate CATPAC's results with data from the 1992 U.S. presidential debates. Incidentally, computing clusters from word co-occurrences also underlies a host of other computer programs, sometimes preposterously called "meaning extractors" or "data miners."

Also without coding or tagging, communication network researcher James Danowski uses a computer program to extract and map all word pairs occurring in the answers to a set of survey questions. The word networks that such an analysis produces can be huge, far exceeding the human capacity to notice patterns in them. Danowski uses a traveling salesman algorithm, which computes the shortest paths from A to B via important nodes in that net, to extract the main concerns expressed in a text, here of listeners to a radio station in one study and the most compelling arguments for selling cars in another.

Jan Kleinnijenhuis and collaborators have expanded Osgood's evaluative assertion analysis,* which used dissonance theory as its analytical construct. They added several assertion types to Osgood's from which evaluations can be inferred as well and developed a new analytical engine to cope with complex semantic networks that large texts yield. The article included here demonstrates not only their computer-aided coding of Dutch newspaper accounts but also how the vast network of relations found in text is computationally reduced to conclusions about the nature of the economic discourse in the Netherlands.

Earlier in this volume, Best** describes his use of biological models to compute "memes" and explains their reproduction and interaction within e-conversations as an ecology. David Fan and Greg McAvoy identify "infons" in text, which resemble Best's computational memes, and model their dynamics with the help of theories from epidemiology. Fan calls his approach "ideodynamics." His software is designed to simulate how the circulation of infons on a particular issue affects divisions in public opinion about that issue. The analytical construct underlying these simulations is implemented in the form of a complex recursive function of news coverage over time on a chosen issue. It computes the changing proportion of people holding beliefs about it. In their example, Fan and McAvoy used Associated Press (AP) wire service stories to simulate changes in public opinion on whether AIDS would spread to the general populations. The

---

*See reading 3.5, this volume.

**See reading 3.6, this volume.

usually high correlation of results from ideodynamics with available public opinion data suggests that this kind of content analysis can substitute for costlier opinion surveys.

We end this section—and our book—with a recent article reminiscent of propaganda analyses during World War II* as well as of Allport's use of personal documents for gaining insights about the psychology of their authors.** In James Pennebaker and Cindy Chung's article, the source of the data for their computer content analysis and the target of their inferences is Osama bin Laden and al-Zawahiri, leaders of the terrorist group Al-Qaeda, using texts from other terrorist groups as controls. Pennebaker's Linguistic Inquiry and Word Count (LIWC) program counts words pertaining to more than 70 variables of social-psychological significance, only a few of which are explored in this article. LIWC enables the researcher to define analytical constructs in the form of regression equations, which have led to many interesting inferences.

---

*See reading 1.5, this volume.

**See readings 1.6 and 7.1, this volume.

7.1

Some Characteristics of Genuine Versus Simulated Suicide Notes

Daniel M. Ogilvie, Philip J. Stone, and Edwin S. Shneidman*

The Notes and the Problem[1]

Thirty-three genuine suicide and 33 simulated suicide notes were made available to members of the research team by Edwin S. Shneidman. The genuine notes were selected from 721 suicide notes collected from folders of suicide cases in Los Angeles County for the ten-year period of 1945 to 1954. This sample included only those notes written by suicide victims who were male, Caucasian, Protestant, native born, and between the ages of 25 and 59. For comparative purposes, simulated suicide notes were obtained from nonsuicidal individuals who were all also male, Caucasian, Protestant, and native born, and who were matched with genuine note writers with respect to age and occupational level. The simulated note writers were instructed to make their notes sound as real as possible, to write as if they were actually planning to take their own life. Through the use of the *General Inquirer,* we were able to distinguish between genuine and simulated suicide notes.

The Dictionary

The dictionary used in this study was the Harvard II Psychosociological Dictionary. That category system, like the Harvard III Dictionary, was divided into first-order tags (discrete, independent categories) and second-order tags (non-independent categories). The first-order tags were subdivided into *ROLES, OBJECTS, EMOTIONAL STATES,* and *ACTIONS.* All *things* were either *ROLES* or *OBJECTS and* all *processes* were either *EMOTIONAL STATES* or *ACTIONS.* The second-order tags were classified as referring to either *INSTITUTIONS, STATUSES, QUALITIES,* or *SYMBOLIC REFERENTS.*

---

*From Ogilvie, D. M., Stone, P. J., & Shneidman, E. S. (1966). Some characteristics of genuine versus simulated suicide notes. In P. J. Stone, D. C. Dunphy, M. S. Smith, & D. M. Ogilvie (Eds.), *The General Inquirer: A computer approach to content analysis* (pp. 527–535). Cambridge: MIT Press.

First Inspection of Tag Score Differences

The genuine and simulated notes were processed separately. The tags that appeared to differentiate between the sets (total difference of .03 percent or greater) are presented in Table 1.

Roughly summarizing the differences revealed, in Table 1, we found that the genuine suicide notes are slightly more diversified in their use of the eight general categories in our theoretical scheme. With the exception of *EMOTIONAL STATES* and *INSTITUTIONS*, the genuine notes have relatively higher counts on some tags under all categories. On the other hand, the simulated notes do not have any higher scores in the following categories: *OBJECTS, STATUSES,* and *QUALITIES.* Moreover, the simulated notes make relatively little use of the *ROLES* category.

More specifically, the greatest difference seems to be that the genuine note writers concentrate more heavily on tags referring to *things* (*ROLES* and *OBJECTS*) and *qualities,* whereas the simulated note writers have their heaviest concentration on tags referring to *processes.* The use of tags under *things* and *qualities* by genuine note writers appears to

Table 1 Tags That Discriminate Between Genuine and Simulated Notes

First-Order Tags

Things

ROLES		*OBJECTS*	
Genuine	*Simulated*	*Genuine*	*Simulated*
SELF	SELVES	ARTIFACT	
OTHER		PLACE	
MALE ROLE			
FEMALE ROLE			

Processes

EMOTIONAL STATES		*ACTIONS*	
Genuine	*Simulated*	*Genuine*	*Simulated*
	ANXIETY-FAIL	COMMUNICATE	THINK
	ANXIETY-UNABLE	POSSESS	SENSE
	DISTRESS	GET	IF
		ATTACK	NOT
			MOVE
			AVOID
			DIRECT
			GOALS

Second-Order Tags

INSTITUTIONS		*STATUSES*	
Genuine	*Simulated*	*Genuine*	*Simulated*
	ACADEMIC	HIGHER-STATUS	

QUALITIES		*SYMBOLIC REFERENTS*	
Genuine	*Simulated*	*Genuine*	*Simulated*
QUANTITY-REFERENCE		SEX-THEME	DEATH-THEME
BAD		MALE-THEME	UNDERSTATE

NOTE: Tags that appear in this table are those which had comparatively "high" counts for the set (genuine or simulated) under which they are listed.

represent a greater emphasis on specifics. On the other hand, the high counts on tags under *processes* might well reflect a more general use of words indicating the operation of cognitive processes for the simulated note writers (words such as think, sense, if, goals). Another difference between the two types of notes is the tendency for the genuine notes to use sentences with words referring to themselves in the first person and to others (male and females), whereas the simulated note writers tend to refer more to themselves and others simultaneously by using the word "we." Equally interesting is the complete absence of tags under *EMOTIONAL STATES* for the genuine notes. This reflects a relative lack of direct references to emotion. Also, we find that the genuine notes are high on the symbolic tags SEX-THEME and MALE-THEME, possibly indicating an underlying concern with sex, which is not recognized on the conscious level.

Leftover Revelations

The words that were not found in the dictionary and thereby were printed out as leftovers were reviewed. First, it was found that the dictionary defined a higher percentage of words in the simulated notes (92 percent) than were defined for the genuine notes (86 percent). In other words, eight-percent of the words in the simulated notes were not defined, whereas 14 percent of the words from the genuine notes went without definition. In addition to this finding, the words in the two lists differed in content. Specifically, 64 percent of the leftover words from the genuine notes could be classified in one of the following five categories: proper names, places, objects, numbers, and time. By contrast, only 32 percent of the leftover words from the simulated notes could be classified under these categories. This finding supports one of our initial interpretations of the differences on tag counts between the two sets of notes. That is, the genuine note writers used very specific, concrete references in their messages.

Retrieving and Judging Sentences

Before processing the genuine and simulated notes, they had been coded and syntax marked. For our purposes, this was important in two respects. First, pronouns could be identified. If the writer referred to his sister by using the pronoun "you," the information that "you" meant sister and sister meant female was not lost. Second, since sentence "parts" (subject, verb, object, and so on) had been specified, initial tag-score differences between the sets of notes were further divided into differences with respect to parts of speech. For example, the summary score for the tag FEMALE-ROLE revealed that genuine note writers referred to females more frequently than did simulated note writers. Further inspection of the printout revealed that the greatest difference lay in the genuine notes' references to females in the *subject* position of the sentence (154 occurrences of female as subject for the genuine notes compared to 64 occurrences for the simulated notes). Making use of this rather substantial difference, we retrieved all sentences from both sets of notes that matched our Female-as-Subject specification.

Working from the printout of the retrieval of these sentences, we found that all sentences from both genuine and simulated notes could be classified under one of the following three categories:

1. Writer is making a request or is giving an instruction or command to a woman.

   Examples:

   You (female) get in touch with Mary Jones (female) at once.
   You (female) please get a lawyer.
   You (female) be happy.
   You (female) teach him (son) to grow into a fine man.

2. Writer is giving information or expressing opinions (given as information) about a woman.

   Examples:

   She lives close by.
   Soon she (daughter) will dominate you.

She packed her bag.
Mother meant good.

3. A woman has acted upon the writer, over and above straight information.

Examples:
She kept after me.
Helen (female) gave it (pen) to me.
And (wife) left me.
But she (mother) drove me to my grave.

Table 2 gives the percentage distribution of sentences retrieved and classified from both genuine and simulated notes with respect to these categories.

Table 2 Classifications of "Female-as Subject" Retrievals

	Genuine	*Simulated*
Instruction	29%	45%
Information	55%	50%
Female acting upon writer	15%	6%

We see that genuine note writers gave a smaller percentage of instructions to females, but they had a higher percentage of sentences giving information about women and sentences implying that a woman had directed action toward the writer. The latter two findings seemed reasonable, but the first finding created difficulties insofar as it was incongruent with our evolving notion of a suicide victim's terse concreteness. An investigation of those sentences in which the writer was giving commands or instructions indicated that they could be further classified into two relatively clear categories. These categories were

1. Instructions are of a specific nature.

Examples:
You (female) tell my folks.
You (female) please take care of my bills.

2. Instructions are of an unreasonable or vague nature.

Examples:
You (female) do not be mean with me, please.
You (female) find a new life for yourself.

Three judges who were not familiar with the materials independently judged these "instruction" sentences as belonging either in the *specific* or *vague* categories. There was complete agreement among raters. The results showed that when genuine writers gave instructions, 55 percent of these instructions were specific and direct. Only 25 percent of the instructions given by the simulated note writers had this quality; the other 75 percent were of a vague, non-instrumental nature.

Moving away from the women in the lives of genuine and simulated suicide note writers, we recall that another difference between the two sets of notes appeared when we considered tags under the *processes* division of first-order tags. The simulated notes were overrepresented by tags falling under this division. Quite generally, we remarked that this might reflect a greater use of decision-making words on the part of the pretenders. To investigate this possibility further, we chose to concentrate on sentences that were retrieved, based on containing words that had been defined by the tag THINK. Fifty-nine sentences were recovered from the genuine set compared to 54 sentences from the simulated set. It was noted from these retrievals that two types of words were responsible for raising the tag count for THINK. The first type included words such as think, recall, reason, remember, explain, consider, decide, and so forth. The second type included the words know, knew, known. Normally when words in the first list are used in a sentence they serve to indicate that the writer is attempting to solve a problem or is using his reasoning processes in some way, for instance, "I am thinking of all the problems we have shared." On the other hand, when "know" is used in a sentence, it indicates that a problem has been solved, knowledge has been gained, a decision has been made; for example, "I knew that if I went to the doctor, I would. . . ."

This distinction within the category THINK differentiated between the genuine and simulated notes in the following manner. Fifty-eight percent of the genuine notes originally retrieved as matching the specification THINK contained a form of the word "know." When the distribution is viewed in a slightly different manner, 19 of the 33 genuine notes contained sentences using a form of the word "know." By contrast, only 8 of the 33 simulated suicide notes contained "know" sentences.

We may conclude that the simulated note writers tended to use words indicating the operation of problem-solving modes, whereas the genuine note writers' use of the word "know" reflects the fact that a final decision has been made. Partial substantiation of this view is gained when we recall that, along with the tag THINK, other tags referring to intellectual processes (SENSE, IF, ACADEMIC) were more frequently used by the simulated note writers than by the genuine note writers.

Discussion and Summary

Before summarizing the results of our analysis, it is instructive to review briefly the results of these same paired notes in an analysis conducted by Gottschalk and Gleser (1960). By using a hand method of classifying words into objects, processes, spatial relations, and so forth (a method similar to our computer method), they summarized that the categories of words that typify genuine suicide notes include a relatively high percentage of references to people and things, places or spatial relations, and a relatively low percentage of references to cognitive processes. We too found that genuine notes had a relatively high percentage of references to people, places, and things when we (1) compared the frequencies of tags under *ROLES* and *OBJECTS* and (2) compared the two lists of leftover words. The results of our analysis of *specific* versus *vague* requests made by the note writers using "Female-as-Subject" warrant us to note the possibility that the genuine note writers not only made more specific mention of names, places, and objects but they were much more specific in their entire final communicative attempt than were the simulated note writers. Again, in line with Gottschalk and Gleser's findings, we pointed out that the simulated note writers used a large number of words that were defined by the tags indicating the use of cognitive processes. The results of the analysis of the tag THINK and the high counts on tags SENSE, IF, and ACADEMIC for the simulated note writers added support to this finding. Contrasting these results for simulated note writers, we found that the genuine suicide note writers tended to use the word "know" more often. This finding can also be viewed as another example of the genuine note writers' specificity as opposed to the generality of the simulated notes.

As a demonstration of the usefulness of these findings in discriminating between the genuine and simulated notes, Stone carried out the following procedure. First, he developed a discriminant function for distinguishing between the first 15 pairs of notes. The three factors that, when combined, best discriminated between these pairs were

1. References to concrete things, persons, and places (higher for genuine notes).
2. Use of the word "love" in the text (higher for genuine notes).
3. Total number of references to processes of thought and decision (higher for simulated notes).

The first and third criteria were taken from the findings just discussed. The addition of the second factor (use of the word "love") was the result of further exploration of the text word differences between these 15 documents.

The discriminant function developed from these factors was simple and straightforward: The score on the third measure was subtracted from the sum of the scores of the first two measures. This index correctly discriminated 13 of the 15 pairs of notes.

Stone, who was not familiar with the remaining 18 pairs of notes, then applied the discriminant function to them. After making his predictions based on the index scores, we found that he had correctly separated 17 of the 18 paired notes.

More elaborate functions for discriminating between real and simulated suicide notes could be obtained by combining stepwise multiple regression techniques with tree-building procedures. Our further explorations have shown that the task becomes much more difficult, however, if the notes are not available in matched pairs, as they were for Stone. Assuming that age and socioeconomic information is available, a more realistic procedure would be to collect more notes and develop separate discrimination formulas and norms as needed for each major age and socioeconomic group.

In summary, the question asked at the outset of this study was "Can we find differences between genuine suicide notes and simulated suicide notes by using the General Inquirer procedures?" We found that we could find differences and that those differences were substantial. More often than was true of the simulated notes, genuine notes contained specific information, used names of people, places, and things, made frequent mention of women, and gave instructions to others that were concrete enough to be actually carried out. By contrast, the simulated suicide notes contained a greater percentage of "thinking" words, suggesting that the issue of suicide was being pondered, reasoned with, and probably rationalized.

Note

1. Shneidman, E. E., & Farberow, N. L. (1957). *Clues to suicide.* New York: McGraw-Hill.

Reference

Gottschalk, L. A., & Gleser, G. (1960). An analysis of the verbal content of suicide notes. *British Journal of Medical Psychology 33:*195–204.

7.2

Analyzing Maps of Literary and Non-Literary Texts

Michael E. Palmquist, Kathleen Carley, and Thomas A. Dale*

This article describes a methodology for representing mental models as maps, extracting those maps from texts, and analyzing and comparing them. Drawing on a computer-based cognitive mapping procedure developed by Carley (1986, 1988; Carley & Palmquist, 1992), we illustrate the methodology with an analysis of 27 works of science fiction in which robots play a significant role. These works were published between 1818 and 1980. Results indicate that by the 1980s robots were portrayed much more positively than they were prior to the 1940s. We conclude with a discussion of potential applications of this methodology.

Depictions of Robots in Science Fiction

This study analyzed 27 works of science fiction by 20 authors. In each of the selected plays, short stories, and novels, robots play a significant role. The texts ranged from Shelley's *Frankenstein* and Capek's *R.U.R.* to Asimov's *The Robots of Dawn* and Anthony's *Robot Adept,* with particular attention paid to texts published during the past five decades. In all, 30 robots are depicted in the texts.

The texts were selected using a three-step process. First, an electronic database search of the holdings of Hunt Library at Carnegie Mellon University was conducted using the terms *Science Fiction* and *Robot$,* with the *$* denoting a wild-card character. Second, the results of the search were screened to produce a preliminary set of 65 texts that matched the search criteria. Finally, the researcher selected a subset of 27 texts based on their representativeness and, to a lesser extent, on the relative importance of the author. Mary Shelley's *Frankenstein,* for instance, was selected because it is one of the first literary works that explores the implications of creating an

*From Palmquist, M. E., Carley, K. M., & Dale, T. A. (1997). Applications of computer-aided text analysis: Analyzing literary and nonliterary texts. In C. W. Roberts (Ed.), *Text analysis for the social sciences: Methods for drawing statistical inferences from texts and transcripts* (pp. 171–189). Mahwah, NJ: Lawrence Erlbaum.

artificial being. Several of Isaac Asimov's works were selected because he is both a seminal science fiction writer and a writer well known for using robots as central characters in his stories. Because no attempt was made to create a random sample of works of science fiction in which robots played significant roles in the plot, we present the results of this study strictly as a demonstration of the ways in which such texts can be analyzed, rather than as generalizable findings.

Our analysis of these texts was designed to explore whether we could measure differences in attitudes exhibited toward robots by authors writing at different times. To pursue that goal, six questions were addressed.

1. Do the types of robots that authors describe (e.g., android, metallic humanoid) change over time?
2. Do the features of robots change over time?
3. Do the actions in which robots engage change over time?
4. Do the emotions that robots exhibit change over time?
5. Do the attributions that characters in the play, short story, or novel make to the robots change over time?
6. Does the overall depiction of the robots in each work of fiction (i.e., positive or negative) change over time?

Method

Grouping the Texts

To determine whether attitudes toward robots changed over time, the texts were placed into three groups. The two dividing points were chosen in light of two important milestones in the U.S. space program. The first, 1960, marks the beginning of the decade in which the United States, spurred first by the Soviet success of Sputnik and then by John Kennedy's challenge to send a mission to the moon by the end of the decade, firmly committed itself to the space race. The second point, 1969, marks the successful lunar landing of Apollo 11. The 1960s is seen as a pivotal decade not only for the development of the U.S. space program but also for the national self-image of the United States as a high technology culture. Using 1960 and 1969 as demarcation points, the 30 maps of robots can be grouped into one group of 12 robots in texts written before 1960, one group of six robots in texts written between 1960 and 1969, and one group of 12 robots in texts written from 1970 to 1988.

Creating the Concept List and Relationship Types

Cognitive maps are networks of statements, where each statement consists of a pair of related concepts. Thus, prior to encoding statements, one must determine the concepts and relations according to which texts are to be encoded. The concept list and relationship types for this study were developed empirically; that is, they were established during and after the texts were read rather than prior to reading the texts. (For a more complete discussion of issues related to creating concept lists, see Carley & Palmquist, 1992.) Following an initial reading of the texts, six types of relationships were established:

1. The type of robot in each text (e.g., "Robot <IS OF THIS TYPE> metallic nonhumanoid")
2. The features each robot possessed (e.g., "Robot <HAS FEATURE> eyes")
3. The actions each robot engaged in (e.g., "Robot <DOES ACTION> walking")
4. The emotions each robot experienced (e.g., "Robot <HAS EMOTION> anger")
5. The attributions made to each robot by characters in each text (e.g., "Robot <HAS CHARACTERISTIC ATTRIBUTED BY CHARACTER> pride");
6. The author's apparent attitude toward each robot, ranging from very negative to very positive (e.g., "Robot <IS EVALUATED BY AUTHOR> positive").

In all, the researcher coded 412 concepts as being related in one of these six ways to the robots in the set of texts.

Creating Maps

To answer each of the research questions, the texts were coded and subsequently analyzed using MECA, or Map Extraction Comparison and Analysis.[1] One researcher coded the entire set of texts, producing maps of 30 robots (three texts contained two major characters who were robots; the others contained one). (To establish reliability, a second researcher coded a subset of three texts. . . .

After the coding was completed, a separate set of four coders ranked the emotions and character attributions identified by the primary coder. The various emotions and attributions were ranked as negative, neutral, or positive. These rankings afforded the three-level ordinal measure on these variables used in subsequent statistical analyses.

Creating Modified Maps Using SKI

Because the goal of this study was to represent the depictions of each robot as accurately as possible, a software program, SKI, was used to make implicit statements explicit. SKI accepts two files as input, a map file and what might be termed an implicit knowledge file. A fairly simple illustration may clarify the manner in which SKI operates. Imagine that the implicit knowledge file contains a statement amounting to "if something has ears then it can hear." Then, if a map file contained the statement that a robot has ears, SKI would add two additional statements: if a robot has ears then a robot can hear, and a robot can hear. When creating modified maps, SKI adds concepts and statements that explicate the implicit knowledge. SKI does not delete concepts. It can add concepts and add relations among existing or new concepts, thus creating statements. Although SKI cannot overcome gross coder error, it can overcome some of the most frequent coder errors, such as neglecting to fully specify all implied statements in the text. The modified maps generated by SKI are thus larger than those generated by novice coders. SKI-modified maps tend to be closer to maps coded by individuals who are experts in the domain from which the texts are selected. Carley (1988) described SKI in detail and demonstrated how its application to texts coded by novices actually improves the coding so that it more closely resembles coding by experts.

A comparison of agreement on features of robots between unmodified and SKI-modified maps indicates that the modified maps allow more common features to be identified. Similar results were obtained for emotions, actions, and character attributions. Because of this, the subsequent analyses are based on maps modified using SKI.

Analyzing Maps

After each map had been modified by SKI, all maps were analyzed statistically and depicted graphically. To prepare the maps for statistical analysis, software was used to produce data matrices for each map in which the rows were either concepts or statements and the columns were the names of the other maps. The cells in the data matrices indicated whether each concept or statement was found in that map. Summary matrices were subsequently produced in which the rows were individual maps and the columns were variables indicating the total numbers of concepts and statements in each map, the intersection of concepts and statements across the set of maps, the number of concepts and statements in each map not found in each of the other maps, and the number of concepts and statements that were unique (i.e., not found in any of the other maps) to each map.

Maps were also depicted graphically. A modified map of Harry Harrison's short story, "Arm of the Law," is presented in Figure 1. To read the map as a series of statements, begin at the central concept, "robot," read a phrase such as DOES ACTION as the relationship between robot and another concept, and read one of the concepts linked to DOES ACTION by a line as the second concept. The arrow on each line indicates the direction in which the statement should be read. For example, you could read "Robot <DOES ACTION> Fights" as a statement meaning that the robot in "Arm of the Law" fought. In a more detailed map, concepts such as "fight" might be linked to still other concepts, such as the person or thing being fought, the type of weapons (if any) used in the fight, and who won the fight. The reader should note as well that a map of a longer text, such as Robert Heinlein's novel, *The Moon is a Harsh Mistress,* would be more detailed than the map of "Arm of the Law."

Results

Comparisons of the maps of the three time-periods indicate only one trend in robot types, features, or actions. Over time, fewer authors depicted robots as nonmetallic humanoids, and more authors depicted robots as metallic humanoids. This trend is mirrored by the presence of one feature, circuits, in the second and third periods, which does not appear in the first period.

Clearer trends over time can be seen in the emotions that robots exhibit during the three periods, the attributions made to robots by characters in the texts, and the overall evaluations of robots by the authors of the texts. In general, the characterizations of robots in texts written after the 1960s are more positive than those written prior to or during the 1960s. In the texts written prior to 1960, consensus exists only on the emotions "disdain" and "intelligent." In the 1960s, the emotion "disdain" is joined by "anger" whereas "fear" is not present, and the character attribution "disdain" is joined by "anger" and "pride," but "fear" is not present. In the 1970s and 1980s, "fear" is present but is counterbalanced by the

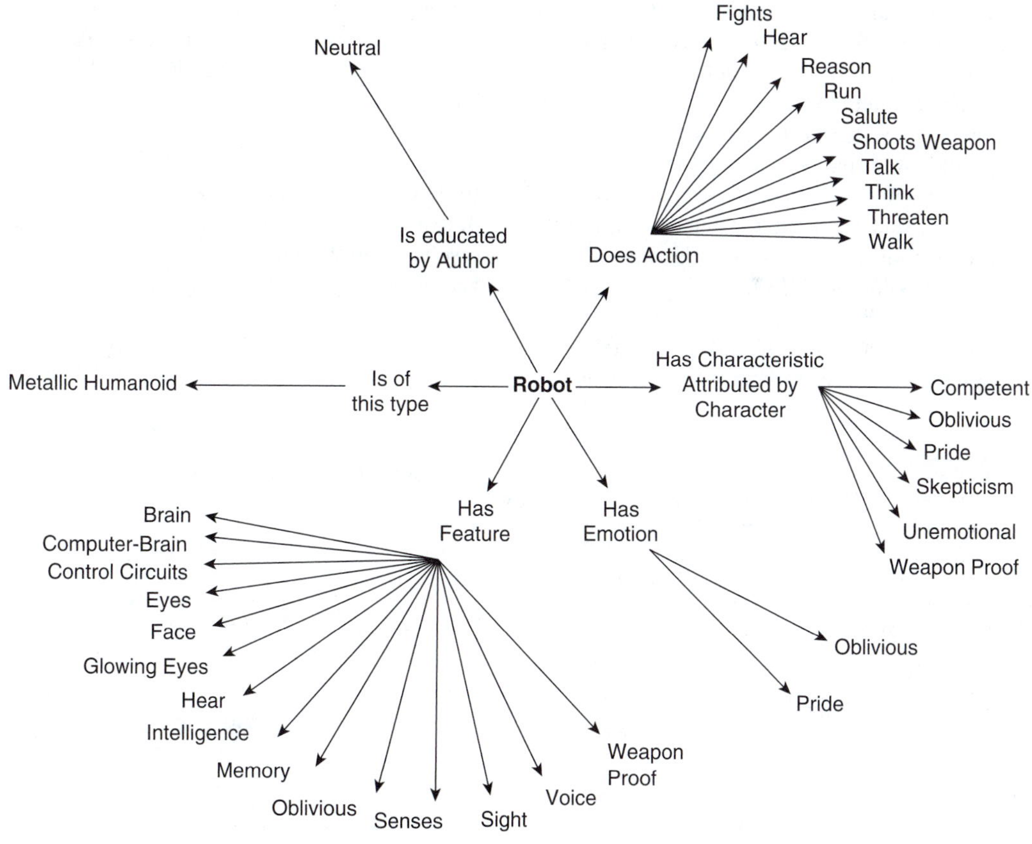

Figure 1 Map of "Arm of the Law"

more positive emotions of "loyalty," "trust" and "friendship," emotions that authors do not attribute to robots in the first two periods. Similarly, in the 1970s and 1980s, the character attribution "fear" is present but is counterbalanced by the more positive character attributions of "loyalty," "trust," and "friend," qualities that characters do not attribute to robots in the first two periods.

Statistical analysis mirrors these trends. Positive and negative robot emotion, character attribution, and author evaluation scores were calculated for the modified map of each text, the first two of which were based on rankings by four raters. Table 1 presents the results of three analyses of variance that showed significant differences among the three time periods in the mean percentage of science fiction texts in which positive emotions were exhibited by robots and in which positive attributions were made by characters. The table also lists the mean author evaluation score. The mean scores for positive emotion statements, character attributes, and author evaluations were significantly higher for texts written in the 1970s and 1980s than for the other two periods.

A Pearson correlation between the percentage of positive emotion statements and publication year (excluding *Frankenstein,* which was published in 1818 and which served as a strong outlier) also indicated a significant positive trend ($r = .468$, $p < .01$). As publication year grew more recent, the percentage of positive emotion statements increased. Similarly, a Pearson correlation between the percentage of positive character attribution statements and publication year (again excluding *Frankenstein*) also indicated a significant positive trend ($r = .380$, $p < .05$). As publication year grew more recent, the percentage of positive character attribution statements increased.

Discussion

Results

These results illustrate change over time in the depictions of robots by the authors in this set of texts. Although the actions and features of robots have remained relatively constant during the periods studied, robots' emotions, characters' attributions, and authors' evaluations have shifted from largely negative to largely positive. By the 1970s and 1980s, robots were considered capable of inspiring loyalty, trust, and even friendship within their human counterparts.

Because the texts were not selected randomly, however, we cannot generalize these findings to depictions of robots in science fiction in general. Despite this limitation, these results suggest that a more ambitious investigation of texts in which robots play a significant role might reveal changes over time in writers' presentation of robots and, by implication, of changes over time on a societal level.

Table 1 Temporal Changes in Statements Indicating Robot Emotions, Character Attributions, and Author Evaluations That Are Positive

	Pre-1960s (12 texts)	*1960s (6 texts)*	*Post-1960s (12 texts)*	*F*
Robot emotions	28.1 (20.9)	29.5 (24.1)	55.0 (17.8)	6.25††
Character attributions	26.4 (18.7)	27.5 (20.7)	47.1 (21.9)	3.58†
Author evaluations	2.0 (1.2)	2.7 (1.6)	4.3 (1.0)	11.43†††

NOTE: Robot emotions and character attributions are in percentages; author evaluations are means on a 5-point scale with 1 being very negative and 5 being very positive. Standard deviations are in parentheses.

†$p < .05$. ††$p < .01$. †††$p < .001$.

Method

This study provides a relatively straightforward example of how computer-aided text analysis can be used to conduct map analysis. However, at least two issues related to the use of the methodology are worth noting: the inherent threats to reliability and validity entailed by the use of human coders and the data reduction problem. First, the use of human raters to code the texts (as opposed to machine coding, which carries with it another set of challenges) raises questions about the reliability and validity.

Second, text analysis necessarily entails some data reduction. The amount of information provided by a statement that a robot possesses a certain feature or exhibits a certain emotion cannot be expected to provide the same amount of information conveyed by an author's careful development of a character or a scene. For instance, a statement that is coded "Robot <DOES ACTION> Attack" does not indicate who was attacked, why they were attacked, or how they were attacked. Map analysis would be able to indicate that the same statement occurred in two or more texts, but it would not be able to indicate, unless it were explicitly coded as such, that in one case the attack occurred because the robot was defending someone whereas in another case the robot was running amok. The data reduction problem can, to some degree, be alleviated by careful and comprehensive coding of a given text. However, it seems unlikely that researchers will always want to create highly detailed maps of a particular text. For the majority of researchers, it seems that at least some data reduction is inevitable.

Conclusion

This study illustrates the power of using maps to analyze and compare mental models. Even simple maps admit empirical analysis and make it possible to address detailed questions about shifts in meaning. We can ask, with these maps: do mental models become more complex or more integrated over time? Under what conditions do novice mental models become more like expert models? What is the content of this change? With map analysis, we can thus focus not only on concept usage but also on meaning and shifts in cognitive structure.

Note

1. MECA is a collection of 15 text analysis programs. The programs can run on UNIX workstations, many IBM personal computers or clones, and Apple Macintosh computers (Carley, 1986, 1988, 1993; Carley & Palmquist, 1992). For availability, see Popping (1997).

References

Carley, K. M. (1986). An approach for relating social structure to cognitive structure. *Journal of Mathematical Sociology 12:*137–189.

Carley, K. M. (1988). Formalizing the social expert's knowledge. *Sociological Methods and Research 17:*165–232.

Carley, K. M. (1993). Coding choices for textual analysis: A comparison of content analysis and map analysis. In P. Marsden (Ed.), *Sociological methodology, 1993* (pp. 76–126). Oxford: Blackwell.

Carley, K. M., & Palmquist, M. E. (1992). Extracting, representing and analyzing mental models. *Social Forces 70:*601–636.

Popping, R. (1997). Computer programs for the analysis of text. In C. W. Roberts (Ed.), *Text analysis for the social sciences: Methods for drawing statistical inferences from texts and transcripts* (pp. 209–221). Mahwah, NJ: Lawrence Erlbaum.

7.3

CATPAC FOR TEXT ANALYSIS

Presidential Debates

MARYA L. DOERFEL AND GEORGE A. BARNETT*

INTRODUCTION

CATPAC is part of the GALILEO program suite produced by Terra Research and Computing (1994).** CATPAC is a set of programs for analyzing text***—open-ended question responses, speeches, company newsletters, etc. It does not require *a priori* categories. Instead, word frequency counts, cluster analysis, and Multi-Dimensional Scaling (MDS) provide a description of the shared symbols and meanings in a text. This facilitates the naming of categories, or themes, in a text, and the description of a culture.

Freeman and Barnett (1994) used CATPAC to analyze the newsletters, promotional materials, and human resource statements of various companies and to describe the culture of those organizations. Jang and Barnett (1994) used the program to analyze the annual letters to stockholders from the CEOs of 17 Japanese and 18 U.S. corporations. Woelfel (1996) used it to develop new customer service programs and to analyze corporate communication.

In this review, we use examples from Doerfel's (1994) study of the 1992 presidential debates and of the subsequent newspaper articles about those debates.

*From Doerfel, M. L., & Barnett, G. A. (1996). The use of CATPAC for text analysis. *Cultural Anthropological Methods 8*:4–7.

**Now available at the Galileo Company at http://www.galileoco.com (accessed January 10, 2007).

***Woelfel (1990–1998) conceptualizes CATPAC as a self-organizing neural network that "learns" to associate words according to their proximity within text. Proximity is measured in terms of the frequency of their co-occurrence within a window of specifiable length. As this window slides over a text, pairs of chief words next to each other are counted more often than words far apart. CATPAC continuously updates the interconnections between these words and ends up representing a body of text as a "network" of associations, which can be entered into several statistical procedures. Here, a result of CATPAC's clustering feature is presented. It exemplifies developing categories from text without human coding—except for the identification of chief words, which are specific to a research question.

Getting Started

After spell checking, proofing, and organizing of data with a word processor, the text file needs to be saved in ASCII format. CATPAC recognizes the full set of ASCII characters, which allows for work in any major European language.

With the user manual (Woelfel, 1993) and the help options available at most stages, the program is easy to run. To customize the analysis, CATPAC, within the GALILEO system, provides the choice of network analysis, cluster analysis, and frequency accounts.

Slides and Windows

CATPAC enables one to specify the "number of unique words," the *n*-most frequent words in the text, not including a list of words whose inclusion is guaranteed by their presence in an *include* file. One can also create an *exclude* file, which guarantees the exclusion of a list of words. The *exclude* file begins with words like articles, interjections, and conjunctions, and grows as one adds to it in the course of analysis.

CATPAC also allows one to choose the "Size of window," *k*-words long, which determines if any pair of nonexcluded words are present. The program then reads the next group of *k* words, depending on the "slide size." If the slide size is 1, CATPAC moves one word further in the text and reads the next *k* words.

In the example:

News polls show (that) Smith (is) ahead (by) twelve points

the words in parentheses are part of the *exclude* file and therefore ignored. With a window size (*k*) of 5 and the slide as 1, the first window contains the words "News polls show Smith ahead" (the words "that" and "is" are ignored). The second window contains the words "polls show Smith ahead twelve" ("that," "is," and "by" are not counted). And so on.

The program premultiplies the words-by-windows matrix and produces a words-by-words, or words cooccurrence, matrix on which MDS and cluster analysis are run.

If the slide size is smaller than the window size, there will be some overlap with the individual words counted more than once. Consider the document's size to determine the number of unique words to use in the analysis, but always begin high. The first few runs are useful in customizing the analysis for each unique data set.

In our experience, there is usually a clear break in the frequency counts, which clarifies the number of useful words. In analyzing the 1992 presidential debates, Doerfel began with 100 unique words, a window size of 5, and a slide of 1. The list of frequencies showed a clear break between 30 and 40 words. After 40, the words (like "inside" and "became") were not relevant to the issues being addressed. Adding the texts from news articles about the debates created a break between 40 and 50 words.

When words like these are among the most frequent, one can lower the cutoff in the "number of unique words" or add these words to the *exclude* file. The latter is best when irrelevant words are scattered *within* the useful, relevant concepts.

Other Units of Analysis

CATPAC lets one treat blocks of text, rather than windows, as unique cases. To define individual responses from interviews, for example, as the units of analysis, place a –1 on the line following each case. Claffey (1996) used this technique to analyze individual customer complaints and to determine categories of complaints. The delimiter tells the program to treat each block of text between each denotation (the –1) in the same way as the window slide. On the screen that asks for window size, simply place a –1.

Likewise, if the analysis examines the differences among individual speakers or specific bodies of text, place a +1 and +2 at the beginning of the block of text to differentiate the individual or group. The case number will then be treated as a unique symbol and *its* frequency, cooccurrence with other concepts, and location in the MDS map and position in the cluster analysis are determined. Doerfel used this to differentiate among the three candidates' discussions of the various topics covered in the 1992 presidential debates.

Outputs and Analysis

CATPAC creates four output files. One file presents the unique words with their frequencies and their percentage of occurrence, along with a dendrogram of the word clusters produced by a cluster analysis of the word coocurrence matrix.

Doerfel used CATPAC to produce a list of the 50 most used words in the 1994 presidential debates and in the corpus of newspaper articles about the debates. Table 1 shows a sample of the word list output from this analysis.

Figure 1 shows a nonhierarchical cluster analysis of the cooccurrence matrix of those words, given a window and a slide value of 1.

If the dendrograms show too few divisions (e.g., only two or three clusters among 50 words) one can decrease the initial window size. If one started at 5, one may try 3; if one started at 7, try 5. If the window is too large, CATPAC will find some relationship among *all* the concepts. If there are too many clusters, then CATPAC is using a very strict criterion for determining which words are connected. Increase the window size. (Too many divisions may also be a function of one's data set. But if one is only getting 2–3 word clusters, one can assume there are too many divisions.)

The network option in CATPAC automatically produces a MDS analysis (in two or three dimensions) of the word cooccurrence matrix. The coordinates from the MDS output are provided as well. One can plot these, using the plot program in GALILEO.

Finally, one can obtain a list of the concepts ordered by their frequency of occurrence, which includes a weight input network, which is needed for running other programs in the GALILEO system.

Limitations

The data must be virtually free from any typos, spelling errors, or erroneous marks

Table 1 Word Frequencies

Descending Frequency List					*Alphabetically Sorted List*				
word	*freq.*	*%*	*case freq.*	*case %*	*word*	*freq.*	*%*	*case freq.*	*case %*
Program	138	4.3	542	17.1	Act	54	1.7	240	7.6
People	127	4.0	509	16.0	American	65	2.0	294	9.3
Bill	117	3.7	465	14.6	Bill	117	3.7	465	14.6
Year	105	3.3	440	13.9	Center	48	1.5	195	6.1
New	92	2.9	405	12.8	Chairman	58	1.8	251	7.9
Committee	88	2.8	376	11.8	Children	69	2.2	244	7.7
. . .					. . .				
. . .					. . .				
. . .					. . .				
Federal	45	1.4	207	6.5	Work	48	1.5	208	6.6
Increase	44	1.4	186	5.9	Year	105	3.3	440	13.9
Legislation	43	1.4	200	6.3	Years	284	2.6	386	12.2

```
A F C C P F N O H M P O P C F U A N N G M P Y P S Y P T W F P L I T E S I B C C G S C P S S U C R E
C U I O U E E V O E E I R O I N M A E O I E E R T E R O O O R E N A C E N I O H E U H R C T N E E N
T N T U B D E E U . R L I S R D E T W V L O A O A A O D R O E G C X O R C L M A N P I O H A I N S E
. D I N L E D R S . C . C T S E R I . E L P R B T R G A K D S I O . N V R L M I T P L G O T T T E R
. I Z T I R . . E . E . E . T R I O . R I L . L E S R Y . . I S M . O I E . I R L O D R O E E E A G
. N E R C A . . . . N . . . . . C N . N O E . E . . A . . . D L E . M C A . T M E R R A L S D R R Y
. G N Y . L . . . . T . . . . . A A . M N . . M . . M . . . E A . . I E S . T A M T E M . . . . C .
. . S . . . . . . . . . . . . . N L . E . . . S . . S . . . N T . . C . E . E N A . N . . . . . H .
. . . . . . . . . . . . . . . . . . . N . . . . . . . . . . T I . . . . . . E . N . . . . . . . . .
. . . . . . . . . . . . . . . . . . . T . . . . . . . . . . . O . . . . . . . . . . . . . . . . . .
. . . . . . . . . . . . . . . . . . . . . . . . . . . . . . . N . . . . . . . . . . . . . . . . . .
. . . . . . . . . . . . . . . . . . . . . . . . . . . . . . . . . . . . . XXX . . . . . . . . . . .
. . . . . . . . . . . . . . . . . . . . . . . . . . . . . . . . . . . . . XXX . . . . . . . . XXX .
. . . . . . . . . . . . . . . . . . . . . . . . . . . . . . . . . . . . . XXX . . . . XXX . . XXX .
. . . . . . . . . . . . . . . . . . . . . . . . . . . . . . . . . . . . . XXX XXX . . XXX . . XXX .
. . . . . . . . . . . . . . . . . . . . . . . . . . . . . . . . . . XXX . XXX XXX . . XXX . . XXX .
. . . . . . . . . . . . . . . . . . . . . . . . . . . . . . . . . . XXX . XXX XXX . . XXX . . XXXXX
. . . . . . . . . . . . . . . . . . . . . . . . . . . . . . . . . . XXX . XXX XXX . . XXX XXX XXXXX
. . . . . . . . . . . . . . . . . . . . . XXX . . . . . . . . . . . XXX . XXX XXX . . XXX XXX XXXXX
. . . . . . . . . . . . . . . . . . . . . XXX . . . . . . . . . . . XXX . XXX XXX . XXXXX XXX XXXXX
. . . . . . . . . . . . . . . . . . . . . XXX . . . . . . . . . XXX XXX . XXX XXX . XXXXX XXX XXXXX
. . . . . . . . . . . . . . . . . . . . . XXX . . . . . . XXX . XXX XXX . XXX XXX . XXXXX XXX XXXXX
. . . . . . . . . . . . . . . . . . . . XXXXX . . . . . . XXX . XXX XXX . XXX XXX . XXXXX XXX XXXXX
. . . . . . . . . . . . . . . . . . . . XXXXX . XXX . . . XXX . XXX XXX . XXX XXX . XXXXX XXX XXXXX
. . . . . . . . . . . . . . . . . . . . XXXXX . XXX XXX . XXX . XXX XXX . XXX XXX . XXXXX XXX XXXXX
. . . . . . . . . . . . . . . . . . . . XXXXX . XXX XXX . XXX . XXX XXX . XXX XXXXX XXXXX XXX XXXXX
. . . . . . . . . . . . . . . . . XXX . XXXXX . XXX XXX . XXX . XXX XXX . XXX XXXXX XXXXX XXX XXXXX
. . . . . . . . . . . . . . . . XXXXX . XXXXX . XXX XXX . XXX . XXX XXX . XXX XXXXX XXXXX XXX XXXXX
. . . . . . . . . . . . . . . . XXXXX . XXXXX . XXX XXX . XXX . XXX XXXXX XXX XXXXX XXXXX XXX XXXXX
. . . . . . . . . . . . . . XXX XXXXX . XXXXX . XXX XXX . XXX . XXX XXXXX XXX XXXXX XXXXX XXX XXXXX
. . . . . . . . . XXX . . . XXX XXXXX . XXXXX . XXX XXX . XXX . XXX XXXXX XXX XXXXX XXXXX XXX XXXXX
XXX . . . . . . . XXX . . . XXX XXXXX . XXXXX . XXX XXX . XXX . XXX XXXXX XXX XXXXX XXXXX XXX XXXXX
XXX . . . . . . . XXX . . . XXX XXXXX . XXXXX XXXXX XXX . XXX . XXX XXXXX XXX XXXXX XXXXX XXX XXXXX
XXX . . . . . . . XXX XXX . XXX XXXXX . XXXXX XXXXX XXX . XXX . XXX XXXXX XXX XXXXX XXXXX XXX XXXXX
XXX . . . . . . . XXX XXX . XXX XXXXX . XXXXX XXXXX XXX . XXXXX XXX XXXXX XXX XXXXX XXXXX XXX XXXXX
XXX . . . . . . . XXX XXX . XXX XXXXXXX XXXXX XXXXX XXX . XXXXX XXX XXXXX XXX XXXXX XXXXX XXX XXXXX
XXX . . . . . . . XXX XXX XXXXX XXXXXXX XXXXX XXXXX XXX . XXXXX XXX XXXXX XXX XXXXX XXXXX XXX XXXXX
XXX . . . . . . . XXX XXX XXXXX XXXXXXX XXXXX XXXXX XXXXX XXXXX XXX XXXXX XXX XXXXX XXXXX XXX XXXXX
XXX . XXX . . . . XXX XXX XXXXX XXXXXXX XXXXX XXXXX XXXXX XXXXX XXX XXXXX XXX XXXXX XXXXX XXX XXXXX
XXX . XXX . . . . XXX XXX XXXXX XXXXXXXXXXXXX XXXXX XXXXX XXXXX XXX XXXXX XXX XXXXX XXXXX XXX XXXXX
XXX . XXX XXX . . XXX XXX XXXXX XXXXXXXXXXXXX XXXXX XXXXX XXXXX XXX XXXXX XXX XXXXX XXXXX XXX XXXXX
XXX . XXXXXXX . . XXX XXX XXXXX XXXXXXXXXXXXX XXXXX XXXXX XXXXX XXX XXXXX XXX XXXXX XXXXX XXX XXXXX
XXX . XXXXXXXXX . XXX XXX XXXXX XXXXXXXXXXXXX XXXXX XXXXX XXXXX XXX XXXXX XXX XXXXX XXXXX XXX XXXXX
XXX XXXXXXXXXXX . XXX XXX XXXXX XXXXXXXXXXXXX XXXXX XXXXX XXXXX XXX XXXXX XXX XXXXX XXXXX XXX XXXXX
XXX XXXXXXXXXXXXX XXX XXX XXXXX XXXXXXXXXXXXX XXXXX XXXXX XXXXX XXX XXXXX XXX XXXXX XXXXX XXX XXXXX
XXX XXXXXXXXXXXXX XXX XXX XXXXX XXXXXXXXXXXXXXXXXXX XXXXX XXXXX XXX XXXXX XXX XXXXX XXXXX XXX XXXXX
XXX XXXXXXXXXXXXXXXXX XXX XXXXX XXXXXXXXXXXXXXXXXXX XXXXX XXXXX XXX XXXXX XXX XXXXX XXXXX XXX XXXXX
XXX XXXXXXXXXXXXXXXXXXXXX XXXXX XXXXXXXXXXXXXXXXXXX XXXXX XXXXX XXX XXXXX XXX XXXXX XXXXX XXX XXXXX
XXXXXXXXXXXXXXXXXXXXXXXXX XXXXX XXXXXXXXXXXXXXXXXXX XXXXX XXXXX XXX XXXXX XXX XXXXX XXXXX XXX XXXXX
XXXXXXXXXXXXXXXXXXXXXXXXXXXXXXX XXXXXXXXXXXXXXXXXXX XXXXX XXXXX XXX XXXXX XXX XXXXX XXXXX XXX XXXXX
XXXXXXXXXXXXXXXXXXXXXXXXXXXXXXXXXXXXXXXXXXXXXXXXXXX XXXXX XXXXX XXX XXXXX XXX XXXXX XXXXX XXX XXXXX
XXXXXXXXXXXXXXXXXXXXXXXXXXXXXXXXXXXXXXXXXXXXXXXXXXXXXXXXX XXXXX XXX XXXXX XXX XXXXX XXXXX XXX XXXXX
XXXXXXXXXXXXXXXXXXXXXXXXXXXXXXXXXXXXXXXXXXXXXXXXXXXXXXXXXXXXXXX XXX XXXXX XXX XXXXX XXXXX XXX XXXXX
XXXXXXXXXXXXXXXXXXXXXXXXXXXXXXXXXXXXXXXXXXXXXXXXXXXXXXXXXXXXXXXXXXX XXXXX XXX XXXXX XXXXX XXX XXXXX
XXXXXXXXXXXXXXXXXXXXXXXXXXXXXXXXXXXXXXXXXXXXXXXXXXXXXXXXXXXXXXXXXXX XXXXX XXXXXXXXX XXXXX XXX XXXXX
XXXXXXXXXXXXXXXXXXXXXXXXXXXXXXXXXXXXXXXXXXXXXXXXXXXXXXXXXXXXXXXXXXXXXXXXX XXXXXXXXX XXXXX XXX XXXXX
XXXXXXXXXXXXXXXXXXXXXXXXXXXXXXXXXXXXXXXXXXXXXXXXXXXXXXXXXXXXXXXXXXXXXXXXX XXXXXXXXXXXXXXX XXX XXXXX
XXXXXXXXXXXXXXXXXXXXXXXXXXXXXXXXXXXXXXXXXXXXXXXXXXXXXXXXXXXXXXXXXXXXXXXXXXXXXXXXXXXXXXXXX XXX XXXXX
XXXXXXXXXXXXXXXXXXXXXXXXXXXXXXXXXXXXXXXXXXXXXXXXXXXXXXXXXXXXXXXXXXXXXXXXXXXXXXXXXXXXXXXXXXXXX XXXXX
XXXXXXXXXXXXXXXXXXXXXXXXXXXXXXXXXXXXXXXXXXXXXXXXXXXXXXXXXXXXXXXXXXXXXXXXXXXXXXXXXXXXXXXXXXXXXXXXXXX
```

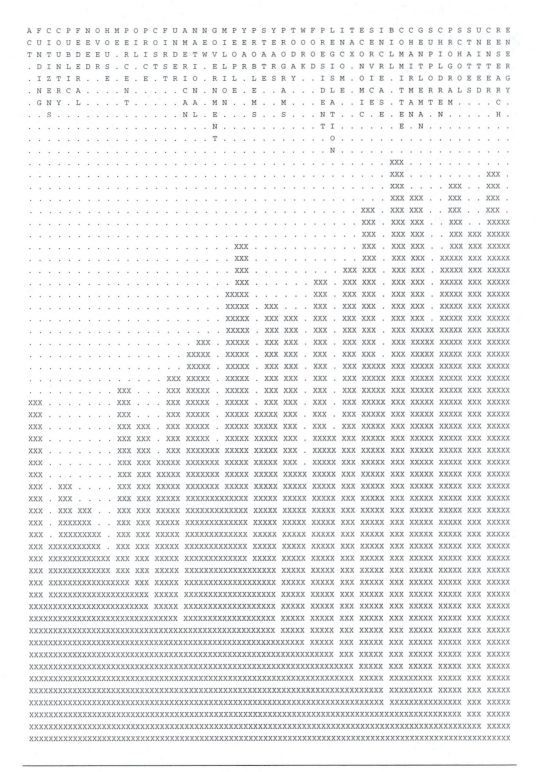

Figure 1 Dendrogram From Cluster Analysis

NOTE: The cluster analysis is Johnson's (1967) diametric method, which is hierarchical. Nonhierarchical cluster analysis is an option and is useful for arranging categories that are not mutually exclusive (see Woelfel, 1996).

since the program reads them as different concepts. Also, CATPAC does not use a concept dictionary, so if concepts of interest have synonyms, the computer treats each synonym as a different concept.

Nor can CATPAC differentiate among different uses of the same word/concept. In the analysis of the presidential debates, "president" was clearly a concept of interest. The term, however, could be used in various contexts: "I want to be president because. . . ." or "Mr. President, how do you feel about . . ." or "President Bush has been in the White House for . . ." and so on.

Different uses of single words, therefore, must be differentiated in the text by creating unambiguous word concepts for the program to recognize. Every time the word "president" was used as a title, a new word was created: "presidentbush." This cleaned up part of the problem, but "Mr. President" was a reference used for addressing President Bush as well, so that was also changed to "presidentbush." This enabled discrimination between the use of "president" as a title versus its use as a role in government ("President Bush" versus "I want to be president").

Changing "Mr. President" to "presidentbush," however, may have lost a potential element of analysis. Perhaps referring to "Mister" Bush rather than to "President" Bush indicated different levels of respect. With the adjustment of the data, there is no way to test this possibility.

The same shortcoming is apparent if one is trying to capture negative and positive connotations of the same concept. Some words carry negative or positive valence in and of themselves. Others need qualifiers to project such meaning. Finally, concepts that require two words to create meaning might be adjusted ("New York" would be changed to "newyork"). Although adjustments can be made in the data, one should be wary of changing too much of the syntax. Will the data still contain the original meaning?

These limitations demand that the user exercise judgment in setting the parameters and in interpreting the results of the analysis. With proper caution and judgment, CATPAC is a convenient set of tools for analyzing and interpreting textual data.

References

Claffey, G. (1996). *Customer feedback: Using content analysis to reduce uncertainty in a changing environment.* Paper presented at the annual meeting of the International Communication Association, Chicago.

Doerfel, M. L. (1994). *The 1992 presidential debates: A new approach to content analysis.* Paper presented at the annual meeting of the Speech Communication Association, New Orleans, LA.

Freeman, C. A., & Barnett, G. A. (1994). An alternative approach to using interpretive theory to examine corporate messages and organizational culture. In L. Thayer & G. A. Barnett (Eds.), *Organizational communication: Emerging perspectives IV.* Norwood, NJ: Ablex.

Jang, H., & Barnett, G. A. (1994). Cultural differences in organizational communication: A semantic network analysis. *Bulletin de Methodologie Sociologique 44:*31–59.

Johnson, S. C. (1967). Hierarchical clustering schemes. *Psychometrica 32:*241–253.

Woelfel, J. (1993). *GALILEO manual.* http://www.galileoco.com/N_manuals.asp (accessed January 10, 2007).

Woelfel, J. (1996). Attitudes on nonhierarchical clusters in neural networks. In F. J. Boster & G. A. Barnett (Eds.), *Progress in communication science 13: Advances in persuasion and attitude change.* Norwood, NJ: Ablex.

7.4

Inferences From Word Networks in Messages

James A. Danowski*

Introduction

Imagine a large group of people talking. Suppose the full text of their messages is available in computer-readable form. How would you represent what they are talking about?

Your first thought may be to use traditional content analysis methods, which categorize text manually or by computer (Krippendorff, 1980; Stone, Dunphy, Smith, & Ogilvie, 1966). They crudely simplify texts by assigning message elements to a limited number of nominal categories.

A network perspective, by contrast, captures the relationships among words within messages. It defines word-pair link strength as the number of times each word co-occurs with another. Every possible word pair has an occurrence distribution, whose values can range from zero on up. This ratio scale of measurement of the strength of the word links in this network allows you to use sophisticated statistical tools. Some enable you to map the structure of the word network. They highlight word groups, or clusters, and quantify the structure of the network at different levels. Using these word-pair data as input to network analysis tools, you map the language region. Figure 1 shows an example of a word-network map from a collection of descriptions of listeners' favorite radio stations. The nodes you see on this map are not cities but words, and their connections are not roads but links among words.

Traveling through the word network are fleets of social objects. These communication vehicles are the concepts, ideas, or physical things that people linguistically describe. As they link words to these vehicles in the course of their everyday informal and formal communication, this propels them through the network. Sometimes these movements are unplanned. At other times, organizations try to manage vehicular traffic. By means of optimal messages, they try to steer vehicles away from certain words or to induce traffic to flow in particular word-link areas (Danowski, 1990).

---

*From Danowski, J. A. (1993). Network analysis of message content. In W. D. Richards Jr. & G. A. Barnett (Eds.), *Progress in communication sciences IV* (pp. 197–221). Norwood, NJ: Ablex.

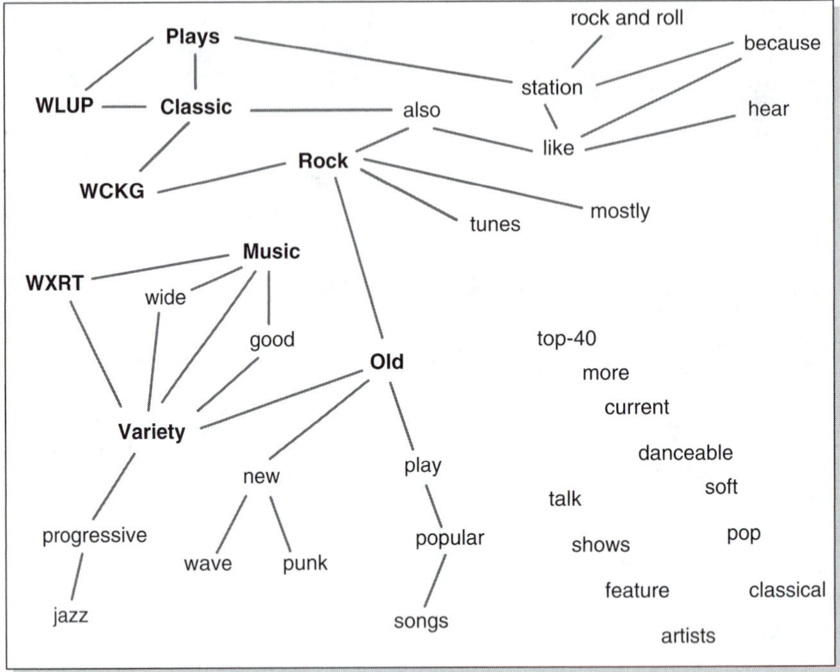

Figure 1 Word Network of Favorite Radio Station Talk, Pilot Study

Mathematically-based procedures have been developed to create optimal messages. These are constructed through systematic analysis of the paths connecting word nodes of interest. The procedures identify the optimal association network across the aggregate social community. The underlying assumption is that messages stimulate associations more effectively when the sequence of words they contain is shorter. This is because people process strings of words linearly over time, encoding and decoding them in sequences. Furthermore, the triggering of associations to words in context takes cognitive time. The most effective message, therefore, optimizes the association networks in the receivers' minds as they read or hear the message.

Network Content Analysis

[N]etwork content analysis enables message scientists to design research serving a range of purposes:

a) Description of communication content,

b) Theory development,

c) Hypothesis testing,

d) Identification of social units and problems,

e) Evaluation, selection, and placement of units,

f) Message creation, and

g) Effects tracking

Network approaches do not occur frequently in the content analysis literature. Existing examples use manual coding of networks of actors represented in the content. Each time an actor appears in the text with another, the pair receives a score. After all content has been coded, then network analysis is performed using actors as nodes. Danowski (1988) coded a set of news stories for relations among all organizations appearing across them, treating them as nodes in defining a focal organization's inter-organizational field. Alexander and Danowski (1990) network analyzed individual actors mentioned in Cicero's letters more than two thousand years ago. While useful for some purposes, manual actor-network coding is not the type of network content analysis of central concern in this chapter.

Here, the focus is on the range of word co-occurrences across texts (Danowski & Martin, 1979; Danowski, 1980, 1982), not just actor names. Although our initial word co-occurrences pilot studies used manual coding, now they are automated. The approach can be thought of as using a window, '*n*' word positions wide, that slides over the text, identifying, counting, and aggregating all word pairs that appear within the window. Then, the word pairs are network analyzed. This identifies an aggregate structure for the whole set of words. It finds clusters or groups of words that frequently occur together. It also finds liaison words, linking groups together. In addition, it computes quantitative measures of the structural properties of the overall network, as well as of sub-areas and of individual nodes.

Once the word-network analysis is completed, the analyst can link the textual representations to other information. Adding such "side data" enables tests of hypotheses about relationships of word network variables to others kinds. For example, message variables can be tied to markets. One example is to correlate word pairs with financial performance data, such as stock price-to-earnings ratios. The associations between the words and the financial valuation metric provide a way to measure the predicted value of any financial message (Danowski, 1991b). A second example uses market share, instead of financial performance. Here, word pairs that the audience uses to describe the marketing vehicles are correlated with their market share: audience ratings data indexing market share are correlated with word-pair frequencies that audience members use to describe the radio stations (Danowski, 1991a).

Steps in Word-Network Analysis

Figure 2 summarizes the primary procedures in this author's approach to word-network analysis of natural language. WORDLINK* is a computer program we developed to process text files into word-pair records.

1. Assemble Textual Corpus

The analyst assembles the text in regular ASCI files. First, it is useful to run a spellchecker and correct errors; even commercial data base records contain them. With respect to text sample sizes, general statistical guidelines suggest that the minimum number of cases should be 30, with numbers in the neighborhood of 300 ideal. A variety of different kinds of text have been analyzed:

a) Electronic mail transcripts;

b) News stories;

c) Advertising copy;

d) Book excerpts;

e) Focus group transcripts;

f) Verbatim responses to open-end survey questions, including:
   - Self-administered paper-and-pencil questionnaire forms
   - Computer-assisted telephone interviewing, in which the protocol appears on the interviewer's computer screen. As the interviewer asks questions, he or she types verbatim responses, which are stored on disk.

2. Do Word Frequency Counts

The next step is to identify the unique words and their frequencies of occurrence. The utility of this includes identifying the total number of words for use as a denominator, should the analyst want to compute proportional frequencies. . . . Normally, WORDLINK strips out punctuation and numerical digits from word strings. An option can stop the window at the end of a sentence. . . . [It also] enables the analyst to choose any set of drop words. . . .

---

*CATPAC (see reading 7.3, this volume) also computes a matrix of word co-occurrences. It then creates clusters of words pairs that shrink that matrix to a more compact representation. However, Danowski's approach preserves the matrix and explores the links between words to find typical paths. Also, unlike CATPAC, this author does not stem grammatical endings of words, which causes word co-occurrence matrices to be much larger than CATPAC's, preserving plurals, verb tenses, and the like.

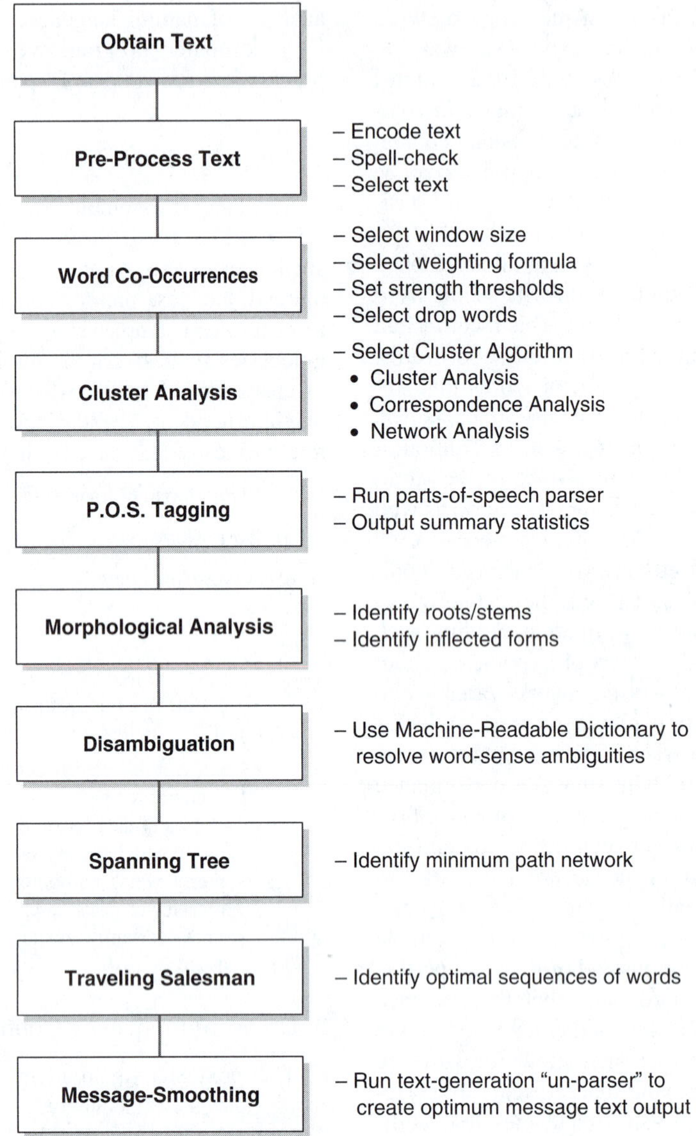

Figure 2 Network Analysis

3. Do Word Co-occurrence Analysis

The next step in the process is to index word co-occurrences. WORD LINK counts (within a window of *n* words) the number of times each word in the text occurs at a certain distance from other words. WORDLINK can be set to treat word pairs as directional or non-directional. In the latter case, an A-B pair is treated the same as a B-A one. In the directional option, these pairs are kept separate. Retaining word-order information is useful in constructing optimal messages. This is a sort of statistical "unparser" to put messages together at an aggregate level, after breaking down large volumes of input text into word pairs.

To conceptualize how word-pairing is done, think of a window sliding through the text. It centers on a word, and each pair of words that appears around it within a specified distance is counted. Then the window moves to center on the next word, and the next word, until it has slid all the way through all the text for all the cases. The window is actually a range over which word-pairing occurs throughout a body of text. It refers to the quantity of link steps spanned for word-pair tallying. The upper limit for the quantity of word pairs is (window size $n - 1$) × (# of words – 1).

Word-pairs within a window can be treated as having the same strength, regardless of their distance from one another within the window. Or, WORD LINK can weight pair strength based on how close to one another words in a pair are. That is, with text "A B C D," A-B may be weighted at 1.0, A-C at 0.67 and A-D at 0.33.

The outcome of this windowing is a list of word pairs and the total number of times each pair has occurred within the window sliding across the text. Table 1 shows the most frequent word pairs for a set of news story headlines about floods in the 1990 National Newspaper Index.

Because WORDLINK has been written to handle text files with up to 1 billion words, sometimes the word-pair output could be so large that it overloads computer system defaults for acceptable file sizes. To get around this problem, a "word grabber" option was implemented. The program can be set to use a file of specified "grab" words. It will grab pairs only around these specific words, using whatever size window is set. For example, if you were interested in scanning corporate annual reports to see how the word "innovative" appeared in context, you could set WORD LINK to turn on its word-pair output generation only when it encountered that particular word. It would then generate output for all word pairs occurring within the window size around "innovative" throughout the text. The current version will output all word pairs appearing within up to 64 words on either side of the grab word.

Table 1 Word Pairs and Frequencies: 1990 Flood Stories

Word A	*Word B*	*Frequency*
flood	victims	17
state	flood	14
flood	response	12
response	activities	12
for	flood	8
p.m.	update	8
washington	state	8
activities	p.m.	6
flood	damage	5
to	flood	5
flood	insurance	4
flood	recovery	4
aid	to	3
approved	for	3
assistance	approved	3
disaster	unemployment	3
due	to	3
flood	control	3
flood	proofing	3
in	flood	3
ohio	town	3
on	flood	3
recovery	tips	3
unemployment	assistance	3
victims	to	3

4. Do Word-Network Analysis

The lists of word pairs and their frequencies of co-occurrence are then fed to network analysis procedures that can identify a reduced structure. Usually, NEGOPY (Richards & Rice, 1981; Richards, 1986) is used because it can handle many nodes, 6000 in the mainframe version, and 3000 on a PC. Other network analysis procedures are limited to an order of magnitude fewer nodes, in the range of 100 to 300 maximum. Correspondence analysis has also been useful (Danowski & Rice, 1989; Freeman & Barnett, 1991) as has cluster analysis. The problem, however, is that most implementations limit the number of variables to no more than 500, not 5000 or more, as in NEGOPY.

5. Identify Minimum Spanning Tree

The next step is to find the structure that provides the minimum number of link steps connecting all nodes in the network, the minimum spanning tree. There are different programs in the operations research networks literature that can do this. Nevertheless, NEGOPY is convenient. It identifies minimum path distances among nodes within a group.

6. Mapping Coordinates of Nodes in Euclidean Space

Before implementing a traveling salesman algorithm* to identify optimal word strings, spatial coordinates representing the dispersion of the nodes in the network are needed. One cannot run word-pair data directly into a distance model without severe violation of assumptions, and highly questionable solutions. This is because word-pairs frequently violate the triangular equality assumptions of Euclidean geometry (Woelfel & Barnett, 1982). Word A may be linked to B at a high rate; B may be linked to C at a high rate: yet, A and C may never appear within the window together. Nevertheless, after the minimum path distance among all nodes is computed by a network analysis program, these distances are perfectly Euclidean. They can be effectively input to a metric multidimensional scaling program such as GALILEO (Woelfel & Fink, 1980).

7. Traveling Salesman Optimal Solution

The traveling salesman algorithm finds an optimal sequence of nodes such that by visiting each in this order, the network is most efficiently traveled. For reasons discussed earlier, this has theoretical appeal for the model of communication vehicles and optimal message creation.

A useful traveling salesman algorithm is Nagel's (1990) implementation of the classic Bell Labs optimal solution. It requires that each node be identified with a set of spatial coordinates. This is what necessitates the previous step of finding the Euclidean distances among all words based on the minimum path distances among them.

The traveling salesman algorithm was applied to a problem with a sample (n = 500) of automobile dealership personnel. The dealerships were stratified into four cells based on being in either the top or bottom quartiles of the J.D. Power "Customer Satisfaction Index (CSI)," and by dealer sales volume. Respondents, representative of main dealership roles, including sales, service, parts, and management, were asked the following open-ended question (plus three probes) in a telephone interview survey: "When you think of 'customer satisfaction,' what comes to mind?" Verbatim responses were captured via a computer-assisted telephone-interviewing laboratory. Human interviewers read questions that appeared on a computer screen, and they typed the word-for-word answers that respondents gave.

The dealerships in the upper half of both the CSI and the sales volume distributions were segmented out for word-network analysis and optimal message creation. Using the procedures described above, the traveling salesman algorithm was applied. It ran on the minimum path distances among the primary group of words resulting from the word network analysis of the verbatim responses in this cell of the design (n = 125).

The traveling salesman algorithm identified the following string of words in this order: "Customer satisfaction: good service on the new car done right the time first." When the order of the last two words is reversed, the message has linguistic validity. It would be understandable to car dealer personnel who might see the message on posters in the dealership, printed on payroll checks, in employee publications, in videos, and in other media.

*The traveling salesman problem has a long history in mathematics. It originated with a salesman's difficulty of finding the shortest or least expensive route to visit all of a given set of cities along the way, one at a time, and then returning to the starting city. In Danowski's algorithm, cities are the nodes of a word co-occurrence network, and distances between words are obtained from their co-occurrences in a body of text; the more frequent, the shorter the distance.

8. Compute Net Value of Messages

Once a body of text has been network analyzed, one can add side data that indexes value. Value data can be diversely conceptualized depending on the problem at hand:

a) Collective-subjective, as exemplified by stock price-to-earnings ratios for organizations;

b) Collective-behavioral, such as market share for products/services;

c) Individual-subjective ratings of value, for example, the Customer Satisfaction Index (CSI) for automobiles and dealerships.

After a value metric has been selected for each case, a record is created, including frequency variables for each word-pair identified from the initial window-scanning step and for the value index. Then, correlations are run to yield a value weight for each word-pair. With the (word) network now value-weighted, messages can be tested for net value by extracting and summing their constituent word-pair weights from the aggregate network.

Any message can then be evaluated for its net value within that particular semantic domain. It is the sum of the *n*-step weighted links activated by the words in the message. There is a decay function across successive *n*-steps. (This decay function can be empirically estimated in an experimental design.) At each step, the value weights are multiplied by the word-pair co-occurrence values to yield a link value/frequency weight. These are summed across all the links for a word within a step-level and multiplied by the step decay value. Values across levels for a word are summed. The result is a sub-aggregate value weight associated with the particular word in the test message. This process is repeated for each word in the message. The sum is computed for the sub-aggregate weights for all the words to arrive at the net aggregate value weight for the message. The formula for net value weight of a message is:

$$NVW = \sum V_i^* V_j \left(\left(F_{ij}^* T_{ij} \right) \left(\frac{1}{m^E} \right) \right)$$

where: V_i = value weight for word *i;* V_j = value weight for word *j;* F_{ij} = frequency of co-occurrence of *ij;* T_{ij} = number of two-step links for the *ij*-pair; M = minimum path distance from trigger word (*n*-step link value); E = activation decay exponent.

This definition of message value, in (word) network terms, takes into account the micro-level relationships among message elements in terms of their associations and relative value. Such an approach allows the analyst to establish a value reference network for a semantic domain against which any messages can be checked. So, the analyst can compare alternative ones using a common standard. This makes it possible to determine whether qualitatively different messages are significantly different in value.

9. Evaluate New Text Against the Value-Weighted Reference Network

There are two main ways to approach preparing the reference network. One is when the target population is clearly known in advance. The other is when the population is not so clearly identifiable but the criterion variables of interest are. For example, an organization may already tag the group of high performers by other procedures, such as quarterly or annual ratings. If a suitable identification of the reference group does not already exist, then the analyst could use a different approach: sample from the whole range of units tested; for example, salespersons. In addition to their open-end question answers, the analyst obtains reliable and valid data on the criterion variable of interest. In this case, the variable would be some measure(s) of sales performance, such as total volume of sales or supervisor ratings. First, the analyst identifies the (word) network for the whole sample. Then, he or she value weights it on the criterion variable. Next, the correlation coefficient for each word pair with the value criterion variable serves as a weight for that pair in the network.

Then, the analyst gathers open-end data from test subjects using the same reference question(s). The test subjects, newly hired prospects, for example, are asked the exact same question as was asked in the reference sample. Their answers are recorded verbatim.

The fit test comes next. Each individual's answers are processed to measure the distance of each word from the center and the reference weights are assigned. The values are summed for each word encoded by the test subject. These total scores represent the closeness of each subject to the reference network.

Decisions can then be made about whatever social unit is being evaluated—a person, an organization, or whatever. There are different decisions possible depending on the overall goals. One goal may be to place individuals into cohesive units. Another may be to identify people to serve as liaisons between groups. Or, a goal may be to introduce change into the organization in which case one would select the more peripheral, rather than the central individuals.

10. Test Predictions

The network analysis of open-end text provides a way to do precise time-series analysis with qualitative data. The actual change in word-networks can be specifically tracked. This testing is useful for two kinds of applications. One is optimal message creation and dissemination. The other is selection of social units according to fit with a reference word-network. By re-administering the same open-ended questions or gathering textual samples from these units, we can see how well the predictions were borne out.

11. Update Reference Population, Sample, and Reference Network

Over time, it would be good to revisit the reference population, redefine it as necessary, sample it again, and update the reference network. This updating can be part of the long-term, over-time research on word networks. The reference network can be revised, based on predictive validity data, or on externally specified changes in the reference population and sample.

Conclusion

This article focused on using network analysis tools (familiar in communication research) to analyze text messages. It . . . outlined the development of a set of procedures for word-network construction and analysis. We conclude by listing some benefits of this approach to text. The word network approach:

- Represents . . . messages in the actual, natural language in which they were originally expressed, resulting in greater external validity
- Reduces errors of translating what is said into its representation, resulting in greater internal validity
- Preserves relationships among concepts (words) . . . , resulting in a qualitative analysis that is quantified, enabling the integration of the two kinds of content analytic traditions
- Retains more information compared to traditional nominal and manual coding, which often reduces rich qualitative information to five to nine nominal categories
- Avoids the unreliabilities (biases) of human coders
- Minimizes the number of coding transformations between the original utterances, and the final representation that is statistically analyzed, thus reducing analytical errors
- Processes large volumes of text, well beyond the capacity of humans to read it (WORDLINK has been written to handle text files with up to one billion words)
- Enables precise quantitative comparisons of qualitative information across different groups of respondents.

References

Alexander, M., & Danowski, J. (1990). Analysis of an ancient network. *Social Networks 12*:313–335.

Danowski, J. (1980, May). *Message content cooccurrence in computer communication networks.*

Invited presentation to the Workshop on Metric Multidimensional Scaling, International Communication Association, Acapulco, Mexico.

Danowski, J. (1982). A network-based content analysis methodology for computer-mediated communication: An illustration with a computer bulletin board. *Communication Yearbook 6:*904–925.

Danowski, J. (1988). Organizational infographics and automated auditing: Using computers to unobtrusively gather and analyze communication. In G. Goldhaber & G. Barnell (Eds.), *Handbook of organizational communication* (pp. 335–384). Norwood, NJ: Ablex.

Danowski, J. (1990). Organizational media theory. *Communication Yearbook 14:*187–210.

Danowski, J. (1991a, April). *Radio semantics: Audience word-networks as predictors of market share changes.* Paper presented to the National Association of Broadcasters, Las Vegas, NV.

Danowski, J. (1991b, February). *Collective semantic network structure and content as predictors of market share changes.* Paper presented to the International Network for Social Network Analysis Conference, Tampa, FL.

Danowski, J., & Martin, T. H. (1979). *Evaluating the health of information science: Research community and user contexts.* Final report to the Division of Information Science of the National Science Foundation, no. IST78–21130.

Danowski, J., & Rice, R. (1989, May). *Correspondences between users' semantic network and computer monitored data on users of voice mail for messaging versus answering.* Paper presented to the International Communication Association, San Francisco.

Freeman, C., & Barnett, G. (1991, May). *An alternative approach to using interpretive theory to examine corporate messages and organizational culture.* Paper presented to the International Communication Association, Chicago.

Krippendorff, K. (1980). *Content analysis: An introduction to its methodology.* Thousand Oaks, CA: Sage.*

Nagel, R. (1990). *Optimal traveling salesman algorithm.* Computer program.

Richards, W., Jr. (1986). *The NEGOPY Network Analysis Program.* Monograph, Simon Fraser University, Burnaby, B.C., Canada.

Richards, W., Jr., & Rice, R. E. (1981). NEGOPY network analysis program. *Social Networks 3,*3:215–223.

Stone, P. J., Dunphy, D. C., Smith, M. S., & Ogilvie, D. M. (1966). *The General Inquirer: A computer approach to content analysis.* Cambridge, MA: M.I.T. Press.

Woelfel, J., & Barnett, G. (1982). Multidimensional scaling in Riemann space. *Quality and Quantity 16:*469–491.

Woelfel, J., & Fink, E. (1980). *The Galileo system: A theory of social measurement and its application.* New York: Academic Press.

*Krippendorff, K. (2004). *Content analysis: An introduction to its methodology* (2nd ed.). Thousand Oaks, CA: Sage.

7.5

REASONING IN ECONOMIC DISCOURSE

A Network Approach to the Dutch Press

JAN KLEINNIJENHUIS, JAN A. DE RIDDER, AND EWALD M. RIETBERG*

This article discusses a method for relational content analysis that is based upon the idea that the explicit or manifest content of a text can be depicted as a network consisting of relations between meaning objects. To map the content of a text into a network, texts are parsed into nuclear sentences, each of which connects one meaning object to another. The network representation enables the formulation of inference rules that reveal implicit or latent content. In addition to providing a rigorous description of text content, network analysis also provides a foundation for various significance tests, for example, for differences over time or between implicit and explicit content. We conclude with an application of network text analysis to economic news, which shows the decline of Keynesianism in the Dutch press.

Usually texts convey more than explicit messages. Part of their meaning is expressed between the lines. In fact, ordinary users of language are quite sophisticated interpreters of unspoken and unwritten meanings. Whereas explicit meanings can be understood by employing the author's and audience's common knowledge of the grammar and semantics of a language, implicit meanings can often be inferred from explicit information within the text by employing the author's and audience's application of inference rules.

The method for text analysis described in this chapter allows not only for an analysis of the manifest content of texts but also for an analysis of their latent content (i.e., the content that can be logically inferred from the manifest content). The first section describes concepts and coding procedures for unraveling (i.e.,

*From Kleinnijenhuis, J., de Ridder, J. A., & Rietberg, E. M. (1997). Reasoning in economic discourse: An application of the network approach to the Dutch press. In C. W. Roberts, B. Jennings, & D. Zillmann (Eds.), *Text analysis for the social sciences: Methods for drawing statistical inferences from texts and transcripts* (pp. 191–207). Mahwah, NJ: Lawrence Erlbaum.

parsing) a text into a list of so-called nuclear sentences. This list of nuclear sentences can then be used to construct a network representation of the analyzed texts. The next section describes procedures, derived from the field of network theory for representing explicit meaning as well as for inferring implicit meaning. The balance of the chapter is devoted to describing an application of this method within a content analysis of Dutch economic news coverage between 1968 and 1984.

The Encoding of Manifest Content

Philosophers such as Ludwig Wittgenstein have suggested that the manifest content of a text can be represented as a list of elementary assertions, or *nuclear sentences,* each connecting one meaning object to another (Wittgenstein, 1921/1973, par. 3.144). Osgood, Saporta, and Nunally (1956) were the first to develop explicit coding instructions to assure that the list of "atomic sentences" would be reliable. They also introduced mathematical formulae for rendering political language according to Heider's (1946) "psycho-logic," a logic subsequently made more rigorous by Abelson and Rosenberg (1958). Holsti (1966) first used the computer in an attempt to automate this approach.* From a different starting point, Axelrod (1976) originated a similar two-place predicate coding scheme to exhibit authors' cognitive maps, which would be predictive of future actions. Amidst these developments, Abelson (1968) was able to show the logic of the underlying psycho-logic to be partially nonsensical and surely incomplete. The next section presents a consistent set of rules for logical inference-rules that meet Abelson's early critique. It is here that we introduce the structure of a nuclear sentence.

The Structure of a Nuclear Sentence

The grammar of a human language enables authors to combine many nuclear beliefs in one complex sentence. The text analysis method presented here relies on the reverse ability of the audience (or, more important, the coder) to unravel complex sentences. A formal method is described here for mapping the logic of texts' nuclear sentences.

A nuclear sentence is defined as a two-place predicate connecting an *i*-object (i.e., its agent or subject) with a *j-object* (i.e., the object influenced or implied by the *i*-object).[1] Optionally, the authorship of a two-place predicate can be attributed to a quoted or paraphrased actor. Two types of quotes are distinguished: the *say-quote* (denoted by ":") and the *order-quote* (denoted by ":!"). In an

Table 1 Structure and Illustrations of Nuclear Sentences

Author *(!)*	*(Quoted Source)* *(!)*	 *(IF*	*i-object* $i_{()}$*-object*	/	*predicate* *predicate*	/	*j-object* $j_{()}$*-object*	 *THEN)*
John:			Anna	/	doesn't like (–)	/	Frank	
John:	Maureen:		Anna	/	has made eyes at (+)	/	John	
John:	Frank:!		Anna	/	ought to love (+)	/	Frank	
John:		IF	Anna	/	has made eyes at (+)	/	John	THEN
			John	/	can date (+)	/	Anna	

Original text:
John said, "Anna doesn't like Frank. According to Maureen, it's John that Anna has made eyes at. From Frank told me, Anna ought to love him—that is, Frank. But if Anna has made eyes at John, he's the one who can date her."

* For an introduction to nuclearizing sentences, see reading 3.5, this volume.

order-quote, the quoted or paraphrased actor orders, wishes, or desires what the nuclear sentence signifies; in a say-quote no such order, wish, or desire is indicated. Furthermore, an author may use an IF-clause to specify under which condition the two-place predicate holds. Table 1 illustrates the core of nuclear sentence structure.

The Two-Place Predicate

Almost any relation established by a two-place predicate can be ranked on a positive-neutral-negative axis. For example, "*i* / enhances / *j*" is a positive connection, whereas "*i* / inhibits / *j*" establishes a negative connection. "To enhance" is a positive predicate because *j* (e.g., unemployment) will be influenced positively, which means that there will be more ups, more prominence, more fortune, or more success for *j*. Note that it is not relevant whether success for *j* is desired by other actors or normatively desirable according to the author (e.g., as "success" for unemployment would unlikely be).

We use the word *quality* to label the degree of positivity or negativity of a predicate. The quality of a predicate takes values along the range [–1 . . . . +1], where –1 denotes *extremely negative* and +1 *extremely positive.* Moreover, the quality of a nuclear sentence can be dampened by its ambiguity. Nuclear sentences are normally assumed to be unambiguous (ambiguity = 0). However, when they include double-edged compliments (e.g., "overly intelligent") or chance words (e.g., "probably attractive"), nuclear sentences are coded as ambiguous ($0 \leq$ ambiguity $\leq 1 -$ [quality × quality]).

The quality of a predicate does not exhaust its full meaning (Abelson, 1968). Obviously, both "to kiss" and "to give $25" are positive predicates, but the activities these predicates refer to are not interchangeable in social life. To capture somewhat more of the substance of relations between *i*- and *j*-objects, predicate types are also encoded.

Meaning Objects and Predicate Types

Both the *i*- and *j*-objects are *meaning objects*—objects that can be classified into a few abstract types. Various types of meaning objects include *actors,* such as individuals, collectively acting groups, organizations, and institutions (e.g., President Clinton, the Supreme Court, the United States); *states,* more or less concrete products of human action or interaction (e.g., "President Clinton's plan for health care reform," "Amendment 5 to the U.S. Constitution," "Iran-gate," "Communism"); *variables* (e.g., the level of inflation, the level of employment); *attributes* (e.g., dichotomous variables such as "being president of the United States"); *values* (e.g., doing good, doing what is desirable); and *realities* (e.g., the economic reality in the Netherlands in 1984).

The last two object types are in need of further clarification. A value is a meaning object that an author uses to evaluate another meaning object. According to the author, the evaluated meaning object has an effect on the value. President Clinton's evaluation (simplified here), "The current health care system is endangering lives," suggests that the "current health care system" has a negative effect on a value (namely, the preservation of human lives). Our approach does not distinguish among evaluations involving different types of values but rather lumps all values under one meaning object labeled *Ideal* (i.e., "good"). Thus, Clinton's evaluation could be coded as "Clinton: health care system / is endangering lives (–) / Ideal." Note that Ideals can only occur as *j*-objects.

A reality encompasses everything that happens within itself. Many different realities may be distinguished by an author (e.g., Ronald Reagan's world in 1981, the world our children will live in), but in almost every discourse, explicit references are made to the author's reality. Obviously President Clinton's sentence, "This new world has already enriched the lives of millions of Americans," should be coded as "Reality / has already enriched (+) / Americans." The same coding also applies to sentences in which Reality is not explicitly stated, such as "The lives of millions of Americans have already been enriched." If an author proclaims an actor's success (+) or failure (–), a state's appearance (+) or disappearance (–), or a variable's increase (+) or a decline (–) but makes no attribution to a specific *i*-object, then Reality is to be coded as the *i*-object. Note that Reality is never coded as a *j*-object.

Different types of meaning objects correspond loosely to qualitatively different types of predicates. Although predicate types may be defined for assignment to nuclear sentence types that frequently occur in one's texts, we describe only five types of predicates that are directly relevant to the research at hand. Illustrative sentences are (often loosely) derived from President Clinton's 1993 State of the Union Address.

- *EVA* predicates are used to evaluate a meaning object (e.g., "The current health care system is endangering lives" is coded as "Clinton: health care system / is endangering lives (-¾) / Ideal").
- *REA* predicates relate a *j*-object to the author's reality (e.g. "The lives of millions of Americans have already been enriched" is coded as "Clinton: Reality / has already enriched (+) / Americans").
- *ACT* predicates are used to code actions (e.g., "We are reducing our budget deficit" is coded as "Clinton: Clinton / are reducing (–) / budget deficit").
- *CAU* predicates are used to code causal relations between pairs of variables (e.g., "The reduction of the deficit will increase savings" is coded as "Clinton: national debt / reduction increases (–) / savings").
- *AFF* predicates may be used to code an affective relation between two actors (e.g., "I salute George Bush for his half-century service" is coded as "Clinton: Clinton / salutes for his service (+) / Bush"). AFF predicates may also be used to code an affective relation from an actor (as *i*-object) toward a variable (as *j*-object). For example, "We will insist on fair trade rules" is coded as "Clinton: Clinton/ will insist on (+) / fair trade."*

Finally, it should be noted that one verbal phrase may be encoded as multiple nuclear sentences. The statement "The increasing debt is responsible for the decline in national savings," for example, should be encoded as two nuclear sentences of REA type ("Reality/+/debt" "Reality/–/savings") and one nuclear sentence of CAU type ("debt/–/savings"). The statement "unemployment is too high" gives rise to one REA type ("Reality / exhibits high (+) / unemployment") and one EVA type ("unemployment / is too (–) / Ideal"). However, such detailed coding may come at a cost to lowered intercoder agreement.

Increasing Coder Reliability

Coding a text according to the method presented here takes effort and time. The coding task is complex, and detailed coding instructions are required (e.g., Azar, 1982; Kleinnijenhuis & Rietberg, 1991a). Nevertheless, careless errors and elaborate coding will decrease reliability among as well as within coders. A few ways to reduce the amount of work and to increase the reliability are discussed here. Most of our recommendations have been tested in reliability research (Kleinnijenhuis, 1990:299–309: Kleinnijenhuis & Rietberg, 1991b).

Coders' attention must be directed by a list of well-defined and intuitively clear meaning objects as they aggregate words into general categories of meaning objects. If the researcher's starting point is curiosity (e.g., "What's in here?"), then the texts to be analyzed should be inductively searched for meaning objects. If the starting point is a research question (e.g., "What's in here with respect to *X?*") and answering the research question requires the analysis of many texts by many coders, then extensive pretests should be conducted to find a good match between the research question at hand, the meaning objects specified thus far, and the levels of abstraction in the texts to be analyzed.

Coders must also be given a clear set of predicate types. Generally, one's substantive research questions should guide the selection of the smallest possible number of types of relations to be coded. In conflict-and-cooperation

*Further explanations of these predicate types can be found in Krippendorff (2004:294–296).

research, for example, Azar (1982) found only relations between actors to be relevant. The fewer (and more mutually exclusive) the predicate types, the greater intercoder agreement is likely to be.

The method presented here uses the nuclear sentence as the recording unit. However, such fine-grained data can be aggregated and analyzed using the paragraph, book, or other text block as the unit of analysis. Data from a sample of events or of a series of events (possibly discussed in multiple texts) might be aggregated into event networks (e.g., Azar, 1982). Likewise, nuclear sentences can be assembled into cognitive networks. Although aggregation will not reduce coders' systematic prejudices, the higher the level of aggregation, the more likely coders' random errors will be smoothed out of the aggregate-level data.

Many coding errors can be prevented by using a specialized computer program to validate the completeness and consistency of codings. Many errors can be detected by the text analyst, if software is used that confronts one's common sense interpretation of the text with the logical implications of one's codings.[2] In this way, errors can be detected, and coders can be retrained during the coding process itself.

Inferring the Latent Content of Texts

Before explaining rules for inferring latent content from aspects of indirect paths between objects, we must first consider methods for preprocessing IF-THEN statements and say-quotes. To interpret a source's IF-THEN statements, the propositional calculus prescribes that coded sentences attributed to that source should be searched for nuclear sentences satisfying or denying the IF part. Whenever the IF part is satisfied, the THEN part is added to the list of nuclear sentences as an unconditional nuclear sentence. However, when the search for satisfaction or denial of the IF part renders nothing, the THEN part is added as an unconditional nuclear sentence with weakened quality and high ambiguity.

An order-quote may be interpreted as a set of two conditional evaluations. The sentence, "President Clinton should reduce the budget deficit." may be interpreted not only as the IF-THEN sentence, "IF President Clinton / ACT reduces (–) / the budget deficit THEN President Clinton / EVA acts appropriately (+) / Ideal," but also as the IF-THEN sentence. "IF President Clinton / ACT increases (+) / the budget deficit THEN President Clinton / EVA acts inappropriately (–) / Ideal."

Statements of neutral actors are presumably impartial and can be trusted, whereas statements of partial actors are indicative of their position. Accordingly, say-quotes attributed to actors who are neutral according to the source are added as unquoted nuclear sentences attributed to the source. On the other hand, an evaluative say-quote attributed to an actor who is partial according to the source is added as an unquoted affective nuclear sentence connecting the quoted actor with the object of evaluation. Thus, evaluations by quoted partial actors are treated according to the rule *s: q*: *i* / EVA-connection / *Ideal*⇒ s: *q* / AFF-connection / *i.* Following this logic, the say-quote in the *Washington Post,* "Clinton: current health care system / is endangering lives (–) / Ideal," gives rise to the unquoted nuclear sentence, "Clinton / attributes endangerment of lives to (–) / current health care system."[3]

Direct and Indirect Relations

Because an object of a first nuclear sentence may be the subject of another, a text may be considered as a concatenated network with subjects and objects as vertices (i.e., nodes, points) and predicates as directed edges (i.e., arcs, arrows). Whereas the direct relations in the network (i.e., links) represent the literal content of the text, psychologists such as Heider (1946) and Osgood, Saporta, and Nunally (1956) purported that the indirect relations (i.e., chains, paths) represent inferences that might be drawn by reasonable, sophisticated users of a language. Unfortunately, these early authors treated predicates as if they were symmetric or applied inconsistent inference rules. The inference rules presented here are based on those discussed by van Cuilenburg, Kleinnijenhuis, and de Ridder (1986, 1988).

These inference rules take the world of one author or the world of one quoted author as the point of departure. As a first step, all nuclear sentences that have the same *i*- and *j*-objects are combined in parallel, thus rendering the *ij-links*.

Let's define f_{ij} as the frequency of *i*'s link toward *j* and q_{ij} as the averaged quality of this link. Equation 1 defines f_i as the relative frequency of nuclear sentences of *i* toward other meaning objects (i.e., the "outdegree" of *i*).

$$f_i = \Sigma_j f_{ij} \tag{1}$$

We define in equation 2 the base b_{ij} of the *ij*-link as the number of nuclear sentences of *i* toward *j* as a proportion of the total number of nuclear sentences of *i* toward other meaning objects. The base, b_{ij}, can be interpreted as the importance of the relation of *i* toward *j* from the point of view of *i*.

$$b_{ij} = \frac{f_{ij}}{f_i} \tag{2}$$

An acyclic or elementary path μ from *i* toward *j* is a sequence of directed relations $\{u \rightarrow v\}$, in which *i* is the initiator, *u,* of the first relation $\{u \rightarrow v\}$, *j* is the target, *v* of the last relation $\{u \rightarrow v\}$, each relation's target, *v* is the initiator, *u* of the next relation within the sequence, and not one initiator, *u,* or target, *v*, appears more than once in the sequence As defined in equation 3, the base, b_{ij}^{η}, of an acyclic path μ from *i* towards *j* represents the importance (i.e., base) of this path from *i*'s point of view, given the importances of the links within the path.

$$b_{ij}^{\eta} = \prod_{\{u \rightarrow v\} \in \eta} b_{uv} \tag{3}$$

The frequency, f_{ij}, of a path from *i* toward *j* is defined in equation 4 as the product of the base of this path and the outdegree of *i*.

$$f_{ij}^{\eta} = b_{ij}^{\eta} f_i \tag{4}$$

The quality of the *ij*-relation for a single acyclic path, μ, is denoted as q_{ij}^{η}. Given a value range of [–1 . . . . +1] to express the quality of separate links, the multiplication operator is used in equation 5 to define q_{ij}^{η} as the product of the qualities of the links that constitute path μ.

$$q_{ij}^{\eta} = \prod_{\{u \rightarrow v\} \in \eta} q_{uv} \tag{5}$$

Multiplication represents the idea of *transitive evaluative transfer.* If *Z* is evil, and *Y* causes *Z,* then *Y* causes evil to occur. However, this idea has been criticized by Abelson (1968). Types of links having an unsure effect on the state of the *j*-object, such as AFFection links, make the quality of a path hard to interpret. The idea of evaluative transfer is also dubious in the case of "scarce" meaning objects. If *A* wants to build a coalition with *B,* and *B* with *C,* but a minimum coalition of only two actors suffices, then *A* and *C* may be rivaling for the scarce affection of *B*. Contrary to the idea of transitivity, *A* may thus not be "on *C*'s side." Our solution is to circumvent Abelson's critique by only inferring evaluative transfer among types of links for which *j*-objects clearly change due to the activities and processes described by the predicates. When path's predicate types consist solely of links of the types REA, ACT, CAU, and EVA, their interpretation is straightforward in the light of evaluative transfer. These are the only predicate types for which we trace the directed relations within acyclic paths.

In a dense network the number of paths between two actors increases exponentially with the number of actors. Bundling all separate paths (of length greater than 1) may be useful to keep track of latent content. This is because a path of at least length 2 is needed for latent content to be inferred. The frequency F_{ij} of a bundle of paths is defined in equation 6 as the sum of the frequencies of the separate paths.

$$F_{ij}^{\eta} = \Sigma_{\eta} f_{ij}^{\eta} \tag{6}$$

The quality Q_{ij}, of a bundle of paths is defined in equation 7 as the weighted mean of the qualities of the separate paths. Paths are weighted by their frequency.

$$Q_{if} = \frac{\sum_{\eta} f_{ij}^{\eta} q_{ij}^{\eta}}{\sum_{\eta} f_{ij}^{\eta}} \qquad (7)$$

The degree of divergence is defined in equation 8 as the variance among the qualities of separate paths. The paths are weighted again by their frequency.[4]

$$D_{ij} = \frac{\sum_{\eta} f_{ij}^{\eta} (q_{ij}^{\eta} - Q_{ij})^2}{\sum_{\eta} f_{ij}^{\eta}} \qquad (8)$$

In sum, inference rules apply only once nuclear sentences have been combined in parallel into a network (via a generalized summation operator). Within separate paths, links between meaning objects are combined serially (via a generalized multiplication operator). Bundles are created by combining paths in parallel (via a generalized summation operator). Once this has been done, it can be proven that the definitions given here of the base and quality of nuclear sentences, as well as of links, paths, and bundles, are consistent with the requirements of a path algebra (Carré, 1979:84–85; de Ridder, 1994a:109–116). As a fortunate consequence, the orders of parallel and serial computations do not alter values of the various measures presented here.

Let us consider the manifest information in a text to be those links in a network prior to the application of inference rules. If the starting point of transitive evaluative transfer applies, then bundles generated according to the formerly specified inference rules represent the text's latent content.

An Application: Economic Discourse in Dutch Newspapers, 1968–1984

This illustration of network text analysis uses data from a research project on economic news coverage in Dutch newspapers between 1968 and 1984 (Kleinnijenhuis, 1990). In the Netherlands, approximately 80% of the adult population reads a newspaper regularly. The two newspapers in our analysis represent roughly 10% of the total readership market share. *De Volkskrant* and *NRC Handelsblad* are the most popular newspapers among the highly educated. *De Volkskrant* is an outspoken left-wing newspaper. *NRC Handelsblad,* emerging from a fusion between two conservative-leaning liberal newspapers, holds the most intellectual image.

The method for content analysis described here has been applied to samples of economic articles in the two newspapers from the months September and October of the even years in the period 1968–1984. In the Netherlands, economics is most newsworthy in September and October. In September, the Dutch government coalition presents its economic forecasts, budget estimates, and major policy proposals for the subsequent year. The Lower House of the Dutch Parliament discusses these forecasts, estimates, and proposals in October.

Texts were assembled from the newspapers using a snowball sampling procedure. Whenever a newspaper devoted one of its editorials to economics or economic policy, all newspaper reports and commentaries with respect to economics and economic policy from the same day and the preceding day were included in the sample. The coding scheme included a variety of meaning objects. Eight political actors (e.g., the government, political parties, employer unions) and 29 economic variables (e.g., employment, interest rate) were included as well as the abstract meaning objects Ideal and Reality.

Texts were coded by 18 students from different disciplines (e.g., economics, political science, law, linguistics). Coder reliability was assessed for a small sample of the news articles (n = 109 were independently coded twice). It turns out that the coding procedure did well to detect which issues (i.e., relations between meaning objects) were at stake. Although not as good, the reliability in the coding of the quality of relations is sufficiently high for one to be confident in tests of hypotheses. Krippendorff's (2004:221–236) α (interval level) for the frequency of a bundle (i.e., for F_{ij} scores) was 0.82 and for the quality of a bundle (i.e., for Q_{ij} scores) was

0.57 (Kleinnijenhuis, 1990:306–309). A total of 14,241 nuclear sentences were coded (*De Volkskrant,* 6,811; *NRC Handelsblad,* 7,430).

The Example: The Return to (Neo-)Classicism

The 1968–1984 period is an interesting one from an economic point of view. In the early 1970s the economic boom of the 1960s waned. The 1980s saw the severest economic recession since the big depression of the 1930s. Also during this period, there was a loss in the authority of the Keynesian doctrine that the government could cure temporary imperfections of the market. The late 1970s and 1980s saw an increasing popularity of theories (e.g., monetarism, neoclassicism, supply-side economics) that claimed the ineffectiveness of Keynesian demand management. Because economic news presumably plays an important role in establishing the cognitive map of decision makers, it is interesting to investigate whether new fashions in economic theory were reflected in economic news. New modes of economic thought are expected to slip into economic news as brute causal assertions on a commonsense level rather than as direct renderings of economists' esoteric journal-bound statistical methods (Klamer, 1984).

What type of causal reasoning would be expected in the news, given our hypothesis of a return to (neo-)classicism? According to the laissez-faire, classical view of economics, the processes of employment and wealth would operate naturally in terms of their own built-in mechanisms without any necessity for the government to intervene. Unemployment would be banned by lowering wages, which would cause an increase of profits and investments in labor (wages /–/ profits; profits /+/ investments; investments /+/ employment, thus wages /–/ employment). An increase in public spending would lead to a finance deficit but not to an increase in employment (public spending /+/ finance deficit; public spending /0/ employment).

According to Keynesianism, government expenditures can alleviate unemployment by increasing demand for government-purchased products (cf. Samuelson, 1967). Business investments would not depend primarily on profits (profits /0/ investments) but on effective demand for the goods to be produced. Public spending and high wages could stimulate effective demand (public spending /+/ employment; wages /+/ employment).

A Network Representation of Changes in Newspaper Coverage

Figure 1 depicts two selections from the economic outlook of *NRC Handelsblad* and *De Volkskrant,* one from 1968 until 1976 (n_1 = 881 nuclear sentences) and one from 1978–1984 (n_2 = 1,025 nuclear sentences) respectively. The omitted year, 1977, can be seen as a turning point in Dutch politics. In 1977 the left-wing coalition government was succeeded by a series of right-wing coalition governments, whose policy rhetoric centered on "clearing the rubbish" created by this left-wing government. Although leftist ideas became popular in the Netherlands in the late 1960s and early 1970s, it was not until 1973 that a left-wing coalition government headed by the social democrat, Joop den Uyl, came into office. Figure 1 exhibits the qualities (q^{η}_{ij}) of the links between eight meaning objects that played a major role in the controversies of the 1970s between the neoclassical view of economics and Keynesianism: government, public spending, the finance deficit, wages, profits, investments, employment, and the Ideal.

The figure for 1968–1976 displays a mixture of classical and Keynesian arguments. According to neoclassical thought, the newspapers maintain that an increase of public spending will increase (+.7) the finance deficit; an increase in wages will diminish (–.7) employment, because high wages will diminish (–.7) profits, whereas increasing profits would have increased (+.7) employment because profits will lead (+.3) to higher investments, which in turn will increase (+.3) employment; high public spending is evaluated slightly negatively (–.2).

Elements of the Keynesian mode of economic thought are present also. Public spending will contribute (+.6) to full employment, and because an increase in wages (and

1978–1984

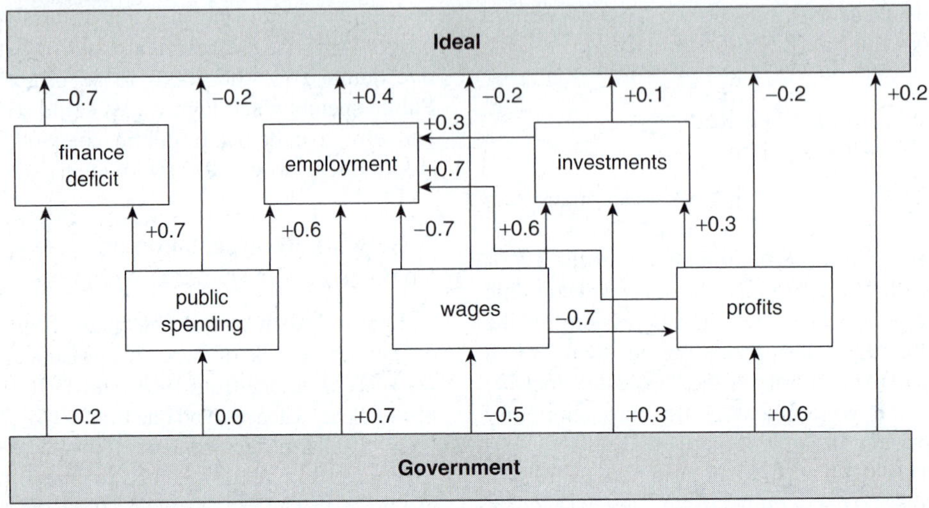

1968–1976

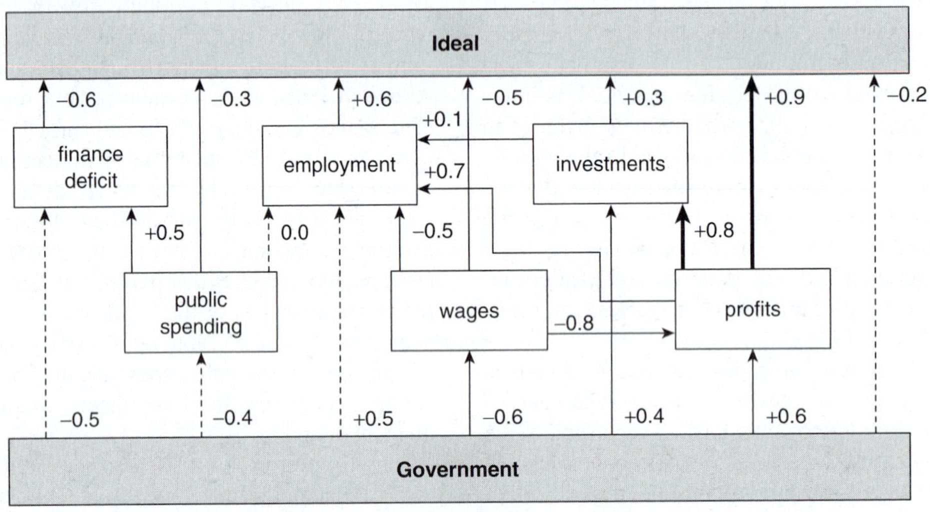

Legend The numbers represent the 'quality' (directional thrust) of a relationship

→ Quality did not change significantly as compared to 1968–1976

→ Quality significantly more positive than in 1968–1976

- - -→ Quality significantly more negative than in 1968–1976

Figure 1

associated demand for products) stimulates investments (+.6), which in turn increase (+.3) employment; high wages may indirectly create employment. High profits are not necessary for a healthy economy but are evaluated slightly negatively (–.2).

In the figure for 1978–1984 a dashed line means that the quality of a relation has decreased significantly in the expected direction ($p < .05$ in one-tailed tests) as compared to 1968–1976, whereas a thick line means that the quality of a relation has increased significantly in the expected direction ($p < .05$ in one-tailed tests) as compared to 1968–1976, whereas a thick line means that the quality of a relation has increased significantly in the expected direction. Because the quality of a link is defined as the mean quality of the nuclear sentences that build up the link, the question of whether a relation changed significantly or not can be judged using a *t*-test for the equality of means.[5] The figure shows that elements of Keynesian thought are nearly absent for 1978–1984. Public spending will not contribute (0) to full employment, higher profits will contribute enormously (+.8) to higher investments, and profits are extremely desirable (+.9). No mention is made of wages' stimulation of investments.[6]

The links between the government and the economic variables show that in the period 1978–1984 the government was depicted as pursuing less Keynesian policies than in the period 1968–1976. According to the two elite newspapers, the government tried harder in the latter period to reduce public spending (0 to –.4) and to reduce the finance deficit (–.2 to –.5) than in the 1978–1984 period. The figure for 1978–1984 illustrates that the government pursued good policies according to newspapers: The chains (i.e., indirect relations) between the government and the Ideal are all positive. Moreover, journalists appear to have agreed by and large with the neoclassical economic theory that underlay government policy.

Chain Reasoning and Latent Content

In the previous section, attention was paid solely to manifest content. The analysis was restricted to links (i.e., direct relations) between meaning objects. However, Figure 1 may also be used to trace the meaning objects that are indirectly connected in the elite newspapers. The principle of transitivity states that every indirect relation from i toward j amounts to a chain argument that provides an implication about i's relation with j. If a newspaper writes that a high employment rate is desirable whereas investments contribute to employment (investments /+/ employment rate /+/ Ideal), then this implies that higher investments are desirable (investments /+/ Ideal). Of course, this chain argument would be invalid when investments have major undesirable side effects (e.g., investments /+/ environmental pollution /–/ Ideal). Even in the case of multiple effects, the direct relation from investments to the Ideal should correspond with the (weighted) mean of the expectations based on separate chain arguments, provided one reckons with all effects and side effects of investments considered in the texts to be analyzed.

We expect that the quality of a direct relation does not differ significantly from the mean quality (Q_{ij}) of the corresponding bundle or chain arguments weighted by their frequency. Chain arguments can be used to expose texts' latent content—content that normally corresponds to the manifest content reflected in directly observed links. In the absence of such correspondence, the reader might find explicit information to contradict conclusions inferred from chain arguments.

T-tests can be used to test the hypothesis that the quality of the links depicted in Figure 1 does not differ significantly from the mean quality of chain arguments. Indeed, this is the case for most relations depicted in the 1968–1976 period. Table 2 lists the four exceptions to the hypothesis. Based on chain arguments derived from the news of the two elite newspapers in the 1968–1976 period, one can only faintly infer that the government promoted business profits and employment (the mean quality of chains is +0.1 in both cases). One cannot infer that the government did anything to reduce wages: it may even have promoted increases in wages (+0.1). One cannot infer that high wages are a major cause of unemployment (–0.2 as compared to –0.7). Each of the four differences is interesting, but here we concentrate on the divergence between the manifest news that the government wanted to increase employment (+0.7) and the latent news derived from chain arguments that the government promoted employment only faintly (+0.1).

Table 2 Significant Differences Between Manifest and Latent Content, 1968–1976

Nuclear Sentence			*Quality of*	*Mean Quality*		
i-object		*j-object*	*Link* (q^{μ}_{ij})	*of Chains* (Q_{ij})	*df*	*t*
government	→	business profits	+ 0.6	+ 0.1	30	3.66
government	→	employment	+ 0.7	+ 0.1	173	9.18
government	→	wages	– 0.5	+ 0.1	20	3.96
wages	→	employment	– 0.7	– 0.2	8	3.09

NOTE: All *t*-values are significant at the .05 level in two-tailed tests using separate variance estimates. Q_{ij} is based on chains that exclude the direct *ij*-link.

Consistency theory argues that journalists will strive for consistent news because they are sophisticated and involved readers of their own news (Wicklund & Brehm, 1976). In the end an inconsistency between the latent and manifest content of economic news (that is, divergence between direct and indirect relations) will predispose journalists to adopt a more parsimonious economic outlook that does not suffer from the earlier inconsistencies. In keeping with consistency theory, news will show long-run changes in links (i.e., direct relations) or changes in chain arguments (i.e., indirect relations) that reflect greater consistency.

Both types of changes occur in our data. Journalists described the government's dedication to full employment less positively in 1978–1984 than in 1968–1976. The quality of the direct link from government to employment decreases significantly (cf. Figure 1). Parallel to this is the finding that Keynesian chain arguments in the newspapers had faded away almost completely by the later period. For instance, the one 1968–1976 chain argument (i.e., indirect relation) that was inconsistent with this positive influence of government on employment disappears entirely. In the 1968–1976 period readers were told that the Dutch government played a negative role (–0.5) in how employment is increased (+0.3) via investments that are stimulated by higher wages (+0.6). Because investments were supposed to increase employment, the policy of the government to reduce wages allegedly had diminishing employment as a side effect. In the period 1978–1984 this could no longer be inferred from the news because no mention was made of wages' stimulation of increased investments. Thus, consistency theory appears useful as a measure for explaining the disappearance of Keynesian chain reasoning from elite newspapers in the period 1978–1984. Although Keynesian theory commends policies for overcoming economic recession, when the Dutch economic recession appeared, the theory was the first victim.

Discussion

This article provides an illustration of network text analysis. Like other relational content analysis methods, it involves the coding of connections between meaning objects, in this case, connections and meaning objects as intended by their author(s). The text analysis method described here allows the encoding of both manifest and latent content, whereby latent content is content that could be inferred by any reasonably sophisticated user of language from statements manifest in texts.

In an analysis of economic news coverage in the Netherlands during the period 1968–1984, a shift was found away from Keynesian economic image to a more consistent neo-orthodox view of government in the Dutch economy. For all but four pairs of meaning objects, manifest and latent depictions corresponded closely. One of these four rated the effect of government on employment negatively "between the lines" (i.e., latently) at a time in 1968–1976 when it was simultaneously rated positively in manifest statements. By 1978–1984 the newspaper journalists had completed their shift from such inconsistencies to a consistently neo-orthodox view of government, although included in this view was a modestly attenuated depiction of the government's positive role in enhancing employment.

Notes

1. When sentences are in passive voice, the *i*-object is the indirect object, not the subject. For example, in "Mary received a letter from John," not Mary but John is the *i*-object. *i*'s activity should always be more relevant for the success of what the two-place predicate describes than *j*'s activity.

2. Many of the advantages listed here are afforded by CETA, a software package developed by Jan A. de Ridder (1994a, 1994b) specifically for encoding texts for the type of network text analysis illustrated here. The program was used to generate the data analyzed in this chapter.

3. The preprocessing of say-quotes is further complicated when latent evaluations by quoted actors are considered according to the inference rules discussed here. The rules to infer whether a quoted actor is neutral or partial according to a source are not treated here.

4. Van Cuilenburg et al. (1986:91–95) provide a somewhat more complex formula to compute the variance within chains. This measure of ambiguity takes into account ambiguities both within and between nuclear sentences that are linked in a particular chain.

5. For example, the sample for the period 1968–1976 contained 361 nuclear sentences with direct evaluations of the government, with a mean quality of 0.16 and a sample variance of 0.55. The sample for the period 1978–1984 contained 476 nuclear sentences with a mean quality of –0.19 and a sample variance of 0.41. This results in a *t*-value of –7.39 ($df = 835$, equal variances assumed), which implies that the elite newspapers came to evaluate government as significantly more negative.

6. The quality of this link could not be computed because no nuclear sentences in 1978–1984 linked wages to investments. It is for this reason that Figure 1 does not display the link during this latter period.

References

Abelson, R. P. (1968). Psychological implication. In R. P. Abelson, E. Aronson, W. J. McGuire, T. M. Newcomb, M. J. Rosenberg, & P. H. Tannenbaum (Eds.), *Theories of cognitive consistency: A sourcebook* (pp. 112–139). Chicago: Rand McNally.

Abelson, R. P., & Rosenberg, M. J. (1958). Symbolic psycho-logic: A model of attitudinal cognition. *Behavioral Science 3:*1–13.

Axelrod, R. M. (1976). *The structure of decision: The cognitive maps of political elites.* Princeton, NJ: Princeton University Press.

Azar, E. A. (1982). *Conflict and peace data base, 1948–1978* [machine readable data file]. College Park: University of Maryland, Center for International Development and Conflict Management.

Carré, B. (1979). *Graphs and networks.* Oxford: Oxford University Press.

de Ridder, J. A. (1994a). *Computer-aided evaluative text analysis: CETA 2.1* [User's manual]. Groningen: ProGamma.

de Ridder, J. A. (1994b). *Van tekst naar informatie: Ontwikkeling en toetsing van een inhouds-analyse-instrument* [From text to information]. Amsterdam: University of Amsterdam.

Heider, F. (1946). Attitudes and cognitive organizations. *Journal of Psychology 21:*107–112.

Holsti, O. R. (1966). External conflict and internal consensus: The Sino-Soviet case. In P. J. Stone, D. C. Dunphy, M. S. Smith, & D. M. Ogilvie (Eds.), *The General Inquirer: A computer approach to content analysis.* Cambridge, MA: MIT Press.

Klamer, A. (1984). *The new classical macroeconomics: Conversations with the new classical economists and their opponents.* Brighton: Wheatsheaf.

Kleinnijenhuis, J. (1990). *Op zoek naar nieuws: Onderzoek naar journalistieke informatieverwerking en politiek* [In search of news]. Amsterdam: Free University Press.

Kleinnijenhuis, J., & Rietberg, E. M. (1991a). *Codeerinstructie politiek-economische teksten* [Coding instruction for political and economic texts]. Unpublished manuscript. Amsterdam: Department of Political Science, Free University.

Kleinnijenhuis, J., & Rietberg, E. M. (1991b). *Experiment codeurbetrouwbaarheid* [Experiment on coder reliability]. Unpublished manuscript. Amsterdam: Department of Political Science, Free University.

Krippendorff, K. (2004). *Content analysis: An introduction to its methodology* (2nd ed.). Thousand Oaks CA: Sage.

Osgood, C. E., Saporta, S., & Nunnally, J. C. (1956). Evaluative assertion analysis. *Litera 3:*47–102.

Samuelson, P. A. (1967). *Economics: An introductory analysis.* New York: McGraw-Hill.

van Cuilenburg, J. J., Kleinnijenhuis, J., & de Ridder, J. A. (1986). A theory of evaluative discourse: Towards a graph theory of journalistic texts. *European Journal of Communication 1*:65–96.

van Cuilenburg, J. J., Kleinnijenuis, J., & de Ridder, J. A. (1988). Artificial intelligence and content analysis: Problems of and strategies for computer text analysis. *Quality and Quantity 22*:65–97.

Wicklund, R. A., & Brehm, J. W. (1976). *Perspectives on cognitive dissonance.* Hillsdale, NJ: Lawrence Erlbaum.

Wittgenstein, L. (1973). *Tracticus logico-philosphicus.* Frankfurt/M: Suhrkamp. (Original work published 1921)

7.6

Predictions of Public Opinion on the Spread of AIDS

David P. Fan and Gregory McAvoy*

Since AIDS reached public awareness in 1982, there has been extensive mass media coverage and public opinion polling. However, most AIDS poll questions are not repeated over time, and as such, it is difficult to construct time series and to perform dynamic analyses (Singer, Rogers, & Corcoran, 1987). This lack of time series data is typical for issues other than the popularity of political figures (Page & Shapiro, 1982). For many topics, polls are very scarce, especially in the case where the same questions are asked repeatedly over time. Furthermore, polling schedules are usually irregular and infrequent. Finally, for a limited number of issues, poll questions are asked annually, yet such data cannot give accurate trends, especially where opinions change rapidly in response to fast-breaking news.

To facilitate the analysis of time trends of public opinion about the spread of AIDS, this article describes a computer methodology which has several important advantages for studies of the impact of the media on public opinion. First, this methodology will permit the identification and retrieval of news stories from an electronic data base, which is much more efficient and thorough than is possible with manual searches. Secondly, the computer method of successive filtrations will also be utilized which leads to the rapid, flexible and consistent scoring of stories needed for the efficient study of different themes in a very large amount of relevant text. Thirdly, the robustness and validity of the scoring instructions will be tested by comparing results using different rules. And lastly, the mathematical model of ideodynamics will also be used, which permits opinion estimates with a *minimal* knowledge of prior opinion.

Combined, these methods will make it possible to estimate opinion time trends about AIDS in the absence of extensive poll data. This feature is significant because it makes the model more powerful than those derived from econometrics, for example, where key parameters cannot be set unless there are preexisting series, with tens to hundreds of poll

---

*From Fan, D. P., & McAvoy, G. (1989). Predictions of public opinion on the spread of AIDS: Introduction of new computer methodologies. *Journal of Sex Research 26:*159–187.

points, spaced evenly in time (McCleary & Hay, 1980). While such voluminous data are readily available in the financial world, such data usually do not exist in the polling realm.

The Mass Media and Opinion on AIDS

The procedures in this paper are an extension of those described by Fan (1988). Fan has previously used Associated Press (AP) wire service stories to calculate successfully the results of public opinion polls for: whether American troops should be sent to Lebanon (1983–1984); whether American aid should be sent to the Contra rebels in Nicaragua (1983–1986); whether more money should be spent for national defense (1977–1986); whether inflation was more important than unemployment (1977–1980); whether the economic climate was improving (1981–1984); and who was the preferred candidate in the Democratic primary (1983–1984).

In brief, the full texts of stories relevant to the polled topics were retrieved by computer from mass media libraries in commercial data bases. The stories were then scored by computer for the extent to which they supported different viewpoints. This content analysis used the method of successive filtrations (Fan, 1988). Finally, the content scores for the mass media stories were entered into another computer program, implementing the equations of ideodynamics to predict opinion time trends (Fan, 1984, 1985a, 1985b, 1988).

Mass Media Information for AIDS Analysis

The present study was specifically designed to test if AIDS news stories could be used to calculate public opinion about whether AIDS would stay in confined, high-risk subpopulations or whether AIDS would spread to the general population. The AP wire service was used as the primary data source. Several factors determined this choice. First, the AP wire service has been widely used by both the print and electronic media. Secondly, AP has tried to remain neutral in outlook. Thirdly, AP stories have been considered the "backbone of the nation's system of news-gathering and dissemination" (Shaw, 1988). And finally, AP stories were previously found to be good news sources for predicting public opinion (Fan, 1988). Therefore, AP stories were considered a reasonable representative of the bulk of the mass media.

The analysis for the spread of AIDS began with the search for AP stories in the Nexis data base using the following command: AIDS and (DISEASE or ILLNESS) and (SPREAD or RISK or TRANSMIT! or THREAT!). This meant that the story had to contain the word AIDS; one of the words DISEASE or ILLNESS; and one of the words SPREAD, RISK, TRANSMIT!, or THREAT! The ! symbol meant that any trailing letters in the word were acceptable so that THREAT! included the words THREAT and THREATEN. The search dates were from January 1, 1979 to July 2, 1987, the day when the analysis began.

This search identified 2,794 stories on AIDS. Among these dispatches, the texts of a random 987 were retrieved by computer in random order. The yield was over 3.2 million characters or 740 pages of elite, single-spaced typewritten pages containing essentially no blank spaces. As in Fan (1988), the retrievals were for text within 50 words of one of the capitalized search words in the previous paragraph. If two search words were separated by no more than 100 words, the entire intervening text was kept. On the other hand, if the topic changed, as would happen during a press conference, the retrieval would stop after the 50-word limit. This limit typically meant that all relevant text was retained with little irrelevant text being collected.

Computer Content Analysis

At this point, the text was analyzed using the method of successive filtrations (Fan, 1988). First, there was a "filtration" step where the computer was instructed to keep only those paragraphs with a word suggesting a possible target population for AIDS. Such words included "homosexual," "doctor," "hemophiliac," "worker," etc. After this step, 93% of the original 987 stories still had at least one retained paragraph mentioning an AIDS target population. However, the text was now reduced to 38% of the original or 280 pages. Therefore, passages irrelevant to the spread of the disease were "filtered" out. Many of those passages still discussed AIDS but focused on aspects other than its spread.

If a word suggesting the concept of "spread of AIDS" was close to a word referring to a target population (i.e., homosexuals, Haitians, hemophiliacs, prisoners or intravenous drug users), the paragraph was scored as suggesting the confined spread of AIDS. If the target population was any other group, the paragraph was scored as supporting the general spread of the disease.

Sometimes it was necessary to consider word clusters, rather than individual words, to obtain the concepts of "spread of AIDS" or "target population." For example, "drug" by itself was sometimes used in the context of a cure for the disease, and "user" by itself had many different connotations. However, "drug" close to "user" almost always referred to intravenous drug users in AIDS stories.

In other cases, single words strongly implied an idea. For instance, words like "AIDS" and "threat" typically connoted the spread of the disease when that word was close to a word (or word combination) referring to a target population.

In addition to scanning for word combinations relating to target populations and the idea of the spread of AIDS, the computer also included refinements such as the safeguard that phrases like "police said" close to a "spread" word would be un-scored even though "police" was clearly a word implying the general "target population." Paragraphs with word clusters favoring both positions were given a 50% score for each position.

During their development, the computer instructions for the content analysis were continually checked to see that they gave acceptable scores for randomly chosen paragraphs. If the computer scores were not consistent with the analyst's reading of the paragraphs then changes were made in the computer instructions. The computer rules were modified until satisfactory matches were found between human and computer scores. At this point, the machine was given the task of scoring the entire retrieved text without further human intervention.

The content scores for each story were structured according to the mathematical model of ideodynamics. In this model, each message or story is divided into different components called infons (Fan, 1984, 1985a, 1988), with each infon favoring only one viewpoint. In the present example of AIDS, each story was divided into two infons, one supporting the idea of general spread and the other favoring the concept of confined spread. Therefore, each story has two infons each with its own score. Both scores are in numbers of paragraphs. For example, a story would have a score of two paragraphs for the infon favoring general spread, and one paragraph for the infon favoring confined spread, if the story had two paragraphs discussing AIDS being of concern to school children (general risk), and one paragraph noting that AIDS was still found mainly in high-risk subgroups (confined risk). If a single paragraph spoke of both types of risk that paragraph was given a score of one-half for each position.

After the analysis described above, 81% of the original 987 stories had at least one paragraph scored as suggesting either the confined or general spread of AIDS. Since scores came from such a large percentage of the retrieved stories, the scoring was applicable to the majority of the text, even though the rules formulation was only based on a portion of the total retrieved.

Display of Message Structure

Once obtained, the AP story scores were plotted as time trends (Figure 1). Each plot has two frames corresponding to the two types of infon scores for each story. The upper frame (Figure 1) gives the persuasive information suggesting that AIDS would stay in confined subgroups from mid-1982 (the time of the first AIDS story in the AP) to July 1987 (the end of the story collection). The lower frame gives the persuasive influence implying the general spread of AIDS.

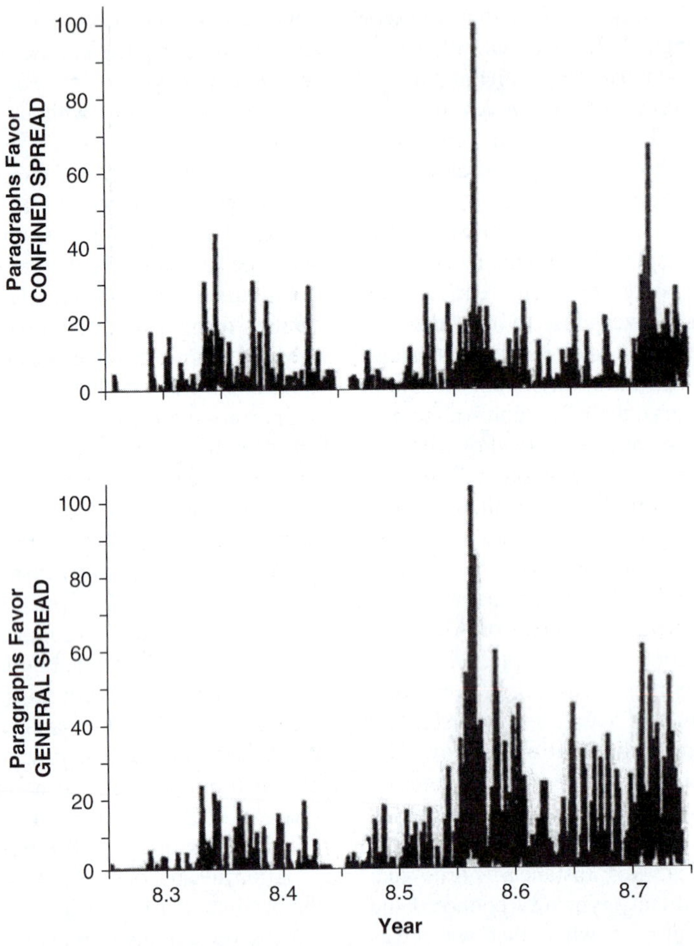

Figure 1 Persuasive Influences From Fan Infon Scores for the Spread of AIDS—From All Retrieved Stories

NOTE: Plots persuasive influences calculated from infons scored by Fan. The infons were scored to favor the idea of AIDS threatening the general population (bottom frame) or the concept that AIDS will spread mainly within the confined subpopulations of intravenous drug users, homosexuals, hemophiliacs, Haitians and prisoners (top frame). The persuasive influences are measured in average AP paragraphs and are assumed to decay with a one-day exponential half-life.

For the plots, each infon was given a height equivalent to the paragraph number on the date of the study. Then the height was assumed to decrease exponentially with a one-day half life. For five out of six issues, this half-life was shown to be the value giving the best fit between mass media information and public opinion (Fan, 1988). For the sixth issue, this short half-life was also perfectly acceptable. Longer half-lives meant that new messages could only have a small effect, since there was so much remembered information. The result was opinion which could not change as rapidly as was found in actual polls. Therefore, six prior studies suggest that one day is a good consensus half-life.

With this short duration, each infon contributes a vertical spike going up to the maximum number of paragraphs on the date of the story and falling back to negligible influence within a week. In Figure 1, each spike actually includes an exponentially decreasing tail, but this tail cannot be seen due to the compressed time scale in the five-year plots. If a second infon arrived before the effects of the first were dissipated, the spikes of the two infons were added together.

The plots in Figure 1 describe the total AP—and by inference other mass media—persuasive forces acting on the public. They are proportional to the *G* functions in the mathematical model of ideodynamics. The top and bottom frames correspond to G_C and G_G describing the persuasive force suggesting confined and general spread, respectively. Both G_C and G_G are functions which change as time proceeds so that $G_C = G_{C,t}$ and $G_G = G_{G,t}$. The time unit *t* of calculation was one day in the studies in this paper.

Figure 1 shows that there was relatively more information implying confined spread before 1984–1985. Later, the information supporting general spread clearly outweighed the information suggesting that AIDS would stay confined to high-risk groups.

Estimations of Opinion on the Spread of AIDS

As noted earlier, ideodynamics can use infon content scores to estimate opinion percentages as time trends. This mathematical model projects opinion better than can be done using a variety of linear time trend models, including those of the vector auto-regressive (VAR) and autoregressive integrated moving average (ARIMA) class (Fan, McAvoy, & Freeman, 1988).

To apply ideodynamics to the spread of AIDS, it is appropriate to include all infon scores without any partition by themes (Figure 1) because all this relevant information can persuade the populace.

The basic postulate of ideodynamics is that people will change their minds in response to message pressures. In the present analysis, information implying that AIDS can spread to the general population is presumed to change opinions among those people feeling that the disease will only strike high-risk groups. Conversely infons supporting confined spread of AIDS should persuade people worried about general spread to believe that the illness will be circumscribed. Note that opinion change can only occur by believers in a position being converted by opposing information. Favorable information might reinforce an opinion, but it will not change it.

To consider ideodynamics as applied to the spread of AIDS, let $B_{G',t}$ be the opinion (*B* for believers) that the disease may become prevalent in the general population. Let $B_{C',t}$ be the opinion that the disease will stay in confined subpopulations. Both of these opinions can change so both B_G and B_C are functions of time *t* in 24-hour units. In actual opinion polls (Table 1), the persons with no opinion ranged from 4 to 18%. They were assumed either to stay ignorant of the AIDS issue or to have opinions in the same approximate percentages as those with opinions. Therefore, $B_{C,t} + B_{G,t} = 100\%$. The removal of the *Don't Knows* is consistent with analyses of other authors (e.g., Page, Shapiro, & Dempsey, 1987).

The ideodynamic equation (see Fan, 1988, for fuller treatment including relationship between discrete and continuous time models) describing $B_{G,t}$ is

$$B_{G,t} = B_{G,t-1} + k_2' \cdot G_{G,t} \cdot B_{C,t-1} - k_2' \cdot G_{C,t} \cdot B_{G,t-1} \qquad (1)$$

This equation states that current opinion B_G is the same as opinion at an earlier time $B_{G,t-1}$, increased by a recruitment term and decreased by a loss term.

The recruitment term $k_2' \cdot G_{G,t-1}$ notes that the conversion of opinion will be greater if the persuasive forces $G_{G,t}$ from infons suggesting general spread (as drawn in Figure 1, top frame) are greater, and if the size of the susceptible target population, $B_{C,t-1}$, is larger. Clearly, the amount of opinion change must be dependent on the population of opponents. For instance, if everyone already believed that AIDS was a general threat, then there would be no individuals in the population holding the idea of the confined spread. In this case, there will be no opinion change, regardless of the power of information favoring general spread, because everyone is already convinced. The amount of change is proportional to a modified "persuasibility" or "volatility" constant (Fan,

1988). The larger the modified persuasibility constant, the more will be the conversion given the same amount of persuasive information and same size for the target population.

The loss term in equation 1 is the equivalent of the recruitment term of the previous paragraph. This loss is simply due to information favoring confined spread $G_{C,t}$ enticing people of the $B_{G,t-1}$ group to change their minds.

Since every entry into B_G means a loss from B_C, the equation for $B_{C,t}$ is

$$B_{C,t} = B_{C,t-1} + k_2' \cdot G_{C,t} \cdot B_{G,t-1} - k_2' \cdot G_{G,t} \cdot B_{C,t-1} \quad (2)$$

Therefore, with a mixed population and mixed messages, equations 1 and 2 permit simultaneous cross movement from B_G to B_C and vice versa.

In its simplest embodiment, ideodynamics uses the same k_2' persuasibility constant for all transitions. Given enough poll points, this parameter can be optimized by minimizing the Root Mean Squared Deviation (RMSD) between ideodynamic estimates and actual poll measurements (Fan, 1988). In addition to the modified persuasibility constant, the only requirement is a set of initial $B_{G,t-1}$ and $B_{C,t-1}$. After specification of k_2', the starting $B_{G,t-1}$ and $B_{C,t-1}$, and the G functions shown in Figure 1, a time trend can be estimated for the B functions using equations 1 and 2.

However, as noted earlier there are many cases where neither the modified persuasibility constant, nor any initial poll points, are available. Yet, even in these cases, opinion can be estimated using a procedure which can be called the CWC method, standing for the method of "convergence from worst cases."

As the name implies, the strategy is to compute a series of opinion time trends assuming the worst possible input conditions, and then determining the time after which the same opinion is calculated, regardless of variations in the starting conditions. Projections beginning with the actual opinion will be between the values computed from the extremes. Once the calculations from the two extremes have converged, giving the same opinion value, projections from the actual opinion, being somewhere in between, will also have the same value.

To use the CWC method for the AIDS example, opinion was estimated using different k_2' values under the two worst cases of 100% and 0% of the population believing that AIDS is relevant to the general population. These conditions would correspond to 0% and 100% of the population feeling that AIDS will stay confined. Tested k_2' values ranged from almost 0, corresponding to opinion being impervious to persuasion, and values so large that calculated opinion underwent extreme fluctuations.

Larger persuasibility constants mean that opinion is more volatile, with larger fractions of the target populations changing their minds for a given amount of persuasive information. This situation would be true for issues far from the core beliefs of the population, so that there is no emotional stake in the opinion. On the other hand, lower persuasibility constants would be characteristic of issues close to core beliefs, so that large persuasive efforts would be needed to change the minds of a few wavering individuals. Low persuasibility constants would also be found for issues where the population is disinterested and paying little attention to the relevant persuasive messages. In addition to this simple interpretation, the modified persuasibility constant measured in these studies also depends on other factors such as the appropriateness of the original search commands for the electronic database. Therefore, it is difficult to compare modified persuasibility constants directly from issue to issue (Fan, 1988).

From a series of paired computations starting at extreme initial B_C and B_G values (Figure 2), it is clear that there is always convergence toward common opinion estimates, despite the fact that initial opinion values are at opposite extremes. The convergence occurred at progressively earlier times as the modified persuasibility constant increased. However, the volatility and instability of estimated opinion also became larger. These results are exactly as would be expected, since high persuasibility means that opinion equilibrates rapidly with the information structure. After opinion convergence, the main consequence of larger persuasibility constants is that there is rapid fluctuation of opinion around the same approximate value.

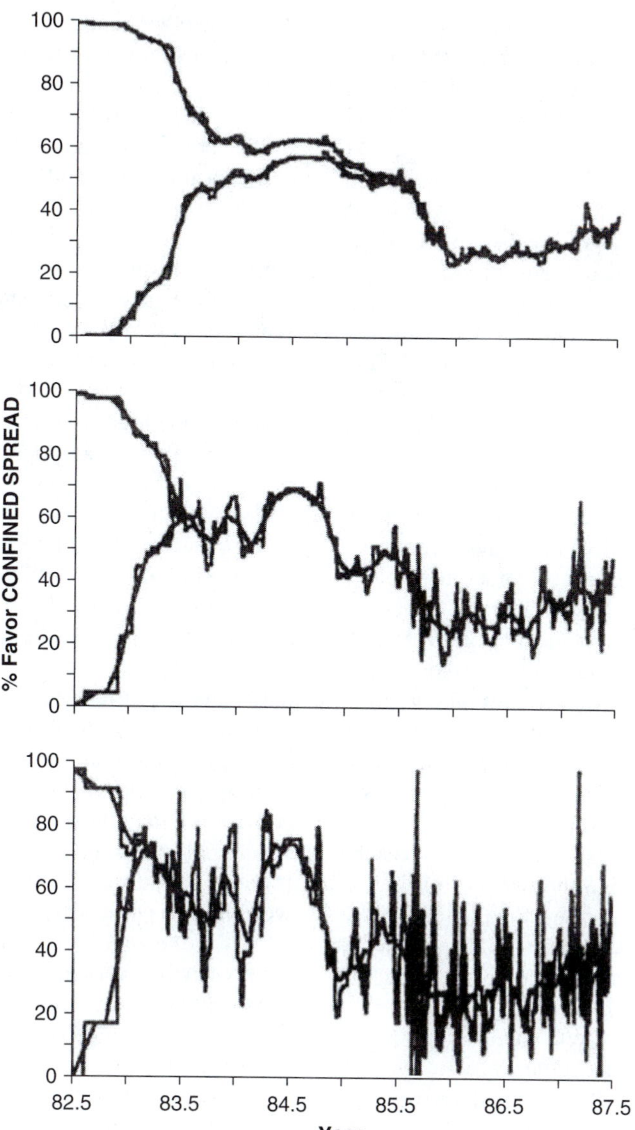

Figure 2 Estimation of Public Opinion on the Spread of AIDS Using the CWC Method

NOTE: Time trends were estimated using the persuasive forces shown in Figure 1. The calculations (see Fan, 1988, for details) began on July 1, 1987, shortly before the first AIDS message, and were made every 24 hours assuming that the opinion was either 0% or 100% in favor of the idea that AIDS would spread to confined populations only. The computations used modified persuasibility constants of 0.05 (top frame), 2 (center frame), and 8 (bottom frame) per AP paragraph per day. The jagged curves are the resulting opinion calculations. The smoothed curves at the centers of the fluctuations are running time averages where each plotted point is the average of all computations from 40 days before to 40 days after the point.

The curves in Figure 2 suggest the following general strategy for implementing the CWC procedure. Opinion values at the earliest time of convergence can be chosen as the starting value for opinion computations. This convergence will occur for the highest persuasibility constants, for which opinion trends can be estimated without having such large fluctuations that all trend patterns are obscured. The highest constant shown in Figure 2 is eight per AP paragraph per day. Opinion converged on March 15, 1983 for this highest persuasibility constant. Under these conditions, 75% of the population endorsed the idea that the spread of AIDS was confined. The choice of these opinion values for starting the calculations meant that the population was assumed to be in equilibrium with the information structure at this early time. This situation was probably valid if there had not been drastic changes in the information structure before that time. For the AIDS case, this assumption was tenable since there was very little prior information of any sort.

With this estimated starting percentage, opinion could be calculated using a variety of persuasibility constants. In order to see the general opinion trend through the calculated fluctuations, it is convenient to perform running time averages where the plotted opinion is the mean of all computed values ranging from 40 days before to 40 days after the plotted time. Such plots show that the opinion projections are relatively insensitive to changes in the persuasibility constant over a ten-fold range.

Therefore, a plausible estimate can be obtained by choosing the persuasibility constant which gives opinion fluctuations in the range of that found in Fan (1988), when the persuasibility constant could be optimized by minimizing the RMSD.

In summary, the CWC method can give an estimate of opinion without reliance on data from opinion polls. The principal assumptions are that opinion for the issue will equilibrate rapidly to the information structure and that the rate of equilibration to the information structure will be similar to those found by Fan (1988). Of course, the appropriateness of these values can only be established firmly by comparison with actual poll measurements.

Ideally, it would be possible to assemble time series with comparable poll points from the same polling organization asking the same questions at different times (see Page & Shapiro, 1982; Singer et al., 1987). However, as in the present case, there is frequently not enough polling by any one organization to gather such a time series.

On the other hand, the closeness in opinion percentages between similar polls will be an indication of the insensitivities of the percentages to question wording and polling organization. For the spread of AIDS, four similar poll measurements can be assembled to make a time series (Table 1). These polls only occurred at two times, in mid-1983 and late 1985. The result is that the time series does not contain many intermediate points. However, the poll percentages are quite similar within the cluster in late 1985, despite significant differences in question phrasing. For example, the question wording specifically assigned different sub-populations to the confined, high-risk subgroup. Nevertheless, the poll percentages are not very different, suggesting that the general public tended to think in terms of whether AIDS was (or was not) a personal threat. Thus, information discussing the spread of high-risk groups was likely to give the majority of the public a feeling that they were not at risk. Similarly, the public at large was likely to pool information about all the major high-risk subpopulations, as was done for the text analyses in this paper. The congruence in poll percentages suggested that all the poll points can be assembled into one time series, despite differences in question wording and polling organization.

When the values in Table 1 are plotted together with the opinion estimates from the CWC method it is clear that the estimates give a reasonable, although not perfect, approximation to measured public opinion. There seems to have been a significant underestimation in opinion appreciating the general spread of AIDS prior to the end of 1985. This phenomenon could have been due to the public reinterpreting statements about AIDS being found in high-risk groups as time proceeded. Rather than interpreting the news as implying that AIDS was only going to strike confined populations, the public may have begun to reinterpret the news as additional evidence that AIDS was going to spread further, potentially to all people, once it began to appear that AIDS was a general threat. In other words, the content of the news might have been interpreted differently at different times, a possibility specifically excluded in

Table 1 Published Public Opinion Polls on the Spread of AIDS

Dates	*Polling Organization*	*Likely Target Population for AIDS*		
		Confined	*General Public (Percent of Responses)*	*Don't Know*
Jun. 15–19, 1983	ABC/Washington Post	52	36	12
Sept. 5–8, 1985	Louis Harris	15	81	4
Sept. 9, 1985	CBS/New York Times	20	61	18
Sept. 19–23, 1985	ABC/Washington Post	18	79	4

the computer text analysis in order to assure uniformity of coding.

Whatever the reasons for the underestimate in opinion on general spread at the end of 1985, the more striking observation is that the CWC method was able to give a reasonable set of opinion estimates. This observation is very important from a pragmatic standpoint, demonstrating that it is possible to obtain an idea about opinion movements based solely on information available to the population.

Although the CWC method was reasonably successful for estimating opinion on the spread of AIDS, very few poll points were available for comparison with calculated opinion. Therefore, there is no assurance that the procedure would always be successful when more points are available. However, the method has also been applied successfully to other cases (Fan, 1988).

Besides being useful for estimating opinion without reference to actual poll measurements, the CWC method gives a good idea of the information structure relevant to a topic, after the time of convergence for the opinion estimates. From Figure 2 it is clear that calculated opinion is the same for all times, after the point at which opinion first converged. This fact means that all calculated opinion in the time period of convergence reflects the information structure. As a result, opinion estimates using the CWC method will give a good indication of the structure of the infon scores. Therefore, if two sets of infon scores give the same projected opinion, those scores will have the same content.

Conclusions

The work in this paper is consistent with previous studies (Fan, 1988) and extends the methodology in three important ways. First, it demonstrates that it is simple to extract threads from complex issues in order to assess the contributions of individual themes to the overall information structure. Second, it is possible to use the CWC method to estimate opinion time trends without reference to measured opinion. (Incidentally, compared to actual poll values, these estimates were found to have reasonable accuracy for the spread of AIDS). Third, the computer text analysis appears to be quite robust.

Turning to the opinion estimates in this paper, the model of ideodynamics was applied in its simplest form with all messages decaying with the same one-day half-life, with all quoted sources and all paragraphs having the same weight, etc. These simplifying assumptions were used because there were insufficient poll data for optimizing the weights. A better fit could have been produced by varying a number of weights, but it was not apparent which weighting was more appropriate. However, as discussed in Fan (1988), the general form of ideodynamics permits variations which can include every message or speaker having its own weight and each message having a different duration.

Nevertheless, the crude assumption of uniformity for all messages does provide estimates of opinion trends which are similar to those from measured polls. Since the

CWC method can estimate opinion without reference to poll data, it will even be possible to make reasonable guesses of opinion shifts decades and centuries in the past, so long as the information available to the population at the time can be studied. The precise opinion values might be questionable, but general trends will usually be accurate.

One major assumption of the CWC procedure is that opinion is in equilibrium with the information structure at the earliest time of convergence. This assumption will probably be valid if the information structure and opinion were changing relatively slowly before the time of initial convergence.

The second major assumption for the CWC method is that the modified persuasibility constant should give opinion fluctuations similar to those found earlier (Fan, 1988). With no opinion measurement, it is not possible to set this parameter precisely. Opinion might change significantly more slowly with a smaller constant value if the issue is close to the core beliefs of the population, or if the population is only peripherally interested in the topic. However, despite these difficulties, the CWC method does permit opinion estimates under conditions where no other method will provide any clues. For instance, many econometric models cannot be applied to compute opinion without reference to actual opinion measurements (McCleary & Hay, 1980). Not only does the CWC extension of ideodynamics permit the calculation of expected opinion, but the resulting estimates can be entirely plausible, as is seen by comparison to actual poll data.

References

Fan, D. P. (1984). Mathematical models for the impact of information on society. *Political Methodology 11:*479–494.

Fan, D. P. (1985a). Ideodynamics: The kinetics of the evolution of ideas. *Journal of Mathematical Sociology 11:*1–24.

Fan, D. P. (1985b). Ideodynamics predictions of the evolution of habits. *Journal of Mathematical Sociology 11:*265–281.

Fan, D. P. (1988). *Predictions of public opinion from the mass media: Computer content analysis and mathematical modeling.* Westport, CT: Greenwood Press.

Fan, D. P., McAvoy, G., & Freeman, J. (1988). *The effect of the media on public opinion: A new mathematical model and computer content analysis applied to the Bush-Dukakis race, etc.* Paper presented at the American Political Science Association Annual Meeting, Washington, DC.

McCleary, R., & Hay, R., Jr. (1980). *Applied time series analysis for the social sciences.* Thousand Oaks, CA: Sage.

Page, B., & Shapiro, R. Y. (1982). Changes in Americans' policy preferences. *Public Opinion Quarterly 42:*24–42.

Page, B., Shapiro, R. Y., & Dempsey, G. (1987). What moves public opinion. *American Political Science Review 81:*23–43.

Shaw, C. (1988, April 3). The AP: It's everywhere and powerful. *Los Angeles Times.*

Singer, E., Rogers, T. F., & Corcoran, M. (1987). The polls—a report: AIDS. *Public Opinion Quarterly 51:*580–595.

7.7

COMPUTERIZED TEXT ANALYSIS OF AL-QAEDA TRANSCRIPTS

JAMES W. PENNEBAKER AND CINDY K. CHUNG*

Traditionally, the analysis of political documents has been done by experts in policy and international relations using a mix of discourse or content analyses (e.g., Hart, 1984; North, Holsti, Zaninovich, & Zinnes, 1963; Simonton, 1988; Walker, 2000; Winter, 2005). The goal of these analyses has typically been to understand the meaning of the documents themselves or, perhaps, the motivation or intention of the authors. Although computerized approaches to text analysis have been around since the 1960s, they have not been widely used. With recent advancements in technology, computational linguistics, and the psychology of language, computerized text analyses are increasingly efficient and reliable.

For the past 10 years, we have been exploring some novel ways to think about people's use of language. Rather than focusing on the meaning of a document per se, we have been studying how the language people use in writing a document (or even naturally speaking) reflects who the authors are. That is, the ways people use language reflect their basic social and psychological state. Others have discovered this as well. Weintraub (1981) hand counted thousands of documents and speech samples and provided compelling evidence that people's use of certain parts of speech was diagnostic of their emotional well-being. Martindale (1990); Mergenthaler (1996); Stone, Dunphy, Smith, and Ogilvie (1966); Gottschalk and Glaser(1969); and others have also contributed to the measurement of natural language use in psychology. Today, there are an increasing number of applications of word analyses in clinical (e.g., Gottschalk, 2000), criminal (e.g., Adams, 1996, 2004), cultural (e.g., Boroditsky, 2001; Tsai, Simenova, & Watanabe, 2004), and personality assessments (e.g., Oberlander & Gill, 2004; Pennebaker & King, 1999).

We have been approaching language use in two relatively independent ways. The first examines people's social and psychological states by analyzing their use of function and emotion words. Function words include

*The authors can be contact via email (Pennebaker@mail.utexas.edu; CindyK.Chung@mail.utexas.edu) or through the Department of Psychology A8000, University of Texas at Austin, 1 University Station, Austin, TX 78712.

pronouns, prepositions, articles, conjunctions, and auxiliary verbs. We find that the use of these word categories is diagnostic of emotional states (e.g., depression, self-esteem, suicide proneness), biological states (e.g., testosterone levels, heart disease proneness), personality (e.g., neuroticism, immediacy), cognitive styles (e.g., complexity of thinking, psychological distancing), and social relationships (e.g., honesty, dominance). Indeed, function words are powerful correlates of demographic variables such as age, sex, and social class (for a review, see Pennebaker, Mehl, & Niederhoffer, 2003).

Whereas the function word approach explores people's writing or speaking styles, the use of nouns, regular verbs, and many adjectives and adverbs reveals the content of their thinking. This style versus content distinction is quite important. Indeed, our second strategy to studying language focuses on groups of content words and how they cluster together in natural speech or writing. Much like recent developments in artificial intelligence (e.g., latent semantic analysis, clustering methods, and other data-mining strategies), we are developing approaches to automatically determining the underlying meaning structures in text.

The Data

The purpose of this project is to apply function word analysis and a meaning extraction method to Al-Qaeda text samples. The function and emotion word analyses provide a sense of the social and psychological dimensions that we see in bin Laden and al-Zawahiri. The meaning extraction strategy allows a way of determining the themes that they are emphasizing in their public statements.

The text samples provided by the Federal Bureau of Investigation (FBI) were cleaned prior to analyses. Only the actual words spoken by bin Laden or al-Zawahiri were retained. Translator interpretations, extended religious or other quotations, or interviewer questions were removed. Spelling was corrected and normalized across texts. The final sample consisted of 58 texts of which 36 were authored by bin Laden, 17 by al-Zawahiri, 3 by both, and 2 unknown. As a comparison sample, we used a corpus of 17 files previously identified by Allison Smith (2004) as representing a sample of terrorist groups. This sample included statements from five different terrorist groups representing a wide range of time periods, ideologies, and geographic locations. Groups represented in this sample include the Sicarii group of ancient Palestine (2 texts), the Front du Liberation du Québec (1 text), the Shining Path (4 texts), Hamas (1 text), and the Army of God (9 texts).

Social and Psychological Profiles: Analysis of Function and Emotion Words

For the past several years, we have been developing a computerized method by which to assess people's use of function and emotion words. The program, Linguistic Inquiry and Word Count (LIWC; Pennebaker, Booth, & Francis, 2007; Pennebaker, Francis, & Booth, 2001), is a relatively simple word-counting program that calculates the percentage of words within several dozen categories that are used within any given text. The underlying logic of the program is that it searches for groups of words that have been predefined as matching the various categories of interest. For example, the program searches for and counts words that are related to the construct of anger. Groups of judges were used who agreed that words such as *hate, kill, angry, outrage,* and so on were all anger-relevant words. The LIWC program looks at each text file separately and simply calculates the percentage of words in the entire text that match the words in the predefined anger dictionary as well as more than 70 other language categories.

The basic LIWC program was used to analyze each of the Al-Qaeda files. Rather than focus on all 70+ LIWC dimensions, the current project examined the 16 or so language dimensions that have been found to be most correlated with social and psychological variables. For example, use of pronouns is closely related to depression, social status, individual and group identity, and insecurity. Certain classes of prepositions are associated with cognitive complexity. Both positive and negative emotion words are linked to the emotional state of the author. We first provide a comparison between the Alison Smith corpus and the two Al-Qaeda authors. A comparison between bin Laden and al-Zawahiri follows.

Al-Qaeda Versus Other Extremist Group Differences

As can be seen in Table 1, simple LIWC analyses paint a striking difference between other extremist groups and the two Al-Qaeda authors. Compared with authors of the Smith corpus, bin Laden and al-Zawahiri focus more on other individuals (as seen in third-person plural pronouns) and are more emotional in their statements. They also pay less attention to past events than other groups.

The use of third-person plural pronouns (e.g., *they, them*) is highly significant. In our analyses of online extremist groups such as American Nazis, animal rights groups, and so on, we find that third-person plural pronouns are the best single predictor of extremism as rated by independent judges (Seyle & Pennebaker, 2004). It suggests that the group is defining itself to a large degree by the existence of an oppositional group. A high usage of words such as *they* and *them* indicates that the speakers are addressing people who they believe share the same worldview and are attempting to bring the audience closer to their worldview.

It is also of interest that the Al-Qaeda speakers are far more emotional in their use of both positive and negative emotion words than authors of the Smith corpus. In natural conversation, most people use almost twice as many positive emotion words than negative emotion words. It is interesting to note the high degree of negative emotions among the Al-Qaeda authors. These effects are due almost exclusively to the remarkably high rate of anger or hostility words (relative to anxiety or sadness words).

bin Laden Versus al-Zawahiri

The analysis of the al-Zawahiri and bin Laden files suggests somewhat different speaking and, by extension, thinking styles. Overall, al-Zawahiri uses bigger words, tends to be more positive in his outlook, and is less time bound, less immediate, and ultimately less analytical than bin Laden. Although there have been some revealing changes in al-Zawahiri's language of late (see below), most of his earlier communications suggest someone more emotionally detached from his topic and audience than bin Laden.

We are hesitant to overanalyze the historical distinctions between the two Al-Qaeda authors at this time. The reason is that al-Zawahiri has been changing his speaking style rather dramatically and progressively over the past year and a half. Most striking has been his changes in pronouns. As can be seen in Figures 1a and 1b, Zawahiri has more than tripled his use of first-person singular pronouns, primarily the use of the word *I*. At the same time, his use of first-person plurals has remained flat, even dropping slightly in comparison with bin Laden. Normally, higher rates of *I* words correspond with feelings of insecurity, threat, and defensiveness. Closer inspection of his *I* use in context tends to confirm this. Indeed, to the degree that bin Laden and al-Zawahiri are in contact, the relative differences in *I* use would suggest a significant change in their relationship.

The analysis of emotion words in Table 1 suggests that both bin Laden and al-Zawahiri share similar levels of both positive and negative affect. However, closer inspection of Figures 1c and 1d reveal some interesting trends over time. Since 2002, bin Laden's use of positive emotion words has risen significantly. al-Zawahiri has used similar impressively high rates of positive emotion since his first works in 2003. Interestingly, bin Laden's use of negative emotion words has been steadily increasing since 1988. Indeed, this effect is due almost exclusively to an increase in anger-related words. When this time factor is considered, it is clear that al-Zawahiri is significantly less negative and hostile than bin Laden.

One other category that we pay close attention to is exclusive words. Exclusive words such as *except, but, exclude,* and *without* signal a person's attempting to make

Table 1 Comparison of Public Statements by bin Laden, al-Zawahiri, and Other Terrorist Groups

	bin Laden (1988–2006) (n = 28)[†]	*al-Zawahiri (2003–2006) (n = 15)*[†]	*Controls (n = 17)*	*(2-Tailed) p ≤*
Word count	2511.5[††]	1996.4	4767.5	
Big words (greater than 6 letters)	21.2_a[†††]	23.6_b	21.1_a	.05
Pronouns	9.15_{ab}	9.83_b	8.16_a	.09
I (e.g., I, me, my)	0.61	0.90	0.83	
We (e.g., we, our, us)	1.94	1.79	1.95	
You (e.g., you, your, yours)	1.73	1.69	0.87	
He/she (e.g., he, hers)	1.42	1.42	1.37	
They (e.g., they, them)	2.17_a	2.29_a	1.43_b	.03
Propositions	14.8	14.7	15.0	
Articles (e.g., a, an, the)	9.07	8.53	9.19	
Exclusive words (e.g., but, exclude)	2.72	2.62	3.17	
Affect	5.13_a	5.12_a	3.91_b	.01
Positive emotion (e.g., happy, joy, love)	2.57_a	2.83_a	2.03_b	.01
Negative emotion (e.g., awful, cry, hate)	2.52_a	2.28_{ab}	1.87_b	.03
Anger words (e.g., hate, kill)	1.49_a	1.32_a	0.89_b	.01
Cognitive mechanisms	4.43	4.56	4.86	
Time (e.g., clock, hour)	2.40_b	1.89_a	2.69_b	.01
Past tense verbs	2.21_a	1.63_a	2.94_b	.01
Social processes	11.4_a	10.7_{ab}	9.29_b	.04
Humans (e.g., child, people, selves)	0.95_{ab}	0.52_a	1.12_b	.05
Family (e.g., mother, father)	0.46_{ab}	0.52_a	0.25_b	.08
Content				
Death (e.g., dead, killing, murder)	0.55	0.47	0.64	
Achievement	0.94	0.89	0.81	
Money (e.g., buy, economy, wealth)	0.34	0.38	0.58	
Religion (e.g., faith, Jew, sacred)	2.41	1.84	1.89	

[†]Documents whose source indicates "Both" ($n = 3$) or "Unknown" ($n = 2$) were excluded due to their small sample sizes.

[††]Numbers are mean percentages of total words per text file and the results of statistical tests (mean square differences) between bin Laden, al-Zawahiri, and controls.

[†††]In any row, mean percentages that differed from each other—on a level of significance indicated in the last column—bear unequal subscripts, a or b. A mean that is not different from either a or b is subscripted by ab. Means that are not statistically different from each other bear the same subscripts.

distinctions between what is in a category and what is not in it. We have found that exclusive word use is associated with greater cognitive complexity, telling the truth, and better grades in classes (see Chung & Pennebaker, 2007, for review). Although bin Laden and al-Zawahiri do not differ in overall use of exclusive word use, Figure 1e indicates that bin Laden's exclusive words have been increasing significantly since 1988. On the other hand, al-Zawahiri continues to think in less complex ways.

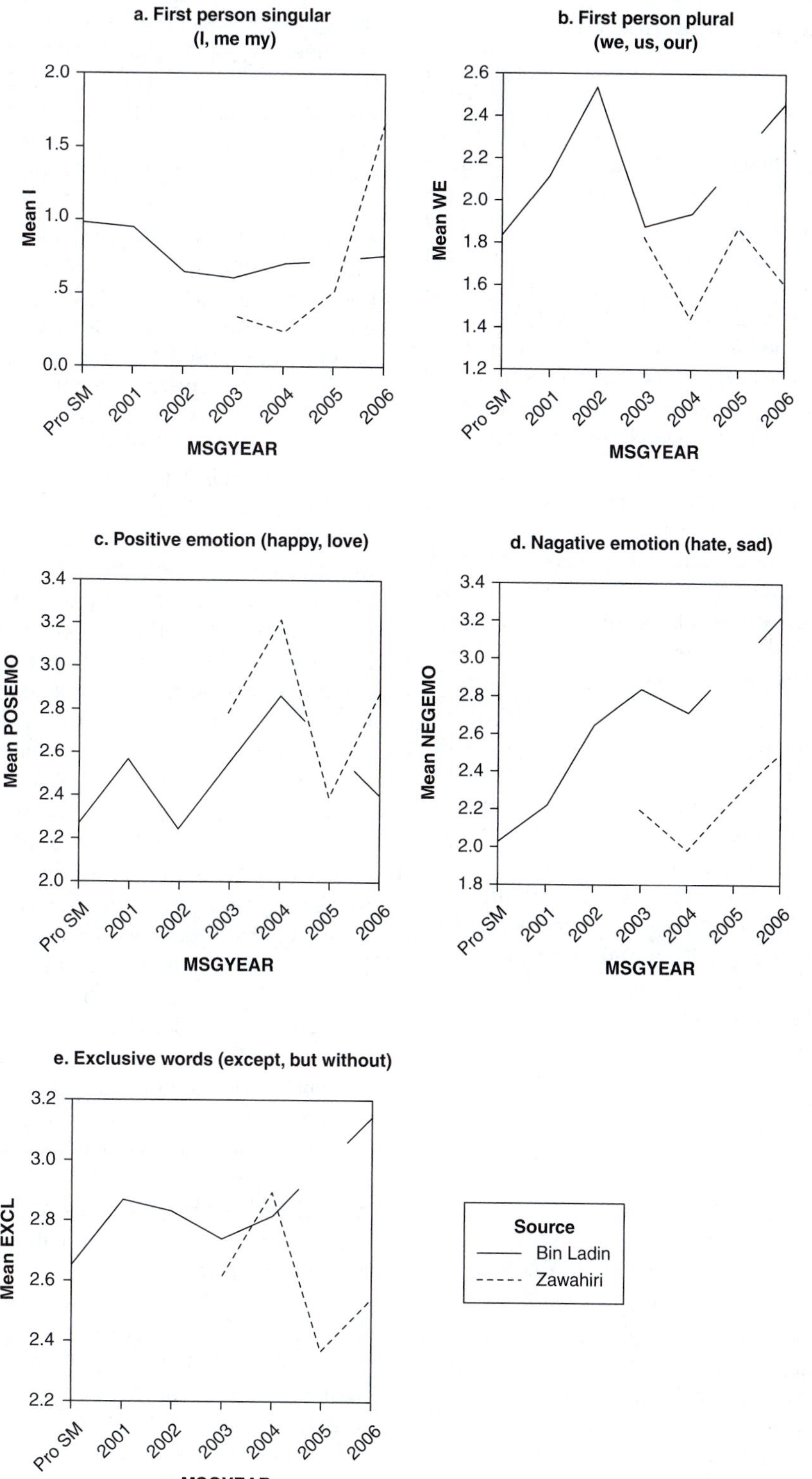

Figure 1 Use of Pronouns and Emotion Words by bin Laden and al-Zawahiri Over Time

Message and Target Analysis

Table 2 includes a basic comparison in word use as a function of the types of messages that bin Laden and al-Zawahiri have used. The table excludes the 3 letters and 3 epistles by the authors and only includes the 10 interviews and 42 statements. As is apparent, the language use is somewhat different among several dimensions. Not surprisingly, interviews result in more personal (i.e., first-person singular) pronouns. Use of second-person (*you, your*) and third-person plural (*they, them*) were more common in statements. The use of second person is generally considered an aggressive form of speaking in one-on-one communications, whereas it is quite common in general statements where the *you* is not specific and personal. The third-person plural effects are less clear and may reflect the nature of the interviewers' questions and perspective.

Target analyses comparing likely audiences of the messages were categorized into predominantly Muslim ($n = 37$), both Muslim and Western ($n = 7$), and predominantly Western ($n = 8$). As can be seen in Table 3, the differences in word use as a function of audience were not particularly striking. As might be expected, the authors were significantly more likely to use *we* (in reference to the speaker and his or her world) and *you* and less likely to use third-person plural when speaking to Western audiences. When addressing fellow Muslims, bin Laden and al-Zawahiri made reference to "them" in reference to Westerners.

Meaning Extraction Method: Pattern Analysis of High-Frequency Content Words

Much like recent breakthroughs in computational linguistics (e.g., Landauer & Dumais, 1997), we have developed a method to determine the major themes that occur in a text sample based on the co-occurrence of high-frequency content words. Content words (or open-class words), such as adjectives, adverbs, nouns, and regular verbs, are more telling of conversational or writing topic than of linguistic style. Our meaning extraction method begins by using a word-counting program that ranks all the content words in a corpus by frequency of use. The most frequently occurring content words across all texts are compiled into a LIWC dictionary, and their patterns of co-occurrence are assessed using a factor-analytic approach. Each resulting factor is made up a coherent group of words that co-occur in the texts. The factors can be used for descriptive purposes or for further analyses both within and across texts. The primary advantage of the meaning extraction method is that it provides intuitively comprehensible themes based on a purely inductive approach.

Instead of imposing a predetermined coding structure on the Al-Qaeda files, the meaning extraction method was used to uncover the major themes in the 57 texts from 1994 to 2006. First, the most frequently occurring content words appearing in at least 25% of text files were made into a LIWC dictionary. Each text file was broken down into text segments of 308 words for analyses. This text segmentation was chosen since the smallest text file had a total of 308 words after the text files had been cleaned. After dividing by 308 words, remaining text segments in text files were included for analyses if they included at least 40 words. This resulted in 519 text segments. LIWC assessed each of these 519 text segments for the occurrence (coded as 1) or absence (coded as 0) of the top 257 occurring content words (including any alternate forms that could be made from their root word). The final data summary, then, can be thought of as a 257 (content word) by 519 (text segment) matrix, with each entry referring to the presence or absence of each content word within each text segment.

A factor analysis on this matrix (principal components analysis with varimax rotation) produced 18 factors with eigenvalues of at least 2.50, accounting for 22% of the variance (see Table 4). Regression-based factor scores were computed for each of the text segments. The means of the regression-based factor scores for each text file are the basis of further analyses over time and by author.

Table 2 LIWC Analyses by Message Type

	Interviews (1994–2005) (n = 10)	*Statements (1988–2006) (n = 42)*	*(2-Tailed) p*
Word count	3329.2	2495.4	
Pronouns	8.26	9.18	
I (e.g., I, me, my)	1.21	0.58	.01
We (e.g., we, our, us)	2.22	1.90	
You (e.g., you, your, yours)	0.32	1.54	.01
Other (e.g., he, hers, they)	2.75	3.65	.01
Propositions	14.7	14.7	
Articles (e.g., a, an, the)	9.35	9.35	
Exclusive words (e.g., but, exclude, without)	2.89	2.89	
Affect	4.55	4.55	
Positive emotion (e.g., happy, joy, love)	2.22	2.22	
Negative emotion (e.g., awful, cry, hate)	2.32	2.32	
Cognitive mechanisms	5.19	5.19	.09
Content			
Death (e.g., dead, killing, murder)	0.48	0.48	
Humans (e.g., mother, people, selves)	0.92	0.92	
Money (e.g., buy, economy, wealth)	0.50	0.50	.06
Religion (e.g., faith, Jew, sacred)	1.79	1.79	
Factor 1: Compassion	.16	−.50	.01
Factor 2: Bush in Iraq and Afghanistan	.20	−.21	
Factor 3: Islam-Israeli conflict	−.03	−.04	
Factor 4: Saudi, Egypt, United States, Holy Land	−.08	.40	.06
Factor 9: Worldwide Islamic conflicts	−.08	.27	.06

NOTE: Numbers are mean percentages of total words per text file. Mean differences between statements (1988 to 2006) and interviews (1994 to 2005) are based on two-tailed independent samples t tests, $df = 50$. Documents whose message type is "Epistle" ($n = 3$) or "Letter" ($n = 3$) were excluded due to their small sample sizes.

Word Factors Over Time and by Author

The meaning extraction approach to content analysis opens new ways of thinking about language. Each factor exists along a continuum where a high positive number reflects the use of words within the factor. Because most factors include words that are only positively loaded, a negative loading on a factor indicates that the text does not deal with this topic. Table 4 lists the actual words that load most highly on each of the 18 factors. Words that are negatively loaded on the factors are in brackets. Note that each word factor suggests a different theme or meaning unit. The factors are centered on themes of religiosity (Factors 1, 7, 17), war and Jihad (Factors 2, 3, 6), emotions (Factor 14), economics (Factors 8 and 16), or Middle Eastern and Western politics and geography (Factors 4, 5, 8–13, 15, and 18). Analyses for Factors 1, 2, 3, 4, and 9 are highlighted for further discussion.

Table 3 Target Information

	Muslims (1988–2006) (n = 37)	*Muslim/West (1996–2006) (n = 7)*	*West (2002–2006) (n = 8)*	*(2-Tailed) p*
Word count	2742.5	2592.4	1343.6	
Big words (greater than six letters)	22.2	22.1	21.4	
Pronouns	8.52	9.49	11.13	.01
I (e.g., I, me, my)	0.61	0.68	1.17	.09
We (e.g., we, our, us)	1.86	1.70	2.77	.03
You (e.g., you, your, yours)	0.94	1.93	3.27	.01
He/she (e.g., he, hers, they)	1.25	1.33	1.16	
They (e.g., they, them)	2.32	2.28	1.42	.06
Propositions	14.7	14.9	16.0	.05
Articles (e.g., a, an, the)	9.10	8.83	8.25	
Exclusive words (e.g., but, exclude)	2.64	2.64	3.15	
Affect	4.83	5.24	5.46	
Positive emotion (e.g., happy, joy, love)	2.49	2.71	2.47	
Negative emotion (e.g., awful, cry, hate)	2.32	2.52	2.95	.06
Anger words (e.g., hate, kill)	1.37	1.47	1.81	
Cognitive mechanisms	4.60	4.20	5.00	
Time (e.g., clock, hour)	2.21	2.03	2.46	
Past tense verbs	2.14	1.77	2.00	
Social processes	10.30	11.06	12.60	.07
Humans (e.g., child, people, selves)	0.77	0.85	0.97	
Family (e.g., mother, father)	0.50	0.41	0.29	
Content				
Death (e.g., dead, killing, murder)	0.42	0.62	0.80	.06
Achievement	0.91	0.88	1.00	
Money (e.g., buy, economy, wealth)	0.36	0.40	0.47	
Religion (e.g., faith, Jew, sacred)	2.22	1.96	1.39	
Factor 1: Compassion	–.02	.15	–.17	
Factor 2: Bush in Iraq and Afghanistan	.08	.09	–.76	.01
Factor 3: Islam-Israeli conflict	.10	–.19	–.34	
Factor 4: Saudi, Egypt, United States, Holy Land	–.15	.72	.47	.01
Factor 9: Worldwide Islamic conflicts	–.03	–.22	–.39	

NOTE: Numbers are mean percentages of total words per text file. Mean differences between Muslim, Muslim/West, and West are based on one-way analyses of variance, $F(2, 49)$. Documents whose target type is "general" ($n = 2$) or "extremists" ($n = 4$) were excluded due to their small sample size.

Table 4 Meaning Extraction Results: 18 Factor Solution

1	*2*	*3*	*4*	*5*	*6*	*7*	*8*	*9*
Guide	Bush	Crusade	Saudi	Palestine	Child	God	Important	Afghan
Companion	Operate	Islam	Region	Occupy	Kill	Pray	Resource	Iraq
Forgive	War	Muslim	Holy	Century	Woman	Almighty	Aware	Sudan
Praise	Iraq	Campaign	Occupy	Liberate	Innocent	Bless	Role	Victor
Message	Qaeda	Zion	Control	[Taliban]	Bomb	Faith	Grace	Chechnya
Family	Evident	Support	America	[Pakistan]	Death	Serve	Major	Palestine
Lord	America	Israel	Land	[Afghan]	Terror	Accept	Victor	Kashmir
Allah	Afghan	Pakistan	Peninsula	(Omar)		Jihad	UN	Somali
Muhammad	Add	Jew	Force	[Mujahid]		[Sake]	Crime	[Situation]
Patient	[Man]	Jihad	Month			[Allah]		
Mercy	[Allah]	Duty	Regime					
Bless	[Life]		Year					
[County]	[Lord]		Egypt					
			Jew					
			State					

10	*11*	*12*	*13*	*14*	*15*	*16*	*17*	*18*
Issue	Banner	Human	NewYork	Sword	Plan	Economy	Ladin	Media
Clear	Lead	Free	Washington	Age	Achieve	Dignity	Usama	Huge
Event	[verify]	Britain	Change	Sacrifice	Resist	Long	Shaykh	Deal
Point	[Friend]	Real	Expose	Head	Return	Oil		State
Sudan	[Unjust]	Begin	Respond	Turn	Egypt	Blood		[Remain]
Act	[Christian]	Destruct	[Abu]	Pride	Small	[Knowledge]		
Conflict	[Belief]	Face	[General]	Humiliate	Policy	[Arab]		
Nature	[Protect]	Day		Heart	International	[Affair]		
[Occupy]	[Campaign]	[infidel]				[order]		
		[Money]				[Abdallah]		

NOTE: All words within a factor are positively loaded except for the words in [brackets]. Only words that have loadings of. 25 or higher are included. Words are listed from the highest to the lowest loadings.

Factor 1, for example, can be thought of as a compassion factor, made up of words such as *guide, companion, forgive, praise, message, family, Lord, Allah, Muhammad, patient, mercy,* and *bless.* As can be seen in Figure 2A, bin Laden's use of compassion-relevant words has increased over the course of his career, peaking in 2002. al-Zawahiri's loadings are not significantly different from bin Laden's and have not fluctuated much in the past 4 years.

The remaining graphs in Figure 2 highlight meaningful trends in the topics that the authors are emphasizing. bin Laden, for example, has been dramatically increasing his references to Bush's involvement in Iraq and Afghanistan (Figure B), whereas he has been dropping his references to other Islamic hotspots such as Saudi Arabia, Egypt, and the Holy Lands (Figure 2C) and Chechnya, Kashmir, Somalia, and Sudan (Figure 2D). In other words, one can easily see how bin Laden's early goals for Al-Qaeda have been co-opted by the American involvement in Iraq and Afghanistan.

Whereas the content dimensions are generally quite similar for bin Laden and al-Zawahiri, the two authors are strikingly different about one issue. As can be seen in Figure 2C, al-Zawahiri is much more consumed by the Islamic-Israel conflict than is bin Laden. It is interesting that this topic is a feature of virtually all of his communications.

Message and Target Analyses

As can be seen in Table 3, Factor 2 (Bush's involvement in Iraq and Afghanistan) is a topic commonly discussed when addressing Muslim audiences but not those in the West. The topics relevant to Factor 4 (Saudi, Egypt, United States, and Holy Lands) are used much more when the target audience includes Westerners.

Table 4 lists the use of the factors according to message type. The differences in use of factors may not be so surprising, considering that interview audiences (e.g., Al-Jazeera, Pakistani newspapers) have included a large Muslim population, whereas statements are intended for a wider audience. For example, Factor 1 (compassion) was much higher in interviews, relative to statements. On the other hand, talk of broader issues, such as control and occupation of various lands (Factor 4) and international Islamic conflicts (Factor 9), was much more common in statements than in interviews.

Discussion and Summary

The ways in which public figures use words give us glimpses into who they are—much in the way that facial expressions, haircuts, and nonverbal gestures do. Because it is difficult for people to control their linguistic styles, the analyses of subtle word use are helpful in gaining insights into the ways people and groups think and relate to their conversational topics, their audiences, and perhaps themselves. The Al-Qaeda findings hint at some of the social and psychological dynamics behind two of their leaders.

The LIWC analyses suggest that bin Laden has been increasing in his cognitive complexity and emotionality since the terrorist attacks on 9/11, as reflected by his increased use of exclusive, positive emotion, and negative emotion word use. Also, since the 2003 invasion of Iraq, both bin Laden and al-Zawahiri have accelerated in their use negative emotion words—especially anger words. In fact, their use of anger and hostility words is much higher than that of statements from other known extremist groups. Also in comparison to other extremist groups, Al-Qaeda's sense of identity is more strongly defined through an oppositional group or government, as indicated by their higher use of third-person pronouns.

The meaning extraction strategy results indicate that Al-Qaeda is increasingly focused on disseminating their interpretations of American involvement with Iraq and Afghanistan, especially to Muslim communities. This increased attention to the West has replaced talk of Middle Eastern holy lands and other Islamic conflicts, which was the one of the group's main concerns in statements before 9/11.

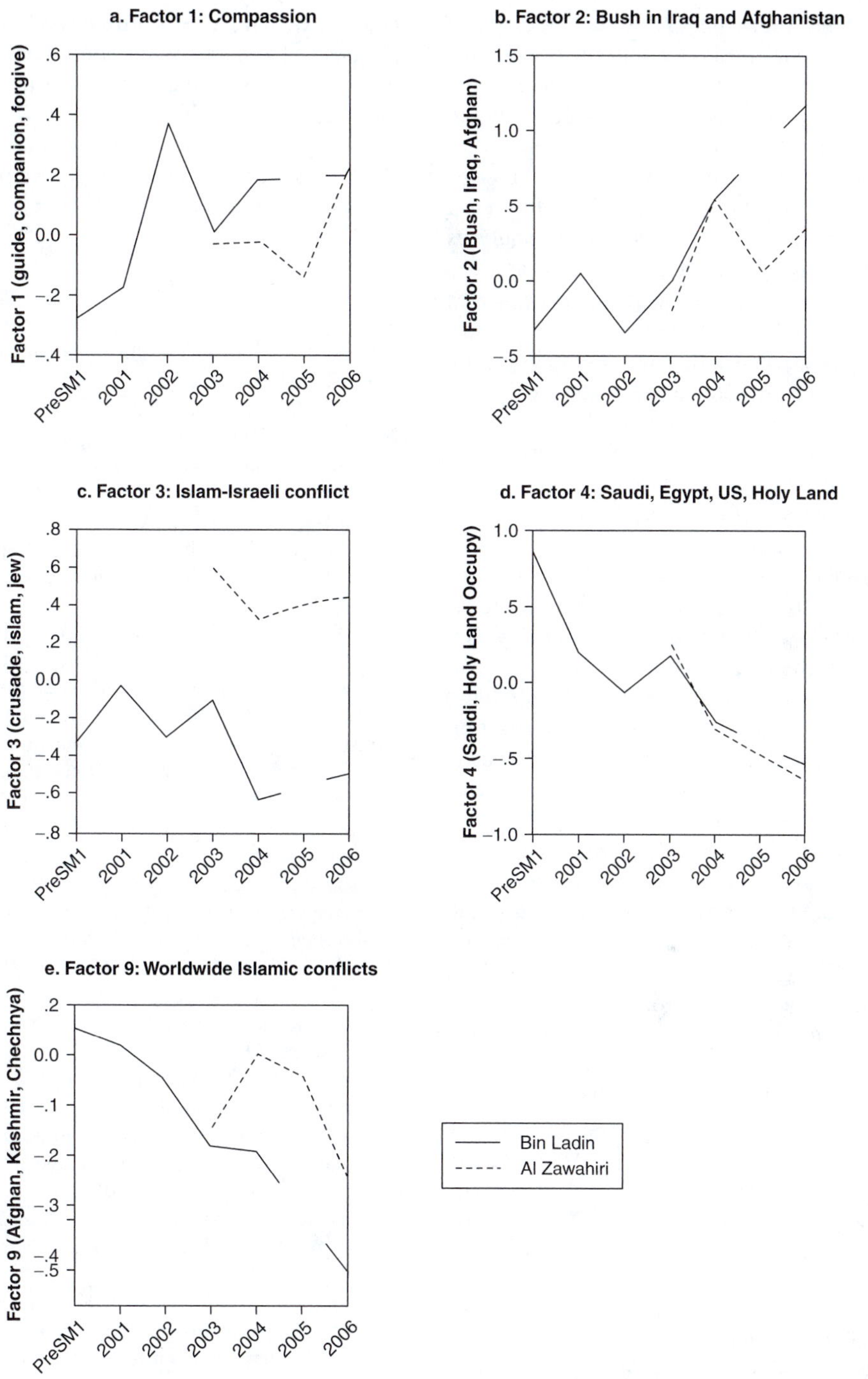

Figure 2 Changes in Content Over Time and by Author

Perhaps more important than the actual findings themselves is the introduction of new computer-based text analysis methods. The text preparation time involved spell checking and the removal of interviewers' and transcribers' comments along with extended religious quotations—a process that took approximately 4 hours. The LIWC analyses of linguistic styles of all 57 texts took approximately 12 seconds. Subsequent data analyses reported in this paper required perhaps 3 additional hours. In short, analyses of linguistic style of a large number of texts involved 7 hours and 12 seconds of work.

The meaning extraction method is much more experimental, is a bit more time-consuming, and involves greater interpretation once the process is concluded. The results reported in this paper involved perhaps 5 to 10 hours of text analysis work. The underlying logic of meaning extraction is to mathematically discover which groups of words tend to co-occur. These word clusters tend to reflect underlying themes. What makes the meaning extraction method appealing is that there is no predetermined categorization made by linguists, operatives, or even translators. Indeed, this method is not language determined. We could do the same methods on Farsi, Arabic, or Korean language sets without being able to read a single word or character. The only time that translators and/or interpreters would be required is at the end of the analytic procedure.

We realize that our interpretations of the meaning extraction results are superficial. This is where the expertise of the intelligence and diplomatic communities is needed. As computer language analysts, we can say which words hang together. Unfortunately, without deep knowledge of the authors and context, we are restricted in knowing what the themes may reflect.

We are at the dawn of a new era in computerized text analysis. Through continued analyses of linguistic style and automated theme-based analyses, it will be possible to follow the individual and group dynamics of Al-Qaeda and other groups over time. Similar analyses can be conducted with almost any text-based documents surrounding Al-Qaeda or other groups. This could include blogs, posters, e-mails, overheard conversations, or public statements. With continued refinements in computational linguistics and cross-language research, it will soon be possible to bypass many problems in translation and examine statements in the language in which they were originally spoken or written.

References

Adams, S. (1996, October). Statement analysis: What do suspects' words really reveal? *FBI Law Enforcement Bulletin,* pp. 12–20.

Adams, S. (2004, April). Statement analysis: Beyond the words. *FBI Law Enforcement Bulletin,* pp. 22–23.

Boroditsky, L. (2001). Does language shape thought? English and Mandarin speakers' conceptions of time. *Cognitive Psychology 43:*1–22.

Chung, C. K., & Pennebaker, J. W. (2007). The psychological functions of function words. In K. Fiedler (Ed.), *Social communication* (pp. 343–359). New York: Psychology Press.

Gottschalk, L. A. (2000). The application of computerized content analysis of natural language in psychotherapy research now and in the future. *American Journal of Psychotherapy 54:*305–311.

Gottschalk, L. A., & Glaser, G. C. (1969). *The measurement of psychological states through the content analysis of verbal behavior.* Berkeley: University of California Press.

Hart, R. P. (1984). *Verbal style and the presidency: A computer-based analysis.* New York: Academic Press.

Landauer, T. K., & Dumais, S. T. (1997). A solution to Plato's problem: The latent semantic analysis theory of the acquisition, induction, and representation of knowledge. *Psychological Review 104:*211–240.

Martindale, C. (1990). *A clockwork muse: The predictability of artistic change.* New York: Basic Books.

Mergenthaler, E. (1996). Emotion-abstraction patterns in verbatim protocols: A new way of describing psychotherapeutic processes. *Journal of Consulting and Clinical Psychology 64:*1306–1315.

North, R. C., Holsti, O. R., Zaninovich, G. M., & Zinnes, D. A. (1963). *Content analysis: A handbook with applications for the study of international crisis.* Oxford, England: Northwestern University Press.

Oberlander, J., & Gill, A. (2004, August). Individual differences and implicit language: Personality, parts-of-speech, and pervasiveness. In *Proceedings of the 26th Annual conference of the Cognitive Science Society,* Chicago, pp. 1035–1050.

Pennebaker, J. W., Booth, R. J., & Francis, M. E. (2007). *Linguistic Inquiry and Word Count: LIWC 2007.* Austin, TX: LIWC.

Pennebaker, J. W., Francis, M. E., & Booth, R. J. (2001). *Linguistic Inquiry and Word Count: LIWC 2001.* Mahwah, NJ: Lawrence Erlbaum.

Pennebaker, J. W., & King, L. A. (1999). Linguistic styles: Language use as an individual difference. *Journal of Personality and Social Psychology 77:*1296–1312.

Pennebaker, J. W., Mehl, M. R., & Niederhoffer, K. (2003). Psychological aspects of natural language use: Our words, our selves. *Annual Review of Psychology 54:*547–577.

Seyle, D. C., & Pennebaker, J. W. (2004, January). *"We're right, they aren't": A linguistic picture of extremism.* Paper presented at Society for Personality and Social Psychology, Austin, TX.

Simonton, D. K. (1988). Presidential style: Personality, biography, and performance. *Journal of Personality and Social Psychology 55:*928–936.

Smith, A. (2004). From words to action: Exploring the relationship between a group's value references and its likelihood of engaging in terrorism. *Studies in Conflict and Terrorism 27:*409–437.

Stone, P. J., Dunphy, D. C., Smith, M. S., & Ogilvie, D. M. (Eds.). (1966). *The General Inquirer: A computer approach to content analysis.* Cambridge: MIT Press.

Tsai, J. L., Simenova, D., & Watanabe, J. (2004). Somatic and social: Chinese Americans talk about emotion. *Personality and Social Psychology Bulletin 30:*1226–1238.

Walker, S. G. (2000). Assessing psychological characteristics at a distance: Symposium lessons and future research directions. *Political Psychology 21:*597–602.

Weintraub, W. (1981). *Verbal behavior: Adaptation and psychopathology.* New York: Springer.

Winter, D. G. (2005). Things I've learned about personality from studying political leaders at a distance. *Journal of Personality 73:*557–584.

Conceptual Cross-Tabulations

Media Analyzed	Methodological Issues										
	Units of Analysis		**Coding Process**		**Analytical Constructs**		**Data languages, Categories**		**Criteria**		*Computer Aides Used or Discussed*
	Unitizing	*Sampling*	*Manual*	*Computer*	*Qualitative*	*Quantitative*	*Separate*	*Relational*	*Reliability*	*Validity*	
In General	3.1, 3.5	2.2, 5.6	4.1, 4.2, 4.3, 4.4	4.3, 4.4	3.2, 3.4	3.1, 3.4, 3.5	4.1, 4.2, 5.4, 5.5	3.1, 3.5, 7.3	4.2, 4.4, 6.1, 6.2	4.2, 4.3, 5.5, 6.2, 6.3	4.3, 4.4
Books/Magazines	3.9, 5.2, 7.2, 7.4	3.9, 5.2	3.1, 3.9	1.7, 5.2, 7.2, 7.4		3.1, 3.9, 5.2, 7.2	5.2	3.1, 7.2		3.1, 3.9	1.7, 5.2, 7.2
Broadcasts/Radio			1.5, 3.1		1.5	1.5, 3.1, 7.4	2.7	1.5, 7.4		1.5, 3.1	7.4
Comics	5.8		5.8		5.8			5.8			
Education Material, Tests	3.9	3.9	3.9, 5.9, 5.10			3.9, 5.9, 5.10	5.9, 5.10			3.9	
Entertainment-Film, TV	2.6, 5.7, 5.10, 5.11, 6.6	5.11, 6.6	2.6, 5.7		2.6	5.7, 6.6	5.11, 6.6	2.6		5.7, 6.6	
Games	5.1		5.1.0			5.1.0	5.1.0				
Historical documents	3.8		3.1, 4.3	3.8, 4.3	3.2	3.1, 3.7, 3.8	3.7, 3.8	3.1		3.2, 4.3	3.8, 4.3
Institutional records		2.1	1.5, 2.1		1.5, 2.1, 3.2				2.1	3.2	
Interactions	2.5		2.5, 6.4			2.5	2.5, 6.4			6.4	
Internet	2.3, 3.6	2.3	2.3	3.6		2.3, 3.6		3.6			3.6
Interviews, Narratives	2.7, 4.1, 7.4	4.1	2.7, 4.1, 4.2, 5.4, 5.5	7.4		2.7, 5.4, 5.5, 7.4	2.7, 4.1, 4.2, 5.4	7.4	4.2, 5.4	3.2, 4.2, 5.4, 6.3	7.4
Letters, Posts	1.6, 3.6, 3.7, 5.1, 7.1		1.6, 3.7, 5.1	1.6, 3.6, 7.1	1.6, 4.1, 5.1	1.6, 3.6, 3.7, 5.1, 7.1	1.6, 4.1, 5.1, 7.1	3.6	5.1	3.7	1.6, 3.6, 7.1
Music, Songs	1.1, 3.7		1.1, 3.7, 5.11			1.1, 3.7, 5.11	1.1, 5.11			3.7	
News, Newspapers	2.4, 2.7, 3.1, 3.5, 4.5, 5.2, 6.5, 7.3, 7.5, 7.6	2.2, 2.4, 2.7, 4.5, 5.2, 5.6, 6.5	2.7, 4.4, 4.5, 5.6, 7.5, 7.6	4.4, 4.5, 5.2, 7.3, 7.6	1.2, 6.5	1.2, 1.3, 1.4, 2.2, 2.4, 2.7, 4.4, 4.5, 5.2, 5.3, 5.6, 6.5, 7.5, 7.6	2.2, 2.4, 2.7, 4.5, 5.2, 5.3, 5.6, 6.5, 7.6	3.5, 7.3, 7.5	3.5, 4.4, 4.5	2.2, 6.5, 7.6	4.4, 5.2, 7.3, 7.5, 7.6
Painting	3.7				3.7					3.7	
Public Speeches, Debates	3.1, 3.5, 7.3, 7.7		3.1, 3.3, 3.5	1.7, 3.8, 7.3, 7.7	3.3	3.1, 3.5, 7.3, 7.7	3.3, 7.7	3.1, 7.3		3.1, 3.3	1.7, 7.3, 7.7

Media Analyzed

Analytical Constructs From	Methodological Issues										
	Units of Analysis		**Coding Process**		**Analytical Constructs**		**Data languages, Categories**		**Criteria**		*Computer Aides Used or Discussed*
	Unitizing	*Sampling*	*Manual*	*Computer*	*Qualitative*	*Quantitative*	*Separate*	*Relational*	*Reliability*	*Validity*	
General			4.5		3.4	3.4				3.4, 6.3	
Biology: genetics, epidemiology	3.6, 7.6			3.6		3.6, 7.6		3.6, 7.6			3.6, 7.6
Cognition: Individual Psychological	1.6, 3.1, 3.5		3.5, 5.4	1.6, 3.5, 7.1, 7.7	1.6, 3.2	1.6, 3.1, 3.5, 5.4, 7.1, 7.7	5.4, 7.7	1.6, 3.5, 5.4, 7.1	5.4	3.2, 5.4	3.5, 7.1, 7.7
Networks: Contingencies, Coocurrences, Semantic	3.1, 7.2, 7.3, 7.4, 7.5	7.5	3.1, 3.5, 7.5	7.2, 7.3, 7.4	3.1, 3.5, 3.6, 6.4, 7.2	3.6, 7.2, 7.3, 7.4, 7.5	7.3	3.5, 7.2, 7.3, 7.4, 7.5		3.1, 6.4	7.2, 7.3, 7.4, 7.5
Indexical, Correlational	1.4, 2.4, 2.5, 2.7, 3.7, 3.9, 5.2, 5.7, 5.10, 6.6, 7.1, 7.3	2.3, 2.4, 2.7, 3.9, 5.2, 5.3, 5.6, 5.7, 6.5, 6.6	2.3, 2.4, 2.7, 3.9, 5.7, 5.10, 6.5, 6.6	1.7, 3.8, 4.3, 5.2, 7.1, 7.3	1.2, 3.2, 3.7	1.1, 1.4, 1.6, 2.3, 2.4, 2.7, 3.7, 3.9, 5.1, 5.2, 5.3, 5.4, 5.7, 5.9, 5.10, 5.11, 6.5, 6.6, 7.1, 7.3	1.4, 1.6, 2.7, 3.7, 3.9, 5.1, 5.2, 5.10, 6.5, 7.1	1.5, 2.7, 4.2, 5.8, 7.3	4.2	3.9, 5.7, 6.3, 6.5, 6.6	5.2, 7.1, 7.3
Political-Economic, Ideology					1.2, 5.8		5.8				
Propaganda, Influence	1.1, 2.6, 2.7, 3.3, 7.7	2.4, 2.7	1.5, 2.5, 2.6, 2.7, 3.3, 4.4	4.4	1.5, 2.6, 3.3	1.1, 2.4, 2.7	2.4, 2.7, 3.3		4.4	1.5, 3.3, 3.7	4.4
Public Opinion Dynamics	1.4, 2.7, 3.8, 7.6	2.7	2.7, 7.6	3.8, 7.6		2.7, 3.8, 7.6	2.7, 3.8, 7.6		4.4	7.6	3.8, 7.6
Representational, Descriptive	2.3, 5.1, 5.5, 5.7, 5.8, 5.11, 6.5	2.2, 2.3, 5.6, 5.7, 5.11	4.3, 5.5, 5.6, 5.8, 5.9	4.3, 5.2		2.2, 5.2, 5.5, 5.6, 5.9	5.2, 5.5, 5.6		2.1	2.2, 3.2, 5.5, 5.7, 6.5, 6.6	4.3, 5.2
Social Psychological	2.5		2.5			2.5	2.5, 6.4			6.4	
Sociological, Institutional	5.1, 6.5	2.1	2.1, 4.3, 5.1	4.3	2.1, 3.2, 5.1	5.1, 6.5			5.1	6.4, 6.5	4.3
Weather Dynamics	1.4		1.4			1.4	1.4				

Analytical Constructs From . . .

Inferences Of	Methodological Issues										
	Units of Analysis		Coding Process		Analytical Constructs		Data languages, Categories		Criteria		*Computer Aides Used or Discussed*
	Unitizing	*Sampling*	*Manual*	*Computer*	*Qualitative*	*Quantitative*	*Separate*	*Relational*	*Reliability*	*Validity*	
Inferences Of . . .											
In General	4.5	4.5	4.1, 4.2, 4.5	4.5	3.4	3.4, 4.5	4.1, 4.5		6.1, 6.2	3.2, 4.2, 6.2	
Attention, Agenda	2.7, 5.3, 5.6, 6.5, 7.6	2.2, 2.7, 5.3	4.3	1.7, 4.3		2.7, 4.4, 5.3, 5.6, 6.5, 7.5	2.7, 5.3, 6.5	2.7	3.1, 4.4, 6.3, 7.6	2.2, 6.5	4.3, 7.6
Attitudes	3.5, 7.6, 7.7		3.5	7.7		3.5, 6.5, 7.7	7.7	3.5	4.4	6.3, 7.6	7.6, 7.7
Authorship / Identity	3.7				3.7	3.7	3.7			3.7	
Biases: Attention, Gender, Political, etc.	5.8, 5.10, 6.5	2.1, 2.2, 5.6, 6.5	2.1		2.1, 5.8	1.3, 2.2, 5.6, 5.9, 5.10, 5.11, 6.5	1.3, 5.6, 5.8, 5.9, 5.10, 5.11, 6.5		2.1	2.2, 6.5	
Economic Variables	7.5		7.5			7.5		7.5			7.5
Historical Events	3.7				3.2, 3.7	3.7	3.7			3.2, 3.7	
Influence, Effects	2.6, 3.9	3.9	2.6, 3.9		2.6	1.1, 1.5, 2.4, 3.9	2.4, 3.9			3.9, 6.3	3.9
Intelligence: Military, Political	3.3		1.5, 3.3		1.5, 3.3	3.3		1.5, 3.3		1.5, 3.3	
Psychological Variables	1.6, 3.1, 4.5, 7.1	4.5	3.1, 4.5, 5.4	1.6, 7.1		1.6, 3.1, 5.4, 7.1, 7.7	1.6, 4.5, 5.4, 7.1	1.6, 3.1, 7.3	4.5, 5.4	3.1, 5.4, 6.3	7.1
Public Opinion	2.7, 4.4, 7.6		4.4, 7.6	4.4, 7.6		2.7, 4.4, 7.6			4.4	7.6	7.6
Relations of Power	3.3	2.1	3.3		2.1, 3.3	3.3		3.3		3.3	
Social or Textual Dynamics	2.5, 3.6, 3.8, 7.6	2.1, 7.6	2.5	3.6, 3.8, 7.6	2.1	1.4, 2.5, 3.6, 3.8, 7.6	1.4, 3.8, 7.6	3.6	3.6	7.6	3.6, 3.8, 7.6
Underlying Structures, Distributions	2.3, 3.5, 5.6, 5.11, 7.2, 7.4, 7.5	2.3, 5.11	3.5, 5.6, 6.4, 7.5	7.2, 7.3, 7.4		3.1, 3.6, 5.6, 7.2, 7.4, 7.5	5.6, 7.2	3.1, 3.5, 5.8, 7.2, 7.4, 7.5		6.4	3.5, 7.2, 7.4, 7.5
Values	5.2, 5.8	5.2	5.1	5.2	5.1, 5.8	5.1, 5.2, 5.11	5.1, 5.2, 5.11		5.1		5.2
Violence, Sex	5.7, 5.11, 6.6	5.7, 6.6	5.7, 6.6			5.7, 5.11, 6.6	5.7, 5.11, 6.6			5.7, 6.6	

Index

About the Editors

Klaus Krippendorff, PhD, is the Gregory Bateson Term Professor for Cybernetics, Language, and Culture at the University of Pennsylvania's Annenberg School for Communication and a Past President of the International Communication Association (ICA). He has contributed more than 100 articles and book chapters on human communication theory, methodology in the social sciences, cybernetics, and design; coauthored *The Analysis of Communication Content, Communication and Control in Society;* and authored *Content Analysis: An Introduction to Its Methodology* (translated into Italian, Japanese, Spanish, and Hungarian and recipient of the 2004 ICA Fellows Book Award), *Information Theory,* and *The Semantic Turn.* His current work focuses on second-order cybernetics, critical (emancipatory) theory, and the role of language in the social construction of realities.

Mary Angela Bock is a PhD candidate at the University of Pennsylvania's Annenberg School for Communication studying with Dr. Krippendorff. She is a former television journalist whose career stretched from the Iowa presidential caucuses to the Lewinsky hearings to the events of September 11. She studies the impact of convergent technologies on photojournalism and television news within the constructivist paradigm. She has contributed to the *Visual Communication Quarterly* and has twice received honors for papers presented at conferences for the International Communication Association.